The "Jewish Threat"

Also by Joseph W. Bendersky

Carl Schmitt: Theorist for the Reich
A History of Nazi Germany

The "Jewish Threat"

Anti-Semitic Politics
of the U.S. Army

Joseph W. Bendersky

BASIC
BOOKS

A Member of the Perseus Books Group

Published by Basic Books,
A Member of the Perseus Books Group

Designed by Rachel Hegarty

Library of Congress Cataloging-in-Publication Data
Bendersky, Joseph W., 1946–
    The Jewish threat : anti-Semitic politics of the U.S. army / Joseph W. Bendersky.
        p.   cm.
    Includes bibliographical references (p.) and index.
    ISBN 0-465-00617-5 (alk. paper)
    1. Antisemitism—United States—History—20th century.   2. Jews—United States—Public opinion.   3. Public opinion—United States.   4. United States—Armed Forces—Officers—Attitudes.   5. United States—Ethnic relations.
I. Title.
DS146.U6.B47   2000
305.892'1073—dc21   00-034330
                                                                                              CIP

First Edition

The paper used in this publication meets the requirements of the American National Standard for Permanence of Paper for Printed Library Materials Z39.48-1984.

00 01 02 03 / 10 9 8 7 6 5 4 3 2 1

For
Carmen

Contents

Illustrations appear after pages 110, 222, and 366

Acknowledgments

As this book grew enormously in scope and ultimately took more than a decade to complete, I incurred debts to a variety of individuals and institutions. Without their professional assistance, financial support, or hospitality and kindness the extensive work required for a book of this kind would have been impossible. The necessary research was very time-consuming and involved travel to archives across the country as well as innumerable trips to the National Archives. A fellowship from the National Endowment for the Humanities allowed me to devote a year entirely to this study. Further research was supported by grants from the American Council of Learned Societies, American Philosophical Society, and Holocaust Educational Foundation. I would also like to thank Virginia Commonwealth University for a Grant-in-Aid and Terry Oggel, former associate dean of the College of Humanities and Sciences, for providing travel funds at an early stage of the project.

Although it is not possible to identify all of them individually, a debt of gratitude is owed to the archivists and staff of the numerous archives listed in the bibliography. All scholars know the vital, though too often unrecognized, role that archivists play in the historical discipline. In this regard, I would like especially to thank Richard J. Sommers, David Keough, and Pamela Cheney of the U.S. Military History Institute at the U.S. Army War College, Carlisle, Pennsylvania. Over a period of years, David Keough in particular provided invaluable guidance, insight, and professional judgment concerning documentation and research strategies in key areas of my work. Numerous archivists at the National Archives were also helpful. However, I would like to express my sincere thanks for the assistance of John Taylor and Richard Boylan. They were both instrumental not only in finding the sources I had identified but also in opening up entirely new avenues of extremely valuable investigation. Every scholar who has had the privilege of working with them knows exactly what I mean. On numerous occasions the Interlibrary Loan Department at Virginia Commonwealth University was very helpful in securing sources for me.

Several colleagues and scholars provided important support, advice, and encouragement. My departmental colleague Melvin I. Urofsky, Athan Theoharis of Marquette University, and George Schwab of the Graduate Center of the City University of New York understood the importance of this study even before much of the most revealing documentation had been uncovered. Their professional support at this early stage of development was crucial. I certainly would like to thank the chairs of my department, George E. Munro and Susan E. Kennedy, for their patience and understanding while I devoted myself to such a long-term project. Nancy Campbell was quite helpful in working out the technological problems of manuscript preparation. Sam Bullock, Krister Johnson, Josh Katz, Lynn Shepherd, and Pat Webber also worked on various stages of the project. The Department of History of Ben-Gurion University of the Negev in Israel, particularly Robert Liberles and Ilan Troen, deserve thanks for offering me the opportunity to present my findings to their faculty and students.

As I approached the publication stage, Benton Arnovitz kindly shared the fruits of his years of experience in the publishing world. I would like to extend my sincere appreciation to my literary agent, Jim Hornfischer, to Don Fehr, senior editor at Basic Books, and to John Bergez, whose incisive reading, commentary, and thoughtful editing greatly enhanced the quality of the book.

Even with the financial resources provided by grants and fellowships the research for this book could not have been completed without the hospitality shown by Mike and Ann Bendersky during my frequent trips to Washington for almost a decade. Machi and Greg Dilworth were equally kind in accommodating me over the years of research. Certainly my wife, Carmen, and my daughters, Karen and Nicole, deserve a great deal of thanks for their understanding during my frequent and often long trips, as well as for tolerating the years I spent in the office writing this book. The essential contribution of George Bock to my work has gone unrecognized for too long; he is an undeniable example that altruistic individuals do exist. I would never have published a single word without his teaching and assistance many years ago.

The Jewish Files

O N MAY 2, 1919, CAPTAIN JOHN B. TREVOR sent an urgent request to the director of military intelligence in Washington under the title "Plans for the Protection of New York in Case of Local Disturbances." To underscore its gravity, he followed up with a telephone call from his military intelligence office at 302 Broadway. In the hysterical atmosphere of the Red Scare just beginning to spread across America, Trevor was convinced that a Bolshevik revolt was imminent in his home city of New York and that "the force available is utterly inadequate to meet a serious uprising in the congested district."[1]

Fearing local troops would be "overwhelmed by a great superiority of numbers," Trevor sought "prompt action" from headquarters. The expedited response from Washington the next day alleviated some, though not all, of his mounting anxiety. The good news was that "6,000 Springfield rifles" had already been shipped from Augusta, Georgia. But he had also asked for machine guns, which he intended to organize "into a Machine Gun Battalion with two motor trucks capable of carrying eight guns and crews." The probable deployment of the desired Machine Gun Battalion was in the area he identified as "most strongly permeated with the Bolshevik movement."[2]

These particular sections of New York were clearly outlined on the secret "Ethnic Map" Captain Trevor had drawn up months before. Pondering these areas of the city, he easily visualized the threat in human form—for he had encountered them personally in the streets for decades and had kept them under intense surveillance for more than a year. Outsiders, alien in appearance, language, and behavior, they threatened, in his mind, not only his country's heritage, culture, and political institutions but the continued predominance of the very race that had created and maintained advanced civilization itself. And these sections of Trevor's "Ethnic Map" specifically denoted "the congested districts chiefly inhabited by Russian Jews."[3]

The very day of his request to Washington, Trevor's secret agent had again confirmed that radical gatherings were "90% Jewish."[4] Accordingly, "it would be eminently desirable," Trevor had notified headquarters, "to have sufficient force available to enclose the area and localize the outbreak."

As a patrician New Yorker, Trevor had watched with dread as waves of new immigrants poured into his city in the decades before World War I. A good part of his wartime service with the Military Intelligence Division (MID) was devoted to surveillance of these newcomers, particularly Jews. After leaving the military, he would become one of the most prominent and influential figures in the anti-immigrant and anti-Communist movement in the United States. Yet Trevor's paranoid nativism and susceptibility to conspiracy theories, though perhaps accentuated by personal experience in New York, differed very little, if at all, from the values and perspectives of career officers throughout the American army in the first half of the twentieth century.

Thus, army intelligence headquarters questioned neither the veracity of Trevor's reports nor the alarmist tone that permeated each paragraph of his request. They contained nothing surprising or unusual. It all fitted quite well into a general pattern emerging from information ascertained through various official and unofficial sources. About the same time, the American military attaché in Switzerland, Colonel William Godson, had sent similar intelligence on the dangers posed by Jewish Bolsheviks in Europe. Godson, one of the army's most valued intelligence officers, wrote from Poland:

> The connection between the Jews and the Bolsheviki at Vilna seems to be proven without a shadow of a doubt. When the Bolsheviki entered the city they were taken to the houses of the wealthy by the Jews and apparently had this matter arranged beforehand.[5]

Even more horrifying than the seizure and destruction of property were eyewitness accounts of barbarism and butchery by these Bolsheviks. Typical of the atrocity stories that filled pages was that of "the man and woman who lived on the estate . . . [who] had been killed and frightfully mutilated. The woman had her head cut off and the man had his eyes gouged out and his ears and nose cut off." Accompanying photographs depicted Bolshevik mutilation of two captured Polish soldiers. Here were naked bodies with butchered flesh, hanging upside down from trees, while "the Bolsheviki soldiers were laughing and grinning and standing about."[6]

That event embedded such an indelible image on the mind that two years later, Godson would write passionately:

> I am so thoroughly convinced of the reality of a Jewish movement to dominate the world that I hate to leave a stone unturned.[7]

Although the precise nature of the phenomenon was still murky and contradictory information impeded definitive conclusions, the evidence had been mounting for more than a year of a "Jewish International" movement. Some "highly reliable sources" and officers indicated a link between Zionism and radical Jewish activity; others argued that wealthy international Jewish bankers financially backed the Bolshevik Revolution. In effect, the accumulating files at MID identified a myriad of institutions and individuals that could be drawn upon and formed into various malleable combinations when necessary to substantiate one theory or another.

The credulity with which much of this information was so readily accepted and manipulated revealed a critical predisposition toward Jews that extended beyond mere prejudice. It was part of a broader worldview in the army officer corps that was quickly becoming institutionalized. This worldview embodied aspects of xenophobic geopolitics, anticommunism, and racial theories. It presumed a superior "true American" society and government of Anglo-Saxon heritage under siege by various radical alien forces and particularly racially inferior Eastern European immigrants. The mixture of biological racism with national security issues would prove instrumental in creating the impression of a Jewish threat at home and abroad. In turn, the need to counteract this alleged danger furnished both the motivation and justification for officers to extend their spheres of operation far beyond the legitimate mission of either the army or military intelligence.

Intelligence officers had created separate classifications for "Jews" to accommodate pertinent reports, memoranda, and correspondence. The MID subject index "Jews: Race" would eventually fill over 200 large index cards, containing citations to close to 2,000 referenced reports on Jewish activities between 1918 and 1941. Scattered throughout related categories in a truly immense records system, these reports were routinely stamped secret or confidential. By policy and established procedure, they went directly to the office of the chief of staff, where intelligence officers decided on their dissemination to interested governmental and military agencies for information or action.[8]

MID File 245, however, was a special central dossier reserved for data deemed, for one reason or another, particularly significant to the "Jewish Question." Compiled primarily in the early 1920s, with a few additions thereafter, this truly remarkable file housed an amazing array of documents ranging from the routine to the fantastic.[9]

During the 1920s, File 245 contained letters between officers, secret agents, state secretaries, and embassies abroad exchanging the latest information on Jews. Among these would be interspersed lists compiled of prominent Jews who supposedly dominated or influenced German banking, industry, and politics. Far more numerous lists would be gathered of Jews supposedly controlling the Soviet government as MID became preoccupied with the link between Jews and Bolshevism. Although Zionism and Palestine received attention, much more concern was displayed toward Jewish refugees and immigration to the United States. Certain prominent American Jews, including Supreme Court Justice Louis D. Brandeis, Felix Frankfurter, and Rabbi Stephen Wise, were considered sufficiently important to warrant individual scrutiny. Most incredible, though, were lengthy, meticulously documented reports with titles such as "The Power and Aims of International Jewry."[10]

The dubious assumptions and specious arguments manifested in these documents were matched only by the marginalia added as they circulated throughout MID, for officers occasionally punctuated their concurrence by remarking that recent world events seemed to offer proof of these assertions.

Most official reports in File 245, like those indexed elsewhere under the subject heading "Jews," were written or compiled by officers of longtime professional military service. And the attitudes and preconceived notions about Jews that prompted military intelligence to see the necessity, indeed the virtue, of establishing separate investigative classifications for Jews were by no means confined to a relatively small coterie in MID. Neither were they held only by a limited number of anti-Semites in the officer corps generally. Over time, hundreds of officers made direct contributions to this endeavor or worked with this material, including the military attachés in American embassies around the world, who collected and shared a good deal of this information.

Since Military Intelligence by its very nature was the most politically conscious and engaged of any section of the army, it provided some of the most articulate and fully developed illustrations of this perspective. MID's area of expertise (data collection and analysis) also ensured that it would accumulate and preserve the most abundant documentation on this subject.

Nonetheless, no significant differences in attitude are discernible between those officers who spent their entire careers, or substantial portions of them, in intelligence and those from other parts of the army who rotated in and out of MID. And evidence drawn from numerous sources besides MID records suggests how pervasive, institutionalized, influential, and enduring this worldview was throughout the army.

Reaching into the highest echelons of the army hierarchy, such attitudes permeated all ranks of the officer corps. This included the director of military intelligence in Washington, who held the rank of assistant chief of staff and personally handled a considerable amount of the work related to Jews. In MID, few below the rank of colonel or major were actually involved in such endeavors. During the 1920s, reports and analyses relative to Jews were routinely exchanged with top officials at the Departments of State, Immigration, and Justice.

The worldview of the army officer corps predated the Red Scare of 1919, and it persisted long after the anti-Communist and antiforeign hysteria of the nativist 1920s had subsided. Of course, its tenets received more open and fuller expression during these years, for the apprehensive psychological climate of the period added credibility and urgency to policies, laws, and other governmental actions that these beliefs seemed to dictate in the face of foreign danger from within and abroad. But most of these assumptions and characteristics had clearly manifested themselves among officers long before World War I. And once they were reinforced and further developed through additional theoretical studies and historical experience in the 1920s, they were thereafter perpetuated for decades—well into the Cold War era—through attitudes and institutions within the army.

The careers of many officers that extended into the 1940s attest further to the continuity of these viewpoints. Many of those who participated in these Jewish investigations in early or midcareer, or who left traces in other historical records of anti-Semitic attitudes expressed when it was acceptable, even fashionable, to do so, subsequently rose to important positions. Some became generals in World War II. If new generations of officers entering the military after World War I did not already hold such ideas or attitudes, they would have ample opportunity to absorb them in the army either through direct instruction or from the general institutional culture to which they were expected to adapt themselves.

For most of this century, these significant dimensions of the army's past remained unknown to all but the participants themselves. File 245 and other MID records on Jews were kept classified until the mid-1970s and stored with tons of other military intelligence material until recently examined.[11] Yet when studied in conjunction with an abundance of evidence from other sources, the Jewish files reveal that a racial anti-Semitic worldview persisted in the officer corps of the army through World War II and affected the perspectives and activities of some retired officers long thereafter. There was an enduring susceptibility to Jewish conspiracy theories on the part of certain officers. Indeed, biological-racial anti-Semitism had not, as historians generally contend, "virtually disappeared from the American scene" after 1924.[12] For Jews continued to be perceived in racial terms.

Thus, while focusing on the army and specifically on officers in the first half of the twentieth century, this book makes a contribution to the broader debate over anti-Semitism in American history. The pre–World War II historiographical tradition had been to view anti-Semitism as outside America's mainstream and as a problem attributable to fringe groups or declining social classes, with limited impact on major developments. Other historians have since challenged these assumptions, arguing that the persistence and pervasiveness of anti-Semitism had important ramifications for Jewish social progress in America.[13] But even among these recent scholars, there are still serious disagreements over the extent to which anti-Semitism explains the failure of America's response to the Holocaust.[14] Many of these interpretive differences are due to the peculiar nature of American anti-Semitism, which, as David Gerber noted, has been less visible and reputable than European versions and has never been sanctioned by government or official ideology.[15]

Such distinctive features have made American anti-Semitism both insidious as a social force and problematical to study. This is particularly true regarding anti-Semitism within the institutions of government, where documenting prejudice and then demonstrating its effect on policy have proven exceptionally difficult.[16] The Jewish files and other extensive evidence have, however, provided the foundation for a fully documented case study of a functioning anti-Semitic worldview within an American governmental institution.

This documentation shows that even though anti-Semitism never became official policy or law within the American government, its pervasiveness within the culture of the army officer corps affected much more than the direction of intelligence gathering. The anti-Semitism of army officers had an important impact on critical legal and policy decisions concerning immigration, the fate of European Jews during and after the Holocaust, and the establishment of the state of Israel.

Varying from simple prejudice to theoretically sophisticated dogma, the anti-Semitism of army officers fluctuated with changing times, circumstances, and historical experiences. At certain points it manifested itself through sweeping condemnation and dread of all Jews. At other times it was more nuanced, distinguishing between the acceptable assimilated Jews and the "dregs" from Eastern Europe. Changing American sensibilities after World War II and the Holocaust also altered attitudes and their expression. The vehement racial anti-Semitism flaunted so arrogantly by many officers in the 1920s would later be expressed only privately or in more subtle forms after Nazism made such views disreputable within an increasingly progressive American society. Often, anti-Semitism appeared under the guise of patriotism and seemingly sound assessments of national interests at home and abroad.

Although in some respects the anti-Semitism of these officers reflected the prejudices of Americans generally, army views lagged far behind changes in societal attitudes. Indeed, the army, particularly its senior officers, remained a bastion of both racial and other forms of anti-Semitism much longer than indicated by either popular memory or previous historical studies. The persistence of such anti-Semitism would have serious ramifications.

CHAPTER 1

The Officers' Worldview, 1900–1939

The trouble is, the "Master Race" is on the decline and gradually ceasing to be master in its own house; it is being swamped by . . . Mongrels, greasers, whelps, and hounds.

—Colonel William A. McCain to
Colonel Gordon Johnston, May 20, 1920

ALTHOUGH COLONEL MCCAIN WROTE THESE WORDS IN 1920, he was actually expressing a trepidation that had been widespread among officers of the United States Army since the late nineteenth century.[1] Like him, many in the officer corps feared that the "true Americans" were losing control of something they rightfully possessed by conquest, merit, heritage, and even divine providence.

This fear was rooted in a set of attitudes that, by the early twentieth century, constituted nothing less than a worldview among members of the officer corps. They had been imbued with a common set of general assumptions, beliefs, attitudes, and values related not only to their military avocation but to the broader context of human behavior. Officers shared definite ideas about their American heritage, contemporary events such as the rise of Bolshevism, human motivation and psychology, the characteristics of racial groups, and the nature of politics and government. They believed these ideas to be well founded. Their validity could easily be demonstrated by "common sense" and "experience" or, if more elaborate proof was required, by studies of the day in the natural and social sciences. Such knowledge pertained as much to individuals as it did to social classes, nations, or races.

Like most worldviews, this had its internal contradictions, extremist and moderate gradations, and differences among adherents and interpreters. Not all of its followers accepted, or were even aware of, every tenet; for that matter, many did not necessarily consider that what they naturally believed constituted a worldview at all. Nor were all of its aspects explained uniformly or precisely in an organized and detailed manner. Its general outlines and components continued to evolve over time. This is also true of most worldviews, including those of Christianity, Judaism, and Marxism. They too were characterized by diversity, ambiguity, and incompleteness and evolved as they adjusted to changing circumstances. Although these officers lacked an official canon, their worldview had theoretical foundations and formulations. These are easily discernible in the voluminous books and articles they read, cited, and used, with further substantiation coming from the extensive correspondence, memoranda, and memoirs these officers left behind. Prominent in these writings is an overriding concern with protecting the Anglo-Saxon legacy that officers associated with being "American."

"American" Character: The Anglo-Saxon Legacy

Army officers in the first decades of the twentieth century were primarily Anglo-Saxon and Protestant, products of the middle and upper classes. As they understood history, through centuries of struggle, toil, and perseverance, their people had conquered and tamed a continent. Through inherent ingenuity and applied moral virtue, they had transformed a vast colonial wilderness into a world power. They had achieved impressive levels of material progress; the land of yeoman farmers and small businessmen had taken its place among the industrial giants. But just as their country had reached these heights, it was deluged by an incessant flow of immigration by Jews, Italians, and Slavs—Colonel McCain's mongrels and greasers. This influx, together with a degeneration of the indigenous stock of Americans, held out the prospect of a future in which the inferior newcomers would numerically overwhelm the great race that had created this country.

For these officers, though, much more was at risk than continued domination by their own kind. They rarely, if ever, articulated their concerns solely in terms of the economic, cultural, or political self-interest of their social class, profession, or ethnic group. They elevated the fear of their decline to a universal problem of the survival of civilization and the continuance of human progress. To many of them, it was an article of faith, vindicated by science and historical experience, that only their race created and maintained higher culture and advanced civilizations. Its decline imperiled an entire array of cherished values, creations, and institutions of Western civilization, not the least of which were democracy, science, technology, and even rational thought.

The pedigree of this special people was Anglo-Saxon. Over time, however, Anglo-Saxon became a rather fluid designation encompassing more than those tracing their ancestry to the British Isles. Ethnically—or, in the language of the day, racially—this expanded category included all Northern Europeans, particularly Germans or Scandinavians. Some officers used the term "Nordic race" to describe this broader grouping, and it became interchangeable with "Anglo-Saxon" in their writing or discourses. Anglo-Saxon did retain a primary, distinctive status by signifying the unquestionable British origin of the language, cultural values, and institutions that constituted the essence of the United States. The Anglophile perception was that their Nordic cousins assimilated easily these British cultural traits and adapted to their institutions.[2]

Officers' self-image stemmed, in part, from their vivid historical consciousness, extending back to the colonial period and beyond. In the American context, proper origin and lineage seemed almost the equivalent of what noble bloodlines meant in Europe. In public statements, private letters, official documents, and memoirs, some written as late as the 1970s, officers emphasized pride of heritage. Although few could claim, as General Bradford G. Chynoweth would, to be "a direct descendent of William Bradford of the *Mayflower*," many had their own variant of that legendary story. They typically boasted: "[M]y last ancestor . . . came here in 1793, and . . . two of them came here in 1634"; or "I come from old New England stock . . . [and for] more than three centuries the Smiths have dwelt in New England." Occasionally, the blood of the original settlers could be reinvigorated by an infusion from the mother country. "I was born," wrote General George Van Horn Moseley, "of a fine New England father and a wonderful English mother." For others, Nordic countries such as Switzerland were equally distinctive as the tribal "home of the forefathers."[3]

Often entwined with the Mayflower mentality was the frontier myth, for if their heritage bequeathed special social and economic status to them, it was definitely deserved. Officers stemmed from a true meritocracy of self-made families, if no longer always of self-made men. Theirs was the story of apprenticed servants of the colonial era acquiring education and property, thereafter founding new towns. Later they tamed the West. "Born in a log-cabin in the woods of Southwest Wisconsin," General Amos A. Fries recounted how "following the terrible blizzard of early March 1888," his family moved on to Oregon. Subsequent generations of officers learned from military journals of this grand historical saga of "blood and suffering, bravery and endurance," of "adventures, and progressive settlers" subjugating the "hordes of savages" who spread "death and terror." Rapidly, the "forests, plains, and even the deserts and mountains, [became] the homes of thousands of free and Christian people."[4]

"Like the wandering knights of old," the army itself played a central role in the drama of conquering the wilderness. "Fighting many battles, suffering massacres, campaigning under the torrid sun of the southern summer and the ice and snow of northern winters," the army protected the settlers against "the crafty and merciless savages." Some, like sixty-five-year-old retired brigadier general Conrad Babcock, could boast of an unbroken family tradition of patriotic service in every war since the colonial era. "I am crazy to do a soldier's part in this war," he wrote, asking for a commission in 1941.[5]

This historical consciousness was personified in the 1930s in the novels of Kenneth Roberts. In *Northwest Passage* and other historical romances, Roberts brought the colonial experience to life and perpetuated Anglo-Saxonism into the 1950s. Few officers had difficulty identifying their ancestors among the heroic English settlers Roberts characterized in accounts of the French and Indian wars. Roberts often modeled these characters after his own Maine forebears, whom he idolized, and whose legacy and blood he attempted to protect fiercely from non-Nordic immigrants. His stories offered an incarnation of the Anglo-Saxon values and ideals that accounted for American greatness. Courage in the face of adversity and enemies, like fortitude and self-reliance while in the midst of nature's hostility, tempered the laudable Anglo-Saxon traits brought from England into the unique American character. In the process, a wilderness was turned into a civilization coveted around the world. In 1946, when Douglas MacArthur had himself risen to legendary heroic stature, it was an inscribed copy of Roberts's *Rabble in Arms* that an officer selected as the appropriate gift of appreciation for the general.[6]

Any effort to criticize, broaden, balance, or deviate from this orthodox picture of historical reality was, at best, suspect and, at worst, viewed as "liberal," possibly subversive, and certainly un-American. Owing to rising anti-American currents, the Warner Brothers 1934 production *See America First* was, retired General Fries noted, "most urgently needed." The American Legion, Sons of the American Revolution, and other patriotic organizations would support this film only if it emphasized "the good points in American history and . . . the development of our great country." Revealing a rather simplistic view of what constitutes a significant historical event, Fries suggested a focus on shibboleths like "Tippecanoe and Tyler, Too," "Old Hickory," and "The Rail Splitter." The filmmakers should discard the "mud hole[s] in the great highway of American advancement" like the "exception of 18 witches" who were burned. These "few bad spots" would only play into the hands of those trying to "tear down the ideals of America."[7]

In the context of American society of the day, there was nothing unusual, or even noteworthy, in such outlooks. Officers essentially shared the same cultural vista as the majority of their fellow countrymen. Despite diversity in individual background and early life experiences, officers, for the most part, fit the subsequently stereotype of the proverbial WASP. Although a good many officers stemmed from small-town and successful farm families, part of the officer corps could still be recruited from the established Eastern elites. The latter felt quite at home at the Harvard Club on West 44th Street in New York City, where generals and other officers mingled socially, exchanging views with business and government leaders of similar class and background.[8]

Easterners and Midwesterners were joined by the sons of Southern patricians and remnants of the Old South planter class. Officers who came from the Mott and McCabe families of Richmond, the Hagoods of South Carolina, or the McCains of Mississippi revived the earlier Southern tradition of the gentleman officer and warrior. Although perhaps not on a par with the Eastern elites, they had their own distinctiveness, coming as they did from the "quality" people of the Old South. Their variant of Anglo-Saxon history highlighted the Civil War and regional pride. They were more concerned with the "Negro question" than about being overrun by inferior immigrants from Eastern Europe; but they were no less zealous in investigating the newcomers.

Although they formed a very small, tightly knit professional elite within American society, army officers had acquired most of their values, attitudes, and views long before they underwent military training. The military reinforced their deeply embedded beliefs, ideals, and biases. This was particularly true for second-generation officers; and among the con-

siderable portion of officers who had attended West Point, many followed
in their fathers' footsteps. If anything, officers regarded themselves as the
guardians of true Americanism as defined by Anglo-Saxon society. The
army would be the "school for citizenship" for the rest of the nation.[9]

As these officers remembered it, the America they grew up in was an
idyllic setting difficult to recapture today. Some lived in "a village where
many homes lay well back from the street, each surrounded by beautiful
grounds." Or their childhood "paradise" sat

> high on a hill from which we could look down on beautiful Mendota Lake.
> In winter, the street was hard-packed layers of snow. Family buggies were
> mounted on sleigh runners and the harness jingled with merry sleigh bells.
> We had snow fights and snow puddings flavored with vanilla. In early fall,
> the ground was covered with leaves. In every yard the leaves were raked into
> piles and the fragrance of the bonfires was heavenly.[10]

Whether this childhood vision of a simpler, secure world of commonly
accepted values and behavior ever corresponded to the reality experienced
by the adult world of the time is perhaps irrelevant, since romanticized
memories or longings for a lost past that might never have existed are
often the foundations for powerful beliefs. What mattered was that this
world of childlike innocence and incontestable truths was threatened by
the very transformations in American life that raised the country to world
power status and economic greatness. Incessant industrialization and urbanization, generated in part by millions of immigrant workers, undermined rural, small-town America, as well as Anglo-Saxon purity and
domination. Under such circumstances, these more immediate memories
merged with the traditional Anglo-Saxon legacy. Together they became an
important component in the mental framework through which officers
perceived and judged the rapidly changing world around them.

In the late nineteenth century, two new elements significantly elaborated
this evolving worldview. Each would validate and embellish the firmly entrenched Anglo-Saxon legacy. The first was an idealistic self-image of America and Americans vis-à-vis the rest of the world. While already existing in
American culture, this now came into clearer focus as America broke from
its isolation to join Europeans in imperialistic excursions. The other element
emanated from the cold, harsh realism of Social Darwinism. Depending
upon the issue, officer thinking might involve one of these new elements as
opposed to the other. But normally they worked in tandem. Now and then,

a few officers might identify evident or potential contradictions; yet most considered Social Darwinism, with its alleged scientific basis, as a vindication of the more idealistic image of American uniqueness.

American Idealism

The debt to England, of course, never faded from recognition. Into the 1930s, officers still attributed America's stability and greatness to the fact that "the national institutions and the individual characteristics of the average citizen are derived more from the Anglo-Saxon than any other racial stock." But there was much more to Americans. With the proper balance between rigidity and malleability, Americans retained the customs and institutions of their forefathers but adjusted them to changing conditions. Stability was preserved while progress ensued as a result of the American historical experience on the new continent.[11] Freedom and individualism, together with the harshness of a frontier life of challenge, danger, and self-reliance, forged an American character greatly improved over that inherited from Britain.

American character, as most officers envisaged it, combined down-to-earth attitudes and mannerisms with a devotion to higher ideals. Unpretentious, "indifferent to formal courtesy" and "saving face," Americans were "abrupt and direct," "very demonstrative," "impatient and impulsive"; they were "not especially excitable" and had a "good sense of humor." "Constructive and inventive," they excelled in originality and technological innovation. Their "patriotism [was] based on historic ideals and belief in American institutions of government." But such ideals were expressed in a way the "common man" could easily grasp, if not always precisely articulate. Thus, respect for "fair play" and the "golden rule" were invoked as often as reverence for higher ideals like "liberty" in describing laudable American attributes.[12]

Americans "never sought war and have only resorted to it when reluctantly forced to do so." Never did they "conquer and rule the people of any other territory against their will; America only desires to help other nations." Their selfless goal in the Philippines was to create for this "alien and recalcitrant oriental people" a government based on the principles that made the United States "foremost among the nations of the earth."[13]

Although there was disillusionment on the part of some during the 1920s and occasionally officers complained that Americans were "too idealistic," the positive identification of the United States with idealism continued throughout the first half of the century. In World War I, "that splendid army of Americans, highly trained, thoroughly equipped and imbued with the highest ideals," wrote General J. S. Kuhn, "appeared in the field to champion the cause of liberty and justice." During the 1950s, General Robert L. Eichelberger could still assert in all sincerity "the Red world had little or nothing to fear from the United States [because of] our decency, our love of truth, [and] our unwillingness to get into war."[14]

To many soldiers, the way they withstood the strains and tensions caused by the horrors of war and the behavior they witnessed among Europeans undeniably verified the nobility of this unique American character. Writing to his former commander in 1921, a medical officer, vacillating between confessing and boasting, acknowledged that "the only thing that saved me in the end was the athletic spirit of fair play learned upon the sport fields of American schools and colleges." Shocked by the actions of soldiers from other civilized countries, he imputed that "brutality is a European Military characteristic. . . . To us this thing is horrible . . . we cannot see things in the same light. We have a really superior humanity than any European can understand."[15]

Some officers naively assumed the rest of the world shared this egotistical perception. On August 17, 1918, General Johnson Hagood wrote in his diary that the French now "regard Americans as the highest type developed by modern civilization. They regard us as idealists who put principle above material, a semi-fanatical people bent on a crusade in which all personal interests must be sacrificed to the accomplishment of an unselfish end." Hagood's vanity appeared boundless, as he declared that "without exception every woman in France with whom I have come in contact regards the American man as superior to the man of her own nationality." Even most French males told him that "they want their boys to be raised according to the American standard."[16]

Within such celebrations of American virtues could sometimes be detected the residue of a puritanical past that partially accounts for a sense of moral superiority. As a boy, General Bradford Chynoweth was "not simpatico" with his Filipino schoolmates, because they "seemed preoccupied with sex and obscenity." Writing to his wife in 1918 about immorality in Paris, Fries remarked that "British officers are perfectly brazen," whereas "our boys are immeasurably better . . . because they are built and taught differently and also because that business [prostitution] is outlawed."[17] Far more indignant were several U.S. military observers in Berlin after World

War I, who, in numerous reports to Washington, poured out their revulsion at the newly unleashed cultural freedom of the Weimar Republic. Unrestrained artistic expression and public toleration of a sexual revolution in values and practice particularly shocked them.

One officer portrayed all of Germany as

> a bursting dam . . . a deluge of reckless living, talking and writing. The motion pictures depict noxious vampire studies of all gradations of nudity. The spoken stage presents a picture of the illicit relations of two women . . . prevalent in man-impoverished Germany. A newspaper is published to further relations between men . . . The cabarets flourish on the nude dancer. The streets at midnight swarm with girls in short dresses. The men dress in gaudy colors, the women undress. Bathing is neglected . . . disease is spreading. . . . Queues line up . . . to sign the separation-from-the-church agreement. . . . Gambling dives are raided so frequently as hardly to arouse interest. The ministers are openly accused of being profiteers.[18]

Religious heritage was an important strand in this image of Americanism. That American moral virtues and ideals were founded upon Christianity was a truism. Officers also presumed any dilution of religious influence in society would begin the dangerous corrosion of the pillars of American civilization from the family and public school to the system of government. Despite lip service to religious freedom and toleration, the deeply held conviction that America was and must remain a Christian nation prevailed. Some spoke of an atheistic radical element destroying "belief in God and country, home and virtue . . . [so as to] overthrow American ideals." These "faithless pariahs" offered nothing "save unbridled license and lust."[19]

Christianity provided a bulwark against this "moral breakdown" by fostering loyalty and obedience to "the basic principles underlying our government." Even when chaplains were absent on the frontier, army posts still evidenced a "moral and religious tone." "The Christian, or rather the devout soldier, will surely do his duty far better than he who has denied all save what he can see and touch." Officers occasionally spoke before religious groups, urging them to "build up Christian character . . . [and continue] the spread of its aims and ideals."[20]

Officers frequently used Christianity to justify and legitimize everything from defensive wars to imperialism, and even a warrior culture. "Civilization has reached the point and the character of our government is such," one officer argued in 1927, "[that] the United States will not—can not—engage in a war of aggression for purely materialistic gain. There must be a moral issue involved, and of such a character as to be predicated upon the teachings of the Christian religion." Without the slightest vacillation, he then claimed "religion formed the basis, and the only basis, of our recent wars."[21]

At the same time, officers condemned pacifist tendencies among Christians. "It is a mistake," said Colonel Benjamin Bailey in public lectures in the 1920s, "to believe that Christianity is incompatible with the military spirit. It is the thought of a decaying people, no longer vigorous thru whose veins red blood has ceased to flow." If this false and dangerous pacifist interpretation of Christianity ever succeeded, it would signal the destruction of "the virtues of courage, patriotism, devotion to home, fireside and native land."[22]

Other officers noted that in the Old Testament, "religious ideas are generally expressed in warlike terms [and clearly] Jehovah is the God of Battle." Basically, "the history of the human race has been, and always will be, a history of battles. When the All-wise creator put the spark in the human soul, in the human body, he created a machine that prospers only by doing." Certainly, "it was the doctrine of extermination that shaped the rise of the Jewish race. . . . Then, as now, the sword was the supreme arbiter of the nations." These officers cited "Christ's cleansing of the temple" and other New Testament references to explain American military actions in terms of idealistic crusades for right and justice; they chastised pacifists for "lacking in moral fiber."[23]

The fates of Western civilization, Christianity, and American military power were inextricably intertwined. As Colonel Bailey reminded listeners, the overwhelming majority of the inhabitants of the world had not achieved the level of enlightenment and civilization of 350 million Christians; thus, pacifism meant certain doom. Blending religious with geopolitical and Malthusian demographic imagery, he prophesied that "if these Christian people allow their military spirit to wane . . . they face the deadly peril of annihilation" by the billions "who have not reached the mental and moral stage that is necessary to insure peace for any extensive period of time." Such self-evident truths required little elaboration for those like General Leonard Wood who considered American imperialism an indispensable defense of both Western civilization and Christianity against biologically and religiously inferior peoples around the globe.[24]

Questions of spirituality, devotion, dogma, or religious rituals had little, if anything, to do with all of this. Whereas Protestantism clearly predominated and anti-Catholic prejudice endured, no specific Protestant denomination overshadowed others; and the officer corps did include a portion of Catholics. Christianity, preferably in Protestant form, meant, in effect, that the Bible and religious tradition were sources of moral values and a code of proper social conduct founded in truth handed down from God. It was a type of pragmatic deism, a civil religion in which Christianity, state, and society were forever intertwined. Others were free to believe and worship as they pleased, so long as they never challenged the Christian monopoly in government and society.

In general, officers lived by a commonly accepted and uncomplicated, essentially unspoken, code of behavior devoid of affected airs. It was a simple vision of human activity with a rather small gray area between the poles of right and wrong. Americans took a stand and did the right thing, without letting pretense or formalities interfere with getting the job done. When necessary, they found a quick solution through justifiable force. These special attributes were often expressed in trite American cultural clichés—the "team player" against the "flashy" one; the "square deal" versus selfishness; or simply the "good sport."

Among these, officers relished, in particular, the cult of manliness and the fist. When asked to speak before the American Legion on a pressing contemporary issue, Colonel Bailey composed an entire lecture with the title "Americanism and 'Guts.'" More than anything else, "guts" best distinguished the real American soldier from other kinds. But this "right kind of Americanism . . . [had] to be bred in him and kept under cultivation daily from cradle to the grave. We have got to start breeding and rearing men who just naturally have: Guts enough to fight for the country whether it is right or wrong."[25]

Living in a cultural milieu that valued a good left hook, officers had a fondness for regaling their readers or listeners with stories in which decisive action precluded conflict or brought it to speedy resolution. In turn, these tales divulged much about the social perceptions of these officers, of what they respected and expected. Revolutionaries could not succeed in the United States, wrote Colonel Gordon Johnston in 1920, because "the bulk of red blooded Americans would snatch a paling from the front yard fence and whang the bunch of them on the head."[26] This philosophy of just "smack[ing] him once and end[ing] it" surfaced in various forms, from a "tall strong Texan corporal" punching the knife-wielding Communist in New York to General Moseley deterring Ku Klux Klan rallies in Illinois by ordering machine guns positioned and ready to fire.[27]

Such decisiveness was certainly the proper response to radicalism, espe-cially if it involved labor or immigrants. Quite simply, the principle was: "[I]f any man hauls down the American flag, shoot him on the spot." Dur-ing labor struggles in 1919, General Leonard Wood supposedly thwarted further disturbances in Gary, Indiana, by a simple blunt warning to a rad-ical editor: "If you utter or publish inflammatory matter tending to stir up these people to the point of where they disregard law and order and resort to violence, you will be promptly suppressed and, if necessary, shot." The circulation of the Wood story into the 1930s indicates how widespread and persistent such attitudes were among officers.[28]

As much as they acclaimed these virtues, officers simultaneously feared that these special American attributes were gradually vanishing. Traditions were being undermined by modern ideas, homogeneity was being threat-ened by immigration, and the physical vitality and virtuous character pro-duced by frontier and rural living were degenerating within a "sedentary" urban, industrial existence. The environment that "bred courage, patience [and] endurance" had disappeared; there were concerns about "effemi-nacy." Although the "real Americans," with the "right stuff," still resided in the small town, a physical and moral breakdown, as well as a crisis of patriotism, seemed to have arisen throughout the nation.

Many felt the army could help reverse a degeneracy caused in part by industrial work and in part by the comforts of a prosperous economy that made Americans soft and self-interested. Articles in the *Infantry Journal* in 1913 left no doubt that prosperity also accelerated "Our Military De-cline." Compulsory military training through a universal draft would re-store the health and stamina of America's youth while teaching traditional values and patriotism. Pondering the future of the country in the midst of crisis in 1919, one officer noted that "the conservatism and steadfastness of our farming classes will hold the ship of state fast. Much may also be expected from the soldier element, 2,000,000 of whom at least have had in-culcated a higher measure of patriotism through their experience abroad."[29]

Although officers perceived themselves as defenders of the American system of government and its way of life, they had a deep-seated mistrust of democracy, especially as practiced in big cities or among non-Anglo-Saxons. Certainly, they were absolutely loyal to the American Constitu-tion and political institutions in whose name they were willing to sacrifice their lives. But while they spoke proudly of democracy as the "only kind of government ... under which the people ... can get what they want," they interpreted it very narrowly. To them, self-government and liberty meant individual freedom, resistance to oppression, rule by law and order, and protection of private property. Many were also convinced that the entire political and legal edifice of the country could only be sustained by preserving the Anglo-Saxon values and attributes of Americans. Any exercise of constitutional rights deviating from "well-established traditions and ideals" was quickly labeled illegitimate and subversive. Reformist political parties advocating social or economic change, as well as labor unions, interest groups, or "organized minorities," had no place in this system; in fact, they threatened it with destruction.[30]

Many officers were sure that "big-city" politics and society spawned the evil of "mobocracy." Urban radicals abused constitutional rights to manipulate the political process to advance their own selfish ends to the detriment of true Americans. The sections on "citizenship" in the widely used 1928 reserve officers' *Training Manual* tellingly defined democracy as

> a government of the masses. Authority derived through mass meeting or any other forms of "direct" expression. Results in mobocracy. Attitude toward property is communistic—negating property rights. Attitude toward law is that the will of the majority shall regulate, whether it be based upon deliberation or governed by passion, prejudice and impulse, without restraint or regard to consequences. Results in demagogism, license, agitation, discontent, anarchy.[31]

Politicians and the press ranked among the most insidious elements precipitating this slide toward anarchy. Epithets such as "[P]oliticians the world over are ready to resort to any means or to give an adherence to any policy that will put them in office and keep them there" suggest both suspicion and contempt. Officers were just as sure that "American newspaper men . . . are frequently biased, many being pink or red" and that "the press [is] the most valuable asset the radical elements have in this country." This required, some officers contended, action "to abridge freedom of the press."[32]

So ingrained were these suspicions that into the 1950s, retired general William D. Connor would still passionately declare that the inherent fatal flaw in democracy was popular government by majority vote. In such a system the demagogue easily ascends to power by irresponsible promises to the 51 percent of voters who are the "lower half of the electorate in intelligence, plus" a few "mildly pink" others. With his blood pressure rising, Connor wrote, "Don't stir me up too much."[33]

In essence, officers in the 1920s and 1930s feared that the urban lower classes, misguided, infected with radicalism, and consisting more and more of non-Anglo-Saxon immigrants, were on the verge of overwhelming traditional society and government. They threatened to turn a stable republic of limited government by responsible leaders into a mobocracy, or worse, to overthrow it by revolution. Officers during the early decades of this century attributed everything from the growth of pacifism to the popularity of communism to "a misunderstanding of American ideals among the very element which now causes our greatest anxiety, the unassimilated immigrant."[34] Foreigners with "unscrupulous ambition for leadership," especially the kind known as "the born talker, writer, and agitator," exploited this situation to further their political aims or foment revolution.[35]

The antiforeign, anti-immigrant paranoia fitted in perfectly with the nativist American propensity for discovering subversive foreign conspiracies lurking behind various societal problems and historical movements. At one point or another since colonial times, international conspiracies of Freemasons, Catholics, Abolitionists, Communists, and others had supposedly been exposed by self-styled guardians of pure Americanism.[36] Following this well-established tradition, several educated officers of high rank and responsibility, particularly among the pre–World War I generation, manifested a marked degree of susceptibility to such beliefs.

The Russian Revolution provided both a stimulus and a rationale for conspiracy-minded thinking. Generals Amos Fries and Eli A. Helmick, inspector general of the army (1919–1927), expounded the theory of Bolshevism as the continuation of an international conspiracy that originated with the European Illuminati of the eighteenth century. They captivated public audiences and readers with chilling accounts of how in pursuit of their Communist goals, the Illuminati incited the great French Revolution of 1789 and "were the influence which led to the bloodshed during the reign of terror," just as a century later, Karl Marx carried on the conspiracy through the "the terrible bloodshed in the Paris Commune after the overthrow of the French Government in 1871." The modern form of this conspiracy was the Communist International of Lenin and Trotsky, from whom no less bloody destruction could be expected.[37]

This legacy partially explains why perhaps the most invidious and pernicious twentieth-century conspiracy theory—the theory of an international Jewish conspiracy—received serious consideration among American military intelligence officers. Already predisposed by a suspicious, antiforeign frame of mind and widely shared assumptions of a beloved America under siege, many officers had little difficulty believing in the nefarious plots of "International Jewry."

Scientific Racism and Social Darwinism

Army officers' attitudes toward "alien" groups in general and Jews in particular were rationalized and exacerbated by the "scientific racism" promoted by Social Darwinism in the late nineteenth and early twentieth centuries. As eclectic as it was broad in scope and content, Social Darwinism had multiple uses and meant different things to various writers. Its most common form denoted the application of Darwinian theory, which explained biological evolution in the natural world, to the study of human history, culture, and society.

As molded by certain sociologists, anthropologists, psychologists, historians, and popular writers in Europe and America, Social Darwinism purported to establish scientifically that various races of humanity had evolved through natural selection into distinct groupings. Each race was the equivalent of plant and animal species in nature. But whereas Social Darwinists originally emphasized that species change by continually adapting to their environment, many others argued that permanent racial features, once evolved, remain impervious to change caused by environmental factors. Some Social Darwinists combined hereditary and environmental theories.[38]

Due to differing genetic makeup or environmental influences, or both, each race was considered inherently different from every other, not only physically but culturally and intellectually as well. The differences between Asians and Europeans in physical stature and appearance were merely the most evident, outward manifestations of deeply rooted biologically inherited and unalterable differences in the way each race thought and behaved. Social values and behavioral characteristics, levels of intelligence and cultural development, civilized and uncivilized peoples, architecture and religion all were attributed (by one Social Darwinist or another) to inherited racial traits passed on genetically from generation to generation.

Neither education nor improved social circumstances could significantly transform those inbred features distinguishing one race from another. A true Social Darwinist would no more expect an African child raised in England to instinctively think and act like an Anglo-Saxon than believe in the possibility of a canary building its nest, feeding its young, and hunting prey after the fashion of a hawk. Nurture, through culture, experience, or environment, could not alter, except superficially, what nature had already determined with firmness.[39]

One Social Darwinist trend explained all human history according to biologically determined levels of intelligence and peculiar innate racial traits that had evolved in particular types of peoples. The existence or deficiency of particular traits divided humanity into superior and inferior races. Those with the right inherited qualities could create higher culture and civilization, whereas others could not. Complementing this interpretation was the older concept of "survival of the fittest," which considered the entire evolutionary process as a harsh, merciless struggle for existence by species against their environment and each other.

In the context of history and society, this meant that all groups, nations, races, and so on were constantly engaged in a struggle in which the fit would survive and the weak perish. Backed up by abundant scientific data and countless publications by prominent biologists, anthropologists, and sociologists, such theorizing allegedly explained the rise and fall of nations, in fact, of whole civilizations. It accounted for the appearance and passing of great historical epochs.[40] But such theories, though bolstering long-standing presumptions of Anglo-Saxon superiority, likewise contributed to the alarm caused by the migration of inferior breeds into the United States.

Among the Darwinian works with a wide readership in Europe and America, William Ripley's meticulously documented 600-page study, *The Races of Europe*, published in 1899, ranked prominently in the minds of Army officers. A professor of economics and sociology at MIT who lectured on anthropology at Columbia University, Ripley espoused the theory that Europeans actually constituted three distinct racial types. Each could be identified scientifically through a cephalic index that measured ratios between breadth and length of a skull. Longheaded types (an index below 75) he labeled dolichocephalic, roundheaded (above 80) brachycephalic, and in-between types (75 to 80) mesocephalic. Dolichocephalic, constituting the Teutonic or Nordic race of Northern Europe, were tall, light-skinned, and light-haired with long faces and narrow noses. The short, stocky, broad-faced, roundheaded brachycephalic race included Southern Germans, Slavs, and Celts, whereas the mesocephalic types were a Mediterranean race with long heads but dark skin and hair.[41]

Ripley's hefty volume seemed to verify claims of a Europe divided into inherently different racial groups rather than one race with diverse cultures. Photographs of carefully measured human skulls, graphs of the cephalic index of MIT students, maps of worldwide race distributions, sketches of racial types, and a vast array of scientific scholarship created the overall contours of the apparent racial reality of the Western world. Into the 1930s, the components and overall vision of Ripley's book were widely accepted as scientific gospel throughout the officer corps and used routinely in analyses of other nations.

The military attaché at the Warsaw embassy in 1921 was well versed in Ripley's craniology, knowing the exact formula for measuring skulls to determine cephalic index and the standard proportions distinguishing dolichocephalic, mesocephalic, and brachycephalic. He thus questioned whether Poles were of an "Alpine race [because] their dark blond hair and complexion, stature, and cephalic index are characteristics of the Slavs as well as of the Alpines." In page after page of statistical data and calculations, he painstakingly explained how the Poles of different classes, regions, and gender varied according to skull type and stature, as well as eye, hair, and skin color. With equal precision, he statistically surveyed the ethnic minorities within Poland after the Versailles Treaty. Carefully delineating the cephalic index of male White Russians (81) from that of Ruthenians (83), he cautioned against confusing these two groups.[42]

Meanwhile, the emergence of social psychology and the Eugenics movement in the late nineteenth century fortified the division of humanity into rigid racial categories. By emphasizing the unalterable nature of innate characteristics inherited from racial forebears, they assisted the advance of racist social and political theories. When British psychologists like William McDougall and William Trotter or American eugenicists like Charles Davenport argued that "great differences between races . . . have been persistent throughout thousands of generations," they referred to much more than physical appearances. To them, "innate tendencies" determined the intelligence, morality, religion, and political institutions of each race. Science had supposedly proven that "Asiatic fatalism" was as inbred as "the negro . . . happy-go-lucky disposition [and] unrestrained emotional violence" or the phlegmatic temperament of the English.[43]

McDougall and Davenport also concurred that since nature had established the "inequality of races," preserving the purity of the higher Nordic race must have absolute priority in this age of mass demographic migrations. Miscegenation, like crossbreeding in nature, produced inferior hybrids and the certain decline of the higher race. The "Nordic type" they wanted so desperately to preserve was, McDougall insisted, an anthropological fact. It was "characterized physically by fair colour of hair, skin, and

eyes, by tall stature and dolichocephaly . . . and mentally by great independence of character, individual initiative, and tenacity of will." Evolving
through brutal Darwinian struggle, it "underwent a prolonged severe
process of . . . group selection" in which its peculiar qualities of body and
intellect ensured its survival and dominance.[44]

In the twentieth century, this superior race was, McDougall warned,
being overcome by the faster-breeding inferior races. In his view, unless
this trend and the collateral problem of interbreeding could be reversed,
"the civilization of America is doomed to rapid decay."[45] Officers who read
these writers took special heed of that warning.

The European social theorist of race degeneration with greatest appeal
to American officers was the turn-of-the-century French thinker Gustave Le Bon. Into the late 1930s, officers used, recommended, and praised
his books more frequently than perhaps any other studies on race, social
psychology, and national character. Le Bon's extraordinary reputation,
within his native France and internationally, rested upon his widely acclaimed prolific publications on group psychology, which also suited the
needs of many elitist and racially minded politicians. A strident racist, anti-
Democrat, and defender of France's military caste, Le Bon postulated the
necessity of maintaining racial purity in order to preclude the unavoidable
decline that occurs through interbreeding.[46]

U.S. officers described Le Bon's *The Crowd* and *Psychology of Peoples*
"as a sort of basic manual," insightful, "profound and accurate." As late as
1928, a committee of officers compared his concepts to Admiral Mahan's
theory of "sea-power," adding that Le Bon "blaze[d] the most certain path
amidst the facts of history and human conduct to some understanding of
the psychological principles that underlay the actions of men in mass or in
national organization." They agreed with Le Bon that "inherited racial and
national characteristics are highly important, [since] there is nothing so
stable in a race as the inherited ground-work of its thoughts."[47] Le Bon's
contention that the stability of British institutions and society could be attributed to the purity of the English race also fitted in quite well with their
cherished notion of Anglo-Saxonism.

Fears of race decline aroused by Le Bon and others were spread and perpetuated within the American officer corps by its own Darwinian theorist,
Major Charles E. Woodruff. Among the extensive writings of this army
surgeon were books entitled *The Effects of Tropical Light on White Men*
and *The Evolution of the Small Brain of Civilized Man*. In his lengthy
magnum opus, *Expansion of Races* (1909), he expounded a grand theory

of human development that rivaled, in tone and anthropological breadth, the master works of Social Darwinist literature. But he humbly remarked in the preface, his theory "merely applies to man the natural laws that are known to govern the spread of all other species of plant or animal."

Writing in the chilling, stark scientific style of the laboratory, Woodruff told a grim tale without "right or wrong." He refused "to hide the awful brutality, suffering, poverty and mortality which have been part and parcel of man's evolution to the present point in which modern civilization makes the suffering of a new kind." A cruel natural world had forced man, like all living organisms, into a ceaseless "struggle for existence" according to the governing law of "survival of the fittest." Woodruff accentuated these points by endlessly interjecting the most horrifying statistics: 7,000,000 Chinese drowned by floods, 1,000,000 killed in an ancient Sicilian uprising, 200,000 starving daily in modern Tokyo.[48]

Woodruff drew analogies with ant colonies and schools of salmon to prove that the perpetual struggle against limited resources and overpopulation forced human societies to customarily use murder, euthanasia, infanticide, and suicide when demanded by "self-preservation." His style of comparison and description is itself illuminating:

> Works on anthropology refer to the universal custom in a certain stage of civilization to kill the infirm, crippled, sick and aged. . . . When a monkey is ill its companions worry it to death or will kill it . . . and in some species they drown the sick by throwing them into streams. . . . In human herds of savages the same law holds good. The natives of Fiji buried their old men alive. . . . In many parts of the world the aged were killed and eaten. . . . Destruction of the aged and infirm was a dire necessity among the Teutons and Slavs, even up into historic times.[49]

Although Woodruff believed these practices had been eliminated in advanced modern civilizations, the brutal Darwinian struggle had not diminished significantly. "Man began his existence by murder of competitors and has continued it ever since, if not one way then in another." Ancient wars were wars for the total physical "extermination of competitors"; war had not disappeared in the modern world, because "the real basis of war—overpopulation" remains an inescapable fact of life. Moreover, war still facilitated the natural selection of the fittest within a given population: "The stag engages in personal combat every autumn and the best fighters survive, the worst are ruthlessly killed. This survival of the best fighters produces warriors by instinct. . . . [And there is] inconsistency in advocating that man should and could repress his nature inherited from untold thousands of ancestors." He chastised critics for "forgetting war and civilization have ever traveled hand in hand, each dependent upon the other, that peace develops the advantages gained by war, and then rots it until another war oxidizes the stagnant impurities."[50]

When humanitarians and moralists cringed at the rawness of this beastly description of human existence, Woodruff had a blunt response: "Ethics never bothers nature."[51]

When Woodruff applied these naturalistic arguments to "higher and lower races of man," he did so as the dogmatic champion of Nordic supremacy. Following the common practice of his day, he used the terms "Nordic" and "Aryan" interchangeably to describe the tall, blond, superior Northern European race responsible for advanced civilization. The source of American culture and greatness, these higher beings still constituted the country's best leadership and its warrior class. Nordics reached heights only by exploiting the lower Alpine and Mediterranean races, whose natural inclination was for manual labor or trade. Throughout history, these Alpine and Mediterranean breeds had, in return, enjoyed some of the benefits of higher Nordic civilization that they otherwise would never have known.

The unabashed manner, bordering on insolence, in which Woodruff described this relationship suggests confidence not only in the scientific validity of such racial interpretations but in an anticipated concurrence among his readers:

> All lower races in civilization, then, are actually a species of animal under domestication, increased in number hugely by the sanitation forced upon them and kept up by the Aryans.[52]

Like many of his era, Woodruff felt compelled to address the bleak, though inescapable, "evidence as to the deterioration of Northern European types in America." The disappearance of the "blond type" and its replacement by "broad-headed Alpines" and dark-skinned Mediterraneans could only be prevented by a continual influx of immigrants from Northern Europe to replenish the Nordic stock and by precluding any inbreeding with the lower European races. Dismissing the very notion of a distinct "American type" of man emerging from the "melting pot," he cited recent eugenic and biological studies to verify that "the history of civilization shows that racial stocks are never mixed with profit."[53]

In fleshing out the fundamental outlines of this racial mosaic, Woodruff was joined by Homer Lea, Madison Grant, and Lothrop Stoddard. The historical panorama they created significantly molded and confirmed the worldview of army officers whose careers extended into World War II and beyond.

On December 7, 1941, wrote retired general Moseley, "I left the radio a minute, went to my study, and took down . . . *The Valor of Ignorance* by Homer Lea." That was Moseley's immediate reaction to the Japanese attack on Pearl Harbor. His former commander, Major General Jesse M. Lee, had given him the book in 1909, and, Moseley recalled, it "made a deep and lasting impression on me. I read it and studied it, carrying it . . . to the Army War College where I went the following year." Moseley found Lea's work replete with "historical facts" about "races, breeding and war that are everywhere in evidence throughout the world today and particularly so in the United States."[54]

Lea's 1909 prediction of a future Japanese attack no doubt explains his renewed popularity in 1941, when even Secretary of War Henry M. Stimson quickly remembered this particular aspect of the book. But many officers, like Moseley, had long been persuaded by Lea's broader wisdom. General Chaffee declared it more important than most military literature. "Masterful, . . . the military and navy . . . owe him a debt of gratitude," stated the *U.S. Cavalry Journal* in 1910. Seven years before Pearl Harbor, George S. Patton had relied upon *The Valor of Ignorance* as an important source for a military report entitled "The Causes of War." It also "formed the bases of plan and counterplan in military and naval circles," noted General Douglas MacArthur's intelligence chief, General Charles A. Willoughby.[55]

Oddly enough, Lea, though often addressed as general and photographed in a military uniform, was never a soldier. A dejected hunchback in chronic pain who died young, he did live out some romantic military fantasies. After associating with revolutionary Chinese students in California, he went to China, where he apparently advised Sun Yat-sen. Lea used his rank of lieutenant general in the Chinese army to establish his "professional" credentials as a strategic military thinker. Whether based on actual experience or only conjured up in his imagination, Lea's works made captivating, though distressing, reading.[56]

The Valor of Ignorance and its sequel, *The Day of the Saxon*, grafted geopolitics onto Darwinist principles to create a grandiose vision of "the rise and decline of nations." Like all human associations, Great Powers were governed by stern biological and natural laws recently uncovered by science. There existed "no line of demarcation between peace and war . . . [since] everlasting struggle forms the necessary *motif* of human aspiration. . . . Nations as individuals exist always in a state of potential combat." It was a cyclical epic of ascendancy to national greatness through war, followed by decline as success and the fruits of victory bred laxity and softness, leaving the old power prey to the newly arising hungry competitor: "In the first struggles of a race the tendency to expand is most dominant. . . . But when expansion, and the military that has made it possible, ceases, then the nation approaches the end of its political existence."

Since Anglo-Saxon Britain and America had passed their expansionist military phases, they stood vulnerable to the inevitable onslaught of more ruthless, militaristic, and potentially stronger imperial Germany and Japan. The United States faced an impending catastrophe because the Anglo-Saxon warrior race that conquered America had turned into an effete, decadent business and industrial population.[57]

Officers retained their fascination for Lea because he illuminated what they had already internalized in their hearts and minds. But Lea the man never impressed them, whereas the pedigrees of Madison Grant and Lothrop Stoddard were impeccable by officer standards.[58] More important, these conservative patricians offered a more complete picture encompassing the danger presented by inferior races and not merely the hazards presented by decadence within the master race or challenges from newly ascending races.

Two of the most influential racist publicists of the twentieth century—Grant and his protégé Stoddard—proudly traced their roots to colonial America. Grant's interests and activities exemplified the intermixture of natural science and historical consciousness that characterized the Social Darwinism of the day. A wealthy Park Avenue resident who belonged to New York's most exclusive social elite, he read extensively, wrote American history, pursued genealogy, and was a charter member of the Society of Colonial Wars. A skilled hunter, amateur naturalist, and chairman of the New York Zoological Society, he was a guiding force behind the development of the Museum of Natural History, where prominent exhibits still bear his name. Through his writings, the racist ideas of many prominent natural scientists, with which he remained closely associated, reached a wide popular audience.[59]

A Harvard Ph.D. and lawyer, Stoddard brought the crusader's zeal to his work. Far more prolific than Grant, he attracted a broader readership for a longer period of time, publishing some twenty books and numerous arti-

cles for *Collier's, Forum,* and the *Saturday Evening Post* between the two
world wars. Too often dismissed as a fringe theorist, the well-connected
Stoddard retained public respect until America's war against Nazism.
Through his books and lectures, Stoddard exercised continuous influence
on the thinking of American officers in the twenty years separating the
two world wars.[60]

Books by Grant and Stoddard had foreboding titles: *The Passing of the
Great Race, The Rising Tide of Color Against White World-Supremacy*
and *The Revolt Against Civilization: The Menace of the Under-Man.* Rife
with the arguments of "natural selection," "survival of the fittest," and
"the supreme importance of heredity," these works argued that

> the backbone of western civilization is racially Nordic. . . . [And] if this great
> race, with its capacity for leadership and fighting, should ultimately pass,
> with it would pass that which we call civilization. It would be succeeded by
> an unstable and bastardized population, where . . . a new and darker age
> would blot out our racial inheritance.[61]

Acknowledging their debt to Ripley's racial study, they depicted the
Nordic as the

> purely European type . . . the *Homo europaeus,* the white man par excel-
> lence . . . [with] blondness, wavy hair, blue eyes, fair skin, high, narrow and
> straight nose, which are associated with great stature, and a long skull, as
> well as with abundant head and body hair.

Together Grant, Stoddard, and Woodruff told a gripping tale of epic proportions, constituting nothing less in scope than a racist history of the
world. The Nordic race appeared on the grasslands of Eastern Europe and
Central Asia about 3,000 years ago, spreading to Greece and India, whose
people and great civilizations were originally Nordic. Over centuries of
brutal warfare, the Nordics were driven back to Western Europe by the numerically larger Mongoloid hordes of Asia. Race mixing on the frontiers
bastardized many Nordics, creating the Slavic races of Eastern Europe and
Russia. Ripley's Alpine and Mediterranean races were likewise "western
extensions of Asiatic subspecies."

During the Middle Ages, Charlemagne abated this Asiatic onslaught
through his Christian empire, "the nucleus of the civilized world of today." On its eastern and southern frontiers, he erected buffer zones against

Asiatic incursions. The culturally "Nordicized" Alpines, Mediterraneans, and Slavs who inhabited these regions benefited from a superior Nordic civilization they could never create themselves. The influx of Nordic blood, leadership, or influence among their ruling classes led to the establishment of political states among these inferior races. These races eventually pushed the "pure Nordic race" back to Northern Europe and England.[62]

But by the time of the modern world, "natural selection" allowed the great Nordic race to reverse this historical trend and acquire world domination. The severity of medieval life and centuries of attacks by "brown-yellow" races had hardened the Nordics, ensuring only the fittest and superior among them would survive. Consequently, the "white man," already possessing "inherent racial aptitudes," "could think, could create, could fight superlatively well." The "redskins and negroes feared and adored him as a god, while the somnolent races of the Farther East, stunned by this strange apparition rising from the pathless ocean, offered no effective opposition." Since "the Nordics are . . . a race of soldiers, sailors, adventurers, and explorers, but above all, of rulers, organizers, and aristocrats," they were well suited for conquest and empire building. "The white man stood indubitable master of the world."[63]

The conquest of the New World by "Protestant Nordics" stood out prominently among the key chapters of this racial epic. "The Indians had been ruthlessly swept aside," since "a few hunting tribes could not be allowed to possess a continent," and a truly great and unique American civilization reached its zenith by the late nineteenth century. Ever since, however, this higher civilization was seriously threatened by the "rising tide of color."

Motivated by illusory democratic ideas of racial equality and lusting after the material rewards of advanced civilization, the nonwhite and inferior white races started revolting while the Nordic race lapsed into decline. Race envy also motivated them (e.g., from time immemorial "members of the colored races . . . regard[ed] the possession of a blonde woman as an assertion and proof of racial equality").

America's "altruistic ideals" and extension of democratic equality to inferior races facilitated its own demise. That "absurd fallacy"—the melting pot—accelerated that disastrous consequence by lowering the higher races forever rather than elevating the inferior ones. For "the offspring [of miscegenation] is a mongrel—a walking chaos, so consumed by his jarring heredities that he is quite worthless. We have already viewed the mongrel and his works in Latin America." Now the United States was being swept "toward a racial abyss." Soon the descendants of the original colonists would be "as extinct as the Athenian in the age of Pericles, and the Viking in the days of Rollo."[64]

When urbanization was added to the equation, it touched a nerve among officers already alarmed by assimilationist, melting-pot philosophies who looked with dread upon America's big cities. Grant, Stoddard, and Woodruff claimed that everywhere Nordics suffered depletion through war, low birth rates, interbreeding, and urbanization. An adventurous class of explorers, pioneers, and warriors, Nordics were first to fight and lead; the "big blond fighting man" sustained greater losses. This "high standard" man, requires "healthful living conditions," which are denied him by industrialization and congested urban existence. In America, the Nordic was being replaced by the short dark Mediterranean and Slavic-Alpine races, better suited genetically for a low standard of existence. "The Nordic native American has been crowded out with amazing rapidity by these swarming, prolific aliens, and after two short generations he has in many urban areas become almost extinct."[65]

To arrest this decay, these theorists favored a racist political agenda to avert miscegenation and end completely the immigration of lower races. The long-term security of civilization also demanded that Nordics in Europe and America cooperate in their common racial self-interest. In this regard, Grant, Stoddard, and Woodruff envisaged a future Darwinist Armageddon reminiscent of Homer Lea's grandiose prophecies of a racial showdown with the "Yellow Peril." And many officers agreed with their prediction that "the Nordics [were] again confronted across the Pacific by their immemorial rivals, the Mongols." The Far East would be the ultimate battleground "between these two major divisions of man for world domination and the Nordic race in America may find itself bearing the main brunt."[66]

Social Darwinism Among the Officers

To the army officers who read these eloquently narrated grand scenarios, their meaning was as self-evident as it was portentous. They accepted their major points as cogent arguments and their detailed descriptions of historical and contemporary racial struggles as accurate depictions of reality itself, as it always had been and always would be.

Those who experienced West Point culture before World War I had direct exposure to Darwinian racist history through several of their assigned readings at the military academy. In their studies of civilization and government, they learned of the "harsh and cruel" struggle for survival through racial conquest and domination. It was also impressed upon them that "superior races" cannot mix with "inferior" ones, for whom "extinction not absorption is the ultimate fate."[67]

Cadets read that the "leading part in the great drama of the world's progress" had always been played by the Aryan branch of the "dominant" white race. The Aryans had reached the point where "the world is now practically subject to their power." The Semitic Hebrews had, of course, contributed the "true religion" of monotheism and its exalted moral code. But otherwise:

> [T]hey have not, like the Aryans, been the planters of new nations; and they have never attained a high intellectual development, or that progress in political freedom, in science, art, and literature, which is the glory of the Aryan nations.[68]

Although some of these racist interpretations might have been offset by progressive historical works added in the early twentieth century, many officers clearly internalized these Darwinian arguments and images.[69] The army propagated these views well into the 1930s. Stoddard's books were standard reading for officers at the Army War College, where a review by one faculty committee referred to his *Racial Realities in Europe* as: "a comprehensive discussion of the ethnological foundation of European populations, describing the migrations and intermingling of the Nordic, Alpine, and Mediterranean races with their resulting effect upon the character of existing nationalities."[70] An army manual titled *Psychology of the Filipino* recommended Stoddard's *Rising Tide of Color* as "well worth reading by American officers, it being their duty to understand the problems of the United States in the . . . Far East and thus prepare themselves to intelligently assist in the solution of these problems."[71]

These were also the authors they read privately and recommended to each other. In 1920, when Colonel Johnston suggested his friend Colonel McCain read a piece by Theodore Roosevelt, the latter replied, "[A]nd so I will just so soon as I finish 'The Day of the Saxon.' You read 'The Passing of the Great Race,' if you have not already done so. I have just finished it! Quo vadis? Quien sabbe?" Twenty years later, General Moseley not only quoted Grant extensively in his memoirs but entitled an entire chapter "The Passing of the Great Race."[72]

Walking among the ruins of ancient Rome in 1919, a troubled General Hagood mused about the barbarian destruction of that great civilization.

He then jotted in his diary: "This, in my judgment, is the danger in which the white race now stands before the yellow. The conflict must come, whether it be in the present century or five hundred years hence." Even years after the devastating defeat of Japan in World War II, Hagood still argued that as a Mongolian race, the Japanese had "a code of ethics different from our own." They remained, as always, "a cruel, treacherous and barbaric people" pursuing slyly the same "five hundred year program to get the white man out of Asia."[73]

This racist political biology permeated the thinking of the officer corps from General Leonard Wood, chief of staff before World War I, down to those writing for military publications or delivering lectures at army institutions. Wood, "a great believer in heredity," found his views readily adopted by younger officers to whom he acted as mentor and who in turn idolized him, for they, too, saw in the natural world a reliable guide to understanding behavior among various human groupings.[74] "Dogs bite with their teeth. Alligators slap with their tails. Wild boars, elephants, rattlesnakes, and other beasts of the field all have their own particular method of making war," wrote Hagood, "but we Americans, in our innocence, expect all the beasts in human form to behave themselves as we do."[75]

Moseley drew a similar naturalistic analogy while lamenting America's social burdens:

> Watch a herd of animals. If a member of the herd becomes unfit . . . the unfortunate is recognized at once and driven out of the herd, only to be eaten by the timber wolves. That seems hard—but is it, in fact? The suffering is thus limited to the one. The disease is not allowed to attack the others . . . With us humans, what we call civilization compels us to carry along the unfit in ever increasing proportions.[76]

General Connor also relied on such illustrations to explain natural selection and survival of the fittest through "intelligence and strength." He asked his fellow officers "to remember the monkeys in the Philippines and how they grabbed food and filled their mouths and pouches; if you remember how your dog carried off a bone or everything he can grab and goes off and buries it [this pertains to] every other form of animal life, whether it be fowl or quadruped—of fishes I do not know—but right down to your own dear children."[77]

Before World War I, writers for the *Infantry Journal* and the *Journal of the Military Service Institution* popularized the "significance" of "Darwinian theory," particularly the connection between "natural selection" and "race struggle." Primitive man "killed and preyed upon the weak in order that he might live; nature had taught him that life was continual warfare, in which the fittest survived." Brutally, he acquired "by force, wealth and power." Modern man "still follows the instinct to beat down his opponent," because the "great and immutable . . . law of self-preservation" will "always govern man." Indeed, "war is but . . . an agent of progress . . . in the development of civilization."[78]

Through such Darwinist spectacles, officers viewed and analyzed the peoples of the world. "Scientific theory" had validated for them hierarchies of superior and inferior racial traits, including "superior mental and moral qualities." Natural selection had permanently elevated whites above non-whites, as "in succession the black, brown, and yellow races have succumbed to the white, which now dominates, the exemplar of the highest type of civilization yet evolved."[79]

"The Filipino lives in a mental world of his own," stated an interwar army manual. "His mind is different in quality and process from that of the American. This quality of mind is crystallized into racial character. Both are relatively low grade according to the white man's standards." The environmental impact of civilization through education and the imposition of American culture could little alter these "inherent," "ineradicable" characteristics of these people. "They are faults of heredity, and hence cannot be corrected beyond certain points by any of the stimuli so effective in energizing the white race to military act and industrial progress."[80]

As late as 1968, retired general Albert C. Wedemeyer told of how fragile the veneer of civilization was among even educated Filipinos, who at the first chance quickly reverted back to their natural "rung in the ladder of progress which was just one huckleberry bush above the chimpanzee." He went on to describe his Negrito guide as a "dog," similar to the one he had back on the farm.[81]

One of the scientific explanations for this permanent subordinate position for Asiatic races was their limited mental capacity and "brain growth." Using statistics on brain weights and measurements gathered by the Japanese themselves, the American military attaché in Tokyo reported in 1920 that "the adolescence of the Japanese is not only somewhat earlier than that of the Nordic race, but the development of the brain capacity apparently terminates sooner."[82]

Comparable scientific data were employed to confirm that Northern Europeans were by nature superior to Southern and Eastern European types.

The Italians and French were inferior in "brain characteristics" and "intelligence," though not in artistic creativity, to the British and Americans. The "dark races" were generally noted for their "submissiveness to authority" and becoming "hysterical under excitement."[83] Russians were also "inferior mentally and morally." The infusion of Mongol blood meant that the "racial characteristics of the Russian [had become] fundamentally more Asiatic than European." Consequently, the Russian suffered from "fatalism, mysticism, lack of culture and reasoning logic."[84]

Despite the disdain for the "Hun" or "Boche" so widely evident among officers during and after World War I, there lingered a respectful, in some cases even admiring, attitude toward the Germans. Like other Northern European nations, their negative traits were counterbalanced by the inherent high intelligence and attractive physical features provided by their "race and environment." Therefore, although the Germans (and the British also) still had to be handled as potential enemies, they remained racially, nonetheless, Anglo-Saxon kin.[85]

To officers trained in these ways of thinking, history appeared an unending saga of rising and falling nations and races, "all engaged in a desperate struggle for advancement or for sheer existence." They cited Woodruff's *Expansion of Races* and the demographer Malthus about the interaction of "economics and biology" as the real underlying source of political conflict. Whether at the level of the individual, small village, or modern nation-state, all "life is a struggle for existence." The "progress of civilization has not seemed to affect these primitive relations," because the primary motivating factor—the "instinct of race preservation"—remained immutable. But "to preserve the race and have it occupy its allotted place in the world, there must be expansion. This expansion—following the birth rate—is controlled by the food supply."[86]

Here was the unsolvable dilemma at the root of most wars. The earth contained insufficient land and resources to accommodate "the indefinite expansion of all competing races." Few officers believed that population control would work or that nations and races could ever be satisfied with their territorial possessions. It was, after all, a "biological fact that when any body stops growing it starts dying"; and the "immutable law of life [dictates] that when a nation or individual ceases to grow it starts to die."[87] In the larger scope of human history, it was simply a question of "which race shall stay to spread its own peculiar civilization and religion at the expense of the others?" Although by the early twentieth century, America's "area of inexhaustible free lands for a growing population has passed forever," the country's "greatest danger is not our own expansion of population." The real challenge would be defending "ourselves against the other nations who have such serious problems."[88]

Although a strong army and navy, supported by industrial power and an efficient system of national defense, could effectively repulse overt challenges by other states, arms alone furnished little protection against a more insidious threat to the survival of the race, for the Old World, East as well as West, incessantly discarded its excess population on the United States. This threatened a now fully settled continent with oversaturation and, perhaps even more destructive, raised the real prospect of race bastardization. Degeneracy among the native stock compounded the problem, since "our birth rate is dropping and our people have passed from a hard agricultural people to a soft nation of city dwellers." Some worried also that in the South, the "old 100-per-cent-American stock survived only in the mountains and in the county districts," while others "deplored the fact that the old stock of New England was rapidly disappearing."[89]

As a matter of course, the very idea of interbreeding with nonwhite races was universally condemned as unnatural. "The white man by instinct does not choose to associate with others of different instincts," wrote retired general Edward M. Almond in 1970. In the natural world, "millions of examples . . . from the mollusk to the human" show that "different breeds are inherently different":

> A blooded race horse is just as different "by nature" from the plow horse as the eagle or the hawk is from the blue bird. . . . [H]ow long would a blue bird associate with an eagle or a hawk—they never do! . . . Why does the deer not seek out the society of oxen?[90]

General Leonard Wood probably spoke for the entire officer corps when he wrote to Theodore Roosevelt in 1905 that "we have enough national weakness and humiliation from the Negro to avoid further trouble by the introduction of races [i.e., Asians] with which we can never mingle." America, Wood demanded, must remain a "white man's country," if we are not to turn into a "breed of mongrels." Putting this question in historical perspective two decades later, General Bailey remained equally adamant against yielding any ground: "To submit passively to the unrestricted immigration of the yellow race to Anglo-Saxon areas would be to betray the very principles upon which our forefathers founded this nation."[91]

But in the early twentieth century, casting the assimilation of nonwhites beyond even the pale of discussion still left the question of "how to absorb the essentially different stock from South and East Europe."[92] So long as these non-Nordic Europeans were considered inferior, they too represented the threat of mongrelization. Although almost without exception officers agreed that immigration from areas other than Northern Europe must be tightly restricted and maybe ended altogether, they differed over possible solutions to the problem of aliens already residing in the United States.

Some adhered to an earlier version of Social Darwinism, in which organisms evolved as they adapted to their environment. At least this offered hope that immigrants would gradually lose their detrimental mental and physical traits as the new conditions of America molded them over generations. "Education and environment" might transform these unwanted, even despised, inferior people into something more akin to the higher American type and assimilate them into the body politic by imbuing them with Anglo-Saxon values and mentality.[93]

But many, perhaps most, officers doubted both the desirability and scientific feasibility of altering the physical or behavioral essence of groups through environmental impact. Working under the omnipresent shadow of Le Bon and Woodruff, they could hardly forget the "scientific fact" that racial characteristics of mind and body were both inherited and immutable. The chances of Russian Jews in New York being behaviorally transmuted into Anglo-Saxons were as slim as tigers losing their stripes due to changed environment.

Equally distressing, respected scientists and theorists of the day had claimed that hybrids usually produced inferior, often useless, offspring. Race mixing, rather than merely absorbing the lower into the higher form, would actually drag the higher down to some mediocre level where the special characteristics that accounted for its prior greatness would be diluted or lost altogether. In humans, this also meant confused, volatile types. An army report in 1935 presented the Russians as a prime example of a case where interbreeding between white and Oriental races had produced "contending strains within the individual resulting in a mass of mental contradictions." Russians thus vacillated between "submissiveness" and "arrogance," "meekness and brutality," "communism and extreme individualism." This confusion explained why Russia lacked "military or industrial efficiency." Viewed from any angle, miscegenation meant mongrelization and decline, pure and simple.[94]

Since Le Bon had attributed the stability of English institutions to the purity of Anglo-Saxon blood, officers in the early years of the century likewise concluded that miscegenation held disastrous political ramifications for America. "Nations of British descent," they concurred, "have been remarkably free from revolution," whereas "peoples of mixed breeds notoriously are unstable" and have an inherited psychological predisposition toward revolution. Like the contemporary theorists they read, officers often cited the specious relationship between miscegenation and political instability in Latin America to forewarn the United States of what its future could hold. Americans would be reduced to Stoddard's vision of "a walking chaos" of hybrid races, followed, no doubt, by the erosion of their democratic form of government and conservative social institutions. Then their country would also vacillate between the anarchy and dictatorship typical of "mongrel-ruled tropical America."[95]

Using detailed "anthropometric statistics" on the "Physical Proportions of the American Soldier," Major Henry S. Kilbourne warned his colleagues in the Association of Military Surgeons in 1898 of the broader historical consequences of the new immigration. The physical power of a race was, he confidently assured them, tied to stature, and Americans were a composite of the "homogeneous and compatible" taller races of northern Europe. As such, Americans were superior to others in overall physical efficiency. But, he added:

> Not so the swarthy, low-browed and stunted peoples now swarming to our shores. Absorbed into the body of the people these multitudes must inevitably evolve an inferior type.... [And] the loss of an inch in stature might bring in its train the loss of national ascendancy. Let us take care then that the State shall suffer no injury.[96]

Kilbourne's warning would be echoed in the ensuing decades—particularly with respect to European Jews.

The "Jewish Threat"

Within the evolving worldview of the officer corps, Jews had already acquired a unique place before the advent of Social Darwinism rationalized and deepened anti-Jewish prejudice. Since the Middle Ages, anti-Semitism had been an integral part of Western culture. Negative images of Jews had for centuries become ingrained in many different facets of European society—from religion to economics and politics. When transferred to the New World, these prejudices mingled with new experiences and problems.

American folklore, religious teaching, and an array of published works combined with the European heritage to create a preconceived notion of Jews as an alien, inherently problematical force. Although all Eastern and Southern European immigrants were subjected to various forms of prejudice, Jews became targets of especially harsh treatment, since they supposedly embodied most clearly those characteristics deemed dangerous to established American society and tradition.[97]

Nonetheless, the American attitude toward Jews has been quite ambivalent. Noteworthy characteristics associated with Jews had their counterparts in contemptible ones. For Christian Americans, Jews were both the great nation of prophecy and the Old Testament (God's Chosen People) and Christ killers who still reject the true faith. They were viewed as a people whose hard work and intelligence had brought them economic prosperity; yet many questioned whether they had earned this success honestly. In the popular mind, "swindle" and "Jew" became almost synonymous.[98]

This ambivalence occasionally manifested itself in good Jew–bad Jew allusions. More tolerant Americans explained perceived negative Jewish traits either as reflective of only certain Jews who unfairly tainted their entire people or as remnants of Old World Jewish culture dissipating under the progressive forces of assimilation. Others drew a distinction between educated, Westernized Jews (good citizens of proven loyalty) and uncouth, backward, often poverty-stricken, Eastern Jews, hopelessly beyond the pale of modern civilization and Western values. The Easterners perpetually spawned immeasurable social and political problems, whereas the well-established assimilated German Jewish community in New York offered a model of what miraculous transformations the "melting pot" of Americanization could accomplish. The latter had abandoned Old World culture along with most traditional Jewish ways; they dressed, spoke, and acted like "real Americans" in every respect. Only their private religious faith of Judaism separated them from the dominant culture of Christian America. Still, persistent social discrimination against assimilated Jews indicates that suspicions about even the "good Jew" had hardly vanished from the American mind.[99]

Between 1881 and World War I, those Jews seen as the very physical embodiment of Old World stereotypes were immigrating to America by the millions. These despised Eastern Jews, so different in appearance, speech, and behavior, not only confirmed but augmented negative perceptions already evident in that era. So distinct and offensive were these immigrants that certain German-American Jews worried about being identified with them or wondered whether the very presence of such vulgar masses might engender the European variety of vocal, political, and violent anti-Semitism from which America had generally been spared. Most army officers, like most Americans, definitely saw a stark contrast between themselves as a unique people with high ideals and almost every aspect of the newcomers.[100]

The emotional intensity of this cultural clash was vividly displayed in *Old World in the New* by Edward Alsworth Ross, a University of Wisconsin sociologist and leading advocate for immigration restriction. Published in 1913, his influential book depicted in word and pictures the coming catastrophe of an America overrun by racially inferior people. Americans faced race "extinctions" comparable to what had caused the fall of ancient Rome. This virtual bible of anti-Semitic stereotypes abundantly illustrated the "Jewish problem," with Ross's reputation as a prominent progressive adding scholarly credibility.[101]

Ross conveyed a menacing specter of throngs of illiterate Jews, whose "Ghetto life . . . bred in them a herding instinct." The very "inborn love of money-making [that] leads them to crowd into the smallest quarters" left little hope they could ever leave the squalid and congested big-city slums into which immigrants poured. It was a self-imposed "hideous nightmare of dirt, disease, and poverty," spawning countless social ills burdening the country. "East European Hebrews have no reverence for law, . . . pursue Gentile girls . . . and lower standards wherever they enter." Upon reaching "here, [these] moral cripples . . . [with] a monstrous and repulsive love of gain . . . rapidly push up into a position of prosperous parasitism." Avoiding manual labor, they live off the production of others and have a tendency to take over professional and economic fields. And they contribute more than their fair share to the moral decline of the big cities. "The murders, hold-ups and burglaries committed in the Jewish section by Jewish criminals" underscore that "with his clear brain sharpened in the American school, the egoistic, conscienceless young Jew constitutes a menace."[102]

Ross's section "American Blood and Immigrant Blood" matched the historical perceptions of the majority of army officers. From the higher type of Northern European stock evolved the "pioneering breed," known for its strength, beauty, and character, whereas recent immigrants were "oxlike men, . . . descendants of those who always stayed behind." They had narrow, sloping foreheads and small craniums ("the average Hebrew woman in New York is just over five feet"). "In every face there was something wrong. . . . [S]o many sugar-loafed heads, moon-faces, slit mouths, lantern-Jaws, and goosebill noses that one might imagine a malicious jinn had amused himself by casting human beings in a set of skew-molds discarded by the Creator."

"On the physical side," Ross wrote, "the Hebrews are the polar opposite of our pioneer breed." They are "undersized and weak-muscled . . . shun bodily activity and are exceedingly sensitive to pain." By comparison, the American type is "of great physical self-control, gritty, uncomplaining, merciless to the body through fear of becoming 'soft.' To this roaming, hunting, exploring, adventurous breed what greater contrast is there than the denizens of the Ghetto."[103]

Ross described the Northern "blond" type from whom Americans stemmed as morally superior "truthtellers" possessing an "innate ethical endowment." Jews he depicted with phrases such as: "[H]e can scent his profit," "[s]ubtle Hebrew brains," or "keen-witted Jews." In contrast to the fair-minded, self-sacrificing American, "the last thing the son of Jacob wants is a square deal." Whether from a physical, behavioral, or moral standpoint, "you can't make boy scouts out of the Jews."[104]

Ross provided illustrative photographs of black-suited Russian Jewish men at Ellis Island, with morose faces, sullen eyes, and huge dark beards. These pictures indeed conveyed the image of totally alien, mysterious, and inferior, though no less insidious, beings incompatible with Americans and their way of life. He further enhanced the effect with maps detailing how they were forcing the "native white stock" out of the very Eastern regions of the original thirteen colonies.[105]

Most officers would certainly concur with this pessimistic prognosis of the relationship between the Jewish question and the future of America. While undoubtedly sharing the ambivalent attitude most Americans had toward Jews, officers as a rule accentuated the negative. They displayed their tolerance and fairness by drawing distinctions in their language and analyses between the "high class Jew" or "fine type of Hebrew" and the "low class Jew." They might also thereby immunize themselves against the stigma of anti-Semitism. But references to "the vulgar, characteristically Jewish type" far outnumbered such cautious attempts at balanced judgments.[106]

The distribution of such remarks throughout the historical documentation further establishes the common perspectives on Jews across the officer corps. Reports written years apart by U.S. military attachés spread across Europe showed amazing similarities in perception and terminology. They identified and evaluated the activities of "the hard headed, calculating Jew[s]" exploiting "fertile fields for their shrewd and keen qualities," or "the impulsive Jewish publicist [who] is naturally good at polemics." Easily recognizable by his "appalling cynicism and maliciousness," "egotism and gross materialism," and "unscrupulous sensualism," the Jew appeared as the reverse mirror image of the noble American type.[107]

Warnings about the serious implications of Jewish success always followed acknowledgments of positive attributes. It was conceded that hard work, together with "the qualities of diligence, economy, [and] organization . . . make the Jew great in business." However, "as constructive and necessary are the Jews" economically, wrote the military attaché in Hungary, "so destructive and repellent are they as a social factor." Besides their usual repulsive characteristics, they use profiteering and opportunism to usurp control wherever they gain a foothold. Unless someone "put[s] a stop to their dangerous expansion," Jews will monopolize entire economic and professional spheres to the detriment of the native inhabitants who tolerated their advance.[108]

Reservations about Jews existed among officers at home as well. In a 1927 public lecture entitled "Correct Human Relations," General Eli Helmick made Jewish history sound like a morality play of tragic decadence and decline. While accepting "The One True God," Old Testament Jews otherwise retained those cruel practices that kept ancient man close to his "animal nature." "Human life was held in little esteem; slavery was common; wars were frequent, and were conducted with great cruelty." Monotheism uplifted the Jews spiritually and intellectually, but "prosperity and power" led to "weakness and corruption . . . and disobedience to God's laws." After military defeats and captivity, these fallen Jews "to this day have been wanderers throughout the world—a people with no national organization." Redemption for civilization came with Christianity and its "Golden Rule," to which "more than anything else, we are indebted for the progress man has made."[109]

To army officers, America was unique, Anglo-Saxon, and Christian (essentially Protestant) in genesis, foundation, and historical evolution. They believed it must stay that way. Exclaimed retired general Fries in 1950, "Without any 'ands, ifs or buts,'" the U.S. government was the finest in human history. He often pointed out that the "very few Jews" in colonial America had no "particular influence" in the Declaration of Independence, the war against England, or creating the constitution.[110] Not only did Jews contribute little to America's heritage, but they were generally a detriment to it and its religious foundations. Despite the "unprecedented religious liberty" Jews could enjoy in America, wrote another officer: "[W]hen they are in the majority they show a tendency to persecute Gentiles and change the Christian customs of the land. Schoolteachers have referred slightingly to Christ. Such intolerance is already creating intense indignation and may cause political disabilities."[111]

The convergence of these attitudes with concerns about cultural decline in America's urban centers led military attachés in the 1920s to state bluntly "that this Jewish movement to America presents a serious menace to our civilization." "By nature inclined to business," Jews avoid agriculture and the manual labor necessary for building the country. Congregating in overcrowded cities, they "form filthy Jewish quarters" as horrendous as the disgusting Jewish ghettos in Europe. Their unsanitary habits make them "carriers of typhus and other diseases."[112] Some officers complained that "daily we are nauseated with the stench arising from the parasitical mob that regards this land not as a great republic whose resources are to be developed and conserved, but as a place in which to batten and grow fat."[113]

Despite possible contradictions, these same officers believed the disease-ridden, congested slums were the breeding ground of an assortment of radical movements. Officers envisaged "an unwieldy multitude . . . of frenzied masses of low brows" subverting the nation with anarchy and socialism.[114] The earlier fear was of old Jewish wealth unduly influencing or usurping American power from the top. Now the apprehension was that beginning in ghetto streets, the newly arriving lower-class Eastern European Jews would destroy the system from below. The concept of the Jew as radical agitator and revolutionary took its place alongside the more traditional Shylock image or its modern equivalent, the exploitive, unprincipled Jewish capitalist.

In general, Jews were depicted as the antithesis of the "great Nordic race which founded and built up our civilization and who settle as small farmers and quickly become good, clean, conservative, hardworking American citizens, willing to fight and, if necessary, die for their adopted country."[115] Here, once again, resonated age-old suspicions of questionable Jewish loyalty. It revived accusations of the "international" orientation of Jews and their allegiance only to other Jews, no matter where they reside or what citizenship papers they might hold.

That reproach had particular saliency for military men. When added to other suspicions—Jews as physically weak, selfish, dishonorable, cowardly, and so forth—it held out the prospect of a major problem in wartime. Those misgivings were enhanced by the belief that "thousands of the foreigners who come to this country do so to avoid military duty abroad. The patriotism of a man who expatriates himself for this reason is doubtful. . . . [And] by what means are you going to coax these people to die for a country which they regard only as a refuge against military duty." Failure to rally to the cause when called, like any hint of antimilitary attitude, would, of course, offend anyone with an officer's avocation. But probably just as important, the American cultural panorama simply did not include the image of Jews as soldiers. As retired general Moseley boasted in 1947, "[W]hen I was a Cadet [at West Point], there was one Jew in my class, a very undesirable creature, who was soon eliminated."[116]

When the American Jewish Committee (AJC) complained about anti-Semitism in the army before World War I, a colonel unleashed a barrage of epithets against its director, Louis Marshall: Jews like Marshall had the hereditary instinct for money but knew nothing about the military. Put bluntly, "the Jew never was and never will be a soldier." A lowly degenerate "dirty malingerer" who avoids danger, the Jew is a "disgrace to the flag" of the very country that has given him "too much freedom." Constituting the biggest prostitutes, pimps, and criminals in America, Jews were the only people in the "world without moral honor or character."[117]

Until March 1918, the Army Manual of Instructions for Medical Advisory Boards stated clearly

> The foreign born, and especially Jews, are more apt to malinger than the native born.[118]

And after the war, officers continued to report that Russian Jews

> came to this country for the purpose of making money and oppose Military or any other service which is not profitable to themselves. A large number intend to return to Europe after enriching themselves in this country and resent any interruption of their prosperity.[119]

Major J. S. Richardson informed General Staff officers in 1920 that New York divisions had caused the most severe troubles. They had large numbers of foreign born, and "many of the drafted men, mostly of the prevailing New York Semitic persuasion, contrived to slide into the Quartermaster or Medical units" to get soft jobs and avoid combat. To escape duty and danger, other Jews used the offices of prominent legislators; "when this failed, occasionally they would become conscientious objectors."[120]

Recalling his World War I experiences, Colonel Truman Smith, who later held the crucial post of military attaché to Nazi Germany, described the "volunteers from rural Pennsylvania" and even Cajun conscripts from "western and rural Louisiana" as "good soldiers." These "reliable" patriotic men contrasted sharply with the "Jewish and Italian soldiers from New York City's 77th," among whom "were some good men," but for the most part they were a "problem." As combat approached, the "New Yorkers disappeared in droves," returning "days or weeks later, when . . . front-line duty" had ended. Fortunately, America had "Kansas and Nebraska farm boys" during the "fierce fighting of the Meuse-Argonne." These "stolid, loyal, ever reliable" men "from our prairies stood up without flinching to German shell and machine gun fire."[121]

Officers differed over whether disloyalty, un-Americanism, or other repugnant traits of these "undesirables" were permanent features or could be rectified through assimilation. Given the history of Americanization of European immigrants, some officers expected that, over time, the newest wave could be inculcated with the proper ideals and successfully integrated into the existing culture. Criticizing those exploiting "racial and religious prejudices," one officer postulated that "even such poor material as the Russian Jew might lose his offensive characteristics in a few generations if deprived of Yiddish newspapers and rabbis." But this required that "all foreign activities should be sternly repressed and the objectors assisted to leave the country."[122]

Far more prevalent, though, was the view that "these Jews do not 'melt' in the 'melting pot' and will, later, form a troublesome racial minority." Many officers, in fact, questioned the very idea of absorbing these particular people. Assimilation could be a monumental mistake, since it would dilute and bastardize the pure American stock they wanted to preserve. "The infusion of alien blood" in itself contributed greatly to "the degeneracy of the American Republic."[123]

These anti-assimilationists found powerful support in Social Darwinism, the harsh reality-conscious component of the officer worldview that counterbalanced the more idealistic elements. Of all the polluting blood migrating from Europe in the early twentieth century, that of the Jews caused officers the most apprehension. Contemporary racial theorists whom the officers read provided ample evidence that Jews possessed undesirable and problematic genetically fixed physical and mental traits. "The Semitic stock," wrote McDougall, "though widely scattered, seems to present certain constant peculiarities . . . [of] innate racial difference" that can "be accounted for in no other way. These existed in all communities of similar racial stocks, in spite of similarities or differences of history and of present conditions."

To Ripley, genetic traits explained why Jews everywhere congregated in cities and invariably displayed a strong aversion to agriculture, manual labor, and "physical exercise or exertion in any form," preferring "to live by brain not brawn." "Narrow-chested and deficient in lung capacity," Jews were "distinctly inferior to Christians in lung capacity, which is generally an indication of vitality." This physical degeneracy, caused by horrible "sanitary and social environment" over a long period of time, had become an inherited "unalterable characteristic of this peculiar people."[124]

Anti-Semitism, Ripley argued, stemmed primarily from the well-founded fear that Western Europe and America would eventually be overrun by these degenerate types. "Germany shudders at the dark and threatening cloud of population of the most ignorant and wretched description which overhangs her eastern frontier." Ripley's warning that this, too, "is our American problem," sounded as portentous as any specter raised by Grant or Stoddard: "This great Polish swamp of miserable human beings, terrific in its proportions, threatens to drain itself off into our country as well, unless we restrict its ingress."[125]

In *Expansion of Races*, Woodruff argued that Jews were "useful and beneficial when scattered and few, but parasitic in large concentrated numbers." One of the "lower races" domesticated by Aryan civilization, Jews were a necessary urban commercial group of "born buyer[s] and seller[s]—the survivor of the fittest types—of a long process of selection, during which only traders could survive." These same traits, however, of inherent "selfishness" and physical weakness make them, at the same time, a liability to the host society—for Jews are by nature both unwilling and unable to share the burden of national defense or take up arms "to fight for liberty."

As a proud military officer, Woodruff exhibited particular passion when explaining: "[T]he Jew as a race will not fight for its existence, but he demands that other races shall sacrifice themselves for him and preserve him. He now exists because he has been protected by the soldiers of the world from massacre. He will not volunteer as a soldier except in small numbers—a very small percentage of the race." Implying cowardice as well as slyness and duplicity, Woodruff charged that the Jew "survives by the spilling of blood of his protectors."[126]

Most of what filled the pages of this volume completely overshadowed Woodruff's reluctant concession that "many Jews do take an active interest in politics and war [and] many of our best statesmen and soldiers have been Jews." To him, Jews still "do not yet perform their share of civic duties"; they most likely cannot or will not ever do so. He even recounted the story of New York Jews supposedly so "terror stricken" during the Spanish-American War they fled inland, though no hint of danger existed. Woodruff's demeaning mental image of the weak, cowardly Jew was shared by many fellow officers then and in coming decades.[127]

Woodruff's naturalistic analogies were, especially in retrospect, nothing less than alarming:

> The Jew, then, is a typical illustration of a commensal race, welcomed as long as he renders a returning benefit but driven out or killed off as soon as he becomes so numerous that he is a harmful parasite and a national disease. European nations have repeatedly undergone a process of disinfection in this regard. The same law applies to the Jew as applies to a bacillus or any other organism which may be beneficial if few and in place, but deadly if numerous and out of place. . . . [J]ust as soon as he becomes so numerous as to be an economic disease he is eradicated. The persecution of the Jew, then, is and always has been a natural law, because it is necessary for the survival of the supporting organism. . . . It is not a persecution of the Jew as Jew, but an extermination of an invading disease.[128]

Woodruff saw America quickly approaching the point where the invading disease threatened the nation. With Jews already controlling trade and railroad centers in several major cities, Jewish "parasitism and ethnic disease" now posed its most crucial and immediate danger to New York. That great metropolis had become "another Poland," where hundreds of thousands of Jews lived in abject poverty within unsanitary and congested slums. Among this filth, Jews lost respect for religious and social conventions; they thrived on vice, crime, degradation, and perversity to such an extent that an American brand of anti-Semitism would surely result, rivaling any experienced in Europe. Even for his own sake, "the safety of the Jew," Woodruff concluded, "depends upon [his] being in a controlled minority."[129]

The genetic explanation for the incompatibility of Jewish traits and American ideals and interests acquired additional reinforcement from the "Khazar Jew" thesis espoused by Grant, Stoddard, Clinton S. Burr, and others. As the theory goes, Eastern European and Russian Jews were not descendants of Old Testament Semites. They were an Asiatic race manifesting the racial inferiority and peril this implied for Nordic thinkers. The ancestors of the "Ashkenazim or ghetto Jews" migrated to Eastern Europe in the eighth century, where they converted to Judaism the Mongol Khazars dominating the region. Over the centuries, Jews, Asiatic Khazars, and Slavs thoroughly interbred until not "a single drop of the Old Palestinian, Semitic-speaking Hebrew blood" remained. The hybrid Khazar Jews embodied all the "defective" traits racial anti-Semites traditionally associated with Jews. Physically frail with brachycephalic skulls typical of Alpine and Asiatic races, they were "selfish," "uncouth," and cunning, though "far less intellectual" than other Jews. And their immutable moral flaws and hygienic deficiencies would repulse any Westerner.[130]

When requested, American officers could readily furnish meticulously documented racial studies on the Eastern Jews, replete with statistical data. Reporting on "ethnographic characteristics" in 1921, the military attaché in Warsaw attested that "the Semitic race [in Poland] has separate anatomical characteristics; they are all brachycephalic; the West Jews show the influence of their racial sojourn in Western Europe."

In an analysis whose detail on Poland rivaled Ripley's work on European races, this officer documented with precise scientific measurements the minor differences in skull shape and physical stature of Polish, Lithuanian, and Galician Jews, men as well as women. The average cephalic index of the male "Polish type Jew" was 82, with a height of 162 centimeters, as compared to a "C.I." of 85 for a Galician Jewish female, whose height measured 152 centimeters. Lithuanian Jewish males, on the other hand, measured 81 in C.I. and 163.5 cm in height, and so on for other groups. When measured against the formula for determining cephalic indices, these data clearly established that Eastern Jews were brachycephalic (81 to 85.4) as compared to the dolichocephalic Nordic race (75.9). With reasonable exactitude, he could also state that "about 57% of the Jews are brunette, 39% mixed, 10% blond. 84% of the men, 81% of the women, have dark hair."[131]

The Khazar theory introduced a genetic dimension to the existing tendency to distinguish between good Jews (acceptable loyal citizens) and bad Jews (inassimilable alien threats). In sharp contrast to the Asiatic Khazar Jews, German and Spanish Jews of earlier migrations to America over previous centuries at least belonged to a "subspecies of the Mediterranean race." Free of the ghetto Jew's physical and moral debilities, these Westernized types formed a Jewish "aristocracy" with proven patriotism and "an enviable record in the United States." Burr, Grant, and Stoddard never overlooked an opportunity to emphasize that these "true Jews" or "high class types" themselves limited their association to the inferior Easterner solely to religious and humanitarian affiliations. They otherwise assiduously avoided these "despised" and "resented" creatures. Unlike the unwary Nordics, too often negligent in protecting their "racial heritage," the pure-blooded Jews forbade their children even to fraternize with these "kikes."[132]

This racial partitioning of Jews had very diverse, though not necessarily disconnected, ramifications for anti-Semitic theorists and officers affected by their ideas. It clarified how American Jews like Bernard Baruch could achieve prominence through public service, including national defense, and have ties with certain military leaders. Those officers who knew through personal experience or reputation the undeniable patriotism and accomplishments of fellow officers of Jewish descent could in this way likewise reconcile fact and lingering prejudice.

Although this distinction indicated greater acceptance and tolerance of older, assimilated Jewish communities, it simultaneously promoted intolerance, even aggression, against the millions of newcomers. In the process, it furnished relentless anti-immigrant crusaders with protection against the stigma of anti-Semitism. Several writers, and subsequently some officers, invoked the defense that "anti-Semitism in America is a misnomer [since] no question of race inferiority is involved in the case of the better-class Jews"; these writers had merely expressed a highly justifiable opinion concerning the Asiatic easterner devoid of Semitic blood.[133] Among its more enduring effects, the Khazar theory forged an incriminating association between new immigration Jews and the Asiatic peril to Western civilization pervading the works of Lea, Stoddard, and others and which, in various forms, troubled the thoughts of many an officer throughout this century.

And everyone knew that acceptance of even the right kind of Jews had its pronounced limits. No matter what slants different adherents might have placed on the Khazar thesis, they, like racial anti-Semites unaware of it, took an adamant stand against the very notion of interbreeding with even the most fully assimilated and Westernized Jews. "It has taken us fifty years," wrote Grant, "to learn that speaking English, wearing good clothes and going to school and to church do not transform a Negro into a white man." Warning that Jews presented Americans with a similar racial problem, Grant stated unequivocally that "the cross between any of the three European races and a Jew is a Jew."[134]

As late as 1970, retired general Edward Almond would still argue strenuously that it was "an actual and valid difference that prevents the true accomplishment of [racial] integration." Further, "history records that men have always preferred their own," and the cause of "conflicts . . . between Jew and Gentile" has always been the "inherent difference in each group."[135]

Those officers leaning more toward environmentalist interpretations did retain faith in the ability of races to transform themselves by adapting to greatly changing conditions. But they, nonetheless, also wondered whether "Jewish and other lesser elements" could—"through means of education and environment"—be assimilated without the risk that the superior Anglo-Saxon culture "be lost or submerged."[136] More often, echoes of Grant's cries of race suicide emanated from officers affirming the gospel of fixed heredity. Explaining the dreadful moral and social impact of Hungarian Jews on the culture of Budapest in 1921, a military attaché wrote: "It is a biological and psychologic law that bad qualities are more readily transplanted or absorbed than good ones."[137]

A year earlier, his counterpart in Germany applied a similar Darwinian framework to the Jewish role in the Bolshevik Revolution. Events in Russia had, he determined, demonstrated that Jews sought not assimilation but domination by their race. Persecutions over millennia, in conjunction with the

> desperate, pitiless struggle for existence in occupations requiring sharpened mental qualities . . . [have] made the Jews the keenest race of mankind and the best equipped for a successful struggle for a "spot in the sun" in our days of liberal laws and equal opportunity for all.[138]

This exaggerated estimate of Jewish mental capacity contradicted the ideas American nativists disseminated widely across the nation about the low intelligence of inferior Eastern European Jewish immigrants. Such high levels of Jewish intelligence might have offset this aspect of nativist anxiety. Instead, it conjured up the deeply embedded historic stereotype of the inherently intelligent and crafty Jew. In the end, neither perception altered the views or lessened the apprehensions of those already predisposed to anti-Semitism. Fears of Jews degenerating the race from the bottom with inferior blood simply existed alongside rekindled older suspicions, now sanctioned by modern scientific fact, that Jews sought to dominate the country from above through the power of intellect or cunning. In the words of a military attaché,

> [T]hey rule mankind in Russia and are looking for further expansion.[139]

That such obvious contradictions within the worldview of officers received no particular attention is not surprising. Similar contravening variances also characterized much of the prolific Social Darwinist and anti-Semitic literature.

Expressions of Anglo-Saxon racial superiority by Americans had, of course, predated the Darwinism that subsequently placed these ideas in a scientific and biological context. Before and after the scientific validation of their inherent sense of superiority by Darwinist arguments, officers not only classified American Indians, blacks, and Mexicans as inferior but treated them as such in both war and peace.[140] Whether on the Western plains, at the Southern border, or in the rural South, officers found that personal encounters with these groups affirmed their own superiority. Officers serving outside Western Europe acquired a worldwide confirmation of these apparent racial realities. And military attachés had a pulpit from which to observe entire nations and judge them according to standards they knew these breeds could never reach.

When America turned to imperialism at the end of the nineteenth century, the U.S. Army involved itself in the type of racial warfare European colonial armies had long been fighting around the world. The war in the Philippines was the army's most extensive foreign conflict before it entered the great European war in 1917. Since most enlisted soldiers and officers had fought in the Philippines between 1898 and 1902, this war greatly impacted America's battlefield leadership and overall performance in World War I. Its role in molding racial attitudes was no less significant.[141]

In conquering and occupying the Philippines, a good portion of the rank and file, as well as the officer corps, acquired years of experience in thinking, fighting, and ruling like a superior breed—subduing and civilizing, first with krags and then with schoolbooks, an inferior nonwhite race. There was no doubt that behind a profusion of lofty democratic and progressive rhetoric, America's occupation of the Philippines, in policy and implementation, rested on racist pillars.[142] Older officers like Woodruff and Leonard Wood relied heavily upon their Philippine years when espousing racial theories, as did many younger officers who found the war to be a decisive experience in forming or solidifying their racial perspectives. Out of this younger group, such men as Moseley, Connor, and Hagood rose to the rank of general and influenced the officer corps into World War II.

It was, however, only during World War I, when such racial ideas converged with current events, that many officers took a special interest in Jews. A powerful upsurge in nationalistic fervor and revival of nativist xenophobia accompanied America's war effort. And this transformed Jews from pariahs in abstract theoretical thinking into a concrete political and military problem in the eyes of officers. Perceived initially as part of the larger and more general threat of millions of aliens within the United States, Jews were gradually isolated as a peculiar group posing a greater danger than others. Up to this point, the trepidation over Jews had been confined to social prejudice and racial theories expressed verbally or in publications, but now it received institutional sanction and power within the gigantic war machine created for victory.

While economic mobilization and confrontation on the battlefields of Europe remained the focal point, one arm of this vast war machine, the Military Intelligence Division, fought the enemy on other fronts. MID expended substantial resources attempting to counteract not only enemy penetration of the United States from abroad but subversion by enemies within. Here the worldview of the officer corps came into play. Predisposed to discover Jewish influences behind a good many of these suspected threats and enemies, intelligence officers eventually directed their institutional efforts toward the Jewish problem at home and abroad.

CHAPTER 2

Military Intelligence and "International Jewry," 1917–1919

IN EARLY JULY 1919, A SECRET AGENT for the American Military Intelligence Division in Paris listened intensely as a Russian aristocrat recounted an incredible tale of barbarism, destruction, and international intrigue. She spoke of Bolshevik atrocities that surpassed the Reign of Terror of the French Revolution. They had murdered her sister in the most horrible manner and caused the death of seven other family members. Yet her account differed in a significant way from the typical stories that fleeing blue-blooded Russian émigrés told to anyone who would listen, for she divulged to this agent that "[t]he Bolshevist revolution in Russia is the result of a worldwide Jewish plot to ruin the country in retaliation for the persecution of the Jewish race."[1]

Trotsky, Lenin (whose real name was Zimmermann, she asserted with certainty), and most of the Bolshevik leadership were actually "German Jews" hiding their racial origins behind Russian aliases. The non-Semitic Bolsheviks were simply "puppets" with "weak characters" manipulated by the Jews in controlling the Russian masses. The entire movement was "secretly supported by the most powerful Hebrew financial interests in London, New York, and Paris, through international banking channels and by the most underground methods." These "most powerful financial interests in the world" were also manipulating U.S. and British public opinion by exploiting the leftist and capitalist press in the interests of the "Semitic movement." Democratic freedoms and "the scramble for dollars" made the United States particularly easy prey for such secret influences.[2]

When the agent submitted this account to army intelligence in Paris, he added that Jewish opinion in Paris reflected "a remarkable unanimity of opinion in favor of the Russian Bolshevist movement." Jewish pride and identification superseded their national identity and class status, as they "were dazzled by the sudden access to power of their race." Even though they hesitated to state so explicitly, they considered Trotsky "the greatest Hebrew ruler and statesman since King Solomon."[3]

In the years following the Russian Revolution, MID files were filled with such reports, ranging from the seemingly preposterous to the marginally credible. Army intelligence officers frequently read of the hidden hand of Jewish intrigue (Bolshevik, Zionist, or both) reaching around the world, even into the United States itself. Indeed, officers at home and abroad routinely did more than read, process, and pass on such information; they augmented it with observations and warnings of their own. The mindset of many officers made them receptive to "evidence" of Jewish plotting, and this preconception influenced their own perceptions and misperceptions of international and domestic events. In these formative years, the foundations were laid for the later responses of many officers to the coming of the Third Reich and, ultimately, the Holocaust.

MID and International Jewish Conspiracies

Within days of Germany's signing of the Treaty of Versailles and President Woodrow Wilson's departure for America, Colonel Ralph H. Van Deman read his secret agent's "Special Report" on Jews and Bolshevism in his Paris office at the American Commission to Negotiate the Peace. As a General Staff officer attached to the Peace Commission, Van Deman had spent months handling paper hills of cables, letters, and secret reports from around the world, filtering out the most urgent for appropriate action while relegating the others to the category "file." His reaction to this particular report, though, revealed a certain credulity when it came to the subject of Jews. Despite its incredible assertions about Bolshevism as an international Jewish conspiracy, Van Deman did not dismiss what he read. Instead, he forwarded everything to the director of Military Intelligence in Washington, with the following cover letter on the subject of "Bolshevism and Semitism":

I am rather in doubt as to whether the conclusions drawn by this agent are based on observations sufficiently wide to be valuable. However, I am myself convinced that the subject would bear closer investigation and while I am not ready to subscribe entirely to these conclusions, still I am convinced that there may be more than a modicum of truth in them.[4]

This was not the judgment of an inexperienced intelligence officer easily manipulated by the web of intrigues and shady agents that proliferated in postwar Paris. The "father of American military intelligence," Van Deman had years of worldwide service.[5] Eventually acquiring a certain mystique about himself and his work, Van Deman would engage in intelligence activities officially and privately throughout the first half of the twentieth century.

His life fitted the general profile of the generational cohort that joined the officer corps around the turn of the century. Born in Ohio after the Civil War, he earned a Harvard B.A. (1889) and Cincinnati M.D. (1893) while a commissioned officer. After spending several years in Cuba and conducting intelligence operations against Filipino "insurrectionists" and Japanese agents, he struggled until World War I to preserve and expand military intelligence as a separate and significant component of the American army. But personality clashes with superiors and an army with little appreciation for intelligence thwarted his ambitions.[6]

Starting with a staff of only 17 officers and 192 civilians, when America entered the war in April 1917, Van Deman quickly and persistently enlarged the size and competency of the Military Intelligence Division (MID, or G-2). As director of the army's intelligence agency, Van Deman served on the General Staff, whose chief was his immediate superior. By the end of the war, MID had been transformed into an intelligence empire of almost 300 officers and 1,100 civilians, whose bureaucratic arms and surveillance reached throughout the world and across the United States. Although credit for creating the U.S. Army intelligence network belonged to Van Deman, he again displeased his superiors and was transferred to intelligence work in Europe in 1918.[7]

His replacement, Marlborough Churchill, a native New Englander and also a Harvard alumnus, had served in the U.S. military mission in Paris since 1916. Less abrasive and more tactful than Van Deman, Churchill had a patrician air about him, though his aspirations for MID differed little from his predecessor's. In an era when MID and the Office of Naval Intelligence (ONI) were the government's primary spy agencies, Churchill envisaged MID as something similar to the combined institutional structures and functions of the present-day CIA and FBI.

Working with an exceedingly broad definition of military intelligence, both directors extended their spheres of competence to include anything that might remotely bear on military affairs. MID, they believed, must be prepared "at all times to answer the question 'What is the situation today?' and 'What is it likely to be tomorrow?'" for the "entire world." MID operated on the assumption that when properly analyzed, sufficient data could allow for reliable predictions on crucial developments worldwide and on the expected behavior of various nations.[8]

Such lofty goals required that besides concerning itself with codes, combat intelligence, and the like, MID engage in extensive political and ideological activities. Its Collection Section (MI5) gathered information on foreign countries and controlled all military attachés, on which it relied heavily for most data. On average, MI5 processed over fifty reports and letters daily from attachés in over thirty countries. Churchill in particular tended to cultivate the attachés within the intelligence system, since he considered them among the "ablest officers of the army" and the primary "contact with the entire civilized world." Moreover, he wanted to rectify the problem that the army had "neglected to produce in sufficient numbers officers capable of playing a part in international affairs."[9]

The most ubiquitous and insidious MID arm, the Negative Branch's Foreign Influence Section (MI4), counteracted nonmilitary enemy activities abroad and domestically. But MI4 quickly enlarged its purview far beyond espionage and propaganda to "the study of the sentiments, publications and other actions of foreign language and revolutionary groups both here and abroad." Despite postwar assurances of strictly limiting such investigations to groups potentially affecting "military situations" and assertions that "individuals are not investigated," MI4 developed surveillance and secret file systems on American citizens and groups that rivaled those of police states. That all MID sections fell under Negative Branch control during the war indicated just how seriously Van Deman and Churchill took these investigative functions.[10]

They justified MID's expanded domestic role as a "war-time necessity" thrust upon their organization. Starting with German sabotage and sedition among conscripted "enemy aliens," MID devoted enormous efforts to investigating every identifiable group or individual that did not fit neatly into conservative Anglo-Saxon patterns or display 100 percent enthusiasm for the war.

From branches in New York, Chicago, Baltimore, and other major cities, MID, often employing civilian agents, investigated labor leaders and unions, journalists and writers, churches and social organizations. Churchill admitted MID investigated 500,000 wartime cases. Van Deman had also established close working relationships with private civilian organizations, including vigilante groups like the American Protective League (APL), whose 65,000 members across the country pursued alleged and, perhaps occasionally, real spies. Their investigations and reports became an integral part of Van Deman's domestic intelligence network.[11]

All information, from long detailed analyses to short private letters and newspaper clippings, were organized into an immense, incessantly expanding, file system of names and subjects. Almost everything was stamped "secret" or "confidential," granting an aura of importance to such undertakings in general, while transforming the slightest detail into a national security question. Violating constitutionally guaranteed rights of privacy and free expression, MID misdirected, or wasted entirely, much of its efforts, quite often producing data and analyses of highly dubious reliability and usefulness.

As a result, questionable or erroneous information worked its way through the system and influenced the thoughts, concerns, and activities of MID and other governmental agencies. Most of this occurred through close collaboration with the General Staff, military attachés, Naval Intelligence, and the Departments of Justice, State, and Immigration. The most systematized and regularized method of disseminating this information came through the *Weekly Intelligence Summary*, a periodical that MID furnished these agencies.

Some of this activity emanated quite legitimately from the nature of intelligence work or potential serious threats by enemy nations. Moreover, the emotional atmosphere created by wartime nationalism and massive mobilization contributed to the overzealousness of intelligence officers. But the specific presuppositions of what might constitute a threat to America—reflected, for example, in the choice of individuals and groups targeted for surveillance—revealed the important influence of the prewar conservative, nativist, and racial perspectives of officers.

The focal point of most of this intelligence campaign, abroad and at home, changed little in the years after the wartime justification for its existence—sabotage and sedition—had vanished with the devastating defeat of Germany. MI4 pursued "radical and racial organizations, activities and propaganda in the United States and foreign countries," including "labor unrest, negro subversion and the like."[12] The elastic definition of "the like" stretched far beyond socialism and communism to other views and activities deemed contrary to true Americanism. Liberals and leftists of all varieties, together with ethnic and racial groups, were perceived as a threat warranting attention. Any opinion, sentiment, or organization favoring "internationalism" was inherently suspect, even though a major impetus to international cooperation and institutions had been their own commander in chief, Woodrow Wilson.

Anyone who fell into these categories constructed by MI4 was considered a potential enemy of the United States. To officers, they became legitimate and necessary subjects of investigation so as to thwart their subversive activities through intelligence and police action, or in extreme cases through armed suppression. Of special concern, from the end of the war into the 1920s, were Jews, since in the minds of intelligence officers, they were intimately linked with so many of the different sentiments, movements, or organizations deemed detrimental to the security of America.

MID's role in preparing the army and government to meet a threat diplomatically, with force on the battlefield, or clandestinely through MI4 was fulfilled by the Positive Branch. It analyzed and synthesized all relevant information collected by other divisions into situation monographs and strategic indexes. Churchill envisaged these documents as the sound foundations for predicting domestic and international developments so that American military and foreign policy could be formulated accordingly. The situation monographs were extensively detailed manuals on the major political, military, psychological, and economic aspects of most countries, as well as on what MID labeled significant "isms." Constantly updated, these monographs covered hundreds of issues ranging from manpower in the combat section to sexual perversion or inherited racial traits in the psychological part. From these monographs, MID then formulated a strategic index to provide "a brief and highly condensed summary of the *existing* World Situation . . . and to forecast the probable future situation of the countries considered."[13]

Since a substantial portion of the information within these monographs had been collected by military attachés abroad and MI4 domestically, the suppositions and attitudes of officers greatly affected the composition and tone of monographs and strategic estimates drawn from them. Information and advice on pressing issues of world concern furnished the Departments of State, Treasury, Immigration, and Justice, as well as the General Staff, were often essentially conclusions based on these monographs or indexes. Through this process, erroneous information and specious arguments about the power and influence of Jews consistently worked their way for years throughout military and government offices.

Already negatively predisposed toward Jews, military attachés and MI4 officers proved highly susceptible to information—plausible, outlandish, or otherwise—that implicated Jews in a wide variety of contradictory political activities. Incriminating, though inaccurate, raw data forwarded to Washington without any critical comment partially contributed to distortions and falsehoods, as did pure conjectures and untenable inferences from anti-Semitic witnesses and informants that were submitted to headquarters after officers added credence to them by noting that they originated from "reliable sources" or "confidential agents." From MID monographs or the *Weekly Intelligence Summary*, this kind of material eventually received even wider dissemination when it appeared as fact in the confidential bulletins written within the Departments of State and Justice. By this point, no doubt, the credibility of this information had been further enhanced by the very fact that it had been compiled and analyzed by an intelligence agency staffed by loyal, competent, and professional officers.

By June 1918, State Department and military officers abroad began informing Washington of Jewish-German-Bolshevik collusion. Lieutenant Norman C. Stinnes, an American officer attached to the legation in Stockholm, confirmed these stories in a memorandum titled "The Role of the Russian Jew in the Great War."[14]

Initially, "I was anything but an anti-Semite," Stinnes professed in the memorandum. But after working with Russian Jews and "studying their methods" for several years, he became "firmly convinced" that the danger caused by the "internationalist in the shape of the wealthy Jew . . . might happen in any other country."

With this dire warning as a preface, Stinnes detailed that from the early stages of the war, both wealthy and poor Russian Jews, "wholly against the interests of Russia," acted as foreign agents by supplying the Germans; every Russian was aware of this great national scandal. Moreover, the Bolshevik government, where "eighty to eighty-five per cent of all the delegates were Jews, and the leaders practically one hundred per cent . . . was practically engineered by the Jews," and actually worked "wholly in the interests of Germany."[15]

Nevertheless, Stinnes did not affirm accusations about Jewish sentimental attachments and political partisanship toward Germany. Instead, he advanced another, more universal anti-Semitic tenet by viewing Jews as a rootless, international force devoid of allegiance to anything but themselves. For "the Jew . . . [the] sole object has been either the material or the political advancement of his own interests. . . . In other words, he is neither pro-Russian nor pro-German, but 'pro-self.'" Stinnes then reiterated his earlier warning that it was "a certainty" that under similar circumstances of war, revolution, and upheavals, Jews in other "countries will blossom out and play the same role as they play in Russia."[16]

In a vengeful, almost wishful tone, Stinnes predicted a violent, massive backlash as the Russian people learned what destruction and chaos "has been wrought by these Jews." The coming reaction "will undoubtedly end in such massacres of the Jews by the real Russian populations as have never been even thought possible." When this occurred, the United States, he argued, should not intervene. Indeed, Stinnes said he would go "so far as to say that instead of being opposed to the Russians' general treatment of the Jew," he believed "that nothing they can do [to the Jews] is bad enough to fit the case."[17]

Although general State Department reaction to such extreme reports remains unknown, one unidentified reader labeled as "rot" the very notion that Jews deserved their violent fate. "This memorandum fails to differentiate," his marginalia stated, "between the Jews who were followers of Trotsky and those who opposed the Bolsheviks Govt." Only the "bad element of Jews" was guilty of selfishness, betrayal, and Bolshevism.[18] Still, over the next several months, the State Department and Military Intelligence would gradually begin to pay serious attention to this kind of information.

Among its own officers, secret agents, and other sources, MID had a coterie of émigrés from imperial Russia, whose credentials of education and official service (and also blue blood) usually belied the devious self-serving motives and fanatical anti-Semitism of many White Russians.[19] Most notorious of all was Lieutenant Boris Brasol, a highly educated aristocratic lawyer and diplomat.

By 1918, Brasol had become a confidant of Churchill. Through secret intelligence supplied to MID and his prolific publications of books and articles on Jewish and Communist conspiracies, Brasol emerged over the next few years as a leading promoter of anti-Semitic theories and documents in America.[20] Brasol's center of operations was New York City, but his associate, a Lithuanian named Casimir Pilenas, worked right in the heart of MID's counter-insurgency branch in Washington. Sly and insidious, Pilenas managed to avoid acquiring Brasol's public reputation as a blatant Jewbaiter, but his behind-the-scenes deceit and maneuvering reeked of anti-Semitism and opportunism. Uninhibited by conscience or commitments, he betrayed trust, attempted extortion, and, while secretly launching vicious anti-Semitic denunciations, tried for years to sell confidential information to the American Jewish Committee. Through 1919, he remained an important adviser and investigator at MID headquarters.[21]

Not surprisingly, astounding material and theories about international Jewish intrigues began to surface within MID during the summer of 1918. Among the more important sources of information propagating and sustaining suppositions of insidious Jewish conspiracies, Secret Agent B-1 held a place of distinction. Never officially identified, though most likely Boris Brasol, B-1 had direct access to Churchill, who routinely read his constant stream of reports well into 1919. "I have found them useful," Churchill wrote, "as a means of checking against reports on similar subjects received through our regular channels. I think it very important that our usual sources of information know nothing about these additional reports."[22]

Churchill's cautious statement aside, his subsequent MID investigations of Jews indicate a certain receptiveness to parts of B-1's conspiratorial hypotheses. Moreover, information from regular channels often confirmed the gist of B-1's reports, if not their exaggerated details or false incrimination of particular individuals and institutions. That the incredible assertions evident in B-1's early reports did not discredit his veracity was in itself quite revealing about official perspectives.

In a long memorandum of August 14, 1918, B-1 related precise details of an intricate international Jewish web. It linked the Joint Distribution Committee of Jewish War Relief (JDC), the Federal Reserve Board, New York Jewish bankers, and the American Jewish Committee with Jewish financiers in Germany, as well as with the centers of German propaganda and spying. Combining facts about actual Jewish familial or business relationships with conjecture about collusion among Jews internationally, B-1 wove specious arguments about the pro-German activities of American Jewish leaders and institutions:

> The head of the Committee is Jacob L. Schiff and the treasurer is Felix Warburg, the brother of Paul Warburg who just failed to be reappointed by President Wilson as Vice Governor of the Federal Reserve Board, and whose other brother, Max Warburg, is head of the Rhenish Westphalian Syndicate, Germany, and whose brother, Fritz, is the German Financial Attaché in Stockholm, Sweden, and the main financier for the German propaganda all over the world.

B-1 then cleverly played upon preexisting suspicions and biases of intelligence officers. He granted a central role in this international conspiracy to Judah B. Magnes, a Jewish leader already under suspicion and surveillance by MID for his pacifism, and associated him with Dr. Isaac Strauss, a real German Jewish spy arrested when America entered the war. B-1 strongly implied betrayal of America's war effort.[23]

Yet B-1 exposed a still more complex web of Jewish shrewdness and deceit. Jewish organizations involved in humanitarian and charitable war relief (especially the Joint Distribution Committee) served another purpose besides Germany. They were a guise behind which powerful Jewish forces enhanced their control and wealth internationally in their own selfish interest: "The German Jewish financial group in this country is planning to take advantage of the disturbed conditions in Russia and Poland by buying up lands from the peasants and land owners in these countries practically for 'Thirty shekels.'" B-1 alerted MID to the need "to watch very closely the financial transactions of the Joint Distribution Committee so as to prevent further economic disaster and pillage in Russia and in Poland which have already suffered a good deal from the German Jewish enterprises and other philanthropic experiments."[24]

Routinely over the next half year, B-1 furnished MID with similar reports, which were forwarded to Churchill when he moved to the American embassy in Paris in November 1918. Beyond B-1's blatant and vehement anti-Semitism, each report disclosed he and his associates engaged in widespread surveillance of numerous private American citizens and organizations with the knowledge, acquiescence, and possibly the encouragement of intelligence officers. Ironically, officers so obsessed with protecting America from alien subversives allowed foreigners like Brasol to violate the privacy and civil liberties of American citizens with impunity. That questions were never raised about the legality or propriety of such activities was, in part, a result of the wartime atmosphere within military intelligence where officers often displayed a paranoia about German and radical subversion.

Aware that the Allied victory would significantly diminish fears of German power, B-1 began to emphasize another dimension of the Jewish conspiracy theory. Expanding his earlier thesis about "International Jewry," he fleshed out the information on Jews and Bolshevism that had been circulating piecemeal throughout 1918. The Jewish Bolsheviks who had seized control of Russia now conspired to overthrow other governments through either violent revolution or subversion. Jews controlled the lead-

ership and constituted the bulk of the rank and file "of the most dangerous Bolshevist organizations" in America and were linked to "Zionist organizations headed by Justice Brandeis, and the German-Jewish financial
group headed by Jacob Schiff."

To undermine the new Polish state, the Jews supposedly contrived stories about pogroms in Poland. But B-1's confidential Polish sources assured
him, "[T]here is no wholesale massacre of the Jews." The Polish high command had merely "executed a dozen or so rabbis" to deter subversion by
Lenin's agent, the "Jew" Radek, and "this measure immediately stopped
the Bolshevist movement."[25]

It was, however, in "Bolshevism and Judaism," B-1's most foreboding
submission, that he alerted military intelligence of the ultimate goal of
"International Jewry"—world domination. Arguing "there can be little
doubt that the revolution in Russia . . . was started and engineered by distinctly Jewish influences," B-1 identified in outline form, with the word
"Jew" emphatically typed next to each name, specific American Jewish
"persons and firms . . . engaged in this destructive work." Most prominent
among these were Jacob Schiff; the Jewish firm Kuhn, Loeb, and Company;
the Warburg families; and Judah Magnus, all long-standing essential elements in his conspiratorial interpretations. In precise detail, he described
how Schiff in New York conspired with the Warburgs in Germany and
Stockholm, as well as with other Jewish bankers in London, Tokyo, Paris,
and Petrograd, "to finance Trotzky, a Jew, for the purpose of accomplishing
a social revolution."[26]

Having established how "the link between Jewish multi-millionaires
and Jewish proletarians was forged," B-1 added additional proof by revealing the true identity of the top leadership of the Soviet government:

Cover Name	Real Name	Nationality
Lenin	Oulianoff	Russian
Trotzky	Bronstein	Jew
Stockloff	Nackamkes	"
Martoff	Zederbaum	"
Zinovieff	Apfelbaum	"
Kamenoff	Rosenfeld	"
Souchanoff	Gimel	"

The list continued until thirty names were covered, with Lenin the only
non-Jew. B-1 extrapolated from this inventory of the "real powers" behind

the Soviet government that the Jewish triumph in Russia and a Zionist state in Palestine represented just the first stages of "Jewish imperialism, with its final aim of establishing a worldwide Jewish rule." At present, "International Jewry" stood on the verge of seizing political power in Germany and Austria-Hungary, while in the United States, they had "raised almost instantaneously" $1 billion to further these efforts around the globe. In the face of this immense danger, B-1 stated gloomily, "Christendom remains silent, inactive, dull and inert."[27]

With Churchill dispatched to Paris, B-1 began to trace the powerful hidden hand of "International Jewry" to the upcoming peace conference. Ironically, culling as much of his information from Jewish publications as from the secret agents supposedly at his disposal, then filtering this through his own warped perspective, B-1 warned that the Jews have sent "their very suspicious leaders to Paris." Most of them had a "Jewish, international, Bolshevist, radical point of view." All were staunchly pro-German and likely to promote German interests to the detriment of the Allies who had actually won the war. Most noteworthy were "Felix Frankfurter, who, as you know, is in the Administration"; Louis Marshall, head of the American Jewish Committee, "one of the most shrewd Jews throughout the world, one of the most dangerous internationalists who have ever lived"; and U.S. Circuit Court Judge Julian Mack, who "would be as dangerous as Louis Marshall did he possess the same mental capabilities."[28]

About this same time, MID launched an internal investigation into the "basis of B-1's statements and allegations." In Churchill's absence, the impetus for scrutiny of this still-mysterious agent arose from Captains Edwin P. Grosvenor, Carlton J. H. Hayes, and Nathan Isaacs, nonprofessional officers serving in MID's Negative Branch. A progressive Columbia University history professor and preeminent scholar, Hayes recognized the broader dangers inherent in B-1's surveillance activities. In December 1918, Hayes lodged a "vehement protest" against B-1's universal condemnation of all labor movements as Bolshevist.[29]

As to the value of B-1, Hayes could not have been more unequivocal. His "lugging-in of the Jewish question" into every issue "can be viewed . . . as only another sign of the raving tendency of a fanatical if not of a disordered brain."[30] This estimate was reinforced in equally blunt terms the following day by Grosvenor, a civilian lawyer on wartime duty, who dismissed B-1's "Bolshevism and Judaism" as "a jumble of opinions formed by an ill informed, suspicious and biased individual." Since factual errors and preposterous speculations reduced this report to "arrant nonsense,"

Grosvenor recommended MID interrogate this agent. Grosvenor could not find "a scintilla of evidence of any alliance between Jewish bankers and the Bolshevists" or other extraordinary claims about Jewish figures. "Unless the writer appears and substantiates his charges," Grosvenor urged "the matter be dropped as unworthy of serious consideration."[31]

Any informant subjected to such devastating refutation should have suffered immediate and permanent discrediting. This became more likely when Grosvenor's superiors, Colonels Wrisley Brown and Kenneth Masteller, concurred with this assessment of "Bolshevism and Judaism" and also favored interrogation. Masteller suggested Churchill be informed of the actual "value we place upon B1 reports."[32] But MID's acting director in Washington, Colonel John M. Dunn, did "not care to disclose who this confidential agent might be or to produce him here in order that he might be interviewed."

Dunn conceded B-1 "is likely to be somewhat biased in his opinions of the Jews," and this must be considered when evaluating his information "for what it is worth." But Dunn showed no sensitivity to the essential point that B-1 should be dismissed as a valueless bigot and fanatic. Reiterating that Churchill found this source useful "as a means of checking against reports" from regular agents, Dunn returned the entire file to Masteller without agreeing to any action.[33]

B-1 continued his activities without the slightest deterrence or interruption from MID. Into the early months of 1919, and perhaps later, he submitted thirty reports to Washington headquarters, all routinely forwarded to Churchill in Paris. Although new events and figures were added, the essential motifs—"International pro-German Jews" and Bolsheviks, occasionally linked to Zionism—remained unaltered. Other political figures were being manipulated "to play the Jewish game at the Peace Conference"; the political "machine" of a Bolshevik convention in New York was "an entirely Jewish one"; and B-1 vigilantly kept all such machinations and meetings under close scrutiny.[34]

Hayes, meanwhile, persisted in his efforts to discredit and expose this "arrant nonsense [as] the offspring of an imagination untrammeled by fact." Through a series of memoranda to Brown and Masteller, Hayes expressed astonishment at "so many blunders, misapprehensions, mistakes, and errors."[35] By this time, Hayes suspected that the mysterious confidential agent and Boris Brasol were one and the same.[36] Although some of Hayes's analyses were forwarded to Churchill along with B-1's reports, there are no indications what, if any, impact they might have had.

In the meantime, an agent in the Propaganda Section of MID in New York cast "grave suspicion" upon Hayes's own credibility and loyalty. Hayes and a long list of prominent American progressives were accused of being "active in radical circles" or "extremely radical in [their] mode of thinking." These "morbid sentiments" and radical associations posed serious security risks to which military intelligence must be alerted.[37]

Throughout late 1918, secret agents and military attachés abroad, while not addressing B-1's conspiracy theory of Jewish world domination, provided information supporting his more general claims. American officers in different countries informed headquarters that the primary agitators in the Russian Revolution and "most Bolsheviki leaders at present were Jews." Not only did the "Jewish Bolsheviki run everything" in Petrograd, but "Lenin's illness [left] the three most important posts in the Bolsheviki Government in the hands of Jews."[38] The American military attaché in London, Colonel Stephen Slocum, soon furnished strong corroboration from "a British agent who has had exceptional opportunities for understanding the subject," since he had spent twenty years in Russia and was an actual witness to the revolution. The inclusion of this dispatch in the *Weekly Intelligence Summary* ensured wide circulation among General Staff officers.[39]

The British agent's lengthy analysis purported that despite exceptions, "the bolshevik leaders were very largely Jews—not real Russians at all— but Russian Jews who for many years have been nursing their grievances, real as well as fancied." While conceding the harsh oppression Jews suffered under the czarist regime, he added that this treatment "was not entirely undeserved": "[I]f you could have seen the Russian Jews battening on the simple peasants in the villages, as I have, you would have understood" the consequent violent hatred against the Jews. These vengeful, exiled Jews, with "undoubtedly clever brains" but without real loyalty to any country, turned to socialist utopian theories. Motivated in part by revenge and in part by misguided fanatical idealism, they were currently engaged in the "ruthless destruction of whatever civilization existed, which would then allow them to rebuild Russia on a purely imaginary basis." This small group of Jewish exiles that had seized control was "well organized, well financed, and extremely clever (all Jews are that)."[40]

In pursuit of these revolutionary goals, these Jewish Bolsheviks became the "conscious and unconscious" accomplices of a German strategy to destroy Russian power. Through infiltration and subversion, they undermined morale and discipline in the Russian army and through inciting class warfare were now carrying out the "shocking massacre" of educated Russians. Other "clever and unscrupulous" Jews were simultaneously intriguing abroad to advance the revolution in Allied countries.[41]

Other observers sounded similar warnings. "What cannot fail to impress all thoughtful observers," wrote Philip Brown in January 1919, "is the conspicuous role now being played by Jews as critics of the existing order of things."[42] Alluding to "the danger of pogroms on a large scale" across Europe, he noted that the sudden emergence of Jewish activism in so many parts of the world could easily cause an anti-Semitic backlash in the United States.

When American officers read these words in the *North American Review*, they were probably not at all surprised, since in tone and content, this journal usually reflected attitudes and views similar to their own. For decades, active and retired officers, including those of existing or future prominence, conveyed their opinions on a variety of political and military affairs through the pages of this journal. Rarely did an issue lack contributions by military men; there often developed close, lasting personal relationships between officers and editors. And Brown's reasoning paralleled MID's current thoughts and suspicions about Jews.

While not attributing "conspicuously ulterior or sinister" motives to the Jews, Brown nonetheless identified certain behavioral traits to explain "the prominence of the Jew in modern reform movements, particularly in socialistic and bolshevistic attempts to overthrow the existing order of things." Besides "rare intellectual powers" and "natural radicalism," "the Jew is restless and by nature detached from most nationalistic interests because of his sense of racial solidarity that militates against his taking deep root in any community . . . [and] he has not actually become assimilated as a race in any country."

Loyalty, even among the long-established American Jewish community, was at best superficial and seriously suspect. Whether Socialist, Bolshevik, or Zionist, "this thing we term Christian civilization is something alien to him. He would readily welcome a new social order with enthusiasm and erect a new altar to an unknown God." In Russia and Hungary, the Jew wore the mantle of Bolshevism and revived anti-Semitism; activism by American Zionists could have similar repercussions. Palestine was a sacred international site, and Zionists should not attempt to greatly transform the "order of things" in the Holy Land. "There exists an instinctive religious resentment towards the Jews," Brown warned, "which they would do well never to excite."[43]

Brown's image of the rootless international Jew manifesting his inherent radicalism through revolutionary forces would acquire widespread public credence throughout 1919. But whereas Brown discounted a Bolshevik-Zionist link, others did not, as coming events soon provided numerous examples to fire the imaginations of those receptive to conspiracy theories.

The Protocols of the Elders of Zion

Many alarmists pointed to the supposed connection between Jews and Bolshevism, and Zionism seemed to be yet another example of international Jewish solidarity. It, too, raised serious doubts about Jewish assimilation and loyalty, especially in a wartime atmosphere demanding 100-percent Americanism. Thus, when Louis Marshall and Cyrus Adler of the American Jewish Committee joined with other prominent American Jews like Frankfurter and Brandeis in promoting the Zionist cause, the old established Jewish community's loyalty was also questioned.

In late 1918, delegations of prominent American Jews arrived at the Paris Peace Conference to promote the fulfillment of the Balfour Declaration promise of a Jewish homeland in Palestine. They also sought treaty guarantees of minority rights (especially for Jews) in the newly created states in Central and Eastern Europe.[44] Soon, however, Communists in neighboring Germany revolted in Berlin in January 1919. Although brutally suppressed within ten days, this event heightened dire expectations of Bolshevism spreading westward. Only about 7 percent of the German Communist Party and less than half of its leadership were Jews. But their very presence further solidified the association of Jews with Bolshevism.[45] Given the deep mutual animosity between Jews in the Bolshevik camp and those of other political persuasions, no reasonable link could be established between events in Paris and Berlin. Yet shortly thereafter, it was publicly revealed that such a sinister relationship might not be beyond the realm of possibility.

In testimony before the Senate Overman Committee on Bolshevism on February 12, 1919, where he held Lower East Side New York Jews responsible for the Bolshevik Revolution, Reverend George Simons disclosed a broader, more devious Jewish plot. He shocked his listeners with allegations of a secret, organized worldwide Jewish conspiracy to undermine, and then subjugate, Christian civilization around the globe. As evidence, Simons cited a Russian book, still unknown to the American public, entitled *The Protocols of the Elders of Zion.*[46] This revelation, however, came as no surprise to the upper echelons of MID, since months before they had already secretly acquired a copy of the *Protocols.*

Early in 1918, Dr. Harris Houghton, a medical officer assigned to MID at Governor's Island, New York, acquired a Russian edition of this work from his assistant, Natalie de Bogory. A daughter of Russian immigrants, she had procured this copy from an associate who turned out to be none other than Boris Brasol. By June 1918, de Bogory had completed an English translation of the *Protocols* with the assistance of Brasol and another czarist officer. An intelligence officer preoccupied with wartime Jewish subversion during the war and Bolshevism thereafter, Captain Houghton worked with Brasol in bringing this document to the attention of various government officials. It is generally assumed that Houghton is the one who provided Reverend Simons and the Overman Committee with the *Protocols.*[47]

By September 1, 1918, Colonel John M. Dunn, chief of MID's Positive Branch, received one of only four existing copies from Herbert Carpenter of the All Russian American League in New York. Brasol and Houghton possessed two copies, while another remained locked in the office safe at MID's Eastern Division Headquarters. About 100 typescript pages in length, this English translation had the title "Protocols of the Meetings of the Zionist Men of Wisdom." This document outlined nothing less, Dunn noted, than "a policy that is aimed towards the entire overthrowal of the social, labor, educational and economic conditions of the world as they exist today. It purports to be a scheme adopted by a Jewish Congress or Meeting at Kief, Russia, held in 1912."[48]

In page after page of the *Protocols,* the supposed Jewish leaders devised one of the most pernicious plots in history. The scheme could only have been hatched in the minds of treacherous men who were as brutish as they were deceitful. Together covering almost the entire political, social, and intellectual spectrum, each protocol disclosed the ruthless principles and strategy guiding these international conspirators toward their ultimate objective.

Protocol I:

I will formulate our system both from our point of view and from that of the Goys . . . the best results in governing them is obtained by intimidation and violence. . . . Every man aims for power, every one wants to be a dictator if possible, and at the same time few would not sacrifice the good of others for the attainments of their own ends. Right is Might. What has controlled the wild animal, called man? What has directed him until the present time. . . .

Protocol III:
Having organized a general economic crisis, by all underhand means available to us, with the help of gold, which is all in our hands, we will throw crowds of workmen into the street, simultaneously in all countries of the world. These mobs will gladly shed the blood of those whom they, in the simplicity of their ignorance, have been jealous since children and whose property they will then be able to loot. They will not touch our people, because we will know of the time of attack and we will take measures to protect our own. . . .

Protocol VI:
We will . . . artificially and deeply undermine the source of industry by teaching the workmen anarchy and the use of alcohol, at the same time making arrangements to exile all the intellectual forces of the Goys from the countries. That the true situation should not be noticed by the Goys until the proper time, we will mask it by a pretended desire to help the working classes and great economic principles, an active propaganda of which is being carried on through economic theories.

Protocol VII:
We must force the Goy Governments . . . by public opinion to beneficial action in favor of our broadly conceived plan, now approaching its triumphant goal, ostensibly through public opinion which has been build up with the help of the so-called "Great Power" of the Press, which with few exceptions . . . is already entirely in our hands.[49]

MID's Colonel Dunn, however, flatly refused to accept this document at face value. He rejected the idea "that the Jews are actually responsible or were the originators of this plan" or "that this program is an effort of the Jews to obtain domination of the world." Yet he felt the *Protocols* did represent some kind of authentic conspiratorial scheme. It most likely originated either with the Germans or anarchists, Dunn surmised, and was made "to appear as if it were the plan of the Jews." After all: "It is a fact that the present activities of Lenine, Trotsky and other Bolsheviks in Russia so correspond to the system as outlined herewith as to lead one to believe that this is actually the basic plan upon which the Bolshevik control functions."[50]

Dunn's dismissal of Jewish involvement did not end such speculations; the history of this document within MID and America had just begun. For the next several years, information proliferated throughout MID either directly associating the Jews with the *Protocols* or implying a possible connection between this document and Zionism or Jewish Bolshevism. MID even established a separate investigative classification for the *Protocols*—File 99-75. Officers placed into File 99-75 not only a wide variety of information on the *Protocols* but also material on Zionism and Palestine. When Rabbi Stephen Wise and Judge Julian Mack spoke in Washington in March 1919 on the "Aims of Zionism," MID had an undercover agent present. As with similar surveillance reports, this, too, was immediately filed in 99-75.[51]

Even recognition of the bogus nature of the *Protocols* failed, in some cases, to protect Jews from conspiratorial suspicions. By early April 1919, Captain John B. Trevor of MID's New York office notified Washington that he considered "the genuineness of the information [to be] open to question." Well informed of its recent secret distribution from Brasol through the Overman Committee, Trevor acquired a copy from Captain Houghton that was then duplicated in his office. The *Protocols*, Trevor "deduced," "might have been prepared by an Agent Provocateur of the former regime in Russia, possibly using material inspired by Roman Catholic sources as a basis for the purpose of disseminating anti-Semitic propaganda preparatory to the pogroms in Kiev and Kishenef." If this was correct, then in his view "propaganda of this kind is as vicious as Bolshevik propaganda."[52]

Despite Trevor's fairly accurate guess on the historical origins of the fraudulent *Protocols*, he seriously entertained the possibility of a different kind of international Jewish influence. While researching the *Protocols*, his investigator had uncovered a source suggesting that

> Freemasonry is, unknown to most of the craft, managed by five or six Jews who lend its influence in every possible way to the furtherance of the anti-Christian movement that passes under the name of Liberalism. The constant influx into the English speaking countries of Jews and Continental Freemasons must necessarily impregnate the order with all the poison of the Continental sect.[53]

Discrediting the *Protocols*, Trevor maintained, "did not necessarily mean that [this] original thesis on Freemasonry may not have some basis in fact, because Freemasonry on the Continent of Europe is quite a different proposition from Freemasonry in England and the United States."[54]

In the long run, Trevor's attitude would prove among the most consequential of those held by intelligence officers, since he would exercise considerable influence on America's reaction to the Jewish question at home and abroad into the 1950s. Few figures personified the worldview of the nativist Anglo-Saxon elite as did this quite prosperous lawyer turned intelligence officer. Born to a prominent old New York family, he studied at the best prep schools and universities (B.A. Harvard, LL.B. Columbia) and traveled within the most prestigious social circles. A close friend of Madison Grant and other Nordic ideologues, he, too, served on the Board of Directors for the Museum of Natural History; later, he assumed a similar position in the Eugenics Research Association. Another of his close friends and political contacts, Charles Stewart Davison, led the American Defense Society (ADS), a superpatriotic group with pronounced anti-immigrant and anti-Semitic sentiments. By late 1918, Boris Brasol had the confidence of the ADS chairman, who took an immediate interest in the *Protocols*. Around this same time, Trevor assumed command of MID in New York, where he became the center of extensive investigations of alleged radicals, particularly immigrants and Jews.[55]

Trevor enjoyed the trust of Churchill, who in January 1919 sent an urgent wire from Paris to MID in Washington: "It is very important that the results of . . . Trevor's bolshevik investigations be sent to us both by mail and by cable. No one here realizes that there is a bolshevik movement in the United States. I consider this question the most important now under consideration. Definite data concerning the subject most valuable."[56]

What Churchill and others received from Trevor tightened further the linkage between Jews and Bolshevism. Some of his intelligence, in fact, closely paralleled that which B-1 incessantly fed to Churchill. On February 19, 1919, Trevor's sources informed him that the Warburgs, Jacob Schiff, and Kuhn, Loeb, and Company (all interconnected by marriage, international banking, and the political and financial interests of Jews) greatly influenced the Federal Reserve Board and Wilson administration to the advantage of Germany.

Although Trevor submitted this information "for what it is worth," he placed at least some credence in the claim that the German branch of the Warburg banking family financed the Bolshevik Revolution. "Colonel Martin will recall," Trevor pointed out, "that this new information corroborates the matter which I communicated to him in our interview in New York recently, when I quoted . . . the substance of a conversation with Felix

Warburg in regard to Lenine and Trotsky." This same banker, the informant stated, had paid hundreds of thousands of dollars into the "Bolshevik
Secret Service in the United States in 1918."[57]

No sooner had Trevor dispatched this letter to Washington than an "absolutely distinct and separate source" furnished him with "important information [on] . . . the Zionist movement," Justice Brandeis, and the "Jewish
International Movement." At a secret session of a Jewish meeting in Pittsburgh over a year ago, "Justice Brandeis was elected president of the 'Jewish
International,' and Louis Marshall, Secretary of Foreign Affairs. This fact
taken in connection with Justice Brandeis' attitude in regard to our intervention in the Russian situation, when it might have been effective is extremely important." The same group which "backed the Bolsheviki—Schiff,
Warburg, et al."—have now embraced Zionism, and "it is practically certain
. . . they are the financial backers of this 'Jewish International.'"

Trevor drew the attention of Washington to the reference in his earlier
letter concerning Warburg's financing of Bolshevism in the United States,
because his second informant had told him that hundreds of thousands of
dollars had been channeled through Scandinavia to secret Bolsheviks in
the United States and "more money was now on its way."[58] As extraordinary as this sounded, it actually had some corroboration from British Intelligence. Urging an investigation of Zionism, the British also told of large
amounts of Bolshevik funds smuggled abroad and of Bolshevik "agitation
among the Jews working in America."[59]

"The Power and Aims of International Jewry"

While intelligence officers in U.S. cities and embassies abroad had only
limited observations and information, officers in Washington witnessed
the daily accumulation of documents from around the world that, in the
aggregate, gradually provided a fuller picture. The convergence of a steady
flow of references to Jews in so much intelligence data with the mounting
hysteria of the Red Scare during the summer of 1919 definitely heightened the concern of MID officers at General Staff headquarters. A mentality of "Where there's smoke, there's fire" prevailed. Surely, there had to be
something to so much intelligence from so many diverse sources.

The dangers of such uncritical acceptance of raw data, often of dubious
origin or veracity, had already been explained by Carlton Hayes and his
Jewish-American colleague Nathan Isaacs in MI4 almost a year before.

Now, as certain reports implicating Jews in various machinations continually reached Isaacs's desk, he became increasingly alarmed and defensive. His earlier refutation of the blatantly bigoted émigré Brasol had obviously been inadequate; in the months thereafter, there had been no apparent cessation in this brand of intelligence. Isaacs's own fellow officers abroad and across America displayed either similar biases or susceptibility to theories linking Jews to German, Bolshevik, or other anti-American intrigues.

When on June 13, 1919, Isaacs read a report from Europe alleging renewed German-Jewish collusion, he reacted immediately. In a scathing attack, Isaacs exposed the "glaring inaccuracies" and "vicious anti-Semitic prejudice" interwoven throughout a report of a secret German scheme to manipulate Jewish reaction to Polish pogroms so as "to influence the American government against the Poles and in favor of Germany." Infuriated that this source worried more about possible German propaganda than the pogroms themselves, Isaacs condemned "the whole report [as] tainted [by] the assumption that it is a patriotic duty of Americans to conceal and distort facts with regard to the Poles from American Jews and Americans in general until it is too late for America to exert any beneficent influence."[60]

It is doubtful whether Isaacs's rebuttal had any meaningful impact. Accurate or not, suspicions of German propaganda behind news of the pogroms were fairly widespread. His entire approach also ran counter to the general pro-Polish tendency that had arisen in MID since the end of the war.

The very next day, one ardent Polish supporter, MID director Churchill, heard confidentially from Casimir Pilenas that Isaacs himself was a Trojan horse. Repudiating an earlier anti-Brasol letter, Pilenas now confessed he had written it under coercion from Isaacs, who sought to discredit Brasol's important revelations about Jews. Absolving himself of any "prejudice against the Jews as a race," Pilenas claimed that Jews (unreliable, disloyal, and indifferent to any government) constituted the leadership of radical organizations that incite "misguided workingmen to acts of violence"; and "Capt. Isaacs is no exception to this rule."[61]

Even during the perils of wartime, Pilenas wrote, the disloyal Isaacs had criticized America for joining the Allied cause; sympathetic to Bolshevism, he supported the Soviet Union after the Bolshevik Revolution of 1917 "because theirs was a righteous cause" and "praised [its] advantages . . . over a capitalist one." After his attendance at a Bolshevik meeting raised eyebrows in MI4, Isaacs became "very guarded in his language"; but in Pilenas's view, he secretly remained "one of those Jews who would like to see all capitalistic governments overthrown." A "leading Zionist," he met frequently and shared confidential information with "prominent Jews." He carried his intrigues right into the heart of MID headquarters by distorting intelligence analyses and summaries "as a means of commiseration with the Jews and condemnation of the Poles" for "alleged Jewish massacres."

Pilenas had, however, saved his most startling indictment until the very end. "Capt. Isaacs confided to me," Pilenas wrote, "that the Protocol of the First Zionist convention, held in Basel, in 1897 . . . is a genuine document, but after reading a copy which is, I understand, in your possession, he branded it as 'all lies, manufactured by Brasol.'"[62]

By themselves, Pilenas's accusations perhaps had no more credence than Brasol's conspiratorial theories. But his charges did not stand alone. On July 5, Van Deman informed Churchill from Paris that he was "convinced that there may be more than a modicum of truth" in theories relating "Bolshevism and Semitism."[63]

Three days later, the U.S. military attaché in London telegraphed:

> Proofs secured by British Government that the Bolshevik movement throughout the world is an international conspiracy of Jews. Secret agents have been located and evidence secured from letters that the leaders in England, France and America are in touch with each other.[64]

Jarred by this apparent confirmation from a respected ally, Churchill queried:

> What is the nature of British proof of Bolshevik movement? Can it be substantiated? Can you obtain copy of this proof?

The response from the London attaché arrived on July 14:

> British proof of international Jewish Bolshevik conspiracy consists of photographs made of intercepted letters between agents and result of police espionage in bolshevik agency in London, and is substantial. British government still working on case and will eventually furnish proof to American government. Am in close liaison with British authorities on subject. Whole subject must be considered extremely secret.[65]

Shortly thereafter, MID's New York office also related "that there is now definite evidence that Bolshevism is an international movement controlled by Jews."[66]

Despite such rapidly accumulating information, Churchill had still not acquired, with the exception of Brasol's clearly prejudiced submissions, any systematic analysis or even many reliable specifics on this entire question. The deficiency was soon rectified, however, by an office with impeccable credentials in a building not that distant from Churchill's headquarters. By the end of August 1919, Churchill had in his possession a lengthy document written in that office that, though less fanatical in tone than the typical Brasol piece, was equally startling in substance and insinuations. Indeed, rivaling anything concocted by B-1, its title was: "The Power and Aims of International Jewry."[67]

This document had emanated neither from some disgruntled coterie of émigrés or Jew-baiters nor from any overzealous xenophobic American patriotic organization. Rather, it was composed in the U.S. State Department Division of Russian Affairs, under the direction of Allan J. Carter and DeWitt C. Poole, two career diplomats.

Although little is known about Carter, Poole's background, attitude, and outlooks mirrored those of most army officers. "My background is entirely English," he boasted before unveiling his early-seventeenth-century New England pedigree and a family history of "prosperous [Midwestern] farmers" and Bostonian merchants, along with the professional military career of his Indian-fighting father, who "as the only white man in five hundred miles," governed thousands of Sioux "just by moral force." This story, which sounded like a saga from the pen of Kenneth Roberts, was to Poole "simply a typical American experience." This frontier "army background," including his officer brother, exemplified to him a "special aspect of a social discipline that is very pervasive in the United States" but lacking among the "immigration from 1890 to 1920" of "Bohunks" who remained "city dwellers [and] did not go out into the country the way the Germans and Scandinavians did." Ultimately, these newer immigrants reelected Roosevelt—"a calamity." Like many officers, he found his racial views confirmed by a visit to the Philippines, where his brother had acquired a plantation during his military service; Poole took special note of the "flock of [red-headed] bastards . . . a pretty sorry lot," left by the American occupation. Poole retained a lifelong interest in the relationship between radicalism and foreigners in the United States.[68]

In Moscow during the Bolshevik Revolution, Poole upheld this heroic family tradition of courage and independence. Commended for protecting American civilians under fire, he then traveled by cattle car into the midst of the civil war raging in Cossack country, at one point spending days with a Bolshevik army engaged in hostilities. He returned to America as one of the few individuals knowledgeable about Bolshevism and soon directed the Russian desk in the State Department. Bolshevism's anticapitalist revolt disturbed him less than the fact that "we who were on the spot saw clearly that it was anti-civilization," a "lapse into barbarism."[69]

In its secret "Power and Aims of International Jewry," the Russian Division under Carter and Poole came as close to verifying a worldwide Jewish conspiracy theory as would be possible without actually crossing the line into a categorical affirmation of the plot's existence. An expanded version completed a month later, under the modified title "Judaism and the Present World Movement—A Study," added about forty pages of appendices of documents, letters, and photographs as corroboration. The rationale for this study was to understand the involvement of Jews in so many world events; and its thematic breadth encompassed the *Protocols*, Bolshevism, European affairs, and Zionism. The anonymous author's own inclinations were already transparent in the introduction, where he attributed U.S. "public indifference" to these subjects to the fact "that the American press is so largely owned and controlled by Jews."[70]

One need not authenticate the *Protocols*, the author contended, in order for them to be considered a valuable and telling indication of "possible or probable fields of Jewish activities, aims and methods ... [and thus] a point of departure" for his study. Genuine or not, there were too many striking similarities in "fundamental principles and ideals" found in the *Protocols* and the writings of certain "Jewish leaders" to be merely coincidental. After all, he emphasized, "All Jews" (extreme radicals and conservatives alike) were united by a common national and religious identity.

> Once a Jew always a Jew. Neither conversion nor naturalization will change him; Judaism and Socialism are different expressions of the same movement, which in the case of the Poale [leftist] Zionists amounts to sheer Bolshevism. [Equally remarkable, the predictions and aims of the *Protocols* coincided with] the coming of a world war; the chaos of Bolshevism ... ; the red terror; and the breaking down of all religions save their own; [these] are all predicted ... by the Jews as a step toward their world domination.[71]

The State Department, the author noted, had "a vast amount of material" on the problem of Jews and Bolshevism, extending from the father of Zionism, Theodor Herzl, to Judah Magnus and others. Despite attempts to hide behind Russian aliases, appendix C exposed the true identity of the

"Jewish-Bolshevik Commissars," thereby proving that in Russia, Jewish "control ranged from 70 to 90%." The only "predominant non-Jewish figure," Lenin, "is now a virtual prisoner in the Kremlin compelled to do what Trotsky and his faction dictate." In "Hungary the Jews predominated as thoroughly as in Soviet Russia."

In 1917, the Jewish-German Warburg banking family delivered the funds to the Bolsheviks; and the German Communist "leaders in Berlin were all Jews" as "were nearly all" those Communists who seized control of Munich. It has even been said that "fully 75% of [Germany's] present leaders—conservatives and radicals—are Semitic." The American military attaché in Berlin reported that German Jews of every political persuasion were supporting the Jewish-controlled Bolshevik regime to prevent the pogroms that would surely follow its collapse.

Pro-Bolshevik tendencies of Jewish newspapers in England had already produced an anti-Semitic backlash. Despite denials by prominent American Jews like Louis Marshall, other Jewish leaders admitted that "the 500,000 Jews of the East Side [of New York] were Bolshevists."[72]

"Many Jews are sincere and loyal patriots of the particular nations in which they live, *but unfortunately the teachings of certain Jewish leaders and the definite tendency of their present world movement is to undermine all nationalism except the Jewish.*" International Jews and German propaganda organizations had orchestrated the publicity and political campaign in America against the newly created Polish state. Using deceit and manipulation of the news, prominent American Jews (Marshall, Schiff, Mack, and so on) greatly exaggerated recent pogroms in Poland as part of their scheme to acquire special undue and unreasonable "minority rights" for Polish Jews, thereby preserving Polish Jewry as a state within a state and as the national center for world Jewry. A weakened Poland also would be unable to serve as a bulwark against "German economic penetration of Russia." Perhaps, Europe, not Palestine, was the ultimate goal.[73]

In pursuing these objectives, Zionists such as Justice Brandeis and Frankfurter, "autocratic and inclined toward dictatorship," engaged in duplicity in public while working secretly "behind closed doors," as they did when advancing Jewish interests at the Paris Peace Conference. The entire movement was financed by an international group of intermarried Jewish banking families, each of which "has a dominant financial position in two or more different countries." As proof of this "inter-locking family unity," the author cited the familiar Warburgs-Schiffs-Kuhn, Loeb litany, then associated these with the firm of Guggenheim, Untermeyer, and Marshall and its dealings with the multinational Rothschilds, whose financial tentacles stretched across Europe.[74]

Other evidence, in the text and appendices, consisted of lengthy comparative quotations from the *Protocols* and writings of Jewish leaders; letters and speeches of Marshall, Brandeis, Frankfurter, and others; and reports from MID and the American minister to Poland, Hugh Gibson. Appendix E furnished visual proof through "a set of photographs of the Bolshevik Commissars of Hungary which suggests not only their Jewish origin but also the types they appear to represent."[75]

The conclusion of this self-proclaimed "detached study" began with caution and ended with suppositions about the existence of an actual peril. It conceded that the problem was too intricate and that available evidence too limited to state categorically that certain Jews sought "to rule the world." It then forcefully argued the case that a "group of international Jews," employing similar methods outlined in the *Protocols*, were "now, with a remarkable unity of action, exerting so powerful an influence upon world politics."

It was power originating from "the very racial characteristics which have permitted the Jewish peoples . . . to flourish and multiply as a distinct race" during a 2,000-year diaspora of persecution. Jews do not assimilate; and as the "Combined Jewish Committees of the World" led by Marshall so clearly demonstrated recently in Paris, they were "entirely concerned with Jewish affairs to the utter ignoring of the interests and problems of the countries to which they severally owed their national allegiance." Through the "artifice and intrigue" of the *Protocols*, they, together with their "international Jewish bankers," maintain Jewish nationalism at the expense of all other nations. The final sentence affirmed:

> It would seem not at all impossible that this Jewish movement, if permitted
> to develop unchecked to its logical conclusion, might approach an actual
> world control.[76]

The Russian Division further legitimized this interpretation by adding: "[T]his conclusion and its appendices have been submitted most confidentially to the Military Intelligence Division, who are understood to approve of their contents both as to substance and analysis."[77]

In essence, Churchill's reception of this report constituted an exercise in ideological cross-pollination. He was participating in a increasingly routine practice in Washington, whereby MID, the State Department, and other agencies mutually reinforced and expanded speculations until they took on an aura of fact. As a matter of course, the State Department incorporated MID data into its new in-house series, "The Progress of Radicalism in the United States and Abroad," which was, in turn, utilized by army intelligence officers.[78]

Under such circumstances, protests by Captain Isaacs had little chance against the cumulative weight of the mounting incriminating information that continued to arrive over the next few months. By the end of 1919, MID's own intelligence summaries attested to the accuracy of the earlier British government contention that "Bolshevism is an international Jewish movement."[79] The implications of this were quite obvious to intelligence officers, who for the next several years focused much of their attention on the revolutionary Russian threat to the West.

CHAPTER 3

Jews and Geopolitics, 1918–1924

I N 1919, COLONEL WILLIAM A. CASTLE, military attaché in Constantinople, took an extensive trip through Southern Russia, where he observed the savage fighting between Bolshevik and White Russian armies. To him, the struggle for Russia was nothing less than the battle for preserving "civilization" threatened by a "disease," a "moral typhus" that "any nation can contract."[1] What Bolshevik expansion might mean for other countries was illustrated by an anti-Bolshevik underground cartoon from Petrograd, which he later sent to Washington in 1922. In his cover memo, Castle noted:

> The sacrifice of Russia by the Jew Bolsheviks is strikingly depicted, with the cowed people looking on in helpless silence. . . . It is a strong presentation of the real situation in Russia.[2]

Throughout the early 1920s, such grave geopolitical concerns about Bolshevism clearly interacted with perceptions of Jews in the minds of many army officers. This "intimate" connection appeared obvious to both those on the spot in locations such as Russia and Poland and the officers interpreting intelligence reports back home. The conviction that Jews were Bolsheviks not only greatly distorted assessments of communism but intensified antipathy toward Jews. It also embedded in the thinking of many officers a crucial divergence between the interests of true Americans and those of Jews. Collaborating in their own self-interest, American Jews and those in Europe supposedly undermined the strategic policies and national security of the United States. Some officers stubbornly held to this notion until long after World War II. In 1919, it initially led many officers to deny or downplay pogroms, ultimately within a few years expressing a willingness, in the name of national security, to tolerate an anticipated massive pogrom of Jews in Russia.

Bolshevik Russia, 1919

Traditionally regarded as an enigma, Russia became even more mysterious and paradoxical to the outside world in 1919, as the civil war raged between Bolsheviks and counterrevolutionary White Russian armies. The normal confusion of revolutionary upheavals and civil wars was exacerbated in Russia by the sheer geographical expanse of the conflict, which stretched across the Eurasian continent from the Baltic Sea to the Pacific Ocean. Since the fortunes of each side vacillated throughout the year and their conflicting hopes for victory rose and fell accordingly, reliable information was difficult to acquire, especially since both sides habitually directed deceitful propaganda at Russia and the outside world. Atrocity stories of cruelty and slaughter by Whites and Reds alike so barbarous they were mentally and emotionally difficult to comprehend only added to the uncertainty. With each passing month, Bolshevik-dominated territory became more impenetrable.

Despite these disadvantages, American intelligence officers continued to gather intelligence on Russian soil. On the pretext of sustaining the war effort against Germany, President Wilson had in summer 1918 authorized U.S. Army units to join the Allied intervention in Russia. American troops (like those of Britain, France, and Japan) remained in Russia until 1920. Whether the American mission included assisting the White Russian forces in this civil war, thereby enhancing their prospects for destroying Bolshevism, was never fully clarified; the issue sharply divided the American government and the public at large.

To Churchill and DeWitt Poole, staunch advocates of army involvement in counterrevolutionary activities, intervention against Russian Bolshevism constituted the logical complement to MID's antisubversive campaign in the United States and Europe. Social and labor unrest in the West, culminating in actual attempts at Communist revolutions in Germany and Hungary, had made the Bolshevik call for world revolution all the more ominous. With few exceptions, MID officers considered the Whites a necessary bulwark against a major danger to Western civilization itself.

State Department officials in Northern Russia and Siberia not only concurred with the pro-White strategy but emphasized that Jews "played the predominant part" on the other side. Jews furnished the "brains" and "skill" for the Bolsheviks and "direct[ed] all the Soviets." The State Department informed MID that Moscow was under martial law and "an extraordinary commission of the Jews appointed with absolute power."[3]

Admiral Aleksandr Kolchak, head of the reactionary White Russian government in Siberia, cleverly exploited such perceptions to acquire Allied support and to vilify any opponent. To turn local Russian populations against the Bolsheviks, the Kolchak forces maliciously incited anti-Semitism, while saturating foreigners with information on the Jewish nature of Bolshevism. But the intelligent, hardheaded commander of the American Expeditionary Force to Siberia, General William S. Graves, impeded the White Russian scheme. A man of exceptional courage and integrity, Graves resisted all pressures from Kolchak, the Allies, and certain officials in Washington to violate the neutrality of his mission in order to fulfill what MID secretly described as his real purpose—"primarily to support Kolchak against Bolsheviks."[4]

Shortly after their arrival, American soldiers themselves became the targets of Jew-baiting by Kolchak and the British, while Graves suffered vilification from Washington cliques. Over a period of months, White Russians in Siberia, occasionally with British assistance, accused American soldiers of being "infected with Bolshevism," claiming "most of them are Jews from the East Side of New York City who constantly agitate for mutinies." Supposedly, "out of sixty liaison officers and translators with American headquarters, over fifty were Russian Jews, or the relatives of Russian Jews," who influenced army policy contrary to America's real national interests. American soldiers, British Colonel John Ward later wrote in a sinister tone, "had been used by somebody for purposes not purely American."[5]

In reality, Graves's forces, recruited mainly from the Pacific Coast, did not have a disproportionate number of Jews. "I never inquired whether a soldier was a Jew or not a Jew," Graves retorted, "and it made absolutely no difference in my attitude to men under my command. I do not know who at my headquarters came of Jewish stock."[6]

Graves's chief intelligence officer was Major Robert L. Eichelberger, a thirty-three-year-old West Point graduate from Ohio with a long and distinguished military career ahead of him. Decorated with a Distinguished Service Cross for heroism under fire in Siberia, Eichelberger became

Graves's protégé. Nonetheless, Eichelberger shared the cultural attitudes and racial views of much of the American officer corps. "At times I almost think I am living in a civilized country," he wrote to his wife, "then later I realize what a hot bed of murder and oriental intrigue we are lying in." Bolshevik leaders were "cutthroats," while White Russian officers were "worthless" autocrats. "There is however in this country," he lamented in the superior tone of someone well aware of his own Anglo-Saxon heritage, "little of the good, solid blood which characterized the men who settled the United States and I can see little hope for an early settlement of the many problems."[7]

Eichelberger frequently complained that "this 'mongrel crowd' included 'too many' Jews, 'ugly women,' 'Chinks,' and even 'niggers.'" A standing joke with his wife concerned "a little American Jew from Boston." For months, this fur merchant with whom he had done some business was repeatedly humorously referred to only as "that little Jew." And as cable censor for newspaper articles, Eichelberger became an admirer of the journalist Carl Ackermann; he highly recommended to his wife Ackermann's piece on "the last days of the Czar." "I am sorry he has left," Eichelberger declared, because "Ackermann is a mighty bright man & a nice fellow even if he is a Jew."[8]

Quite sensitive to the "denunciation of America" by the Whites and "Allies," Eichelberger felt "like telling the whole bunch to go to h___ & to then embark for the Golden Gate." "They say we are all Jews and Bolsheviks etc. etc.," he wrote. In every conversation or conference with Russian aristocrats and officers, "their conversation always turns to the number of American Jews coming from the U.S., but I always counter by saying they are Russian Jews returning from a brief sojourn in America."[9]

His own sources had informed him that official reports of the British and Canadian intelligence staffs stated: "Of 57 [interpreters] employed by the American Forces there are 55, who are out and out Yids. [And] these Yids are Bolshevik." In his final report to Washington, Eichelberger noted that "many of the best soldier interpreters were Russian Jews who had only been a short time in the United States," but he expressed serious reservations about the "intelligence" and "doubtful loyalty" of others. "Because the Russian Army officer has a unreasonable prejudice against the use of Jewish interpreters it would be best in future expeditions to use very few of this type of interpreter."[10]

Intelligence officers in Siberia told Washington that Bolsheviks enjoyed substantial, though by no means universal, support among Russian Jews.

In Eastern Siberia, Jews favored a stable "conservative republic" in the "interests of Jews and Gentile alike," but elsewhere pro-Bolshevik Jews predominated. "Many exiled Jews returned to Russia, where they immediately became a power in the Soviets"; even in Siberia they "soon occupied the most influential positions among the Bolshevists." In the Ural region, "ninety per cent of the special commission of the Bolsheviks were Jews, most of whom had returned to Russia from London." Inherent contradictions aside, these Jews with supposedly Bolshevik tendencies were also variously described as "hoarders," "speculators," and merchants "who seemingly possessed the ability to secure goods under any circumstances," while the Russian businessmen and "best merchants" were failing economically. Jews could exercise such dominating political influence so immediately after the fall of the czarist regime, MID attested, not only "because they were more highly educated . . . [but] also because of their racial characteristics."[11]

Although intelligence from Siberia indicated that virulent anti-Semitism would probably result in violence against Jewish populations once Bolshevism collapsed, MID in Washington showed a reluctance to believe news of actual occurrences. Churchill informed the chief of staff that "there has not been a single pogrom nor any discrimination against Jews." Such "false reports emanate from certain Jews . . . attempting to evade conscription."[12]

Even while harshly rebuking Graves and cautioning others against "inaccurate news," Churchill had fairly reliable knowledge about the killing of Jews elsewhere. Although it would take almost a year before MID hesitatingly recognized this verifiable condition, Jews in the Ukraine suffered the worst pogroms in Eastern Europe since the end of the Thirty Years' War in 1648. In March 1919, massive violence against Jews was perpetrated by Ukrainian nationalist soldiers, followed by literally hundreds of pogroms in coming months as the civil war raged in that area. Thousands of Jews were slaughtered when the White Russian general Anton I. Deniken reconquered the area. Through the approximately 700 major pogroms in the Ukraine in 1919, various armies slew over 50,000 Jews, with perhaps as many as 150,000 more (10 percent of Ukrainian Jews) eventually dying of related sufferings or disease. Hundreds of thousands of others were orphaned or widowed; and all this was accompanied by raping, looting, and massive destruction of property in Jewish communities.[13]

Since the United States had not intervened directly in Southern Russia, information about events came chiefly through American consuls and military observers in these regions. At the American mission in Constantino-ple, the dissemination center for much of this news, stories of Jewish Bol-shevism were expanded to include Jewish treachery among the French in Odessa.[14] By summer, these sources informed Churchill about anti-Jewish violence, saying only that it occurred in Bolshevik-controlled territories. An American officer at Deniken's headquarters telegrammed Churchill that anti-Bolsheviks within "the interior of Bolshevik Russia" rallied to "the battle cry 'KILL THE JEWS.'" Although this officer doubted the White Russian general had ordered the assault, he did identify this com-mander as "author of the paper 'Kill the Jews,'" and noted that the gen-eral's wife had organized a "Crusader movement . . . against the Jews."[15]

Relying upon information supplied by this same officer, Rear Admiral Mark L. Britol, U.S. high commissioner in Constantinople, cabled the MID director on July 11:

> Approximately ninety per cent of [Bolshevik] army commissary are Jews and people are beginning to realize that the former is managing Bolshevism and living in luxury while rest starve. As a result massacres of Jews grows more and more frequent and have recently occurred in Kief . . . and other towns under Bolsheviki rule.[16]

Certain Red Army units also carried out pogroms; but most of these were by former Ukrainian nationalist or Deniken contingents that had switched sides. The Red Army High Command soon reestablished disci-pline; henceforth, the Bolshevik forces offered the Jewish population of the Ukraine the only security they had experienced since 1918. This protection against slaughter by Ukrainian nationalists and White Russians brought most of Ukrainian Jews over to the Bolshevik side in the civil war.[17]

News of pogroms outside Bolshevik-held regions met initially with de-nial or rationalizations. As an official in Constantinople cabled:

> If there are pogroms of Jews, it will not be because they are Jews, but because Jews are chief among speculators, Bolsheviks and destroyers of the Russian Church.[18]

By this point, several Jewish groups in America, armed with abundant information on the Ukrainian massacres, attempted to alert the world to these catastrophic events and elicit some assistance from the U.S. govern-ment. But as late as the end of September, MID in Washington continued to depict such news as "Jewish propaganda in America" and classify information on pogroms from Jewish groups or the *New York Times* under the heading "Alleged Pogroms." Conceding strong "anti-Jewish feeling," MID's secret intelligence summary still cautioned: "[R]eports of pogroms in the Ukraine must be accepted with reserve. Rumors of pogroms are being circulated by the Bolsheviks, Ukrainians and Rumanians for political purposes." The summary reported that each side was laying blame for pogroms on the other and that whatever the truth might be, "the world must be prepared for serious Jewish persecutions in Russia after the war, [since] . . . Russian patriots will not forget the part the Jews have played in the present tragedy."[19]

Only at the end of 1919, when confronted with incontrovertible testimony by its own officers, did MID acknowledge the reality, though not the magnitude of this "tragedy." "In spite of the fact that it has been denied that pogroms have taken place in the Ukraine," stated a former officer after a recent trip through Western Ukraine, "there can be no doubt that great numbers of Jews have been killed."[20]

The most authoritative confirmation came from General Edgar Jadwin. While investigating Polish pogroms, Jadwin also traveled through the Ukraine. "Jewish situation deplorable but improved," he wired, "best information available indicated probably eleven thousand and possibly eighteen thousand more Jewish civilians killed up to September." Favoring a worldwide front against "anarchistic" Bolshevism, Jadwin tried to lesson Deniken's responsibility: Only four hundred killings could be attributed to his forces, and Deniken had done all he could to restrain anti-Semitism among his soldiers. But Jadwin also posed a rare challenge to the "alleged connection [of] Jews with Bolshevism [which has] probably furnished [the] principle basis for antisemitic propaganda." Although the "prominence of certain Jews in the movement" created anti-Semitic feelings, the percentage of Jews among Bolsheviks was "not very different from proportion of Jews in population."[21]

MID always condemned anti-Semitic violence and demanded its cessation. But in the eyes of headquarters, pogroms in the Ukraine, like anti-Semitism among the White armies in Siberia, were not in and of themselves the essential problem. MID considered the actual killing of Jews far less important than the political repercussions of the pogroms, which it regarded as a national security issue. Officers felt that by making pogroms a political issue at home and abroad, Jews were interfering with, and potentially undermining, an international strategy to contain Bolshevism. Exposes of anti-Semitism and pogroms, they feared, weakened public support for White counterrevolutionary forces, thereby bolstering Bolshevik prospects for victory. This had special import for those officers still strongly suspicious of a Jewish-Bolshevik link.

When confronted with irrefutable incidents, MID attempted to exculpate top White political and military leaders, who supposedly quickly disciplined the real perpetrators—lower-ranking officers or enlisted men.[22] MID also frequently insinuated Jewish responsibility for such outbreaks. Jewish character, the traditional attitudes of Jews toward Christian culture, or their economic and political activities all surfaced as explanations for inciting such wrath against them.[23] But whatever their origin or extent, MID remained adamant that pogroms must not interfere with containment of the real threat—the expansion of revolutionary Bolshevism from its Russian core. This same line of thought determined MID's reaction to the Jewish question in Poland.

The Polish Bulwark, 1919

"It is vital to our national interests," Churchill counseled the secretary of war in January 1919, "that Poland's defensive power be maintained unimpaired."[24] In Churchill's strategic thinking, the newly created Polish state stood as "Europe's bulwark against Bolshevism"; it had become nothing less than "a vital rampart protecting the civilization of the world."

Although others also combined geopolitics and anti-Bolshevism to justify staunch pro-Polish policies, Churchill's underlying suppositions gave his policy paper on Poland a noticeable distinctiveness. He had written a paragon of Social Darwinist theory, which in style, tone, and basic concepts, read like pages composed by racial ideologues of the Madison Grant school. It represented one of the clearest policy applications of core ideas pervading the thought of officers in this era.

Like Major Woodruff, the army's own Darwinist theoretician, Churchill attributed the appeal of Bolshevism to man's eternal striving for survival. The availability of food would determine the success or failure of Bolshevism. No exception to this "maxim," postwar Poland posed a particularly critical problem, for it served as the geopolitical gateway to Europe.

Although "the heart of civilization, culture and material well-being," Europe was "but the tip end of a peninsula extending out from the great Eurasian Continent." Favored by "climate and geology," Western civilization emerged and flourished there only because "from time immemorial, the Teutonic tribes—lately known as the Central Powers," protected it "from the vast hordes of disorder and barbarism living to the eastward throughout the vast Eurasian Continent." Invoking contemporary racial stereotypes as elaborated by American war propaganda, Churchill depicted the Germans as "virile, warlike and indomitable." Historically, they "formed the natural dam against which the glacial pressure of vast human masses, moving westward from the dreary primitive expanses of the Eurasian Continent were checked and held." Previous wars in the West had been merely "the eddying strife of a sheltered people," since "everything to the west of this dam developed in security." Tragically, all this had changed when World War I "destroyed, at least temporarily, this great Teutonic dam."[25]

"The mere mechanics of life" now made the West extremely vulnerable. Through their "physical power of superior numbers, superior physique and a greater lust for aggrandizement," the "Slavic and Turanian races" would inevitably overrun Europe unless checked by the new dam constructed by the Treaty of Versailles—Poland. Unfortunately, the Polish state, "the only barrier remaining between Europe and the hordes of Eurasia" led by the Bolsheviks, is a "weak" dam about to be swept away by this "eastern flood." Unless reinforced by essential food and military supplies, the brave Poles, currently sustained only by "intense patriotism," would collapse.

Among the various examples (German Spartacists, Hungary under Bela Kun, and so forth) proving extensive seepage had already occurred, Churchill cited first of all "the Polish-Jewish-Bolshevists of Poland."[26]

His assessment constituted no mere conjecture, Churchill insisted, but was rather "a terse statement of facts verified by all sources and by unimpeachable evidence." Warning of Bolshevik armies and Eurasian hordes posed to sweep across Europe, he "urgently recommended" massive, immediate civilian and military assistance for Poland. While not suggesting sending American troops, Churchill did advise providing American "staff officers." The dire prospects further warranted immediate agreements among the United States, its allies, and the League of Nations "for concerted military support of Poland."[27]

This Western counterpart to Churchill's anti-Bolshevik strategy in Siberia and Southern Russia soon became complicated by the Jewish question. The new Polish state had already been blemished by the Lemberg pogrom of November 1918, when Polish troops went on a three-day rampage of murder and destruction after capturing the city from Ukrainians. Sealing off the Jewish quarter with machine guns and armored cars, the troops went house to house, robbing, shooting, and burning; seventy-two Jews were killed, with over 400 wounded, and numerous buildings burned to the ground.[28] Lemberg strengthened the resolve of Jewish American leaders to oppose recognition and assistance to Poland unless that state guaranteed minority rights and protection against pogroms.

While these issues were debated in the press and at the Paris Peace Conference, Churchill received dire predictions from American officers in Poland that recent victories of powerful Red armies had opened the path for their advancement to the West. It was a conquest that officers attributed in part to internal subversion. Routinely referring to the Jewish "seizure of power in Russia," officers noted that in Poland "the Bolsheviks receive great help from the Jewish population."[29] U.S. diplomatic and military circles expected continued strife and additional violent outbreaks against Jews.

Returning to Paris after a trip to Central Europe, Hugh Gibson, soon to be appointed American minister to Poland, wrote in his diary:

> Practically all the worst and most powerful of the Bolsheviki and the like are Jews and this is bound to react against them before long. Some Gov't is going to see in this a way of taking its people's mind off other troubles and turn them loose on the Jews. Just as likely as not the war will wind up with a gigantic pogrom.[30]

Hardly a week passed when on April 5, about seventy-five Jews in Pinsk, a city liberated by the Polish army a month earlier, met to discuss the distribution of relief from America. Although the city commander had authorized the assembly, Polish soldiers assumed the group was Bolshevist and suddenly arrested, robbed, and then marched the Jews to headquarters. After scant examination, thirty-five were lined up against the cathedral wall and shot; three of these found alive the next morning were quickly executed. The soldiers stripped and severely beat the rest of the men and women. Lieutenant Foster, the American officer sent to investigate, concurred with British and French officers that the "shooting . . . was not a pogrom." While conceding the evidence could be interpreted differently, he wired: "[A]ction taken by Pole commanding officer was pardonable in view of critical military situation but only for that reason."[31]

Two weeks later, after the Poles drove the Bolsheviks out of Vilna, they attacked and robbed Jews, killing over 100. Believing Jews had fired on them, Polish soldiers broke into homes and stores, beating the inhabitants and stealing even the shoes and blankets of poor Jews; they also mutilated the sacred scrolls in the synagogue. "Hundreds of Jews were arrested and deported from the city. Some of them were herded into box cars and kept without food or water for four days."[32]

Colonel William F. Godson, who entered Vilna shortly after its capture, denied a pogrom had occurred. Born in England and raised in Canada, Godson joined the American army in his early twenties; he saw action in the Philippines and taught military science before becoming U.S. military attaché in Bern in 1917. Official MID history highlighted Godson as one of its most "impressive" operatives; among other "feats," he "completely demoralized" the German secret service in Switzerland through infiltration and arrests.[33] Redirecting his talents toward new enemies—Bolsheviks and Jews—Godson proved particularly receptive to versions of events acquired from the Polish general staff. Distinguishing between the "harmless Polish Jew[s]" (who really "had become Poles") and the "extremely dangerous" "Litwak or Russian Jew," Godson declared that "the Jewish question is the most important one" for the entire country.[34]

"The connection between the Jews and the bolsheviki at Vilna," he informed Washington, "seems to be proven without the shadow of a doubt." Jews constituted at least 80 percent of every Bolshevik organization; urban Jews collaborated in the Bolshevik takeover and engaged in "terrific speculation in foods and goods." Neither in Pinsk nor Vilna had pogroms occurred, since General Josef Pilsudski strictly prohibited even the appearance of "abuse of the Jewish element."

Allegations of pogroms originated with "vigorous propaganda from German and Jewish sources to throw every aspersion possible upon the Poles and their army, which was not at all borne out by observations made on the spot" by Godson himself. The facts showed that Jewish Bolsheviks had fired on Polish soldiers, who fought back and carried out some unwise executions. Godson personally attended the funeral of thirty-one Polish soldiers killed by the Jewish-assisted Bolsheviks; one of these Polish "victims" was, he pointed out, a boy scout. He never mentioned the Jewish dead.[35]

Completely neglecting the plight of Polish Jews, Godson had plenty of gruesome details about what these Bolsheviks had in store for civilization. "Misery is written on every face"; the city was "comparable to an orchard which has been visited by a swarm of locusts." His chilling testimony painted dreadful images of starving women cooking "green shoots and buds off the trees and bushes"; he had actually witnessed people scrambling to eat the oats that fell from a horse's mouth. Yet the savagery of the Bolsheviks far surpassed even the unimaginable suffering and desperation caused by famine. Total devastation by robbing, looting, and the destruction of all livestock was just part of their barbarism. He described at length ghastly accounts by Russian émigrés of Bolsheviks executing and mutilating civilians; they cut off ears and noses, nailed boots to faces, and disemboweled the living. The photographic evidence he enclosed in his report to Washington typified, for Godson, the true nature of Bolshevism and the peril to civilized life. After stripping and mutilating two Polish soldiers, laughing Bolsheviks hung them upside down on large trees, with one impaled through the anus.[36]

The effects of Godson's version of events would ripple through official American circles for the next year. Returning to Warsaw, he briefed Hugh Gibson, the new minister to Poland. "The stories he tells," Gibson noted, "are disheartening when they are not maddening."[37] With values and viewpoints similar to those of American officers, Gibson readily internalized Godson's account. Gibson's response to an inquiry a few weeks later from the American Commission to Negotiate the Peace in Paris deviated little from Godson's line of argument. "I feel entirely safe in saying," Gibson wrote, "that nothing in the nature of a pogrom took place at Vilna." During the struggle to expel the Bolsheviks, some stores were pillaged by soldiers, "but even according to the Jews, it was not at all that serious." In Vilna that very day, Colonel Godson and his assistant encountered the "outspoken . . . hostility" of Jews toward Poles, whereas "they heard no stories of alleged ill-treatment" of Jews.[38]

Although admitting the animosity of Jews and Poles made establishing the truth difficult, Gibson reiterated reports of Jews as Bolsheviks, shooting at Polish soldiers, or as spies for Germans and Ukrainians. Like Godson, he delineated between "decent patriotic Jews," "Jewish criminal class" (similar to Jewish gunmen in New York), harmless Orthodox (peddlers and smugglers), and the real problem—"Litwaks." Of course, "a large part of the Jews in Poland have detestable qualities," but these resulted from centuries of persecution and the Jews needed "charity" rather than persecution for "these evil qualities." Gibson then wrote in pen at the bottom: "Please do not show this letter as such to any of our Jewish friends."[39]

Within days, however, Gibson was besieged with telegrams inquiring about "alleged massacres of Jews." As he pictured it, "the roof has blown off and we are in the midst of turmoil." Privately, he held that no massacres had occurred, only some suspicious Jews, hostile to the Polish state, had been killed; anti-Polish German propagandists had manufactured the rest. "But the fat was in the fire and Jews all over the world have been excited about the matter ever since." It reminded him of the protests "in the good old days when the Armenians were slaughtered." Repeatedly referring in his diary to "our Jewish friends," Gibson griped, "I can see that we are in for a long siege of Jewish atrocities."[40]

In an expanded version of June 2, Gibson cabled that inaccurate charges of widespread violence against Jews, aggravated by anti-Polish agitation by American Jews, had caused a Polish backlash. Urging patience and cooperation to gradually reconcile both sides, he still denied pogroms had occurred. In "the important incidents in which Jews recently were killed . . . the [Polish] military were involved," in reaction to the "behavior [of certain Jews] towards the troops." The soldiers assumed "Jews are firing on them from houses, carrying intelligence to the enemy, etc." Commanders "are now experiencing great difficulty in controlling anti-Jewish action," especially since many Polish officers had been in Bolshevik Russia, where "they observed the Jew as a Bolshevik or the latter's agent in practices of a nefarious nature."[41]

Gibson also added revealing observations about the attitude of American soldiers in Poland. They intuitively empathized with the Poles, essentially sharing their aversion to the appearance and behavior of Jews. "American soldiers," Gibson wrote,

are first amused by the costume of the Jews, their beards, their habits and are then incensed by their lack of patriotism and speculation. The soldier's sense of justice is aroused easily because of the misery which is on every side.[42]

More callous was Anson Goodyear, American representative to the Inter-Allied Commission, who conferred with Gibson and Polish officials. Thereafter, en route to Prague in a Cadillac with an American officer, he wrote:

Pouring rain, but we made good progress, through what looked like 90% Jew country—long black coats—greasy beards little curls over their ears—round black hats. On with the pogroms.[43]

Within days, the gist of Gibson's explanations had worked its way through the Paris Peace Commission to Churchill in Washington. For months the MID chief had been dealing with data and analyses on Jewish Bolsheviks at home and abroad (a problem further complicated by the secret

Protocols), so he quickly cabled an inquiry about rumored pogroms. Responding from Paris, Van Deman assured him that "there have been no Jewish pogroms in Poland. There were about 32 [illegible word] Jews killed in Pinsk some time ago but it was proven that they were killed because they were engaged in a bolshevist plot and not because they were Jews." He then reiterated Gibson-Godson's version: U.S. Jews had created the false impression that "Poles are going to massacre Jews," German propaganda stood behind it all, and Poles issued strict orders against "persecuting the Jews." "Careful investigations" of Gibson had already explained this.[44]

When someone leaked Van Deman's message to the press, Gibson found himself embroiled in a dispute extending from Warsaw to Paris and Washington. An immediate attack in the New York papers ensued, followed by protests to the State Department by Jewish-American leaders incensed by the denial of pogroms. The State Department and Gibson claimed the cable "had been wrongly attributed . . . to Gibson" rather than to the Paris military attaché. As Gibson exclaimed privately: "Some damphool gave out a statement made by somebody else as coming from me to the effect that there had been nothing of the nature of pogroms in Poland. All the Jews riz up and smote me hip and thigh." Although persistently maintained, these were rationalizations invented under fire, since Gibson had actually written "that nothing in the nature of a pogrom took place at Vilna."[45]

Returning to Paris to confront his three staunchest critics (Brandeis, Frankfurter, and Marshall), Gibson, by his own account, offered a successful counteroffensive. Presenting himself as merely an official of "integrity and fairness" who only "wanted to ameliorate the conditions of the Jews in Poland," he took a combative stand. "Felix tried a little rough talk and I had to do some straight talk back to him"; and Gibson claimed to have refuted all Marshall's charges point for point. "These gentlemen," Gibson wrote to his friend William Phillips, assistant secretary of state, "accepted as gospel the whole fabric of truth and fiction from Jewish sources about events in Poland and I was supposed to swallow it whole."[46]

Gibson began privately to question their real motives and veracity. Even intelligent Polish Jews, he confided in Phillips, "deplore the present propaganda which is made chiefly by American Jews . . . [because] the whole movement is conducted without any regard for the welfare of the Jews in Poland." Relying upon conjecture and the suspicions of "many people, among them some prominent Jews," Gibson reverted to the wartime allegations of pro-German sentiments, collaboration of America's Jews, and recent concerns about Zionism to explain their guiding principles. They sought "to weaken Poland in the interests of Germany who does not desire a formidable economic or political rival in the East." It was "a conscienceless and cold blooded plan to make the condition of the Jews in Poland so bad that they must turn to Zionism for relief." All of this was clearly detrimental to "American prestige" and interests.[47]

By the end of June, the controversy had risen to such a level that the American Commission to Negotiate the Peace appointed a special mission "to investigate Jewish matters in Poland." Its members, Henry Morgenthau Sr., former American ambassador to Turkey, Homer H. Johnson, and General Edgar Jadwin, spent two months traveling over 2,500 miles through Polish cities, villages, and the countryside.[48]

Suddenly, on August 8, Jadwin personally witnessed an outbreak of anti-Jewish violence as Polish armies pushed the Russian Bolshevik forces out of Minsk. Jadwin's presence and awareness that anti-Semitism could compromise American assistance had led Polish generals to issue "stringent orders" to minimize civilian casualties. But even the pro-Polish Jadwin could not help notice the poisoned atmosphere before the assault: "Stories, some true and others greatly exaggerated were rife among the troops as to the relations between the Jews and Bolsheviks."[49]

Since the Poles had completely pacified the city within just a few hours, Jadwin was shocked to find "soldiers breaking windows and carrying off stolen goods." The next day, civilians joined the soldiers in rioting and looting. Despite attempts by commanders to restore discipline, it took three days to stop the violence. About thirty Jewish civilians were killed, almost 400 Jewish shops were robbed, and many Jews were robbed and beaten within their homes. Jadwin determined that "13 of the deaths appeared incident to street fighting or in fleeing arrest"; others were "nonjustified deaths" resulting from "insufficient military cause." Not a single incident occurred "where Jewish citizens had fired on Polish troops." Among all those killed, in fact, only one was a Bolshevik.[50]

Jadwin briefly mentioned in his preliminary notes that "there was some cutting of beards." But this did not strike him as particularly significant, since "this seems to have been looked upon by the soldiers and even by Jewish boys as a lark."[51]

Despite these experiences, Jadwin departed confident that Poles and Jews could overcome their differences.[52] However, within his own commission, it proved almost impossible to reach a consensus. Dissatisfied with Morgenthau's version, Jadwin and Johnson insisted on attaching their own supplement, to which not only Morgenthau but also other Jewish Americans privately objected.[53] The following year, Jadwin told an intelligence officer that there had been "some attempt made to persuade him to eliminate certain passages not especially complimentary to the Jews, but that he had declined to modify his report." The intelligence officer admired Jadwin's unwavering stand, because "presumably the Jews intended to have only Mr. M's report published."[54]

The final presidential report published in January 1920 opened with Morgenthau's part, followed by the Jadwin-Johnson supplement. Unable to agree even on a definition of "pogrom," the commission used the term "excesses" to characterize violent outbreaks against Jews. Morgenthau described in detail the "eight principal excesses" that had occurred in Poland, including the well-publicized events in Lemberg, Pinsk, Vilna, and Minsk. To these he added numerous other forms of pervasive persecutions and discrimination, ranging from searches to beatings and banishment by soldiers and civilians alike. Contrary to Jadwin's earlier reference to beard cutting as a lark, Morgenthau emphasized how painfully sacrilegious it was for Orthodox Jews to have "their beards either torn off or cut off" by Polish soldiers in almost every city.[55]

Among the major causes of anti-Semitism, Morgenthau attached particular importance to the clash between centuries-long Polish nationalistic aspirations and Jewish cultural autonomy. The Poles regarded Jews as "aliens" within their borders and resented Jewish demands for "minority rights" through the Treaty of Versailles. Morgenthau expressed confidence that a democratic Poland that protected "minority rights" could over generations bridge this gap between citizens of all kinds. But the Polish state must also eliminate the source of anti-Semitic aggression by educating the Polish masses. National unity and survival demanded "the Polish nation must see that its worst enemies are those who encourage this internal strife." The world should rally behind Poland, but only after its conduct demonstrated that it merited international moral and economic support.[56]

On matters of fact, Jadwin and Johnson differed very little from Morgenthau; meaningful dissimilarities came in the tone, approach, and conclusions of the two versions. Jadwin and Johnson tilted toward the Poles, citing "the relatively small extent" of the excesses: "[T]he grand total of deaths from excesses in which antisemitism was a factor has not exceeded 300." Rather than dwelling upon the excesses, they preferred to explain the sources of Polish anti-Semitism. For page after page, they reiterated historic and contemporary Polish "allegations" against Jews: religious and cultural separatism, commercial rivalry and Jewish "acquisitiveness," "alien" nature, lack of patriotism, sympathies for Poland's enemies, namely, Germany and Bolshevism, and so on.

Jadwin and Johnson modeled their solution after the American experience with assimilation. All Jews must become Poles socially and politically, though they could retain their religion. Jadwin and Johnson accused unidentified forces in Poland and abroad of keeping the controversy alive on the "dubious grounds" of promoting "better treatment of the Jew" as a separate minority. They also echoed charges of German economic interests exploiting the Jewish question so as to maintain their dominating position between Russia and the West.[57]

Poland, they concluded, deserved the international assistance it so desperately needed. It was a promising democracy, which repressed anti-Jewish violence and protected Jews thereafter. "None of these excesses were instigated or approved by any responsible governmental authority, civil or military." Jadwin and Johnson abandoned the appearance of impartiality and shifted the burden to the Jews. What they previously cited in the form "Poles believe" or "it is alleged" had by the end taken on the quality of fact. After exculpating the Polish authorities, Jadwin and Johnson bluntly stated, "[W]e find, on the other hand, that the history and the attitude of the Jews, complicated by abnormal economic and political conditions produced by the war, have fed the flame of anti-Semitism at a critical moment."[58]

When the Morgenthau Commission submitted its findings, neither the Jewish question in Poland nor the Polish-Soviet war had been settled. About a year had passed since Churchill's policy statement naming Poland as the bulwark safeguarding Western civilization. Meanwhile, information emanating in Europe about suspicious Jewish activities reverberated through military intelligence circles: Jews refused to fight in Polish armies; spies "invariably proved to be Jews"; Zionists waged a propaganda war against Poland; Jewish hoarders and speculators seized control of the food supply while Poland faced starvation.[59]

Under the title "The Jews Again," MID stated that currency smuggling by "Jewish brokers (money sharks)" in collaboration with German interests undermined Poland's financial foundations. "The houses of both usury and prostitution are known to be almost without exception in the hands of Jews." Other MID reports offered images of Jewish Bolshevik leaders engaged in "unspeakable barbarity," while elsewhere Jewish inhabitants of towns "cheered" and "overwhelmed [the Bolsheviks] with flowers."[60]

By September 1919, MID began to interpret such material in the context of a possible "broad international collusion between certain parties and interests inimical to American policy." Now concerned with "International Jewry," officers noticed a "curious synchronization" of Zionist strategy with Poland's enemies, Germany and Bolshevik Russia. The Russian link held particular significance, since "the Jewish-controlled Bolshevik State has always found in the united and nationalistic Poland its most formidable obstacle in spreading toward Western Europe." The tendency of American newspapers and Zionists to promote this anti-Polish hostility ran "flagrantly counter . . . to American foreign policy"; it warranted an investigation to uncover the "actual forces behind" the entire campaign. As one officer queried:

> Is a cabal of international Jews using American public opinion as a lever for pro-German and pro-Bolshevik ends against Poland? . . . [And] what Jewish interests in particular are encouraged in doing this?[61]

A few weeks later, Churchill personally selected and forwarded to MID and the State Department similar information from a Van Deman source. According to this "impartial and intelligent" informant, there existed a scheme to manipulate the controlled world press through exaggerated atrocity stories about Poland, while consciously neglecting the killing of 30,000 Ukrainian Jews. "The only explanation . . . is that the design is to make Poland the commercial Judea from which as a basis European trade will be controlled, especially the coming great market in Russia." The settlement at the Peace Conference of disputed Polish-Ukrainian oil fields "was dictated by Jewish interests." Such events were "the most worth watching," because "world peace" itself was at stake. Unfortunately, "we do not by any means know all the plans definitely made nor would it be very easy to find them out."[62]

Over the next several years, American military attachés in Europe would expend considerable effort attempting to validate suspicions of such plans and activities. To these officers abroad, the Jewish question in Poland and Russia was inextricably connected with events in the rest of Europe and America.

Military Attachés and European Jews

One of the few documents preserved in Colonel William Castle's private papers from his years as attaché in Turkey is an anonymous typed hymn, with certain stanzas conveying an unmistakable meaning:

Internationality

> *To the free and independent Nations of the World. A.D. 1920. . . .*

Here enters the Emperor of the Internationalists, a man with a semitic cast, of countenance and the face of a sphinx. The Multitude prostrate themselves chanting a hymn of praise in honour of their Emperor.

> The Multitude chanting.
> Internationality.
> Lord to thee we bow
> Saviour of our destiny
> Thy name be hallowed now. . . .

The silent spectator, deeply incensed, exclaims with a loud voice:

> Heed ye not his ravings.
> To thyselves be true.
> Internationality!!!
> The "Kingdom" of the "Jew."
> Keep your Nationality.
> His and Mine and Thine.
> Be not driven headlong.
> Like Gadarenian swine.

Unfortunately the blare of the trumpets and the booming of the drums prevent his words being heard but by a few.[63]

This hymn epitomized many of the components of the officer corps' worldview that attachés superimposed on postwar developments. They felt strongly that national identity and loyalty had to be protected from inroads by the internationalist currents fostered by Wilsonianism and the left. They worried lest the realities of an unavoidable class system be undermined by the illusory demands of a labor movement misled by idealists. There was trepidation that the ignorant, easily misguided masses would no longer heed the wisdom or leadership of the ruling elites; the fanfare of mass culture and demagogic politics might overwhelm responsible government. Even the most sacred in their traditional world was not immune, since they believed that the precepts of Christianity itself, the very moral foundation of their civilization, were being usurped and manipulated, naively or cynically, by pacifists and internationalists. Behind it all stood the Jews, who had become a metaphor for the causes of these dangers. Indeed, attachés' patriotism, anti-Bolshevism, and geopolitical views mingled with racial theories and a predisposition to see Jews as alien, rootless, cunning, and powerful.

These attachés were MID's eyes and ears abroad. What intelligence centers in Washington, as well as the General Staff and a good part of the American government, knew about the world's largest Jewish communities originated primarily with these officers and their Foreign Service counterparts in various embassies. In background, careers, and attitudes, these attachés constituted a fairly representative cross-section of the officer corps. Considered among the army's best, their opinions were greatly valued by the General Staff and high offices of the government. The truly astounding views on Jews permeating attaché reports are so revealing that their tone and content can only be fully appreciated by directly encountering them in the words of the officers themselves. The extensive documentation of what American attachés across the European continent thought and wrote about Jews during these years also establishes how representative such views were of army attitudes.

During a tour of American embassies in Europe in early 1921, Marlborough Churchill found his military attachés pursuing the Jewish question with the same enthusiasm, often zealotry, they had displayed since the end of the war. When Churchill reached Bucharest, he wrote to Colonel Sherman Miles, asking to be kept informed "on the 'isms,' Jewry and the like."[64]

To Churchill, these "isms" held significant geopolitical implications for the strategic states along the rim of Bolshevik Russia. He singled out the Baltic states, Poland, and Romania as particularly important. Referring to their respective attachés, he ordered Miles to "give fellows like Hollyday, Farman, and Poillen all you can, even if you have to cut seriously" into France and England. Although Poland remained the keystone of Churchill's geopolitical strategy, he believed all the attachés in Eastern Europe were "sitting on volcanoes."[65]

Warsaw

When Churchill and his wife arrived in Warsaw and other capitals, the American diplomatic missions welcomed the army officer as one of their own, for they had been cut from the same social cloth. "A pretty good club" of upper class, primarily "eastern seaboard Brahmans," the diplomatic corps recruited from Ivy League graduates lured by commitment as well as the excitement, pomp, and culture of European capitals. Like army officers, they shared a worldview that had at its center the magnificent achievements, power, and future of a "western civilization," whose "moral core" emanated from a "faith in Christianity."[66]

Churchill's access had been well prepared by trusted friends of ambassadors and ministers. "Churchill and I were classmates in college," wrote Assistant Secretary of State William Phillips from The Hague, assuring Hugh Gibson he should speak "frankly of anything next to your heart" when dealing with this "old friend of mine." From Washington, Undersecretary of State William Hurley emphasized the importance of Churchill's "mission" and told Gibson that Churchill could be entrusted with messages that the ambassador might be reluctant to put in writing or pass on through others.[67] After Churchill's visit, Gibson wrote Hurley, "I should mightily like to see all the stuff that Uncle Henry Ford has been getting out on the Jewish question, together with anything else that may be printed in connection with the subject."[68]

Although not Paris, Warsaw dazzled and captivated America's diplomats with its aristocratic society and irresistible invitations to sprawling feudal estates and lavish manor houses. The delegation from democratic America empathized not with the downtrodden Polish peasants whose labor sustained these estates but with a Polish aristocracy clinging desperately to a romanticized version of medieval society. The Americans believed Bolshevism threatened this "way of life" by inciting revolution among the contented peasantry of this strategic bulwark of Western civilization.[69]

Empathy rarely extended to Jewish communities of Poland. To Americans and their aristocratic Polish friends, the Jewish question really meant the Jewish "problem." To some, it emanated from the presumed Bolshevik link, while for others, the very existence of a large culturally and religiously disparate Jewish minority endangered the unity, strength, and perhaps survival of the infant Polish state so crucial to the West. Moreover, anti-Semitism was so rampant in the diplomatic service that inserting caustic remarks about Jews provided comic relief in otherwise serious correspondence. Frankfurter was known as "Hot Dog," whereas meeting a delegation of Jews was equated with "being molested by wild geese."

Gibson's assistant, Jay Pierrepont Moffat, wrote sarcastically of his "delightful time holding the hands (figuratively, of course) of our numerous Hebraic friends who are in trouble." Years later, Gibson joked with Colonel Godson about the time "we committed pogroms together in Poland."[70] From the American embassy in Constantinople, Allen Dulles wrote to his friend Gibson, passing on a "remedy" for his Jewish "troubles" as recommended by a British official: "[N]amely, a 'ham bone amulet' to keep off the evil eye of some of our hooknosed friends."[71]

Gibson, like many Americans, found the mannerisms, dress, and customs of Polish Jews either an amusing spectacle or disgusting. He relished capturing his impressions in private notes, often comparing Polish Jews with the "Negro problem." He dismissed pogroms with the quip that "the number of Jews killed in Poland during 1919 was less than the number of negroes killed in the United States during the same period." Gibson recounted a journey with two American officers where

> the villages were awful. Never have I seen nigger villages at home so utterly shiftless and hopeless as the Jewish settlements along the road. The people are filthy and sullen and you wonder why they go on living.[72]

Although by 1922, Gibson conceded he had "never seen anything to prove the existence of a Jewish world conspiracy, or . . . that Bolshevism is a Jewish movement," he still maintained Jews controlled the "Soviet machinery" of government. "The nearest thing to any great national political idea in Russia," he informed the secretary of state, "is that the Bolshevist government is a government of the Jews, by the Jews and for the Jews; that if and when the Russians get rid of the Jews, they will automatically get rid of the Bolsheviks, and vice-versa."

Gibson objected to U.S. involvement in the Polish-Jewish dispute because it might set a precedent for American intervention on behalf of Russian Jews when the Soviet regime collapsed. Then "there will be a massacre of Jews on a scale unprecedented in modern times." And "interference" would not only be ineffective, it "might well jeopardize our national interests."[73]

Such were the prevailing attitudes in the American diplomatic community in Warsaw where Colonel Elbert E. Farman had served as military attaché since 1919. Described by Gibson as "a good quiet little chap who promises well," Farman fitted perfectly into this milieu. A vociferous anti-Bolshevik, he railed against that "band of assassins and brigands" and anyone the least sympathetic to them. "Some of our formerly good American reviews such as the New Republic," he wrote to Miles, "are completely Bolshevik"; and "M.I.D. ought to hang" them. "The Czar's government was [far more] liberal and benevolent towards the working man."

A staunch proponent of immediate substantial assistance to preserve the anti-Bolshevik Polish state, Farman was assiduously courted by an enticing Polish ruling class. Polish expressions of gratitude occasionally reached comic proportions. When Gibson officially introduced Farman to Prime Minister Ignace Jan Paderewski, the renowned composer stood up and sang "Yankee Doodle."[74]

The Poles had clearly found a friend in Farman, who generally took their side while almost without exception portraying Jews in a pejorative light. Shortly after assuming this post, he advised Miles that he needed as his orderly "a reliable soldier who speaks Polish [but] is not under any circumstances a Jew." Farman's most important intelligence source was the anti-Semitic Polish Secret Service, which had provided him with a forty-page version of the *Protocols*. For the next four years, most of what MID learned about Europe's largest Jewish community came from Farman.[75]

Farman also relied heavily upon Captain P. Wright of the British army. In 1919, Wright served on the British mission investigating "the massacres" of Jews. Sir Stuart Samuel, the delegation head, confirmed that "pogroms" had occurred and recommended British pressure on Poland to fulfill the minority rights clauses of postwar treaties. Wright, however, challenged Samuel in a minority report.[76]

Although Wright acknowledged the violence against Jews ("a shocking outrage") and a virulent anti-Semitic movement, he concentrated almost exclusively upon the nature and behavior of Jews he considered the source of these problems. In arguments later decried by Nathan Isaacs as "anti-Semitic," Wright drew sharp distinctions between the "West Jews and East Jews." The former, totally Europeanized and assimilated, were loyal citizens, but Poland contained a very small minority of such Jews. The masses, nationalist (Zionists) and Orthodox alike, having an "oriental character," remained problematical. The "semi-assimilation" of partially Europeanized Zionists "is the very cause of the evil," because they had adopted a Western-style nationalism that was in competition with Polish nationalism.[77]

The Orthodox, on the other hand, still lived in a "small primitive Semitic civilization, so strangely preserved in Europe." "No West Jew I have ever met," Wright stated, "is like the Orthodox East Jew, or even has any idea that such people exist; otherwise, they would be less surprised at the prejudice of the Poles." While chastising those who ridiculed this culture, Wright portrayed the Orthodox as a poverty-stricken alien mass so "physically, mentally, and morally" different that they were exceptionally difficult even to associate with, let alone assimilate.

Orthodox Jews were "not civilized in our sense of the word." They were an unskilled "people whose personal habits are so unclean" that Poles refuse to work with them. They were like the "negroes in the United States, whom a long past in African forests or in American plantations" left unfit for the modern world. "What the enormous mass of Orthodox Jews really required" was Booker T. Washington's "gospel of the toothbrush," "keeping clean [and] learning a trade."[78]

Wright believed the Polish government must ensure "a powerful and just administration" to make the Jews "loyal to Poland, which is what they are far from being now." Nonetheless, he conceded the persistence of an anti-Semitic movement, which included "very eminent Polish politicians," that remained determined to drive the Jews out of Poland. Since most Poles identified Jews as a "national enemy," Jews suffered daily abuse, as well as pervasive and hostile social, economic, and professional discrimination; as Wright noted, "every independent Polish institution is . . . determined to oust the Jews." The "most anti-Semitic body in Poland" was the army, which drew its officers "from the most anti-Semitic class, the nobles and the intelligentsia."[79]

Despite this, Wright still asserted that "the Jew appears not as the most persecuted, but the most favoured, people of Europe." To him, Jews were economic "middle men" and "dealers," who, unlike other groups, produce nothing. In contrast to the "great martial and patriotic traditions" of the Poles, "the Jews evade military service; by bribery, desertion, or some other device they escape all service at the front." Although he denied Bolshevism was a Jewish movement, Wright asserted that in "administration and propaganda," Bolshevism "was largely Jewish," because Jews alone possessed the necessary literacy. Moreover, all classes of Jews profited from Bolshevism:

> Bolshevism spells business for the poor Jews; innumerable posts in a huge administration; endless regulations therefore endless jobbery; big risks . . . but big profits. The rich bourgeois Jew also manages to get on with it in his own way, "Jüdischer Weise" as the Jews call bribery. Many Jews who are by no means poor, try at the present time to escape into Russia, so fine are the business prospects. Such a desirable state of affairs must naturally have charms for the Jews in Poland, and in spite of repeated and constant accusations, the Jewish political leaders have never publicly repudiated Bolshevism, from which I conclude that they must have many sympathizers with Bolshevism among their followers.[80]

When Farman forwarded the Samuel Commission Report to Washington, he praised Wright's section as "a splendid summary of the Jewish situation here, the best that has come to our attention." Farman dismissed Samuel's part as "of little value." MID circulated only Wright's report in its *Weekly Intelligence Summary* under the title "The Jewish Problem in Poland" and with the disclaimer this did "not necessarily represent the opinion" of MID. But MID commended Wright for "a viewpoint and a dispassionate analysis which is unusual."

Meanwhile, Farman continued to criticize Samuel for a "pro-Semitic report, hostile and somewhat unfair to Poles. The chief value of this publication is . . . in the minority report of Captain Wright, which . . . discount[s] most of Samuel's conclusions." The U.S. State Department likewise favored Wright's position; from Washington, Allen Dulles wrote to Gibson that Samuel's report "is a typical bit of Jewish propaganda."[81]

Another Farman source was a 1917 German handbook on the "ethnographic, biological, industrial and cultural aspects" of Poland. From this "important and accurate scientific" work, Farman constructed a racial overview of Poles and Jews that resembled the racist histories of Grant and Stoddard. Farman included pages of statistics of the cephalic indices of Polish skulls to establish that "Poles are brachycephalic," in contrast to the dolichocephalic Nordic/Anglo-Saxon races. The only exception was that the "head and brain types" of the "upper classes, intelligentsia and the aristocracy, tend more to dolichocephalic sculls than the lower classes." The upper classes were physically and culturally more advanced than the lower, but otherwise they constituted a homogeneous racial group at different levels of development.

Polish Jews, none of whom were of the superior dolichocephalic type, formed a distinct race with "separate anatomical characteristics," which could be more precisely differentiated by cephalic index and height, depending upon whether one measured Polish, Lithuanian, or Galician Jews. An outsider was struck particularly by their separateness. Jews were "more clannish . . . and live in closer concentration" and "grew steadily in number because their standard of living was, and is, much lower than that of the Poles . . . and multiply as rapidly as a people with a lower standard of living always do."[82]

Jews, Farman wrote, belonged to a "despised caste" of traders, whom Poles tolerated due to their economic importance; but Jews were certainly not an "oppressed race." "Excesses against Jewish elements in the population were caused in large part by local conditions and the behavior of Jews in individual instances."[83]

Instead of rallying to an infant Polish state in grave danger, he argued, Jews showed persistent disloyalty. In Europe and America, they launched "a violent anti-Polish campaign of lies and exaggerations concerning the treatment of Jews in Poland." During the Russo-Polish War of 1919–1920, many Jews shirked their patriotic duty. When gendarmes in Warsaw arrested draft evaders and deserters, everyone easily recognized that "90 per cent were Jews." Although many Jews—the "assimilators"—joined and "fought as Poles," a good many of these manipulated themselves into desk jobs or noncombatant branches. "The small portion of Jews at the front" was quite evident to every Polish soldier and civilian, which caused great resentment.[84]

More damning, Jews conspired with Poland's enemies, earlier with the Germans and currently with Russian Bolsheviks. "The preponderant role of the Jew in Bolshevik Russia," Farman wrote, "is realized even by the most ignorant Polish peasant." Jews generally "welcomed the Bolsheviks . . . in some cases [greeting] the invader with bands."

To Farman, most assaults on Jews stemmed directly from this collaboration with the enemy. He exculpated Polish soldiers by viewing their behavior as a reaction to this treachery and to wartime circumstances:

The Polish soldier, worn out by weeks of fighting, retreating, saw in every village and town, Jews in their long black robes standing in groups and whispering together in their jargon and casting sly glances here and there. This sight, so familiar to anyone who knows Poland would be sufficient to make any soldier feel that these Jews were conspiring against him and when he was unexpectedly fired upon, he naturally thought that those Jews had done the firing.[85]

All in all, Farman portrayed Jews as an unreliable, fickle people, capable of shifting quickly from allegiance to betrayal depending upon their perceived self-interest. But even under adverse circumstances, the self-centered Jews managed to survive, for the Jew, Farman noted, "is slyer than the Pole and probably better succeeded in escaping losses and harm."[86]

Farman and the entire U.S. Warsaw mission depicted the Polish-Jewish controversy as something essentially exaggerated and exploited, if not artificially contrived, by American Jews. These "foreign agitators" grossly misrepresented the attitudes, characteristics, and interests of "America and Americans." Rarely were Jewish-American businessmen or relief workers considered anything but a serious problem for U.S.-Polish relations. "An unfortunate attitude toward America," Farman complained, "has been created by some [U.S.] business men of undesirable type, chiefly Jews." Gibson described the "stream of American Jews" as "a swarm of swindlers and intriguers"; the Poles, he remarked, wondered "why so few reputable Americans come here."[87]

The worst culprit was the Joint Distribution Committee, a Jewish-American relief agency. Under the guise of humanitarian work, the JDC, Gibson charged, agitated among Polish Jews, creating exaggerated propaganda about bogus pogroms in order to turn America against Poland. Without considering the welfare of Jews, they pursued a political objective "aimed primarily at weakening Poland" while that country struggled for survival. There was "a determined attempt by American Jews to use the American Government to their own ends."

Gibson frequently complained that JDC leaders were not real Americans at all. Born in Poland or Eastern Europe, they supposedly were "more at home in Polish or Yiddish" and extremely "prejudic[ed] against everything Polish." Behind the protection of American citizenship, "the entire crowd are making themselves very obnoxious and conspicuous." Their "machinations" laid the groundwork "for conflicts, intrigues, and agitation . . . harmful to our country and to Poland." He strongly urged that "Jewish relief organizations" include "only native American citizens who are Americans first, last and all the time."[88]

Farman feared that ubiquitous Jewish influence had infiltrated the State Department and MID and seriously compromised regular channels of confidential communication with Washington. Circumventing direct official routes, he told Miles: "I have to write to you personally as I do not trust your personnel on Jewish matters. It appears sure that at the Peace Conference anything unfavorable to Jews became lost."

Only officers like Colonel Alexander Coxe and Van Deman were completely reliable on this issue. Farman divulged to Miles that the Bolshevik Information Bureau, a State Department office attached to the U.S. legation in Stockholm, "is entirely in the hands of Jews," one of whom, a "friend of Lenine," facilitates Bolshevik communication through American government channels. Unknown to the State Department, "all dope is carefully sifted by those interested. It comes out clear of anything injurious to the Jews."

Farman urged an investigation by "a most reliable person fully up to the Jewish question." When Miles checked, he learned this alarmist report rested solely upon a crude and confused concoction of names and events; in all essentials, it proved to be "absolutely false."[89] Yet similar complaints about Jews flowed from military attachés elsewhere.

Bucharest

While the Soviet-Polish War raged to the north, MID in Washington worried about Bolshevik expansion against Romania, that other cornerstone of Churchill's containment strategy—for Romania was the "southern gateway to Hungary which was Bolshevist once during the war, and may turn again. It is a stepping stone to the valley of the Po, where there is likely to be strikes this spring." In this region, officers once again surmised a potentially decisive Jewish presence:

> While the [Rumanian] King is still king, the government is entirely composed of Levantine Jews. This may mean everything or nothing, but in view of the fact that the present government of Russia is a Jewish oligarchy dominating Russia, it is significant.[90]

Since World War I, MID had attributed the Romanian "Jewish Problem" to Jewish separateness, disloyalty, economic control, and Bolshevik affinities. The 300,000 Jews who had migrated from Poland and Russia over the centuries were not considered Romanian at all, as they remained "distinct [in] dress, speak Yiddish, and live clannishly within their own group." Pro-German, they were regarded as foreigners "impassive to Rumanian nationalism." Due to their "inherited talent in business and superior training," they acquired substantial control of the Romanian economy. While "wealth [was] concentrated in Jewish hands," Romanian peasants lived in an "abject condition." Romanians rightly feared that "equal political rights" would make Jews "masters of the country."

The sympathy for Bolshevism by Jews in Bessarabia only fueled the fires of anti-Jewish hatred. To MID, this susceptibility to Bolshevism was "probably caused by the fact that the movement is headed by men of their own race" and apprehension that a "strong nationalistic regime in Rumania" would persecute the Jews for their earlier pro-German allegiance. Economic envy and national hatred might have spawned the reported Romanian "massacres and persecutions of Jews."[91]

Since the end of 1919, Colonel Arthur Poillon, a career officer about whom little is known, occupied the post of military attaché in Romania. Well versed in intelligence—World War I attaché in the Netherlands and Athens—Poillon brought the typical army attitude toward Jews to his new assignment. Only a few months after arriving in Bucharest, he wrote to Churchill linking American Jews to "General Denikin's downfall and . . .

why we have lost cast with the Russians." Not only had the U.S. failed to detail military missions to Denikin as other allies had done, "but most of our missions consisted of Jews all of whom seem to have had their own little affairs and delved into many things that they should not have. I really believe that the Riggs mission [1918], with so many Jews attached, gave us a bad name."[92]

Poillon's early complaints about army uniforms worn by JDC members eventually escalated to suspicions that the JDC itself was possibly only a Bolshevik front. Early in 1920, he cabled Washington that JDC activities extended beyond relief to the systematic encouragement, facilitation, and financing of large-scale Jewish immigration. Given the relationship between Jews and Bolshevism, it was "extremely inadvisable . . . to allow Russian Jews to enter the United States . . . at least until the menace of bolshevism has passed." When Churchill alerted the Departments of State, Immigration, and Justice of this intelligence, he strongly recommended "that all Russian Jews arriving here should be received with extreme caution."[93]

Over the next year, Poillon's staff established a close relationship with the Espionage Bureau of the Romanian General Staff. When the Americans earned their trust, Romanian officers confided they "were positive" about a JDC-Bolshevik connection. During a secret rendezvous at the horse races in Bucharest, an espionage officer told Poillon's assistant:

A society of Jews known as the "BUND," which had for its object a "world revolution and the murdering of prominent citizens in various countries" had been discovered in Bessarabia and that from undeniable evidence . . . [the JDC] under guise of being a welfare society, is in reality a part of the "BUND."[94]

Extensive investigations, culminating in the arrest of certain Jews with supposedly incriminating documents, had implicated a vast array of Jewish cultural, welfare, and political organizations, as well as individuals and newspapers. They constituted an intricate institutional web of international Jewish sedition.[95]

Persuaded by such allegations, Poillon sent a secret report to Washington titled "Jewism." American Jews were as disruptive a force in Romania as Farman depicted them in Poland. The JDC was "undeniably injuring the reputation and prestige of the United States Government and . . . measures should be taken to keep American Jews from coming to Rumania." They violate Romanian laws and refuse to recognize Romanian authorities, which they try to bribe when arrested, all while impertinently demanding immunity because they carry American passports. Considering the "undeniable evidence against the Joint Distribution Committee," neither the Romanians nor Poillon could understand why the American government tolerated this situation.[96]

Poillon charged that "[i]n order to get relatives of American Jews from the interior of Russia," the JDC had made "agreements with the Bolsheviks to take along with them Bolshevik agents and couriers." Although one might detect bias in the Romanian Espionage Bureau report, "there is undeniably a mass of truth in it and the evidence that the Rumanian General Staff possess against the members of the Joint Distribution Committee cannot be refuted." MID passed on Poillon's report to Undersecretary of State Hurley, and American Jews mentioned by the Espionage Bureau were immediately placed on passport refusal lists.[97]

Poillon proved equally susceptible to similar information about Bolshevik Russia taken from Romanian newspapers. The "list of Soviet leaders" who control "Russian destinies," he learned, consisted primarily of Jews; among the top leadership were "3 Russians and 9 Jews." Poillon then used this to confirm long-circulating MID claims that among the 545 "functionaries who really govern Russia, only 30 were really Russians as opposed to 447 Jews."[98]

Budapest

Although Poillon found Washington receptive and appreciative, he initially met with skepticism from his colleague in neighboring Hungary. General Harry Hill Bandholtz, American representative on the Interallied Military Mission, was quite sensitive to the plight of Jews in Hungary and was willing to intervene decisively on their behalf. A Michigander and 1890 West Point graduate, Bandholtz had perhaps the longest tour in the Philippines of any officer, acquiring thirteen years of experience in occupation security and intelligence. Although very race conscious, never fully trusting Filipinos because they were racially different, he had nonetheless learned a great deal about race relations.[99] Arriving in Budapest not long after the overthrow of the Hungarian Bolshevik government, Bandholtz worried that the new government of Count Friedrich was about "to start a reign of 'white terror' that [would] make Bela Kun's reign of 'red terror' look like a billy-goat beside an elephant." While attachés had been generally reluctant to acknowledge pogroms, Bandholtz stated categorically:

"They have been beating and maltreating Jews in Budapest and we now have definite information that many wealthy and prominent Jews in out-lying territory have been killed."[100]

MID in Washington, however, continued to interpret stories of Jewish persecutions as "greatly exaggerated" propaganda from "the Vienna Jew-ish press, which is to-day strongly under the influence of communists." MID described Hungarian Jews as a fickle, unprincipled, selfish, and harm-ful group that would manipulate any idea or circumstance to their advan-tage, which explained the anti-Jewish agitation among rural populations. As war profiteers, Jews "made tremendous fortunes [in foodstuffs] while the people were starving." Although Hungarian Bolshevism was not a Jewish movement, it provided simply another convenient instrument of Jewish self-advancement. "The Jews, who are equipped with a fine nose for coming events apparently foresaw the advent of the Bolshevist era and wanted to be the pioneers in order to profit thereby."[101]

Nonetheless, Bandholtz knew political and physical assaults against the Jewish community continued to mount well into 1920. Hundreds of exe-cutions occurred; anti-Semitic groups demanded the "internment of Jews and confiscation of Jewish fortunes"; and Jewish newspaper offices were destroyed. Unlike other officers in Eastern Europe, he intervened force-fully to end such activities. He threatened the Hungarian government and army with noncooperation from the Allied powers if such disgraces were allowed. After Hungarian soldiers had beaten up a few Jewish boys, Band-holtz called in the Hungarian general and told him he "was damned sick and tired of such conduct . . . and that if it ever got out that Hungarians were permitting such atrocities, it would seriously affect the entire future of the country." Besides demanding punishment of the captain in charge, Bandholtz obtained the general's promise "to take immediate and drastic action to stop this growing evil" and the "pogroms" they spawned.[102]

When Bandholtz left Hungary in early 1920, that post fell into the hands of Major Henry W. T. Eglin, an officer with strong convictions on Jews. Born in Fairfax, Virginia, in 1884, Eglin graduated from the Virginia Military Institute, where he later taught military science. A field artillery officer, he spent years in ordinance and supply before being assigned as military adviser to the American commissioner in Budapest.

Although lacking a background in intelligence, Eglin was evidently well read and possessed a finely developed literary style with which to articu-late his racial and Darwinian views. When called upon by headquarters, Eglin provided elaborate analyses of racial traits and national character that supposedly determined the behavior of various nations. Casting himself in the role of "psychological anatomist," he confidently made "scientific" observations which he favorably "compared to any estimate of a tactical [military] situation." "History may repeat itself," he wrote, "but Central European racial instincts will remain as permanent as those rivers and mountains." In that region, "each nation's brain has been impregnated with the inbred mental rickets of political instability."[103]

Eglin found Hungarians a "warm hearted," friendly people with many admirable national characteristics, but with serious flaws as well. "A tenacious race," they made "excellent soldiers" and "dashing horsemen"; they were comparable to the finest German regiments. Unfortunately, the "national fault" of "indolence" caused by "racial and climatic" factors paved the way for their demise. Unlike the practical Scotsman and hardworking Germans or Americans, Hungary's moderate climate and "bountiful crops for little scratching" had endowed them with an easygoing "oriental" temperament. This racial defect, together with their "unwise liberalism" and toleration of other nationalities, offered a "fertile field for the shrewd and keen qualities" of Jews. "The ruin of many of the finest old families . . . [occurred when] the Jew lessee and the Jew usurer gradually got them into their power and the estates away from them." Although Jews never ceased complaining about anti-Semitism, Hungarians actually welcomed and sheltered "the persecuted Jews of all Europe"; they found a paternalistic government and not the usual segregation of the ghetto and denial of civic rights.[104]

Although this "Jew policy" resulted in economic development and prosperity through the "earnest and competent work" of the Jews, it did so at the cost of allowing Hungary's "whole economic life to be monopolized by the Jews." Even though the country could no longer survive economically without them, hatred was mounting, because Hungarian Jews "have been, as everywhere in the world, irritating the people by criminal profiteering to the point of desperation."

As the "history of Bolshevism" again demonstrated, "the Jew where he comes into power is apt to wield it with his innate arrogance and cynicism." Moreover, the Jews were on the verge of "Semitifying the whole country" in the same manner they had already transformed Budapest into a "denationalized" "un-Hungarian" metropolis whose mentality was "foreign to an agricultural and conservative way of thinking." One had to travel outside the capital to discover the Hungary of the Hungarians. There the "old virtues of an old race are found unadulterated in country towns and the country."

"Appalling cynicism and maliciousness," "egotism and gross material-ism," and "unscrupulous sensualism," were among the worst traits that made the "Jewish race" "so destructive and repellent." Yet it was precisely these qualities Hungarians inherited from the Jews. Why had the qualities that ensured Jewish business success—diligence, economy, and so on—not also passed on to the Hungarians? To this obvious question, Eglin had a Darwinian answer: "It is a biological and psychological law that bad qual-ities are more readily transplanted or absorbed than good ones."[105]

Indigenous peoples, Eglin pointed out, had employed various methods to deal with "an opulent and arrogant Jewry." In Russia and Poland, "where civilization is only a veneer or does not exist at all, there the out-let is a pogrom." In civilized countries, "the Jew is fought" by legal, social, or political means such as "*numerus clausus*" to restrict their numbers in various spheres of public life and the economy. The Germans, Eglin sug-gested, would have long ago used such legal methods to prevent the "dan-gerous expansion" of the Jews and "done everything to remain masters in their own house." Interjecting a classic Darwinian idiom, he also noted that if necessary the Germans would justifiably suppress this foreign threat with "tooth and nail."[106]

In the current situation, old and new grievances engendered the "Awak-ening Hungarians," a virulent anti-Semitic movement over 1 million strong. It created a "great danger" because it destabilized Hungary and its passionate members appeared "ready to break out against the Jews." Eglin seemed more concerned with the outside reaction to such violence than with its victims. As he saw the problem:

> Should in consequence anything happen to only a few insignificant Jews, the ever-ready and watchful Viennese Jewish (or even Semitic-Bolshevistic) Press would lustily sound the big horn throughout the civilized world.[107]

Riga

While Eglin manned the southern flank against Bolshevism, T. Worthing-ton Hollyday, an officer of equally strong convictions, observed events at the northern bulwark in Riga, Latvia. Professionally respected and well liked wherever he served, Hollyday counted among his "intimate friends" the military attaché in Berlin, Colonel Creed Cox, and E. R. Warner Mc-Cabe, future chief of MID. More important for his postwar career, Holly-day and his wife were "warm personal friends" of Churchill who had

known "Tommy" "for nearly twenty years" and considered him "one of
our most efficient military attaches." Although described by Churchill as
"so straight as to be almost guileless," Hollyday was an impassioned, vocal
advocate of the "great Nordic race" theory of American history.[108]

To Hollyday, the superior racial stock from the "British Isles and . . .
North-Western Europe" provided the bedrock of "our civilization." They
had all the virtues usually embodied in the true American as "small
farmer" mythology. "Good, clean, conservative, hardworking," these
Nordics were "willing to fight, and, if necessary, die for" America. In
marked contrast, he envisaged Eastern European Jews as "filthy" lowlife
slum dwellers of the disease and crime-infested metropolis, racially unsuited for the land or productive work of any kind. Clannish, international,
and without loyalty to any country, Jews would "weaken our national
spirit," while the radicalism and Bolshevist proclivities of this "troublesome racial minority" would undermine America's political stability.[109]

This bias led Hollyday to oppose the assignment of an officer he suspected of being "a Jew":

> [W]hether he is or not his parents were German, and he learned to speak
> German before English. I think there are plenty of "Honest to God" Amer-
> icans in our army to represent us abroad without having German- or Jewish-
> Americans on this kind of work.[110]

One has the sense, though, that Germans bothered him far less than
Jews; Churchill, in fact, had to defend Hollyday against charges that he was
pro-German. Later, Hollyday greeted with open arms the marriage of his
assistant, Robert F. Kelley, to "a very nice Riga girl." Even though she
knew only "six words of English," Hollyday saw her as "a real asset to
him." Fluent in "German, Russian, and French," from a good family, she
was after all "a Baltic German with a mixture of Swiss." Such a pedigree
really impressed Hollyday, who considered an end to Jewish immigration
to America necessary for "the preservation of the purity of our race."[111]

While attaché in Copenhagen after the war, Hollyday met witnesses
from various parts of Europe who testified to the Jewish-Bolshevik link.
An American consular official from Kiev told him privately, "[T]here is no
difference between the Bolshevik question and the Jewish question. Every
Bolshevik Commissar is a Jew"; and "every . . . Communist, ought to be
shot." From a Danish officer returned from the northern front against the
Bolsheviks, Hollyday learned that "very rich" "international Jews" had

used their wealth and influence to force the withdrawal of Allied armies from Russia in order to ensure a Bolshevik victory. Meanwhile, Danish businessmen related that the Jewish-Bolshevik connection was at the root of anti-Semitism in Germany. Hollyday supposedly had personally un- covered a group right in Copenhagen that used the Danish Red Cross as a cover. They were, he wrote,

> a particularly virulent clique of Israelites . . . very active in intrigue and do everything possible to make the hotel a sort of local Zion, plotting in every conceivable way against other Russians.[112]

From the beginning, Hollyday denied that any Jewish question existed in the Baltic region except the one artificially contrived by Jews them- selves. Either they raised the bogus specter of Jewish persecution to justify immigration to America or they caused a reaction against themselves by promoting Bolshevism. Rather than suffering "ill treatment," they were "the richest and most prosperous people." That itself constituted a social problem, Hollyday complained, because "in the Summer, the resorts around Riga are so patronized by Jews that it is unpleasant for other peo- ple to go there."

At the same time, he noted, the chiefs of all Soviet missions and most of their staffs were Jews, who, though leaders of the downtrodden poor and working classes, also displayed this opulence:

> The representatives . . . of the present Jewish (Bolshevik) Government in Russia have finer automobiles than any of the representatives of Christian Governments and the Jewish members of these delegations patronize the best restaurants in Riga and Kovno, where they drink champagne and in- dulge in expensive dinners.[113]

Much of Hollyday's intelligence came from sources similar to those tapped by other attachés in Eastern Europe: British missions, refugees, and indigenous government, police, or intelligence services. Few of these ever reflected any degree of objectivity. The chief of the British Military Mis- sion, General A. S. Turner, classified Jews into only two possible types. The commercial Jew had "only two interests in life," he stated, "money and Jews," accepting Bolshevism because "it gives him every opportunity for bribery and corruption" as well as "vast profit." The second type, the "In- ternational Jew," sought only "power"; he was the cause and guiding force of "events during the last few years in RUSSIA."[114] The Lettish and Estonian Secret Services, of course, could always be counted on for corroboration of such claims or to prove that "large numbers of Bolshevik agents," mostly Jews, were sneaking into America and western Europe.[115]

"Existing facts prove," Hollyday argued, that the Bolshevik government was "entirely controlled by International Jews." More disturbing still, "American money and American supplies" helped sustain their regime; for "the International Jews in America are supporting Bolshevism." They channeled their assistance through the Joint Distribution Committee, which had already allowed "$700,000. worth of supplies" to be dispensed under Soviet control. While "many Americans" starved in Bolshevik prisons, "American money is being used to feed the Jews in Russia who are, unquestionably, the backbone of the present Russian regime." The Soviets hampered or prohibited all relief efforts, save those for Jews, so that "such organizations as the Red Cross are unable to do anything for the many Christians in Russia who are suffering under the persecution of the present Jewish Government."[116]

Like many of his colleagues engaged in domestic surveillance, Hollyday had little difficulty suspecting furtive collaboration of Jews from all countries and walks of life, including Jewish capitalists and Jewish Bolsheviks. With the assistance of the Lettish Secret Service, which intercepted telegrams and "watched [suspects] carefully," Hollyday was sure he had uncovered "a connection" between Isaac Don Levine, a Chicago journalist; Felix Warburg, a financier and JDC president in Washington; and "the Bolsheviks in Moscow." To Hollyday, this explained much more than the success of the JDC in Soviet-controlled territory. It demonstrated "the way the International Jews work to support the Jew movement throughout the world."[117]

The German-Speaking World

Behind this Eastern European cordon sanitaire, military attachés in Austria, Germany, and Switzerland were no less vigilant. American officers posted in Berlin, Bern, and Vienna maintained a keen interest in Jewish influence and power. Despite MID wartime suspicions of strong pro-German sympathies among Jews, officers now tended to view Jews as a selfish ethnocentric group at times facing an anti-Semitic backlash for their avarice and pursuit of power while Germans suffered during and after the war. Whether fostering democracy, capitalism, or Bolshevism, most Jews were,

An officer labeled this photo "A Study in contrasts. American Army officers, Philippine Scout soldiers, and Balugas (Negritos): Military and otherwise" (1931). In discussions, writings, and official manuals, officers used Philippine experiences to articulte racialist theories of superior and inferior peoples.

General Ralph C. Van Deman (seated second from left) in Paris as part of the 1919 American Commission to Negotiate Peace with Germany. The "father of military inteliigence," Van Deman denied that pogroms had occurred in Poland after World War I and was one of the earliest top ranking officers to endorse the notion of a Jewish-Bolshevist link. Through World War II the agents in his private intelligence network continued to investigate alleged Jewish Communist activity and influence in America.

General Marlborough Churchill, Chief of Military Intelligence (1919–1921), seriously considered the validity of The Protocols of the Elders of Zion *and other evidence of Jewish conspiracies to dominate the world. An adherent of racialist theories, he promoted MID's major psychology project to racially explain the behavior of the nations of the world.*

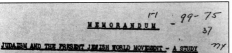

MEMORANDUM

JUDAISM AND THE PRESENT JEWISH WORLD MOVEMENT - A STUDY

A discussion of the so-called Jewish Protocols, and the writings of Theodore Herzl and other Jewish leaders.

An analysis of incidents in connection with Bolshevism, anti-Polish propaganda, and similar developments in Europe and the United States which seem to bear upon the genuineness and the general importance of the Protocols.

Conclusions as to a definite Jewish world movement.

Prepared in the Division of Russian Affairs.

Sept. 29, 1919.

- -

Note: The following is an outline of the most important parts of the Memorandum.
For the complete Memorandum see R. S. #

SECRET

THE POWER AND AIMS OF INTERNATIONAL JEWRY

WAR DEPARTMENT

Introduction:

The recent emphasis in American public opinion placed on the part the Jews have been taking in world events, has caused the current the Department in undertaking a preliminary study of the particular matters in controversy and also the scope of Jewish influence in world affairs ...

I   The authenticity of the so-called ... purport to set forth a Jewish plan, ...

II   The question of how far Jewry as such is ... shevism, not only the Soviet Government ... in all the other countries of the world ... and the United States.

III The various phases of the Polish question:

(a) Whether the Jewish anti-Polish ... United States has been based on actual widespread ... in Poland, or

(b) Whether, on the contrary, ... have been greatly exaggerated as a part ... propaganda to get for the Jews in Poland ... both factions of American Poles published ... to the creation of a state within a state.

(c) How serious is the anti-Jewish ... against all Jews and Jewish guilds recently started by ... can Poles and other Slavic ...

"The Power and Aims of International Jewry," a lengthy report written by the Russian Desk of the U.S. State Department in August 1919 with the concurrence of Military Intelligence, argued that the Protocols of the Elders of Zion offered valuable insights into Jewish aims and activities. Strongly suggesting that Bolshevism was a Jewish movement, the report concluded that the ultimate aim of International Jews might actually be world domination. An expanded version of this report entitled "Judaism and the Present World Movement" added photographs of the Jewish "types" spreading Bolshevism.

Major Robert L. Eichelberger, Assistant Chief of Staff for Intelligence, with the American Expeditionary Force in Siberia reflected the racial worldview of the officer corps. The intelligence reports from Vladivostok denied or downplayed pogroms in the Ukraine while reinforcing the connection between Jews and Bolsheviks. Eichelberger became a prominent general in the pacific during World War II.

Although General Edgar Jadwin (right) personally witnessed a pogrom in Poland in 1919, he emphasized that only 300 Jews had been killed and considered the cutting off of Jewish beards by Polish soldiers merely "a lark." As a member of a Special Mission to investigate the Jewish question in Poland, he traced Polish anti-Semitism to Jewish attitudes.

As military attaché to Vienna in the early 1920s, Colonel Allan L. Briggs attributed anti-semitism to Jews flaunting their wealth while Austrians starved. He was surprised that Austrians did not take more violent action against Jews.

SUBJECT... THE JEW, THE LETT, AND THE RUSSIAN. THEIR RELATIVE

.... ROLES IN SOVIET RUSSIA -- SERVICE REPORT.

From....... GERMANY .... P S Y C H O L O G I C A L

No........ 1074 .... Date.... 14 December, 1920... 19 ·

Replying to No..................................Date............................. 19

                  55   .... AP 10 1921

The relative values of these three elements in Soviet Russia may be expressed in a short formula, as follows:

The Jew is the administrator, the Lett is the policeman, and the Russian is the victim.

JEWS

Of the 14 or 15 Commissaries (Ministers of Departments), only five are Russian: Lenin, Krassin, Tchitcherin, Drgerginsky, and Sereda (Commissary of Agriculture); all others are Hebrews.

Bolshevist governmental offices in Moscow are packed with them. Only the inferior posts: porters, janitors, minor clerks, and such like, are filled by Russians. The same is true of other cities and towns not too remote from Moscow. In the more distant places there is more of the Russian element in governmental offices.

Moscow, formerly a forbidden city to Jews, has been taken by them by storm. It is their Mecca now and they stream to it from the former Jewish concentration zones established by the Tzars.

It is known that in Kopp's offices in Berlin there are among his forty employees only four Russians. All the others, including himself, are Hebrews, most of them of the vulgar, characteristically Jewish type.

How to account for this Jewish "push" to power? The Jews, as a gifted people, have an especial aptitude for mental combinations and for employments requiring this qualification, and thus they easily crept into all the higher positions under the Bolsheviks, leaving the simpler and the ruder work to cruder races.

We must look back into history for explanation, for causes which made possible this unparalleled jump into power of this oppressed people, persecuted, despised and hated by their neighbors throughout the course of their entire existence.

Oppression and persecution called forth reaction, resistance, revolt, solidification into a compact racial block cemented by a religious chauvinism unknown to any other race. Martyrdom and consciousness of injustice endured evoked in

- 1 -

the Jewish race a spirit of exaltation, of heroism and an ardent belief in a brighter future and an eventual triumph. The biblical hope of the Jewish race becoming as numerous as the sand on the seacoast and of its being the ruler of mankind was born in the darkest hours of their miseries and was their guiding star throughout the entire course of their history. It was a part of their religion and they consciously and persistently worked for its realization.

The day of reward has come. Millenia of preparation in the hard school of life, of desperate, pitiless struggle for existence in occupations requiring sharpened mental qualities - since the rougher labor was barred to them in the Middle Ages - has made the Jews the keenest race of mankind and the best equipped for a successful struggle for a "spot in the sun" in our days of liberal laws and equal opportunities for all.

Seen in this light, the Jewish success in Russia and their dominating position there are now comprehensible.

Their Messiah - Trotzky - has arrived. They are numerous as the sand on the seacoast, they rule mankind in Russia and are looking for further expansion.

LETTS

The Letts are one of those simpler, cruder races to whose lot fell the ruder work of Bolshevist Russia. Their role under the Bolsheviks is that of executioners, jailers, policemen, etc. They are a harsh people, cruel by nature, and well adapted for such occupations. Notorious Peters of Petrograd is a typical Lett and Heyduk of Moscow is another one.

It would not be just to cast a general accusation, as above, against a people without citation of causes which influenced the shaping of their character. An observant person who lived among Letts defines them by a somewhat milder formula:

Letts are an industrious, hard working people, harsh of heart and impulsive, devoid of sentimentality and mysticism, - in contrast to Russians.

Originally close relations of Lithuanians, Letts contain in their veins an infusion of Finnish blood through their intermixture with neighbors Lives (or Livons) and Kours, related to Finns. A Finnish-Ugrian race, the Finns have for their cousins the Turk, the Bulgarian, and the Hungarian, a triple racial constellation of an unsavory fame in History, the "Barbarians" of cruel impulses. "Blood is thicker than water". Who knows if the peculiar Lettish-Finnish germ does not contain some of the characteristics of the more pronounced Turkish-

---

Many intelligence officers analyzed the "Jewish Question" from the perspective of the racial worldview of the Officer Corps. They applied Social Darwinist explanations of the survival of the fittest to explain alleged Jewish domination of Russia.

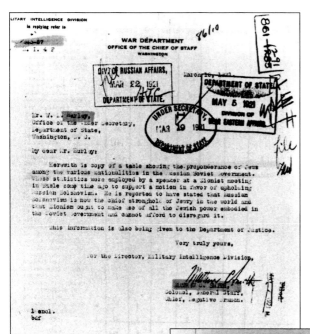

Reports and documents from military attaches supposedly proving the authenticity of the basic principles of the Protocols of the Elders of Zion and Jewish Communist conspiracies reached top officials in the American government.

Top MID officers in Washington in the 1920s analyzed and circulated the Protocols of the Elders of Zion. *Officers believed that their intelligence on Jewish radicals at home and abroad substantiated the basic ideas found in the* Protocols.

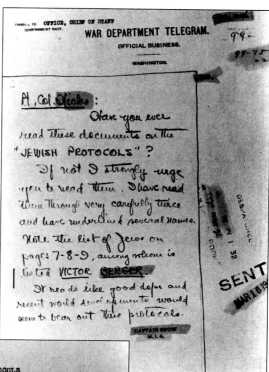

A, Col. Stocks:

Have you ever read these documents on the "JEWISH PROTOCOLS"?

If not I strongly urge you to read them. I have read them through very carefully twice and have underlined several names. Note the list of Jews on pages 7-8-9, among whom is listed VICTOR BERGER.

It reads like good dope and recent world developments would seem to bear out these protocols.

CAPTAIN SNOW
M.I.4.

-7-

EXTRACT FROM PROTOCOLS

6. WE WILL . . . ARTIFICIALLY AND DEEPLY UNDERMINE THE SOURCE OF INDUSTRY BY TEACHING THE WORKMEN ANARCHY AND THE USE OF ALCOHOL, AT THE SAME TIME MAKING ARRANGEMENTS TO EXILE ALL THE INTELLECTUAL FORCES OF THE GOYS FROM THE COUNTRIES.

THAT THIS TRUE SITUATION SHOULD NOT BE NOTICED BY THE GOYS UNTIL THE PROPER TIME, WE WILL MASK IT BY A PRETENDED DESIRE TO HELP THE WORKING CLASSES AND GREAT ECONOMIC PRINCIPLES, AN ACTIVE PROPAGANDA OF WHICH IS BEING CARRIED ON THROUGH OUR ECONOMIC THEORIES.

(Protocol V, page 17.)

SUBSTANTIATION

The following is a list of a few names of the leaders engaged in the promotion of Bolshevism and anarchy throughout the world:

RUSSIA

Cover Name	Real Name	Nationality
Lenin	Oulianoff	Russian
Trotzky	Braunstein	Jew
Stekloff	Nachamkes	Jew
Martoff	Zederbaum	Jew
Zinovieff	Apfelbaum	Jew
Kameneff	Rosenfeld	Jew
Souchanoff	Gimel	Jew
Zagorsky	Krochman	Jew
Bogdanoff	Zilberstein	Jew
Larin	Lurje	Jew
Gorev	Goldman	Jew
Uritzky	Radomilsky	Jew
Kamneff	Katz	Jew
Ganetzky	Furstenberg	Jew
Dan	Gourevich	Jew
Meschkovsky	Goldberg	Jew
Parvus	Goldfandt/Helpland	Jew
Riasanoff	Goldenfarb	Jew
Martinoff	Zikar	Jew
Chernomorski	Chernomordkin	Jew
Solntzeff	Bleichman	Jew
Piatnitzky	Zivin	Jew
Abramovich	Rein	Jew
Zvesdin	Vainstein	Jew
Naklakovsky	Rosenblum	Jew
Lipinsky	Loewensohn	Jew
Bobrof	Nathansohn	Jew
Axelrod	Orthodox	Jew

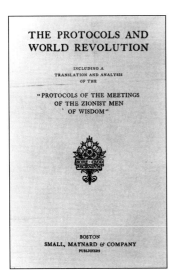

THE PROTOCOLS AND WORLD REVOLUTION

INCLUDING A
TRANSLATION AND ANALYSIS
OF THE

"PROTOCOLS OF THE MEETINGS
OF THE ZIONIST MEN
OF WISDOM"

BOSTON
SMALL, MAYNARD & COMPANY
PUBLISHERS

The Protocols and World Revolution (cover) and MID memo. The Protocols were sent to all Military Intelligence Offices in the U.S. and abroad as a guide in investigating the character and activities of Jews.

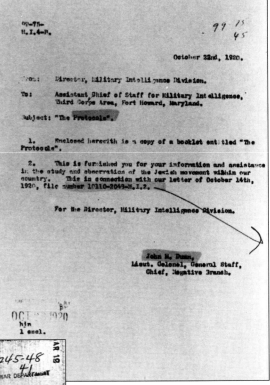

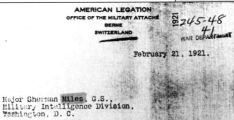

The author of this memo, Colonel William A. Godson, among the army's most respected attaches, steadfastly believed in a Jewish conspiracy to establish world domination. He spent years surveilling Jews in Europe and attempting to validate the Protocols.

in the eyes of attachés, relentlessly advancing their own selfish interests at the expense of the Germans they supposedly so admired and emulated.

The military attaché in Vienna, Colonel Allan L. Briggs, was not only anti-Semitic but so "diametrically opposed" to "democratic" forces that he quickly became "a source of embarrassment" even among American foreign service officers, a group hardly known for its progressive politics. American commissioner Arthur Frazier complained that Briggs, who had served in Vienna under the monarchy, "makes no effort to adapt himself to altered conditions and continues . . . as if nothing has happened since 1914." Briggs reestablished such close relations with the reactionary aristocracy to the exclusion of Austrian republicans that Frazier demanded his removal. Churchill, however, confidentially supported Briggs wholeheartedly—"[Y]ou are doing the right thing"—and preferred the reassignment of Frazier.[118]

Although praised by Churchill for his competent analyses, Briggs remained blind to certain aspects of Austrian society. In Vienna, a city that only a few years before had reelected Karl Lueger mayor on an anti-Semitic platform and whose milieu had provided the young Adolf Hitler with the foundations of Nazi ideology, Briggs could find "no discernible religious or national prejudice."

He denied any "prevalent" anti-Semitism; after all, "Vienna calmly allows the Jews to be their greatest financiers and business men." Briggs never noticed the various kinds of popular, social, and religious anti-Semitism officially and unofficial pervading this society that was so obvious to other observers. Although acknowledging political anti-Semitism, he confined it to "certain of the political parties," without explaining that these included major parties.[119]

Briggs actually expressed surprise at the absence of overt anti-Semitism under conditions he thought should incite such outbreaks. "In the hard economic conditions which obtain," he wrote, "the Jews prosper," while generally industry and business stagnate. They should not, of course, "be blamed for their industry and cleverness," nor for their "incredible accomplishment," since Austria definitely benefited from these. Nonetheless, Jews were still "reprehensible," because "they are grossly selfish," refusing to help the rest of their countrymen living in desperation. Under the monarchy, Jews only contributed to charities when "there was something to be gained—a decoration or baronacy—but today they give nothing."

Briggs painted a stark contrast between impoverished Viennese and insufferable Jews completely insensitive to the human need and "utmost destitution" around them:

Men and boys, barefooted, covered with rags, filthy, and . . . hunting the streets for a moment's pleasure—a discarded cigarette . . . [while] the Jews fill the expensive hotels and restaurants, parade the streets with richly dressed cocottes, roll up to the hotels in splendid automobiles, and this at a time when starvation actually exists.[120]

If Americans really knew what "Viennese Jews" were like, Briggs argued, they would not display such "indignation . . . at the treatment of the Jews in Europe." They were "of a different mentality and caliber" from American Jews; they could not be judged by American standards. Americans who traveled to Vienna faced a rude awakening and quickly became "incensed at the Jews." That the suffering Austrians had not taken "violent measures" against the Jews, Briggs exclaimed, "is a thing to wonder at." He had observed demonstrations in which marchers carried placards with the slogan "Away with the Jews." But then, Briggs added with a sense of incomprehension, the demonstrators failed to act upon their grievances: "[T]he matter ends there."[121]

American officers in neighboring countries "easily noticed" increasing anti-Semitism in Germany. Initially explained as a rightist political ploy to "divert the discontent of the people into anti-Semitic channels" ("to substitute a race war for a class war"), attachés soon interpreted it as a natural reaction to dubious Jewish behavior and affiliations.

According to a reliable Swedish newspaper, one officer reported, "Jews are most cordially hated in Germany," because they "are to a great extent connected with the extreme left parties." Germans believed Jews financed the German Communists and the Red Army. They were also "accused of cheating," war profiteering, disloyalty, and immoral enterprises such as prostitution; "in Berlin most of the forbidden night saloons are owned by the Jews . . . [who] earn great sums of money." The selfish Jew cared not the least for "what will happen to the German citizens"; Jewish "wives go dressed in satin, furs, jewels, etc. while the Germans themselves must starve." While the Swedish author condemned this growing hatred as "incredible and hysterical" and doubted the veracity of many of these stories, the American officer insisted:

The forgoing may be regarded as a tendency of the growing Jewish hatred in Europe, brought on by the unscrupulous dealings of the Jews in all manners and ways. Wherever there has been anything questionable in Europe during the war and after the war, there has in nearly every case been found interested Jews and it is generally believed in Europe that to get to the bottom of the Bolshevik question the Jewish question must be studied in close connection with it.[122]

Most inferences about Jews drawn by officers in the German-speaking world mirrored those of their colleagues in Eastern Europe. The Berlin attaché, Colonel Edward Davis, had already won a prominent place in intelligence history. While in Holland, he had operated "one of the most amazing espionage and counterespionage nets of the entire wartime period" and had penetrated the German General Staff itself. An Illinois native and Cornell University graduate, Davis had also helped establish and pacify the American empire. He fought in "several engagements with the hostiles" during the "Philippine Insurrection" and with the "Army of Cuban Pacification" before spending the war as attaché in Athens and The Hague.[123]

Davis's unpublished memoirs reveal not the slightest trace of bias. The only exception was his mention of two battalions of Jews from Britain who arrived after the capture of Jerusalem in 1917 and on whom others pinned the slogan "No advance without security." That belittling epithet, widely invoked by the British throughout the war to mock the loyalty and courage of Jewish soldiers, circulated for years thereafter among American officers, partly in jest and partly as confirmation of their own low estimates of the military potential of Jews.

In retrospect, Davis told of Jewish British officers dying in heroic charges, as well as of Zionist colonizers turning the desert into productive villages and fertile fields. Recounting major episodes from his Berlin years, he wrote at length of his encounters with German communism, industrial magnates like Stinnes and Krupp, and Generals Ludendorff and Hindenburg, whose political roles had since taken on historic proportions. His failure to mention German Jews belied his true views and intelligence activities during his German tour.[124]

MID was very "interested in the subject of Jewry . . . in Germany." As part of the overall effort against "isms," Miles requested from Davis a broad study of "the weight and influence of the Jew on German politics." Miles needed to know the Jewish percentage of the total population, their occupational classification, and geographical distribution by states and cities. More important, he sought information on "Jewish leaders and their political power and activities," particularly any connection with Bolshevism in Germany or abroad. "To what extent, if any," he also asked, "do the Jews control German finances and industry?" And finally, what was the "strength of anti-Jewish feeling in Germany"?

Among the few surviving responses from Davis was a long "list of Jewish leaders" in various political parties, banking, industry and commerce,
and journalism, as well as in music, art, literature, and the stage. Only here
and there did Davis offer any commentary: Kurt Tucholsky was "the poet
of Socialism"; Hugo Preuss "wrote the German constitution"; "the Jews
control the Bourse and film industry"; and "three-fourths of the big German lawyers are Jews." He also noted that the leader of the German Communist Party, Paul Levi, was "an avowed adherent of the Third
Internationale."[125]

In themselves, these brief remarks do not begin to convey the depth of
anti-Semitism of Davis and his assistant attachés. Davis's office complained about "the heavy representation of Jews among the newspapermen
sent by American newspapers to cover" the Polish-Soviet peace negotia-
tions in Riga. Nor had Germany escaped the long arms of "International
Jewry"; in Soviet "offices in Berlin there are among . . . forty employees
only four Russians. All the others . . . are Hebrews, most of them of the
vulgar, characteristically Jewish type." Indeed, Davis perceived the "eastern" Jews as a horde of unfit, disease-spreading "undesirables" endangering higher American civilization. He warned those back home about the
"poor emigrants" he saw leaving regularly for the new world, "95 percent
of whom are Jews . . . ready to breed." Obstacles must be imposed, he
urged, to halt "the flow of the refuse of Central Europe to the Great North
American dump."[126]

At the same time, a report from Davis's office raised the specter of a
threat emanating not from racially inferior Jews but from inherited characteristics that hold out the prospect of their political domination of other
nations. A blatant illustration of political biology, this remarkable Darwinian interpretation of the Russian Revolution was adorned with all the verifying scientific jargon—"Turkish-Bulgarian-Hungarian species," and so
forth. "With the events in Russia before our eyes," the report noted, "we
see that nature's law of selection, heredity and adaptation to life has already triumphed over the Bolshevist proletarian revolution." Rather than
realizing the utopia of a classless society, the revolution had merely intensified the racial struggle for existence.

Molded by millennia of desperate struggles with discrimination, persecution, and deprivation, "the hard headed, calculating Jew—thus evolved by
life itself—pulls up ahead of the dreamy, care-free Russian and climbs to a
height from which he can dominate him." Through ages of paternalism and
bureaucratic government, the Russians "evolved" into a dependent mass

that, lacking mental skills and initiative, remained unprepared for the modern world. "Therefore, when the gun was fired which opened the revolutionary race, it was the world's best hustlers, the Jews in first place . . . while the Russians contented themselves with the leavings."[127]

This "day of reward" constituted only the initial step in fulfilling the "biblical hope of the Jewish race becoming . . . the ruler of mankind." Current events have proven that "their Messiah-Trotzky-has arrived. . . . [T]hey rule mankind in Russia and are looking for further expansion."[128]

The idea that Jews had seized upon Bolshevism as purely a surreptitious means to expand their own power internationally rather than to fulfill Communist aims resonated across the border in Switzerland. The Bern attaché, William Godson, was the same colonel who had earlier denied pogroms in Poland and more recently distributed copies of the *Protocols*. Although it is unknown whether others in his office held the same paranoid suspicions of a Jewish world conspiracy, they were certainly not immune to anti-Semitism or notions of collusion among Jews internationally.

Assistant Military Attaché Major Ivens Jones seems to have shared Godson's "a Jew is a Jew" mentality. At a luncheon during an official trip to the League of Nations, Jones first met the soon-to-be-famous journalist Walter Lippmann, a former MID officer during the war. Lippmann, himself a third-generation American and a staunch advocate of complete assimilation, urged Jews to abandon all Jewish identity, melt quickly and fully, and become as "inconspicuous" as possible. Nevertheless, Jones immediately judged Lippmann by the heritage the writer thought he had cast off, if he ever possessed it at all.

"There was a Mr. Lippmann of the 'New York World,'" Jones wrote to Churchill, and "the name, I noticed, is a trifle Jewish." By Jones's account, Lippmann then lived up to the worst expectations of a Jewish publicist when "Mr. Lippmann embarked on an eulogistic defense of the Bolsheviki regime and the Soviet Government." Supposedly, Lippmann then not only rebuked Jones for his ignorance in alleging Bolshevik atrocities but defended the Bolshevik "subversion of the children in Switzerland" as "merely carrying out [of] . . . humane ideas." "I wondered," Jones asked Churchill, "if you might tell me just who and what Mr. Lippmann is."[129]

Insisting on confidentiality, Churchill cautioned Jones to be on his "guard against Mr. Lippmann," for his loyalty was questionable: He "is one of the 'New Republic' gang and generally speaking stands for exactly the opposite of what we, as government officers, should stand for." Although during the war MID used this "very clever literary man" in its propaganda section, Churchill confessed he "never trusted him at the time." Moreover, Jones had correctly identified the Jewish angle to Lippmann's politics, for "at the Peace Conference, Colonel Mason caught him suppressing all information unfavorable to the Jewish race."[130]

Since early 1919, officers in Bern had been investigating "Jews with Bolshevik tendencies." Relying upon secret Italian agents, Godson strove to penetrate the intricate clandestine network of international Bolsheviks he believed operated through Switzerland. "Now, the present condition of affairs in Europe is not at all localized," he wrote, "and the ramifications of the conspiracy, which undoubtedly exists, lead to every capital and large city on this continent."

In Bern, "90 per cent" of those attending secret Bolshevik meetings, he informed Washington, "are *Jews*." The annotated lists of Bolshevik Jews compiled by his agents even distinguished the "most fanatic of the lot" from those deemed "too simple to be dangerous." They had uncovered one wealthy Jew who used his "fortune" to "help needy Bolshevists." Like attachés elsewhere, Godson, too, furnished the War Department with his page-length "table showing the preponderance of Jews among the various nationalities in the Russian Soviet Government": 294 Jews compared to only nineteen true Russians.[131]

Like most specious generalizations, Godson's also contained that kernel of fact that, on the surface, appeared to substantiate his case. Bolsheviks had long operated in Switzerland and among them were Jewish activists, some of whom might even have been correctly identified by Godson's agents. Officers and State Department officials in various European countries had also exposed several schemes involving Jewish counterfeiting of U.S. passports and visas. Godson interpreted this as a systematic effort to sneak "undesirable" Jewish masses into the United States and simultaneously provide a cover for the entry of dangerous Jewish Bolsheviks. Each actual incident further confirmed his inherent suspicions.[132]

But his generalizations did not actually emanate from facts. His anti-Semitic biases made him highly susceptible to the most incredible information about a "Jewish International Movement." Godson's agents had allegedly confirmed the existence of a "Jewish National Political Organization" headquartered in Frankfurt with Baron Rothschild as a member. Godson had "very reliable" intelligence that "every important official in the United Press Agency in Germany and other European countries" were "all Jews, without exception."

At the same time, Godson claimed to have uncovered "the most powerful organization in Germany," the Jewish Council of Elders of Berlin
Trades, which provided "millions" for "political assassinations" and the
suppression of opponents. Its power "extend[ed] all over Germany, Frankfurt, Stuttgart and Munich especially."[133]

Godson's paranoia clearly surfaced during his presentation at the 1920
Military Attaché Conference at Coblenz, Germany. Before this gathering
of American officers from most European embassies, Godson announced
his discovery "of a Jewish movement apparently hostile to the Gentile economic system and aimed at the destruction of Christian wealth."

Most analyses erred, he argued, by concentrating on Jewish political organizations, while overlooking the "numerous economic ones" that have
as their real objective "the economic supremacy of Jewry all over the
world." Behind so much of the world's unrest stood "Jewish financiers in
Paris, London, New York and Berlin." Like their relationship with other
political movements, these Jews supported Bolshevism only because they
shared the common aim of destroying "Christian (gentile) property"; "the
Jews have never been and are not now Bolshevists and simply are using
the movement to accomplish their ends." Having seized control of Russia,
they now sought to maintain it.

Jewish financial influence "resulted in the escape of BELA KUHN,"
while the move to acquire Allied "recognition of the Soviet Dictatorship is
being directed by Jewish interests." After siding with the new German
democracy, the perfidious Jews now favored the "enfeeblement of their
foster country [Germany], [since] they know that revolution and trouble
must result to their benefit as it did in Hungary and Russia." To advance
these insidious political machinations, "Jewish money is flowing freely."[134]

As proof of his contentions, Godson presented the following list of arguments:

1) The money power of the world is exerted by members of the Jewish race.
2) The leaders of the Bolshevist movement in Russia, LENINE ex-
   cepted, are Jews.
3) There was constant communication between international Jews
   during the war.
4) Great publicity was given to the alleged pogroms in Poland: none
   to pogroms in Ukrainia, etc.

5) No newspaper in America ever allows the question of Jewish influence to appear.[135]

These "are established facts," Godson told his fellow officers "which
should be carefully weighed in forming an estimate of the situation and
the existence or not of a world conspiracy of Jewish interests against the
Christian civilization."

Although the response of other participants is unknown, Godson's
views definitely coincided with many of those currently circulated by fellow attachés. When, toward the end of 1920, Godson forwarded a copy of
his report to Washington, it made the usual rounds through the bureaucracy, from J. Edgar Hoover to the Russian Desk of the State Department
and Undersecretary of State Hurley.[136]

The cumulative effect of several years of intelligence from attachés
across Europe tended to solidify early MID suspicion of a "dictatorship of
the Jews" in Russia. Some officers might have been uncertain about
whether this domination related to a broader worldwide Jewish plot, while
others, no doubt, dismissed outright the very idea of such a grandiose conspiracy theory. But few, if any, challenged the official MID viewpoint that
"Jewish intellectuals have had the leading and commanding part everywhere," and because of "the growing power of the Jews," they practically
controlled the Government.[137]

Not only Jewish Bolsheviks, MID argued, but Jews generally, profited at
the expense of real Russians. Jews pillaged the old regime's most valuable
riches and smuggled them out of Russia. While the Russians endured hard
work and deprivation, Jews monopolized the privileged government offices
and easy "graft jobs"; they encouraged bribery and were behind "all speculation in foodstuffs." Despite the revolutionary zeal with which they dispatched the Red Army against enemies, complained one informant, "you
never see a damn Jew within two hundred versts of the front."[138]

With the end of Allied counterrevolutionary intervention against Bolshevism in 1920, MID began to speculate that the salvation of Russia, and
perhaps all of Europe, might well spring from within that country.
Throughout 1920 and 1921, MID grasped at every indication that "dissatisfaction" with Jewish control, even within the "Bolshevists own camp,"
would result in either the regime's collapse or overthrow. Either way,
"Jewish pogroms are bound to occur."[139]

As this intelligence worked its way through various government agencies in Washington, MID anticipation took on a sense of imminence. A key

figure in disseminating this information and heightening expectations of pogroms was J. Edgar Hoover, future FBI director and then special assistant to the attorney general. Involved in preparing the *Intelligence Bulletin* on radical activities for the Justice Department, Hoover incorporated MID intelligence into this "Strictly Confidential" publication before personally forwarding copies back to MID directors. This bulletin focused mostly on international affairs, labor unions, Communists, the Industrial Workers of the World (IWW), Negroes, the American Civil Liberties Union, the press, and Japanese matters.

Throughout many of these categories, analysts thought they had easily identified the ubiquitous Jews at work. Tabulations of the "nationalities and races" that composed the leadership of the Soviet government revealed 294 Jews as opposed to only nineteen Russians, as stated precisely in Godson's report on a Jewish world conspiracy. Witnesses attested to the actual existence and power of the International Jew. "The chief investigating judges were American Jews, or rather Russian Jews who had spent long periods of time in America." Arms controlled Russia, and the Jews controlled the armed forces and secret service: "[I]it is solely [due] to their influence that the terror continues to exist in Russia."[140]

"A Report on Bolshevism" appended to the July 31, 1920, edition divided leaders of the Soviet movement internationally into "idealists and crooks." And "75% of the latter class are Jews concealing their real names under fictitious Russian ones." This long report ended with the proof, the by now well-circulated list of top Soviet leaders with the "Nom de plume" column juxtaposed to the "Real Names." After unmasking, only three Russians remained out of forty-seven leaders. Only three "idealists" could be found among the twenty Bolshevik representatives in Estonia; the opportunistic "crooks [who] swing with the pendulum" constituted the remainder. Their wives were "well dressed, wear rings and ... have accumulated wealth." At home, Russians sacrificed and suffered deprivation, while "secret dining halls [were] kept by Jews and bourgeoisie."

Well aware of the vehement resentment they faced, the Jews feared the regime's collapse, when Russian wrath would surely turn against them. And this appeared more likely with every passing month. One anonymous "authority" later conveyed the atmosphere of the day with a contemporary popular Russian saying: "Kill the Jews and save Russia."[141] The intelligence analyst added:

A pogrom of the Jews would be a simple solution to Bolshevik rule.

He predicted that the salvation and regeneration of Russia would rise from a nationalist Russian movement, probably led by a military leader within the country. "Supported by all classes" and crusading on an "anti-Jewish" platform, this leader would seize power through a coup d'état and return Russia to civilization. "It is unfortunate, however, that it is always the poor and inoffensive Jew who gets killed in these pogroms, the rich and dangerous Jew escapes by bribery and influence. If a pogrom does take place it is to be hoped that this time the proceedings will be reversed."

But sympathy for innocent Jews had its limitations. Although "unfortunately a pogrom is probably inevitable," he strongly advised against American or international efforts to prevent this slaughter. Even innocent Jews were a necessary sacrifice for the elimination of Bolshevism and restoration of Russia. He argued against not only armed intervention to preclude or ameliorate this horrible outcome but also against economic measures. The world should assist "any anti-Bolshevik movement" with "trade and peace." "It would be a great pity if outside nations withdrew the support from any new movement on account of a pogrom." By the middle of November 1920, the bulletin foretold "that should the party fall, there will be the greatest Jewish pogrom in history."[142]

While awaiting this outcome, attachés worried lest the true Americans back home fail to act in time to protect themselves against the influx into the United States of this same dangerous "riffraff." The hundreds of thousands of Eastern European Jews immigrating to the United States alarmed attachés. It was a dread matched only by the indignation officers felt upon learning Jewish-American welfare societies were assisting the mass migration of this Bolshevik-infested and racially "undesirable material."

From Bucharest, Poillon suggested an army initiative on Jewish immigration: "Would it not be a wise project to disseminate information of this sort throughout our country with the idea of evidently securing legislation against it!"[143]

Yet MID was already diligently at work on the home front. While attachés acted as America's racial sentinels abroad, military intelligence was equally vigilant toward insidious Jewish penetration of the United States. From suppressing domestic unrest to efforts at erecting barriers against hordes of Eastern European Jewish immigrants, officers waged a vigorous defense of America's "Nordic heritage."

CHAPTER 4

The Nordic Defense of America, 1918–1924

F OR OFFICERS LIKE CAPTAIN JOHN B. TREVOR in MID's New York office, events in Europe following the end of World War I and the Bolshevist uprising in Russia were only the tip of the iceberg. Ever watchful
for signs that revolutionary unrest was spreading to the United States, intelligence officers were quick to relate domestic events to what they
learned from agents and attachés in Europe.

As early as 1918, MID had received warnings from British sources that
the aims of Bolshevist Jews extended far beyond the boundaries of Russia.[1]
Given the postwar collapse of various European governments concurrent
with renewed labor activism and radicalization on the American left, almost any hint of Bolshevist subversion was treated with the utmost seriousness by U.S. government officials. A trusted confidential agent for the
Justice Department Intelligence Office in Milwaukee wrote that the Bolsheviks "in this country are composed mostly of Russians of Jewish descent." Since they had found in Lenin and Trotsky the "Moses who
[would] lead them out of the wilderness," they engaged in subversion to
hinder any action against Bolshevik Russia. "The Chicago Federal bomb
explosion," the agent confided, "is a direct outcome of the Bolsheviki
movement in this country."[2]

MID informants and officers in other cities did much more than cor-
roborate this information. Their descriptions of meetings where radical
leaders made fiery speeches to crowds of impassioned zealots helped create

a psychological atmosphere of imminent danger and a perception of wide-spread revolutionary activity. As they depicted these emotional gatherings, the bands played "revolutionary songs, [while] red flags were waved at every point." Only a large police presence maintained public order, especially when patriotic Americans, usually led by soldiers, challenged the un-American symbols and rhetoric of these "Reds." Whether at Madison Square Garden or the Brownsville Labor Lyceum in Brooklyn, Socialist meetings were characterized as "Hebrew practically to a man" or "composed principally of the lower type Russian Jews."[3]

As rumors of Jewish disloyalty, pro-Germanism, and Bolshevik affinities persisted into early 1919, the president of the American Jewish Committee, Louis Marshall, strongly refuted such accusations. Reacting to Senate testimony that Russian Bolshevism was caused by "the activities of Yiddish agitators from the east side of New York City," Marshall stated that "the Jews of Russia, as a mass, are the opponents of Bolshevism, both because they belong to the bourgeoisie and because they cherish their religion. . . . Everything that real Bolshevism stands for is to the Jew detestable." According to Marshall, the Jews among the Bolshevik leadership were themselves self-acknowledged apostates. Indignant, he then confronted the aspersions cast on Jewish patriotism by citing the percentage of Jews serving in the military and their record of distinction. "Attack Bolshevism as much as you please, and the Jews of America are with you," but there was absolutely no justification for such illogical and unsubstantiated assaults as were currently circulating.[4]

Unfortunately, this was not to be the end of a brief and ignoble event in American history, but merely the prelude to a longer, more frantic affair. The AJC failed to dispel suspicions about Jewish Bolsheviks among a good part of the public or MID. Rather than waning, MID's interest intensified in the coming year, as a relentless stream of intelligence about radical Jewish activity at home and abroad flowed into Washington. The AJC's credibility and loyalty came into question when British intelligence informed MID that its leaders, Louis Marshall and Cyrus Adler, were "suspect." The British were also concerned about their involvement in another emerging international Jewish movement—Zionism. A British intelligence agent in the United States who routinely shared his reports with MID complained, "[T]his Zionist business is rapidly turning what little hair I have gray." He then recommended "closest surveillance of all Hebrew movements."[5]

Although MID would oblige this recommendation, its efforts to defend America did not stop with domestic spying. Homegrown radicals and recent immigrants were problematic enough, but officers also confronted the imminent prospect of hordes of new arrivals to American shores. In the nativist, anti-immigrant climate of the early 1920s, army officers significantly influenced the formation of immigration policy and legislation. Predictably, their efforts to defend America's Nordic heritage against contamination by inferior foreigners singled out one group in particular: "the unfortunate race of Jews."

Revolution in New York

In the years following World War I, many recent young Jewish immigrants in cities like New York and Chicago found either socialism or Zionism inspiring popular movements. Although Jewish public opinion, within older established communities and immigrant groups alike, remained strongly anti-Bolshevik, some young Jews joined the radical left wing of American socialism in supporting the Bolshevik seizure of power.[6] But increasingly obsessed with Bolshevism, many MID officers and informants rarely distinguished between Socialists and Bolsheviks or variances in Jewish attitudes. The left—whatever shade of red or pink—threatened America; and Jews appeared intimately connected with it.

To officers still experiencing wartime anxiety and anticipating problems at home, a series of recent developments appeared to have meaningful relationships to the Jewish question. At a Chicago mass meeting in January 1919, left-wingers in the Socialist Party expressed jubilant support for Bolshevik Russia; at a New York conference on February 15, most prominent left-wing Socialist Party leaders voiced similar admiration for Bolshevism. The latter meeting, in Trevor's own city and attended by the notorious John Reed, who had just returned from Leninist Russia, made the menace appear all the more immediate. Meanwhile, a general strike in Seattle lasted for a few days in early February until it was quickly ended by federal troops and a public backlash. Although a routine American labor dispute, the strike was depicted by the sensationalist press as Bolshevik inspired, and the press exploited the event for all it was worth.[7]

There were, in fact, comparatively few radicals in the United States, and the possibilities of a Communist revolution were almost nil. In principle and practice, organized American labor never deviated from its nonrevolutionary tradition; and a revolutionary Communist Party had not yet been organized. The American Socialist Party, with only 100,000 members, was likewise reformist, and the Communist parties organized later in 1919 at their peak reached only 70,000.[8]

But Trevor was convinced that extensive violence and perhaps a Bolshevik uprising in the streets of New York were quite probable. His preparations for the defense of the city against revolution showed that he expected this turmoil to emanate from alien forces. And here, fact and biased conjecture worked in tandem—for even though the overwhelming majority of radical left-wing socialists consisted of foreign-speaking immigrant proletarians from various countries, Trevor's fixation on one particular group suggested a strong negative predilection toward them no matter what the facts might indicate.

In early 1919, Trevor directed investigators in MID's New York office to research and design an "Ethnic Map of New York" to guide army officers in the suppression of "an organized uprising." Starting with a long, detailed street map of Manhattan and the Bronx, Trevor's men identified every "ethnic district" with colors and an explanatory alphabetical key:

C = Germans
B = Italians
D = Austro-Hungarians
E = Irish
J = Negro

The largest of all these districts stretched across sizable sections of the Bronx, the northeast corner of Central Park, and almost the entire Lower East Side. They designated it

A = Russian Jews

The map's "accuracy has been [rechecked] in several ways," Trevor later attested, "and even in small details we are confident it gives an accurate representation of [the] ethnic distribution." The presuppositions behind creation of the map, like subsequent inferences drawn from it, however, were clearly distorted by Trevor's Anglo-Saxon nativism and that of the officer corps in general. They denied the social and legal equality, as well as the loyalty and political reliability, of American-born citizens of immigrant parents. Trevor's sweeping definition of an inherently unreliable and probably radical "ethnic" population extended beyond those "persons of foreign birth" to include "those born in the United States with one or both parents of foreign origin."[9]

Superimposed on the map were designations of "radical meeting places," with the number of actual gatherings at each. But, Trevor informed Washington, these figures represented "probably only 10–20% of the number now held every day in this city and the percentage shows a steady increase." Despite the inclusion of other ethnic groups in this scheme, Trevor focused his sights mainly on Jews. The sections labeled "A = Russian Jews," especially the Lower East Side, overwhelmingly had the most circles and those indicating the highest number of meetings. As he later noted, "the district most strongly permeated with the Bolshevik movement [was the one] indicated on our ethnic map 'A.'"[10]

"It is not our intention to convey an alarmist view of the situation in New York," Trevor stated, "but there is an undeniable feeling of unrest in the congested districts." Further, "a great deal of property damage and loss of life could be averted through preparation of a plan to adequately cover the situation." He advised distributing this map to all commissioned officers of federal troop detachments that might be deployed to suppress a revolt in New York.

Washington headquarters commended the plan, looked forward to a similar one for Brooklyn, and ordered the master plate secured at MID, New York, for reproduction on short notice.[11] Within a month, Trevor also distributed the map to the commander of the National Guard, the Adjutant General's Office, the New York City police commissioner, and even the New York Chamber of Commerce, all of them expressing intense interest in the foreign population, as the police commissioner put it, "in view of the existing restlessness among the radical element of this city, and . . . throughout the world."[12]

Within days of Trevor's circulation of the ethnic map, his foresight appeared prophetic, as Communists led by the Russian-trained Béla Kun seized control of Hungary and established a Soviet-style party dictatorship in March 1919. This shocking event also vindicated, in the minds of many, the Jewish-Bolshevik theory, since the principal leaders (and thirty-one of forty-nine commissars) of this Hungarian Soviet Republic were of Jewish heritage.

In the 133 days of this Hungarian regime, it destroyed or outlawed all national symbols, socialized property, collectivized agriculture, attacked church and family, and executed hundreds of opponents. The fact that Jews had been well assimilated in Hungary, had played an important political, social, and cultural role before the war, and had been the leaders in the country's capitalist development was overshadowed by the extremism of an apparently Jewish regime. That the Communist leadership consisted of apostates hostile to Judaism itself who terrorized traditionalist Jews was also overlooked. To anti-Semites, then and for decades to come, Béla Kun's regime represented an unmistakable example of rootless "International Jews," uninhibited by any identification with existing society, who sought the annihilation of life, property, family, and nation.[13]

Meanwhile, on April 7, leftist intellectuals, among the most prominent of whom were idealists of Jewish heritage, had taken over Munich and declared a Bavarian Soviet Republic. Although the German army brutally crushed the regime within less than a month, this episode likewise embedded in the minds of the German right and many outside that country the image of the Jew as Bolshevik.[14]

The suppression of the Munich Communists coincided with May Day unrest in the United States and talk of a summer general strike. In Cleveland, riots ensued when soldiers tried to disrupt Socialist May Day marches, while clashes resulted in Boston after policemen blocked a leftist street parade. Most cities, though, including Chicago, remained orderly; those instances where violence erupted hardly threatened domestic tranquillity, since these confrontations involved, at most, several hundred people. However, Americans opened their morning newspapers on May 1 to learn of a nationwide bomb plot directed at prominent government officials and economic leaders. The discovery of thirty-six bombs in the mail created an immediate sense of danger; the police instinctively branded this a diabolical IWW-Bolshevik scheme.[15]

These were hectic days for Trevor's office in New York. Two of his agents observed a May Day meeting at Madison Square Garden protesting imprisonment of Thomas Mooney, a West Coast labor leader. No surprise to Trevor, they reported that of the "three or four thousand people present . . . the greater proportion of them were Russian Jews," whereas a third agent outside estimated "the audience was 90% Jewish." Supposedly, the real "American labor unions" had withdrawn "when they discovered the character of the audience."[16] In reality, only two speakers were Jewish, and the most radical aspect of the meeting, a call for general strikes in support of a new Mooney trial, emanated from non-Jewish leaders. Judah Magnes, in fact, vigorously denounced "violence and bloodshed," condemning the mail bomber as "a brutal cowardly criminal . . . an ignorant fool . . . [who] has hurt the cause of labor." But when analyzed subsequently by MID's Chicago office, Magnes's speech suddenly became a furtive attempt to foment a Soviet-style "Revolution against Capitalism" in the United States.[17]

Contemporary news accounts, however, emphasized Magnes's peaceful tone and the stark contrast between the orderly meeting within Madison

Square Garden and the violent disorder outside by opponents of the rally.[18] But here, too, Trevor's agents put a particular spin on events, duly noting that the "Internationale" and "Hymn of Free Russia" were sung spontaneously before the "Star-Spangled Banner." When the night ended without any disturbance, these investigators inferred, in a somewhat disappointed tone, that

> the crowd was very much disgusted at the orderly tone of the meeting and it was quite apparent that they expected Mooney to be used as camouflage for a radical outburst and good old fashioned Bolshevik denunciation of the Government of the United States and Americans in general. The presence of the Stars and Stripes on the stand must have been very offensive to those devotees of the red flag. One woman selling pamphlets of the Mooney trial—a Russian Jewess—kept saying "Only fifteen cents for American Justice, I'm selling it that cheap."[19]

A third Trevor agent outside observed that only 1,000 policemen shielded the "Bolsheviki" inside from outraged patriotic groups of "soldiers and sailors," who were beaten by police nightsticks and charged by their horses. "Infuriated at the action of the police," these soldiers and sailors said, "[W]e have been overseas fighting and come home to find all the democracy we have being hogged by a lot of Jew bastards, and the government is giving them protection; [i]f we ever have another war I will not go into the service."[20]

Now in a mood of heightened expectation, Trevor spent the next day, May 2, engaged in intense activity. The cause of the previous night's disorders, he informed Washington, was "minority-radicals-shouting down with the government, bring on the revolution, etc. etc., [who] irritate the average citizen . . . to a degree that he is ready to resort to violence to suppress a movement which he regards as being inefficiently dealt with by the authorities." Sharing this sentiment, Trevor directed attention back to the "real danger of trouble"—an anticipated "general strike." If the strike materialized, he stated "with confidence," then "anything may be expected, and on the promptness with which it is dealt with depends the safety of the city."[21]

Working closely with the New York Guard in recent weeks, Trevor had drawn up "Plans for the Protection of New York in Case of Local Disturbances." Expecting the worst, he painted a gloomy picture of widespread disorders, a general strike, and a "sudden rush on any given armory with bombs blowing in the door [that] would result in the distribution of the arms and ammunition to the rioters." Since "the force is utterly inadequate to meeting a serious uprising in the congested district," he pleaded with Washington to expedite the delivery to the New York Guard of pistols, rifles, pump shotguns, machine guns, and ammunition. The plan further involved the deployment of regular army units so that 10,000 soldiers could defend Manhattan, with another 4,000 stationed in Brooklyn.

In intricate detail, Trevor described the number of troops and officers in each infantry and artillery regiments, deficiencies of available types of weapons, the exact city blocks to be occupied by each unit, the security of each armory, and the precise hours required for mobilization. He proposed a special mobile Machine Gun Battalion to be detailed "to the points where the emergency demands," which "as indicated on our ethnic map" were "the congested districts chiefly inhabited by Russian Jews."[22]

Trevor alerted headquarters that coordination of federal and state military units, together with "prompt action . . . will probably result in saving many lives and millions of dollars worth of property." Within a few days, Washington responded with confirmation that 6,000 Springfield rifles were en route but that the state guard had not requested any machine guns.[23] Yet such military preparations for the armed suppression of civilians, native-born Americans and recent immigrants alike, proved unnecessary. A general strike, or even disturbances of the magnitude Trevor envisaged, never materialized.

After dispatching his "Plan" on May 2, Trevor immediately forwarded a report on "Jewish Influence in the Radical Movement." Here was another variant of a now quite familiar theme: German Jewish "Internationalists" under the guise of Bolshevism have conspired to dominate the "Russian people and [force] the Slav world into [the] economic slavery of the aggressive German Jewish Capitalists." Pursuing these goals "with all the vigor and audacity particular to the Jewish race," these international Jews had also enlisted the "whole Jewry of America" in exculpating "the Red murderers" in Russia.

Although judging from its "style and character" Trevor correctly guessed Boris Brasol as the probable source, he still treated this information as "extremely interesting . . . regarding the character of the Bolshevik movement." Trevor also admitted such amazing assertions might contain verifiable aspects. Referring to the implication of Jacob Schiff and Kuhn, Loeb as Bolshevik financial backers, Trevor stated that "our information points directly to another source, but that fact does not exclude the possibility the persons mentioned may be in the background."[24]

Within a matter of weeks, as it turned out, Trevor's own investigator learned that Nathan Straus, head of Macy's, was maneuvering to become the Soviet Union's banker. Straus collaborated with "Louis Marshall, who is related to Judah L. Magnes, the radical, . . . the aim being that the Kuhn-Loeb and Strauss interests would oust the Rothschilds from banking control in Russia."[25]

Trevor's return to civilian life the following month as part of a general army demobilization signaled neither the end of his involvement with the Jewish question nor a cessation of investigations of "subversive" forces by MID's New York office. Well into the next year, his fellow officers relentlessly pursued these surreptitious forces.

Spying on America

In early September 1919, Major Thomas B. Crockett, an intelligence officer in the Chicago office, traveled covertly to New York City. There he confided in a select group of MID officers and prominent civilians about the "sinister . . . agitators [who sought] to create a state of chaos out of which would spring a revolution" in America. The true purpose of his secret mission was to "discreetly and quietly get together an investigative organization" whose network of "official and semi-official bodies" across the United States would expose these radicals and "bring them to a deserved justice." Crockett had already established similar organizations in Michigan, Illinois, and Ohio by reviving the wartime American Protective League under various new titles.[26]

Crockett's first contact in New York was with Major H. A. Strauss, a driving force in MID's investigations of radicals and Jews. Described by a colleague as "quite a live wire" who had difficulty realizing "that some wartime intelligence methods won't hold water in the . . . present," Strauss quickly embraced Crockett's plan.[27] After telephoning MID chief Marlborough Churchill for approval, Strauss arranged meetings with Nicholas Biddle and John Trevor, both of whom since leaving the military had been privately promoting the anti-Red campaign of the New York legislature's Lusk Committee. They found Biddle and Trevor "perfectly willing" to collaborate in the MID scheme.

Over the next few months, Crockett and Strauss traveled throughout the East and Midwest trying to expand the organization and arrange a meeting of various regional group leaders.[28] At MID Boston headquarters, they got an enthusiastic reception from Colonel E.R.W. McCabe, who believed no matter what legal or financial constraints Congress placed on MID, it "must have some sort of an organization to cover the country." In frustration, he wrote to Churchill: "I am not sure that it is the desire of the War Department for us to appear too active except along our own lines of strictly military intelligence . . . but I feel that the present situation demands most careful watching, especially in certain places where radical and labor element predominates."

McCabe requested permission to establish groups in the state capitals and larger cities of New England as "clearing house[s] for intelligence information."[29] Churchill approved "thoroughly" but insisted that such activities remain clandestine and unofficial. He cautioned MID officers "against letting [their] activities be known"; they must offer "assistance without going on record." From Churchill's perspective, the army's politically neutral and selfless efforts to defend America from internal and external enemies were thwarted by certain unnamed forces in the country that "fear any agency which cannot be bought or . . . controlled by blackmail or politics." "The element in this country which sympathizes with the radical element is very powerful and very alert." If "they get any inkling" of MID's surreptitious activities, "they would come down on us and exert pressure in the White House." Nonetheless, the proposed state and civilian intelligence organizations were both justified and necessary, "so that in time of emergency as soon as martial law is declared you will know exactly what tools you have at your disposition."[30]

While these officers conferred, the Red Scare hysteria built to a climax, as the government planned and executed a variety of actions against a perceived revolutionary threat. In the fall of 1919, the General Staff had prepared the infamous "War Plans White" for simultaneous military campaigns to suppress revolutionaries across the United States. Under these "White Plans" officers devised a contingency strategy for every army corps area in the country.[31]

Working with paranoid intelligence that "pointed clearly to a well-organized movement to overthrow our government," the army anticipated the need for military forces sufficient to combat an estimated 600,000 to 1.5 million revolutionaries. They would attempt to seize power through the same methods employed by the Bolshevik minority in Russia. As the army saw it, "out of the criminal dingy alleys of Lower East Side, New York, came Leon Trotzky and his misguided horde," for "it is known that the Bolshevist leaders are German and German Jews, and many of them are former German agents."[32]

On November 7, the Lusk Committee, violating numerous civil liberties, launched raids by hundreds of policemen on alleged radical centers, arresting 500, of whom 246 were ultimately deported. This action was surpassed by raids on January 2, 1920, instigated by Attorney General A. Mitchell Palmer. In numerous cities across the country, approximately 4,000 alleged radicals were swept up and incarcerated during the Palmer Raids. Often conducted without warrants, these raids, which completely ignored constitutional rights in the name of national security, were accompanied by similar actions at the state and local level.[33]

By early 1920, the efforts of Crockett and Strauss had also come to fruition. MID and civilian organizers agreed that working through the Americanization Committee of the United States Chamber of Commerce and its local affiliates offered the best prospects for both success and cover from public scrutiny. After lunching with leaders from the Americanization Committee, Churchill "felt fully justified in cooperating to the fullest extent." But Churchill "suggested that in order to keep the relation between the two organizations secret, . . . the Chamber [should] designate someone in Washington with whom M.I.D. could communicate verbally." Toward the end of the year, this working covert alliance received some official sanction from the acting secretary of war. Under the pretext of assisting the U.S. Chamber of Commerce in combating subversion, the secretary authorized MID to provide confidential information and advice. Through the Americanization Committee, civilians from New York to San Francisco were secretly collecting and exchanging information on fellow Americans.[34]

One of Churchill's "best civilian contacts," John B. Trevor, used his wartime rank of colonel for the rest of his life. Acting on behalf of the New York Chamber of Commerce, Trevor secretly exchanged intelligence with MID over the next few years. Written records indicate Trevor had eclectic interests, including army enlistment, officer selection, war plans, emergency plans for protection of New York, German propaganda, and registration of citizens and aliens. What passed verbally and remained unrecorded will never be known.[35]

In January 1920, Trevor composed a lengthy analysis of "Conditions and Agencies" creating radicalism in America, which Churchill considered "one of the best pieces of work . . . along this line." Two root factors causing the "disease" threatening "the continued existence of our body politic," Trevor wrote, were "RACE" and "MONEY," both of which could be identified with the "unassimilated or partly assimilated" immigrants— "our greatest anxiety." As clearly proven by his attached "Ethnic Map of

New York," among the most radical were the "Russian Jews . . . permeated with Marxian socialism of German provenance"; and he also pointed out that the lists of financial supporters of radical agencies "are crowded with German, German Jewish and Russian Jewish names."[36]

Although Trevor's obsession with radicalism and alien forces paralleled the concerns of most intelligence officers, MID now had to operate under very strict limitations imposed by Secretary of War Newton D. Baker in reaction to the excesses of the Red Scare. In March, Churchill suspended all investigations of U.S. radicals, even though through unofficial private networks and actual violations, MID never fully complied with these rigid constraints.[37]

There was, however, internal "diversity of opinion" over whether MID should risk a hostile public and political backlash that might hurt its funding or reputation. And could, or should, it continue gathering nonmilitary intelligence, given substantial postwar reductions in personnel and appropriations?

In a memorandum to Churchill, Colonel Charles H. Mason, one of MID's wartime creators, strongly opposed any "change in the present doctrines of M.I.D. in this connection." Not only did the situation in each country deserve comprehensive coverage but a "final picture" of the "world situation" necessitated an understanding of international movements transcending national boundaries—"that is to say the 'isms.'" According to Mason:

> In order for us to know whether or not we are going to have a change in the present social order in America to one of Bolshevism, or of socialism, or of Jewish Despotism, it is necessary for us to know what the ends and aims and processes of international Bolshevism, international socialism and international Jewry are.

He then went on:

> If we do not focus our consideration of Bolshevism in each country into a single consideration of that of the world, we fail in our work. We have the husks and not the essence; and yet it is proposed to eliminate the so-called "isms" from consideration by M.I.D. It is these "isms" that are the actual thing that M.I.D. should know and should primarily consider.[38]

Mason's faction prevailed. By early summer 1920, MID sent a policy directive on "International Movements or Isms" to all military attachés and intelligence officers. Despite its exceptionally broad scope, this policy focused particularly on "important international intrigues," among which "International-Jewry" received equal status with Japanese, German, and Bolshevist intrigues. MID followed these "as closely as possible" and urged officers "to keep well up on them."

A few months later, Colonel Dunn, who had received the *Protocols* in 1918, issued a revised directive to which he attached a descriptive sketch of each "ism": anarchism, Bolshevism, Islamism, Jewry, labor, pan-Latinism, pan-Orientalism, and socialism. An "intrigue" he defined as any combination of these and noted, "[T]here are many adherents to these various movements in our own country."[39]

To Dunn, Bolsheviks were "a small group of international demagogues" spreading out from their Soviet base in pursuit of world domination. At the head of the socialist experiment in Russia stood "the German-Asian Lenine and the person of Trotsky a Jew." Moreover:

[T]he intimate connection of the Jews and Jewry with Bolshevism is well established; it is also known that the principal agents of dissemination of Bolshevistic as well as other radical propaganda in the United States are Jewish newspapers.[40]

The section called "Jewry" concentrated almost exclusively on the "International Jew," a concept receiving widespread publicity throughout the year. Dunn's guide described the "International Jew" as

generally a brilliant, egotistical radical, sometimes an idealist dreaming of ultimate world domination by the Jews, but more frequently a thorough-going rascal, using his keen wits for purely personal gain; thus are to be found in the first ranks of Bolshevist leaders, large numbers of Jews. Many of the keenest minds among the Bolshevist leaders, not only in Russia, but in practically all other countries are Jews. It is this intimate connection of the Jews with Bolshevism and Socialism that calls for our close study and attention.[41]

This revised directive of October 1920 distinguished among different types of Jews. In contrast to the real culprit—the "International Jew"—Dunn now excluded from condemnation the Nationalist and Zionist Jews, worthy of only "minor concern." "Conservative, high class citizens of the countries in which they reside, their aims and ambitions are laudable."[42] However, up to this point and often thereafter, MID made no such distinctions. Despite lip service to the merits of assimilation and assertions that loyalty to America was the key to acceptance, many officers never fully trusted or accepted the so-called "national" or patriotic Jews. As a matter of course throughout 1920, intelligence officers treated Zionism as a dangerous movement intimately connected with suspect international currents, including Bolshevism.

At MID's New York office, the ever-vigilant Major Strauss carried on the wartime tradition of collecting data on such prominent Zionists as Justice Louis Brandeis, Felix Frankfurter, and Louis Marshall. "It is interesting to note," Strauss's aide Captain William A. Moffat informed headquarters, that Marshall, who was lobbying Congress on behalf of foreign-language newspapers, had recently traveled to Europe "as a representative of the Zionist Convention." Equally suggestive, he subscribed to a Soviet publication.[43]

Hearsay evidence also identified Brandeis and other delegates to a Zionists' conference as pro-Soviet propagandists in America, while others alleged that Santeri Nuorteva, an actual important Soviet agent in the United States, "had succeeded in reaching Justice Brandeis in Washington." Most apprehension related to Brandeis's position on the supreme court, from which he might alter American law or policy to advance radical or Zionist causes. Regarding Brandeis's "connection with the Zionist movement," wrote Moffat, "enclosed is a clipping . . . showing that Justice Brandeis has again dissented in the conviction of members of the Socialist Party." Favorable coverage in the leftist *New York Call* of Brandeis's dissenting opinion in this free-speech case, like his earlier argument for repeal of the Espionage Act, further solidified the case against him. Officers overlooked that these cases involved civil liberties for all Americans with no direct relationship to Jews; and usually the distinguished Justice Oliver Wendell Holmes concurred with Brandeis. Still, officers classified such information under the subjects "Jewish International Movement" or "Zionist Movement." They placed it in File 245: Jews.[44]

In pursuing figures like Frankfurter, MID had the cooperation and encouragement of the State Department and J. Edgar Hoover, then special assistant in the Justice Department investigating radicals. They were as concerned with Frankfurter's radicalism as with his Zionism. Considered "dangerous," Frankfurter was linked to the Amalgamated Clothing Workers ("the worst outfit in the U.S.") and the Inter-Collegiate Liberal League, "a nucleus for a nation wide organization of parlor bolsheviki and self-styled 'modern intellectuals.'"[45]

In June 1920, Hoover learned that Frankfurter would attend the International Zionist Conference, and "in view of the activities of this subject in this country," Hoover solicited MID assistance. Colonel Miles notified the London military attaché that "three prominent American Jews, Brandeis, Mack and Frankfurter," were attending this Zionist conference in England and requested a "complete report . . . on the proceedings of this conference." At the end of the year, Hoover also anxiously sought an overview of MID "files concerning the ZIONIST MOVEMENT."[46]

Meanwhile, Colonel Gordon Johnston, MID officer in Chicago, sent similar information to his friend Colonel William A. McCain, current head of the Negative Branch in Washington. Although McCain had graduated from West Point and Johnston from Princeton, both were proud Anglophile Southerners; Johnston was the son of a confederate general and McCain had received the Medal Gold from the Daughters of the Confederacy. Each had proven himself in battle; McCain had earned a Distinguished Service Medal in World War I, whereas Johnston, an authentic Teddy Roosevelt "Rough Rider," had won the Congressional Medal of Honor in Philippine action. McCain, an admirer of racial theorists Homer Lea and Madison Grant, also shared a concern with Johnston over the alien threat to America.[47]

Johnston tried to allay McCain's fears of imminent revolution, though he himself felt the situation still warranted a comprehensive study of all "foreign racial organizations" in America rather than limiting such to only "radical" groups. Like Trevor, Johnston counted among the "foreign population" of Chicago not only immigrants but also any natural-born citizen "with one or both parents born in foreign countries." Johnston privately encouraged civilian patriotic organizations to investigate alien racial organizations and furnished these civilian groups with confidential intelligence.[48]

Johnston's secret agents, identified only by code numbers, singled out Jews as the radical core at revolutionary, anti-American rallies and demonstrations. "As usual," wrote "operatives" No. 1431 and No. 1449, "Russian Jews predominated in the audience and they were worked up to a wild enthusiasm by the various speakers," who "aroused bitterness and hatred" that will certainly culminate at some point "in a violent outbreak." At a rally with "a large proportion of Russian Jews in attendance," seven undercover agents noticed the American flag was conspicuously absent, and these radicals shared an unspoken "mutual understanding" about revolution.[49]

By May, McCain possessed amazing information supposedly obtained from "a friend of Trotsky's." Reminiscent of B-1's fantastic allegations, it related how Trotsky had confided in his friend "that in his lifetime the Russo German Jews would dominate the world"; the "final plans" had already been activated. While Jews took control of Soviet Russia and Jewish money financed "anarchistic agitation . . . in civilized countries," German Jews in America would implement their part of the scheme behind the idealistic cause of Zionism. Most instrumental were Brandeis and Bernard Baruch, former German propagandists now secretly inhibiting U.S. intervention against the Soviet Union. Through various methods, "generally women," they "framed up" Wilson and his administration. Supposedly, the "brain and body" was a Chicago man who controlled the entire plot.[50]

Instead of reacting with the incredulity this memo warranted, McCain eliminated the paragraph on Wilson's frame-up and forwarded it to Johnston for relevant information. "Particular attention," McCain wrote, "is invited to the fourth paragraph . . . in which is mentioned the head of the movement" in Chicago.[51] Within two weeks, Johnston responded with an equally fantastic report by Agent No. 8 regarding "Jewry and the Zionist Movement" from an American Protective League member just returned from Russia.[52]

This informant had likewise learned that "an international body of Jews under the guise of the Zionist movement . . . plans to dominate and secure control of the governments of the world." The Jewish question had absolutely nothing to do with religion; it concerned Zionist schemes "to enslave the Christian and Mohammedan world" through economic control. Communicating in codes and acquiring Lenin's pledge of assistance, German, English, and Russian Jews signed secret treaties to exploit Russia economically and from that base the whole world. They had infiltrated the British Secret Service and dominated the American press through ownership, editorship, or advertising; they had elaborated their plans and tactics in "some Jewish document called *Protocols*," which the informant had read in Russia.

All of this revealed the inherent Jewish racial characteristics of "cunning, deceit, lies . . . and the utilization of every base motive" as a means to their ends. The "Princes of Jerusalem" in America were the prominent Zionist leaders, in particular "Justice Brandeis of the Supreme Court and Judge Mack of Chicago."[53]

The *Protocols* Again

Continued references to the *Protocols* from so many quarters nationally and internationally left MID in a quandary. The previous summer, the

State Department's Russian Desk had strongly suggested their major significance. Then, in February 1920, a reputable London publishing house caused a great sensation by releasing the first English edition of the *Protocols* under the title *The Jewish Peril*. This coincided with an anti-Semitic campaign in the British *Morning Post*.[54] Yet the American embassy in London, which now challenged the validity of B-1's "Bolshevism and Judaism," suddenly could not get the British to verify the significance or the authenticity of the *Protocols*. The embassy backed away from earlier assurances given Churchill that British intelligence had "secured proof" that Bolshevism emanated from an international conspiracy of Jews. The new line was that the evidence remained, at best, "circumstantial" and, at worst, constituted pure anti-Semitic propaganda.[55]

But Churchill persisted. On February 27, he sought out Harris Houghton, who initially brought these documents to MID's attention. Aware that Houghton had seen a photostatic copy of "the protocols of the Wise Men of Zion" in the British Museum, Churchill requested whatever information he might furnish "concerning the authenticity of the protocols." Houghton forwarded English translations with the commentary that "this evidence is quite important. . . . In other words, current events have furnished the proof."

Although never mentioning a Jewish conspiracy or Bolshevism, Houghton assured Churchill that "many qualified to judge" regarded the *Protocols* as "a basic document of some sort." Colonel Dunn had drawn that very conclusion in 1918, and ever since, others had as well. The strong belief that the *Protocols* must have some meaning kept the issue alive within MID.[56]

Through a stream of cables and correspondence in February and March, Churchill requested more information from Oscar Solbert, military attaché in London. MID already had various versions of the *Protocols*, but Churchill was "anxious" to examine an original 1905 edition in the British Museum; and he again sought the "opinion of the British as to its authenticity." While Solbert's reply dampened Churchill's hopes for clarification, the veil of secrecy surrounding the issue only heightened his curiosity. The American embassy was "very jumpy" about this matter of "extreme delicacy." Very nervous about any publicity that the American embassy might be conducting investigations of the *Protocols*, State Department officials requested that MID "make no inquiries." "All the information available" on the "Jewish Protocol" had already been sent in a previous dispatch marked "most secret." The embassy, stated Solbert, was even "afraid of any report going from here to America that any one here is interested."[57]

Undaunted, MID persevered in its quest for information and in its analysis of what it already possessed. Intelligence on Jews was circulated and discussed internally, especially within MI4, where most of this material crossed the desk of Captain Robert T. Snow. Among the most active counterintelligence officers, Snow became particularly intrigued by an analysis circulated internally comparing extracts from the *Protocols* with postwar radical currents.

An excerpt from Protocol V described how the "goy" working classes must be deceived by "great economic principles" into undermining industry and producing anarchy. Juxtaposed to this stood the "SUBSTANTIA-TION," a list of "leaders engaged in the promotion of Bolshevism and anarchy throughout the world." The three long pages that followed outlined the "cover name," "real name," and "nationality" of the alleged leaders of radicalism in Russia, South America, Poland, the United States, Germany, and France. Next to each name, in a long column down the entire right hand side of these pages, was typed over a hundred times without interruption "JEW, JEW, JEW, JEW, JEW, JEW."

Despite the countless non-Jews prominent on the left in these countries, the only non-Jew on the list was Lenin. Whoever compiled the list then referred readers to another part of his analysis "for further substantiation of the Jewish character of the revolutionary movement."[58]

After reading these extracts, Snow sent them to Colonel William W. Hicks, a fellow MI4 officer quite sympathetic to his concerns, with the following handwritten cover note:

> Have you ever read these documents on the "JEWISH PROTOCOLS"? If not I strongly urge you to read them. I have read them through very carefully twice and have underlined several names. Note the list of Jews on pages 7–8–9. . . . It reads like good dope and recent world developments would seem to bear out these protocols.[59]

While MID pursued this secret campaign into the spring of 1920, one of America's most prominent and admired citizens, Henry Ford, prepared to bring the entire issue into the public eye more forcefully than ever before. On May 22, Ford's newspaper, the *Dearborn Independent*, launched an anti-Semitic crusade with the sensationalist headline "The International Jew: The World's Problem." Each subsequent issue carried a lengthy section on the "International Jew," which, in overall perspective and precise detail, paralleled the material MID had been accumulating on Jews for years.[60] Ford; his secretary, Ernest G. Liebold; and his editor, William J. Cameron, displayed the same prejudiced attitudes toward Jews so prevalent among army officers. It was a perspective based, in part, on assumptions about inherent Jewish characteristics that were antithetical to those of true Americans. Beneath the headline stood the highlighted quote:

> Among the distinguishing mental and moral traits of the Jews may be mentioned: distaste for hard or violent physical labor; ... the courage of the prophet and martyr than of the pioneer and soldier; remarkable power to survive in environments, combined with great ability to retain racial solidarity; capacity for exploitation ... shrewdness and astuteness in speculation and money matters generally; an Oriental love of display and a full appreciation of the power and pleasure of social position; a very high average intellectual ability.[61]

Ford's paper lambasted the Jews for spawning everything from modern cultural decadence to international financial dictatorship and revolution. Jews made significant inroads into the United States at the top through banking, the Federal Reserve Board, and influence over President Wilson, while from below millions of unassimilated Eastern European immigrants threatened the distinctive nature of American culture through racial bastardization and undermined the government through radical propaganda and revolution. Throughout history, immoral "International Jews" had deceived and exploited the Christian world to advance their own race; at present, they continued to amass and exercise power according to a predetermined plan for world domination. Behind the 1905 Russo-Japanese War, the Bolshevik Revolution, and current world unrest stood the hidden hand of Jewry.[62]

Not only did Ford's themes mirror secret MID files but the actual culprits he cited (Schiff, the Warburgs, Baruch, Brandeis, and the rest) and their alleged schemes were also identical. Indeed, his editors relied upon several of the same sources and individuals involved in MID investigations of the Jewish question. Ford opened an investigative office on Broad Street in New York City, headed by C. C. Daniels, a former Justice Department official. Several of his assistants, known only by secret code numbers, had until recently worked in military intelligence. Among Ford's confidants and sources belonged Russian émigrés, including the ubiquitous Boris Brasol and Harris Houghton, the former MID captain whom Churchill still consulted on the *Protocols*.[63]

Ford significantly heightened anti-Semitic nativist paranoia across the country. Despite a widespread backlash against his campaign, many found his harangues convincing. The industrialist's national prominence, together with a paper circulation of hundreds of thousands, helped spread and perpetuate Jewish conspiratorial theories. Among those supporting what they considered Ford's brave patriotic efforts was Colonel Charles S. Bryan of the War Department, who thanked him for taking on the Jewish immigrants in New York, or, as Bryan phrased it, the "East Side Scum."[64]

Within two weeks of the *Dearborn Independent's* first anti-Semitic edition, MID headquarters in Washington telegrammed Johnston in Chicago for all issues. Johnston also attached a letter to the editor of the *Chicago Tribune* by Rabbi Abraham Hirschberg attacking Ford for a malicious attempt to inflame "race hatred and religious bigotry." Ford merely reiterated, Hirschberg argued, the centuries-old "stock in trade generalizations of the anti-Semite that have never been proven to be true"; and "not a single count in Ford's indictment" could be established by fact. Widely divergent in everything from politics to religion, Jews lacked international unity; certainly no conspiracy existed. Appealing to the "American love of fair play," Hirschberg referred readers to the refutation of Ford in the June edition of *Metropolitan* magazine.

As the Ford file made the rounds through MID in Washington, one intelligence officer, probably Hicks or Snow, added the following marginalia next to Hirschberg's letter:

> *Purely denunciatory.* Appealing to gentile not to persecute Jews on account [of] religious difference. Old line of *Bunk.* A Jew is a Jew whether orthodox or apostate.[65]

This view offered a classic example of anti-Semitism by universally prejudging and condemning every Jew on the grounds of common heritage. It did not consider individual worth or behavior; the great diversity among Jews in class, politics, national identity, and ideology were irrelevant. This attitude presumed an inherent and unalterable Jewish nature unaffected by culture, education, or personality. The tone of the remark left the unmistakable impression that this fundamental Jewish nature embodied few laudable characteristics. An officer with this mental framework could find it plausible that the American financier Bernard Baruch, orthodox Zionists in an impoverished Galician shtetl, the Warburg banking family in Germany, and the atheistic destroyer of the bourgeoisie and capitalism Leon Trotsky shared a fundamental common interest based on ethnicity or religion.

Under émigré influence, Ford's editors had in June 1920 added the *Protocols* to their exposition of an alleged Jewish worldwide scheme. By this time, Brasol and Houghton were each working quickly to complete their own separate English translations of the *Protocols* for U.S. publication. And the British *Morning Post* started an eighteen-part series on the *Protocols* under the headline "The Causes of World Unrest."

Despite disclaimers that "Jewish participation in the plot against christendom was confined to a small number of Israelites" and references to the laudable acts of "prominent patriotic Jews," the paper surged ahead with sensationalist claims about "evidence," the *Protocols* as the "Bolshevik Bible," the German Jewish connection, the secret exercise of power, and so on. "To describe the unofficial activities of the Jews in Paris would be to describe the work of the Conference," the paper stated without equivocation. "Mr. Wilson was surrounded by them; even M. Clemenceau had his watch-dogs."[66]

While Solbert mailed copies of each issue from London, the fruits of Brasol's labors, *The Protocols and World Revolution* appeared at the end of the summer. Published anonymously by Small, Maynard, and Company in Boston, it contained the disclaimer "that the vast majority of the Jews in this country have never heard of the Protocols and would denounce the plan which they set forth." Nevertheless, Brasol's entire thrust was to prove the actual existence of such a worldwide Jewish plot involving Zionism as well as Bolshevism. He repeated the method he had followed in "Bolshevism and Judaism," which the State Department Russian Desk had also followed in the "Power and Aims of International Jewry." He drew "parallels" between specific protocols and Jewish writings, Zionism, and Bolshevism. Through such "substantiation," a reader could easily grasp the unfolding of this plot in the development of current world events.[67]

Although Brasol's book was a commercial failure, it found immediate buyers in MID. Officers, who months before had acquired partial drafts, awaited the complete volume. On August 23, MID in Washington instructed the intelligence officer in Boston to purchase thirty additional copies of *The Protocols and World Revolution* for distribution, and soon MID needed more. At the end of September, Colonel William B. Graham, an avid Bolshevik hunter and Positive Branch chief, "requested that each Corps and Department Intelligence Officer be furnished with a copy of the 'Protocols.'" As Graham explained to Dunn, his branch "needs the assistance of these Corps and Department Intelligence Officers in the matter of the study and observation of this subject [Jews] within our own country."[68]

After ordering MID in Boston to purchase another twelve copies at $1.00 each, Dunn sent copies to the intelligence officers in Maryland,

South Carolina, Indiana, Illinois, Nebraska, California, and New York, as well as Hawaii and the Panama Canal Zone. He expected officers to use the *Protocols* in fulfilling the objectives outlined in the revised policy on "Isms," which had presented Bolshevism and Jewry as inextricably intertwined in the form of an "international Intrigue" labeled "International Jewry." The *Protocols* were provided, Dunn explained, "for your information and assistance in the study and observation of the Jewish movement within our country."[69]

Rather than dismissing it out of hand, MID now actively propagated an infamous historical forgery containing a preposterous conspiracy theory. MID did so not as a means of verifying or refuting its authenticity, but to provide a guide for investigating Jews. By merely circulating the *Protocols*, respected professionals in MID's hierarchy implied that the document had some value. And the gist of Dunn's memo definitely suggested they had much more to offer. When shortly thereafter MID acquired publications exposing the bogus nature of the *Protocols*, it made no effort to circulate these among officers at home or abroad.

On December 2, Colonel William Godson, military attaché in Switzerland, requested "as many copies of the Protocols as can be spared." Although MID had depleted its supply, Major Sherman Miles, attaché section chief, promised to secure additional copies, if Godson deemed it necessary. "I can well use the Protocols," responded the attaché from Bern: "It is an interesting propaganda and I have purchased in Paris at my own expense eight copies, which I have loaned and given to various people. If you can send them I would appreciate it."[70]

While awaiting a reply, Godson learned of Henry Ford's "campaign for investigation of Jewish activities." The same zeal that prompted Godson to publicize the *Protocols* in Europe ensured his enthusiastic embrace of Ford's crusade; he amended his request for more *Protocols* to include a subscription to Ford's paper. The Jewish question, he wrote to Miles, "is a subject in which I am keenly interested." Godson went on:

> I am following it up as best I can, and this information from America may give me leads to follow up. I am so thoroughly convinced of the reality of a Jewish movement to dominate the world that I hate to leave a stone unturned. I will greatly appreciate your assistance.

Godson then questioned whether Miles knew of *The Causes of World Unrest*, a book on the *Protocols* published by the *Morning Post*. "It is extremely interesting and should be read in connection with the Protocols of Zionism."[71]

The candor with which Godson, an experienced intelligence officer skilled in breaking German spy networks, justified his second request suggested he expected a sympathetic ear at MID headquarters. Surely his colleagues would find nothing unusual, let alone questionable, in his attitudes or inferences. Given the bonds of trust and common outlooks within intelligence circles, officers could speak frankly to each other. Directives from Washington and intelligence gathering on Jews in Europe over the past two years had definitely created the impression such views were well founded and shared widely among fellow officers.

Godson and Miles had conferred the previous summer at the military attaché conference in Coblenz, where the Bern attaché explicitly outlined his case for a worldwide Jewish conspiracy. As late as the end of November, Miles was still instructing attachés that "it is desirable" to collect "all information obtainable on the general subject of "Jewry."[72] During Churchill's recent visit to Bern, Godson had discussed all confidential matters with him personally at some length, including the Jewish question.[73]

One can imagine Godson's surprise when Miles suddenly reneged on his earlier commitment and took a stance diametrically opposite to the entire thrust of MID's approach to the Jewish question. Ignoring the original response to Godson, Miles's second letter downplayed the significance that MID had clearly placed on the *Protocols*. Miles now wrote:

> In view of the fact that this office has come to no definite decision concerning the Protocols, and has taken no further action than merely to send copies to the various Military Attaches for their information, it is not deemed advisable to act as a further agent in the purchase and distribution of same. For this reason no more copies are being sent you.[74]

This cautious act of disassociation had much more to do with changing reactions in America than with any fundamental reconsideration of the Jewish question by MID. A public backlash against domestic surveillance by MID and the hysteria created by the Palmer Raids had gained momentum throughout the year. MID had also been alerted that Jewish organizations were about to launch a public campaign challenging Ford and the entire *Protocol* literature.

In New York, Colonel Raymond Sheldon had already started to backtrack. Earlier he had acquired five copies of the *Protocols* on his own and had sent Washington a five-page document entitled "Protocols of the Zionists" from a "reliable source." It asserted that the "preconceived plan of the Protocols bears too close analogy to the passing events in America not to be considered as of utmost importance." Now Sheldon suggested the *Protocols* "may be of Catholic origin and anti-Semitic."[75]

When these denunciations began in late 1920 and continued through 1921, MID closely followed the national and international press coverage of them and started collecting relevant publications. Among these were "An Exposure," released by the Anti-Defamation League and "The 'Protocols' Bolshevism and the Jews," a pamphlet by the American Jewish Committee, both of which systematically debunked the *Protocols* as "a base forgery."[76]

These publications refuted all accusations that "Bolshevism is a Jewish movement." Contradicting information that officers had accumulated for years, the pamphlets pointed out that Bolshevik Jews represented only a small fraction of both Russian Jews and Bolsheviks. The list of fifty Jewish leaders published to prove their domination of Soviet Russia was misleading, since most of these held obscure positions; the few like Trotsky who wielded power were apostates hostile to traditional Jewish religion and culture. Bolsheviks, in fact, identified the bourgeois and capitalist Jews as their class enemy, while condemning Zionism as counterrevolutionary. In return, Orthodox Jews deplored Soviet atheism. Where Jews did predominate was among the Mensheviks, the "sworn foes of Bolshevism" and the proponents of constitutional democracy. The absurdity of the conspiracy theory was that if successful, Bolshevism "would lead inevitably to the destruction of Judaism."[77]

Distributing over 250,000 copies of its pamphlet, the American Jewish Committee reached a wide audience and received favorable press coverage. But its counteroffensive rested on the faulty premise of anti-Semitism as a foreign importation of European émigrés rather than a prejudice that had long taken root in America. To well-educated, assimilated, Progressive Era Jews like Louis Marshall and Cyrus Adler, "American anti-semitism [was] a contradiction in terms; anti-Jewish feeling was for them an aberration in the stream of American history." Their "abiding confidence in the spirit of Justice and fairness that permeates the true Americans" led many Jewish Americans mistakenly to assume that the anti-Semitism of Ford and others would be soundly rejected in a land that had "no room for injustice and intolerance."[78]

Jewish Americans appealed to the country's democratic values and institutions, unaware as they were of the negative and often hostile attitudes among U.S. government officials and army officers. To disassociate immigrant Russian Jews from Bolshevism and demonstrate their loyalty to

America, Jewish Americans pointed out that tens of thousands of these newcomers had "served so faithfully under our colors that they gained the unqualified approval of their officers."[79] In reality, army officers usually belittled such men as unreliable shirkers during the war and potential revolutionary destroyers of America thereafter.

When Jewish-American organizations sought the assistance of Secretary of War Newton D. Baker to prevent Harris Houghton from capitalizing on his former MID affiliations to promote his *Protocols* book, Baker expressed regret, but would not interfere: "Houghton is no longer connected with the military service, [and] the War Department has no jurisdiction." Not only had MID actually drafted this letter for Baker's signature, but at the time, MID and Churchill still remained in contact with Houghton.[80]

An unsuspecting Cyrus Adler of the American Jewish Committee often defended MID against insinuations and warnings from Jews in London that this American institution was actively involved in spreading anti-Semitic information. Unable to imagine the susceptibility of American officers to anti-Semitism, Adler wrote confidently that "there is no question but that so far as America is concerned, the whole matter was planted here by Boris Brasol." Later, a surprised Adler became indignant upon learning that the *Protocols*—"such fraudulent papers"—had made their way into the government at all.[81]

Whatever expectations Jewish-American leaders had of government institutions like MID, the only tangible impact of their counteroffensive against Ford, Brasol, and company seemed to be more caution by some intelligence officers. The publicity surrounding the scathing refutations of the *Protocols* had not led to a cessation of MID interest in these fraudulent documents or its investigations of that dangerous "Ism" and "intrigue" they called "International Jewry."

Intelligence gathering on Jews remained, at a minimum, one-sided and distorted. MID never informed its officers of the serious doubts these exposés created about the reliability of such documents and veracity of the "sources" promoting them. Apparently nothing was done to counterbalance the original impression that the *Protocols* had intelligence value. Not surprisingly, many attachés continued to treat them as quite significant.

Outright disavowal of one of the most outlandish conspiracy theories in history would not have been difficult by this point. But in rejecting Godson's request, Miles only stated that MID had "come to no definite decision concerning the Protocols." A politically astute young officer like Miles understood quite well the dangers of institutional embarrassment, as well as the grave political consequences publicly and within the army, if these documents were bogus and the public learned MID had been so gullible. It would be far more damaging if MID's link to this forgery led to exposure of its investigations of Jews.

Yet MID concerns about Jews proved sufficiently strong to override such serious risks. Miles directed Godson merely to cease distribution of the *Protocols*, not to abandon his investigations. And despite everything, Miles did send Godson a copy of Ford's *The International Jew—The World's Foremost Problem*, together with a subscription to the *Dearborn Independent*. Miles's only reservation was to charge these to Godson personally, since a "Government subscription for Military Attaches" should not include "any 'specialist' paper, so to speak."[82]

Although MID began to backtrack on the *Protocols*, the early focus on them had an enduring impact. Their serious consideration had contributed significantly to lingering suspicions of international Jewish conspiracies. For decades to come, individual officers would note that, whether authentic or not, the *Protocols* contained fundamental truths about Jewish interests and activities. The investigations and classifications of Jews as radicals were of similar import. They added credibility to the notion that a Jewish threat actually existed. In fact, the surveillance of Jews at home and abroad would continue for several years as the army became involved in the historic debate over immigration.

The Red Scare had strengthened the general postwar isolationist and nativist tendencies in America. Increasingly, immigrants from Eastern and Southern Europe were perceived as radicals or racially objectionable. Employers' fears of communism, American working-class concerns about cheap foreign labor, and apprehension over the country's racial heritage led to calls for major immigration restrictions. The congressional hearings on immigration held throughout 1920 were merely a prelude to the legislative decisions that would determine America's ethnic makeup and immigration policies for the next half century. And from the very beginning, many army officers acted as the nation's racial guardians in influencing enactment of laws to halt the influx of "undesirables."

The Army and Europe's Immigrant "Scum"

When the U.S. Senate Committee on Immigration reconvened its hearings on January 11, 1921, its first witness was Congressman Albert Johnson of Washington. A staunch restrictionist, Johnson had for months pushed "emergency immigration legislation" in Congress. His bill would temporarily suspend immigration and then greatly restrict the number and kind of immigrants admitted into the country. On this morning, he came well prepared to strengthen his case with a new piece of evidence. Facing his senatorial colleagues, he held up a long sheet, which he described as "a map of New York City . . . showing the location of the principal colonies of alien and foreign-born peoples there."[83] Drawing the senators' attention to the "large red splotches" on various parts of the map, Johnson said that these areas

> show those whom we know as the Russian Jews, or Russians, or Poles. It is immaterial from my standpoint whether they call themselves Russians or call themselves Jews. I have not the time to make the distinction between orthodox Jews, racial Jews, and Russians. They are of that type we call Semitic.

Suddenly, as if to preclude misunderstanding about what he actually meant, Johnson quickly added: "I do not criticize the race or the religion. I call attention to the congestion." But the struggle over the current bill was essentially a fight over Jewish immigration.

Briefly mentioning the brown areas as Italian, Johnson moved directly to his major point—alien subversion. Blue stars represented "foreign language newspapers"; white dots designated centers of "communist and radical socialist" activity. He reminded his colleagues that "there are over 1,000,000 unnaturalized aliens in New York City alone."

Johnson then turned to the authoritative witness from whom he had secured this map. A reputable attorney with intimate knowledge of the radical alien threat, this public-spirited citizen had voluntarily traveled to Washington to testify on behalf of immigration restriction. Most important, he had experience and closely guarded secret information acquired as "chief of the Military Intelligence Service of New York during the war."[84]

From his opening statement, this witness, Captain John B. Trevor, often invoked his MID background and expertise when warning of the "perils to our country" posed by aliens within and the "hordes of people" moving across Europe toward America. Elaborating on this ethnic map, which he had composed for MID in 1919, Trevor attributed 90 percent of radical activity to those areas "marked in red." These were the districts he had, while in MID, identified as "chiefly inhabited by Russian Jews." In his "Plan for the Protection of New York," Trevor had prepared for the military suppression of these Jewish neighborhoods. But Jewish congressmen had strongly protested the "offensive" allusions to the Jews in Johnson's earlier report, characterizing them as designed to arouse prejudice. Thus,

Trevor now disassociated himself from the "insidious propaganda" that attributed Jewish radicalism to "racial tendencies."

Instead, Trevor shifted the focus from race to urban congestion and historical oppression as the root of Jewish radicalism, thus contradicting his own reports and those of MID that more often than not highlighted the racial factor. This shift was, to say the least, disingenuous. In fact, Trevor collaborated closely with the advocates of racist political biology such as his friend Madison Grant, the anti-Semitic American Defense Society, and the eugenics movements; in the 1930s, he joined the Eugenics Research Association Board of Directors. Johnson had also earlier made it categorically clear that inherent characteristics of the "Semitic race," as well as their overwhelming numbers (75 to 90 percent of immigrants by his count) constituted the main problem.

Johnson was able to buttress his restrictionist arguments with material from other army officers besides Trevor, as well as diplomatic and relief officials in Europe. Since the end of the war, they had indeed painted a gloomy picture of massive hordes of inferior dangerous aliens about to overrun American civilization. Foreign service officers and military attachés considered themselves America's first line of defense. They stood as sentinels signaling the first warning of imminent racial "peril" from abroad.

The language used by American officials conjured up images of an inferior race, often comparing the issue of the Jews with the "negro problem." Eastern European Jews, wrote one consular official, emitted an "aroma no zoo in the world can equal"; "repulsive" parasites, "living by their wits on the labor of others," they were aliens "by their own act." "You cannot see the Jew of Poland in his black skull cap and his curly beard without admitting that he is not a pleasant companion. . . . a first step must be the giving up of that hideous costume." Such depictions were especially prevalent among those charged with issuing visas. Before going on to describe smelly long beards "full of soup," another consular official asked: "Well, what have you done with your Yids? I sent you a whole new flock."[85]

An American soldier picked up the following verse composed in the U.S. consulate in Warsaw:

THE PASSPORT OFFICE

The day begins, and the office
Stinks with the crowd of Jews
Of various shapes and sizes,
In cloths of various hues.

I see the line of God's "Chosen"
Stretch in an endless queue,
Demanding passport visas
In words neither lovely nor few.

I see in front of the counter
The form of Mr. Babtiste,
Whose endless volley of questions
Is fluent—to say the least.

I hear the pen of the stripling,
Writing the answers off,
While the air grows thick with herrings
And the T.B.'s start to cough.

I see the perspiring typists,
Pounding away on the keys
Their speed interrupted only
To swat some offending fleas.

I see the Hebrew children—
A wide eyed, unwashed band—
Brought in by their doting parents
As the hope of the "Promised Land."

(One mother confesses mildly
That her baby, short of a meal,
Mistook the thing for candy,
Chewed up the passport seal.)

I see the faithful Heyear
In his own original way,
Paying the wives and mothers
Drafts sent from the U.S.A.

I'm sure that St. Peter's duties,
To choose the good from the rest,
Are naught compared with the labor
Of sifting the Jews to go West.

It may be some day we'll have comfort,
But one thing I know full well
That if there is a Jew in Heaven,
We'll visa him straight for Hell.

The soldier who carried this piece back home believed this "regular flood" was part of a systematic JDC plan "to transplant three million undesirable Jews from Poland to America." In total frustration, he exclaimed, "Why in the dickens don't the Senate pass some restriction on the emigration?"[86]

While never explaining how such involvement related to their constitutional authority or military mission, some officers deplored the failure to impose strict immigration limits based upon racial criteria. They suspected liberals in the administration were endangering America by intentionally keeping the floodgates open. As one lamented, we can expect "a further influx of Jews—arranged with the concurrence of Depts of State and Labor!"[87]

Military attachés across Europe had already initiated their own campaign against "Jewish Migration." As they saw it, America had much to lose and little to gain by a "wholesale immigration of Jews," especially those from Poland and Romania—"the worst specimens of the race in Europe." Since the "Jew is not a producer," he would most likely be a Bolshevik or "a parasite of the economic variety." Attachés could not "recommend too strongly that these people be kept from the States," but they felt helpless, because American laws made "no distinction between Jews and Gentiles." Greatly disheartened, all attachés could do was "report the matter."[88]

But that helped more than they might have realized. Representative Johnson incorporated extracts from their dispatches into his December 1920 report, "Temporary Suspension of Immigration." Members of Congress read that officers on the scene considered "95% [of the Jews] . . . undesirable from the American standpoint." Jews congregated in overcrowded city slums and spawned most of the "political and labor agitators"; their attitude "toward orderly government" itself was questionable; and among them were "many Bolshevik sympathizers." And there were other dangers, since "they are filthy and ignorant and the majority are verminous." Of the "decidedly inferior type, physically, mentally, and morally, and because of their insanitary habits [they] constitute a menace to the health of all with whom they come in contact." Regarding public health or public safety, "it was impossible to overestimate the peril of [this] class of emigrants."[89]

While Johnson crusaded in Congress through the early months of 1921, attachés enthusiastically rallied behind the cause with a stream of reports on "the necessity of rigid passport control and effective legislation to stop emigration of undesirables." Resorting to gross exaggeration and dubious sources, MID warned about a serious miscalculation in estimating the actual magnitude of the problem. According to MID, to estimate the number of Jewish immigrants at "500,000 is very low," since in Poland alone they were departing at a "rate of one million, two hundred thousand per year," with perhaps another 850,000 waiting in Romania. America "is looked upon as the dumping ground for all the undesirable material." In Warsaw, Polish officials "openly boasted" to Major Hollyday "that they have solved their Jewish problem, as all of their Jews will soon be in America."[90]

Although intelligence officers recognized that postwar upheavals prompted immigration, they also believed that behind this massive migration stood the power and goals of international Jewry. Money, organization, and leadership from American Jews, operating through the JDC and Hebrew Sheltering and Immigrant Aid Society (HIAS), induced the migration of millions. Disregarding the country's welfare, American Jews displayed loyalty to their Jewish brethren abroad. Radicalism and Bolshevism, like public health threats, were immaterial, given the "chief mission" of "getting Jews to America . . . [simply because] they are Jews."[91]

The JDC and HIAS were accused of illegalities, bribery, passport fraud, and deceiving the American public. "Stories of persecution," noted one attaché, were "pure fabrication"; Jews were the least persecuted in Russia and "most prosperous" in the Baltic states. "These societies use this so-called mistreatment of Jews for propaganda purposes in order to arouse sympathy in the United States and prevent popular opposition to the . . . most undesirable element of emigrants."[92]

But neither abiding by lawful procedures nor actual distress and persecution were what really concerned these officers. By facilitating immigration, for whatever reason—humanitarian or otherwise—the JDC and HIAS increased "the danger to our country from this scum of Europe." The sufferings of those far away, particularly of so racially alien and despicable people as the Jews, might warrant American relief efforts. But Americans had an obligation to defend their own institutions, way of life, and racial integrity. America must "prohibit emigration entirely from Central Europe."[93]

Current immigration policy "was only storing up future trouble for the country," one officer wrote. American cities would degenerate into crowded ghettos like those despicable Jewish quarters of Vilna and Warsaw, because these "filthy" Jews have "none of our ideas of sanitation and are carriers of typhus and other diseases." A typhus outbreak in New York while Congress wrestled with the Immigration Bill led the Berlin attaché to repeat his earlier warning of inadequate quarantine of Danzig Jews.

In the view of attachés, Americanization could unlikely alter European Jews' way of life. Clannish, with a strong racial identity, Jews would not assimilate into the "melting pot"; their "international tendencies" precluded any allegiance to America or "willingness to fight and, if necessary, die for their adopted country." Indeed, "a large portion of our radical agitators in the United States are Russian and Polish Jews." Unlike "desirable emigrants" of the "great Nordic race," Jews had inherent characteristics that threatened the "purity of our race" and its civilization.[94]

Throughout these months, MID continued its domestic surveillance of Jews. Intelligence officers wanted to know the "vote cast by the East Side Jews" who might elect politicians unsympathetic to army interests. "It is a known fact . . . that Jews . . . are absolutely opposed to all military measures." The U.S. Communist Party and "the backbone of the labor movement in this country" also were "coming more and more into the hands of the Jews," whose racial solidarity with "their blood brothers" internationally ensured the betrayal of the real "American" worker. Colonel Parker Hitt, the intelligence officer at Governor's Island, New York, learned that the Third International in Moscow financed communism with "large sums of money" brought secretly into America "by some of the Jewish bankers in New York."[95]

Suspicions about alien forces made the foreign-language press a prime target for scrutiny. The Yiddish press (leftists and Zionists alike) had a reputation as a seedbed of radical agitation and anti-American currents. "This is an excellent illustration of the necessity of translating Jewish language papers," responded the MI4 chief to an article in the *Jewish Daily News* regarding a Jewish World Congress. The article "shows their undoubted efforts to establish an International Jew body for control of all Jews on an extranational basis." It "fully warrants the work necessary to turn it out," wrote Major Charles Mason in a long commentary; "it provided "a most interesting insight into what is "being fed the East-side Jews in the Yiddish papers."

As this translation circulated through headquarters, officers disagreed over its significance. Major Gilbert Marshall doubted it revealed "any conspiracy" or that Jews would unite internationally. But his reasoning was curious: Jews would not risk sacrificing the "intangibility of Jewry" that had always frustrated anti-Semites. As Marshall explained:

> The Jew has always been a rebel. . . . this intellectual Jew is bucking against the control of the practical, hard-headed successful one. In what will the strength of Jewry lie if not in the strength of its Rich members? Without the Rich Jew what control can 15,000,000 people exercise over the world when 15,000,000 negroes can not run one country. Note the threat, "No one dared to make enemies of the Jewish people."[96]

But Major Charles Mason, a key figure in MID, expected the Jewish World Congress to materialize and "tend towards extreme radicalism," because it would consist of "Western Jews of the intellectual class and Eastern Jews of the proletariat." A confident Mason thought it "entirely safe and reasonable to consider this movement and watch its development as one phase of the world Bolshevist movement."

The congress might coincide, Mason speculated, with the pogroms against Russian Jews following the Soviet regime's anticipated collapse a few months from that time. The congress was "but one of those perennial schemes of the intriguing 'submerged tenth'"; and "because it is a Jewish movement, the probabilities of its growth into greater importance are greater than usually adheres to such schemes." Still, in and of itself, the congress would never achieve "more than tertiary importance" in major world affairs. Its real significance was in advancing radicalism, in tightening the bond of Eastern with Western Jews, and above all, in politically "affecting . . . the immigration of Eastern Jews to America."[97]

Secret agents attended meetings sponsored by the Hebrew Sheltering and Immigration Aid Society to rally public opinion against the Johnson bill. Antirestrictionist opinions expressed by judges, congressmen, and other public officials were duly noted. At one HIAS gathering, Alderman Fiorello La Guardia and Congressman William Chandler of New York criticized the bill as "discriminatory against Jews and Catholics," condemned the exploitation of immigrants, and depicted Jews as good industrious citizens. "The whole affair," MID concluded, "was an eloquent tribute to the Jew and a severe condemnation of all who wanted the passage of the bill to restrict immigration."[98]

Although surviving files do not indicate whether Johnson was privy to this domestic surveillance, Trevor almost certainly conveyed to him the tone and substance, if not all the details, of MID's overall estimate of America's "Jewish problem." And the State Department, which furnished Johnson with documentation from consuls and military attachés, received timely copies of all domestic surveillance and the weekly *Intelligence Summary*. Just two weeks before the congressional vote on the Immigration Bill, MID's summary of world events again depicted the racial and cultural characteristics of the "Eastern Jew" as a "special problem for the United States." Owing to "his extremely primitive religion and moral code, his Asiatic point of view and social customs," "that type of Jew" constituted a "menace to Anglo-Saxon institutions."[99]

In the midst of postwar anxieties created by labor unrest, leftist agitation, and continued turmoil abroad, Johnson's use of official reports made a strong impression on Congress and the American public. With the feeling of uncertainty heightened further by rising unemployment and a business depression in late 1920, Johnson and other isolationists successfully exploited nativist fears as well as latent anti-Semitism. Among other things, the Immigration Bill promised to save America from a catastrophic deluge of inassimilable and dangerous Jews.

Despite a pocket veto from President Wilson in his last days in office, a compromise Senate-House Immigration Bill was signed into law by President Harding on May 19, 1921. The bill instituted the nation's first national quota system, one that intentionally discriminated against the allegedly inferior racial types from Southern and Eastern Europe. By design, this race-conscious quota system reserved most allotments for Northwestern Europeans.[100]

To many officers in military intelligence, however, the new legislation offered only a brief respite from a persistent danger hovering over America. Although it favored Nordic countries and limited total immigration to 350,000, these emergency provisions had a life of only fourteen months. The ink was barely dry on the bill before some officers took the initiative to promote much more restrictive and permanent legislation.

At the American Military Attaché Conference in Coblenz, Germany, on June 21, 1921, officers acted as partisan political advocates of Nordic racism. Twenty attachés from across Europe were joined by Major Robert Eichelberger from Siberia and Major Philip Bagby, MID chief with the American occupation forces in Germany. MID's crème de la crème, this august body included respected old hands (Edward Davis, Elbert Farman, William Godson, and T. Worthington Hollyday) and rising stars. Among the latter, Oscar Solbert would become President Coolidge's military aide and Warner McCabe MID chief in the crucial years leading up to World War II; Eichelberger would become a prominent general in that war, while James Ord would serve as aide to his friend and classmate Douglas MacArthur.

Churchill briefed the group on the European inspection he had undertaken that year, and each attaché summarized conditions in his host country. They spoke mostly of routine matters—finance, courier service, and the like—with one significant exception: immigration. Normally the purview of diplomats rather than soldiers, immigration received more attention than other issues. Disturbed by inadequacies in the new law, these officers felt duty-bound to bring immigration "again to the attention of our legislative body and to all of our officials in Europe," for immigration had "an important bearing on the future of our country and our race."[101]

The final conference report never mentioned the word "Jew," but it had an obvious unwritten presence. Attachés reiterated, often with the exact phrases, the descriptions of, and warnings about, Jews they themselves had been writing for years. They completely eschewed the contentious issue of Italian immigration in order to focus solely upon "those countries bordering on Russia"—for these spawned the "most undesirable" immigrants and their governments were "only too willing to dump their undesirables upon the United States."

The officers depicted these immigrants as a "herd" of "inferior" people "of a different racial stock," clinging clannishly to their native language, customs, and habits. Rejecting assimilation, they isolated themselves in the congested "slums of our large cities," where they spread "radical ideas" and "social hatreds." Since the European experience demonstrated "the bad effects of a racial minority," these undesirable immigrants "form a decided menace to the future welfare of our country." The officers concluded, "[I]t is against this type that legislative action should be directed."[102]

Slamming the doors shut quickly and forever against Eastern European undesirables was only half the officers' goal. The other objective involved a eugenics policy aimed at the demographic propagation and migration of a special race. While denigrating Eastern Europeans, officers applauded, often in romanticized language, "northwestern European races, that is, those of approximately our own race." This "best class" of immigrant displayed the same qualities and pioneer spirit of America's early colonizers by settling and cultivating "undeveloped parts of the country where they are rapidly absorbed." Relying upon the "observations of its members in Europe," the Military Attaché Conference Report recommended:

Efforts should therefore be made to pass legislation to facilitate immigration to the United States from the states of Northwestern Europe and the British Isles, where the Nordic Race predominates.[103]

Over the next year, MID collaborated with the Departments of State and Justice to build the case for stringent discriminatory racial quotas. "Reliable sources" and military attachés attested that since passage of the 1921 Immigration Bill, the dangers posed by "Jewism" had lost none of their potency. From the State Department's Division of Russian Affairs, DeWitt Poole and Allan Carter played the Jewish-Soviet card. Returning American prisoners, they informed their superiors, had testified that every Soviet commissar and judge they saw was a Jew; and "the Jews have secured the control of practically all available capital in Russia."

In Riga, meanwhile, Major Hollyday worked prodigiously to prove that American Jews systematically initiated and facilitated the immigration of undesirable Russian Jews. MID made sure Hollyday's reports reached the commissioner of immigration and Undersecretary of State William Hurley. Hollyday, like attachés in Poland and Romania, relentlessly attacked JDC and HIAS members for misrepresenting themselves as American government officials, while ignoring or circumventing the recent Immigration Act. On numerous occasions they allegedly assisted known Bolshevik agitators and even official Soviet couriers.

Barely able to contain his indignation, Farman wrote from Warsaw that if they were "not knowingly guilty," their "poor judgment" certainly "borders on the criminal."[104]

Suddenly, in the midst of its restrictionist campaign, MID found itself confronted with a potentially explosive revelation. The most conspiratorial minded among the officers suffered a severe blow to their astonishing theories as well as their credibility. Starting on August 18, 1921, and continuing for several days, the London *Times* hit the newsstands with the headlines: "The Protocol Forgery" and "Historic Fake." In scathing exposés, the paper debunked conclusively the myth of a Jewish world conspiracy.

The *Times* proved that *The Protocols of the Elders of Zion* was a case of "clumsy plagiarism." The original 1905 Russian document by Sergei Nilus, purporting to be transcripts of an actual Zionist meeting, was actually a copy of *Dialogues in Hell*, published in 1865 by the French writer Maurice Joly. American attachés in London, recognizing a scandal in the making, immediately rushed copies to Washington with the comment:

"[T]hese articles . . . endeavor to prove that the so-called 'Protocols of the Elders of Zion' are forgeries."[105]

Whereas earlier challenges to the *Protocols* by British and American Jewish organizations had only limited effect, the *Times* exposé was devastating. Widespread news coverage in both countries ridiculed the myth and the forgery's promoters. Editorial commentaries with such titles as "A Piece of Malignant Lunacy" and "Everybody Is Laughing over the Exposure" were bitter news to officers who held that MID's "accurate, timely intelligence" was America's first line of defense.

At the extreme end, certain officers had embraced the *Protocols*, supposedly discovering evidence to authenticate them. But even more cautious officers had seen some importance in them. They embodied the Bolshevik plan or at least significant clues about international Jewry. There were also those copies MID had distributed to officers as a reference work in studying the Jewish question.[106]

Apparently, MID now pursued a strategy of silence, dropping the matter without further comment. After an inquiry by Churchill in late August about whether MID had "received an article in French concerning the authenticity of the Jewish Protocols," the paper trail in the Protocols File 99-75 ends abruptly. The entire embarrassing affair remained buried in classified secret files for the next half century.[107]

Still, the attitudes of officers toward the Jewish question remained relatively unaffected. Churchill never disassociated himself from those tainted by the affair, especially an avid proponent such as Harris Houghton, who had toiled assiduously since 1919 to disseminate and publicize the *Protocols*. A month later, Churchill requested the MI4 chief to provide whatever assistance he could to this former MID captain. "For some years Dr. Houghton," Churchill wrote, "has been a student of the Soviet regime in Russia and has specialized in the Semitic influences underlying the revolution." He now sought MID's "opinion as to the value of the publication financed by Mr. Henry Ford in connection with this matter." Around this time, Houghton joined Ford's anti-Semitic crusade. A year later, Houghton again tried to warn MID about the plot "between Jewish-Americans and Socialists in Germany and Bolsheviks in Russia to bring about the overthrow of the U.S. Government."[108]

Most attachés remained in place, feeding Washington the same kind of intelligence they had for years. When, in late 1921, financial exigencies forced the elimination of an attaché in Switzerland, Godson, perhaps the most convinced of a worldwide Jewish conspiracy and most compromised by the *Protocols*, was reassigned as chief of the New York Organized Reserves. Churchill personally saw that Trevor would keep Godson abreast of "intelligence matters" and integrate him into the network of former MID officers, citizens' groups, and "influential citizens" with whom Churchill and Trevor collaborated privately. By 1925, Godson would return to Europe as attaché for the Balkans.[109]

The forgery exposure had not in the least slowed the momentum of the nativist campaign against immigration. In May 1922, Congress extended the 1921 Immigration Act for a two-year period, during which nativists prepared an unassailable case for a permanent and highly restrictive immigration law. Among the crucial guiding forces constructing these arguments, rallying public opinion and steering the legislation through Congress were Congressman Johnson and "Captain" Trevor.

After his 1921 testimony, Trevor became one of the most influential unelected individuals affiliated with the U.S. Congress. As Johnson's adviser, confidant, and connection with prominent Eastern restrictionists, Trevor established himself as a permanent feature in informal congressional meetings. Often he provided the ideas and impetus for legislation, eventually personally drafting reports and laws themselves. Throughout this period, Trevor maintained his secret MID liaison, especially with Churchill, who did the "civilian contact work in New York" into 1922. The two men met clandestinely and exchanged confidential information on alien registration, foreign spies, and the political activities of the New York Chamber of Commerce. As late as 1926, Trevor supplied MID with opinions and information on the cases of individual immigrants and alleged radicals.[110]

Despite Trevor's earlier denials, the restrictionist movement had definitely acquired an expressly racist tone in its confidential meetings as well as its public justifications. A circle of Johnson's own acquaintances, expanded by those brought in by Trevor, formed a kind of "racist brain trust" that included Madison Grant, Charles Stewart Davidson of the anti-Semitic American Defense Society, and Harry H. Laughlin, a prominent eugenicist and proponent of scientific racism. Over the next several years, this coterie met together in Washington and New York not only to advise Johnson and Trevor but also to discuss the particulars of the drafts of legislation on which they themselves had already testified as supposed detached expert witnesses.[111]

Among the evidence submitted to Congress were studies emanating from the army itself. In 1923, Princeton psychologist Carl Brigham published *A Study of American Intelligence*, based upon the results of intelligence tests prominent American psychologists administered to hundreds of thousands of World War I draftees. These data appeared to provide irrefutable scientific proof of the Nordic race's inherently superior intelligence and the gravely deficient IQs of the inferior Eastern and Southern Europeans flooding into the country. Although subsequently thoroughly debunked (Brigham later repudiated his own study), these tests did significant social damage in the 1920s and beyond. Brigham personally brought these test results to the attention of Congressman Johnson, while others presented them authoritatively before both houses of Congress.[112]

Through their publications and testimony, this racist intelligentsia persuaded large segments of the public and Congress that new legislation was imperative to the survival of American civilization. The Nordic thesis popularized by Grant's *The Passing of the Great Race* received further elaboration and credibility through a plethora of racist publications appearing in the early 1920s. Some of the most significant came from the pen of Grant's disciple Lothrop Stoddard, who likewise testified before Congress. But in the 1920s, Stoddard's *Rising Tide of Color* and *Revolt Against Civilization* made the alien peril appear greater and more immediate than in Grant's original work. And Grant and Stoddard now inserted the worldwide Bolshevik threat into the dynamics of their political biology. That addition again highlighted Eastern European Jews as a special racial problem.[113]

Referring to the "momentous biological discoveries" underpinning his analyses, Stoddard identified "racial impoverishment" as the cause that "destroyed the great civilizations of the past and which threatens to destroy our own." America must institute laws and social policies to decrease the various "inferior" races while expanding the size of "superior" Nordic groups within its borders. He presented the Bolshevik Revolution as an "instinctive reaction" of the inferior "Under-Man" (non-Nordic masses) against both civilization and the civilized behavior that he is inherently unable to achieve. Fundamentally, "Bolsheviks are mostly born and not made."[114]

Whereas Slavic races constituted the revolutionary masses that overthrew the Nordic Russian aristocracy, Stoddard wrote, international Jews assumed the radical leadership. The "Jewish mind, instinctively analytical, and sharpened by the dialectic subtleties of the Talmud," had ensured such pivotal positions for Jews in all revolutionary movements since Karl Marx. After identifying the "largely Jewish Bolshevist regime in Soviet Russia today," Stoddard subsequently described most Bolshevik leaders as racially inferior, "sinister types." The atrocities perpetrated by some of these "'tainted geniuses,' paranoiacs, unbalanced fanatics, unscrupulous adventurers, clever criminals, etc." indicated "homicidal mania or the sexual perversion known as sadism." Unless counteracted, their vengeance awaited the entire civilized world. As Grant phrased it in an introduction to Stoddard's work, Mongolized "Asia, in the guise of Bolshevism with Semitic leadership and Chinese executioners, is organizing an assault" on the West.[115]

The racist propagandist reaching the broadest audience, Kenneth Roberts, was also among the most influential. After serving as an intelligence officer in Siberia, Roberts took two long journeys across Europe in 1920–1921 for a series of articles on immigration in the *Saturday Evening Post*. He kept the issue in the public eye during this period with no less than nineteen prominently displayed articles, which he compiled into *Why Europe Leaves Home* just in time for the campaign to restrict immigration permanently.[116]

Roberts's writings had a distinctiveness that enhanced their persuasiveness. He, too, juxtaposed the epic of "tall, blond, adventurous" Nordic pioneers developing America into a great nation against the danger of "immigrant inundations that submerged, mongrelized and wrecked the great nations and civilizations of the past." But he synthesized these anthropological and historical racial theories with firsthand observations and official information obtained from American ambassadors, consular officials, and military attachés across Europe. Many of the notes for his articles were actually summaries of information from reports American officials had confidentially submitted to Washington since the end of the war. In essence, Roberts assumed the role of unofficial mouthpiece through which U.S. officials conveyed their views and concerns about the immigrant menace directly to the American public. Jews were singled out as the main problem.[117]

Worried about "national suicide," one consular official stated "factually" that with the United States about to be "overrun by foreigners . . . the American people is in danger of losing its identity." He suspected either that Washington did not fully understand or that its failure to act was political, since "Jewish immigrs. in America exercise an influence disproportionate to numbers." This official imagined the scene back home with a "line of Senators and Congressmen raising hell over some little squirt Jew who has broken a dozen laws to get to America."[118]

Wherever he went, Roberts heard, in emotion-laden detail, the official litany against Jews: lice-infested, disease-ridden "scum" of Europe; a cowardly, selfish lot incapable of loyalty to any country; radical and opposed to all governments; and urban-dwelling, unproductive "human parasites" who live by "underhanded means." Sneaky, "it's their nature" to lie about anything. Cowardly and weak, they are "all very fearful of pain," crying "Oi Yoi" at the very sight of a doctor and releasing "awful wails of Yoi Yoi" when given shots, whereas other ethnic groups "don't give a damn."[119]

Roberts's personal observations confirmed such views of these "Kikes," as he often referred to Jews in his notes. His descriptions of ghettos were unmistakably intended to conjure up images of "a den of wild beasts" wherein screeching, "filthy" Jews, covered only in "horrible rags," were crammed fourteen into four rooms, with "children jumping around like goats." Outside, an "awful odor" rose from the "street covered with crap," helping to explain the widespread typhus and other epidemics. Passport offices were depicted as symbolic bastions of an America under constant siege by "a howling mob" of tens of thousands of screaming Jews, trampling and clawing each other; "the stench which rose from the struggling, squirming bodies was sickening." The book version reinforced these disparaging images through photographs of wretched-looking men dressed in rags destined for America.[120]

Roberts jotted in his notebook, "All Bolsh leads back to Jewish societies. Pictures shows Jews as Bolsheviks. Radical leaders Jewish." Later, he informed his readers that "almost every American government official in the north of Europe received repeated proofs" that America "was letting [Bolsheviks] in by the thousands."[121]

"You're a patriotic American," Edward Davis, military attaché in Berlin told Roberts; "see what you can do for your country" about the waves of Polish Jews embarking for America.[122]

Davis then allowed Roberts to copy his recent MID report, "Emigration of Undesirables to America." Roberts wrote quickly that the entire migration, within which the Bolsheviks hid, was being stimulated and financed by the Joint Distribution Committee and HIAS. Passport and visa fraud, as well as other illegalities and unsavory manipulations, pervaded all such activities. Under financial arrangements with the governments of Poland and Danzig, "Jew societies . . . expedite scum of Europe, etc." Roberts quoted Davis' figures verbatim: "70% are females and males under 18. 95% are Jews: all but 30% are ready to breed."

Davis undoubtedly leaked this information with the intention of affecting politics back home. Referring to the recent election of Warren Harding, Davis remarked: "This administration had four years ahead of it, approval of [the] country behind it, and a great chance to do a few things of great good to [the] country—and couldn't start on anything better than an honest immigration law."[123]

Indeed, prospects were quite good. Month after month, Americans across the country, most of them far removed from the immigration scene of the large Eastern cities, had the Jewish question thrust upon them through Roberts's graphic style and alarmist message. With a circulation of two million, the *Saturday Evening Post* was the most widely read magazine in America. Through its patronage of Roberts and its editorial policy, it became an effective weapon in the restrictionist arsenal.[124]

Upon returning to America, Roberts immersed himself in the political battle as Washington correspondent for the *Post*. He spent the next two years lobbying Congress, exhorting Immigration Committee members in particular to read and endorse his articles and books. He was even known to intimidate and bully those lacking his deep convictions. And he testified before the committee as an expert witness with personal experience in immigration matters.[125]

While the racist intelligentsia saturated the public with dire predictions, officers on active duty entered the debate. Throughout the 1920s, officers spoke on behalf of various political causes, even expressing support for congressmen on specific issues and votes. This practice grew more widespread after 1922, when General Pershing issued an order granting officers equal rights of political expression with civilians and encouraged them to be openly political. In public schools, colleges, universities, and other public forums, officers spoke extensively on such favorite topics as the instinctual causes and inevitability of war and "Communists and Pacifists."

Since peace movements were considered inherently un-American, pacifists were linked logically with alien ideas and undesirable groups incapable of assimilation. While Colonel Walter C. Sweeney frequently delivered his "Reds and Pinks" speech around the Boston area, General Amos Fries, a well-known advocate of chemical warfare, spoke to audiences in New York and Washington on the topic "The Menace of Pacifism." Fries also recommended speakers from the American Defense Society, which was then heavily engaged in the restrictionist offensive.[126]

In lectures with such blunt titles as "Aliens" and "Americanism," other officers alerted their countrymen that unless immigration was "restricted we will soon be overrun by an unwieldy multitude . . . [and] depredations of the frenzied masses of low brows," who "will saturate the nation with anarchy [and] Socialism." Even more detrimental than the danger to "our free institutions" was the "degeneracy of our sons and daughters as a result of the infusion of alien blood."[127]

Over the years, the widely read and respected *Infantry Journal* carried editorials and articles on the "scientific selection" of immigrants and the "Red Menace." It noted various conspiracies to dump on America the "most undesirable" and "unassimilated aliens." These disease-ridden and radical "cast offs of the poverty stricken pest holes of Europe" engaged in "much of the conspiring against the Government."[128]

In 1921, the *Infantry Journal* explicitly linked Jews to "a real conspiracy of world revolution." It published the long lecture delivered by Mrs. Arthur Webster before the British Royal Artillery Institution on the "secret forces" pursuing "world power." These she identified as the "German-Jew Company" that had been active for over a century and now controlled Russia:

> Bolshevism, therefore, is largely Jewish, and we cannot wonder that to many people the whole world revolution seems to be a Jewish conspiracy. I have heard our officers returning home from Russia saying, "I am convinced . . . this movement is a Jewish plot to destroy Christianity," and in all countries we see Jews playing a leading part, in our own country we see them inciting to violence, . . . as interrupters at patriotic meetings and filling the Albert Hall at the Red Flag Meetings. But . . . I do not think . . . it entirely a Jewish conspiracy, for it is also largely German.

Mrs. Webster ended by exhorting soldiers to defend the "honor of women," "happiness of children," "freedom," and "Christian civilization." For similar reasons, the editors of the *Infantry Journal* urged their members to read her lecture carefully, noting:

> It is, therefore, most important for officers and soldiers to be fully informed of the history of the world-wide revolutionary movement that is being undertaken under the guise of Bolshevism in Russia and Communism in this country. It is our duty to be acquainted with these things in order that we may deal with them understandingly when the time comes for us to combat them.[129]

A national propaganda and lobbying campaign by the American Legion further strengthened the restrictionist movement. Through the *American Legion Weekly*, *Annual Reports*, and newspaper articles, the Legion organized a vigorous, systematic effort over a period of years to rally the country and Congress to action. About to emerge as one of America's most esteemed and powerful institutions, the Legion fought a tenacious political battle for 100-percent Americanism and against alien influences.

The Legion started editorializing in 1919 about deporting "alien slackers" who "fattened on American clover, but had not grown American souls." These parasites "stood smirking while American mothers sent American lads off to war. They took the vacant jobs. They rolled in rich rewards." The Legion then began identifying the poisonous "virus of Bolshevism" with the "unbalanced temperament of virulent Slav radicalism." Soon, it was demanding the numerical limitation or total exclusion of the "alien hordes of Europe" and "diverse racial stocks," who were quickly becoming America's "human liabilities." A Legion publication title, "What Cannot Be Fused Must Be Refused," expressed the prevailing attitude.[130]

In 1923, the Legion publicized the eugenic arguments of the "noted biologist" Edwin Conklin of Princeton. "It is the wonderful persistence of heredity that makes immigration such a menace," he wrote. In "Is Immigrant Labor Really Cheap?" and "The Price We Pay," Conklin warned Legionnaires of the damage caused by America's historic search for "cheap labor." The first attempt—"Negro slaves"—cost a bloody civil war and bequeathed "a racial problem that can never be solved short of amalgamation or extermination." Had the second effort—"millions of Orientals"—not been suspended, the "high level of white civilization" would have been lost as America, in the words of Theodore Roosevelt, became "Chinafied."

In Europe, Conklin argued, there were now individuals "whose entrance into the United States would constitute as great a danger as would the opening of our doors to any of the colored races." With the influx of Eastern and Southern Europeans, citizens again were "deciding the fate of America as no enemy can ever decide." The "lowered hereditary qualities" were responsible for dramatic rises in crime, insanity, poverty, and "backward school children" plaguing America's cities. "If we debase the heredity of our people by admixture with inferior stock we commit the unpardonable sin for which there is no atonement."[131]

The Legion brought the message of the racial intelligentsia directly into the homes and lodges of its members and their families. These media efforts, together with fiery speeches at national conventions and local groups against the alien and Bolshevik danger, further intensified this campaign, as did testimony before Congress and direct lobbying of politicians. With over 300,000 members functioning within a national network and united solidly behind a single issue, the Legion wielded considerable political force.[132]

Under pressure, Congress was on the verge of passing a new immigration law by early 1924. The bill would cut in half the number of immigrants allowed under the 1921 act that had already reduced immigration from the high of 800,000 to 300,000 per year. And it would make permanent the extremely low quotas for Southern and Eastern Europeans. However, Jewish-American organizations and congressmen, in alliance with liberal groups, challenged the law's very premise, branding it a defilement of American democratic ideals of justice, equality, and fairness. In congressional hearings, prominent Jewish leaders charged that the anti-Semitic and discriminatory bill rested upon "an unfounded anthropological theory" of a mythical Nordic race for which "no scientific evidence worthy of consideration was introduced." Lambasting Grant and Stoddard for espousing nonsense, they refuted the image of immigrants as inherently inferior, disloyal, radical, or incapable of assimilation. Basically good, industrious, law-abiding people, immigrants had during the war "indicated their desire to fight for the country." Through "acts of valor and bravery," they earned congressional medals and distinguished service crosses. It was, after all, Abraham Krotishinsky, "a little barber from the East Side," who saved the famous "Lost Battalion."[133]

Congressmen realized the effectiveness of appeals to Americans' democratic ideals and sense of fairness. Despite all that had been said and printed for years, restrictionist congressmen now amazingly denied all charges of racism and anti-Semitism. Yes, restrictions were designed to preserve "the basic strain of our population" and "the form of government" that rested on this "stock," but the law was in no way "directed at the Jews," nor did it favor "any particular type of immigrant." Neither had committees "dwelt upon the desirability of a 'Nordic' race" or "devoted its hearings to that end."[134]

The political spin and hypocrisy were obvious. Months earlier, Johnson, writing as chairman of the House Committee on Immigration, had published an article clearly explaining that the "fundamental reason" for restricting the "vast influx of aliens" was not economic but "biological":

We are infinitely more careful in the selection of animals which we import for breeding purposes than we are in the selection of our incoming aliens. . . . No abnormal or diseased animal is allowed to mix its blood with that of our breeding stock . . . an unfit animal is an unfit animal, whether it be a man or woman, horse or sheep. Bonds are powerless to make a fit American father or mother out of a feeble-minded alien.

To Johnson, the proposed legislation definitely "aims to ... cut down the numbers of aliens ... from southern and eastern Europe. In other words, it is recognized that northern and western Europe furnish the best material for citizenship."[135]

To overcome some congressional reluctance and assuage parts of public opinion, Johnson needed to disguise the legislation's racial goal behind an appearance of ethnic neutrality and fairness. Once again, the cynical maneuvers of Trevor proved decisive. Trevor had worked long and diligently researching and formulating elaborate statistical evidence on the current composition and ancestral heritage of Americans. From these statistical tabulations, he contrived a formula for immigration quotas based on the census of 1890 rather than that of 1910, which had been used in earlier laws. This change clearly ensured overwhelming favoritism toward Northwestern Europe. Thus, the nativists could achieve their Nordic objectives while maintaining a semblance of fairness.

Captain Trevor had come a long way since he first composed his ethnic map in 1919 and testified with it in hand before a Senate hearing in 1921. He had over the years moved from witness and advocate to pivotal manipulator. The bill that Johnson's committee guided successfully through the House rested upon Trevor's arguments; even parts of his text were included verbatim, and his statistical tables were appended as explanation and evidence.

When David A. Reed of Pennsylvania encountered difficulty over the bill with his Senate colleagues, he, too, found it necessary to resort to Trevor's scheme. As the renowned immigration historian John Higham remarked, "Without Trevor's statistical tables to show how national origins quotas might work out in practice, Reed would never have succeeded in persuading the Senate of their feasibility."[136]

The 1924 National Origins Act was a watershed. It limited total European immigration to 150,000 annually, allocated proportionally to the percentage of each nationality in the United States in 1890. In effect, about 70 percent of the quota was reserved for those of Nordic origin, and soon immigration of the so-called inferior races dropped from its height of hundreds of thousands to less than 15,000 per year.

While still heavily engaged in the final heated debates over the bill, Congressman Johnson extended his "personal thanks" to former MID Captain Trevor: "If it should happen it will have resulted from your table, of which both House and Senate have made considerable use."[137]

CHAPTER 5

Educating Officer Elites: The Army War College, 1919–1933

IN EARLY OCTOBER 1921, CHARLES DAVENPORT, America's leading eugenicist, opened his mail at the Genetics Research Institute at Cold Spring Harbor, New York, to find an irresistible invitation. The Army War College had asked him to lecture on a subject "possessed of military significance"—"the racial factor in war and international relations." Considering Davenport's work of "great value," the army sought his views on "racial consciousness and inherited racial characteristics," especially those affecting future wars, alliances, and observance of treaties.[1]

To Davenport, this meant army recognition of his eugenic research as well as its understanding of the calamitous price of the nation's neglecting the "racial factor" in history. Described by one historian as a "driven man," Davenport combined the fervor of a scientific zealot with nativist social and racial prejudices. From his well-endowed Eugenics Record Office and Department of Genetics at Cold Spring Harbor, this respected biologist and former instructor at Harvard and the University of Chicago directed a crusade to save American "Protoplasm" from contamination. Making America shorter and darker would be only one result of the infusion of the blood of "undesirable" immigrants. Their inherent behavioral traits would cause national degeneration socially and morally, as these alien races were "more given to crimes of larceny, kidnapping, assault, murder, rape, and sex-immorality." Naturally, America's soldiers would be affected accordingly.[2]

What Davenport would say for the edification of the class of 1921–1922 would be reiterated in various forms by other prominent speakers at the War College until America's entry into World War II. These lectures, together with certain aspects of instruction, readings, and projects assigned to student officers, made the War College an important center for the institutionalization and perpetuation of a racial worldview within the officer corps between the world wars.

Institutionalizing the Worldview

A few weeks after receiving his invitation from the Army War College, Davenport opened his lecture at the college in Washington with a memorable demonstration of racial distinctions. Standing before the class of officers, he summoned to the front of the room for racial examination three "representatives of different European types." Davenport classified the first specimen as "a very good representative of the Nordic" and asked the gentleman whether he "comes from Sweden or is it Scotland." As a Nordic, he was "characterized by tall stature, by light hair, by blue eyes and by a low cephalic index."

Davenport then taught the officers the proper scientific technique for measuring skulls to determine the cephalic index of each race. Initially identifying the second person as "a good representative of the Mediterranean race . . . short stature, dark hair, dark eyes," Davenport quickly revised his taxonomy when closer scrutiny disclosed he lacked the requisite "long head." "Intermediate" in stature and color, the third subject, "from Lithuania, on the Baltic Sea," also proved to be a "less pure type than the Scotchman, of the Nordics."[3]

Discernible physical racial variations would have been less troublesome for Davenport had it not been for the recent report on the Army Intelligence Tests by his former student, Major Robert M. Yerkes, for these tests confirmed extreme "differences in average intellectual capacity" among soldiers of different races. The "percentage of foreign born" soldiers of the Mediterranean and Alpine races scoring in the lowest category (D and E) was extraordinarily high. Of those born in Russia and Poland—who, Davenport emphasized, "must have been . . . largely jews—there were 60 to 70%c who fell into the classes of D and E," whereas of those born in England, "about 9% only" graded so low. The obvious "military bearing" was that army officers, "the men who have to do the thinking, do the intellectual work," must be drawn disproportionately from races with higher levels of intelligence.[4]

Next, Davenport turned to the widely varying "instinctual and emotional traits" illustrated by his study of New York high-school girls of different "racial origin." Measuring them according to ten traits used for "rating [the] capacity of officers," he found those of German origin rated first in "all of the good" traits; they "stood first in leadership, in pertinacity, in humor, in loyalty, and in generosity." The "Jewish girls," though "first in generosity and patriotism," rated "second in suspiciousness, last in coolness, [and] very low in leadership." Switching to a comparison of breeds of terriers and collies, Davenport said scientific studies of "dogs, guinea-pigs, and poultry" had shown such behavioral traits are embedded in the "inheritable substance of the germ cells." "Man is animal," subject to the same laws of nature that "have been worked out in related animals that are lower on the scale."[5]

To demonstrate the military relevance of genetics, Davenport permeated his talk with naturalistic analogies and historical examples. Admiral Horatio Nelson was both "one of the world's greatest tacticians" (hypokinetic traits from the "clergymen on his father's side") and a "dare-devil fighter" ("lively temperament" from his mother's line). Nomadism, "a true racial hereditary trait," ensured that such peoples as American Indians and Bedouins, and the like, though "furious fighters," could neither "organize great armies" nor ever be settled on the land.

Among Davenport's more striking claims was that many of the "causes of wars" and revolutions "have a biological base."[6] "There are hereditary racial qualities," he said, "which may cause social unrest," culminating in upheavals like the French and Russian Revolutions, where the more numerous "lower stratum," led by malcontented intellectual types, killed off "the most capable" classes. Social unrest results when the traits of the "paranoic" blend with "the tendency to reform, . . . also a hereditary one." Although making no reference to Jews, he echoed exactly the charges made by critics of Jewish activism, referring, for example, to born radicals who were dissatisfied even under fortunate circumstances. His list of the paranoiac's inherited qualities left a similar impression; "suspicious" types suffering from a "persecution" complex, they believe they are "abused" and denied their "rights." Earlier in his lecture, he had identified these traits as characteristic of Jewish and Irish schoolgirls.[7]

On the international scene, Davenport foretold of future "starvation, epidemics, and war" caused by overpopulation and the natural antipathies arising from clashing racial instincts. He advocated control of human reproduction to limit wars caused by insufficient space and resources but rejected eliminating race differences "by universal intermingling." The latter would produce an inferior hybrid in which both the race and civilization would be "reduced to the level of the lowest." Davenport implied that polices and wars to preserve the higher race were preferable to such an outcome: "The cost of peace by [miscegenation] is in the minds of many too great."[8]

The institution at which Davenport and others lectured had been established in 1901 as a modified version of the German Kriegsakademie. The U.S. Army War College trained selected officers for both war planning and positions of high command. Entry usually depended upon graduation from the General Staff School at Fort Leavenworth or the Army Industrial College, buttressed by strong recommendations from commandants. Only captains or above under the age of fifty-two (after 1933, under forty-four) showing great promise for upper echelons were deemed worthy of this coveted career path. Among the nine officers composing the first class (1904) were Captain John J. Pershing and Captain Ralph Van Deman. After World War I, classes normally contained eighty students (about thirty colonels and lieutenant colonels and fifty majors.)[9]

Intentionally designed to study problems beyond tactical or strategic military questions, War College courses emphasized the relationships among world powers. Officers formerly trained in conventional "military" skills found themselves guided into the realms of politics, economics, and psychology; they were strongly encouraged to view their mission of national defense in the broadest possible way. The planning and conduct of war required a grasp of industrial systems and manpower, as well as the behavior of nations as determined by environment, history, or inherited racial proclivities.

Opening exercises for each class involved addresses by the secretary of war and chief of staff. Instruction came from twenty officers detailed to the War College for specific periods, supplemented with invited lectures by officers, government officials, and civilians with special expertise or experience. Churchill spoke on MID, Inspector General Eli A. Helmick, on leadership, and the still unknown Major George C. Marshall on the General Staff. The class of 1924 heard Captain H. S. Schofield of the navy lecture on the Washington Naval Conference and Colonel O. L. Spaulding's lecture, "Applied History." That same class was instructed in graphics and signal communications by Colonel Parker Hitt, reassigned to the War College from MID in New York, where he had spent the early 1920s ardently surveilling Jews.

Civilian lecturers included industrialists, ambassadors, university professors, foreign dignitaries, and mainstream labor leaders such as Samuel
Gompers. Among these were occasionally prominent Jewish Americans
such as Bernard Baruch and Ambassador Henry Morgenthau, who spoke
respectively on wartime industrial mobilization and foreign policy. Nevertheless, within this wide range of diverse speakers, students were continually exposed to political biology and racial ideology. And officers were far
more susceptible than resistant to these ideas.[10]

In general, attending the War College was an educational and professional experience that developed or strengthened perspectives not all that
different from mainstream, socially and academically acceptable American
nativism of the 1920s. But whereas America gradually evolved intellectually and politically away from the nativist hysteria as the interwar period
progressed, the curriculum, objectives, and atmosphere of the War College
stood unchanged up to 1940. The army sought to train decision makers for
command and staff positions who shared common outlooks and approaches. As one historian assessed its overall institutional mission and
practice, "the War College attempted to reinforce the army point of view."
The vantage point perpetuated was actually that of the "old army," whose
ideals and "atavistic attitudes" had been formed and firmly entrenched
long before World War I. Jealously guarding its institutional autonomy
and ingrained beliefs, the officer corps emerged as a "subculture"; its "values and outlooks" became increasingly out of touch with changing American society.[11]

The year spent at the War College meant the completion of "the officers' socialization process." Graduates were prepared to become an integral
part of the General Staff—the "brain of the Army." In the interwar years,
a total of almost 2,000 officers would undergo such education, which was
a substantial number if one considers that at any given point, the entire officer corps only had about 14,000 officers on active duty. For most, the career paths materialized as expected. Over 50 percent of all War College
graduates during these years became General Staff officers, and of the
1,000 generals on active duty at the end of World War II, more than 600
were War College alumni. Among these were some of America's most distinguished wartime commanders: Dwight D. Eisenhower, Omar Bradley,
George S. Patton, Robert Eichelberger, Richard Wainwright, Leslie J. Mc-
Nair, and Walter B. Smith, among others. Hundreds of others functioned
as leaders throughout the army, where their decisionmaking was also undoubtedly affected by the ideas and assumptions they brought to their

commands.[12] For many, these ideas and assumptions were inculcated or reinforced by the institutionalization of racial thinking in the War College.

Teaching Racism

The themes enunciated in Charles Davenport's 1921 lecture were echoed in the presentations by other speakers at the War College well into the 1930s. Just a few days after Davenport's lecture, another scholarly authority espoused the wisdom of scientific racism. During his lecture, "Racial Problems Involved in International Relations," Dr. Clark Wissler, an anthropology professor at Columbia University, underscored the consequences of ignoring ineradicable "inborn behavior" and the enduring power of racial identity. He told the future leaders in his audience: "We are dealing with something here almost as constant as a physical law."

In defense of the race, Wissler maintained, its members "will die to the last man." Displaying some lingering residue of wartime sentiments, Wissler used German Americans as a prime example of the difficulty, if not impossibility, of truly assimilating alien races.[13] Although the war was over, "national safety" was still at risk, since America's multiracial makeup strongly suggested that history would repeat itself: "In time of war there may be an enemy within vastly more dangerous than the one without." More complex than disloyalty or subversion, the problem also related to the "moral and mental fiber of racial groups" from which the army might be forced to recruit its manpower. Certain races lacked the "mental efficiency" to handle the sophisticated technology that would determine victory in future wars.

Like Davenport, Wissler cited the dire implications of the Army Intelligence Tests in order to demonstrate the necessity of seriously assessing "the racial constituents of American citizenship." He urged the army not to wait for other institutions to accomplish this crucial task; it must forge ahead on its own. The Army Intelligence Tests, expanded to include other behavioral characteristics such as inherited emotions and temperament, should lay the foundation for a "mental survey" of the entire country.[14]

The notion of an insidious racial danger lurking within America was a fairly persistent theme among academic lecturers at the War College. In *Is America Safe for Democracy?* (1921), William McDougall of Harvard, a renowned social psychologist, had argued for a national eugenics program. This was imperative to save the country from the "most immediately urgent evil" of the fast-breeding "inferior half of the population" over-whelming the superior segments. Unless abated by sterilization and segregation, these demographic patterns would guarantee that "the civilization of America is doomed to rapid decay."

In this book and his classic study of national character, *The Group Mind* (1920), McDougall emerged as an staunch exponent of the Nordic race theory of higher civilization. Addressing officers in the lecture "Race as a Factor in Causation of War," he advised a "dispassionate" consideration of the issue, particularly when comparing "civilized white races" with "inferior . . . colored peoples."[15]

"You gentlemen, as leaders of the Army," he said, confront "this problem of race" more directly than other Americans, because racial differences constituted a major cause of war. Drawing historical analogies with the Hindus and the ancient Greeks, McDougall attributed certain social upheavals and wars, even the survival or collapse of civilizations, to the natural "tendency of a race to prefer its own stock" and struggle to perpetuate it as a pure and distinct entity.

McDougall identified the "dominant feature" of the previous two centuries as the quest for "racial homogeneity." Differences in culture, religion, and language were substantially race based, as were "moral differences" and significant gradations of such characteristics as willpower, tenacity, and trustworthiness. "Most of you have heard of the Army intelligence tests," he interjected; they proved the existence of different levels of intelligence, thereby justifying the sense of superiority some races rightly felt toward others.[16]

According to McDougall, no country could sustain itself through misguided, idealistic policies of accommodating greatly diverse races or by attempting to "override and obscure" persistent racial dissimilarities through educational and cultural assimilation. Such efforts would ultimately fail because of the hard scientific fact that racial homogeneity was the sine qua non of every stable nation-state. The "only wise policy" was "segregation" into nation-states internationally and among different races within a particular state.[17]

Although McDougall joined with most American racial theorists in condemning the cult of Germanic superiority, he did not abandon the Nordic thesis. In his view, World War I was, in part, due to the Germanic myth unequivocally refuted on the battlefield by many of the officers present. But when McDougall repudiated the exclusive German claim to superiority espoused in Houston Stewart Chamberlain's *Foundations of the Nineteenth*

Century, he did so without criticizing this theorist's overall racial philosophy of history. Chamberlain had erred primarily by defining the great race too narrowly. For McDougall, the Germans, Danes, English, and so on (including Anglo-Saxon Americans) were all part of the Nordic race and embodied its special qualities. Although "open to much criticism," Chamberlain's magnum opus received a strong recommendation from McDougall.

Ironically, on April 1, 1924, just two weeks before McDougall's lecture, a new champion of Germanic superiority, Adolf Hitler, had entered Landsberg prison, where, unknown to McDougall or these officers, he was about to compose *Mein Kampf*. In creating this first systematic exposition of Nazi ideology, Hitler would rely heavily for inspiration, philosophy, and historical information upon the authority and erudition of Chamberlain's *Foundations of the Nineteenth Century*.[18]

Nonetheless, it was with mainstream American Nordic racists in Madison Grant's circle that McDougall identified. In recommending theories and books for the officers to continue their study of race, McDougall endorsed Madison Grant's *The Passing of the Great Race* and writings of eugenicists like the renowned biologist and president of the Museum of Natural History, Henry Fairchild Osborn. McDougall also highly recommended *America: A Family Matter*, in which Charles W. Gould described the pivotal role of racial purity in the rise and fall of civilizations. For Gould, the contemporary challenge was whether the creative Nordic race could save civilization by retaining its control of America.

In closing, McDougall spoke of the convergence of "race friction" and acute economic rivalry predicted by the notable Harvard geneticist Edward M. East in his recent *Mankind at the Crossroads*. By ending with East, McDougall left his audience with the dire future prospect of an overpopulated world of perpetual struggle among races varying widely in capacities.[19]

Into the 1930s, class after class heard this message reiterated by yet another notable eugenicist, Professor Henry Pratt Fairchild of New York University, who won national attention for his *The Melting Pot Mistake* (1926). America had saved itself from the brink of catastrophe, he argued, only by finally appreciating the lethal folly of the assimilation myth and closing the gates against alien types through the Immigration Act of 1924. As part of his annual War College lectures on population, Fairchild took officers on a lengthy scientific journey full of sober lessons about man and nature. He delved into species multiplication, amoeba reproduction, and human female ovum maturation rates before reaching the complex statistical level of calculating the billions of people likely to overwhelm the earth's space and resources by the end of the century.[20]

Fairchild shattered any illusions of a benevolent nature as he described a Malthusian world of unlimited reproduction and restricted food supply in which starvation, like "slaughter" and "wholesale killing," was the norm. It was no different for the human animal governed by the same "factors and forces that control the existence of any animal." Man's fate remained the perennial Darwinian group struggle for survival through the acquisition and defense of space and food. The only escape was interposing artificial checks on population through eugenics, birth control, and sterilization. All of this was quite relevant to the army because "overpopulation" was "the great underlying cause of international war the world over, not only today, but in every previous phase of human history."[21]

Speakers unaffiliated with the eugenics movement conveyed similar race-based ideas. Clayton Lane of the Commerce Department invoked anthropological and ethnographic scholarship in 1927 to explain the economic effects of racial traits. Emotion, great excitement, and panic in crisis situations were "characteristic of some races . . . particularly of the Latin and Mediterranean type." Italians had a "racial disposition toward national hysteria," which would have been "disastrous" had Mussolini not kept it under control.[22]

The Princeton Orientalist Herbert Adams Gibbons, though a Wilsonian progressive, was an adherent of instinct theory.[23] Considered an honorary faculty member of the War College, Gibbons delivered the opening lecture on military intelligence by providing an overview of the world situation. When asked to elaborate on Soviet Russia in 1931, Gibbons responded that "Asiatic instincts" caused resentment of the organization and social discipline necessitated by modern society. This doomed the Soviet experiment to failure, as the "weakness" in the Bolshevik system was "the [human] material they are using." "The natural instincts of the people," he thought, will surface and rebel against civilization.[24]

Another frequent lecturer, Robert F. Kelley of the State Department, reinforced this view in his own thirty-page analysis of why the "Bolshevik Regime" could not succeed without adaptation to Russia's peculiar racial characteristics. By nature "emotional" rather than "intellectual," these careless, indifferent, undependable and erratic Asiatic Russians—lacking in initiative, determination, and staying power—remained an impediment to modern economic development.[25]

Following one of Kelley's lectures, the War College commandant, General William D. Connor, delivered a long monologue attributing the fatal flaw in Bolshevik theory to a more universal "trait in human nature." A distinguished leader in World War I, "Bull Durham" Connor had a reputation as a hardworking intellectual type. He directed the War College from 1927 to 1932, becoming the mentor and lifelong friend of Eisenhower. For most of the 1930s, he would serve as superintendent of the U.S. Military Academy. Some critics found him ill suited for such positions, because he seemed to have closed his mind to most post-1918 military thought.[26]

When lecturing, Connor assumed the role of a history teacher well versed in vulgar Darwinism and sociological theories of elites. He walked to the blackboard and drew a diagram to illustrate all of humanity. Cutting the figure in half, he designated 50 percent as "the strongest," who, due to a combination of strength and intelligence, "are going to get what they need from the weaker." Quickly again and again, he created, then subdivided, into successively smaller units each new dominant group while explaining the process of continual struggle for survival and domination that allows the fittest to rise at each stage. Ultimately, out of the final group at the top, "you will have a small percentage that will represent those who get and those who hold."[27]

Throughout his extemporaneous sermon, Connor glided from religion and politics to fish, fowl, and children. Erasing as much as possible any differences between the "human being" and "animal life," he asked officers to recall their experience in the Philippines and to compare the behavior of the monkeys they observed with that of their own young children. "They both grab everything they can." Natural history as well as human history provided incontrovertible proof of a perpetual struggle for acquisition and power.

By defying natural laws and historical experience, Connor argued, Bolshevism had condemned itself to a foolish sociological experiment. Since Stalin recruited most of his ruling group from the "day laboring classes," Connor felt "justified" in presuming it was only a matter of time before "that class of ignorance" succumbed to reemerging natural elites.[28]

Over the years, various classes had heard one rendition or another of Connor's pet theme. In a formal lecture on American foreign policy in 1929, he could not have been clearer:

[S]uccess went to the side with the greatest battalion. The survival of the fittest is the rule in biology and nothing has happened very much in the history of the world that would lead an unprejudiced and cold blooded reader or student to judge that that law has been suspended.[29]

The lexicon of various military instructors and speakers contained similar Darwinian metaphors to be invoked when needed to enunciate one argument or another about the centrality of race and perpetual struggle. In this spirit, the deputy chief of staff, General George Van Horn Moseley, demanded "a more drastic selective system" for officers being groomed for general staff positions. Human beings required constant competition in order "to be kept healthy." Out of this testing and rivalry, those best suited for leadership in the upper echelons would distinguish themselves, while "the unfit must be left by the wayside."

Colonel Preston Brown, a War College instructor for several years and a former Pershing aide, applied similar metaphors to elucidate international relations, noting in 1920 that "the great laws of nature which govern" the "human or national soul" cast serious doubt upon the Versailles Treaty's viability. Attempts to maintain peace and the "international status quo" by treaties or other means was illusionary and naive; "national life, like human life, is growth and change." He also mused about a future showdown between the "white and yellow races" of the "United States and the Japanese Empire."[30]

In an earlier lecture, Brown had extensively cited *Expansion of Races* by Woodruff, the army's own Darwinist theorist. Brown offered a Malthusian interpretation of the interrelationships between population, food, and the causes of war. The law of survival dictated that "either the species will eventually overrun the earth, crowding out all competitors, or else it dies out." Since man, too, was subject to the same laws as every other organism, "the instinct of race preservation" remained the unalterable dominant factor in human evolution. Man's quest for food and space to sustain the race "has been the great compelling factor in his history."[31]

Brown's main objective was to raise the historical consciousness of officers. They must grasp the entire question from the sweeping perspective of "man's transition from the primitive savage . . . to the highly civilized and complex inhabitant of an industrially developed state." They needed to understand that the population explosion was unique to the modern world. And since the earth's land mass and resources were finite, demographic saturation spurred colonization, migrations, and imperialism, all of which had a consequential relationship to "potential enemies or allies" of the United States.[32]

The notions about race, space, resources, and demographic pressures inculcated gradually, though certainly not subtly, by civilian and military lecturers had immediate relevance to army concerns in the 1920s. War planning concerned the distant future, whereas immigration and radicalism put the enemy at the gates and perhaps already within fortress America. As a consequence, when lecturers from Military Intelligence in the early 1920s attributed the revolutionary situation in America to the immigration of racial aliens, the perceived threat coincided perfectly with the racial theories officers had imbibed.

Major William W. Hicks sounded the warning in a lecture in December 1920. From his opening remarks, Hicks, then heavily engaged in the Jewish investigations across town at MI4, left no doubt as to who composed the leadership and rank and file of the "revolutionary movement." Among the anarchists, he said, "the brains ... were BERKMAN and EMMA GOLDMAN, Russian Jews, who were deported to Soviet Russia." The Communist Party, "mostly foreigners and ... dominated by Russians and Russian Jews," had as its "prominent members ... all Jews." Within the Socialist Party, only Eugene Debs was a native-born leader, whereas its other most prominent members were "VICTOR BERGER and MORRIS HILLQUIT, who are Jews."

Although confident that the army could presently crush these revolutionaries, Hicks stated, "[T]heir numbers are increasing, due to the unprecedented immigration, consisting mainly of Italians, Poles, [and] Russian and Rumanian Jews" and to agitators. The long-term national interest demanded that officers face "the cold hard fact" that these immigrants were the most resistant to assimilation and Americanization. Most of them were, by nature or principle, opposed to the current government. These immigrants "will be sympathetic to the new revolutionary movement here and will undoubtedly furnish many of the recruits and add numbers to a movement which is already too large." As a visual aid, Hicks displayed a large MID map of the United States on which he designated "those areas likely to be involved in Revolutionary Activity." The "most dangerous localities"—Chicago, Cleveland, New York, Seattle, and San Francisco—all had heavy ethnic and immigrant concentrations.[33]

Like so many speakers, Hicks concluded on a cautionary note that made it appear he knew more than his position in intelligence allowed him to reveal. The army, he said, needed to be especially vigilant. Attempts had been secretly observed of increasing propaganda and agitation among the troops by the Reds, as they tried to establish clandestine Communist cells within every military unit.[34]

Such lectures were much more than a pro forma obligation for officers. Over 150 copies were usually made of each lecture. These became an integral part of the curriculum and educational resources from which every future class would benefit. The organizational format of War College courses forced officers to study the themes and content of various lectures. Many of the lectures were bound into the course books on certain subjects. When speakers or subjects struck a chord, officers took their lectures with them for future use. One future general, Frank J. McSherry, kept Fairchild's 1936 lecture, "Population," while another, Ralph C. Smith, retained and lent to others a 1939 lecture by Stoddard.[35]

Most work by the officers in the college was done in committees, which were each assigned a particular problem deemed significant by various divisions within the military. Committees were expected to research and write complete reports on all military, socioeconomic, political, and psychological facets of subjects such as the strategic relationships among the Great Powers. Each officer also had to prepare an individual report or thesis. The topics approved for G-2 courses on military intelligence reflected the broad interests and peculiar views dominating MID thinking in these years. Alongside climatology, war, press, and the Monroe Doctrine were listed religion, the dangers of pacifism, Bolshevik influence, European minorities, and the "International problems of colour and race."[36]

The army further oriented officer education in desired directions by requiring or suggesting certain kinds of information be studied in conjunction with these projects. Army faculty selected various works from the library as relevant student reading assignments and references on the subjects for committee and individual reports.[37] The standard readings appearing repeatedly on these bibliographies relating to race or the Jewish question were in harmony with the overall worldview of officers and general images created or reinforced by War College lecturers. Ripley's *The Races of Europe* stood out as the authoritative anthropological guide for officers. Its division of Europe into Nordic, Alpine, and Mediterranean races as determined by dolichocephalic or brachycephalic head types appears to have been treated as gospel truth. For the sociological, political, and historical implications of racial anthropology, officers were directed to works by Gustave Le Bon and Lothrop Stoddard, as well as McDougall's *Group Mind*. Each emphasized the decisive effects of inherited intellectual, cultural, and moral traits on the nature and behavior of nations.[38]

Occasionally, these basic authorities were supplemented with works such as Paul Kammerer's *The Inheritance of Acquired Characteristics* or Earnest Sevier Cox's *White America*. After the mid-1920s, John B. Trevor's *Analysis of the American Immigration Act of 1924* and the Senate committee report "Selective Immigration Legislation" also appeared on these reading lists.

Among those recommended, *Military Intelligence: A New Weapon of War*, was published in 1924 by a War College alumnus (class of 1920) who returned as an instructor in 1925. The author, Colonel Walter C. Sweeney, held that war and civilization were inextricably interconnected; postwar Wilsonian fanfare about morality in international relations and peaceful resolutions of conflict were illusions. The "conception that life is a struggle for existence" for individuals and great powers stood unshaken. History had not indicated any change in the "fundamental relations which existed between men before civilization started" down to "the nation of modern days."[39]

Officers cited such works in their group and individual papers, now and then commenting on specific theorists and their studies. This evidence indicates that many officers internalized such racial ideas, especially the mass psychology in Le Bon's *The Crowd, The Psychology of Peoples*, and *The World in Revolt*. Since his ideas appeared directly applicable to war at home and abroad, this French racial theorist received a good deal of attention. Impressed by the "profundity" of his thought, some officers felt the proliferation of psychological studies after World War I had discovered "few factors" or new ideas not already conceived by this genius, who would remain their authority into the 1930s.[40]

Officers regarded "his fundamental conceptions of the race mind, the crowd mind, and the national mind" as particularly significant to the army's intelligence division. Le Bon had shown, wrote one officer, that fixed, inherited racial characteristics were "highly important." National behavior, in peace and war, acknowledged another group of officers, was greatly determined by "inherited or ancestral characteristics of nations"; even national "feelings and instincts" such as "kindness" and "cruelty" were inherited. Le Bon also taught that the survival of higher civilization demanded the preservation of inherited racial distinctions and the purity of the dominant creative races.[41]

Le Bon's long-standing argument that miscegenation meant inevitable race decline found its contemporary American variant in Earnest Cox's paranoia about a mongrelized population of the United States. In *White America* (1923), this disciple of Madison Grant constructed a scenario of the historic degeneracy of earlier white civilizations as racial purity fallen prey to race "interminglings" and hybrids due to migrations. As a Southerner, Cox focused mostly on the "negro problem," but he also believed that "all members of the white race do not have equal value in establishing and perpetuating civilization." Since the millions of immigrants "from southern and southeastern Europe" constituted a serious problem, America must devise a plan for "the selection of a desirable type of European immigrant" and repatriation of these undesirables.

After reading *White America* as part of his course work, one officer remarked that it "shows by a study of history that mongrelization has been the basic cause of the decline and fall of past civilizations." It "also confirms that conclusion by an extended personal study of the effects of contact between the white man and the negro in all parts of the world." Since the G-2 faculty included this review within the annotated bibliography it compiled on the War College library holdings, it served as the basic introduction to Cox's work for future classes.[42]

Long after McDougall had ceased lecturing at the War College in the mid-1920s, officers also continued to learn from his *Group Mind* that evolution had created "Nations of the Higher Type." These had been scientifically identified as "the Northern races of Europe, more particularly the Nordic."[43] It was through Lothrop Stoddard that officers were exposed to the most elaborate articulation of this theory. The acclaim and criticism accompanying his *Rising Tide of Color* and *Revolt Against Civilization* established his credentials among War College officials. In late 1924, Stoddard published *Racial Realities in Europe*, "a pioneering sketch" of the scientifically discovered "vital importance of the racial factor in human affairs." A War College bibliography praised it as "a comprehensive discussion" of the effects on national character of the "migrations and interminglings of the Nordic, Alpine, and Mediterranean races."

Central Europe remained in turmoil, Stoddard wrote, because of the "violent and recent" mixing of races. Eastern Europe was far worse due to "powerful Asiatic elements," namely, "Huns, Mongols, Tartars, Turks, Jews, Gypsies." America had narrowly escaped this disastrous fate when it decided with the 1924 immigration legislation "to remain predominantly Nordic in race, ideals, and institutions."[44]

Racialist Views of Jews

It was perhaps mostly from Stoddard that officers learned how Jews fitted into this historical scenario and theories of racial characteristics. While the Northern European immigrant was, he wrote, "predisposed by his heredity" to understand American civilization, those of Southern and Eastern European stock were not. The "pull of heredity" made the American way of life "not only incomprehensible but positively distasteful" to the non-Nordic. They could become "American citizens but not Americans." Frustration at remaining alien would invariably lead to "aggression" against America and its traditions.

Of all aliens, the "Asiatic" Jew caused Stoddard the most concern. To the usual epithets of Jews as radicals, Bolsheviks, or disloyal internationalists, Stoddard added the concept of a hybrid race of "disharmonic combinations" and conflicting tendencies. In particular, the influx of a variety of Asiatic and other racial strains separated Russian and Polish Jews physically and in temperament from Western Jews. The "old Semitic Hebrew blood" of the biblical Hebrews was irretrievably lost in the East. While the mixture of various Alpine stocks produced some round-skulled Jews, Khazar blood endowed the average Eastern Jews with their "dwarfish stature, flat faces, high cheekbones, and other Mongoloid traits."[45]

Officers cited Stoddard most frequently on racial issues, European minorities, and colonization. They augmented Stoddard with authors affiliated with the American Geographical Society (AGS) of New York, through which Madison Grant spread his nativist gospel. In his introduction to Leon Dominian's *Frontiers of Language and Nationality in Europe* (1917), Grant assailed the assimilationist theory that environment could "transform or change one race into another." As he put it, "the oak tree and the poplar tree are both wood, but the one can be polished by rubbing, while the other cannot." Where two races compete within the same area, the race already best suited by nature for that specific environment "tends to increase at the expense of its rival." The alternative to the survival of the fittest was miscegenation.[46]

Doubts about the wisdom of assimilating racial aliens also surfaced in *New World Problems in Geography* (1924) by Isaiah Bowman, New York director of the AGS. Here, officers read that the new immigrant posed an undeniable threat to Anglo-Saxon American civilization. "Our democratic institutions and ideals meant little" to these newcomers; their loyalty belonged to the old country, to which they retained their ties by segregating themselves in the congested ethnic slums of the great cities. "Often wholly immune to American ideals," Southern and Eastern European immigrants transplanted age-old European political and ethnic strife to America. Besides divisiveness, these immigrants brought the perennial problem of radicalism, which endangered democracy itself.

Beyond these political concerns, Bowman worried that this wave of immigrants "affects not merely our political forms and social institutions, but also the quality of our people." Assimilating large masses of "peoples far more ignorant and restless in disposition" than those from Northwestern Europe portended profound changes, possibly the loss of those qualities that accounted for American greatness and uniqueness.[47]

For Bowman, the Jew occupied a "peculiar position" among the new immigrants. Religion, social customs, and "strong racial characteristics," combined with legal constraints and persecutions, ensured that "wherever he has gone, the Jew has formed a race apart." Induced by "local law or the instinct of the Jew," he has always congregated in urban ghettos and "maintained a certain aloofness" while pursuing his own narrow economic interests. "Indeed, a great deal" of anti-Semitism could be traced "to his exclusive devotion to trade and personal gain and his success therein." As "powerful merchant" and "banker" in Hungary, the Jew had "a strangle hold upon the peasant . . . [and] commercial system of the town"; for similar reasons, "Vilna is often called the Jerusalem of Lithuania." In Russia Jews' separateness, their "success in business, particularly money-lending," and their attempts at gaining special "privileges as a distinct race" had made them "an object of persecution"; they formed an "element of weakness rather than strength" for that country.[48]

In Poland and Romania, Bowman maintained, Jews became "so numerous and powerful" that these countries enacted strict laws denying "equality to the Jew." To Bowman, "the problem looked much as the Japanese problem appears to a Californian"—the fear was that without such measures, "all the land would be owned by the Jews." In all these countries, "the main difficulty . . . springs from the lack of national feeling among Jews," who always seek to secure special rights and privileges as a minority rather than identifying with the countries where they reside. "The disorders at Vilna and elsewhere"—Bowman's euphemism for the 1919 pogroms—were a "natural" reaction of the "patriotic Pole" to Jewish resistance to Polish nationalism. Bowman criticized postwar treaties guaranteeing "minority rights" in Central Europe as unwarranted interference with "national sovereignty." A solution to "the most serious racial problem in Poland" was possible only "if religious freedom is guaranteed and the Jew attempts to seek no special political rights." Unfortunately, the opposite was occurring as Jews now constituted "a powerful central European organization [that could] force the League of Nations to take account of future persecutions or restrictions."[49]

Officers read something similar in the work of Archibald and Ethel Colquhoun, prewar authors without nativist affiliations. The title of their

1914 book, *The Whirlpool of Europe*, itself conveyed the image of turmoil and permanent instability within the multinational Austro-Hungarian Empire. Their account was one of explosive ethnic conflict of all against all, in which the Jews could prosper.

Although the Colquhouns mentioned the "great poverty and distress" of the masses of Jews in regions like Galicia, they dwelt mostly upon the Jewish acquisition of wealth and power at the expense of the indigenous nationalities. Through "special qualities of brain and character" lacking in the other races, including the universally recognized "commercial talents of his race," Jews rose to positions of dominance over the press and political parties. In some regions, they slowly and insidiously enticed poor Slavs through liquor and usury into a trap of indebtedness "until the wretched peasant is a mere serf," whose land now fell into Jewish hands. Elsewhere, they monopolized capitalism, industry, and banking, controlling the stock exchange and "practically regulating the market." Under their influence, capitalism itself became a foreign and international enterprise without any accountability or loyalty to anything but the selfish interests of those wielding this financial power: "Indeed in the whole civilized world, the operations of the various stock exchanges, controlled by a narrowing ring (chiefly Jewish), are influenced far less than might be expected by national or political considerations."[50]

Such developments would be less troublesome, the Colquhouns contended, "were the Jews not so peculiar a people, [or] were it possible to assimilate them." But since they remained separate racially and in economic interest, there was bound to be a backlash from those "most injured by the Jewish predominance." Thus, Austrians sought to defend Christian culture, as well as workers, peasants, and small businessmen, from large capitalists ("almost invariably Jewish") through a type of Christian socialism. Greatly "alarmed" by this development, Jews "used their influence with the press" to denounce and eradicate socialism. When this failed, the Jews next tried to dissipate the outrage against them by introducing international socialism "as the only way of stemming a rising tide which threatens their interests." Not only could the international Jew "most easily subscribe" to this type of socialism, but it undermined the national focus of the original socialist movement. Throughout this vast European whirlpool, Jewish separatism and domination had already brought developments "over the threshold of one of those periodical waves of irresistible anti-Semitism."[51]

Apparently, the only alternative interpretations of Jews to which officers at the War College were exposed came from American progressives like Herbert Adams Gibbons and John Spargo, though neither had a great deal to say on the subject. In various works stretching back before the Great War, Gibbons lambasted nativist paranoia, insisting that American education and environment—those "irresistible influences of assimilation"—would turn generations of immigrants (including Germans, Jews, and Poles) into loyal and exemplary citizens.[52]

But even Gibbons had his reservations. To him, the only reasonable and acceptable path for immigrants was complete, unconditional assimilation in Europe or America. According to Gibbons, "there had never been strong anti-Semitic feelings in Poland" until Russian intrigue and the great influx of Russian and Lithuanian *Litvak* Jews. Polish anti-Semitism emerged as a reaction against the newcomers, not as an outburst against the loyal nationalist indigenous Polish Jews.[53] Gibbons had no toleration for Jewish insistence "upon their separate nationality" or reluctance to assimilate, whether in Poland or the United States. An ardent and vocal anti-Zionist, Gibbons argued that Zionism would surely reawaken anti-Semitism, possibly unleashing pogroms in Europe, and would most certainly reverse the progress made in Jewish emancipation and acceptance in Europe and America. Zionism was a last effort "to preserve the Ghetto for those whose religion cannot thrive outside the Ghetto." He demanded that "native-born and immigrant" alike adopt "one allegiance—to the Government of the United States."[54]

Spargo had no such reservations. In *The Jew and American Ideals* (1921), he forcefully attacked the "cruel and vicious" Jew-baiting in Europe and America, singling out Henry Ford's *Dearborn Independent* for particular criticism. Spargo rebutted charges of Jewish world conspiracies, the authenticity of the *Protocols*, and the Jewish-Bolshevik link. Not only was anti-Semitism inhumane, it was "alien and hostile to our Republic" and to American ideals. It belonged among those hateful cultural and political currents endangering "American civilization and democracy." Spargo regarded his book "not as a defense of the Jew . . . [but as] a plea for Christian civilization."

Spargo's influence is impossible to ascertain from existing evidence. It is perhaps suggestive that in contrast to Stoddard's works, *The Jew and American Ideals* was listed on only one surviving War College bibliography (1924). Although Spargo's earlier works on Bolshevism (which did not address the Jewish question) were occasionally cited, neither references to *The Jew and American Ideals* nor any resonance of its ideas are discernible in student or committee reports.[55]

MID's Racial Psychology Project

In addition to books and lectures by outsiders, the military generated its own important sources for student readings and research. MID files and monographs on various subjects were deposited at the War College as course resources. Intelligence data constituted a considerable part of a wide range of student committee work, extending from "Strategical Estimates of Italy" to "European Colonization," "Bolshevism," and the "Political Situation in the United States." Among these sources were attaché reports from Europe on race, Jews, and immigration that filled in the gaps left by lectures and publications.

In all likelihood, officers regarded these sources as more authoritative than the work of scholars. Military records projected an aura of official sanction; the designation of "secret" or "confidential" stamped on every page of many documents only enhanced the sense of significance and reliability. The writers of some documents had been friends or colleagues of the officers reading these reports; many of them would probably serve together in the future as well.[56]

The MID documents most relevant to race and Jews were contained in the psychological sections of attaché reports and monographs. Stimulated by the importance that propaganda had assumed for all belligerent countries in World War I, psychology became institutionalized in military intelligence. By 1917, the army added psychology to military, economic, and political indices as a basic factor in its "Strategic Equation," which was utilized in estimating an enemy's current or potential war-making capacity.

After the war, the national prestige of psychology surged enormously, and MID was swept up in the growing overconfidence in this new field. As a mass of new practitioners arose in areas extending from education to advertising, top intelligence officers seized upon the promising scientific techniques of psychology as a means of evaluation, manipulation, and control.[57]

Under Churchill's prodding and guidance, MID undertook a grandiose psychological project in 1920. For three years MID psychologically analyzed most peoples of the world, with particular focus on the Great Powers. Excited by the prospect of a key role for military intelligence in national decisionmaking circles, MID aimed at producing a manual on each country from which accurate predictions could be made of national behavior. Officers also hoped to manipulate national psychologies to achieve American foreign policy objectives. "Not only may the reactions to certain stimuli be predicated but the stimuli to be applied to produce certain desired reactions may be ascertained and the most efficacious methods of application determined."[58]

Remarkably, MID did not engage psychologists to conduct these studies. The substance of each psychological manual would be derived from information compiled and interpreted by American military attachés. MID headquarters and attachés alike agreed unanimously "that the attaché is in a very favorable position to make a psychologic study of his people."[59]

These attachés were also among the most articulate spokesmen for the racialist worldview. Moreover, the detailed manual written to guide attachés in their psychological work, though highly eclectic, relied heavily upon the racial psychology and anthropology of the day. Attachés were instructed to consult "authorities on the subject" and read widely about their host country's race, culture, and history. The manual contained 121 specific categories for examination, covering subjects from science, education, and ethics to religion, sensuality in art, sexual perversion, and nervous derangement.[60]

Some of the most telling aspects of the mentality of those who composed the project guide came in the annotations and detailed lists of sundry questions accompanying many of the 121 categories. Le Bon's long shadow was evident in the interest in psychological suggestion, psychosis, and hysteria, especially as these pertained to crowds. Under Category 41, "Brain," were these questions: "Do they go into trances? How do they behave in crowds—orderly or disorderly—dangerous or not? Are they easily led? Are they easily swayed by words? Do they make good subjects for hypnosis? Do they run amuch? Do they suddenly go insane?"

Much of the manual had an anthropological or sociological orientation, as in Category 36, "Expression": "Discuss their architecture? Do they indulge in extravagance in dress? . . . Do these people mutilate their persons by any such customs as Chinese foot binding, slashing of the face? . . . Do they indulge in orgies or other practices where hysteria is developed in a crowd?"[61]

In addition, officers were explicitly instructed to learn as much as possible about the "racial stock" of each country. Were the people racially homogeneous or heterogeneous? What was the "predominant race or tribe?" Race was to be specifically correlated with social class: "From what stock or mixture of stocks is each class descended?" And which stock engendered the "governing class?"[62]

It was in search of the "National Brain" of each country that political biology manifested itself most clearly. Attachés had to identify the characteristics and intelligence of the national brain as evidenced by the "predominant anatomical type of head," "brain weight," and environmental factors. Data were requested on the various head types and brain weights for fourteen different social classes within each country. "Physiological/mental" features of urban professionals had to be distinguished from those of rural professionals; those of peasants from yeoman farmers and landed gentry; and those of city laborers from the bourgeoisie and high bourgeoisie. Scientific exactitude dictated still more specificity. "What is the brain power, characteristics, and amount of actual intelligence exhibited by each of the above classes as regards each of the following subdivisions: (a) man (b) woman (c) children (d) youth (e) adults?"[63]

As clarified by Churchill, "the national brain is a composite; and its reactions are a composite of the reactions of all the brains" that constitute a country: "The racial classification gives an opportunity for discussing the anatomical brain itself, the shape of head, the average brain weight of the people of the race in the environment under consideration." Heterogeneous countries with "different brains racially" were more complex. Churchill cited "an exaggerated example . . . [of] a small group in the United States composed of an uneducated high class Jew merchant; a Jew lawyer and a shoestring peddler; an Irish American politician, an Irish literary man and a day laborer; a high class Anglo-Saxon business man and two farm hands of the same ancestry."[64]

Attachés were told that the national brain determined the "national intelligence" and anticipated reactions of a country. After calculating a country's national intelligence, officers were expected to compare it with the "native intelligence" of Americans and people of other nations. A summary of the "more prominent or peculiar racial or national traits" was to include how these affect "the attitude of the subject towards other nations, races, and 'isms' such as Bolshevism, Anarchism, etc." Such analyses should make it easier to predict responses to significant developments nationally and internationally so that the United States would be prepared to establish its policies accordingly.[65]

Major Gilbert Marshall of MID's Psychologic Section tried to extend this project to America, urging a similar "psychologic monograph be written for each Corps Area" of the United States. Applying psychological analysis to the home front was necessitated by the likely use of the army in "domestic difficulties" and "serious troubles" caused by class and racial antagonisms. A commander must know "the inhabitants are either for you or against you"; at home, too, "potential allies" must be distinguished from "potential enemies," and the behavior of both anticipated correctly. Marshall argued that the fundamental Anglo-Saxon psychology of the country was no longer universal among the population; within America's geographic vastness, diverse environmental influences had "caused marked differences in psychology," a problem aggravated by the influx of "certain racial stocks" resistant to Americanization. Churchill, however, categorically rejected Marshall's proposal.[66]

For several years, MID made an intensive effort to produce "a monograph on the psychology of each nation and issue." Attachés dispatched report after report on countless subjects—"Polish stock," the intelligence and influence of French women, instinctual German hypocrisy and treachery, among others—as these supposedly illustrated brain power, emotions, reactions, and other psychological aspects of populations.[67]

One of the most Darwinian reports originated with Major Charles Burnett, military attaché in Tokyo. Relying upon studies of hundreds of brain weights conducted by Japanese and foreign doctors since the nineteenth century, Burnett furnished specific anatomical data on Japanese heads and brains. Among the largest brains weighed, approximately a 300 gram difference consistently separated males (1585–1790 grams) from females (1260–1432 grams). He also found considerable class disparity among brains and resultant intelligence. "The lower classes . . . show more definitely their connection with the Mongolian race," he wrote. In contrast, "the aristocracy of Japan presents a much more developed type," racially, anatomically, and intellectually; "their cranial measurements are larger . . . and the brain weights appreciably more." Naturally endowed with "keener and finer intelligence" than Japanese laborers descended from racially inferior Chinese, aristocrats had purer Malay blood running through their veins. Ethnographically they should be classified closer to the higher "'brown' races than the 'yellow.'"

In Burnett's estimate, however, even Japanese aristocrats failed to measure up to Americans, since the "development of [Japanese] brain capacity apparently terminates sooner" (two to four years earlier) "than that of the Nordic race." Retaining their youthfulness longer, Japanese were also "more responsive to stimuli" than the "fully developed races of Northern Europe."[68]

Such reports usually reflected American ethnocentricity and the prevailing racially anthropology of the era, as well as the fondness or contempt individual attachés felt toward their host countries. Lingering hostility toward the enemy, enhanced by susceptibility to the barbaric image of the Hun and Boche generated by wartime propaganda, almost guaranteed crude racial caricatures of the Germans. Central European races, while individually possessing certain laudable qualities, when taken together offered a rather hopeless picture of a mishmash of clashing heterogeneous races with doubtful prospects for political stability or progress. The Francophile attaché in Paris, on the other hand, was infatuated with French culture and character.[69]

The one constant among the diverse attitudes of attachés in Europe involved the Jews. With the exception of a few positive or neutral references from places like Italy and the Balkans, Jews were, as a matter of course, portrayed negatively. The vocabulary of the anti-Semite's lexicon—racial inferiors, economic parasites, Bolsheviks, inassimilable and disloyal aliens—was invoked far more often than not. What attachés had written for years about Jews in their other dispatches was repeated, sometimes with elaboration sometimes verbatim, in their psychological observations.[70]

Although monographs were written on several countries, the plan to create a usable manual for each nation and movement never reached completion. By 1922, major reductions in the military's size and funding ended the project. Most completed monographs, including one on Jews, were at some future point either lost or destroyed. Nevertheless, much of this psychological information had already been integrated into the standard monographs MID composed and routinely updated on the major countries of the world. And for years thereafter, attachés continued to provide intelligence under the rubric of psychology.[71]

Responses of War College Officers

In various forms—some specific, others more general—the gist of this effort at racial psychology filtered down to officers at the War College. Evidence that the racial worldview took hold in the minds of officer-students can be found in the work produced by committees and individual officers. Into the 1930s, for example, committees referred to cephalic index when distinguishing Alpine Southern Germans—"broader-headed, darker types"—from "North Germans who are more nearly akin to the Anglo-Saxons." Italians, as "a Latin race with an extremely temperamental mind" were found to be deficient in logic and discipline. Historically and currently under Mussolini, they could be "roused to an extraordinary degree" by charismatic, popular leaders, only to lapse into indifference when faced with adversity or reversals. History and psychology had determined that Italians were simply "not a military race."[72]

Russia, by comparison, was potentially a "great menace to the future of European peace." The founding of the Soviet Union had induced the convergence of race, traditional Russian geopolitics, and the "fanatical desire" to expand communism around the world. "Racial instincts" ensured that Bolshevik foreign policy would ultimately aim at recapturing the Russian Empire. Moreover, psychological estimates of Russia written by committees and individual officers disclosed the price of racial hybridization. Already ranking below other European races on nature's hierarchical scale, Russian Slavs suffered from a significant infusion of "Asiatic blood," widening the gap separating Russians from European civilization. "Fundamentally more Asiatic than European," Russians were depicted as a "fitfully ferocious mass," who, though "in bodily force and size" stood above the average European, remained "inferior mentally and morally." Capable of enduring great physical hardship, punishment, and the suffering that accompany the horrors of war, this massive population was depicted as having low average intelligence. Docile, yet impressionable and temperamental, the Russian "lacks energy, initiative and self-control—the capacity to get things done."[73]

One committee compared the impact of "national psychology" on the potential military effectiveness of various countries in "a war of great magnitude." Racially and linguistically homogeneous countries with a "strong sense of national spirit" were rated "excellent" (England, France, United States) or "very good" (Japan, Germany) in their psychological capability for war. States comprising mixed races or containing large racial minorities were designated "fair" (Poland) to "poor" (Russia, Turkey).[74]

To various committees throughout the 1920s, the tumultuous postwar history of the former Habsburg Empire offered incontrovertible proof of the debilitating effects of racial, ethnic, or linguistic diversity. The prime example, Poland, had failed "to assimilate races not purely Polish." Its "lack of homogeneity . . . in race, religion, and customs" caused "extreme unrest."

Not surprisingly, such racial analysis singled out Jews. Of all the "disturbing internal factors" disrupting Poland, "the most serious menace seems to be . . . the Jewish question." And officers again emphasized that "the principal advocates of Bolshevism are Jews."[75]

Nor were the struggling new states of Austria and Hungary immune from this "perplexing question." No matter how various Jews (including those already assimilated) perceived their own identity or nationality, many officers tended to view all Jews as a separate, unified group. By nature distinct from others, they supposedly acted in concert in pursuit of their own group interests that conflicted with those of the majority of the country. Assaulting the system from above as capitalists and from below as Socialists, Jews sought political and economic domination.

Several committees argued that through their peculiar "mental characteristics" and high level of education, Hungarian Jews exercised "great influence" over the country and controlled "many large commercial enterprises." In Austria, "the Jewish element is quite large and controls banking, the press, the learned professions, higher education, and many of the leading industries to an extent which gives them a power in the state vastly out of proportion to their numerical strength." Since the new Austrian government had been "very liberal towards the Jews, . . . their influence is increasing" even further. Despite such influence and power, the Austrian Jew was viewed as completely devoid of national or political loyalty, as basically a fickle "opportunist, willing to side with the winning party if it furthers his large business interests."[76]

Devious Austrian Jews allegedly even denied or disguised their Jewish identity in pursuit of opportunistic political objectives. When, after World War I, Jews detected "the drift of Austrian public opinion toward Pan-Germanism and political union with Germany," they jumped on the bandwagon, exerting their "great influence" through the "press and educational institutions under their control" to promote the Pan-German cause. Jewish insincerity seemed quite obvious to officers on these committees as well as to those on the scene in Austria who furnished some of these data. They were both sure that in supporting German unity, the Jews concealed their own interests and real objectives "by posing as Germans rather than as Jews."[77]

These officers attributed anti-Semitism to "the prominence of the Jewish minority in business and politics" and simultaneously to the identification of Jews with socialism and communism. Austrian anti-Semitic parties were reactive attempts to protect Christians against "Jewish religious influence" and the small gentile businessman from "the great Jewish businessmen." In Hungary, the "claim that the Jews are profiteers" led to demands for the "confiscation of all Jewish fortunes to pay for the cost of the war." Supposed Jewish pervasiveness on the left was equally worrisome. In Austria, "the Socialist parties [were] controlled to a great extent by Jews," whereas in Hungary "all of the Commissars under the Bolshevik regime were Jews," causing confusion in the "popular mind between the Jewish race and the Communist Party."[78]

In the early 1920s, officers harbored similar ideas about Bolshevism. The general notion seemed to be that Lenin, "father of Bolshevism and its guid-

ing spirit," was the only "real Russian" and "idealist" within the entire Soviet hierarchy. If the truth be known, "most of the Bolshevik leaders are Jews
and they hold most of the important State and local offices." These "self-
chosen" leaders were not even members of the Slavic race they pretended to
represent. Internationally oriented, they were alien in language and culture
from real Russians, with whom they had only the most cursory contact.
These Jews "have a German dialect as their mother tongue" and had spent
most of their lives in exile "nursing their grievances against the old governing classes." Russians were ruled by "a tyrannical few who are not of them
except in name."[79] Bolshevik propaganda and idealistic rhetoric aside, these
Communist leaders were essentially "opportunists of the most extreme
type." Their only real doctrine, which changed as expediency dictated, "is to
get the Communist party in power and keep it there by any means." Thereafter, their intent was to foment worldwide revolution.

For this reason, officers in the class of 1920–1921 felt the need for the
"most stringent immigration laws . . . to keep the 'Reds' out of the United
States." Among all potentially subversive groups, the officers singled out
by name only "Russian Jews . . . [as] an especially dangerous class of
immigrants."[80]

Student officers throughout the 1920s looked with dread upon America's major urban industrial centers, "where these foreigners . . . congregated." In Cleveland, Chicago, Detroit, and New York, these foreigners
"live segregated in groups, speaking their native language, following their
ancient customs, eating their native food." Assimilation was unlikely, since
they "make little contact with the forces of Americanization"; in fact, they
preferred to perpetuate the old country in the new.[81]

The Jewish religion, in particular, "is an influence tending to retard
amalgamation of the race with the native stock." A committee of officers
described Judaism as the only "truly racial church" in America; its adherents consider themselves the "chosen of God," "whose race will one day be
gathered in a great nation." Rather than reaching out to the rest of society,
religious Jews believed, in principle, "that all Gentiles are but fit subjects
of exploitation." Over several generations, however, other Jews shifted
from religion to "indifference or free-thinking." Since only a few adopted
Christianity, the overwhelming majority of these apostates were left without any of the moral grounding or restraints of religion. And freethinking
was synonymous with radical social views, and was perhaps the first step
to socialism or communism.[82]

The very idea of assimilation might be problematic, officers warned. "By
tradition, training, and heredity" Southern and Eastern Europeans were of

"different stock" from the "Northwest European wave." Their rapid rate of immigration and "larger fecundity" posed a danger to the original American stock and their unique Anglo-Saxon society and cherished system of government. Before the gates were closed in 1924, many officers wondered whether Americanization through "education and environment" could sufficiently alter inherent differences. Could the country assimilate

> the Slavic, Jewish and other lesser elements in such a manner that the inherent value of Anglo-Saxonism be not lost or submerged?[83]

The likelihood of eventual Americanization aside, these immigrant communities remained, at present, the "hotbed of revolution." While conceding that some leaders and members of radical organizations were Anglo-Saxons, officers argued that "it seems to be established . . . that immigrants from Eastern and Southeastern Europe are the more active participants in, if not actually the fomenters of, overt revolutionary acts." Even some of their schools, churches, and other cultural institutions established "for the ostensible purpose of teaching English and religion" were fronts "in reality for teaching revolutionary doctrine."

At the height of the Red Scare, one committee studying internal unrest concluded that America was on the verge of a full-scale civil war along class lines, with the immigrants leading the way. Although another committee discounted an imminent revolution, it, too, identified the "unassimilated foreign population" as a major source of unrest.[84]

In the view of officer analysts, a prolonged war would aggravate an already precarious situation, since the draft of native-born men would leave the home front increasingly vulnerable to attack or subversion from the foreign enemy within. Well into the 1920s, officers warned that "undoubtedly the most dangerous element" were "the so-called Russian and Austro-Hungarian immigrants [who were] chiefly Yiddish and Polish." Wherever they mass in large numbers, "there is industrial and social unrest and danger." Any sector of the country where this situation exists "must be regarded as potentially as dangerous as if it were exposed to foreign attack." Given the likelihood of internal subversion, sabotage, or seizure of arms by these immigrants, national security dictated that "large storehouses, arsenals, and munitions plants should be kept out of such sections, or at least, carefully protected."[85]

Although officers complained of the injustice of drafting native-born men while aliens escaped the hardships and sufferings of war, they were uncertain about the wisdom of conscripting large numbers of immigrants. Radicalism aside, these immigrants were inherently inferior—mentally, physically, and socially—to Anglo-Saxon Americans; they were genuinely poor material from which to build soldiers. "The experience of the draft shows a considerable factor of physical efficiency in favor of the native born, increased by the fact that the rural population is better physically than the urban and that 72% of the foreign born is urban." Moreover, military planners also had to take into account that "there is twice the insanity among foreign born than native whites, over 50% more blindness, four times the pauperism, double the number of criminals in confinement and double the illiteracy." In these circumstances, to draft or not to draft was a real dilemma. These same ethnic epithets, long the coinage of racial theorists and nativist crusaders, also enhanced the general ambivalence about the desirability of assimilation and Americanization.[86]

Such were the ideas, values, and attitudes on race and ethnicity inculcated upon officers at the War College. Certainly not all were influenced equally. For a variety of reasons, including background and personality, some officers may have been impervious to such thinking. Others probably shared Eisenhower's middle-of-the-road stance; while not disagreeing with the ideas as presented, he shied away from anything implying extremism or controversy, often relegating these questions and attitudes to the political arena, beyond the purview of military professionals.[87] Yet, exceptions aside, the pervasiveness of this racial worldview would be difficult to deny. There is no evidence available suggesting any attempt by officers or instructors into the 1930s to challenge, modify, or counterbalance the dominant viewpoints expressed in lectures and readings that advanced racial ideologies, often to the detriment of Jews.

It would be this generation of War College–trained officers who would eventually have to respond to the problems and challenges posed by the Third Reich. Then, the "Jewish Question" would take on far greater significance than it had after World War I. Officers in Washington and various theaters of war would make crucial decisions regarding Jewish immigration and refugees, ultimately confronting the problems of relief and rescue during the Holocaust. Of course, at the time the War College cultivated these future military leaders, no one could have foreseen these events. And beginning in the mid-1920s, the army entered a deceptively quiet phase of greatly reduced political engagement.

CHAPTER 6

Quiet Continuities, 1925–1936

I N 1925, COLONEL WILLIAM GODSON, one of the most ardent promoters of Jewish conspiracy theories, returned to the field as military
attaché to the Balkans. He had learned little from his earlier blunders on
the *Protocols* and thus assured Washington that if allowed, MID could still
"clearly demonstrate . . . that Communism is a despotism of a small national Jewish minority."[1] But Godson would be frustrated in his efforts to
acquire official sanction and resources to pursue this cause—for this old
hand now faced the realities of enormous postwar retrenchment. By mid-
decade, the paucity of resources that typified the lean 1920s and a changing national mood had undercut the army's anti-Communist crusade.

Godson's pleas had little impact on an institution that had shrunk to a
mere skeleton of its wartime greatness. Paring the army down to 137,000
soldiers required the discharge of over 1,000 career officers, and MID suffered severe cuts. Scared by adverse publicity, the War Department had
also prohibited the army from continuing domestic surveillance. Further,
passage of the Immigration Act of 1924 proved to be a watershed for the
military as well as the country in general.[2] The nativist frenzy propelling
the army's antiradical, anti-alien, and anti-Semitic activities through the
postwar era quickly dissipated.

But adjustments to legal and budgetary constraints should not be confused with attitudinal changes. There were few, if any, major shifts in army
thinking in the interim between the volatile years after the first world war
and the events leading up to the next. And by the early 1930s, the instability of the Great Depression, together with deep suspicions about the

Roosevelt administration, would once again heighten concerns of many officers. With this turn of events came the renewal of official domestic surveillance by the army as well as its collaboration with the investigations of thousands of American citizens via a vast and secret private network.

Retrenchment Without Change

Even during the period of low-level army activity characteristic of the late 1920s, however, interest in Jews at home and abroad had not disappeared. Arguing that "the dangerous radical activities" in the United States were "assisted and directed from Moscow," MID chief Colonel William K. Naylor, warned the chief of staff: "[T]here is some evidence that the financial interests affiliated with the German-Jewish bankers who financed Lenin and Trotzky in 1917 are going to exert pressure on the Administration for Russian recognition."[3]

Even the *Protocols* would not stay dead and buried. Despite public exposure of the forgery, certain high-ranking officers acted as if this issue had not been already resolved for all time. In 1926, Colonel William Graham inquired about the "M.I. conclusion on the authenticity of 'The Protocols.'" His old colleague, Walter O. Boswell, then G-2 executive officer, responded: "[O]ur records fail to disclose any definite information as to [their] authenticity . . . or any G-2 conclusion pertaining thereto." However, the officer who searched Protocol File 99-75 for the answer had reported that "page 13 of this file appears to give the best argument as to the authenticity of the 'Protocols.'" That page was the letter to Churchill in which Harris Houghton attested that the "Protocols" were "quite important," as they constituted "a basic document of some sort," and that "current events furnished the proof" of their authenticity.[4]

Similarly, army surveys on race still reached the desk of Secretary of War Patrick J. Hurley as late as 1932. A study called "The Caucasian in Hawaii" read like the Nordic epic of an intellectually superior and courageous white race with an instinctive pioneering spirit spreading progress and civilization. Even though a numerical minority in Hawaii, there, "as elsewhere, the adventuresome originality, clear foresight and determination to achieve regardless of obstacles have again brought the Caucasian to the fore." Developing this isolated territory "into a progressive outpost of the United States," Caucasians again demonstrated "the Occidental capacity to pioneer throughout the far-flung places of the world." But considering "the difference in cultural and temperament," as well as "race and physiology," it remained an open question whether the "white man can superimpose upon the Oriental, through education and environment, the essentials of American ideals and institutions."[5]

The army also stretched a loophole permitting collection of press information on radicalism to include material from other departments and "voluntary informants." With and without the acquiescence of corps commanders, individual officers—often working with reserve officers or various patriotic organizations—circumvented regulations or snubbed them outright.[6] Early in 1927, Colonel Raymond Sheldon met secretly in Detroit with William J. Cameron, the Ford Company executive who had actually written most of Ford's *The International Jew*. They discussed at length Communist, radical, and labor union activity.[7]

Military intelligence hid part of its activities within the Chemical Warfare Service, whose head, General Amos A. Fries, proved to be a lifelong zealot highly susceptible to the most paranoid conspiracy theories. An 1898 West Point engineering graduate, Fries championed chemical weapons as the most humane way to conduct war. To him, pacifists or anyone opposing chemical warfare, militarism, or armaments engaged in "treason," since behind such people lurked the subversive hand of communism. From the early 1920s, Fries fancied himself a specialist on communism, laying the foundation for a post-army career as an anti-Communist publicist and witch-hunter into the 1950s.[8]

Even though a second explicit directive in 1923 again forbade such work, Fries continued for years thereafter to collect and disseminate information as he saw fit. He exchanged confidential and often illegally obtained information on private citizens and politicians with active and retired officers across the country involved in "patriotic" freelance intelligence or political activities. He maintained a close liaison with organizations like the American Defense Society that were also privy to his intelligence.

Although not as preoccupied with Jews as some of his colleagues, Fries found the Jewish-communism link "of sufficient importance." Polish officers, Fries told MID's chief in 1926, believed "extremely clever and absolutely unscrupulous" Jewish leaders, most disguised behind Russian names, really controlled the Soviet Union: "[O]f the Russian Congress some 70% were Jews and the remaining 30% were largely figure-heads ... real power ... was entirely in the hands of the Jews who were in it ... for what they could get out of it, and very few members ... really believe in the doctrines which they preach."[9]

MID immediately consulted Captain Trevor W. Swett, a recent military attaché to Poland. While avoiding Fries's cynicism and apparent exaggeration, Swett affirmed his central point. Only half the "total party membership may be considered reasonably sincere and loyal Communists"; and among these, real control rests in the hands of "a very small group of professional politicians and their supporters." Swett concurred that "the relative strength in the Congress of Jews and others noted, 70% and 30%, is about correct." But "there are fewer Jews now than two years ago" because of the "marked anti-Semitism arising in Russia."[10]

By the late 1920s, domestic intelligence activities had tapered off considerably. During this brief hiatus, references to Jews, so ubiquitous for almost a decade, were remarkably absent from domestic intelligence reports. But deeply embedded images of Jews had not disappeared from the minds of certain officers who shifted their focus to moral and cultural subversion.

As they saw it, insidious forces were gnawing away at American civilization and national defense from within. Officers across the country collaborated in getting the "facts" out to civilian society, with the expectation that patriotic groups would deal with these problems, "at the same time keeping the army in the background." Officers foresaw a growing cultural decadence in which atheism acquired public recognition while the Bible and "religious instruction in schools and colleges" were prohibited. Teachers and college professors undermined patriotism by teaching disrespect for parents, the flag, and government. Simultaneously, the "destruction of the home"—the foundation of society—was to be realized through "change in marriage and divorce laws; promotion of free love; promotion of immoral literature, plays and motion pictures."[11]

In public lectures throughout the East, the army's inspector general, Eli A. Helmick, dwelled on the problems of "home, religion, country, God," always linking these to the establishment and preservation of freedom, progress, and civilization. Among his favorite themes was the centrality of "good Christian doctrine," wherein he presented the history of the Jews as the "reverse side of the picture." Although originally God's chosen, they eventually degenerated into disloyalty, disobedience, "weakness and corruption." "Loyalty and obedience" were not only the cornerstones of the army and society, he said, but sound "Christian principles."[12]

The revival of labor and other political activity with the onset of the Great Depression quickly aroused latent army fears and suspicions. As one officer noted, "The situation was made-to-order for rabble-rousers and Communist agitators who made the most of the distress that was on every hand." Although Communists in the United States and elsewhere had intensified their activities, the army exaggerated the threat and overreacted to actual political activity.[13] With renewed domestic surveillance in the early 1930s, the specific linking of Jews to various problems resurfaced immediately.

In mid-1931, the new chief of staff, Douglas MacArthur, allowed MID to reactivate its subversive hunting. Working with police departments and reserve officers, G-2—as MID was more commonly called in this period—had little difficulty uncovering a plethora of subversive activities.[14] The discovery of damaged airplane engines at Langley Field, Virginia, made it "reasonable to assume" Communist infiltration of the air corps for the purpose of sabotage. One of the most enthusiastic officers, Colonel J. C. Pegram in Baltimore, alerted the entire corps area about the distribution of "subversive literature" to soldiers by New Yorkers of "Semitic extraction." Reporting a week later on a "subversive demonstration," he pointed out that the headquarters of the group had been raided earlier by the police "when Jewish women and Negro men were found dancing together." Pegram felt "satisfied" that "the lone policeman present when the trouble started did well as one radical has a fractured skull and one or two had teeth knocked out."[15]

The chief of military intelligence in New York City, Colonel Kenyon A. Joyce, started a "systematic inquiry into the Communist Party," which he extended to very broadly defined "sympathetic groups." A veteran of the Philippine campaign, former military attaché to England, and 1930 War College graduate, Joyce was assigned to the city that more than any other symbolized the worst nightmare of American nativists. In unpublished memoirs written at the height of the Cold War, Joyce described his work as a necessary vigilant struggle against "subversive" Russian communism. His "true stories" contained no references to Jews, foreigners, or aliens; at most, he briefly mentioned an amorphous class of "agitators" and "rabble-rousers." Joyce also later socialized with Bernard Baruch, praising his character and accomplishments as he did few others. However, the "Subversive Situation" reports Joyce sent to the adjutant general in Washington showed another side of the officer and his work.[16]

"The Metropolitan Area of New York City," these stated, "is the natural centre and fountain-head of all radical and subversive activities in the United States," because "the large foreign born labor element . . . furnishes a natural and fruitful field for the impregnation with radical doctrine." As his office informed Washington, the Communist Party "consists mostly of foreigners, Jews predominating"; in fact, the ratio was "probably not less than 70% Jewish, and less than 10% American born christians." When discussing particular leaders, Joyce made sure he was referring to "a Jew." And what did Joyce think of these Jewish immigrants? They were, in his words, "the dregs from Russia," who poured into the country before immigration restrictions had shut off the valve. Augmented annually by a stream of illegals, they constituted "a veritable cesspool of indigestible foreign elements."[17]

It was in this atmosphere that events during the winter of 1931–1932 culminated in a military-civilian confrontation. A hunger march on Washington and deadly shoot-out between police and radicals in Detroit was followed by the famous Bonus March on the capital. Beginning in May 1932, veterans from around the country began arriving in Washington, demanding immediate payment of deferred bonuses to help them survive the Great Depression. On May 24, the G-2 chief, General Alfred T. Smith, and MacArthur met to consider defending the capital by activating Emergency Plan White, designed years earlier for suppressing domestic unrest. Charged with preparation and implementation of this plan was MacArthur's old friend, his "most trusted subordinate," deputy chief of staff General George Van Horn Moseley (West Point 1899; War College 1911). A fanatical, conspiratorial-minded anti-Communist, in coming years Moseley would reveal himself as a notorious political and racial anti-Semite. To Moseley, communism and Jews were basically synonymous.[18]

On the very day of the MacArthur-Smith discussion, Moseley privately described to Herbert Corey his own chilling estimate of "present trends and conditions in our country" and what "governmental measures should be considered." Moseley made no reference to Jews, but his future statements leave little doubt whom he had in mind. Beginning with a long discourse on eugenics and politics, Moseley warned of the permanency "of those things which affect the blood and breeding of the nation . . . [and] determine our national destiny." Although these "inferior components" might be killed off in war, "they cannot be bred out" in peacetime. This was "a well known fact, established by the historical record," a lesson of the past that Americans ignored at their peril:

> We pay great attention to the breeding of our hogs, our dogs, our horses, and our cattle, but we are just beginning to realize the . . . effects of absorbing objectionable blood in our breed of human beings. The pages of history give us the tragic stories of many one-time leading nations which . . . imported man-

power of an inferior kind and then ... intermarried with this inferior stock ... [T]hose nations have either passed out of separate existence entirely, or have remained as decadent entities without influence in world affairs.[19]

He continued, "Intensive investigations of the past months" have disclosed "we are harboring a very large group of drifters, dope fiends, unfortunates and degenerates of all kinds." Always a national "embarrassment," they had in the crisis of the depression become a "distinct menace" to the body politic:

> For years we have been breeding and accumulating a mass of inferior people, still in the minority it is true, but tools ready at hand for those seeking to strike at the very vitals of our institutions. Liberty is a sacred thing, but ... it ceases to be liberty when under its banner minorities force their will on the majority. An active minority, well financed for good or evil in America, can accomplish more today than any inactive and ill-informed majority."[20]

Moseley recounted his experience in the Philippines, where he believed the army had successfully employed dictatorial measures to bring order and civilization to "our little brown brothers." To eliminate insurrection, "undesirables" were rounded up and deported to distant islands. This historical example held "the germ of a simple plan that in case of need could be applied to cure the ills now threatening to destroy ... the United States." Although Moseley quickly added "certainly we do not want any dictators," he essentially proposed a pseudo-constitutional presidential dictatorship of emergency decrees. This would be accomplished with the assistance of "carefully selected military governors installed in all our States," and this regime would have to cover the entire country "for quite a considerable period." Then "the good people of this nation would immediately rise" and take back their government from the corrupt, inferior, and disloyal elements.[21]

Moseley, MacArthur, and others were convinced that Communists had infiltrated the Bonus movement and had seized control of its leadership to incite insurrection. Top army commanders stirred up among themselves a type of political hysteria reminiscent of the 1919 Red Scare. Disregarding initial reports from various quarters of quite limited and peripheral Communist involvement, the army sought confirmation of its own suspicions through its military apparatus across the country. Again, the responses were mixed, as some found no evidence of Communist subversion. Others, like Colonel Joyce in New York, shared Moseley's certainty of "a sinister, organized . . . communist conspiracy." As part of a larger surveillance project, Joyce "had dossiers and photographs of every communist of importance in [the] New York" vicinity. "I can say," he wrote later, "that every group from that area was communist led."[22]

Moseley tried to persuade MacArthur to clear the capital with force. Transferring soldiers, support vehicles, and reserves to Washington for this purpose, Moseley finally got his wish in late July, when the army used tear-gas bombs, cavalry charges, sabers, and bayonets to drive the Bonus Marchers violently out of the city. Two officers involved in the attacks on the veterans were Dwight D. Eisenhower and George S. Patton. When this event turned suddenly into a political fiasco in which soldiers appeared to have attacked innocent protesters, the Hoover administration and army claimed they were only responding to Red-inspired revolt. Subsequent investigations by various local and federal agencies, including the FBI and the army's own military intelligence, could provide no evidence of Communist inspiration or leadership of the Bonus March.[23]

Unlike 1919, no efforts were made at the top levels of the army or its intelligence service to discover a Jewish conspiracy behind the Communist one. But residues of earlier identifications were still manifested in reports from Pennsylvania to Texas. "He looked like a Russian Jew" and "talked of drastic action," including killing the president if necessary, wrote army interrogators of one suspected Communist marcher. Meanwhile, charges of bogus discharge papers for veterans led the army to believe that a systematic Communist plot was operating in every major city. Such suspicions warranted, urged one colonel, an investigation of "the pawn shops in the Hebrew and Negro sections of Philadelphia."

Simultaneously, unverified reports spread about Metro Goldwyn Mayer furnishing truck transportation and expenses for Bonus Marchers from Los Angeles. This information immediately jarred the memory of Colonel James Totten, adjutant general at Fort Sam Houston, Texas. "Metro-Goldwyn-Mayer Picture Corporation," he notified his commanding general,

is known to be 100 per cent Jewish as to controlling personnel, and that high officers of this company are in politics. An unconfirmed rumor circulated many months ago, stated that agents of U.S.S.R. had contacted motion picture companies in California, and contributed to some of them with a view to insuring propaganda and support of U.S.S.R. policies.[24]

Military Attachés Persevere

During the years of retrenchment of the late 1920s, the flood of information on Jews flowing from military attachés in Europe had slowed to a trickle. The restrictionist legislation of 1924 had calmed attaché anxieties of hordes of Jews overrunning America. Attachés and other officers could now joke about the performance in Palestine during World War I of two Jewish battalions from Britain. "They were known in the Near East," Major Sherman Miles wrote facetiously, "as the 'Jordan Highlanders,' and their regimental motto was 'Never Advance Without Security.'"[25]

But America's racial sentinels abroad had not changed their basic anti-Semitic characterizations or political interpretations of Jews. Despite relief that America had been saved, attachés continued to emphasize the seriousness of the Jewish problem in Europe. In doing so, they helped perpetuate the anti-Semitic worldview of the officer corps. Equally important, they provided a continuity between the alarmist intelligence on Jews that attachés had provided Washington after World War I and the antagonistic stand that attachés would take when America again confronted the immigration issue as hundreds of thousands of Jewish refugees tried to flee Nazi Germany.

Before taking up his duties as attaché in Constantinople, Colonel Robert C. Foy toured Palestine in December 1925. He returned with deep admiration for British rule and apprehension regarding "the rising tide of Zionism" and this outside intrusion into the Arab homeland. The British now recognize their "mistake" in permitting "a Zionist home in Palestine," Foy observed, but "they do not dare to reverse their attitude." The situation had somewhat improved with the appointment of Lord Plummer as high commissioner for this region. "There is a general understanding that the Jewish element no longer receives preferential treatment, as it supposedly did under the previous High Commissioner, who was himself a Jew." After America shut off immigration in 1924, the systematic transfer of thousands of emigrants each month out of Eastern Europe had been redirected toward Palestine. Although the settlements built with money from American and British Jews were "very respectable looking," Foy commented that "the majority of the immigrants are Jews from Poland, Roumania and Russia, the most repulsive form of humanity."[26]

The military attaché in Vienna, Major Harry N. Cootes, concurred with Foy's opinion of Eastern European Jews and the discord inevitably stirred up wherever they migrated. "There are some good types of Jews here," he wrote, "but on the other hand there is the Polish and Galician Jew who came here during and after the war, who are responsible for most of the trouble." This "type of Jew" was "entirely different from the American Jew." The Eastern Jews "are rapacious, grasping, unscrupulous . . . [and rely upon] sly and cunning methods." After having been "run out of Hungary and Czechoslovakia [they have] found a heaven here." They "control the Banks, the Press, most of the large industries, the political parties and in fact about own Austria."

A "reliable Austrian" told Cootes that through war profiteering and speculation, the Jews had expanded their real-estate holdings in Vienna from 14 percent "in prewar time" to 82 percent. "Only Jews and war profiteers are seen in the night life places, no people of any social prominence attend." While Austrians suffer, "the Jews fill the best cafes, night life places, race tracks, automobile meetings, and own the best property." The instincts and "non-European temperaments" of these Jews make them oblivious to "how much Jewish influence a non-Jewish public will tolerate." By their very nature, these Jews "seemed destined to arouse the passions of those with whom they come into contact." In Vienna, as well as the provinces, they "are openly hooted at and called 'Schiebers' (nick name for Jewish war profiteers)." Given the rising tide of Austrian anger against them, "there is no doubt that some day a serious 'Pogrom' will occur."[27]

Cootes's successor, Major Henry Eglin, had as attaché to Hungary already established himself as one of the most articulate anti-Semitic ideologues in the officer corps. During 1925, his last year in Budapest, Eglin summed up the ethnic situation in Hungary by contrasting the "considerable German element" in the capital, villages, and countryside with the Jews. The former "have always been considered good citizens"; nowhere did these Germans form "a solid mass"; they were "rather dispersed and mingled with Hungarians." But Jews congregated in urban centers, where "general absorption," though evident, was occurring "rather slowly."

To Eglin, "the general anti-Semitic trend" in Hungary was a natural reaction against an array of Jewish activities that were in one way or another hurting or threatening the country. Hungarians saw "the active participation of the Jewish element in the Bolshevik revolution of 1919" and "immigration during the war of rather low-grade individuals from Galicia, living and getting ahead by profiteering." Yet anti-Semitism had not arrested Jewish progress or success, as they continued to usurp most wealth and power. In cities, Hungarians watched "the increasing occupation of the leading posts in commerce and industry by Jews," while in the countryside, they witnessed Jewish purchase "of an ever-increasing amount of agricultural land."[28]

The attaché in Warsaw, Colonel Richard I. McKenney, considered "the conflict between Poles and the Jews . . . the most intricate interior problem of Poland." But he insisted that anti-Semitism was "a new factor in Polish social life." The widespread conception of a "long continued oppression of Jews in Poland" was erroneous, since it did not exist before 1870. He learned from "an excellent authority" that "there is practically nothing in the Laws of Poland which arbitrarily discriminates against the rights of the Jews." McKenney admitted, however, that "racial, religious, and commercial enmity," intensified by postwar economic crises, had caused "considerable hardships for the Jews."[29]

In McKenney's account, Poles merely reacted to the problematic nature and activities of the Eastern European Jews. Yiddish ("an incongruous German barbarism" written in "Hebrew characters") symbolized the alien nature of Jews while simultaneously accenting their cultural and historical affinity with Poland's German enemy. Until recently, Jewish loyalty remained rightly suspect, since through World War I, they sided "with both Russia and Germany against the interests of the Poles." Fearing retaliation after the war, Jews resorted to rumors of pogroms and "alleged Polish persecutions without actual substantiation in fact."[30]

Neither in war nor peace had Jews fulfilled their patriotic duty. "The Jews habitually avoid military service in this as in other countries." When conscripted, as much as 90 percent of them "at the last minute discover physical disqualifications or forms of illness" exempting them from service; "some become suddenly insane and others do themselves serious injury in order that they may avoid service." Abetting this was the "dishonest military doctor," who when exposed turned out to be either a Jew or working for Jewish organizations designed to keep Jews out of the army. Those finally forced into the military spared no effort "to become coiffeurs, shoemakers, tailors, musicians, or members of the Medical Department, anything but service as a regular soldier." McKenney claimed he could identify only one Jewish career officer in the entire Polish army, a "colonel in a Supply Department."[31]

The Poles were further antagonized by the "lack of hygienic conditions in Jewish homes and streets and the low level of education and culture in the Jewish proletarian masses." But the greatest source of hatred and dissension emanated from the "predominant characteristics" and "ability" of the Jews in commerce and finance. Efforts by American-Jewish social organizations to uplift and economically reorient the Eastern Jews through job training and relocation on farms were inevitably doomed to failure by inherent Jewish characteristics. When one Jewish association boasted of thousands of Bessarabian Jews working only in agriculture, McKenney wrote to Washington:

> It is needless for me to state what I think of the folly of such an enterprise. The Jew has never in the history of the world worked with his hands and his natural bent is business, in which he exerts the cleverest brain of modern times. Every Pole hates every Jew. From infancy a Russian child was taught to hate the Jew. At the present time about six Jews control all of Russia.[32]

By the end of his tour in 1928, McKenney had somewhat modified his opinions. Recovered from the tumultuous 1920s, Poland was economically and politically fairly stable. Faced with these circumstances, "the Jewish attitude became more respectful [as] they abandoned intrigues and commenced to show devotion toward Poland." He even noticed "spontaneous patriotic manifestations" among Warsaw's Jews. Various economic and tax policies had ensured that the Jews were "no longer dangerous competitors"; many were actually "abandoning trade to become artisans." Political and economic accommodations had changed Polish attitudes toward the Jews. Repatriation of many Polish Jews recently from Palestine, in McKenney's view, offered "the best proof that Jews are not unhappy in Poland." The "Jews admit themselves" that aside from a few local exceptions, "there is no anti-Semitism in Poland."[33]

McKenney's last accounts were full of inconsistencies and outright contradictions. Still insisting that "Poland has never persecuted the Jews nor limited their citizenship rights," he continued to assess the problem as one of Poles antagonized by Jewish qualities and behavior. "Poles regard the Jews as cowards, devoid of the spirit of chivalry, dishonest in business dealings, and above all, a people of strong international feeling as opposed to Polish patriotism and nationalism." Language and history had made them the "natural allies of Germany," for which "they very often acted as spies." While Poland fought against Russian Bolsheviks, "Jews showed much sympathy toward Bolshevism" and currently "Communist propaganda is carried on in Poland mostly by young Jews." In McKenney's final words, "at present . . . Jews are regarded as friends of the Soviets."[34]

Far more adamant on the subject of Jews and communism was Major Emer Yeager, attaché to Warsaw during 1929–1931. In many respects, including an affinity for the Polish elite, he resembled the army's first at-taché to Poland, Major Elbert Farman.[35] Yeager's primary bond with the Polish ruling class was anticommunism. "I feel very strongly," he wrote, "that the controlling powers of the Soviets are the most dangerous ene-mies of civilization that have ever been loosed in the world."[36]

"Controlling powers" was Yeager's euphemism for Jews, which he even-tually abandoned in favor of unabashed identification. In an effort at "forced humor," Yeager used jokes about "the differences between the Jews, Georgians, and Russians" to illustrate the significance of "Jewish In-fluence in Soviet Russia." His more sober analysis, however, conveyed the same message. Russians, basically good-natured though not known for their intelligence or initiative, were "fools," as were most soldiers in the "preponderantly Russian" Red Army. The Jews, by nature plotters, now joined by Georgians like Stalin, were preying upon these submissive Rus-sians and governing the country by controlling institutions like the Cheka and Politburo.[37]

Despite "growing dissatisfaction" with having their country "governed by foreigners," neither the Russian population nor the Red Army was likely to "turn out their masters" in the foreseeable future. "Slav psychology" would, Yeager reminded Washington, ensure that the tractable "Russian masses" remained incapable of overcoming their historical docility by trans-forming deep discontentment and thoughts into logical political action.

"To properly understand the significance of many events . . . in Soviet Russia," Yeager contended, "it is necessary to understand the mental habits of the Slav as well as Asiatics and more particularly the combination of the two." Thus, his criteria for intelligence specialists on Soviet Russia included knowledge of the "historical background and an understanding of the psychological factors." Psychology was of "greater importance" than skills in Slavic languages, which were still certainly of "paramount importance." A specialist on Soviet Russia must "have had experience with oriental peo-ples" and these "psychological factors," because "there is a strong oriental tinge in the mental make-up of the Eastern European Slavs." Here were clear echoes of War College teachings on Russian thought and behavior, as well as MID's project on the psychology of nations.[38]

Yeager also kept alive into the early 1930s some of the more dubious views that had permeated military thinking in the Red Scare hysteria but had long been discredited. He forwarded to Washington a translation of an article from the "most reliable newspaper in Poland," claiming that "offi-cial Soviet statistics" themselves proved not only the broad representation of Jews in Soviet society and government but also the notion that "everywhere the Jews hold leading positions." "If the above is true," Yeager wrote, "and from my observations I believe it is so, approximately, it shows that the Jews wield considerable influence in the direction of affairs in the present Soviet regime." Yeager went on to claim:

> [T]his, in a way tends to support the theory advanced by some students of subversive movements throughout history that the present one at least is of Jewish origin.

If this contention, in itself, were not remarkable enough, he concluded by taking a step further backward into the conspiratorial thinking of the previous decade:

> In short it tends to support the arguments of those who maintain that the "Protocols of the Old Men of Zion" were not so far wrong after all, despite their origin.[39]

Not long after Yeager's comments on the *Protocols*, Major Gordon R. Young arrived at the American embassy in Berlin. A graduate of West Point and General Staff School, Young was destined for the War College in 1934, followed by important posts in Panama and Washington. As part of his "Overseas Summer 1931," Young made the grand tour of Germany and neighboring countries, visiting museums, cathedrals, and other sites. Daily, he drew sketches and wrote notes in his diary on his experiences, including what he heard from the attachés he sought out whenever possible.

In Berlin, Young lunched at the Buccaneers Club—"quite a place"— with George Reinberg, U.S. military attaché for air; afterward, they walked through the city's famous Tiergarten. Reinberg struck Young as "very fond of the Germans." He quoted Reinberg as saying that "the French are bleeding Germany badly . . . their black troops on the Rhine behaved abominably. . . . Some day, they'll be licked." Reinberg also predicted that the "Hitlerites will get stronger [and] may get control [as the] Jews have all the money, and are hated." During another walk through the Tiergarten the next day, the military attaché, Colonel Edward Carpenter—a "nice egg"—confirmed the estimate that the Germans would eventually knock the wind out of France.[40]

Young then set off to Prague, where he mourned the collapse of the Austrian Empire and his diary entries began to reflect his own feelings. "Politically, these new states *must* be Balkans," he wrote before jotting: "A Balkan = an unkempt & mongrel nation, whose past is hard luck & whose future is intrigue." Upon returning to Germany, he described a restaurant proprietor as a "fat rather Jewy bird" and complained about his terrible misfortune during a bus trip on which the "Americans included [the] usual lamentable gang: New York Jewess; [and] 20-yr-old with hair and pimples."[41]

It was, however, during a return sea voyage that Young frankly confronted the Jewish question. He shared a table with a man named "Feingold or thereabouts," "a German-born(?) Jew," about whom Gordon immediately noticed certain stereotypical features he "didn't like": "Feingold" was an "extensive talker, Socialist & anti-French tendencies . . . no doubt a decent enough person of his sort but may become a pest with encouragement."

The very next day, the two men clashed when Feingold shifted the conversation to "Jews, anti-Semitism & Zionism" and lent Young a copy of Ludwig Lewisohn's recently published *The Last Days of Shylock*. Through various episodes in Lewisohn's novel, Jews appeared helpless in the face of the power and political intrigues of the dominant Christian or Muslim cultures. Facing repeated historical cycles of persecutions, the only recourse for the Jews was flight or attempting to buy their freedom and security. "They see only their side," Young wrote privately, as he grappled with these issues. The Jews have been persecuted "for 20 centuries; & they say the outrages are outrageous, which is correct." But it never occurred to the Jews "to ask *why* they're outraged. I don't claim to know the answer; but nobody else seems even to ask it."[42]

Young's next passages suggest strongly held views on that answer. Starting a train of thought that would lead from natural science to philosophy, Young complained, "Mammals spend much of their time looking for someone to blame it on." This was "humanity's worst vice; this tangle of ethical judgment, self-justification, all that in place of a cold search for truth." Young quoted Lewisohn's Shylock, "For more than 13 centuries now, Israel had not touched the sword. Nay not wholly because of its weakness." He then repeated: "Not wholly."

To Young, this frame of mind was indicative of "Nietzsche's 'sclavenmorral' a rationalization of the attitude into terms of 'Faustian' thought." For what "has run thru the blood of west-Europe from the beginning. The heart of our tradition," he continued, "is aggressive fighting"—"He is dead who will not fight." Without mentioning Jews, he pursued the argument to yet another highly suggestive stage:

A race that will not fight is a base race, a slave race, says the heart of our thought; and when, not fighting, they still find weapons—of passive resist-ance, and calculating intelligence—they become a monstrous *evil in the eyes*—[43]

How Young finished this line of thought will never be known. History was left with this abrupt ending to what might have been a most revealing resolution of Young's argument with himself. For the following page, the last in Young's diary, containing the continuation of this sentence, was at some later date mysteriously cut out. It is the only page missing from this document.

Almost a year to the day after Young made these notations, the Nazi Party won over 37 percent of the popular vote, setting the stage for Hitler's later appointment as chancellor on January 30, 1933. Less than a month later, as historical coincidence would have it, Hitler's nemesis, Franklin D. Roosevelt, was inaugurated president of the United States. Although the po-litical regimes of Hitler and Roosevelt would parallel each other chronolog-ically, it would not be until several years after their assumption of power that each set his country upon the path of confrontation. Their early years would be preoccupied by the enormous tasks of coping with the immense domestic political and economic problems of the Great Depression that had brought them to power. In the United States, army officers would have much to say about these problems and about their commander in chief.

Generals Against Roosevelt

Army officers normally expressed serious reservations about the New Deal and its leader. There were exceptions and Roosevelt had his defend-ers, but most opinions ranged from general aversion to downright disdain and loathing, especially among the older generation of officers.

Of course, in public, as well as in the performance of professional duties, officers remained quite respectful. Among themselves, or with their trusted civilian political friends and associates, their demeanor was entirely different. Some spoke of the "coronation in Washington" and creation of a "Roosevelt Party." Others were much more personal. "Whatever else may be said of President Franklin D. Roosevelt," exclaimed General Hagood, "no one could say that he was an honorable, straightforward, and truthful man." Another officer wrote "General Moseley . . . hates the President &

so does Gasser [the Deputy Chief of Staff]." Years later, the wife of Colonel Truman Smith recounted the "exultation" and "fierce delight" in their social and political circle upon hearing the news of Roosevelt's death. Finally, in her words, "The evil man was dead!"[44]

In the minds of many officers, the New Deal brought various anti-American tendencies into the political mainstream, and indeed to the seat of government itself. At home and abroad, the new administration appeared too close to the Reds and Pinks. To some, New Deal economic policy was creeping socialism that undermined the work ethic and bankrupted the country. Politically, it reeked of labor, radical, and minority influence. It all rested, wrote General Chynoweth, upon an irresponsible and reckless "TAX-SPEND-ELECT" formula. In terse language among friends, New Deal electoral support was "bought and paid for." Roosevelt's foreign policy damaged American long-term interests and security; granting independence to the Philippines weakened America's Far Eastern presence; recognition of the Soviet Union aided a future enemy that threatened "our government, our homes and firesides and our religions." Other officers, however, criticized Roosevelt from the opposite direction, believing "the essential features of fascism are in the New Deal."[45]

Whether seeing the New Deal danger to American institutions and values as leftist or rightist, most of the army strongly resented the massive influx of funds into social programs. Although Roosevelt provided the army with more funds than the military had secured from Republican administrations, he did not meet army requests. Officers were annoyed further by their forced participation in the Civilian Conservation Corps program. Although some saw the potential of disciplining America's youth through the program or even using the CCC to train reserves, the army generally worried that the corps' work camps would become centers where Communists, Pinks, or pacifists corrupted America's young.[46]

The army no longer felt a part of official Washington once the brash New Dealers moved in. The upper echelons of the army lost the ear of the president and the intimate access to the White House they had enjoyed when their personal friends Hoover and his secretary of war, Patrick J. Hurley, had held power. Feeling alienated, often snubbed, the army turned inward. Harboring serious mistrust of the newcomers and their dangerous policies, officers quickly became quite cautious in their public statements and official reports. This was especially true by 1935, when Roosevelt replaced MacArthur as chief of staff with General Malin Craig and forced General Johnson Hagood into retirement the following year. "I have seen little of Washington," wrote Moseley in 1938, "only going there when I am compelled to do so."[47]

Although no particular incident prompted MacArthur's removal, Roosevelt's action against Hagood came in the midst of a public clash over New Deal spending. An 1892 West Point graduate, Hagood came from a distinguished South Carolina family that included a Reconstruction governor. Against the New Deal answer to the Great Depression, Hagood projected a romanticized version of the Reconstruction South pulling itself up by its own bootstraps. As he proudly remembered it, his family recovered "after Sherman's March through their plantations, all without one penny of outside help."

An early critic of army mismanagement and spending, Hagood unleashed a vehement barrage against the New Deal in confidential congressional testimony in 1935.[48] When his testimony surfaced in newspaper headlines months later, Roosevelt acted swiftly and forced him into retirement. Hagood's removal sent a clear message to career officers about voicing political opinions, even in secret committees among sympathetic political friends. Life was difficult enough for officers in the interwar army without risking a future promotion or assignment. Moreover, the army's institutional interests might suffer from disagreements over politics and policies.[49]

Once released from official constraints, ex-officers lost most inhibitions. For years thereafter, Hagood remained a thorn in Roosevelt's side, attacking the New Deal "orgy of spending" in the Saturday Evening Post. Although a steadfast and rather emotional anti-German, Hagood lambasted Roosevelt's foreign policy even after the outbreak of World War II; he preached isolationism and the concept of fortress America almost until Pearl Harbor.

Pershing's old deputy chief of staff, retired general James G. Harbord, followed a similar course of relentless criticism. Harbord, a president of RCA, went so far as to suggest in one speech that Americans were losing their freedom under a Roosevelt administration that bordered on totalitarianism. Meanwhile, retired general Charles H. Martin, elected to Congress on the Democratic ticket in Oregon (subsequently elected governor), voted against virtually every New Deal budget and program.[50]

Retired generals across the country reacted similarly in 1936, when Congressman John J. McSwain of the Military Affairs Committee solicited their counsel on defense and preparedness. Through their lenses, the New Deal military appeared plagued by excessive costs, waste, bureaucratic nightmares, and irresponsible politicians. Intertwined with their visions of a costly yet inadequate national defense were concerns about international subversion. The old guard had clearly lost none of its nativist paranoia about aliens, especially the proverbial "undesirables."[51]

There was also continuity in Darwinian thought, illustrated by the un-published manuscripts written by Hagood into the 1940s. Under titles such as "White Faced Cattle," "White Man's Country," and "Race Prejudice," Hagood offered a spirited defense of racism and the struggle to maintain racial purity. Contesting the trend toward greater racial toleration and pos-sibly assimilation, he actually lauded racial prejudice as a primary law of nature, necessary for preserving the species. "Man could not have ad-vanced from protophlasm to his present high state of civilization without it." History, he wrote, had shown that "nations once powerful [were] now on the decline, because of mongrelization." The "birds, the beasts, and the fishes" instinctively "exclude all intruders" and fight to the death defend-ing their domain against them; "the weak go down before the strong." So, too, all the human races—Japanese, Filipinos, Negroes, Jews, white Euro-peans, and so on—must remain segregated. "So long as the United States shall have the mental, moral and physical courage to defend these princi-ples, so long and no longer, shall we survive."[52]

As a member of the old South Carolinian elite with years of Far East ex-perience, Hagood focused on blacks and Asians. In Charleston, there were so few Jews "you rarely heard the word." Besides, Jews "are a very fine people, and what would we have done without them?" he said, praising their contributions—the Bible, Christianity, "the moral uplift of man," and a variety of "great men." Jews were not the "most universally despised people on earth" because of religion; "the prejudice against Jews is purely economic."

But even Hagood's praise of the Jews involved the concept of race. What was most admirable, in Hagood's eyes, was the way Jews throughout his-tory had kept "their race pride, their prejudice against other races and sur-vive[d]"; they proved "true to their blood and their faith." But the instinctive prejudice of one race against another meant that despite great Jewish contributions, "every man in the United States, perhaps through-out the world, has some prejudice against a Jew, although he may not be willing to admit it."[53]

Regarding their persecution in Nazi Germany, Hagood never doubted the Jews would, as in the past, survive and ultimately prosper again. Nei-ther did the Nazi doctrine of German racial superiority cause him any difficulty, since it was natural for each country, including America, to boast of its innate superiority over all others. Hagood derided Secretary of State Cordell Hull for even taking the time to condemn Hitler's racial claims. In any event, what the Nazis said or did, Hagood advised, "should be of no concern to us. We have our problems to solve in this country, and the less we bring Hitler into the matter the better."[54]

Out of the public eye, some active-duty officers expressed candid political opinions and racial concerns among loyal colleagues and lifelong friends. Late in 1934, Moseley urged his friend MacArthur to take up the "serious problems" of America's racial future with the secretary of war. Moseley had compared a company of "southern lads" of "good Anglo-Saxon stock" with soldiers in a Northern company, most of whose names "indicated foreign blood [and were] . . . difficult to pronounce." A problem for the army, these same types caused the serious labor problems in the North and were responsible for "so much trouble in our schools and colleges." In the South, which remained immune to these outside forces and their "isms," American institutions were safe, but "the problem is clear." As Moseley posed it to MacArthur, "It is a question of whether or not the old blood that built this fine nation, which became famous throughout the world, is to continue to administer that nation, or whether that old stock is going to be destroyed or bred out by a lot of foreign blood which the melting pot has not touched." MacArthur promised to raise the issue with the secretary of War, noting, "I am in entire accord with the inferences you have drawn from the situation."[55]

Army anxiety ran deep when it came to American youth—the source of military manpower as well as the heirs to the country's cherished institutions and culture. Ever vigilant about the education of America's future elite, officers looked askance at the depression era political and social currents on the nation's college campuses. Student activism, particularly liberal or leftist, immediately conjured up suspicions that the nation's youth had fallen prey to anti-American influences. Student demonstrations and strikes were viewed with the utmost seriousness, while the increasing popularity of antiwar sentiments among students raised alarms. The army secretly followed, occasionally through surveillance, the course of student activities on and off campus. Participants at one University of Chicago meeting were described as "of foreign appearance with the Jewish type predominating."[56]

One of the most detailed appraisals of Jewish influence in student unrest had been voluntarily submitted by a professor at Cornell University to Colonel John J. Fulmer, in charge of military instruction at that institution. A Russian émigré with a U.S. Naval Reserve commission, this professor brought the worst cultural baggage of the old country into the new. Although he denied categorically any personal anti-Semitism (he had, he said, Jewish friends), he drew upon the centuries-long experience of his native czarist Russia in laying out the alternatives facing America as either restrictions on Jews or pogroms. Biology endowed the Jews, he argued, with extreme "aggressiveness" and "other peculiarities" that aggravated the dominant American race to such an degree that a "bloody" backlash would soon be inevitable; czarist pogroms and Hitler's policies would pale by comparison.[57]

In the professor's observations, the rise in campus resistance to military training and service at Cornell corresponded directly to the great influx of New York Jews into the student body. There were, admittedly, some gentile students and church groups involved, but behind these stood the resolute leadership and "brains" of the Jews. Born with a complete lack of courage and an "aversion to physical exertion of all kind," Jews were by their very nature antimilitary; unlike the youth of all other races, Jews could not be expected to fight or even engage in competitive sports. Yet he suspected something far more sinister. As disloyal internationalists without a country of their own, Jews sought to break down all national barriers so they could, as in the past, exploit the confused conditions of civilization. Military preparedness and patriotism impeded these objectives. America must awaken to the "menace" of a possible Jewish ascendancy through such intrigues.[58]

Officers in important positions did not dismiss such ranting out of hand. Colonel Fulmer, executive officer of the Army War College until 1929, endorsed the fundamental arguments in this document before forwarding it up the chain of command, where it stopped only one step short of the chief of staff. "The letter," Fulmer wrote, "sets forth what appears to be the underlying cause of the present anti-military propaganda in this country in a very clear and able manner."

Fulmer added that his own study of the situation at Cornell over the past two years had "indicated this [same] cause but many restrictions confronting [his] Department compelled the abandonment of many leads and the uncovering of many subversive efforts." Fulmer had no doubt that the "fountain head" was New York City, and he intended to spend the next two months preparing for an anticipated new wave of activities.[59]

Well into the second Roosevelt administration, the old guard watched with dismay what many of them perceived as the degeneration of America through the convergence of New Deal politics, loss of control by the old stock of true Americans, and the spread of Communist influences. Late in 1938, Moseley wrote to MacArthur in the Philippines that since the latter had "left America, the problems among our people have been increased . . . [through] labor problems, graft, disease, and problems of that kind." He ranted against the appalling conditions in the American army, as well as against Roosevelt's foreign and domestic policies. "In case of an emergency," he wrote, "you and I had better get together again and pull Uncle Sam through." MacArthur professed himself very happy to hear from his "dear and cherished friend." "As usual," he "agree[d] with every word . . . with regard to our internal and external problems." MacArthur also worried that "the utter disregard of fundamental common sense and the profligate abuse of power in the United States at the present time may eventually result in that almost impossible thing—the shaking of the very foundations of our country." He sincerely hoped that "America will awaken to the true situation before it is too late."[60]

Actually, after MacArthur's departure, the army not only maintained its vigilance but prepared for dealing with domestic disturbances. Under orders from General Craig, officers across the country drew up new contingency plans similar to the original Emergency Plan White and expanded their contacts with private intelligence groups run by big corporations like U.S. Steel and General Motors. Part of the impetus for a renewal of intensified domestic intelligence emanated, ironically, from the much-maligned Roosevelt himself, who had a penchant for secret intelligence gathering as well as concerns about radical groups on the left and right. Nevertheless, though the army would investigate the latter, the enemy in its view stood on the left, where most of its efforts would be devoted.[61]

By the outbreak of World War II, the Army War College library contained less than forty entries on Nazism compared to almost 400 for "Communism." As part of its "contribution to Emergency Plan White," the War College class of 1937 classified "subversive activities" as essentially an internationally oriented leftist phenomenon, while categorizing the radical right as "those forces that strive [merely] to supersede our form of government." Limited in strength, the right constituted not even a "distant threat [and] serve . . . partially to curb subversive influences." Inherently patriotic, the right would be expected to "rally to a nationalistic doctrine in the event of a decided leftist threat against our government."

The real subversive forces, "more specifically Communism, . . . unless more effectively curbed, gives promise of being able to seriously threaten our form of government at some future time." The "more effective" methods proposed by this study pointed implicitly in the direction of Jews. Officers demanded tighter "immigration restrictions" and "naturalization requirements," accompanied by "prosecution of dangerous agitators and the deportation of undesirables."[62]

A month later Colonel C. L. Clark, G-2 in Baltimore, made the same argument without the subtleties or euphemisms that, more and more, characterized officer writing in the 1930s and beyond. Identifying the Socialist Labor Party as "led by the Jewish Marxian, Daniel de Leon," Clark informed Washington "that Jews are apparently completely or almost completely in control of the Socialist Labor Party." Clark cited the executive committee, which consisted of "Thal, Feinberg, Kowarsky, Gerold, Herzel, Smiley, Moskowitz, Lasker, Orange, and Rosen." Equally suggestive was the "Talmudic logic of de Leon," who "is being built up as the 'Moses' or 'Lenin' of the American Labor Movement."[63]

The view was obviously the same from Pittsburgh, where an agent had secretly attended a meeting of a group the army believed was the largest Communist front organization, the American League Against War and Fascism. Its "ten-point plan" called for security through international efforts, total disarmament, and resistance against militarism. Especially irksome for the military, the program linked war and fascism as interrelated. As a last barb, the agent wrote, "the majority of the crowd was Russian Jews. There wasn't an American present, outside of myself."[64]

Van Deman's Secret Network

Lacking sufficient resources for the surveillance of radicals, the army welcomed private efforts from "patriotic organizations." These right-thinking groups were readily identifiable by the average group of officers: the American Coalition, American Legion, Daughters of the American Revolution, Reserve Officers' Association, National Security League, and Veterans of Foreign Wars (VFW).[65] Yet perhaps one of the most important private contributors to domestic intelligence in the 1930s and 1940s was nearly invisible.

Sitting at home in San Diego, an old wiry and determined man of great experience in these matters began a remarkable freelance intelligence operation in 1932. Frantically working ten hours a day, he sustained a pace matching his earlier wartime routine. Day after day over the next twenty years, he solicited information from old and new sources, which he then disseminated carefully throughout his wide network of private and government contacts. In return he received extraordinary support for a private citizen engaged in intelligence work. But retired general Ralph H. Van Deman, father of military intelligence, was no ordinary citizen. Of the countless thousands of pages Van Deman read, clipped, and filed, most dealt with communism; among these were articles with titles such as "The Jews as the Apostles of Communism." But the range of categories of individuals and subjects he considered worthy of investigation was exceedingly broad. Interspersed with files on Russian or American Communist leaders were those on churches and movies, labor leaders and union activity, congressmen and liberal causes, all cross-referenced in an elaborate card index.

Unlike most Red-hunting patriots, Van Deman enjoyed immediate access to the highest levels of the intelligence community, several of whose members he had personally mentored in their craft. At various points, the army furnished some funding and assistants, as did state and local governments. Before his organization ceased functioning, it had amassed about 200,000 files with references to some 125,000 individuals and groups.[66]

By 1940, Van Deman's close working relationship with the FBI, though still known to very few, became official. "I want you to know," wrote J. Edgar Hoover, "that the officials of the Federal Bureau of Investigation officially and personally have the utmost admiration, respect and friendship for you. We value your cooperation, assistance and counsel most highly."

The intelligence community reciprocated by regularly providing Van Deman with classified material, along with military personnel as secret agents and informants. In addition to the FBI and G-2, his group worked with the Office of Naval Intelligence, the National Guard, the Reserve Officers' Association, and the San Diego and Los Angeles police departments.[67] Van Deman's illegal activities, directed against thousands of innocent American citizens, never bothered government agencies. In their eyes, he did what was necessary but what they could not because of fiscal, legislative, or constitutional restraints.

Throughout the 1930s and 1940s, intelligence officers at the Presidio in San Francisco sent Van Deman information on various labor leaders or suspected radicals. Special vigilance was maintained for immigrants and foreigners. When a group of Russian engineers visited California, G-2 forwarded its complete dossier of the case to Van Deman. "Please return the file," requested Major Thomas J. Betts, "when it has served its purpose."[68]

Although never focusing specifically on the "Jewish Question," the Van Deman files were peppered with anti-Semitic stereotypes, usually involving the familiar identification of Jewish and Communist. To the Office of Naval Intelligence, a "prominent Trotskyite" appeared to be "a very brilliant Jew," while another struck G-2 as "having an unmistakable Jewish cast of face," though the subject spoke with "a hardly perceptible Jewish accent" and was "a very likeable little fellow."

Responding to Van Deman about a "labor adviser," Major Betts noted that though American educated, "in appearance he is a typical Polish Jew." San Diego police officers could not identify a man disseminating "communist literature" but surmised from his description—"small build . . . dirty gray hair . . . [and] Hook nose"—that he "may be a Russian-Jew." Occasionally, targets of investigation denied being Jewish, only to be met with skepticism because of "facial appearance."[69]

Assuming an irrefutable racial pedigree of communism from "Karl Marx and Friedrich Engels, two apostate Jews," down to contemporary Red subversion, Van Deman's military contacts often invoked descriptions like "ex-German Jew-Communist agitator" or "active Jewish Communist."[70] A Legionnaire and "old warrior" acquaintance of Van Deman's noticed "occasional strangers of Hebrew and possible red persuasion playing about" with the Communist Party. Investigators of "communist activities" at UCLA and USC, while uncovering "no definite information" on the politics of two professors, classified one as "Questionable," because of being "married to a Polish Jewess." The Russian film *Deserter* was shown not at just any theater but one in the "Jewish & Communistic Quarters" of the city. Van Deman's contacts just as quickly pointed out that the "crowds" at radical meetings were "predominantly Jewish." After typing up his report on a joint surveillance with Naval Intelligence, a police officer wrote in by hand: "Meeting well attended by Jews."[71]

To some informants it seemed self-evident that "the revolutionary movement is gaining momentum through the energy and force of the Jews." Anyone serious who looked at subversion in the aircraft industry knew that "if it were not for the Jews we would have little or no Communist agitation in the United States." One Methodist minister was branded as "an agent of Moscow" because Van Deman's reliable source believed that despite his Anglo-Saxon name, he was "of Russian Jewish ancestry . . . and belongs to a clique of radicals (of Jewish Russian ancestry) or pacifists."

Van Deman forwarded to G-2 a report on international financial intrigue linking the Mexican government, the stock market crash, and the fact that "New York Jews who speak Spanish and English brokenly handle the stock exchange in Mexico." His source revived old suspicions of collusion between capitalist and Communist Jews, arguing that in Mexico "some wealthy Jews are backing Trotzky."[72]

Most telling was a document procured by Agent B-11 entitled *B'nai B'rith: An International Anti-Christian, Pro-Communist Jewish Power*, by one John Merrick Church. To someone not already predisposed to its line of thought, this work held as much validity as any other run-of-the-mill anti-Semitic diatribe. To a true believer, though, it constituted a well-documented treatise proving that "Communism and Jewry are linked." Whereas other intelligence offered only bits and pieces, it coherently synthesized other scattered comments, examples, and suspicions into a cogent argument encompassing a wide variety of evils. From politics and religion to sex, the B'nai B'rith supposedly spearheaded a full-scale assault against the culture and institutions of Christian America. Startling revelations about lectures at the New School for Social Research "on degenerate and unnatural sex subjects" were followed by attacks on former ambassador to Germany William E. Dodd and "his Red Son."[73]

Someone, if not Van Deman, then perhaps B-11 or another member of their secret inner circle, found such arguments and "facts" sufficiently credible to devote time to underlining and marking "significant" passages while he read. A big X was placed next to "Jews Foremost in Communist Party" and heavy underlining appears beneath "Is Jewry Communistic?" Infiltration of the American government received similar scrutiny: "Jews in the New Deal," "Felix Frankfurter, a Roosevelt Red advisor and power," "Morgenthau Controls U.S. Gold," and the Communist "activities of 7 out of 10 . . . Jewish Congressmen."[74]

Moreover, Van Deman worked closely with, confided in, and vouched for the veracity of Red-baiters like Margaret Kerr, whose writings about Jewish conspiracies equaled, if not surpassed, the bizarre anti-Semitic paranoia of B-11. As secretary of the xenophobic Better America Federation, Kerr carried out a zealous crusade to unmask the Red Hydra and urge true Americans to recapture their government. Not content with accumulating intelligence and working through contacts, she personally went undercover within a Communist cell in Los Angeles; and when the opportunity arose, she traveled to Washington to testify before congressional committees. Throughout the 1930s, Van Deman read numerous submissions by Kerr purporting, among other things, to offer "proof of the sinister ties between Jewry, Bolshevism, and Freemasonry."[75]

MILITARY ATTACHÉ CONFERENCE AT COBLENZ, JUNE, 1921

Top Row—Lieut. Doherty (M. I. D.). *Second Row*—Major Bagby (G-2, A. F. in G.), Major Ord (Holland), Major Colvin (Sweden), Major Villaret (France). *Third Row*—Lieut. Col. Briggs (Austria), Lieut. Col. Allen (Egypt), Lieut. Col. Castle (Turkey). *Fourth Row*—Major Holmes (Sweden), Major Eglin (Hungary), Major Hollyday (Finland and Baltic Provinces). *Fifth Row*—Major Van Natta (Spain), Lieut. Col. McCabe (Czecho-Slovakia), Lieut. Col. Cox (Turkey), Lieut. Col. Thomas (Belgium), Col. Johnson (Italy), Lieut. Col. Davis (Germany), Lieut. Col. Poillon (Roumania), Lieut. Col. Coffin (Germany), Lieut. Col. Godson (Switzerland), Major Shallenberger (Greece and Jugo-Slavia).

Most military attaches were racial anti-Semites who for years investigated alleged Jewish subversion and power across Europe. Attaché reports demonstrated the racial anti-Semitism of the Officer Corps. At this 1921 attaché conference, these highly respected officers strongly advocated legislation to halt immigration of the "herd" of inferior races from eastern Europe in order to preserve the purity of America's Nordic Race.

Colonel Sherman Miles as instructor at the Army War College in 1918. He was a major participant in the Military Intelligence investigations at home and abroad of Jewish Bolsheviks and other Jewish conspiracies in the early 1920s. As Chief of Military Intelligence in the early phases of World War II, he reinforced the national security arguments against admitting Jewish refugees from Nazi Germany.

The U.S. Army War College in Washington, D.C. (1932) prepared the elites within the army for the upper echelons of command and the general staff. Between the two world wars, the War College was a key institution in the development and perpetuation of the racial worldview of the Officer Corps.

The Army War College Class of 1924 which was instructed in racial theory, civilization, and war by the renowed Harvard psychologist William McDougall, a leading advocate of Nordic racial supremacy. Until America's entry into World War II, War College officers received similar lectures from other prominent racial theorists and eugenicists.

General George Van Horn Moseley, Assistant Chief of Staff, (far right) watching his close friend President Herbert Hoover bestow a service medal on a fellow officer in September 1932. A rabid Social Darwinist, Moseley later articulated racial and anti-Semitic ideas virtually identical to Nazi ideology. In 1938, Moseley, one of America's most decorated officers, would advocate the sterilization of Jewish refugees from Nazi Germany.

Colonel Charles E. Loucks, attaché in Paris during the French collapse in 1940. While processing visa applications for Jewish refugees fleeing before the German armies, Loucks was surprised to find that they did not "look very Jewish" or like "Kikes." He believed that admitting radical refugees would endanger American democracy.

Into the 1930s and beyond certain military attaches and other officers claimed that Jews dominated the Soviet Union and that, even if a forgery, the Protocols *still revealed basic truths about Jewish aims and radical activities.*

General George van Horn Moseley (front, third from right), General Douglas MacArthur (third from left) and their close friend Secretary of War Patrick J. Hurley (center) in January 1933. At this point, Eisenhower whom Moseley had mentored, hoped that Moseley would become Chief of Staff. Eisenhower never lost his respect for Moseley, defending him as a misunderstood patriot long after Moseley's vicious anti-Semitic crusade.

General Amos A. Fries, Chief of Chemical Warfare Service (1918–1929), remained one of the most influential spokesmen and lobbyists for anti-immigrant organizations until the 1950s. Denying Nazi anti-Semitic measures, Fries was a proponent of a rearmed anti-Communist Germany. His restrictionist activities were pivotal in keeping America closed to Jewish refugees.

11 The Prado
Atlanta, Georgia

October 23, 1940

Mr. R. Douglas Stuart, Jr., Director,
America First Committee,
1806 Board of Trade Building,
Chicago, Illinois.

Dear Mr. Stuart:

If I am to acknowledge the receipt of your letter dated
October 11th, I must, in keeping with the principles which have
always governed me, write you very frankly.

At the outset, I must say that I am happy to know that
your organization has chosen such a vital mission. But I wonder
if you realize the difficulties of such a campaign and the real
strength of the enemy - and are you prepared to go to battle with
him and with his tribe? A number of organizations have started out
bravely with a mission similar to yours, but too often they have
melted away before the enemy.

I have had considerable experience on this subject, for
I tried to arouse the American people from their apathy, pointing
out the dangers confronting us as a nation. But I stated the truth
too frankly and so, for many months now, my pen and my voice have
been silenced.

Early in my endeavors, I received an invitation to speak
before the Union League Club of Chicago, an organization I remember
from boyhood, which always marched in step with the Republic. No
date had been fixed but when the enemy went after me in the public
press the heroic Union League Club evidently lost their nerve and
they did not renew their invitation.

What prevents America from being first today? Let me
be frank and point out the enemy who would themselves be first in
America today, and that is the Jewish nation, a nation within a
nation. If you will investigate, as I have - crime, graft, filthy
publications and unsavory movies, the liquor and drug traffic, the
red light district, white slave traffic and WAR - you will arrive
headon against a pack of Jews in control.

I am not going to take your time to discuss in this letter
the age old problem of the Jew, but if you are interested, you can
get all the evidence concerning his plans for world domination from
the writings of Jews, themselves. You do not have to rely on the
statement of any Gentile. Suffice it to say, however, that they have
been driven out of every country in which they have been domiciled,
and for good reason, and EVENTUALLY THEY WILL BE DRIVEN OUT OF THE
U. S. A.

The Jew may tell you that there are only some four and a half
million of them in the United States. The fact is, there are over thirteen
million of them in the United States today. Formerly I felt sorry for
the Member of Congress who could not face this problem frankly on account
of Jewish influences in his district, but now I find the influence of the
Jew extends to every field. The banker, who may agree with me on principle
just one hundred per cent, dares not touch this problem, for some of his
biggest depositors are Jews; many a lawyer will not face it for some of
his big clients are Jews; the press cannot touch it, for so many of the
big advertisers are Jews, and it is the advertiser who makes the paper
pay. If we lack the character to face this problem squarely and solve
it, we will experience the tragedy which overtook France.

I shall be glad to join your organization, assisting it as far
as I am permitted to do so -

1. If you eliminate from your organization all Jews and all
Jewish influences (they join all organizations and buy in on both political
parties; thus they keep themselves fully advised, and control or ruin);

2. If you will come out before the nation with a definite
statement against the Jew and all he stands for, including the closing of
our doors to all refugee Jews, of whatever nationality;

3. If you will take a definite stand against the control by
Jews in local, state and national affairs;

4. If you will advocate the restoration of our REPUBLIC,
bringing back in the written and spoken language throughout the United
States the words, "Republic, Christ and Christian".

If you will take the stand that I have suggested above, millions
of Gentiles will rush to your banner. But if you fail to meet this issue
squarely, your organization will accomplish nothing, except possibly to
support a certain overhead, including perhaps several Jewish secretaries,
placed with you for the purpose of spying upon you and your work.

You may not agree with me in what I have written above. Perhaps
you will give this letter no consideration whatsoever, but may I ask you
to preserve it, so that as the years roll by you may again read it, with
the perspective of, say, ten or fifteen years. May I ask also that you
make acknowledgment of it, for I plan to give copies of this letter to
individuals over the land who know this problem and agree with me just
one hundred per cent.

Enclosed herewith is a copy of a letter inviting me to meet
Mr. Lewis L. Strauss of Kuhn, Loeb & Company, and my reply.

Very sincerely yours,

George Van Horn Moseley

The vehement anti-Semitism characterizing this letter was typical of the thinking of retired general George Van Horn Moseley, former Deputy Chief of Staff. In his mind, the world was in danger of being undermined and dominated by sinister Jews.

Colonel Truman Smith, American military attaché in Berlin (seated left) and Charles Lindbergh (seated right) during a tour of German military installations in 1938. Smith and Lindbergh later worked closely with the America First Movement to keep the United States out of a war with Germany.

Colonel Percy G. Black (right) receiving the Legion of Merit for his wartime service in military intelligence. As attaché to Nazi Germany (1939–1940), Black favored U.S. nonintervention. He opposed immigration to Palestine during the Holocaust and later accused President Truman of selling out American strategic and economic interests in the Middle East for New York Jewish votes.

*General George V. Strong, Chief of Military Intelligence (1942–1945)
was the most powerful intelligence figure in Washington and an influential opponent of opening Palestine to Jewish refugees. Strong
even attempted to get the secretaries of state and war to prevent
meetings and demonstrations by American Jews on the Palestine
issue.*

By early 1933, Kerr started writing to MacArthur, warning the chief of staff of various subversive activities. Since the chief of the Operations Branch, Colonel F. H. Lincoln, regarded her as a troublesome "crank on the subject," he shielded MacArthur from any association with her. Lincoln soon recommended completely ignoring her letters as "embarrassing to the Chief of Staff." And MacArthur concurred.[76] Undeterred, Kerr continued writing to a leader she considered one of America's last hopes. In her "absolutely secret" reports, Kerr identified an intricate web of incongruous political and economic forces including Kuhn, Loeb, and Company, Rockefeller banking interests, the Soviet Union, and the Roosevelt administration. Behind all this stood "the Jews in the East and/or the international Jews."[77]

Unaware that MacArthur's subordinates had already rebuffed Kerr, Van Deman urged her to go to Washington and speak directly with the chief of staff. Given his increasingly close interaction with military and naval intelligence, as well as the FBI, Van Deman had no reason to assume that his personal intervention would fail. And there was an old personal relationship; Van Deman had started his spy career as the intelligence officer for MacArthur's father in the Philippines. Van Deman wrote to MacArthur in December 1934: "I consider [Kerr] the best informed person on the West Coast on matters Communistic. You may rely absolutely upon her discretion in every way."[78]

When Van Deman's letter reached Lincoln's desk, he dismissed it with a terse "no response necessary." Two weeks later, however, Kerr received an enthusiastic endorsement from another retired general active in anti-Communist circles. Amos Fries informed a fellow officer that Kerr "has the most comprehensive and complete story of Communism . . . in this country." Through their exchange of information over previous years, Fries had acquired "a keen appreciation of [her] fine work for Americanism; he could also attest that every aspect of her meticulously prepared case rested upon "original documents." To Fries, superpatriots like Kerr and Van Deman were a critical part of the Americanism campaign against "Communism, Pacifism and Internationalism," which were "all one and the same thing."[79]

Among veterans, however, anti-Communism and Americanism were by no means monopolized by rightists like Fries and Van Deman. Throughout the 1930s, these were among the most important issues for the Jewish War Veterans (JWV) of the United States. At every annual convention since 1932, the JWV passed a resolution urging governmental action against "the insidious attacks made by the agents and sympathizers of Moscow against our beloved American institutions." The JWV eventually founded its own "Americanism Committee" to rejuvenate the "spirit of American-ism." The organization sustained these efforts well into the 1950s.[80]

Beyond demonstrating Jewish loyalty, the JWV sought to establish Jews as integral parts of American history and society. Drawing upon references to the Pilgrims and Founding Fathers, the JWV asserted that "democratic principles and institutions stem from a twin root—the Jewish Bible and the folk-ways of the Anglo-Saxons." But the prejudice the JWV was com-bating had twin roots as well: Deeply embedded suspicions of a Jewish-Communist connection exacerbated the anti-Semitism inherent in so many other patriotic groups. Thus, the JWV trumpeted its anti-Commu-nist message as Americanism.[81]

"The truth is," stated the JWV's magazine, "that Communism and Ju-daism are fundamentally incompatible—just as fundamentally incompat-ible as Americanism and Communism." Aggressively lambasting both Communist ideology and the brutality of Stalinist Russia, the JWV argued that "to be a Communist and to keep faith with the ancient Covenant of Israel is a moral *impossibility*." Russia's Jews, the majority of whom fought against the Bolshevik seizure of power, were oppressed under So-viet rule. Contrary to the myth of Jewish domination, "Jews constituted only 3.5% of the Communist Party membership"; only two of Stalin's chief aides were "of Jewish origin." Finding it "deplorable" that the rank and file of the American Communist Party contained some Jews, the JWV described them "as almost exclusively callow youths, embittered by the hardships of the depression." This "blind" youth revolt by a minority con-stituted an attack "against Jewish tradition as well as against American in-stitutions." They were vigorously condemned by the "overwhelming majority of American Jews of all classes as *renegades to Judaism* and *trai-tors to America*."[82]

The JWV also tried to use patriotic ideals to fight anti-Semitism, con-tending that anti-Jewish prejudice was as un-American as communism. The JWV naively expected that the government and other patriotic organ-izations would follow its lead in combating anti-Semitic movements in the United States. It was equally resolute in declaring that American ideals de-manded active opposition, at home and abroad, to the threats posed by fas-cism and Nazism.[83]

These positions indicated serious differences between the JWV's per-spectives on Americanism and those of patriots associated with Fries and Van Deman. While obsessed and uncompromising regarding communism, such retired officers, like some on active duty, displayed a distinct ambivalence toward Nazism and fascism. These foreign doctrines were, of course, unsuited for America and antithetical to its ideals; but their values and systems might be quite appropriate to other countries, especially if the alternative was communism.

"Why," asked Fries, was there "such a furor by the communists about Fascism in the United States?" It was, he answered, merely a "smoke screen" for the Communists while "they planned [and] plotted" to overthrow the American government as they had unsuccessfully attempted to do in Italy and Germany. "*Dictatorships were the only immediately effective means* Italy and Germany could find to stop the infinitely worse dictatorships of Communism, under which every human right is destroyed." Had the Communists succeeded, these countries would have become a "blood-soaked land," "where homes, family life, private property, religion, [and] virtue in women [would] be as dead as the dodo." Threatened by a Communist uprising within and Soviet military power from without, Germany "had no alternative but to go to dictatorship." Even then, Fries continued, Hitler only assumed power after acquiring "a majority of the German nation."[84]

Fries's erroneous historical account was intended to establish the Hitler dictatorship as both legal and necessary. Hatred of Communist ideology and fear of Soviet military might had led Fries to welcome a resurgent, rearmed Nazi Germany as the salvation of civilization. In Fries's own words: "Were it not for the powerful Military forces of Italy and Germany, all Europe [would fall under] a black pale of death."[85]

Fries's geopolitical argument was shared by other retired officers as well as many on active duty. It was the same line of reasoning that officers had used after World War I to justify support for Poland despite widespread pogroms. In the mid-1930s, the new anti-Communist bulwark, a resurgent Germany, was to be afforded similar consideration despite Nazi persecution of Jews and others. Such geopolitical rationalizations had been made easier by the groundwork laid by military attachés, who for fifteen years had continually emphasized the problematic nature and activities of Jews in Eastern Europe and Russia. Attaché reports took on additional relevance when pressure mounted for America to admit large numbers of Jewish refugees from Nazi Germany.

Among the vocal opponents of admitting more Jews, Fries and Moseley would acquire places of distinction. Although Fries channeled his restrictionist crusade through various patriotic organizations, Moseley's anti-Semitic declarations would cause a major public scandal for the army. The restrictionist cause would be strengthened further by Van Deman's private network, whose surveillance heightened the sense of danger from insidious alien forces. Working ever closer with MID and the FBI in the coming years, Van Deman's informants also underscored the connection between Jews and communism.

When President Roosevelt ignored these kinds of geopolitical rationalizations and also empathized with the plight of Jewish refugees, he increased the antagonism toward him already prevalent in the army. Some officers began to suspect him of jeopardizing American domestic and foreign policy interests to accommodate Jews. Many officers at home and abroad were convinced that Roosevelt was pursuing the wrong course toward Nazi Germany for the wrong reason. Thus, Roosevelt had to be ever vigilant against giving credence to charges that he sacrificed American interests on behalf of alien Jews or was acting under pressure from Jews within his administration.[86] Such political caution hampered the efforts of the president and others to assist Jews.

CHAPTER 7

The Officer Corps
and the Third Reich,
1933–1939

JUST A FEW MONTHS AFTER HITLER'S ACQUISITION OF POWER, Major John H. Hineman, acting military attaché in Berlin, and his assistant, Captain Hugh W. Rowan, informed Washington that Jewish and liberal American reporters were distorting Germany's image abroad. These newspapermen had, Hineman and Rowan argued, swayed the Association of Foreign Press Correspondents in Berlin "to adopt an antagonistic attitude toward the Hitler government." The "articles on Germany in the foreign press since that time" clearly confirmed this bias and the cause of this animosity could be traced to the "prominent and influential positions" occupied by Jews. Even if all these journalists were not Jews, the effect would be the same, because "they are at least men of strongly liberal, if not to say radical tendencies." Although it was "quite natural that such men . . . would be decidedly unfriendly towards the Hitler Government," Washington must understand that "personal prejudice played an important part in . . . this attitude" by the foreign press.[1]

From the beginning of the Third Reich, many American officers, in fact, worried that Nazi persecution of German Jews might become a major disruptive factor in German-American relations. To such officers it was crucial that America realize that there existed other (more important) aspects to the country's relationship with the new Germany than what was revealed by supposedly biased accounts overemphasizing anti-Semitism. Although individual attachés in Europe, like fellow officers back home, might

227

condemn Nazi brutality toward Jews, realistic foreign policy considerations took precedence.

It was a stance also conditioned by decades of institutional racial and anti-Semitic thought, for even after personally observing the human consequences of Nazi repression, attaché attitudes toward Jews did not change appreciably from the views of earlier generations of officers. And such preconditioned attitudes and perspectives definitely colored the lens through which current officers viewed the characteristics and plight of European Jews. Throughout the Third Reich, attachés left the distinct impression that little could, or should, be done to change the conditions of Jews in Germany. Certainly no American action should risk jeopardizing key U.S. interests. Nor should America address the problem by opening up its shores to provide a place of refuge for Jews, as this would only transplant the Jewish problem from Europe to America.

The View from Europe

"Upon my arrival here in August 1933," wrote Captain James C. Crockett, "I at once perceived there were two definite schools of thought among the military attaches." One treated Germany as a nation conquered by "a victorious allied force"; the other "viewed Germany as a rising great power not to be permanently restricted by the Treaty." There were, in essence, "the enemies of Germany and the friends of Germany." Since Crockett belonged to the latter, he earned "much unpopularity, except in the German Army, where [he had] made many good friends."[2]

The attitudes of one side were, in part, a reaction against Nazism and fascism. "Intolerable" was the way General Robert C. Richardson assessed the Hitler and Mussolini regimes.[3] Many in this group were also Anglophiles, tilting almost instinctively away from things German. These sentiments were reinforced by memories of the sacrifices of World War I and the lingering effects of anti-German wartime propaganda.

Those supportive of Germany, on the other hand, were rarely, if ever, pro-Nazi. Their sympathies rested with the "old Germany" of admirable cultural and scientific achievements. American officers perceived the Nazis as radicals from below who threatened respectable society and institutions. "It was the German civilians from the 'lower depths' not the army officers whom we had to fear."[4] Without hesitation, American officers condemned Nazi brutality and repression as acts of barbarism unacceptable in civilized society.

Still, these officers recognized, occasionally admired, certain of Hitler's accomplishments. Economic recovery had ended despair and the depression; resurgent nationalism had renewed pride; but, above all, Hitler had saved the country from communism. And concerns about a rearmed Germany turning westward were offset by the prospect of a stronger Germany protecting Europe from Soviet military might.[5] The Germanophiles hoped that traditional German society could restrain the radicalism of the Third Reich, perhaps eventually topple the regime. Diplomats and generals might temper Nazi extremism in foreign policy, while social and religious leaders curbed the uncivilized treatment of German citizens, Christian and Jew alike.

The American military attaché in Berlin until 1935, Colonel Jacob Wuest, always bluntly described the "terroristic methods" and nature of the Third Reich. Unlike other observers, Wuest dismissed as "childish arguments" the anti-Semitic claims that Jews were not really Germans and were at the root of Germany's "woes." The "fanatical attack and . . . hatred against" Jews in the early months of the regime was sop to "satisfy the mob"; the "better classes in most cases [were] emphatic in their disapproval of the cruel treatment of the Jews." In a lecture at the War College two years later, he would condemn the "terroristic handling of their own people."[6]

Nonetheless, even Wuest was optimistic about the future. Confident in the "better classes" and "saner members of the party," he expected a less radical regime; for years, he kept alluding to a possible monarchist restoration. Writing in 1933, Wuest commented, "Hitler himself is more moderate now that he has responsibility for the nation. . . . [W]ith proper control [by Göring and Goebbels], these outstanding men can serve Germany well, in restoring its old discipline and national pride." He described early Nazi Germany as "more cheerful," disciplined, and "united than ever before, in a strong centralized government of force—a thing which the average citizen understands far better than liberal rule." Even after the Night of the Long Knives in June 1934, when the bloody purge of Storm Trooper leaders exposed the murderous nature of Hitler's rule, Wuest kept his faith in the moderating forces of traditional German society.

Wuest's inclinations did not escape the notice of William E. Dodd, American ambassador to Germany, who appraised the colonel as "a good man with many contacts, but to whom the German "military appeal is strong." Dodd, a liberal New Dealer, complained that Wuest "instinctively approves of the army drills and demonstrations—contradictory as these are to the interests of the United States."[7]

Wuest's replacement, Colonel Truman Smith, though born at West Point, graduated from Yale and did graduate work in history at Columbia. Smith belonged to the old-stock American elite. His family had resided in New England since the seventeenth century, his grandfather was a Connecticut senator, and his father, a career officer, died fighting at Cebu, in the Philippines. Intelligent and competent, he arrived with both fluency in German and extensive experience in the country. As a young officer, Smith had served as assistant military attaché in Berlin (1920–1924), and he would soon emerge as the army's expert on Germany. While he had "extreme difficulty" with Dodd, Smith "worked in the closest harmony" with Hugh R. Wilson, who became ambassador in 1937. The two men had earlier established a friendship while serving together in Germany during the early 1920s and appeared to have mutual professional admiration for each other. They shared reports; and Wilson revised certain dispatches after consulting Smith.

Generally fond of Germany, Wilson fell into that category of Foreign Service officers who "viewed Nazi Germany through the filter of communism." A supporter of appeasement even after Munich, Wilson favored turning Hitler eastward to "take care of" Soviet Russia. He opposed those "certain elements" in America trying to get the United States into the war against the wishes of the majority.[8] Wilson also admired Hitler's social programs for diminishing the appeal of communism.

Wilson's attitudes were fairly typical of the American embassy. Colonel Smith's wife, Katharine, complained that upon her return from Nazi Germany, Americans always expected one "to describe horrors" about that country, because U.S. newspapers only "stressed Jewish troubles and warlike preparations" while ignoring the "favorable side" of Germany. Under Hitler, she attested, German cities were safe again because "all the drunks, bums, homosexuals, etc. had been put in concentration camps." As she explained it, "this was the original purpose of the concentration camp, to house arbeits scheu (. . . those who did not want to work)."[9]

Colonel Smith already knew a good deal about Nazism before his arrival in Germany in 1935. He held the honor of having been the first American to interview Hitler. In November 1922, almost exactly one year before the famous Nazi Beer Hall Putsch in Munich, Hitler had spoken frankly to him about the early goals of the National Socialist movement: a national dictatorship to replace democracy, a war against Bolshevism, and withdrawal of Jewish citizenship. But Smith doubted Hitler possessed the "political genius" to become master of Germany,[10] and he remained skeptical until Hitler actually seized power. As a student at the Army War College in December 1932, Smith helped write a lengthy strategic survey of Germany, predicting that the Nazis had passed their peak and were unlikely to succeed. A month later, the Weimar Republic collapsed when Hindenburg appointed Hitler chancellor.[11]

In his individual spring 1933 report, Smith reversed himself, making Weimar's doom appear inevitable and German democracy a historical anomaly. "The Hitlerite revolution," Smith wrote, "constituted in no way any radical departure from historic trends of German political thought." Nazism merely took Germany "from unaccustomed Democracy to accustomed authoritative government . . . [which] is best suited to the political genius of the German people." He now expected Hitler to "establish a personal dictatorship," eliminate all political opposition, and "reduce the Jewish influence in all phases of German life." But "no radical changes in her foreign policy" were anticipated, because of Germany's weakness and the constraints the army would exercise on Hitler.[12]

Contrary to popular ludicrous portrayals of Hitler, Smith regarded him as a "Mohammed and not a Charlie Chaplin." Driven by a fanatical sense of destiny, backed up by German power and determination, Hitler had to be handled with extreme caution. Smith urged what soon became known as appeasement rather than resistance by the West, for he was convinced that "Hitler, the Army and the Party want an understanding" with England and France. "Once the Western European nations sit down around a table, a solution of most of the world ills will not be difficult to find." The alternative would be too catastrophic for Western civilization itself to even contemplate. Smith cautioned:

> I believe very firmly that if the British or anybody else try a policy of intimidation towards Germany, such a policy will only result in a blood bath and with the dissolution of society as we know it.[13]

Smith was aided by several assistant attachés and American officers studying at the Kriegsakademie (German War College). Smith and his assistants renewed old contacts and established new ones with their German counterparts until most had "many friends and acquaintances in the German army." Smith cultivated German officers he had known at Fort Benning, Georgia, whereas Crockett, on his own time unofficially attended the Kriegsakademie. Many of these close friendships endured through World War II. The mutual professional admiration and respect American and

German officers had for each other reinforced prevalent sympathies of U.S. officers for traditional German society. These relationships strengthened the desire among American and German officers to maintain good relations between their countries and to keep the United States out of any European conflict.[14]

Although all of those Americans at the Kriegsakademie would rise to the rank of general, most noteworthy was Albert C. Wedemeyer, who became a close friend of Smith. Young Captain Wedemeyer was certainly influenced immensely by his German teachers and his two years in Nazi Germany. "Not that I approved of the Nazi regime or condoned its brutalities," he later wrote, but "I had come to see Germany in a different light from most of my contemporaries."

Even after World War II, Wedemeyer placed responsibility for the rise of Nazism on England and France, vengeful victors of World War I who "denied justice, self-respect, and opportunity" for economic survival to the Germans. While condemning Hitler's methods and "treatment of the Jews," Wedemeyer credited the Nazi dictator with overcoming this "repression" and restoring Germany to dignity and power. Wedemeyer recognized as pure propaganda much of what was taught at the Kriegsakademie about the "Bolshevik menace," but he also learned "a great deal of truth about Communist aims, practices, and methods unknown or ignored in America." His instructors convinced him that Nazi expansionism posed a far lesser threat to the West than "the world-wide Communist conspiracy centered in Moscow."[15] When barred from lectures by the renowned geopolitical theorist Karl Haushofer at the Kriegsakademie, which the Wehrmacht kept *geheim* (top secret), Wedemeyer acquired "appropriate reading material" on Haushofer's geopolitical thought from a German general who had befriended the American captain. Although he later downplayed Haushofer's influence on his own strategic thinking, Wedemeyer's explanation of the Nazi doctrine of *Lebensraum* clearly bore the intellectual mark of Haushofer, from whom Hitler borrowed this concept.

Wedemeyer completely ignored Nazi racial ideology and the extermination of European Jewry, as well as the destruction, exploitation, and enslavement in Nazi dominated eastern Europe. As late as 1958, he explained *Lebensraum* as merely "a national movement to win 'living space,' meaning sources of raw materials and markets, territory sparsely inhabited by more backward peoples." Consciously or unconsciously, Wedemeyer drew the same historical analogies Nazi theorists and propagandists used to justify *Lebensraum*. He compared the eastward expansion of the Germans "to Americans whose forefathers had wrested half a continent from the Indians, the Spanish, and the Mexicans, [and] to the British who had conquered an empire 'upon which the sun never set.'" The "compulsions" for empire, Wedemeyer argued in Haushoferian terms, grew directly out of "the dynamic force of self-preservation."[16]

The image Americans had of Germans as the "most belligerent of peoples" Wedemeyer also berated as "propaganda" emanating from "superficial or prejudiced articles by popular journalists." There were those "who wanted to make us fear and hate the Germans in order to get us into war and [bring about] the destruction of Germany." To Wedemeyer, "the fevered imagination of Roosevelt and his speech-writers" greatly exaggerated the threat of Nazi Germany: "All that I had ever learned in my studies of history . . . caused me to oppose an untimely American intervention in World War II."[17]

Officers with limited experience in Germany, such as Major Ralph C. Smith, also came away quite favorably impressed by the Third Reich. While serving together at Fort Leavenworth, Truman Smith and Ralph C. Smith (military attaché in Paris after World War II) established a close lifelong friendship. After studying at the Army War College in 1934–1935, Ralph C. Smith was detached the following year to the École Supérieure de Guerre, the French equivalent of the Kriegsakademie. While Germany hosted the Olympics in August 1936, Ralph C. Smith and his wife, Madeleine, departed on a long auto tour through Germany into Eastern Europe.[18]

Wherever they traveled, from small towns along the romantic Rhine to densely populated industrial cities in the North, the Smiths were greatly impressed by the achievements of Hitler's regime. Again and again, they encountered only a united, "wholesome," "healthy and vigorous" people who loved nature; there were "fine shops" and an abundance of good food. Neither could one fail to appreciate the uniform manifestations of order, efficiency, and cleanliness. Unlike England, the German industrial centers of Essen and Hanover were "very clean," with "an amazing number of parks"; the Smiths were "struck by the fields of grain and gardens" in the midst of factories.

Germany was the land of natural "blondes like Jean Harlow," of organized groups of boys and girls who "march and sing and seem as happy as can be"; indeed, "all the people look well-dressed, happy and contented." Always friendly, Germans greeted Americans in particular with warmth and hospitality.[19]

When the Smiths visited the German family with which Major Smith had been billeted during the American occupation of the Rhineland, they found the Hermans "very delighted with the regime." They kept "a beautiful crayon picture of Hitler." Frequently, the Smiths also saw "the straight-arm salute, but there is certainly nothing offensive about it." The Smiths felt the Germans "have greater liberty, in their disciplined way, than we have seen in some countries where liberty has become license." They summed up their overall assessment of the current system as to be avoided if possible but felt that it worked "well in Germany for Germans."[20]

The Smiths certainly preferred these conditions to those in chaotic France with its Popular Front government, where a car with the American flag was met with the Communist salute. Other striking contrasts became immediately apparent when they left East Prussia and journeyed into Poland. Although the rich soil was the same as on the German side of the border, the Smiths observed the fields and roads showed serious neglect. They judged this a consequence of a negligent Eastern European society, further evidenced by the reliance upon horses and wagons, and "many barefoot," "poorly dressed" people. When they reached Breslau, the Smiths exclaimed: "[W]e were so happy to be back in Germany again."[21]

The Smiths noticed surprisingly little about the conditions of Jews during this monthlong trip through Nazi Germany. Evidently, the only Jew they spoke with was "a Jewish engineer, one of the acceptable type," who was not German. All they mentioned about him was that he had come from Palestine and was driving a big Buick on a tour similar to theirs. The Smiths remembered Jewish stores in Essen and "a Jewish school and Synagogue and many Jewish shops" in Hanover. The only hint of Nazi anti-Semitism was one sentence in a report Smith filed after returning from Bavaria: "Propaganda against Jews was noted in all villages and such posters as 'JEWS NOT WANTED HERE' were seen."[22]

Military couriers who traveled routinely from Paris to the major capitals of Europe also attested to German contentment with the Third Reich. But the information that couriers provided on the plight of Jews, though sparse, left no doubt of the hardships inflicted by policies such as the Nuremberg Laws, which withdrew citizenship from Jews and made racial segregation the law of the land. "The situation of thousands of young Jews in Germany today" was typified by the end of a promising career due to the "stigma" of one Jewish parent.[23]

The former military attaché to Vienna, Colonel Joseph Baer, saw the Austrian-Jewish question in a much broader context. Baer belonged to the old school within the officer corps. Born in 1878 and a 1900 graduate of West Point, where he taught for several years, Baer was a veteran of Cuba and the Philippines. His postwar career had been divided between the Army War College (student, 1920–1921; instructor, 1923–1924) and the General Staff. And his observations from Vienna were colored by the racial perspectives so prevalent at the War College and other military institutions of the 1920s.

In 1933, Baer informed the MID chief that the Jewish question contained the seeds for sweeping political upheaval in Central Europe, which would then cascade across the continent. He equated the magnitude of *"Jew Question"* with the volatility caused by the Versailles Treaty. These alone were the "two questions" that could upset the peace "not only of Central Europe but of Europe itself." While Versailles was discussed endlessly, he believed "the question of the *Jew* ... [was] not understood outside Europe, [even though] it affects all other questions and problems in Europe."

In Baer's historical account, no Jewish problem existed in Central Europe prior to the twentieth century. Earlier, numerous "rich, influential and respected Jewish families" inhabited the region; "the cleverest bankers, physicians, lawyers and artists were Jews [who] were not only tolerated but were given a definite place." This long-standing social harmony and acceptance changed drastically when persecuted Russian Jews fled Galicia in "a continuous migration" into Central Europe. Baer explained that the success of the well-established "old Jews" had derived from "their innate cleverness," which allowed them to be social and economic contributors, whereas "these later Jews, these Galician Jews, are merely parasites."

The modern Jewish problem in Austria originated thereafter, he argued, when the "older Jews helped the new ones to gain a foothold"; thus began the insidious Jewish takeover, as "innate Jewish cleverness took advantage of this situation." The problem became so acute that a graduate of Vienna University, "unless he is *a Jew*, will find it impossible to make a living in law, medicine, journalism, finance, music, or art, no matter how talented. He merely just doesn't get a show."[24]

Ignorance of this real economic and social situation, Baer said, initially led him to completely misconstrue events in Vienna. Thus, he "had made light of the anti-Jewish riots in the University of Vienna." These outbreaks struck him as mere youthful "effervescence"—"a good football season could have wiped them out." Gradually he discovered that "the disturbances were entirely political," for they were always an aggression of Christian students against Jewish ones. This was the key to understanding Hitler's "extremely popular" reputation in Austria.

Hitler's "solution of the *Jew question* was . . . to solve by force a [similar German] condition." His program "to throw out the Jews and give their jobs to Christians" immediately resonated across Austria, since "in no other way could the white-collar jobs fall into the hands of the present young Christian generation." Soon, "the Jew question will be serious" and, together with economic hardship and nationalism, would probably bring Austria into the German orbit.[25]

Baer indeed painted a bleak picture for the future. The prevailing idea everywhere, he wrote, was that war held the only solution to the "scrambled" racial polyglot of Central Europe. The League of Nations ("pasteboard sanctions"), like "altruism," were illusions; "force only will prevail," and with it "racial oppression." "All hesitate to precipitate a war" for one reason only—the "stark fear that in the next war, the loser will be wiped out as a nation, absorbed if not exterminated." In this region, Baer concluded, "racial hate is again almost medieval." He added ominously that "a silly overt act may precipitate a world catastrophe."[26]

Baer's replacement in 1933, Colonel Martin C. Shallenberger, Pershing's former aide-de-camp and son of a Nebraska governor, had little to say on the subject of Jews. He suggested that the "better class jewish element" ("bourgeois Jews" and "rich ones") had accommodated themselves to the authoritarian regime that governed Austria after 1934. Accommodation was the lesser evil and offered "protection against the Hakenkreuz type of anti-Semitism" exhibited by the Nazis. Shallenberger's information, though brief, reflected better the complexities of Austria's Jewish community than Baer had intimated. "The rich Jews," he noted, preferred the "anti-Marxist policies of the present government," which freed them from social welfare taxation and protective labor laws. The socialist Jews, primarily "the smaller and poor type Jews," lost out completely in every respect. Whether he was cognizant of it or not, Shallenberger's brief explanations contained an implicit refutation of the myth of Jewish solidarity and Communist proclivity at the root of so much anti-Semitism.[27]

Yet Shallenberger's estimate of the basic Austrian attitude toward Jews differed only slightly from Baer's. The "final solution of the Austrian Jewish problem," as proposed by the right-wing Heimwehr, he wrote in 1934, called for denying citizenship and equal rights to the Galician Jews who immigrated after 1914. It would clearly be the approach preferred by "the best thinking Austrians . . . were it feasible to attempt a solution" directly.[28]

While the General Staff learned about the Jewish question in Austria, Truman Smith remained silent about developments in Germany, deliberately eschewing the issue for most of his four-year tour. In his view, the Jewish question belonged properly within the competence of the State Department; as a rule, he "de-emphasized political reporting to avoid a possible conflict of views with the Embassy." The one exception was if Nazi anti-Semitism "breeds hostility or friendliness to Germany in foreign countries which, perchance, may be of military-political significance to her."

Smith was far from ignorant on the subject. From his earliest analyses at the War College in 1933, he recognized that Hitler's anti-Semitic policies could cause a serious breach in German-American relations. "Germany is liable to do all in its power," Smith forecasted, "to conciliate America, short of changing her Jewish cosmetic policy," for he believed that Hitler was ardent in his racial and anti-Semitic ideology.[29]

To Smith, anti-Semitism "contributed materially" to Hitler's success because "Germany's Jews rapidly increased both their political and financial power in the unsettled post war period." Although the Nazis greatly exaggerated how much Jewish bankers and speculators profited from the Great Inflation, he argued, "there can be no doubt that by 1926 [Jews] possessed financial and industrial power far in excess of their numerical strength." They further antagonized Germans by "display[ing] their wealth throughout Germany's years of misery (1921–1924) in anything but an unostentatious manner," so much so that the "profiteer" was usually caricatured "as a Jew."

In politics, "their representations [were] also important," including "the father of the Constitution" and "Jewish leadership in the Communist Party." Thus, Hitler definitely intended "to reduce materially Jewish power and influence in Germany," though initially he might not be as radical or impetuous about it as party programs and propaganda exhorted. It appeared highly improbable, in Smith's words, "that the power of International Jewry will prove strong enough to alter materially the Hitler anti-Semitic measures."[30]

Actually, there was much more to Smith's perspective on the Jewish question than such official reports indicate. He personally believed that international Jewish power extended to the United States, where Jews exercised considerable "control" in American society. He later became convinced it was "that crowd" who tried to destroy his military career after he returned from Germany. In the 1950s, he expressed admiration for the writings of John Beaty, whose anti-Semitic works attempted to prove Jewish control and subversion of America.[31]

Smith had high regard for and kept a personal copy of Houston Stewart Chamberlain's *The Foundations of the Nineteenth Century*. That was the same work that the racial psychologist McDougall had recommended to officers at the War College and that provided a theoretical foundation for Nazi ideology and *Mein Kampf*. Urging Beaty to read Chamberlain, Smith praised the lengthy section on the Jews as "authoritative." He was referring to the passages in which Chamberlain condemned the Jews as an eternally "alien Asiatic race" and natural enemy of the Aryans and all their higher ideals. By modern times, Chamberlain argued, this insidious Jewish foe was on the verge of enslaving the Aryans by controlling "our government, our justice, our science, our business, our literature, our art." Aryans and Jews were engaged in a decisive racial and spiritual war for the survival of higher Western civilization.[32]

As already noted, Wedemeyer, perhaps Smith's closest friend among the military personnel in Berlin, likewise had strong convictions about Jews. It was only his attendance at the Kriegsakademie in 1936, he later said, that opened his eyes to the number of Jews in the American government. Only after reading *Die Frankfurter Zeitung* and *Die Berliner* in Nazi Germany did he fully comprehend the implications of the Jewish advisers around Roosevelt.[33]

The Nazis had subjected German Jews to barbaric persecutions, Wedemeyer later conceded, but the media had exaggerated their extent. And Jews collectively and individually provoked part of this repression by their own behavior. To Wedemeyer, Jews had historically displayed inherent abrasive, obnoxious, and selfish traits that made them eternally "suspect or distasteful and incompatible" with other groups.[34]

In July 1937, while commenting on the Hitler-Mussolini alliance, Wedemeyer noted that, despite Nazi anti-Semitism, in Italy "Jews provide gold" for Italian armaments and expansion. That November, Wedemeyer tied the current German food shortage to the Jewish question. Writing to friends on embassy attaché stationery, he dismissed public explanations of poor weather and disease in favor of a cause only "whispered" about. Jews in other countries, including America, he wrote, had apparently bought up enormous quantities of food and grain and intentionally redirected their sale away from Germany. While admitting such Jewish action seemed "fantastic," Wedemeyer was very receptive to its probability, since he had learned this from a "level-headed" American banker with extensive experience in Germany.[35]

One year later, on the night of November 9, 1938, the Nazis suddenly unleashed an organized pogrom across Germany, destroying most synagogues and hundreds of Jewish businesses. Physical assaults on thousands of Jews resulted in about 100 murders; around 30,000 Jews were temporarily incarcerated in concentration camps. This infamous Kristallnacht (Night of Broken Glass) pogrom was followed by some of the most oppressive anti-Semitic policies of the Third Reich. The critical response abroad to this state-sponsored violence was immediate and harsh. American ambassador to Germany Hugh Wilson wrote in his diary: "The full tale of these Jewish attacks becomes known and one experiences a sensation akin to nausea."[36]

Roosevelt's vigorous protests against the Nazis received strong support from the American Legion and CIO. Herbert Hoover broadcast a statement condemning the "outrage" against civilized behavior, which had its equal only in Bolshevik violence. When Roosevelt recalled Ambassador Wilson, the public at large gave its general approval.[37]

The anti-Nazi backlash in the United States caused by Kristallnacht brought Smith's intelligence work to a standstill. The previous years of valuable cooperation of German officers ceased, the special privileges long enjoyed by American officers "were abruptly curtailed," and Smith's "espionage system" collapsed. "From that moment," Smith thought, "both Hitler and the German Army reckoned with the probability of America's entry into a European conflict."[38]

The Jewish question he had neglected for the past six years was now in Smith's purview. "The United States is unfriendly to Germany because of Anti-Semitism," and this had serious long-range military consequences. In his reports to Washington, however, Smith emphasized this catastrophic outcome did not have to materialize. Implicit in his arguments was that the "Recent Anti-Semitic Measures of Germany" should not interfere with America's real national interest, which dictated accommodation rather than war with Germany.

Between the Munich Agreement's ceding the Sudetenland to Germany in September 1938 and Hitler's illegal occupation of the rest of Czechoslovakia in March 1939, Smith still maintained that Germany posed no threat to the West. The United States and the Western Hemisphere were in no danger, despite alarms sounded by the Roosevelt administration. "Hitlerian Germany is pursuing to-day a 100% Eastern Policy," he tried to persuade Washington. Hitler really sought an economic empire of satellite states in Eastern Europe, and ultimately land for German colonization in Russia. Germany, Smith reported, "has given up totally the plan, if she ever had had such a plan since 1919, of attacking France, Great Britain, South America, Australia, or Mars."[39]

' Whether dealing with Nazi foreign policy or anti-Semitism, American journalists in Berlin had, Smith emphasized, overlooked a crucial factor. "Anti-Semitism has been in America neither respectable nor good form," but it was "a powerful force" in Eastern Europe and perhaps the "most trenchant" weapon Hitler had in advancing his Eastern-oriented policy. Smith speculated that several governments in the region could not survive without exploiting anti-Semitism. Over a period of months, he repeatedly made the point that "the advantages accruing to [Germany] from Anti-Semitism in Eastern Europe" outweighed the "losses this policy will bring" or the "hostility engendered" in the United States and England.[40]

Under these circumstances, Smith sat down and wrote his first lengthy analysis on "Anti-Semitism in Germany." In contrast to the "American 'melting pot theory,'" Nazi racial ideology classified the Jews as an Asiatic race "incapable of assimilation by the German people." Smith likened the Nazis to "the average white inhabitant of Alabama or Georgia, but with a racial feeling towards the Jew, who exists in Germany alongside the German in large numbers, rather than towards the Negro."

When Smith then moved on to explain Nazi perceptions of Jewish characteristics, he abandoned the tentativeness and qualifications of his 1933 War College paper, in which he had made it clear that he was merely repeating Nazi "beliefs" about Jews. Now his unqualified descriptions of Jews in German political and economic life were conveyed more definitively and forcefully.[41]

After introducing the Nazi concept of the Jew as an unredeemable economic "parasite" that "must live off the labors of some other race," Smith underscored that the historical "facts" seemed to support such an interpretation:

It is a *fact* that whereas during the World War and in the decade following, the German people became impoverished, the Jewish element in Germany succeeded in markedly increasing their wealth, in gaining influence within the government, in the intellectual professions and in control of the German cultural institutions such as theaters, universities, the kino and the arts. . . . Equally important was the role of the Jews in the Russian, German, Bavarian and Hungarian revolutions. . . . Furthermore, the international tendencies of Communism appeared to cover exactly with the international tendencies of Jewry.[42]

Smith traced the origins of the Nazi Party to a widespread reaction in Germany against "this sharp and rapid increase in Jewish influence." This response had not emanated merely from Nazi prejudice, for "the political power of German Jewry in the Weimar Republic was self-evident to foreigners as well as to Germans." To support this historically inaccurate contention, Smith claimed that "in the Democratic Party . . . Jewish Influence predominated, and in the Socialist, Independent Socialist and Communist parties, Jewish power was scarcely less important."

The position of German Jews was so "unassailable and their racial allies abroad were even more formidably entrenched," Smith argued, that the Nazi struggle had been a difficult one. More astounding still, Smith attributed the "mild" anti-Semitic policies in the early years of the Third Reich to the fact that Hitler "recognized the international power of Jewry." Nazis efforts to force German Jews to emigrate by gradually increasing pressures on them failed because Jews wanted to "preserve their property" and expected the regime either to collapse or "be crushed militarily by the Western Democracies." It was the Nazi belief—which Smith noted "may have been incorrect"—in an international "Jewish war plot" against Germany during the Czech crisis that largely accounted for Kristallnacht. In response to this real or imagined plot, Hitler finally decided "to proceed with his long planned Jewish surgical operation."[43]

The "national security" against foreign interference acquired at Munich, however, finally allowed Hitler to seek "to liquidate the Jewish problem once and for all." When, in the post-Kristallnacht atmosphere, Smith referred to "the liquidation of that non-German element," he meant specifically the Nazi goal "to expel the Jews finally and completely" and not genocide. But on this point, Smith informed Washington, "no amount of foreign pressure will force" Hitler "to deviate one iota from this *fundamental* element" of his racial ideology.[44]

While never condoning Hitler's actions against the Jews, Smith—the army's eyes and ears in Germany—indicated that Jews were indeed a real problem for Germans. He seemed to convey the idea that there did exist some root cause to which the Nazis were responding. One could not read Smith's dispatches without getting the sense that the Jews, in Weimar and internationally, actually possessed the economic and political power the Nazis attributed to them. It was an impression whose erroneous nature could easily have been detected by any astute observer. Yet Smith used such explanations of Nazi policies to buttress his case against U.S. involvement in a situation he believed America could not hope to change. More important, any U.S. attempts to interfere would be counterproductive and injurious to American national interests.

Smith had little to fear. The American outrage against Germany caused by Kristallnacht never rose beyond verbal condemnation and media protests. Although Nazi violence, followed by the seizure of Jewish property, shocked the American public and sent reverberations throughout the country's social and political institutions, the only discernible effect was a more negative American attitude toward Germany. It was a change in tone that never implied a willingness on the part of most Americans or Congress to initiate any U.S. action against Nazi Germany. Most Americans resented the very thought that Jews, at home or abroad, would increase the chances of war.

American sympathies for the plight of German Jews also stopped abruptly at U.S. borders. Most Americans remained adamantly against admitting Jewish refugees fleeing Nazi Germany. The dramatic events of November 1938 had not changed the negative attitudes toward refugees that Americans had held since the beginning of the Third Reich.[45]

Refugees and Restrictionist Officers

Kristallnacht had certainly not altered the basic view of Jews held by Smith's fellow officers back home. Army officers were no more receptive to refugees than they had been almost a year before, when the Nazis had launched vicious attacks on Austrian Jews. Most officers had long doubted the need for and wisdom of American involvement in the refugee question. They had tenaciously held to this position since the very first American demonstrations in March 1933 against Nazi anti-Semitic actions. The G-2 in New York, Colonel Kenyon A. Joyce, in fact, saw this demonstration as another indication of the "subversive situation" in that metropolitan area. Joyce informed Washington that the protest was against the "alleged mistreatment" of German Jews.

As part of the anti-German protest, however, 20,000 New Yorkers filled Madison Square Garden, while another 35,000 overflowed into nearby streets. Although the American Jewish Congress had organized the rally, that evening cheering crowds also heard long speeches from governors, senators, and Catholic bishops. Other rallies across the country drew 1 million people.[46] But suspecting both the motivation and sincerity of the participants, Joyce classified it among "many demonstrations" staged by "subversive groups." The Communists and Socialists, he surmised, were attempting to organize "liberal and radical political elements against Fascism." Without noting the presence of most prominent speakers, Joyce simply described "the most interesting occurrence [as] the booing and hissing" when the "religious intolerance" of Soviet Russia was mentioned. To Joyce, "this was a clear indication that the assemblage was present to demonstrate for radical doctrine rather than against racial or religious oppression."[47]

When similar demonstrations soon included demands for admitting refugees, restrictionist officers balked. Their ingrained anti-Communist and racist hostility toward immigrants was continually reinvigorated by attachés, who portrayed Jewish immigrants throughout the 1930s as an invariably destabilizing force wherever they resided or migrated.

From the early 1930s, military attachés in Central America complained about the influx of "a large number of Polish Jews"—the "*Polacos.*" These immigrants were "an entirely different type from the native Jews." The older class of "well-to-do, hard-working and intelligent Jews" had mixed racially and socially with the "better class natives," earning respectability in the "highest society." The newcomers were wandering peddlers who cheated ignorant peasants and undercut local businesses. A parasitic, clannish, inassimilable group, they "make no contribution to an increase of national wealth." They "cling to their customs and language" and could "best be described by the term 'Kike.'"[48] Among these "kikes" were "active communists," who created an anti-Semitic backlash against the "whole [Jewish] race for the evils that only the '*Polacos*' typify."[49]

On the refugee question, sentiments like these within the army were in close step with most of American public opinion. Xenophobia, depression-era unemployment, and a strong sense that charity begins at home, together with apathy and callousness toward the sufferings of strangers in a faraway place, only partially explained the American attitude. There was also a resurgence of anti-Semitism, ranging from expressions of traditional ethnic and religious prejudice to virulent, well-organized anti-Semitic crusades by populist extremists.

Although far less socially acceptable in public discourse among the country's elites and the corridors of government, anti-Semitism had not disappeared from private discussions among America's middle and upper classes. At the popular level, it could still captivate and incite readers and audiences across the country. More than 15,000 joined William Dudley Pelley's Fascist Silver Shirts, while hundreds of thousands regularly tuned in to the anti-Semitic radio broadcasts of Father Charles E. Coughlin. Around 100,000 read *Defender Magazine*, in which Reverend Gerald B. Winrod warned of the Jewish-Communist conspiracy to dominate the world.[50]

Public opinion polls in the late 1930s revealed that 53 percent of respondents believed that "Jews were different and should be restricted"; three-fifths attributed undesirable traits to Jews, such as selfishness, dishonesty, and clannishness; 72 percent opposed increasing the number of Jewish refugees allowed into America. Drawing upon this sentiment, restrictionist groups repeatedly thwarted all efforts to alter immigration laws, make exceptions, or otherwise allow America to play a leadership role in the rescue of Europe's Jews.[51]

In this struggle to maintain the tight racial quotas they had helped create in the 1920s, restrictionist officers could not take an active part. The time had passed when officers could, with impunity and encouragement, submit reports to the highest levels of government full of anti-Semitic invectives. The blatant prejudice and routine anti-Semitic jokes that had characterized State Department and attaché reports of the 1920s gave way to an air of professional detachment when dealing with the Jewish question. Yet, their "factual" observations and interpretations conveyed the unmistakable inference that they were still really dealing with the Jewish "problem."

Now, however, Roosevelt was at the helm, and Jews served prominently in his administration. One of Roosevelt's friends and advisers, the foreign-born Felix Frankfurter, had long been regarded by military intelligence as a dangerous Jewish radical. Frankfurter's role in the New Deal, like his controversial appointment to the Supreme Court in 1939, signified to the old guard that they had lost their predominance, perhaps forever. These new political realities deterred even the most racist army officers, particularly those facing promotion or retirement, from engaging in political activity on behalf of restrictionists.

Meanwhile, Nazi racial ideology was under attack in the press as pseudo-science and fanatical bigotry. Attachés were unlikely to hold an attaché conference, similar to the Coblenz gathering in 1921, to urge resistance to dumping the racial inferiors of Eastern Europe on America and to defend the racial purity of the nation's ruling Nordic race.

But some retired officers stood in the forefront of the restrictionist movement, often representing various patriotic or military organizations. Most prominent, relentless, and effective was the American Coalition (an umbrella for about 100 groups), led by Captain John B. Trevor, creator of the 1924 racial quota system. Following its slogan "Keep America American," the American Coalition vigorously resisted the slightest legislative or bureaucratic move to assist refugees, including providing refuge for a mere 250 Jewish children.

Trevor was assisted by retired general Amos Fries, who also held positions with the Sons of the American Revolution, the National Sojourners, and the Military Order of the World War. Both men spent twenty-five years publishing, speaking, and lobbying against immigration. Permanent features on the Washington scene, they testified routinely before every relevant congressional committee. Besides persuasive depression-era economic arguments, restrictionists exploited xenophobia. Relaxation of immigration laws—even facilitating visa applications—would be tantamount to dropping a formidable American defense against Communist infiltration.

When Rabbi Stephen Wise pleaded for admission of persecuted German Jews, Fries argued the Nazis were only persecuting known Communists and their sympathizers. Since such types should definitely be barred from America, the emerging debate on immigration laws had, in his mind, nothing to do with the Jewish question.[52] In public, Trevor and his associates usually eschewed the buzzword "Jew," though proponents and opponents alike knew this was always the issue.

In contrast to earlier immigration debates, the term "Nordic"—now so tainted by its Nazi identification—was no longer uttered by many of its former exponents. But restrictionists had not abandoned their racial views. Fries and Trevor still referred to "blood" affinities when describing American ideas and institutions springing historically from a "homogeneous people," but now diluted and endangered by "new stock immigration" and "the hordes of foreigners that have been admitted prior to 1924."

American political institutions, Fries testified in 1935, could not "stand a wide influx of people who know nothing about our institutions and care less for them." Maintaining current national quotas against pressure to admit refugees was insufficient; the countless undesirable immigrants already residing here must be deported. And immigrants from racially heterogeneous countries must be reduced, so as to return America "to that homogeneity that we had in 1860, in 1776."[53]

The presumed inferiority of recent immigrants was also pointed out to Congress and the public. They came to America because their native land considered them "undesirable" politically, morally, or physically. At one congressional hearing, Trevor had a New York clinical psychologist certify that "mental and social inadequacies" in certain foreign types, were "a serious menace to our civilization and future population."[54]

Although based in Washington, the American Coalition sought support across the country. Fries, Trevor, and other members reached as far as the West Coast in soliciting the assistance of General Van Deman's espionage network. One of Van Deman's major sources in the East, Trevor kept him informed of his work to undermine any effort to admit more German Jews than existing quotas allowed. Discussions with State Department officials, Van Deman was told, had established fundamental agreement with the Coalition on the necessity of resisting mounting pressure from Jewish groups to accommodate refugees.[55]

Someone in Van Deman's network wrote a lengthy report on Samuel Untermeyer, a prominent public figure and refugee advocate. This zealous piece of research and surveillance described him as "the lowest type of human that ever lived" ("a reptile"). Untermeyer supposedly exercised enormous "influence . . . on state, national, and international affairs," especially with regard to "naming co-religionists to key positions in government" such as Louis Brandeis' appointment to the Supreme Court by President Wilson in 1916. The informant alleged that Untermeyer was "organizing international Jewry for a boycott against Nazi Germany" and was also involved "with pro-Communist activities in America."[56]

Some of the Coalition's strongest and most important support came from the American Legion, which opposed any change in immigration laws and lobbied Congress accordingly. The Legion's message for congressional committees on immigration in 1934 was personally conveyed by the chairman of its National Defense Committee—retired general Amos A. Fries. On the eve of World War II, the national commander of the Legion, Stephen F. Chadwick, would still express "heartily" that America "should not become the dumping ground of the political and religious persecuted of Europe, nor even an un-checked receiving station for the helpless persecuted children."[57]

Although hopes of further limitations on immigration remained unfulfilled, restrictionists did thwart all efforts to open America to refugees from Nazi Germany. Despite mounting persecution by the Third Reich and the lack of places of refuge for emigrating Jews, relaxing immigration laws "never received serious consideration in Congress." In the end, the United States admitted proportionally fewer refugees than did England and France. "The primary reason for the failure" to open the gates even a little wider, wrote a prominent immigration historian, "was the opposition of groups traditionally hostile to immigration."[58]

As already noted, restrictionist sentiments within the army would not even change with the intensification of Nazi repression of Jews in 1938. In March of that year, the Germans occupied Austria, and the Nazis immediately launched a campaign to force tens of thousands of Jews out of the country. Austrian Jews were physically abused, arrested, and forcibly deported; almost 2,000 were sent to concentration camps.

In the face of this brutal persecution and the prospect of tens of thousands of additional refugees without care or refuge, the Roosevelt administration took the initiative to have the international community assist in the emigration of Jews out of the Nazi Reich and in resettling them elsewhere. While plans were made for an international conference on the problem at Évian, France, the administration organized a presidential advisory committee on refugees. Roosevelt also tried to soften America's opposition to immigration through a publicity campaign emphasizing the country's idealistic and humanitarian tradition of offering asylum to the oppressed.[59]

Restrictionist officers, however, saw the situation differently; and military attachés increased the doubts about the wisdom of Roosevelt's initiative. Colonel Joseph B. Pate, attaché in Central America, continually reiterated that public opinion and government policy in Costa Rica were staunchly against "the entry . . . of a large number of Jews." Pate apparently had little difficulty with 'high-type' Jews," but he shared the widespread antipathy among officers toward lower-class Easterners. Later, he strongly opposed American and British support for a Palestine solution to the Jewish question. Privately, he expressed the crudest form of vulgar racism, describing a certain politician as the "radical, 'Nigger loving' present incumbent." To Pate, the New Deal represented "varieties of Communism."[60]

Efforts by Roosevelt and Jewish-American organizations, Pate insisted, were counterproductive in Costa Rica. Even the "better class" German Jews possessing financial means were unwelcome. Only "local German Nazis" benefited from attempts to settle Jews there. As late as March 1939, Pate was recommending that "only time and a complete abstention of efforts to have refugees admitted to Costa Rica could, in time, change the situation."[61]

The attaché in Mexico City related similar stories of university students organizing against Jews and of vocal public opposition to "the immigration of German and Austrian Jews," as well as "Polish Jews." Mexican newspapers, Major William F. Freehoff stated, had charged that "these Eastern European Jews"—"undesirables"—were "rapidly absorbing" small Mexican businesses and industries. A Mexican banker told Freehoff (in confidence, since "50% of his clientele are Jews") that "Jews are gradually getting into their hands the commerce of Mexico." Freehoff confirmed press claims that most Jews entered Mexico illegally through graft and bribery. Subsequently, a scandal occurred in Chile, where Jews were accused of bribing and corrupting the Chilean Foreign Service to acquire visas.[62]

In the tense months following the Munich Conference, Major Lowell M. Riley, military attaché in Prague, informed Washington that in Hitler's mind, "the most difficult and serious question between Germany and

Czechoslovakia is the latter's treatment of the Jews." By elevating the Jewish question to such central importance over more pressing political and ethnic tensions tearing the rump Czech state apart, Riley created a grossly distorted picture of events and their causation.

Riley also claimed "60% of the country's wealth" was "in the hands of the Jews" and that only economic control, combined with threats of a "boycott from certain quarters," was restraining the Czechs from enacting "serious measures against the Jews." So far, the Czech government, under pressure from indigenous forces and Nazi Germany, had only taken some "mild" steps by reviewing the citizenship of Jews and outlawing Jewish teachers in schools and universities.[63]

Two days before German troops marched into Czechoslovakia on March 16, 1939, Riley reported that "the Jewish population is extremely nervous . . . and those who can get out of the country are continuing to depart." Although immigration was one of the few options for escaping Nazi oppression, Riley, like many fellow officers, doubted it was in the interest of another country to accept large numbers of Jewish refugees. To him, the Czech case illustrated how foreign and domestic tensions could be unnecessarily aggravated by an influx of these immigrants, thereby shifting the Jewish problem from one arena to another. "The Czechs at large," he wrote, "are rather tolerant to the Jews, rather too tolerant, it might be said." They have "complicated their present situation" by allowing "vast numbers of Jewish refugees from Austria and Germany to enter the country."[64]

Two years earlier, Riley had argued the same point about Poland. Anti-Semitism heightened "as the possibility of transplanting them to some other land decreases."[65] By 1937, the military attaché in Poland, Major John S. Winslow, noted that popular pressures were forcing government action on the Jewish question. The Medical Association banned new Jewish members, while the Bar Association called for a limitation on Jewish lawyers. Strikes and demonstrations by university students coerced the official segregation of Jewish students into the "Bench Ghetto."

There was also violence and intimidation in the streets. "Window-breaking; beating of Jews . . . and other forms of hoodlumism" became common occurrences. All of this was exploited and aggravated by "Jew baiting" political parties. He reported that the Polish government "openly deplores" this spiraling anti-Semitism but never "uses the necessary force to suppress it."[66]

Winslow downplayed these incidents as "anti-Semitic rowdyism" and "minor but open lawlessness." He believed that Jews overreacted to such incidents and was not greatly disturbed by Poles "sticking needles into bearded rabbies." "Chased out of certain parks," he wrote, Jews "shriek that they are being murdered (very rarely true)." Yet Winslow character-ized the situation as so explosive that it could at any moment erupt into widespread violence and destruction. The right provocation could be "the signal for minor pogroms all over the country."[67]

Meanwhile, similar intelligence out of Paris indicated that the influx of Jewish refugees had created "an anti-Jewish movement ... gradually spreading" in parts of France. These ubiquitous foreign Jews, wrote Colonel Sumner Waite, tend to take over: "A year ago in Strasbourg there were 500 Jews, now there are 15,000, many of whom control lucrative commercial enterprises and occupy important positions in the town." The anti-Semitic "undercurrent" and "tension" were so strong that the French army was compelled to police the "entire Jewish section." In Nancy, reac-tion against the newcomers culminated in outbreaks of "serious distur-bances in the Jewish quarter and a Polish Jew was killed."[68]

Resurgent French anti-Semitism had been aroused by more than the large number and activities of immigrant Jews. Age-old suspicions resur-faced about the character and courage of indigenous Jews as well, especially regarding their loyalty and willingness to fight for France. "It was re-marked by many," Waite stated, that the noncombatant support units of the French army, "such as those charged with making issues at the mobi-lization centers, were mostly Jews, while comparatively few were noted in the combat echelons."[69]

Given the long-standing anti-Semitism of many officers, there was nothing really new or distinctive about such depictions of Jews in secret dispatches. However, such secret or privately held notions, together with other racial components of the officer corps' worldview, were about to re-ceive public exposure in their crudest and most extreme form. The reaction against this disclosure would force the army to publicly rebuke one of its most distinguished leaders. It also compelled the army to dispel suspicions that it might as an institution harbor anti-Semitic prejudice or tolerate such attitudes among its officers.

The General Moseley Scandal

The origin of this political storm for the army was the convergence of two seemingly unrelated events. As it happened, Roosevelt's 1938 initiative on refugees coincided with a medical military training course for inactive re-servists at Tulane University in New Orleans. And a guest speaker in that course was the opinionated commander in Atlanta, General George Van

Horn Moseley. It was the wrong time to provide Moseley with a platform. Unable to restrain himself any longer, Moseley bluntly related eugenic ideas he had been expressing for years, but which were now shunned in public discourse of the day.

Moseley, though, felt safe. He was "addressing a group of doctors" who would understand his scientific analysis of "American manpower." And he just naturally placed the refugee question in the dismal context of America's social and hereditary degeneracy: tens of millions suffering from venereal disease, insanity, and feeble-mindedness or engaged in crime. The economic and social crises of depression-era America were "simply by-products of our human frailties." The military consequences were ominous, as "we have the most defective manpower today of any first class nation." The survival of the country and its founding principles were at stake.[70]

Moseley was not a completely cold-hearted Darwinist. Humanitarianism, he said, demanded that America take its fair share of these unfortunate refugees and not allow them to suffer. But since America could ill afford any further degeneracy of its population, this charity stopped at the "individual lives" of the refugees. The country could not take the risk that those thrown out of other countries as "undesirables" would reproduce their own kind in America. Thus, refugees should be accepted only "with the distinct understanding that they all be sterilized before being permitted to embark. Only that way can we properly protect our future."[71]

When Moseley's private talk leaked to the press, the reaction was mixed, with strong feelings on both sides.[72] Moseley put the numerous letters of condemnation, mostly from Jews or other ethnics, in his collection of "disapproval," while he thrived on the abundant individual and organizational support from others. The Reserve Officers' Association in New Orleans praised Moseley for trying to rehabilitate the country's manpower and hoped his initiative would succeed. Herbert Hoover's former military aide, General Campbell B. Hodges, told his mother that Moseley had merely clarified his "stand regarding the refugees and American man-power." It was neither a matter of surprise nor concern, since Moseley was "always very outspoken in his views." On the extreme side, retired colonel Pearson B. Brown, commander of the Protestant War Veterans, wrote of the alien Jewish-Communist conspiracy to enslave America.[73]

Considering what Moseley had said and the protests that flooded the office of the secretary of war, the General Staff response was low-keyed. Initially at least, Moseley could count on his old friends near the top.

Sending along an article, General Lorenzo D. Gasser joked about Moseley "still belong[ing] to the head-line folk" and praised him for the "great success" he always achieved. Although not sharing Moseley's extremism, Gasser came out of the same tradition. He had attended the Army War College when instruction in racism and eugenics was at its peak; occasionally, Gasser expressed such views himself. But stationed in Washington, and perhaps lacking Moseley's self-righteousness, Gasser made his personal gesture but risked no more.[74]

General Malin Craig, chief of staff, also took a lighthearted approach— for a few days at least. Craig informed Moseley that quite a stir had been created over remarks he had made "about refugees who might be shipped to this country." As Craig phrased it, the uproar concerned "a certain surgical operation which should be performed upon these refugees before they should be allowed to enter this country." And there were strong demands that Moseley "be taken to task." After joking about a letter from New York, Craig merely requested that he be informed sometime of what had really been said. How little importance Craig attached to the whole affair surfaces in his last sentence: "I just wish to be prepared to continue to poo-pooh the alleged ideas expressed and published by the papers. Good luck!"[75]

Two days later, Moseley apologized to Craig. But on the very next line, he exclaimed: "Why is it when anyone goes after the Communists, Jews here and there rise up with the feeling that they are being attacked? Does the charge fit?" The refugees were not all Jews, and he was positive that he never used the word "Jew"; he had a lifelong Jewish friend in Chicago. Moseley then basically confirmed the newspaper accounts of his lecture, concluding that "America will stand or fall according to the virility, dependability, loyalty and patriotism of her people." As unyielding and self-assured as ever, Moseley told Craig: "I am perfectly willing to go to jail."[76]

Although the army contained this first Moseley incident, it had sustained publicity damage. Henceforth, the military determined to protect itself against charges of anti-Semitism that might sully its reputation or cause it political problems. Roosevelt's secretary of war, Harry H. Woodring, was certainly in no mood to tolerate anything similar from military personnel.

The following month, a retired officer, Captain Hunter McGuire, was discovered in Washington distributing an anti-Semitic leaflet ("The Truth About Jews in Germany") and allegedly "customarily uttering" the following: "This is a good day to kill a damn Jew." Woodring reacted swiftly. He ordered MID chief Colonel E.R.W. McCabe to have McGuire "cease such activities," which were "entirely inappropriate to a retired Army officer and may bring discredit upon the service."[77]

The army projected itself as an institution that would tolerate neither racism nor anti-Semitism. As Colonel McCabe explained in his memorandum to the adjutant general, "in the opinion of this office, the inciting of racial prejudice and hatred by a retired Army officer is distinctly reprehensible." Yet policy statements aimed at redeeming and protecting the army were hypocritical. Due in part to a racist worldview, the military maintained a racially segregated army and vigorously resisted any talk from progressive political circles about altering this situation in the slightest way.

Until the end of his life, McCabe himself remained a resolute defender of "white supremacy," who, when among trusted fellow officers and friends, expressed his own racial prejudice in the most vulgar terms. Son of a Civil War hero and notable educator from Richmond, Virginia, McCabe remarked that labor leaders and integrationists constituted a greater threat to America and the white race than Stalin. Using images reminiscent of Stoddard's *Rising Tide of Color*, he urged segregationists to awaken to the need to keep the South a white man's country rather than allow it to decay into a land of half-breeds. As G-2 chief, McCabe opened his annual lecture on military intelligence at the War College with the same racist story about "colored divisions," complete with derogatory humor and accents.[78]

A 1931 War College graduate and former attaché to Mussolini's Italy, McCabe belonged to the old guard of intelligence officers who served at the center of that division during the height of its nativist and anti-Semitic phase. In fact, he ran the attaché section in 1922, when some of the worst racist and anti-Semitic material was requested from and submitted by officers abroad. At the end of 1938, he could still tell the chief of staff, "actually it is difficult to distinguish between the various Slavic races."

But like most of his class and profession, McCabe found religious intolerance and anti-Semitic violence repulsive. While attaché in Prague, he had expressed outrage at the destruction of synagogues by anti-Semitic mobs. Similarly, he related easily to certain assimilated Jews of equal or superior social standing. McCabe had the greatest admiration for the American minister in Prague, Lewis Einstein. Nonetheless, when praising Einstein, McCabe still felt compelled to alert his fellow attaché that Einstein "is a Jew," and then added, "but his wife is a Gentile."

Later, when Moseley neared the peak of his anti-Semitic crusade and was speaking across the country about Jewish conspiracies, McCabe reassured the general of their cherished friendship. He completely agreed with Moseley that certain "enemies from within" had created an "extreme dangerous situation" for America.[79]

The army had not silenced Moseley for long. On September 30, 1938, the day of his mandatory retirement, Moseley issued a veiled attack on the New Deal as a disastrous path toward dictatorship and ruin reminiscent of the fall of Rome. The current government, Moseley said, was manipulated by the "alien element in our midst." Americans must awaken to the "sinister" motives of these wrong sorts of immigrants, who seek to replace "our system with their own un-American theories of government." Against these subversives, the army "stands firm as the one stable element in an unstable and shifting domestic scene."[80] Although Woodring again publicly reprimanded Moseley in the harshest terms, he failed to contain this affair as he had the sterilization episode. Neither Moseley nor the press would let the incident die.[81]

Public reaction and press coverage of the latest Moseley controversy was extensive and mixed. While many felt satisfied by Woodring's swift, forceful rebuke and his assurances that Moseley did not reflect the sentiments of the army, the general had his supporters. The annual convention of the Military Order of the World War in New Orleans adopted a resolution commending Moseley's military service. Retired general Johnson Hagood, who after his own earlier showdown felt himself a Roosevelt victim, congratulated Moseley "for what you did and how you did it." Former president Herbert Hoover commented that Woodring's smear attacks made his "blood boil" and warned Moseley not to expect those in power to act in any other way. Hoover then welcomed Moseley to the class of those devoting "the balance of their lives to trying to save the Republic."[82]

The prestigious *Army and Navy Journal* rose to the defense of Moseley's "carefully considered" views, devoting a good deal of space over the next several months to his distinguished military career and speeches. Woodring had been "compelled" by political reasons to rebuke Moseley, the editors said, but he privately had not lost his admiration for the general. And perhaps they were well informed on this point.[83]

Three days after the Moseley-Woodring confrontation, chief of staff Craig informed the general that his public chastisement had been a politically necessary sham. Moseley's replacement (an old friend and classmate), General Stanley D. Embick, would tell him "exactly what happened, which will obliterate . . . any feeling that the War Department, which includes Mr. Woodring, has in any way changed or is not devoted to you both personally and officially." Craig went on, "Never since I have known you, have you ever been anything but a dependable, clear-headed friend and supporter." Craig's loyalty and friendship remained as strong as ever; he offered whatever information or help Moseley might need in the future.[84]

A few months later, General Gasser—soon to be deputy chief of staff—told Moseley that his own current experience within the government left him amazed that American democracy had survived. He wondered how long it would continue. "Organized minorities," Gasser wrote, were increasingly dominating the entire government and manipulating it to acquire preferential treatment in their selfish interests and to the detriment of the nation as a whole. Not only had Gasser confirmed the core of Moseley's public assertions, but his foreboding as well. From Gasser's inside view, things had progressed so far as to make him deeply pessimistic that this "dominant influence" could ever be checked.[85]

The criticism at the Officer's Club in Fort Sill, Oklahoma, was not of Moseley's views, but that he challenged the administration. As explained by Colonel Bailey, an officer worried about his own advancement, Moseley had done "a very unwise and unwarranted thing that will do the army no good." During the 1920s, that same officer had given numerous public talks similarly decrying the decay of America caused by the inferior blood, self-serving politics, and subversion of immigrants. Bailey had urged the same political call to arms to save America from these insidious alien forces. But then such sentiments were in perfect tune with the currents of the time.[86]

An undaunted fighter and dogmatic thinker, Moseley would not be silenced; if anything, he had been unleashed. His burgeoning political ambitions were only encouraged by his sudden demand as a speaker across the country. Here was an illustrious national figure, willing to confront the administration, who might rally popular support. Recognized by even his staunchest critics as a brave soldier and brilliant general, Moseley had twice won the Distinguished Service Medal. His fearless courage was legendary. But his admirers would soon discover that his personality, charisma, and speaking ability fell far short of his reputation.

Initially sought by reputable New Deal opponents, as he progressed down the extremist path, Moseley would become the hope of radical rightist, anti-Semitic, and Fascist groups. At each step he became more explicit in identifying the source of America's problems and its real domestic enemies.

Speaking before the National Christian Convention in Cincinnati on Armistice Day 1938, Moseley called for the restoration of American democracy against government by the "political dollar." He demanded a greater role for the church in renewing the family and community. He lashed out at Roosevelt for a wasteful military buildup and the "war hysteria" justifying it; and he urged nonintervention in Europe. Moseley reiterated these same points before leading industrialists of the New York Board of Trade, where John Trevor spoke as well. He was then off to Boston and Philadelphia.[87]

As emboldened by his popularity as he was indignant by mounting criticism, in early 1939 Moseley became overt in his anti-Semitism. At the National Defense Meeting in the City of Brotherly Love, he said: "The war now proposed is for the purpose of establishing Jewish hegemony throughout the world." While "your sons and mine" would fight side by side with Christian-killing Communists, only the Jews would profit. He then interjected what had been widely circulated by MID in the 1920s: The Jewish firm Kuhn, Loeb, and Company had "financed the Russian Revolution." Americans must not let history repeat itself.[88]

Vacillating between claims that he was only reacting to recent Jewish attacks on him and assertions that he had "studied this problem of the Jew for a long time," Moseley revealed a deep obsession with Jews. They controlled the media, possibly the cities of New York and Philadelphia, and were about to dominate the federal government. They had "attempted to kill one of our most important [though unidentified] citizens" and were leading America into war to reinstate their power in countries that had banished them.[89]

In its vehemence, vulgar articulation, and theoretical framework, Moseley's racism and anti-Semitism were virtually identical to Nazi ideology. He was, in fact, deeply inspired by Hitler's racial prophet, Houston Stewart Chamberlain. And when Germany invaded France in May 1940, Moseley wrote privately that while he held "no brief for Hitler," there would be no peace in Europe until British domination of the continent was broken: "After all, the Germans, who are bringing into Central Europe each year well over a million babies, have a right to live some place. A nation breeding its race up, as the Germans are doing, cannot be crushed out of existence." Indeed, America must "breed up" its own decaying population by copying Nazi eugenics practices. The United States must immediately begin "selective breeding, sterilization, the elimination of the unfit, and the elimination of those types which are inimical to the general welfare of the nation."[90]

Moseley's prolific correspondence and *One Soldier's Story* (a multivolume memoir written over twenty years) read like an anti-Semitic anthol-

ogy. These works embody every kind of anti-Semitic argument ever manifested in the history of Western civilization. Among the general's papers
are over fifty boxes of his hateful letters and writings.

Endowed with "objectionable" hereditary traits preserved by strict inbreeding, a Jew, Moseley wrote, no matter how assimilated, will always remain a Jew, a permanent "human outcast." Describing Jews as "crude and
unclean, animal-like things," he exclaimed, "it is like writing about something loathsome, such as syphilis." Insidiously, Jews rise from the under-
world to control the economy, then government, making themselves
"all-powerful." Using international finance simultaneously with communism to further their selfish ends, they know no loyalty to any country. In
the modern world, their ultimate goal is the "destruction of Christian civilization as we understand it in America today."

In Europe today, Moseley wrote in December 1941, the Jews were "receiving their just punishment for the crucifixion of Christ," whom "they
are still crucifying at every turn of the road." Jesus Christ was the "greatest anti-Semite" in history. Since the "Jew ruins everything he touches . . .
he has been thrown out of every land." The most humane solution to the
Jewish question, Moseley suggested, was a "worldwide policy which will
result in breeding all Jewish blood out of the human race."[91]

Congressmen gaped in amazement when this celebrated American general testified before the House Un-American Activities Committee (HUAC)
in June 1939. America, he stated, must learn from the experience of other
countries. In Hungary and Russia, the "murder squads" of the Jewish Communists Trotsky and Béla Kun killed "millions of Christians." But in Germany, "fortunately, the character of the German people was aroused"
against the "internationalists" who sold them out at Versailles. "We should
not blame" the Germans, he continued, "for settling the problem of the Jew
within their borders for all time." In developing its own refugee policy,
America could fortunately "benefit" from the German response.

Totally shocked, the committee deleted his statements from the official
record. But not all found Moseley's remarks so absurd. Senator Robert R.
Reynolds of North Carolina, a leading nativist and restrictionist, requested
a copy from Moseley and maintained a working political relationship with
him thereafter.[92]

Moseley's testimony was a watershed. He had stepped beyond the
bounds of the acceptable political discourse of the time and atmosphere. He
had destroyed any chance of emerging as a presidential candidate in 1940
as the rightist "man on horseback." There was a marked shift away from

him over the next year by those on active duty or engaged in politics; more and more of them considered him a man to be handled cautiously.

The zealotry that made Moseley a pariah in mainstream politics ingratiated him to true Fascists and fringe elements across the country. Although he distanced himself from them politically, many of his ideas surpassed their most extreme visions. Quite aware of his increasing isolation, Moseley never moderated his views or toned down his rhetoric. "The truth" was that as he "located the real enemy and stood up and faced him and his tribe, many old friends and supporters deserted [him] on all sides." His experience as a soldier had taught him to expect nothing less; "it is the old story—few advance to the firing line—few stick when reaching it."[93]

What was definitely on the minds of many across the country after Moseley's first round of speeches, followed by his fantastic testimony before HUAC, was whether he reflected army attitudes. He had certainly raised eyebrows when, in one speech, he went so far as to justify, under certain circumstances, military resistance to the president. The army "is your salvation today," he assured his listeners. "If the administration went too far to the Left and asked our military establishment to execute orders which violated all American tradition, that army would demur."[94]

Within days of Moseley's congressional appearance, many felt relieved when one of the country's most progressive voices, the *Nation*, assuaged concerns about Moseley and the army. "I can say with certainty," wrote Kenneth G. Crawford after consulting various sources, "that General Craig and other responsible army leaders take Moseley seriously only as a menace to the prestige of the service." Crawford created the very comforting impression that Moseley was a "ludicrous" loner, a loose cannon the army tried to restrain and then from whom it disassociated itself.

Keeping Moseley at arm's length, Craig supposedly only answered his letters in "coldly cryptic acknowledgement and nothing more." Through an army emissary, the military had privately "suggested that he hold his irresponsible tongue in the interest of preserving the dignity of the army." Thereafter, supposedly only the personal intervention of Roosevelt himself had prevented the War Department from imposing "disciplinary measures" on Moseley. Crawford was "less clear" about Moseley's relationship to the Republicans and the political fringe. But "the attitude of the army toward the whole affair has been reassuring."[95]

This confidence in the army was unwarranted. Often sounding like a fanatic or even a quack, Moseley made it easy for the army to publicly dismiss him as an oddity, completely unrepresentative of their revered institution. And in many respects he was different, particularly in the vehemence of his expressions at the time and his ultimate political paranoia. But in fundamental arguments he was articulating what had been standard Darwinian racial thought in the officer corps through the 1920s. The same was true of his assertions of Jewish-Communist subversion. Such political and racial anti-Semitism still affected the perspectives of many officers, especially those of the military generation immediately following Moseley's own. Moseley's shocking statements differed very little from the depictions of Jews by General George S. Patton after World War II and from the views some retired generals would hold into the 1970s.

How lightheartedly the upper echelons of the army reacted to his initial anti-Semitic outbursts strongly suggested that they saw this episode primarily as a political problem. Only a few years earlier, Moseley had been a serious contender for chief of staff. Throughout the period of his anti-Semitic tirades and even after his death, prominent officers would privately continue to express their admiration for Moseley as a military leader; and among these were Eisenhower and Marshall.

The army would sustain a consistent record throughout the first half of the twentieth century of opposing Jewish immigration on racial and anti-Communist grounds. While not resorting to Moseley's vile anti-Semitism and eugenics arguments, most officers in 1938 probably viewed Jews as a problem and opposed their immigration as well as what was believed to be Jewish interference with American foreign policy. During the very years in which Moseley's public anti-Semitism was creating such outrage, the War College was still educating officers in racial thinking and political biology. And lecturers and student officers alike took strong stands against the immigration of "undesirables."

CHAPTER 8

War College, War Clouds, 1933–1941

P URE BUNK," PROFESSOR HENRY FAIRCHILD told the War College
class of 1937. That's what he thought of the very idea of America as
"a haven for the downtrodden" or the notion that U.S. immigration laws
should be affected by "philanthropy."

Since every class for two decades had heard something similar from this
prominent racist intellectual, Fairchild's reputation had preceded him. His
audience had already read his more extensive papers on the worldwide
Malthusian struggle for food and space on an overpopulated globe.
Fairchild then related these to contemporary questions of German, Italian,
and Japanese expansion. Although America had prudently closed its gates
against the "enormous horde of foreigners" before it was too late, these
nations, in their "search for survival and existence," had no alternative but
to pursue aggressive expansionism. Since that demographic fact superseded any "ethical or moral proposition," a "turbulent explosion" was "inevitable."

Among the student officers listening to Fairchild that day were Frank
McSherry and Mark Clark. As generals after World War II, both men
would be charged with coping with the tremendous problems of refugees
and displaced persons in Europe. And McSherry kept his copy of Fairchild's
lecture on population.[1]

Lectures of this kind revealed much more than merely the continuation
of racial education at the War College through the 1930s. They interconnected several elements of the officer corps' worldview and established
their paramount relevance for contemporary America. Within such lec-

tures, as well as the reports of various officers at the War College, racial thinking and geopolitics were clearly linked to immigration and the possibility of war between Germany and the United States. Many officers expressed a surprising degree of understanding about a resurgent Germany and a strong conviction that a war with that country was not in America's national interest. The general sentiment within the officer corps was non-interventionist, with some officers becoming actively involved with the isolationist America First movement.

One cannot fully comprehend the views of such American officers without taking into account the Jewish question, which was interwoven throughout so many of these issues. Concerns over immigration, communism, and anything enhancing the likelihood of hostilities with Nazi Germany made many officers wary of American involvement with the plight of German Jews. Some officers were also suspicious of what they believed was a strong Jewish political influence that might lead America down the path to war. Two decades of institutionalized anti-Semitism played at least a partial role in establishing and reinforcing such ideas.

Racial Education, Jews, and Germans

Across town a few months after Fairchild's lecture, another leading authority concluded his lecture, lit a cigarette, and readied himself for questions from a class at the Army Industrial College. Designed to prepare officers for planning and command positions in the upper ranks of the service branches, the Industrial College sent its best graduates to the War College. The lecture—"The Racial Factor as a Determinant in National Policies"—was one the speaker had already "given off and on before the Naval War College at Newport." Like Fairchild, Lothrop Stoddard needed no introduction. He was arguably America's foremost racist intellectual, whose books had long been standard reading at such military schools.

Although Stoddard eschewed the entire Jewish question in his lectures of the late 1930s, his anti-Semitic credentials, earned through numerous books on the racial peril to Nordic America, were impeccable. Particularly in "The Pedigree of Judah," an article for *Forum* magazine, he had expounded "the biological foundations of the Jewish problem." Stoddard introduced this piece with a portrait "GALLERY OF JEWISH TYPES" displaying stereotypical page-length drawings of several "Ashkenazi," "Sephardic," and "Disharmonic" Jewish heads and faces. Captions identified anthropologically the "Mongolian eye" and "absence of the Jewish nose" in one "Ashkenasic Type," the "negroid traces in lips" of another.[2]

"Now race," Stoddard told these officers, was "no mere invention of theorists or propagandists." Race was a "very deep-going instinct that is shared not only by men but by animals far down in the animal kingdom"; it inhibited interbreeding and fostered racial aggression. "Deadly enemies, the gray rat drives out the black rat."

Social experiments like those in Communist Russia to eradicate inbred "metaphysical, mental, and psychological" differences among the races through "training and education" would certainly fail.[3] More logical and reasonable was the "very interesting experiment" in Nazi Germany, with which he sympathized. This marked the first historical attempt of a national policy "guided by racialist and eugenic considerations." Germans would "weed out the unfit, the moronic, and the persons afflicted with certain diseases, by sterilizing and thus removing their strains from the populations." The ultimate goal, Stoddard said, quoting a Nazi theorist, was "what we shall become by the constant elevating and purifying, bettering of our stock generations hence."[4]

Responding to an officer's query about the American "Color question," Stoddard proposed legalized segregation and stringently enforced anti-miscegenation laws. Otherwise, "the loss of the peculiar identity of the white man will be a terrific biological loss."[5]

Lecturing on "World Affairs" at the Industrial College until the outbreak of World War II, Stoddard often opened his talks by stressing "that the increasing knowledge of the true nature of race by modern sciences: biology, anthropology, etc. had important results such as . . . our immigration laws." This knowledge had now "validated and put on a scientific basis matters which were considered in former times mere prejudices, the prejudices against the intermarriage of races [and] the effect of the competition of races."[6]

In foreign affairs, Stoddard urged a policy of "realism" that did "not mix up ideologies and interests." America's "idealistic, forward-looking minority" helped create an illusionary postwar order based on the "rotten foundations" of the Versailles Treaty and League of Nations. Americans were victims of their own wartime propaganda. They came to believe "there was something uniquely vicious about Germany," which had to be "disarmed and kept down." But peace could only be preserved by dispelling these illusions and adjusting to the legitimate needs and power of the dissatisfied countries. The true realist was Neville Chamberlain, whose "policy of understanding" (which Stoddard preferred to the word "appeasement") allowed for such prudent changes.[7]

Even after Hitler violated the Munich Agreement by occupying all of Czechoslovakia in March 1939, Stoddard told the officers in his audience that tolerating a revived German empire in Central Europe was preferable to another war, which would be "collective suicide" for Europe. He painted a horrifying picture of the next war as involving "such terrific destruction, such tremendous loss of life," among civilians as well as soldiers, that entire countries would lapse into chaos and anarchy. There would be "neither victors nor vanquished," only universal famine, epidemics, and economic collapse.[8]

Discounting threats to the Western Hemisphere, Stoddard spoke as an apologist for Fascist Italy and Nazi Germany. Their "real motives" were "scarcity [and] immediate danger." Economically deprived and "surrounded by enemies," they felt it necessary to organize themselves with "rigid efficiency" and "submit to the rule of one gifted man" who worked for the "national good."[9]

After the outbreak of war in 1939, Stoddard studied Nazi eugenics policies for several months in Germany. Since Nazi racial anthropologists and eugenicists had long cited Stoddard as affirmation of their own ideas, he was able to meet with such leading figures as Himmler and von Ribbentrop. Particularly impressed by Nazi sterilization practices, Stoddard returned an avid defender of German racial hygiene programs that he hoped his own country would emulate.[10]

Not only was Stoddard's racial science erroneous, it was—despite his assertions to the contrary—out of step with the major trends in science and scholarship. Advances in biology and anthropology had not, as he boasted, offered new scientific knowledge vindicating racial theory; quite the contrary. With evidence mounting against the racist assumptions of an earlier generation, mainstream scholarship in the natural and social sciences had clearly rejected "race as an explanation for human social difference," substituting a cultural interpretation in its place. "By the 1930s," noted the historian Carl Degler, "it was about as difficult to locate an American social scientist who *accepted* a racial explanation for human behavior as it had been easy to find one in 1900." Fairchild, Stoddard, and their ideas were anachronisms. However, the two anthropologists most responsible for the shift from racial to cultural theory, Franz Boas and Alfred Kroeber, were, despite their renown, never invited to lecture at the War College.[11]

Officers of the 1930s also apparently remained behind the times, as various aspects of the earlier scientific racism continued to resonate throughout their studies and thought. Invoking the "Malthusian Doctrine," an officer at the Army Industrial College attributed war to "economic and biologic" causes; the "struggle to live is basic." The "law that has governed so much of our commercial and physical expansion" was "Let him take who has the power, let him keep who can." As late as 1940, officers at the War College could still write that "the natural instincts of the race evolved by centuries cannot be eradicated in a generation or two." Some officers still studied Le Bon and Ripley's *Races of Europe*.[12]

Such assumptions undoubtedly affected officers' perceptions and expectations. That officers often based their analyses on information from widely dispersed attachés strongly suggested these views were shared far beyond the War College. Russian racial characteristics, asserted a 1935 War College strategic survey, were "not conducive to military or industrial efficiency," because they were a mixture of the "Orient and the Occident—the white race with the yellow." Their "lack of culture and reasoning logic . . . show the Mongol blood." Russians remained unreliable, shifting from one extreme to another—"communism and extreme individualism, meekness and brutality"; the "contending strains within the individual" of this mongrelized race resulted "in a mass of mental contradictions." All of this paralleled Stoddard's theory of "disharmonic racial groups" caused by interbreeding.[13]

Four years later, Captain Bonner F. Fellers stood before his classmates and declared the "strange blend of European and Oriental traits" in the Russians made it unlikely they could ever realize their immense military potential. Soon to play an important role in military intelligence during World War II and Republican national politics afterward, Fellers described the Russian as a naturally suspicious, intriguing, unfaithful "Oriental killer who settles things in a way which only Asia understands—death to opposition without the slightest mercy."

The question seemed to be whether the advantages of population, natural resources, and technological modernization could compensate sufficiently for inherited racial deficiencies. One officer said in the discussion period: "It does not matter how many planes you have if they are not kept in proper shape. Russians are Orientals and, like all other Orientals, they will use wooden rivets and paste things together so that they will not work when the time comes. . . . [N]o matter how many planes they have, they don't fight."[14]

An officer committee in 1935 did challenge the validity of biological racism for differentiating Central European nationalities. "It might be well to mention," they wrote, "that any references to Slavic, Teutonic, or Latin race does not necessarily imply blood relationship. We are considering these different peoples . . . as linguistic groupings . . . and not an ethnic type." Yet even these officers still held that "racially the Poles are an East Baltic people with an eastern substratum and Nordic and Mediterranean accretions." Other points sounded remarkably familiar as well: Poles had "contradictory" national characteristics; "they have the psychology of the Eastern World . . . in the Western World."[15]

The most significant change by the 1930s was the complete absence of references to the earlier theories of Jewish-Bolshevik conspiracies or domination of the Soviet Union. Officers now wrote of the "heterogeneous characters" of the Russian government. They only noted that "Jews . . . are remarkably well represented in proportion to their number both in party and Government. They are no longer looked upon with open animosity by the Russians, because this attitude is officially regarded as bourgeois and reactionary."[16]

But the Jewish question had not disappeared. Although lacking the vehemence of earlier expressions, jokes and stories about Jews, as well as blacks, still lightened up lectures or discussions. General Peyton C. March, a legend in army circles, reminisced about a dinner at the White House when Senator Henry Cabot Lodge complained to Theodore Roosevelt about his treatment at the hands of the Russians. "T.R.," recalled March, "showed all his teeth and said: 'Cabot, they probably took you for a Jew— Henry Cabotski Lodgstein.' . . . The whole table shook with laughter." To illustrate a point during a discussion, an officer interjected: "Two Jews were walking down the street and one said, 'this anti-Semitic movement will never get anywhere until they get a smart Jew at the head of it.'"[17]

Writing in the late 1930s, committees of student officers noted that the "problem of minorities and racial differences" remained "a very important one." They attributed Poland's "faltering" democracy to the presence of "so many antagonistic minorities." Progress had occurred in diminishing "inter-racial friction," "except in the case of the Jews." Because "Jews constitute a serious problem in the economic life" of Poland, they predicted "adverse consequences for them." The church and government had already sanctioned economic boycotts against Jews, and the state was unable to contain the "increasing number and seriousness" of anti-Semitic "outbursts" and "riots."[18]

Although acknowledging the "many very poverty-stricken Jews," with "at least a million on the verge of starvation," officers identified a major source of anti-Semitism as the "predominance" of Jews in Polish economic life. Citing German statistics, they described how these urban-dwelling non-Poles controlled "nearly half the commercial enterprises" and a substantial part of the professions. "Some estimate that more than half the real property in Warsaw and other cities is also Jewish." Moreover, "it is said that the miserably poor peasants are exploited by the Jewish traders."

Since Polish Jewry was "unassimilated," the alien nature of the Jew only aggravated these economic animosities. The influx of Jewish refugees from Nazi Germany, these officers believed, heightened the tension by accentuating the foreign nature of Jews and exacerbating other problems.

In almost every respect, Poles viewed Jews as detrimental to their society and culture. They alleged Jews had been "hostile to the Polish state" and "unpatriotic" in wartime. Even the primate of Poland claimed "that the Jews support free thought, godlessness, Bolshevism, pornographic literature, embezzlement, usury, and the white slave traffic."

Although the Polish government was "gravely concerned" about U.S. and British reactions, a committee of officers studying the Polish situation in 1939 advised against intervention. "The feelings of the mass of the Poles toward the Jews . . . probably cannot be changed by any foreign influence."[19] Quite sympathetic to the Polish government, the officers believed that it took reasonable measures to deal with a complex racial question. As they saw it, Poland faced the age-old problems of economic and racial conflict caused by "overpopulation" that War College studies had long emphasized. The government's "solution" was increased "Jewish emigration," together with a reduction in Jewish economic predominance. But neither Palestine nor South America were adequate outlets. And "many Jewish leaders" opposed mass emigration from Poland, the officers argued, because they did not want to relinquish "their last stronghold in Europe."[20]

Reorienting Jews toward labor, crafts, and agriculture was also unlikely due to Jewish physical and behavioral characteristics. In their report, the officers depicted Jews as physically weak, lazy, "radical and difficult to handle." While tens of thousands of servant jobs went unfilled, Jewish girls were not "available," despite the masses of unemployed poverty-stricken Jews. Even "Jewish industrialists" were "unwilling" to "employ Jewish laborers," preferring instead "Christians in better physical condition and willing to perform hard work." Pressured by coreligionists, these industrialists employed some Jews for "light work."[21]

For similar reasons, the Polish "army does not consider the Jews as desirable material for the military establishment." And suspicions about Jewish loyalty were so strong among Polish officers that they wanted to exclude "them in the zone of the interior during wartime." The American officers explained the Polish attitude by resorting to the old charges that Jews had sided with the Bolsheviks against Poland in 1919–1920. "Bitter experiences during the Polish-Soviet War," these officers argued, "taught the [Polish] Army not to trust them." Concern about a Jewish threat to national security in wartime prompted the Polish army to seek "a complete evacuation of the Jews."[22]

Central European ethnic strife taught War College officers in the 1930s important lessons about protecting America's homogeneity. Their determination to do so only hardened as they continued to learn from Le Bon about the predisposition to revolution in the "psychology of certain peoples" and that "mixed breeds" were "notoriously unstable." The "outstanding characteristics" Le Bon attributed to those of Anglo-Saxon "racial stock," which accounted for the "remarkable" vitality and stability of "nations of British descent," were threatened by heterogeneous groups and "ideas".[23]

In order to "increase stability" in the United States, these officers recommended sharp new restrictions on immigration, specifically to exclude the "undesirable" types who "retain alien ideals," "do not assimilate rapidly," or lack the "capacity for self-government." America had long "exhausted" its ability to absorb such immigrants without grave damage to the body politic.[24]

Like Poland, the United States faced potential threats to national security from undesirables. "In any war," asserted one officer committee in 1938, "we will have our alien problem" among those "whose loyalty to the United States is very doubtful." In fact, "in addition to possible future enemies, we may expect a loud and well organized minority within the jurisdiction of the nation, hampering the efforts of the War Department in peace or war, by every possible obstructive method."

A more open-minded committee still ended up identifying the same alien danger. "Experience has shown," these officers wrote, "that generally foreign born whites readily adopt the American customs, become imbued with the national spirit, and their loyalty can usually be depended upon in case of war." Although they had no use for "foreign born non-whites," officers argued that the army could raise the "combat value" of white immigrants by mixing them with "native born Americans." These officers cautioned, though, that "74% of the foreign born are in . . . areas which contain vital industries and will have to be watched to prevent sabotage or instigation of strikes, as one out of every ten workers in the manufacturing and mechanical industries is an alien. The Japanese in California also present a problem." They concluded that "concentrations of alien and foreign born populations . . . will in time of war cause a serious problem."[25]

Racial thinking and concerns with minority problems also affected the attitudes of War College officers toward Nazi Germany. For years, War College teaching had promoted racial ideas that fostered a natural affinity for Northern Europeans and a strong antipathy toward Jews. Often overtly, at other times only thinly disguised, officer committees in the 1930s displayed admiration for the German people. While condemning Nazi oppression, these officers also showed an appreciation of the accomplishments of the Hitler regime. Above all, however, they appraised Nazi Germany in terms of American foreign policy interests and avoiding war. These officers, therefore, assessed the persecution of German Jews and attempts by American Jews to assist them from the perspective of these overriding considerations.

War College reports from the time of Hitler's seizure of power to the outbreak of World War II show amazing uniformity of opinion on almost every point about the Germans, except whether they were inherently aggressive. Officer committees still employed racial interpretations to explain German characteristics and behavior. These American officers accepted the scientific validity of the concept of race, in its biological and cultural sense, applying it without reservation. The only Nazi racial doctrine rejected outright in these committee reports was that Germans alone constituted a superior race.[26]

Otherwise, year after year, class after class of War College officers described the Germans as a product of racial heredity and environment. Although not a pure race due to "Slavic admixtures" in the East, the "old teutonic element has persistently predominated" and Germans were "a fairly homogeneous people," which officers highlighted as one source of their continuing strength. Contemporary Germans inherited not only their "tall, fair" racial characteristics and "strong physique" but also mental and behavioral characteristics (high levels of "native intelligence" and "stubbornness").[27]

"Environment and education" contributed "a strong nationalism," a "military mind," "discipline, obedience, love of orderliness, cleanliness, [and] extraordinary ability in technical and scientific matters." Germany's "temperate zone" created an "energetic people of a high degree of activity," while centuries of warfare kept "the race fit and virile." Devoted to home, church, and Fatherland, Germans would fight and sacrifice as long as necessary to defend these. And Germans possessed "great moral stamina and fortitude."[28]

These same officer committees classified the Nazi regime itself as a fanatical and ruthless "totalitarian state at full bloom." In explaining Nazi rule, however, they also credited the regime with a number of accomplishments.[29] Projecting a slide of Hitler on a screen, one officer told his classmates: "This 'Charlie Chaplin-mustached' man, given to insomnia and emotionalism, is . . . to millions of Germans a saint. He fills them with love, fear, and emotional ecstasy. He is irrational, contradictory, and complex." Then the officer quickly qualified his assessment: "On his behalf, it must be said that he has accomplished much that he promises the German people."[30]

It was generally acknowledged among War College officers that Hitler had saved Germany from domestic turmoil and depression. In rescuing Germans from communism and defeat, he had restored stability and "national pride." Drawbacks existed for the "upper strata" and Jews, but conditions for the masses "very definitely had been improved."[31]

The Nazis certainly deserved credit for the admirable new Wehrmacht. While "we hold no brief for German political doctrine, we have been forced to conclude," admitted one colonel, "that within a remarkably short period, under most difficult circumstances, Germany has created the finest army in the world." In addition, the "lack of organized minorities" and "effective opposition" made this one-party dictatorship "an excellent type of government for the conduct of war."[32]

The Nazi dictatorship, in the words of a 1938 committee, had "not changed basic [inherited German] characteristics." It "more firmly molded these into the channels which marked the German people of history as an outstanding race."[33] A year earlier, other officers had argued that the Germans only sought "a security signified by the world's respect for her political, economic and military positions, which constitute the very life of a respected, accepted, stable, progressive and modern nation." Under Hitler, these officers anticipated that Germany would "emerge as one of the world's real and respected powers."[34]

Such views persisted among members of the officer corps right up to the eve of the war. "Following the armistice," said one major during a discussion in January 1939, "I spent two pleasant years" in "intimate contact" with Germans. "During that period I gained the very strong impression that the German people are rather a peaceful and home-loving people." Germans were, he said, "more like the Americans than any other of the nationalities of Europe."[35]

This major had difficulty reconciling his experiences with the "general belief that the German people now have been transformed into a rather belligerent nation" or were "wholeheartedly behind Hitler." The officer leading the discussion responded that the Germans had not changed substantially. Most Germans disapproved of certain Nazi "methods" such as the Secret Police and "brutalities," and supported Hitler's foreign policy only if it did not result in war.[36]

From the early days of the regime, War College officers' appraisals of Hitler's intentions downplayed the threat Nazi Germany posed to the United States. As late as 1937–1938, these officers depicted Hitler as a cautious realist and "opportunist." They never doubted that his expansionist foreign policy, "clearly stated" in *Mein Kampf*, was "directed towards the East" and constituted little danger to the West.[37]

In the mid-1930s, American officers urged recognition of Germany's legitimate "vital interests" in continental Europe. They felt it only natural for Germany to seek restoration of "lost territories" identified as the "Polish Corridor," "Upper Silesia," and "the Saar Basin" and to unite Austria with Germany. Indeed, officers emphasized that "these interests do not conflict with those of the United States." While conceding that Germany, pursuing its legitimate objectives, might have to resort to war at some point, officers argued that there were no "basic issues which [could] serve to provoke armed conflict between these two countries."

Since 1919, Germany had always displayed great "respect" for Americans, especially after their "sympathetic cooperation" and assistance during Germany's "economic troubles." Into 1938, officers held that "Germany evidenced no animosity against the United States" and was unlikely to take actions that would jeopardize this relationship.[38] German rearmament and remilitarization of the Rhineland were neither unexpected nor particularly menacing from the perspective of War College officers, who still maintained that "Germany does not want war." From the annexation of Austria in 1938 through the Munich Agreement, officers insisted that the Nazis sought war only with Russia.

When Chief of Military Intelligence Colonel McCabe addressed the class of 1939, he brought with him Major Percy G. Black, who had personally observed the German scene as a recent military attaché in Berlin.[39] Asked about Hitler's intentions, Black answered: "I am certain German foreign policy is faced toward the East." But what about "guarantee of the German-French border?" queried another captain. The Germans, Black responded, would definitely honor the guarantee, because "the Hitler regime has had no interest whatsoever in aggressive action to the West."[40]

Black's assessment received academic reinforcement through the War College lectures delivered in 1938 and 1939 by Harvard historian William Langer. Hitler was unlikely to start a war, Langer asserted, because he wanted to spare his people the horrors that he himself had experienced during World War I.

Langer's optimism surpassed even that of the officers in his audience. He dismissed *Mein Kampf* as that "silly little book" and discounted the likelihood of a German-Russian war or "aggressive purposes" toward Czechoslovakia. Like military experts, he discounted a war against France. After the 1938 Munich Agreement ceding part of Czechoslovakia to Hitler, Langer retained the optimism of the appeasers, predicting that the Germans would be "content with their gains."[41]

Meanwhile, the Roosevelt administration was sounding the alarm about Nazi aggression in Europe and attempting to overcome the paralyzing effects of American isolationism. When Roosevelt told Congress in January 1938, "Our national defense is inadequate," the army was supportive. Officers knew that war could very well materialize. Throughout the 1930s, War College officers worked on plans for war against various combinations of Germany, Italy, and Japan. If called upon by their president, these officers would do everything in their power to confront and defeat these enemies.[42]

The one war that War College officers wanted to avoid, however, was with Germany. While committees devised war plans for a conflict with this respected adversary, officers strongly believed that such a war was neither necessary nor in America's national interest. They were quite confident that should a war occur, America would prevail; but as late as 1938, one committee noted that "Germany has evidenced no animosity against the United States."[43]

What seriously concerned many officers, however, was whether Roosevelt's policies might actually precipitate an unnecessary war. They were particularly wary of Roosevelt's scare tactics about Nazi threats to the Western Hemisphere. Although War College officers were ordered in 1938 to plan for this military contingency, their own studies consistently showed that Hitler would not violate the Monroe Doctrine. In 1939, Captain Bonner Fellers criticized Roosevelt and other "public officials" for creating a bogus "war scare" and threatening force to defend Latin America.[44]

Throughout the 1930s, one worrisome problem for German-American relations was Nazi anti-Semitism. Initially, officers perceived this as somewhat troublesome, though insufficient to cause a breach in foreign relations. As one committee noted in January 1935,

> Some annoyance has been created in the United States because of anti-Jewish activities of the Nazis. But it is hardly probable that the United States would

permit herself to be involved in any purely European problems, unless peculiar conditions should arise, which do not seem probable at this time.[45]

A few months later, however, other officers foresaw a situation in which Jewish influence would involve the United States in a war against Germany contrary to America's true interests. They envisaged a scenario of a war between Germany, France, and Italy that could seriously affect the U.S. economy by substantially curtailing trade with Europe. In this view, Americans—who were ripe for manipulation—failed to realize that Japan, not Germany, was the "real threat." In the projected scenario, as Americans looked for someone to blame, "Jewish and other anti-Nazi propaganda already active, seized on this opportunity to make Germany and her allies the scapegoat." Anti-Nazi newspapers "dwelt upon" the cruelty of German warfare as "Jewish money interests in the United States used all available means of increasing the resentment against the Nazis."[46]

The issue of the effects of Nazi anti-Semitism on American policy simmered beneath the surface for years. Gradually, officers concluded that Nazi "hatred of the Jews" and anti-Semitic policies had done more than anything else to alienate public opinion outside of Germany. By the late 1930s, Nazi anti-Semitism, when combined with Roosevelt's vigorous protest against Nazi expansion, became a real point of contention between the two countries.[47]

Every officer knew the "intensely anti-Semitic . . . Nazi Party proceeded against the Jews the moment it came to power." Despite Nazi vacillation between "Jew-Baiting," legalistic methods of persecution, and outright violence, by the eve of Kristallnacht in November 1938, officers realized that the ultimate goal was to make Germany "racially pure" by "forcing" Jews "out of Germany."[48] Although otherwise extensive War College analyses of Hitler's Germany devoted comparatively limited coverage to this question, they did document the nature and effects of Hitler's "anti-Semitic campaign against the small Jewish minority." As one committee wrote in 1936:

As "Non-Aryans" they have been denied citizenship, their property confiscated, their opportunities for making a livelihood curtailed, and they have been removed from the professions and positions of financial and industrial power. Many have been imprisoned and many have fled from the country. They are forbidden to marry or consort with the Aryan population, and their descendants of mixed marriages of two previous generations have been penalized proportionately.[49]

That these policies had "the unqualified approval of the great majority of the German people" did not mean that Germans were imbued with Nazi ideology. Most Germans did not "approve, or even condone, the excesses" of Nazi fanatics and "deplored the pogroms and the other unbridled persecutions." Some officers attributed the popularity of anti-Semitism and "Jew-Baiting" to "jealousy," since after World War I, "Jews were the first to fit themselves into the new conditions and gain success." As a consequence of these "persecutions," "some of Germany's best talent—writers, scientists and teachers, have been removed and their uplifting influence will be missed for generations."[50]

Other officers, however, suggested that some anti-Jewish grievances might have serious merit. "The fact remains," one committee argued in 1939, "that the German people are convinced that they have a strong case against the Jew for his exploitation of Germany in the years immediately following the World War, and that, when Hitler rose to power, the insignificant Jewish minority controlled the country economically and politically to a degree that amounted to enslavement of the Gentile majority."[51] In trying to understand the Jewish question, these officers cautioned that students of the situation "must remember that the point of view of the Jewish-controlled press of the United States is no more impartial than the sources of the propaganda of the Nazi Government."[52]

Someone subsequently edited the typed report in pen to read the "Jewish-controlled *portion of the* press." But committees during other years held similar views. As one group of officers expressed it in 1935, Nazi anti-Semitism had "done much to alienate Germany to other nations, particularly those where banking and markets are strongly under Jewish influence, as in Great Britain and the United States."[53]

To some officers, the "primary basis" of the "Jewish Problem" was "the influx of eastern Jews during and after the World War." The "majority, natives of Galicia," could not be repatriated in 1919, because the Polish government refused to accept them. "They were regarded, even by native German Jews, as most unwelcome guests, since . . . the Ost-Juden completely crowded out all others." The Nazis found a powerful political issue in alien outsiders detrimental to the economic well-being and cultural survival of true Germans.[54]

In a long commentary on the twenty-five points of the 1920 Nazi Party program, one officer reaffirmed that the key issue was Eastern European Jews "who flocked into the country." He acknowledged that the Nazi racial criterion of "German blood" automatically excluded all Jews from being "members of the nation" and that the Nazis had removed "all known Jews" from public offices. But ignoring this, he still argued that Nazi policies were "aimed primarily at Jewish refugees" and "non-citizen Jews." The Nazis attempted to solve the economic crisis through work, public assistance, and "other means." Withdrawing citizenship rights from those lacking "German blood," deporting Jewish immigrants from the Reich, and preventing future immigration of "foreign nationals" were "believed necessary" to protect the welfare of the German people under difficult circumstances.[55]

Over the years, American officers recognized the thoroughness of such actions. By 1939, officers were acknowledging that "the Jew, the former pariah of the nation, had been stripped of his goods and of his rights as a citizen, and now exists in a persecuted ghetto class." "All in all," they wrote, "Hitler has applied himself so assiduously to the Jewish question that it remains a problem only to the Jew."[56]

In reality, every officer knew that Nazi anti-Semitism continued to aggravate German-American relations. A colonel at the War College asked William Langer to account for "our great misinformation and misconception in this country of the actual German situation," adding that "all one hears is hostility for Hitler and for Germany." Langer ascribed these misconceptions, in part, to "elephantine" German efforts to explain and promote their own interests. Langer started to give the "other reason," but hesitated briefly. He then said, "I see no reason why it should not be stated here," and continued his candid explanation:

> I think the Jewish influence has a great deal to do with it. You have to face the fact that some of our most important American newspapers are Jewish-controlled, and I suppose if I were a Jew I would feel about Nazi Germany as most Jews feel and it would be most inevitable that the coloring of the news takes on that tinge. As I read the *New York Times*, for example, it is perfectly clear that every little upset that occurs (and after all many upsets occur in a country of 70 million people) is given a great deal of prominence. The other part of it is soft-pedaled or put off with a sneer. So that in a rather subtle way, the picture you get is that there is no good in the Germans whatever.[57]

In January of 1939, MID director McCabe told a War College class: "Up until a year ago, the Germans were making every effort to be friendly. We found that in relations with the German army and with the German Government, they were going out of their way to show us special favors."

More recently, things had changed, and "our relations have not been quite so cordial." The reasons for this sudden cooling, McCabe said, were the "American press attacks on Germany" and events since Munich. Although he did not know where things might lead, McCabe remained confident that Germany posed no threat to America and wanted to avoid any further rift. "I think," he said, "that our relations with Germany will depend more upon the United States than on Germany."[58]

That prognosis was what worried many officers at the War College and elsewhere—for they were convinced that the Roosevelt administration and other political forces, especially Jewish ones, were determined to undermine even a pragmatic relationship with Germany.

Officers and Isolationists

A few years after World War II, General Albert C. Wedemeyer, then deputy chief of staff, wrote to his close friend retired colonel Truman Smith that the British, Zionists, and Communists made American entry into the war "inevitable." They were motivated by selfish interests rather than the welfare of humanity. In his private notes a few years later, Wedemeyer stated that "most of the people associated with Communism in the early days were Jews." He also claimed that the president's Jewish advisers (Samuel I. Rosenman, Frankfurter, Morgenthau) "did everything possible to spread venom and hatred against the Nazis and to arouse Roosevelt against the Germans." Breaking his promise to keep America out, the Machiavellian Roosevelt, with "much help from the Jews," manipulated the country into the conflict.[59]

Despite the tradition of institutional anti-Semitism, it is difficult to determine how many officers, especially after the war, would draw this kind of direct connection between Jewish influence and America's drift toward involvement. However, those with Wedemeyer's mentality held major positions of responsibility and interacted in significant ways with other decisionmakers within the army. Ironically, Wedemeyer himself would in 1941 be charged with developing the army's Victory Plan for World War II. Moreover, the objectives of those officers harboring anti-Semitic views and those less susceptible or immune to this kind of thinking converged in their common strong opposition to intervention.

While attaché in Berlin until 1939, Smith had warned against allowing the Jewish question to interfere with German-American relations. By spring 1939, not only had Smith become General George C. Marshall's major German specialist in Washington but he was a respected army proponent of nonintervention, simultaneously advising Charles Lindbergh, a leader of the isolationist movement. Smith's replacement in Berlin, Major Percy Black, also belonged to the Wedemeyer-Smith circle. Equally understanding of Germany's Eastern-oriented foreign policy, Black advised against U.S. intervention even if Germany attacked Czechoslovakia or Poland.[60] Colonel Raymond Lee, attaché in London, strongly concurred even on the eve of World War II, arguing that the United States must be guided by self-interest, "not emotion."[61]

The most outspoken isolationist general in 1939, former deputy chief of staff Stanley D. Embick, was Wedemeyer's father-in-law and longtime mentor in political theory and geopolitics. Among the army's most respected thinkers, Embick, like the current General Staff, envisioned a "colossal European catastrophe" of massive intercontinental destruction, destitution, and postwar upheaval. A year before, Chief of Staff Malin Craig said it "would mean the end of civilization."[62]

Writing to Deputy Chief of Staff George C. Marshall in April 1939, Embick identified himself with America's major isolationists and vehemently denounced interventionist "political leaders" and "newspapers."[63] Marshall and Craig were "impressed" by Embick's assessment and shared his frustration, as they too felt the army's advice was not heeded by the Roosevelt administration. "I am afraid that if you were up here," Marshall told Embick, "you would have a hard time keeping your temper."[64]

Embick represented the views of a substantial portion of the American army. As Forrest Pogue, Marshall's noted biographer, has explained, these officers believed that true patriotism demanded standing up for American interests and resisting those pressures at home or abroad that might involve the country in foreign wars. While intervention abroad risked catastrophe, a well-prepared fortress America could adequately defend itself. With numerous gradations in between, the other major segment of military opinion favored aid to Britain, but only after American needs were met. As chief of staff, Marshall sided with those who favored supporting British assistance but keeping America out of the war, at least until late 1941.[65]

The poisoned atmosphere in which the debate over intervention occurred only heightened suspicions on both sides. Manipulating public opinion through the press, Hollywood, and the FBI, the Roosevelt administration tried to increase America's sense of danger, while discrediting isolationists as pro-German, pro-Fascist, anti-Semitic, and antidemocratic. In

turn, the isolationists saw themselves as the besieged true patriots standing against an autocratic president who infringed on their freedom of expression and moved them closer to a war that would undermine American
democracy. Many within the isolationist camp, though not always willing
to state so publicly, tended to juxtapose American interests with those of
the British and Jews. From their perspective, non-American interests and
forces were driving America toward a disastrous and unnecessary war.[66]

Lindbergh, the symbol and most popular figure of the isolationist
movement, was a great admirer of Germany. In private, he also expressed
anxiety that "British and Jewish propaganda" were pushing America into
war. Lindbergh and other prominent isolationists were, he noted in August
1939, "disturbed about the effect of the Jewish influence on our press,
radio, and motion pictures. It may become very serious."[67]

In addition to the destructiveness of modern war, Lindbergh's isolationism was motivated by racial thinking similar to that held by the army officers with whom he collaborated. Lindbergh believed that the West was
about to "commit racial suicide" by entering "a war in which the White
race is bound to lose." To him, white racial superiority, characterized in
particular by modern scientific creativity, was a "priceless possession" on
which civilization depended. But now it was challenged by a "pressing sea
of Yellow, Black, and Brown" inferior races. Instead of a fratricidal racial
war among whites, the West should unite against the real threats: "dilution" of "European blood" within each country and attack by armies of the
"teeming millions of Asia." We must "guard our heritage from Mongol,
Persian and Moor."

Lindbergh looked beyond Soviet Russia spreading communism to chilling visions of barbaric hordes pouring out of the East, overrunning the
"treasures of the White race." With "Oriental guns . . . turning westward,
[and as] Asia presses towards us on the Russian border, all foreign races
stir restlessly." Speaking of "White ramparts," Lindbergh pleaded for a
"Western Wall of race and arms" to defend against a "Genghis Khan or the
infiltration of inferior blood." He envisaged an international racial alliance
based upon "an English fleet, a German air force, a French army, [and] an
American nation."[68]

The officers with whom Lindbergh worked closely for years, including
G-2 chief Warner McCabe, were also "very apprehensive" about the country's future, especially regarding recent trends under Roosevelt and "this
race problem." Joined in common cause with these officers, Lindbergh
worked with MID, visited American air installations, advised the military

on German aviation and European affairs, and served on the board to improve the U.S. Air Corps.[69] Most important was the intimate friendship that grew between Lindbergh and Truman Smith in Berlin between 1935 and 1939. Establishing lifelong ties, their families lived together for weeks in London, Paris, and Berlin, working, socializing, and touring.

Smith used Lindbergh as an invaluable source on the Luftwaffe. Hermann Göring's presentation of a medal to Lindbergh, together with Smith's early high estimates of the Luftwaffe, however, led to dubious charges that both men were pro-Nazi. In their defense, they dismissed the Göring presentation as an unfortunate surprise and denied that their estimates of German air power were intended to scare the West or the United States into appeasement. But these criticisms remain contentious points among historians.[70]

After diabetes forced Smith to return to the United States in April 1939, the two men privately worked together in political opposition to Roosevelt's interventionism. By this point, Smith had the confidence of Marshall himself, who personally intervened to keep the ailing G-2 on active duty as his valued adviser on German affairs in an army with "few German specialists." Marshall trusted and admired Smith for his "thorough understanding of things German," praising his attaché reports as "most remarkable."[71]

During this time, Lindbergh conferred on politics and military affairs at the Washington offices of Smith, McCabe, and Colonel Hamilton McGuire, then heading G-2's German section. All the while, he continued his isolationist radio broadcasts.[72] Two weeks after the German invasion of Poland, Smith arrived at Lindbergh's home with a confidential message. As Lindbergh recalled, Roosevelt offered him a cabinet post in aviation in return for ceasing his isolationist broadcasts. After conveying this serious message, as duty required, Smith joined Lindbergh in a good laugh. "So you see," said Smith, "they're worried."

Over the next few weeks Smith conferred with Lindbergh on the content, emphasis, and timing of his broadcasts urging the maintenance of the U.S. embargo on arms and credits to belligerents. The two men were heartened by the public response as they sat together opening Lindbergh's mail—"ninety-five per cent favorable, and most of them from people of a good type."[73]

At the end of November 1939, Smith's former assistant attaché in Berlin, Major Percy Black, arrived in Washington. Since Black had actually accompanied the German army into Poland, the War Department anxiously waited to debrief him. Within days, Black delivered a confidential lecture on Germany at the War College.

Black deviated from his planned talk to correct the "false impression" about Germany and the war that had been "created in the United States in the press." Like his mentor Truman Smith, Black spoke optimistically of prospects for a negotiated settlement before the war spread. "There is, among the German people, from top to bottom and among the leaders, a very sincere desire for peace in the West," since Germany's real "fear" was Russia. If Britain and France would only sign a peace "which would not humiliate the German people," Germany "would turn against Russia within six months."[74]

With Black suddenly in demand, Marshall wanted to send him on "a brief tour to several installations" around the country. However, the uproar caused by Black's early public statements derailed Marshall's plans, since Black's comments upon disembarking in New York contained not the slightest criticism of Germany's actions. German morale was good, he said: "Remember any people who go to war feel their cause is just and that they are being attacked." The Germans believed they were acting defensively; they were afraid of another defeat and Versailles that would "be the end of Germany."

More disturbing, Black discounted stories of Nazi brutality and the terrorizing of civilian populations through massive urban bombing. Traveling with the German army outside Warsaw, he observed that the "Polish population was demoralized . . . and German soldiers rounded up women and children and fed them in soup kitchens." Black did "not believe any of the atrocity stories."[75]

To those generals requesting conferences with Black, Marshall responded, "[I]t is not advisable to initiate these discussions at the present time." The real reason for pulling him off the circuit, Marshall noted "confidentially," was that "Black had made statements to the press that have produced a violent Jewish reaction; so we are not advertising him."

A month later, Black was quietly sent on the postponed "rounds of the Divisions." Although "not to be publicized," Marshall wrote, Black, like Truman Smith, "would interest any formal gathering" regarding Germany.[76]

In May 1940, however, Black's assessments of Nazi intentions proved grossly inaccurate and German armies swiftly overwhelmed French and British forces. The mood in American political and military circles ranged from pessimism to panic. Shocked by the unprecedented German success, both sides in the interventionist debate were more determined than ever of the righteousness of their cause and the need to pursue it more vigorously.

At the same time, a national hysteria quickly swept across the country, reaching a psychological level not seen since the Red Scare of 1919. It was an atmosphere partially created by Roosevelt, who for years tried to overcome public apathy and discredit isolationists by stigmatizing them as un-American or as subversive agents of Germany. The White House had become the center of a "fifth-column scare campaign," and Roosevelt warned of a "Trojan horse" infiltrating America just as Nazi fifth columnists had undermined European countries from within. Later, Roosevelt shocked reporters by stating that pro-Germans had infiltrated the American army and navy.[77]

In this climate, the relationship between Truman Smith and Lindbergh came under hostile scrutiny. On May 29, 1940, Smith's wife, Katherine, phoned Lindbergh with the distressing news that the Roosevelt administration was attempting "to injure" Lindbergh by removing her husband. Behind it all, supposedly, stood Henry Morgenthau, one of the most prominent Jews in the administration, who used the Lindbergh association as grounds for demanding Smith's discharge. Marshall refused, but he advised Smith "to avoid the appearance of such a close friendship."[78]

As Truman Smith recalled it, a constant barrage of press attacks then condemned him as a ghostwriter for Lindbergh. These were "instigated," Smith's "G-2 comrades" informed him, by Justice Frankfurter and Secretary Harold Ickes, though Smith also attributed his troubles to Morgenthau. Years later, Smith would angrily state how that "crowd," with Frankfurter using all his influence, tried to ruin him.

Sufficiently "disturbed" by the weekly attacks, Marshall now told Smith to leave Washington "until the political heat cooled." The Smiths fled to Fort Benning, Georgia, living in temporary exile with Wedemeyer. Smith later returned to headquarters and also resumed his association with Lindbergh and other isolationists.[79] But the incident only reinforced impressions of powerful Jewish influence in the government.

Although in reality a fifth column never existed, the new chief of G-2, General Sherman Miles, was absolutely "convinced" of it, and intelligence officers again reverted to widespread surveillance.[80] As concerns about a German-American confrontation increased, MID investigated a wide variety of rightist, Fascist, or just plain noninterventionist groups. It probed extensively into the affairs of numerous German-American individuals and organizations, as well as the activities of groups like the Protestant War Veterans and the Christian Front.[81]

For the first time, certain intelligence officers began to regard anti-Semitism as a manifestation of un-American and possibly subversive trends. Although army interest in the matter remained limited in scope, the very fact that a few officers perceived the problem in this light marked a dramatic change. Several reports were submitted on anti-Semitic meetings and propaganda, often linking these with pro-German or isolationist activities. Some disclosures were indeed ironic, considering MID's own history of involvement with the Jewish question, because the anti-Semites under investigation associated Jews with un-Americanism, internationalism, and communism. And intelligence officers of Miles's generation had earlier promoted those same views.[82]

While investigating the Christian Front in Boston, an officer dug up an incriminating skeleton that old-guard intelligence officers would have preferred to leave buried. The guest speaker at the Hibernian Hall, a former captain named George Moriarity, made claims that probably sounded fantastic to the undercover officer, though perhaps not to some of his superiors: The Russian Revolution had been led by "New York Jews." And Moriarity had proof. As a former MID officer in World War I, he had served on the Overman Committee investigations of communism in 1919, whose report had documented this. Unpersuaded, the local G-2 officer classified Moriarity "dangerous," because he could attract those "easily swayed by emotions."[83]

There were other ironies. Several of the individuals and groups occasionally identified as warranting investigation had long-standing affiliations with army officers. Major David G. Erskine now placed John Trevor and the American Coalition under suspicion as "anti-Semitic [and] anti-New Deal." Among those the FBI alerted G-2 to investigate for automatic arrest in time of war was the same Lothrop Stoddard who until recently had lectured at the Army Industrial College and whose books officers still read and cited. Another target, Lawrence Dennis, a prominent opponent of intervention and Roosevelt, was in contact with Truman Smith, who had introduced him to Lindbergh.[84]

The shift in G-2 was, in part, due to progressive changes in America and Roosevelt's campaign to discredit isolationists, rightists, and anti-Semites as un-American forces linked to foreign powers. But the broadening of G-2's scope to include the right, and to a more limited extent anti-Semites, also reflected the growing diversity of an expanding army. More and more, the army mirrored the complex makeup of America in contrast to the homogeneous old officer corps. At least part of the new officers were more broad-minded than their predecessors; among them, no doubt were also New Dealers and a variety of ethnics, including Jews.

Still, in the upper echelons of G-2, the entrenched old guard was soon reinforced by the return of badly needed experienced officers. Miles recruited his former MID friends and mentors who had retired or scattered to other branches. As attachés or counterintelligence officers, several of them had been involved with the earlier surveillance of radicals and Jews.

Miles unsuccessfully sought an appointment for Colonel Oscar Solbert, the attaché to England during the infamous *Protocols* affair. For the chief of G-2's Liaison Branch, controlling attachés, and relations with the State Department, Miles tapped his old friend Colonel Elbert E. Farman. Although he knew Farman was a zealous anti-Semite, Miles considered him "the man for the job," because "it's an important one and requires savoir-faire, vision, initiative and executive ability." Farman's former assistant attaché in Warsaw, Major Trevor W. Swett, served as acting chief of G-2's Eastern European Section. And Colonel Ralph C. Smith, former Germanophile military attaché to Paris and friend of Truman Smith, became G-2's executive officer in Washington.[85]

The new index MID drafted in 1940 for collecting and categorizing military information also indicated continuity as well as change in army thinking. The categories for examining Jews now reflected the real problems they encountered, including "restrictions of their political and civil rights" through the secret police, pogroms, purges, and penal camps. But they were also classified under "aptitude for military service and loyalty of immigrant groups" and "effect on stability of government," alongside revolutionary movements, communism, radicalism, and fascism.[86]

Miles brought back to Washington the two grandfathers of MID— Colonel Alexander Coxe and Van Deman. Both actively participated in highly confidential conferences, and Van Deman acquired official sanction and funding for his private network.

MID, including Miles, exchanged intelligence with Van Deman, while army and navy officers conducted investigations for him. Van Deman's apparatus now cast its nets rather widely to cover anything of foreign appearance. His intelligence on Italian Fascists, the German-American Bund, American Nazis, and Japanese mounted with each passing month.[87]

Yet old habits and identifications persisted. Some of Van Deman's agents opened their reports on the "typical Communist gathering" by routinely declaring that "75% were Jews," "almost all Jewish," "seventy per cent appeared to be foreign born," or "only two of whom were Gentiles." The year before, Van Deman's agents arranged meetings and security for Moseley's speeches. One agent wrote of Moseley, "[M]ore power to him . . . and all others who recognize the existence of the Jewish menace."[88]

The old frame of mind within the army certainly survived among intelligence officers at Governor's Island, New York. They informed Washington in November 1940 that New York Jews engaged in systematic subversion of the minds and values of students in the primary and secondary schools. Jews sought to weaken allegiance to America and willingness to defend the country. Behind their "liberalism," teachers "are usually found following the 'Party Line.'" The damage done by having the "most ardent radical members . . . in charge of high school classes" was compounded by their "teaching emigrants from Europe" and "refugees."[89]

Most teachers, the intelligence report went on, graduated from Hunter College and the City College of New York, which were "decidedly more to the left than is healthy" and emphasize "sociology with a 'left wing' approach." The officers clinched their argument by pointing out that both colleges were "attended predominantly by Jewish students." Equally incriminating, one of the Board of Examiners for Teachers had made a "pacifistic speech in a city school" during World War I and "four of the seven members of the Board . . . are Jewish."

Not all of these suspect Jews were easily identifiable, since Jews often adopted Anglo-Saxon names, hiding their ethnicity and true politics.[90] In reality, "sixty percent of all New York City High School principals were Jewish." One "dangerous type"—"very 'Pink'"—"spent his summers in Russia"; another "urged the young men never to . . . take part in a war, even in defense of the United States." And one was "reported to be a Communist." The officers declared that less than half of city teacher organizations were "soundly American." Taken together, all of this disclosed rather serious political and social problems in light of the fact that "the Jewish population in New York City appears to be particularly susceptible to the influence of the Communist Party."[91]

The fifth-column scare, however, was gradually shifting public opinion toward Roosevelt's side. This drift toward war brought about the coalescence of disparate noninterventionist forces into the America First Committee (AFC) in September 1940. Although never fundamentally anti-Semitic, the AFC did have its share of anti-Semites, while attracting only a couple of Jews nationwide.[92] And in the end, it would be Lindbergh's accusations against Jews that almost destroyed the AFC.

As a prominent spokesman for the AFC, Lindbergh could count on the support of Truman Smith and Major Bonner Fellers, who shared his concerns with Jewish influence. Present at the creation of AFC, the staunch isolationist Fellers was about to become the American observer with the British forces in North Africa. A relentless critic of Roosevelt and the British, Fellers eventually had to defend himself against charges of pro-Nazi sympathies.[93]

Among its top leadership, America First boasted three prominent retired generals: Hugh Johnson, Thomas S. Hammond, and Robert E. Wood, who chaired the committee. Of these three figures, Hammond and Wood each had strong opinions on the Jewish question. Like Lindbergh, Hammond saw Jews as a powerful interventionist force and wanted to make this a major public issue, whereas Wood, though privately agreeing, wanted to avoid any hint of anti-Semitism.

Wood's position was as unusual as his personal views were ambivalent. As chairman of the board of Sears Roebuck, Wood enjoyed the confidence of its Jewish family owners, the Rosenwalds. He had also earned the deepest admiration, loyalty, and friendship of Sidney J. Weinberg of Goldman, Sachs. Moreover, Wood lent his name to Jewish charity campaigns. After the war, Wood claimed that he purged any anti-Semites he found in AFC. But he also said that Lindbergh "was telling the truth about the Jewish people . . . [being one] of the principal forces leading us into war."[94]

Along with Lindbergh, Wood claimed that his noninterventionist activities had the best interests of his "Jewish friends" at heart, since surely they would become the "scapegoats" for a horrifying war and its "inevitable" terrible aftermath. "What astounds me," Wood told Weinberg, "is that for a race as brilliant as the Jewish race is, there are so few who can see ahead and see what is bound to happen." Yet this was the same Wood who could write to Lawrence Dennis that the Jews were "one minority which may try to make trouble." And when asked later about a procurement scandal while he had been quartermaster during World War I, Wood responded: "Those garment manufacturers in New York, they were mostly recent immigrants . . . and most of them hadn't any ethics. . . . Of course, today, when the sons of those men—who were mostly Polish Jewish immigrants—have grown up and earned a good education and different outlook, some of them are pretty fine."[95]

America First's strongest media support came from the "Colonel of Chicago," Robert McCormick, owner-editor of the conservative, ardently anti–New Deal *Chicago Tribune*. McCormick had earned the rank of colonel as an intelligence officer in France during World War I, where he established a lifelong friendship with Moseley. A "White-Man's Burden" variety racist, McCormick shared Lindbergh's fear of Western civilization overrun by Asiatic hordes. The *Tribune* urged France and Britain to make peace with Germany so that "civilization" could unite in a war against the "Asiatic barbarism" of Soviet Russia. Although the *Tribune* employed Jews and was circumspect on the Jewish question, McCormick was known to mimic and mock American Jews. Privately, he considered Jews a powerful force behind America's anti-German policy, suggesting after the war that Jews had America bomb Germany into rubble.[96]

Although upon the AFC's formation, Lindbergh and Smith thought it "inadvisable" to meet, by spring 1941 Smith was again discussing antiwar strategy with Lindbergh while simultaneously serving as G-2 expert on Germany.[97] And these were nerve-racking months for the General Staff, with serious British reversals as the Germans launched successful offensives in the Balkans and North Africa. Secretary of War Stimson complained about Miles's "unduly pessimistic" reports, expressing general disappointment "at the narrowness of the viewpoint of G-2 on these matters."[98]

On April 15, Marshall asked Stimson into his office for a briefing with Smith, whose attitude annoyed the secretary. Smith had "made it about as bad as it could be in the Mediterranean," Stimson wrote in his diary, and his entire view was "so anti-British" that Stimson immediately consulted privately with Marshall. Upon Stimson's insistence, all those in G-2 who concurred with Smith were "summoned" and forbidden to repeat any of this intelligence. "I couldn't stand it anymore," Stimson said, when just two days later Marshall gave him a new G-2 estimate. It "was so gloomy and so evidently influenced by the officers whose heads have been lost almost . . . by their contemplation of German efficiency." In a heated exchange with Marshall, Stimson complained about "the German-educated officers—notably Truman Smith and Ratay," and instructed that "G-2 must be toned up against pro-German influence."[99]

Meanwhile, Smith continued to advise Lindbergh on his speeches. "Kay and Truman," wrote Anne Lindbergh in her diary, "want him to reiterate all the points he has used. They think his speech from Minneapolis was the best yet." Lindbergh also arranged a meeting between Smith and the "silent partner" in America First, Herbert Hoover.[100] The next day, Smith spouted secret military and political intelligence to Hoover, arguing that the British should "make a peace" and that "an expeditionary force to Europe is crazy." Smith said that no one in G-2 "could see any point of our going to war" and that "no member of the General Staff wants to go to war but they can bring no great influence to bear on the situation."[101] The political "pressures on

General Marshall were so great" that if questioned publicly, the General Staff "would be compelled to issue some kind of equivocation."[102]

A few months later a medical board forced Smith to retire, freeing him for America First affairs at a crucial turning point, for on September 11, Lindbergh delivered his infamous radio address at Des Moines, Iowa, which played into the hands of critics and almost split the AFC apart.

Of the "three major groups" Lindbergh identified as "agitating for war," two had long been part of the public debate: the British and the Roosevelt administration. Lindbergh's interjection of the "Jewish people," however, was explosive. He empathized with their sufferings and desire to destroy Nazism: "No person with a sense of dignity of mankind can condone the persecution of the Jewish race in Germany." But then he attacked "their pro-war policy," which would "lead our country to destruction."[103]

Most troubling, however, was not his identification of Jews with interventionism but how he described American Jews. It was a clear-cut case of "us and them," with Lindbergh drawing a line between a separate "Jewish race" and real Americans. To him, Jews in America, Germany, and elsewhere had "their own interests" quite distinct from "ours." This "Jewish race" acted "for reasons which are not American." Yet they had immense power and control over public life: "Their greatest danger to this country lies in their large ownership and influence in our motion pictures, our press, our radio, and our Government." Intervention would be disastrous for the Jews themselves, as they would be the first victims of the "war and devastation" that would quickly destroy the "tolerance" Jews enjoyed in times of "peace and strength."[104]

Despite AFC damage control, the stigma of anti-Semitism was thereafter impossible to cleanse. MID, which had followed AFC activities for some time, noted that Lindbergh's "interjection of racial prejudice" had shifted the support of many isolationists to the "administration's foreign policy."

Among Lindbergh's staunch defenders was retired general Thomas S. Hammond, the Chicago chairman, who urged unqualified support. The Jewish race's "prejudiced and disproportionate influence on today's affairs" warrants public discussion, Hammond said, especially since "the Jews do constitute a definite problem and a threat to our peace." Besides, Lindbergh actually sympathized with the Jews; his warning "should be regarded by them as a real service to their very existence."[105]

The Lindbergh-Smith relationship remained unaffected. Since his retirement, Smith had openly associated with AFC leaders and gatherings. In early November, Lindbergh and Smith traveled to Chicago for meetings with General Wood and others, including McCormick of the *Tribune*. Although a harsh critic of Lindbergh's ill-advised speech, Wood privately agreed with him.[106]

By this point, though, Smith and Wood not only struggled against the tide of public opinion, but they confronted shifts in army attitudes. Increasingly, many officers concluded the "American cause is inseparably linked with the British cause." While noninterventionists like Embick and Wedemeyer never wavered, recent events had, many felt, already created a "state of undeclared war." Economic and military assistance through Lend-Lease had been extended to Britain, then Russia; American draftees had their service extended by eighteen months. When American ships were fired upon in the Atlantic, merchant vessels were armed and the navy was ordered to "shoot on sight" enemy warships.

More and more officers believed that the decision for war had already been made. They were at the point of "right or wrong, my country."[107] When the Japanese bombed Pearl Harbor, the isolationists united wholeheartedly behind the war effort. And Truman Smith was immediately ordered back into service as Marshall's trusted adviser on German affairs.[108]

Although isolationists in the army had lost this battle, they had increased the doubts about the wisdom of fighting a war in Europe and the part that Jews had played in taking American down this path. Certainly officers like Smith, Wedemeyer, and others believed Jewish pressure was significant. Ever since the beginning of the Third Reich, they, like many officers at the War College, had warned against this outcome.

In fact, concern about adding credibility to certain popular sentiments that this was a war over Jews also inhibited Roosevelt in relief efforts or even in focusing attention on the destruction of European Jewry. Ever since 1933, the Roosevelt administration had to dispel notions that it placed the needs of foreign Jews over those of Americans. In wartime, such undercurrents took on additional gravity. Thus, the president and other governmental agencies were ever careful to avoid creating the impression at home or abroad that American boys were dying for Jews.

The conscious decision to downplay the Jewish question during the war was reinforced by advice from, among others, Roosevelt's military leaders, who informed him that Nazi propaganda was exploiting susceptibility abroad to claims that this was a war for Jews.[109] Throughout the war, even in the face of the Holocaust, many officers remained suspicious of Jewish influence and interests working against the wartime needs of America.

CHAPTER 9

Officers and the Holocaust, 1940–1945

O N June 17, 1940, Colonel Charles E. Loucks was simply too busy to eat lunch, for that day he was overwhelmed by the work in the visa section, where all available personnel at the American embassy in Paris had been reassigned. It was a necessary but unusual job for someone with his background and expertise. A chemical and munitions specialist posted as assistant attaché, Loucks typified the rising officer of his generation in career path and attitudes. Commissioned during World War I, he had served with the Siberian Expeditionary Forces in 1919, done his Philippine tour, and attended the Army Industrial College. Now he was processing the throngs of people besieging the U.S. consulate in search of visas. As French military resistance quickly collapsed in the face of the approaching German armies, the lines of visa seekers had grown enormously.

Loucks worked hard to facilitate the exit of Americans and their relatives. He truly commiserated with the plight of certain foreign refugees frantically pleading for consideration, describing them as "sad cases," "hopeless!" Some worried about their daughters; some threatened suicide; some merely collapsed.[1]

Those failing to find escape or refuge were, Loucks wrote, "largely Jewish." Among these, he distinguished between the "desirable" ones and the "others." What Loucks often found particularly striking about certain petitioners was that "they did not look very Jewish." He described such types as "cultured and reasonably attractive—refined in speech and definitely not 'kikes.'"

Later, Loucks reacted similarly to Jewish refugee businessmen and scientists in London who offered their services to America. He felt they
would do anything to defeat Nazism. Upon learning that companies in
several countries were owned by the same Jewish family, however, Loucks
noted in his diary: "Clever, these Jews."[2]

While a "refined Jewish couple" might be deemed acceptable, the "agitators and trouble makers" (whom he could apparently readily identify from
a brief encounter) constituted a danger to the American way of life. Loucks
envisaged among them the future radicals who would seize the first opportunity to "abuse" American freedoms. He compared them to radical American labor leaders, German-American Bundists, and fanatical Coughlinites,
and even to some in Roosevelt's administration. "None have even American
parentage," Loucks emphasized; they assaulted American democratic ideals
with the radical doctrines of class struggle and European hatreds. Of course,
as a humane and idealistic American, Loucks stated that he would, nonetheless, help these pathetic people if he could, though always realizing that as
soon as they were well fed, "they would slit my throat."[3]

To Loucks, the French experience offered America an excellent "lesson"
about the necessity of a "strong conservative democracy." He attributed
the French military debacle to the "collapse of ideals and patriotism"
caused by years of leftist governments. While condemning Nazi totalitarianism as equally unacceptable, Loucks was impressed by the Germans he
saw occupying Paris, whom he described as "reasonable" and "unoffen-
sive." Unlike the shamed and defeated French, they were "disciplined" in
appearance and behavior. "Good looking and young—First line troops,"
they were, Loucks exclaimed in admiration, "the German Army."[4]

The triumphant German army that heightened the refugee crisis in the
West would also set the stage for the Holocaust by its equally impressive
conquests in the East the following year. Nevertheless, when the American
officer corps confronted the desperate need for refuge at the outbreak of
war and later learned of the real magnitude of the Holocaust, it proved as
hesitant to deal with the plight of European Jews as it had been reluctant
to enter the war. The arguments sustaining its previous resistance to Jewish immigration and refugees were expanded to include the dictates of
wartime necessity, for throughout the war the Jewish question overlapped
with the perceptions and realities of national and operational security.

Since policy decisions in such matters often lent themselves to wide-rang-
ing interpretations, the attitudes and preconceived notions of officers making or affecting such judgments were vitally important. Thus, what appeared

to be legitimate military needs and concerns too often became rationalizations for inaction or opposition to relief and rescue. Geopolitical and strategic arguments of this kind helped keep Palestine closed to Jewish refugees and, together with questionable logistical reasoning, prevented the army's serious consideration of the bombing of Auschwitz. Meanwhile, fear of subversion or Jewish influence justified greatly restricting refugees to America as well as renewed surveillance of Jews at home and abroad.

Officers and Refugees

Although the German army had elicited great respect from Colonel Loucks, it incited widespread fear in America, where the presumed invincibility of the German army was explained, in part, by fifth-column treachery. The fifth-column hysteria conjured up by Roosevelt and others to bolster the case for intervention had come back to haunt them. It became a major obstacle to Roosevelt's efforts to assist refugees fleeing Nazi persecution and, soon, annihilation. The fifth-column threat added a new twist to the problem Loucks and others felt they faced in separating "desirable" refugees from the rest. Supposedly the Soviets, Nazis, and Vichy government used refugees to infiltrate espionage agents into the United States. Either agents posed as Jewish refugees or Jews were blackmailed into spying.[5]

Although some rumors of Jewish refugee spies originated with State Department officials, this illusionary threat was mostly created by the FBI, ONI, and G-2. Intelligence reports issued by these agencies not only raised public misgivings about refugees but convinced government officials and Roosevelt himself of the existence of this hidden danger. When asked at a press conference whether the government could not do more to lessen discrimination by allaying suspicions that refugees from Nazi Germany were fifth columnists, Roosevelt responded that "unfortunately" he could not. There were, he said, "some spies" among those fleeing to America, just as in other countries where the Nazi fifth column operated, there were among "especially Jewish refugees . . . a number of definitely proven spies." By noting that they were "spying by compulsion" and that the government had the "story . . . rather fully," the misguided president presented the dubious hostage theory as a fact based upon sound intelligence.[6]

Two figures prominent in perpetuating the refugee spy alarm were J. Edgar Hoover and General Sherman Miles, whose agencies provided much of U.S. intelligence on security matters at home and abroad. While German armies were rolling across France in June 1940, Hoover informed Miles by "special messenger" that "German Espionage Agents . . . in the guise of German-Jewish refugees" were already in America and more were on the way. Throughout that year, Hoover and Miles forwarded to the president and State Department similar disclosures from "confidential sources." Meanwhile, Miles intensified his efforts to tighten immigration controls and encouraged legislation requiring registration and fingerprinting of all aliens.[7]

The actions of Miles and Hoover concerning "German-Jewish agents" cannot be explained merely as a reaction to imminent danger and impending war. Nor can their groundless allegations of Jews as instruments of foreign subversion be attributed to "faulty surveillance," as has recently been claimed.[8] The FBI and MID had a long history of inherent suspicion, prejudice, and political action against Jews. Miles and Hoover had personally been involved in the surveillance of Jews (native born, immigrant, and foreign) during the early 1920s.

At that time, their agencies were already predisposed to view Jews as racially undesirable alien types with subversive tendencies. After World War I, the intelligence community had invoked the authority of "reliable confidential sources" innumerable times to associate Jews with pro-German and Bolshevik sympathies and subversion. After the Nazi-Soviet Non-Aggression Pact of August 1939, they again discovered Jews as German and Communist agents.

It was assumed the Nazis and Soviets blackmailed Jewish refugees by withholding exit papers or holding families hostage. Yet, amazingly, some Jews were suspected of acting out of loyalty to Germany. That Jews also willingly worked for the Communist cause was a long-standing institutional view. In 1918, MID had accused reputable Jewish relief and rescue organizations of collaborating with the Germans and Bolsheviks either out of commitment or in exchange for Jews. Now, the intelligence community revived charges that the Hebrew Immigrant Aid Society and Joint Distribution Committee were knowingly infiltrating spies into America.[9]

These assumptions led to policies making it more difficult for Jews to enter the United States in the early stages of World War II, when more Jews could have escaped than later. New regulations and hardened sentiments ensured that far fewer visas would be issued Jewish refugees than were actually authorized under law. Some in the State Department and MID wanted to suspend all immigration from Axis or Soviet occupied territories but had to settle for new procedures eliminating security risks and "undesirable immigration."

Henceforth, visa applications would be screened by Interdepartmental Committees representing the State Department, Immigration Service, FBI, MID, and Naval Intelligence (ONI). This crucial change in policy gave the intelligence agencies a decisive voice in immigration. They had "to clear sponsors and immigrants through their own record sections" for "derogatory information," thereby influencing significantly reactions to visa applicants with their data and interpretations. If need be, they could simply outvote State and Immigration members. Army policy was that "in the present emergency risks cannot be taken"; in case of doubt, "visas should be withheld."[10]

Major Charles R. Mabee, the G-2 in charge of formulating policy, and his superior, Major Carter W. Clarke, considered the new procedures "mild restrictions." Not to admit that the country faced a "critical subversive situation," Mabee argued, would constitute a dereliction of duty, since "historical fact" showed the countries conquered by Axis powers had for months or years "been softened by the infiltration of enemy agents, fifth columnists, and Axis sympathizers."

Yet Mabee and his associates thought far beyond the immediate wartime emergency. Tracing the problem back long before the Nazis had come to power, Mabee again clearly revealed the continuity in MID's thinking since World War I. The source of the current "acute" danger, he wrote, was the "innumerable undesirable aliens and subversive elements" who had entered the United States "for the last twenty years."[11]

When an advisory committee to Roosevelt complained about the veto power of the intelligence community and the number of visa applications rejected, Mabee responded with speculative, highly dubious examples of Jewish refugee agents. Typical was the case of one "Jewess" suspected of being a "German agent" for no other reason than she had "ample funds" and the intelligence officers thought she endeavored "to contact Wright Field employees for future subversive activities." Mabee saw "a mounting volume of subversive activity" by such refugees that neither military intelligence at the time nor subsequent studies have substantiated. But such claims by those experienced in security matters continued to convince Roosevelt, who merely established an Appeals Board with two presidential appointees.[12]

There soon developed a struggle between Interdepartmental Committees and the Appeals Board, which reversed twenty-five per cent of the negative decisions. Finding even this ratio unacceptable, Mabee's replacement, Colonel George D. Dorroh, favored counterbalancing the presidential appointees with retired military men to "minimize reversals."[13]

The anxiety of intelligence officers never abated. On October 22, 1942, the Director of Naval Intelligence sent a lengthy memorandum to all District Intelligence Officers, as well as the FBI, MID, and State Department. It concerned the "great danger to our National Security" posed by the "Refugee Problem."[14]

The assumptions and allegations permeating the entire document were variations on long-standing anti-Semitic beliefs about the questionable loyalty of Jews and their unscrupulous pursuit of money. Capitalizing on their humanitarian reputations and "anti-Fascist tendencies," the American Joint Distribution Committee and HIAS "arouse public sympathy and obtain privileged treatment" for refugees. But there existed "convincing proof" that these organizations were vehicles for infiltrating those engaged in "espionage and sabotage for the Axis powers."

In their "eagerness" to assist fellow Jews, such organizations disregarded American national interests. They were "willing to strike a bargain with Nazi authorities whereby certain of the alleged refugees would agree to act as Nazi agents in return for permission granted them and perhaps other groups to leave Germany."[15]

Part of this "danger to the security of the Western Hemisphere," ONI argued, emanated not from humanitarianism or ethnic allegiance but from selfish economic motives. Much of this refugee activity was simply a Jewish "racket." Not only would certain Jewish individuals and organizations sell out the United States, but, ONI claimed, they consciously collaborated with the Nazi persecutors of the Jews if the price was right. According to Naval Intelligence:

> a very large proportion of the agencies and individuals engaged in the refugee traffic appear to be moved by purely commercial considerations. These reports reveal a complicated interlocking of Jewish welfare agencies, travel agencies, both legitimate and shady, and officials of various Latin American countries, all of whom see the present situation merely as an opportunity for making a large amount of money. The danger to security lies in the fact that these many agencies are so eager to bring over refugees, on each one of which they are able to realize a substantial profit, that they have little interest in the connections of the individuals whom they are "importing," and not only do they fail to make any careful investigation of the in-

dividual's bona fides, but there is evidence that if the price is high enough they will overlook suspicious circumstances. Inasmuch as many genuine refugees are without the funds to pay the exorbitant fees demanded, obvious opportunities for profit lie with agents posing as refugees who are financed by the Nazi Government.[16]

In practice, cases were frequently decided on the basis of biased presuppositions or caprice. One German refugee scholar personally sponsored by the librarian of Congress and supported by the Rockefeller Foundation was initially rejected. Although he eventually won approval, MID and the FBI dissented vigorously, because he had relatives in Germany and these agencies had "derogatory information" on his other sponsor, the New School for Social Research.[17]

Sponsorship had its own risks. When several Jewish soldiers signed a petition for a prominent Jewish leader in Vienna, all were immediately investigated. The "State Department's refusal to issue a visa," in itself, led an investigating officer in North Carolina automatically to assume that a sponsoring soldier's "loyalty appears to be in question." The signature of another Jewish soldier stationed in Illinois raised suspicions among intelligence officers of his possible "Nazi sympathies or activities."[18]

The Appeals Board seriously questioned whether "hostage pressure" or other means could force persecuted Jews into the "Nazi cause" or whether Nazi agents would risk dealing with refugees. Assistant Secretary of State Adolf A. Berle concurred that policy should not be based upon unfounded fears of refugee subversion. But policy and practice remained relatively unaffected.[19]

The burdensome process of investigation, disapproval, and appeal continued, significantly slowing rescue efforts through legal immigration. The War Refugee Board (WRB) later estimated that in 1943 only 11,737 immigrants were admitted, while 142,142 quota slots went unfilled, the lowest immigration rate since 1862. This was partly due to wartime conditions, which greatly limited immigration from occupied Europe. Nevertheless, the WRB pointed out if the United States admitted Jewish refugees already in non-Axis territory, from Spain to Palestine and South America, these countries would be more willing to admit additional refugees who could escape. This could be greatly facilitated merely by "a more realistic and sympathetic attitude" by the Interdepartmental Committee.[20]

Besides the newcomers, the military remained exceedingly worried about the "unpatriotic and dangerous minorities" already in the United States. Although ever vigilant against German, Italian, and Japanese groups, by 1943 officers conceded that subversive activity among them was almost nonexistent. More and more, the army's search for subversion turned to communism, which once again focused attention on Jews. A substantial number of visas were denied on grounds not of Axis espionage but alleged Communist affiliations or sympathies. Thus, while continuing to report on anti-Semitism, the army conducted surveillance of Jewish groups.[21]

Jewish conferences and rallies supporting the Soviet war effort and Russian war relief, including those attended by Rabbi Stephen Wise of the American Jewish Congress, were still categorized under "subversive situation," as was the convention at the Waldorf Astoria of the American Jewish Conference dealing with Zionism. When 500 Jewish rabbis traveled to Washington in 1943 to petition the president and Congress to "rescue the Jews of Europe," army counterintelligence agents followed their every move, even filming part of the events. As late as 1944, the army opened a new file on "Jewish Groups." Its first entry, drawn from "reliable" MID and FBI sources, claimed "Communist Control" among "high leaders" in the B'nai B'rith who "dictate the policies . . . in conformance with the Party line."[22]

Van Deman's agents in New York also suspected the B'nai B'rith and Anti-Defamation League. Citing communism as "absolutely the last stronghold for the international Jew," one "special report" linked these groups to an intricate web of Jewish business, financial, and political interests reaching up to close Roosevelt advisers such as "Judge Roseman" and "David K. Niles." The "Jewish element in the motion picture industry" bribed the House Un-American Activities Committee "to the tune of $100,000" to go easy on "Jewish interests in the east," while Jewish manipulation of the press and other government officials protected the "intellectual reds and radical Jews." These were the types of reports Van Deman routed to the FBI, ONI, and G-2.

From coast to coast, Van Deman's network infiltrated organizations and meetings related to Russian war relief. Regarding "some of the 'Big Shots'" on a list of "500 Writers of Red-Pink-Yellow Hue" who demanded a second front to relieve the Soviet Union, an agent added, "Notice a number are refugees." Other agents observed that of the 12,000 people at a Hollywood Bowl Tribute to Russia rally, "95% of them were Jews"; at another "spectacle," "negro and white people associated with one another." A Communist convention in Los Angeles ("about 90% Jews") brought to light a particularly worrisome trend, as "approximately 25 members of the

U.S. Army" attended: "Most of the men in uniform appeared to be Jews and definitely were with Jewish companions."[23]

Jewish Soldiers and Anti-Semitism

Of all areas of subversion, infiltration of the army concerned many officers the most. As in World War I, such officers looked askance upon the large percentage of ethnics, recent immigrants as well as second generation, as the country mobilized its manpower for war.[24] Where did their loyalties lie? Would they fight? What would be the impact on unit cohesion and effectiveness of the very presence of these heterogeneous groups?

In early 1940, Colonel Dean Hudnutt addressed this concern in a War College study titled "Political and Racial Reasons for the Collapse of the Polish Army." Among various factors contributing to Poland's debacle such as peasant oppression and class conflict, he included the fact that the "problem of the Jews was unsettled." Relying heavily upon earlier War College studies of Poland, he reiterated depictions of troublesome Jewish characteristics as well as the dissension and suspicions they engendered. "While Christians would perform hard labor," 78 percent of Jews were in business; very few were "farm workers." The mass of ordinary Jews were "radical and difficult to handle"; even "Jewish industrialists would not employ their own." Poland considered them "a grave menace to the stability of existing institutions" and facilitated their emigration, while the "Army did not trust them."[25]

From the Polish experience, Hudnutt drew certain "Lessons of value" to the U.S. Army concerning the importance of citizenship training to create a bond of identification and loyalty between soldiers, their military leaders, and their country. He warned against those who might not fit within this community of identity. The military must "exercise great care in the selection of recruits in that we do not accept those who are agents of foreign governments." Precisely whom he had in mind came through when he immediately conjured up nativist images of earlier decades by insisting that "the American Army should not be made up of the scum of Europe."[26]

Paradoxically, there surfaced at the same time widespread complaints about large numbers of Jews evading military service. Such allegations, which had been quite prevalent during World War I, conformed to traditional stereotypes of inherently selfish, weak, and cowardly Jews shying away from anything physically strenuous or dangerous and being antimilitary almost by nature. In hearings on compulsory training before the House Military Affairs Committee, one congressman stated bluntly:

> There are great classes in this country who never have enlisted, who will be forced under this bill to assume their responsibility of serving their country. It is largely racial in my opinion. I do not think there are many Jews who would fight, and I do not think they should be left to go scot free and we should have all of them in there.[27]

The recruiting officer in St. Louis charged that escaping the draft was the "chief interest" of many young men. He told the press that "he had made a special appeal to Jewish leaders for more recruits from that race, [since] only one man of the Jewish race enlisted for service in August." In actuality, Jewish enlistment was close to 8 percent of the total. Meanwhile, a West Coast supervising officer "instructed a Draft Board confidentially that it was to examine the Jewish claims for deferment very carefully inasmuch as Jews were making improper claims and Jews and Italians were the worst offenders." Throughout Pennsylvania and New Jersey, popular anti-Semitic sentiments were aroused by rumors that "Jewish physicians serving on local draft boards were favoring the exemption of Jewish draftees."[28]

The counterpart to charges of draft evasion was the accusation that Jews who could not escape conscription avoided infantry service and combat duty. One friendly old man in Missouri gave a lift to a soldier; upon learning the soldier was Jewish, the man said quite abruptly, "I hear that all the Jewish boys in [Camp] Crowder are tying to get into the hospital to keep from going overseas." Marine paratroopers from the Pacific on leave in North Dakota told their friends that "in all their experiences they had never seen a Jew in the combat zones or the names of Jewish boys on any casualty lists." Most American soldiers had the same experience with Jews, these marines asserted, for they "had talked to Servicemen back from the North African and Italian theaters who had reported that they had never seen any Jews in the combat zones."[29]

Such accusations made some Jewish soldiers quite self-conscious about perceptions of their behavior, achievements, and assignments. A Jewish soldier recalled his mental anguish after hearing an officer ask, "Why are there so many Jewish Majors in the Medical Corps?" In one infantry unit, educational level, language skills, and high test scores led to the transfer of a high percentage of Jews for specialized training. A Jewish officer in that unit felt certain that the natural resentment against any soldier who got out would manifest itself in anti-Semitism.[30]

In fact, hundreds of thousands of Jews served during World War II; their percentages of combat dead and wounded approximated their proportion of the American population. Tens of thousands were decorated; several rose to the rank of general and admiral. Among these were old and recent Jewish immigrants who served not only loyally but enthusiastically. Some, like Gerd S. Grombacher, arrived in the late 1930s as refugees, quickly assimilated into American culture, and made the army a career; Grombacher retired as a major general. Another young refugee from Germany expressed his pride, as an American and a Jew, in fighting for his country. He denied that "most Jewish boys were behind desks," as many "served in the Infantry . . . as I did" and "fought and died in every theater."[31] What is most notable about the soldier's statement is that he felt the need to make it.

But prejudice persisted throughout the war. An officer from Mississippi made a practice of inquiring where the parents of his soldiers came from. Upon reading the Army Classification Card and discovering that 50 percent of his men were Jewish, "he complained that there were too many 'foreigners' in the outfit."[32]

In the middle of the war, a lieutenant wrote to his former commander that his new unit was the first he "ever saw that didn't have a bunch of Jewish officers in it, as we do not have a one. Thank God for it." Later, he wrote that though the "few enlisted men of Jewish persuasion" could usually "be handled," he had to "read the riot act to" his Jewish sergeant major. If a two-week furlough "to think it over" did not change his attitude, the lieutenant intended to have "him reassigned and stripped of his stripes." When the colonel who received these letters was subsequently asked to account for the anti-Semitic remarks, he responded that "he did not interpret either of these statements as indicating any prejudice . . . towards the Jews."[33]

At the level of individual soldiers, encounters with anti-Semitism during wartime service varied greatly. Some recalled no incidents at all; some felt "Army life was less anti-Semitic than civilian life"; others found it an embittering and humiliating experience. Perhaps the most common view was that the army mirrored American society; anti-Semites in civilian life carried this attitude into military service and acted accordingly.[34]

Many Jewish soldiers went into the war believing in cherished American ideals and had these ideals challenged by the prejudice they encountered but ultimately found their ideals reaffirmed by living and fighting closely with non-Jews. Such Jewish soldiers believed themselves among the most committed to fighting to preserve the "American way of life" and constitutional rights. During and after the war, many such Jewish soldiers spoke proudly of the special American values of democracy, equality, "tolerance and fair play." They found that their non-Jewish fellow soldiers were equally devoted to the same ideals but that their commitment to such principles did not preclude anti-Semitic attitudes or expressions.[35]

Perhaps most widespread were general anti-Semitic talk, anecdotes, and jokes, often in front of Jews themselves. Most consisted of age-old epithets. Jews were all rich bankers or parasitic middlemen living off the work of others, producing nothing, and contributing nothing to Western civilization. "There must be a catch somewhere," said one soldier; "I don't know of any Jew who don't make money." Such remarks often came from soldiers who had never met Jews before nor knew very much about them. They were surprised to learn, wrote one Jewish soldier, that "we weren't all bankers, and didn't have horns growing out of our heads." There was some preoccupation with long noses ("a sign of greed and avarice"). Some were shocked upon discovering that close buddies they really liked were, in fact, Jews, especially if they had short noses.[36]

Other expressions ranged from pointed remarks ("A damn Jew!" "Jew-York") to persistent mockery aimed directly at Jews as individuals and as a group. Some Jewish soldiers remembered the frequent "pointed finger," of being "singled out for repudiation and ridicule" merely because one "was a Jew." A "Jewish-sounding name" was often free game, a magnetic target too tempting to resist. One sergeant always put a big smile on his face while "pronouncing a Jewish name with an exaggerated accent on a syllable." To "some Army officers," under whom another Jewish soldier served, "no matter what the name, if it smacks of Jewishness, then it's funny."[37]

Apparently more rare, though perhaps more stinging by their very nature, were barbs with contemporary political relevance. They were particularly painful to refugees or those with relatives in concentration camps. Sometimes they came in the form of repeated jibes. As one soldier stated so bluntly, "I don't agree with Hitler except for one thing . . . the way he took care of the Jews. . . . The Jews owned practically all Germany, and it was about time the Germans got rid of them."

Neither had the army remained immune to the latest conspiracy theory. Certain soldiers insisted this was really a "Jewish war"; Americans were fighting and dying "merely to maintain Jewish business interests not democratic ideals."[38]

The responses of Jewish soldiers were as varied as their personalities and specific circumstances. At one extreme, a "certain percentage . . . tried to conceal and deny their Jewish identity or play it down." A few changed their names; Cohn became Clarke. Others eschewed any behavior that might be construed as revealing typical "Jewish characteristics." At the other end of the spectrum, "many a Jewish GI settled the problem . . . with his fists." When reasonable and feasible, fighting back seems to have been a sure means of achieving broad respect, even "cheers," since standing up for yourself and winning through "fair play" were considered admirable American characteristics. Usually, though, reactions were confined to discussions and arguments; there were instances of successful persuasion.[39]

Except among incorrigible types, familiarity arising from living together diminished overt anti-Semitism at the unit level. As time passed, men realized they were bound to a similar fate and shared common interests as soldiers, including the same complaints about army life. To the extent that a true esprit de corps gradually evolved as a potent unifying bond within a unit, it reduced accordingly rancor and confrontations growing out of religious and ethnic differences. The longer soldiers lived together away from civilian life, and then the farther from home they traveled, the less prevalent anti-Semitism seems to have been. One Jewish soldier recalled that it "made the men more understanding and tolerant towards each other."

Battle provided the ultimate bonding. Jewish soldiers frequently attested that "there were no anti-Semites at the front line." In combat, the "Jew shared the same fox hole with his Christian buddy"; they "all hugged the ground and sweated blood." Under fire, a soldier's comrade was like "his own brother." As recounted by a Jewish infantryman, "it was never a question of going out there to save a Catholic, Jew or Negro, it was going out there to save John, David, or Jimmy. . . . It was this UNITY that gave us VICTORY."[40]

Within an institution fully engaged in fighting for freedom and democracy against Nazism, there was always the option of pursuing recourse through official channels. The segregation of African-Americans notwithstanding, official army policy condemned any form of racial or religious prejudice. A letter to a congressman, a word with the chaplain, or a complaint to superior officers usually brought some reaction. How sincere the commitment or effective the response depended upon the individual officer. Even though "open discrimination of any sort was not countenanced," stated a Jewish chaplain, when officers took action on such matters the problem was usually "submerged rather than eradicated."

Many Jewish soldiers suspected that anti-Semitism was far more prevalent among older soldiers and "regular army officers," especially "higher
officers." And at "higher levels," anti-Semitism was "the subtle kind that
made counter-action impossible." Although Jewish soldiers sensed this
only from limited experiences with individual officers (and some Jews
thought such suspicions groundless), the history of an anti-Semitic culture
within the officer corps tends to bear out their hunches.[41]

Manifestations of anti-Semitism in the officer corps ranged from the mild
to the vicious, from the cultural-religious slur to the political and racial perspective. Some of this stemmed subtly, perhaps even unconsciously, from the
residue of Darwinian theories about race and ethnicity inculcated in the preceding decades. In the *Command of Negro Troops*, the War Department felt
compelled to instruct officers that "effective command cannot be based upon
racial theories" and that Nazi theories of inferior and superior races were
"nonsense." Since the War Department worried that "RACIAL THEORIES
WASTE MANPOWER," it clearly believed that a serious problem existed.
Although directed at commanders of African-American troops, such directives had relevance to ethnic minorities generally.[42]

As certain officers matured, broadened their experiences or were re-
pulsed by the extreme consequences of Nazi racial theory, they overcame
or tempered their earlier views. But the extent and sincerity of such transformations are difficult to identify and assess. In light of Nazi barbarism,
the wartime devastation itself, tens of millions of civilian and military
deaths, and revelations about death camps, some were definitely converted,
whereas others simply preferred to forget their own past attitudes.

After fighting his way across Europe, Colonel Benjamin A. Dickson
chastised Nazi racial ideology, the fanatical bigotry of its young adherents,
and the bestiality of the extermination camps. His wartime journal made
such racism, hatred, and brutality seem incomprehensible. Yet as a young
officer in Siberia in 1919, Dickson himself had proclaimed the racial superiority of whites and American civilization over that of Russians, Orientals, and others: "Russians are lazier than our niggers." He appeared in
these years to be quite concerned about "race mixing" and "race suicide,"
and took note when his commanding officer married a girl of mixed Russian and Mongolian heritage. The young Dickson also saw the necessity of
violence in the suppression of domestic enemies: "In the states the people
who are Red or anarchistic should be shot down like dogs. Believe me I
would have no compunction at all about massacring such devils as the
American Bolsheviks."[43]

The past followed some officers right into the war. Floyd L. Parks had served as aide-de-camp to former chief of staff Malin Craig during the Moseley sterilization controversy, so he was undoubtedly familiar with, and perhaps took part in, the anti-Semitic banter among officers of that time. Parks himself invoked stereotypes for humorous effect, describing a man "with a rather Semitic Cast of Countenance." And his wife? Well, Parks would "know her nose anywhere." After graduating from the War College in 1940, Parks rose to the rank of general and later military governor in Berlin.

In the middle of the war, Parks established a good relationship with Hersh Livazer, a Jewish chaplain under his command, going so far as to attended Jewish services. Although this gesture won Livazer's profound admiration and respect, it struck General Craig as hilarious. For at least a half year, Craig needled his friend and former aide about how rabbis performed ("rattling good talkers") and about baptism with a "pair of scissors," speculating that perhaps "my Hebrew friends . . . are not so bad after all." In the spring of 1944, while the army was being requested to take some action to hinder Nazi genocide, Craig continued his quips. Could the rabbi be "one of those birds with straggly long black whiskers in which the bats hang, or fly in and out. Or perhaps . . . a nice looking young fellow with a goatee, or maybe he has no hair on his chest at all."[44]

While fewer officers were willing to convey such ideas in writing than before the war, certain ones felt highly justified in continuing to express their earlier views. The reason Truman Smith had not already been awarded the Distinguished Service Medal, General Wedemeyer told General Marshall in 1944, was that Smith had wrongly "received a lot of unfavorable publicity, sponsored, I believe, by the Jews."[45] There was, however, a definite feeling among some officers at home and overseas that the political climate created by the Roosevelt administration had forced them into silence, particularly concerning Jews and Communists.

The "Secret Americans"

While the Germans were attacking France in May 1940, Colonel Henry C. McLean, former G-2 chief in the Philippines, traveled through Palestine on his return home. The impressive growth and modernization in Palestine did not surprise him. He saw it as a natural consequence of the "recent reentry of the Jews." Wherever he journeyed thereafter—Hong Kong, the

Philippines—he always noticed Jewish businesses and their success. In Jerusalem, McLean had a "delightful" time with Vice Consul Blatchford, a man "very fond of telling jokes, particularly on the Jews." McLean recorded several of these in his copious diaries: Zionism as rich American Jews persuading poor Jews to emigrate to Palestine; a grossly distorted sense of Jewish business "ethics" and honesty; stupid Irish Catholics afraid to bear "Kike children."[46]

Reassigned to MacArthur's intelligence staff when the United States entered the war, McLean spent the duration of the conflict in the Pacific, far removed from the Jewish question. Yet he retained his keen interest in Jews, whom he usually identified in such terms as the "aggressive Jewish businessman" or "a Jewess, very pushy and with ambitions both social and political." In his mind, Jews (American and foreign, at home and abroad) were getting whatever they could out of the war, even at the risk of American lives, while contributing very little.[47]

At headquarters, he was "suspicious" of "some of the elements," especially an officer from New York—"a Jew"—whom he believed continued his business intrigues as a "scavenger for Lehman Brothers." This Jewish officer allegedly had sufficient political influence to force General Marshall to relieve his competitor. Using "any rank for purposes of his own," this "very ambitious" officer sought "military titles and recognition," even though "he had never had a gun in his hand." "One of the Jewish refugees" from Nazified Austria was arrested for selling "deadly liquor" that killed numerous soldiers and blinded others. "He is really a murderer."[48]

Perhaps McLean's most startling diary entry implied that Jewish greed was behind the reluctance of the British Shell Oil Company to furnish the air force with the "80% octane gas" it needed, whereas the Standard Oil Company willingly supplied whatever the military required. The British company, McLean wrote, would only provide "60% gas," because paying for higher "lead content . . . reduces their profits." He attributed this selfish business decision in wartime, in part, to the "fact that by far the great majority of the Shell Company is Jewish." The consequences were potentially disastrous for Allied airmen, he noted, since the "poorer gasoline reduces the efficiency of our planes and increases their danger."[49]

McLean described "from good authority" a similar case of Jewish interests taking precedence over the lives of brave American soldiers. An officer from Washington allegedly told him that while the Allies fought in North Africa, the United Nations Relief and Rehabilitation Administration had suggested that "practically all of the bed spaces in the American Army hospitals in North Africa be turned over to Jewish refugees from Europe on their way to Palestine." Only threats to expose it to the press foiled the plan. McLean predicted indignantly that "if the American public should learn that their wounded and sick sons were being neglected there would be a big reaction and an irresistible one."[50]

By late 1943, McLean learned more about the un-American forces affecting policy from Colonel Bonner Fellers, who had been transferred from Washington to MacArthur's intelligence staff. The situation had become so bad, this old acquaintance told him, that those officers "looking after the interests of their own country" had to "keep it quiet" or face official or unofficial retaliation or silencing. Back home, they started humorously referring to themselves as "Secret Americans."

Within military intelligence, there formed a clique of established officers in Washington and abroad who embodied such feelings and acted accordingly. Some, like Fellers, had earlier affiliations with the America First movement, while others were distressed by what they believed were detrimental American wartime policies formulated in the interests of the British, Jews, and Soviet Communists.[51]

The clique to which Fellers belonged included Marshall's German specialists (Truman Smith and Percy Black), Colonel Ivan D. Yeaton, a "Russian Specialist" and chief of G-2's European Branch, and Colonel Carter W. Clarke, chief of G-2's code-breaking operations. Behind the scenes, Smith and Fellers maintained their political connections to former America First friends Robert Wood, Charles Lindbergh, and Robert McCormick of the *Tribune*. They also leaked secret information to Roosevelt's opponents, such as Herbert Hoover and Supreme Court Justice Frank Murphy.[52]

The circle extended to Frank E. Mason and William LaVarre, two officials convinced of insidious Jewish power in America and Communist infiltration of the government. A former intelligence officer and vice president at NBC then serving as special assistant to the secretary of the navy, "Colonel" Mason retained his close contacts with his G-2 friends in Washington. This confidant of Herbert Hoover and Ambassador Hugh Gibson stated that he had learned in the 1930s of the tremendous economic and political power of the Jews, who only "look out for Jewish interests." Mason found "their penetration . . . incredible"; however, it was not until the 1970s that he felt comfortable enough to speak out against the "corruption that American Jews—some of them at least—are sowing on Capitol Hill." "I have reached the stage in life," he wrote, "where organized Jews can no longer hurt me."[53]

LaVarre was a journalist serving in the State Department during World War II. At that time, he leaked information from military intelligence, which he believed was being systematically suppressed by "pro-Communist officials in Washington" and other un-American forces. In the 1950s, he would become editor in chief of the conservative *American Mercury Magazine*. Alarmed at supposed Jewish penetration of the White House during the 1960s and 1970s, LaVarre would compile a thick dossier of documents and exhibits to prove the pernicious behind-the-scenes expansion of Jewish and Zionist power over Washington and the presidency, from Wilson to Roosevelt.[54]

Within such circles, the prevailing attitude throughout the war appeared to be that Felix Frankfurter and Henry Morgenthau had "tremendous power with Roosevelt" and were "responsible for many of the President's moves," including military strategy and objectives vis-à-vis Germany and the Soviet Union. In 1943, Truman Smith complained to Herbert Hoover that the "President was headstrong and not disposed to listen to any of his military advisers." Fellers, Smith, and Yeaton were more concerned about the prospect of an ultimate Soviet victory assisted by American economic and military power than they were about achieving a quick defeat of Nazi Germany. Yeaton's uncompromising anti-Soviet attitude and interference with Lend-Lease had already led to his removal as military attaché to Moscow. Smith had serious reservations about Roosevelt's policy of strategic bombing of Germany, total destruction of the German army, and unconditional surrender.[55]

Fellers and Yeaton believed that the Russians constituted a backward, "temperamental" Slavic race lacking "the stability of the Teuton and Anglo-Saxon"; psychologically, the Slav "is incapable of the intense sustained effort demanded by a prolonged war." Still, Yeaton feared an anticipated postwar surge in Soviet power and shuddered at the thought of a "western advance of the atheist-led, Oriental-minded Eastern Slav." Fellers also worried about the "Yellow Peril," as Japanese domination of the "Oriental Billion" turned them against the "White Man" in a racial war in Asia while the United States concentrated on Europe.[56]

In Feller's geopolitical thought, the keys to American postwar security and the "peace of the world" were air power and oil, which necessitated bases in the Philippines and Middle East. For this reason, "without delay the United States must secure the friendship of the Moslem world." A major obstacle, however, was "the Jew-Arab Problem" that had concerned Fellers since his Cairo assignment. "Jewish colonization of Palestine," he wrote, "creates the only barriers to a British-Arab agreement. Immediate settlement of this controversy is of utmost importance to the United States."[57]

While in the Pacific, Fellers had little chance to affect policy, whereas Yeaton was in charge of a G-2 section that would be called upon for intelligence regarding Jews and the Middle East. A nativist who proudly traced his ancestry back to a Revolutionary War hero, Yeaton developed his anti-Communist zeal in Siberia in 1919. Ever paranoid about conspiracies, he thought Communists had infiltrated the White House and MID, seriously compromising security. He also believed in notions of a strong Jewish-Communist connection.

Yeaton claimed that his experience as a G-2 Soviet expert had shown him that Jews and homosexuals made the best targets for KGB recruitment. It was this mentality that later permitted him to seriously consider that presidential adviser Henry Kissinger might actually be a Soviet agent. Although Kissinger was not a homosexual, Yeaton argued, he could, as a foreign-born Jew with a fondness for women, have been recruited or blackmailed while serving as a G-2 officer in Germany.[58]

Colonel Carter Clarke, previously involved in the military scrutiny of refugee passports and visas, became highly regarded by the upper ranks of the army hierarchy. As chief of the newly established Special Branch in G-2, he was entrusted with one of the greatest secrets of the war, the code-breaking machine Ultra. Some of the analysts and most famous cryptographers in Clarke's branch were the very kind of Jews that officers automatically suspected. At least one was the son of Russian Jewish immigrants, while others had graduated from the "Red" City College of New York. But it is unknown whether they were the ones that certain intelligence officers referred to when claiming that Soviet agents infiltrated this branch and that all information (in some cases as much as 80 percent) unfavorable to communism or the Soviet Union was suppressed.[59]

What Clarke thought of Jews and the Jewish question during the war is likewise not evident. At the time, however, Fellers described him as a close friend for ten years and an associate of this intelligence political circle, a "true-believer" in whom they could "place complete reliance." Fellers recommended that the "exceptionally well-informed" Clarke brief Herbert Hoover; and LaVarre later stated that Clarke had been a major source of information. According to Frank Mason, Clarke complained bitterly in the 1970s about America's subservience to Israel. As Mason related it to others in the clique, Clarke had written to him: "If, and a big—damned big IF, as the Jews claim the Protocols of the Elders of Zion were f—— cooked up by the Russian Secret Police, why is it that so much they contain has already come to pass, and the rest so strongly advocated by the *Washington Post* and the *New York Times*."[60]

While earlier supervising the G-2 section's handling of visa policies, Clarke had used national security as grounds for tightly restricting the entry of refugees. As G-2 deputy director in the late 1940s, he would submit a major "Top Secret" report strongly opposing Jewish immigration into Palestine and the creation of Israel. Clarke would argue that Jews and Arabs were irrelevant to American interests, which must be determined solely by geopolitics.[61]

As the example of Clarke strongly suggests, the "Secret Americans" were much more than merely a clique of discontented officers with strong opinions and prejudices. During and after the war, they held positions that affected American policies and actions relating to Jews. Black and Smith would regularly advise Marshall and assistant secretary of war John J. McCloy on wartime developments. Black would eventually be reporting for G-2 from the Middle East on the Jewish-Arab problem. During the period in which the army and the government would have to make crucial decisions regarding responses to the Holocaust, Yeaton headed the G-2 section providing intelligence on the destruction of European Jewry. Yeaton would also be influential in the army's struggle to counteract efforts by Jewish groups and others to convince the American public and Roosevelt administration to support Jewish emigration into Palestine during the Holocaust.

Upper Echelons and Jewish Policy

The intelligence officers who characterized themselves as "Secret Americans" ultimately reported to the "most powerful intelligence figure in Washington," General George V. Strong, G-2 chief from 1942 to 1944. A graduate of West Point (1904) and the War College (1924), Strong had started out as a cavalry officer fighting Ute Indians and went on to participate in the army's actions against labor activists. He taught law at the military academy before rising within the War Plans Division and intelligence. Often given to self-deprecating humor, Strong humbly described himself as "only a plain country boy," whereas around Washington his self-confident mannerisms and toughness earned him the title "King George." He was known as a "master of sarcastic memorandums and committee warfare."

A hard-liner on domestic and foreign policy, Strong long complained that "pacifistic, religious and other pernicious organizations" were forcing a limitation on armaments. "If profits in the shape of foreign trade are desirable," he wrote, "then you have got to run the risk of war or be prepared, cold-bloodedly, to wage war for the sake of profits."[62]

Strong would write some of the most influential reports affecting American wartime policy toward Jewish refugees and Palestine. In these, he always projected the image of an unbiased professional, who, while empathizing with Jewish suffering, was constrained by wartime security needs. But other evidence suggests a different attitude.

In his earlier correspondence with his close friend Hugh Gibson, former ambassador to Poland and Herbert Hoover confidant, Jews were a fairly regular source of amusement. Between Gibson and Strong, the Russian minister was always "Litvinoff, ne Finkelstein"; and Strong wrote jocular marginalia such as "a Hebraic steno's idea." Neither could Strong resist entertaining Gibson with the old army story about the kind of soldiers Jews make: the "Jordan Highlanders" from the East End of London, a "Hebraic outfit" whose motto in Palestine was "No advance without security."[63]

As chief of the War Plans Division in 1940, Strong had requested a "loyalty" check on, among others, Albert Einstein. Neglecting his scientific significance, G-2 concluded:

This office would not recommend the employment of Dr. Einstein on matters of a secret nature, since he was *'an extreme radical'* . . . [who] has been sponsoring the principal Communist causes in the United States.[64]

G-2 virtually embraced (without attribution) the Nazi Party line on this distinguished scientist. Einstein, the report attested, had been "ousted from Germany as a Communist." Neither the word "Nazi" nor references implying any connection between Nazis and Einstein's case appeared in this document. No mention was made that the Communist label originated with the Nazis as a pretext for persecution and possible arrest of someone they considered a racial and intellectual enemy. As a Jew and political opponent of the emerging Hitler dictatorship, Einstein had become persona non grata. Using as its source the "Berlin Conservative press," G-2 referred only to events in Germany before Hitler's seizure of power, when supposedly "the Einstein home was known as a Communist center" and "hiding place of Moscow envoys, etc." His wife and daughter "were always prominent at all extreme radical meetings and demonstrations."[65]

The German government, G-2 noted, hesitated "to take any action" against the Einsteins' Communist activities for fear of being branded "Anti-Semites." And when emigrating to the United States, the Einsteins tried to circumvent normal State Department procedures by calling upon the assistance of "prominent Jewish women in New York," who started an unsuccessful "press campaign" to pressure President Roosevelt. Einstein, it seems, initially refused to sign "an affidavit that he is not a member of any radical organizations." Einstein's case warranted "much more careful investigation," because "it seems unlikely that a man of his background could, in such short time, become a loyal American citizen."[66]

There are other indications that those near the top of the military hierarchy harbored negative views on Jews. These ranged from suspicions and erroneous assumptions about Jewish wealth and power to vulgar anti-Semitism. After the war, Rabbi Judah Nadich, then Eisenhower's adviser on Jewish affairs, was "really startled" when he suddenly discovered General Walter Bedell Smith's "way of thinking" about Jews. By that point, Nadich and Smith, Eisenhower's deputy, "had become rather good friends." After traveling to Poland and learning of the Warsaw ghetto, Smith "seemed stirred to the innermost parts of his being." Although intending to express deep-felt compassion for Holocaust victims, Smith imparted something else to Nadich when he asked the rabbi essentially:

I can't understand it. In Germany—alright, at least the Jews here were wealthy; they were in positions of power; they were in journalism and banking, and so I can understand it a little bit at least. But why in Poland? The Jews there were poor, and the Jews there had no power. Why was there such hatred of them by the Poles?

"So here, you see," Nadich later said, "was a man who felt that there could be some justification for anti-Semitism because of the fact that Jews were wealthy in Germany and had positions of power." To Nadich, this incident demonstrated "that even with our so-called best friends we mustn't expect a complete understanding."[67]

Others in the upper echelons of the army apparently lacked Smith's sensitivity and articulated their feelings in the crudest fashion. General Alfred M. Gruenther, Eisenhower's close friend, bridge partner, and deputy chief of staff in London, was often referred to as the "brain" or Ike's "right arm." He served as General Mark Clark's chief of staff in North Africa, Italy, and postwar Austria, later becoming chief of NATO. Up to the eve of the war, Gruenther continued to express his deep-seated animosity toward a particular Jewish reserve officer he knew for some years who had done well in the New York real estate business. "He always impresses me," wrote Gruenther, "as a prosperous, fat, greasy, Kike."[68]

There is nothing even suggesting that Marshall or Eisenhower ever resorted to vulgar references to Jews. Given their personalities and styles of command, it is unlikely that they would have treated Jewish officers or enlisted men with anything other than respect, dignity, and fairness. But in the broader context of racial thinking, as well as the relationship of the Jewish question to the policies and mission of the wartime army, their perspectives are less clear.

This was especially true of Marshall, whose taciturn character and impenetrable aloofness often left those around him wondering about his real thoughts. And the documentation on Marshall's thoughts before 1932, when he was already over fifty years old and the army had passed its blatant nativist phase, is indeed sparse. There was also little in Marshall's background or career to distinguish him from his generation of officers. He had come out of the same pre–World War I army milieu as such strongly opinionated officers as Craig, Embick, Gasser, and McCabe, with whom he served on the General Staff in the late 1930s. The army's two most notorious Darwinist racial thinkers, Moseley and Johnson Hagood, were among his most influential mentors.

Marshall apparently never lost his immense respect and "affection" for Moseley. After Moseley's "sterilizing the refugees" affair and controversial retirement in 1938, Marshall wrote to him: "I know you will leave behind a host of younger men who have a loyal devotion to you for what you have stood for. I am one of that company, and it makes me very sad to think that I cannot serve with you and under you again."[69]

Through all of Moseley's infamous years of political Jew-baiting, Marshall neither rebuked nor ignored him. In late 1940, as Moseley's anti-Semitic crusade reached its peak, Marshall not only kept him informed of army manpower plans but "trusted" him "in extreme confidence" with the real reasons behind particular General Staff appointments. Marshall continued to write substantive responses to Moseley's inquiries until the end of the war.[70]

On the character and use of African-American soldiers, Marshall's position differed very little from the racial thinking of his colleagues. He referred to a "darkey soldier" and a close friend complained to him about a "regular 'nigger' town."[71] Although sincerely concerned about the training and welfare of African-American soldiers, Marshall advanced their cause solely within the confines of a strict system of separate but equal treatment. Hostile to integrating the army, he warned that such proposals were pushed by the Communists. Marshall's reservations about the potential of African-American troops stemmed in part from his low estimate of their inherent capacities. The disastrous performance of the African-American Ninety-second Division in Italy only further solidified his views.[72]

Marshall's lecture before the Army War College in the early 1920s indicated that his thinking on immigrants, labor, and urban America resembled that of most officers. Since "strong feelings regarding labor questions and similar matters" had made it quite difficult to recruit effective National Guard units "near large cities," Marshall said, enlistment should be confined to "very young men." Such problems did not exist "in those sections of the country where the bulk of the population is of pure American stock." As an example of the difficulty he cited the "27th Division in New York."[73]

That Marshall had little to say on the Jewish question is not surprising. His life in a political fish bowl as chief of staff only reinforced his natural reserve and caution, especially in light of the difficulties he had had after the "violent Jewish reaction" against his German specialists Truman Smith and Percy Black at the beginning of the war. Marshall also had to tactfully deal with Treasury Secretary Morgenthau; and he took particular pains to cultivate Bernard Baruch's political support.

Marshall was undoubtedly aware of the existence and impact of anti-Semitism within the army from his long years of service and incidents brought to his attention. In one case, an officer Marshall knew rather well appealed to him about a controversial reassignment. The appeal was unsuccessful, for when Marshall looked into the matter, he learned about "another reason . . . which could not be brought out officially": "That is . . . complaints of the enlisted men in the 174th Infantry . . . that there were too many Jewish officers assigned to that regiment and, correctly or incorrectly, Lieut. Col. Ritchel was assumed to be a Jew."[74]

On army policies related to the rescue of European Jews and the Middle East, Marshall never deviated from military thinking in general. On geopolitical and strategic grounds, he was a long-standing opponent of wartime Jewish immigration to Palestine. As secretary of state in 1948, he argued ardently against U.S. recognition of Israel. To Marshall, the pressure for recognition was a clear-cut case of Jewish political power. In a heated exchange with Truman, Marshall accused the president of disregarding American national interests for no other reason than to win New York Jewish votes in the upcoming election.[75]

Eisenhower also became politic and cautious as he rose to higher rank, along the way acquiring a reputation as a middle-of-the-road sort with "no strong views on race or politics." But excluding the eugenic aspects, some of his political opinions sounded remarkably similar to ideas articulated by Moseley when Eisenhower served as his assistant. Having high expectations for Eisenhower, Moseley had helped advance his career; in turn, Eisenhower never ceased to have "great admiration and esteem" for the general. "Among the senior officers," wrote Eisenhower in his diary, Moseley "has been my most intimate friend." In these sincere private notations from which he could not hope to curry any favor, Eisenhower described Moseley as a "mentally honest" man of "great moral courage . . . well equipped for any task this gov't can possibly give him." Eisenhower considered Moseley the best candidate for chief of staff in 1934—"he'll be a peach."[76]

During the early 1930s, Eisenhower concurred with Moseley's views that Herbert Hoover must pursue an authoritarian solution to America's depression-era ills. As Eisenhower wrote privately and argued openly with others: "For two years I have been called 'Dictator Ike' because I believe that virtual dictatorship must be exercised by our President." Only then will there be recovery "and we will be freed from the pernicious influence of noisy and selfish minorities."

Initially, he had similar hopes after Roosevelt's victory and felt that "individual right must be subordinated to public good, and that the public good can be served only by unanimous adherence to an authoritative plan. We *must* conform to the President's program regardless of consequences. Otherwise dissension, confusion and partisan politics will ruin us."[77]

The following year, Eisenhower wrote Moseley from the Philippines:

> I miss the talks we used to have on such subjects as "the state of the nation"—and all included matters. So much is happening that is going to be of the utmost significance to our country for generations to come—that I would like very much to discuss with you the motives, purposes and methods of some of the actors now occupying the national stage.[78]

Although Eisenhower did not share Moseley's racial dogmatism, neither did he totally reject such thinking. To Eisenhower, American paternalism had turned the Philippines into "an outpost of European civilization." He discounted "any racial defect" as an explanation for his frustrating failures to develop an "intelligent and efficient" Filipino officer corps. After all, he said, Genghis Khan succeeded and his "only material . . . was nomadic tribes-

men of Central Asia," thus a "powerful military organization" did not require an educated population and "a high level of civilization." However, he
told Moseley that these "comforting reflections" aside, he was still troubled
by the possibility that the problem might, at least in part, emanate from
some inherent Oriental characteristic. The "difference in basic character" between the Oriental and the American and the "peculiar traits" of the Filipino, Eisenhower believed, "impede progress."[79]

Like Marshall, Eisenhower never repudiated or ignored Moseley. Apparently not greatly disturbed by Moseley's 1940 anti-Semitic campaign,
Eisenhower merely commented at the time that "in spite of his retired activities," Moseley always had been "a shrewd judge of officers." In late
1942, Eisenhower wrote to Moseley:

> My mind has been turning back more and more to the things you used to
> tell me when we were in the War Department together. . . . There are many
> times when I wish you could drop in here for a chat. It would not only be
> refreshing to me, but helpful in the actual determination of proper courses
> of action.

Until Eisenhower became president, they kept up their intimate correspondence, with Eisenhower replying to the substance of Moseley's letters
while ignoring his vile anti-Semitic comments. Even after Moseley was
long dead, a retired president Eisenhower described his former commander
merely as a misunderstood "patriotic American unafraid to disagree with
a consensus." Moseley's "outspoken reaction to public questions," Eisenhower claimed, "got him a bad press," creating a "distortion" of what the
old general really stood for.[80]

While in the Philippines, Eisenhower acquired a reputation as a vocal
anti-Nazi who eschewed the anti-Semitic talk so common at the Army and
Navy Club. According to Eisenhower, he had such a good rapport with the
small Jewish community in Manila that they offered him a very lucrative
job as director of an organization for resettling Jewish refugees in Asia.
Ironically, the offer was made just as his close friend Moseley had
launched his tirade against Jewish refugees to America. He later recounted
being reared on the Old Testament, "believing that the Jews were the chosen people, that gave us the high ethical and moral principles of our civilization."[81] Commenting on the invasion of Poland, Eisenhower wrote that
"Hitler's record with the Jews . . . is as black as that of any barbarian from
the Dark Ages."[82]

Otherwise, Eisenhower rarely said or wrote anything on the Jewish question. Concerning wartime policy on race or army involvement in relief and rescue of European Jews, no distinction could be detected between his positions or sensitivities and those of his peers in the older officer corps.

Two crucial figures in policymaking were Secretary of War Henry Stimson and his assistant secretary, John J. McCloy. A close friend of Frankfurter, McCloy exhibited no animosities toward Jews and was quite wary of the army's overzealousness regarding communism and subversion, which he tried to restrain. In turn, the G-2 clique seriously mistrusted McCloy, even suspecting he took his directives from Morgenthau. Yet in many wartime matters, McCloy had to defer to army data and judgments.

Early in the war, Truman Smith and Percy Black routinely briefed McCloy on Germany. Strong remained in daily contact, while Carter Clarke and other intelligence officers advised him on a fairly regular basis. McCloy proved rather susceptible to army arguments when it came to those things couched in the language of "military necessity," which one member of the clique admitted "covered a multitude of sins." McCloy acquiesced in the army's plan to incarcerate Japanese Americans and, though sympathetic to the plight of Jews, he accepted the military's arguments against rescue efforts.[83]

Stimson, "the colonel," was cut from the same cloth as the old officer corps. As governor general of the Philippines, secretary of state, and then secretary of war, Stimson exhibited the same "ethnic prejudices" and sense of "racial superiority" toward African-Americans, Jews, and Orientals as his close friend General Leonard Wood, former chief of staff and paradigm of the Darwinism imperialist. Ever conscious of the "race question" in America and the "Negro problem in the army," Stimson believed the "social equality" sought by "foolish leaders of the colored race" was an illusion "because of the impossibility of race mixture through marriage." After Pearl Harbor, he determined that second-generation Japanese-American citizens were the "most dangerous elements," because "their racial characteristics are such that we cannot understand or trust" them.

Stimson's relationship with Jews was more complex. He could befriend Frankfurter, but otherwise he shared the genteel anti-Semitism of his class and generation. He complained about the "tremendous Jewish influence" at Columbia University and after the war accused Morgenthau and Baruch of succumbing to racial "impulses," calling their behavior "semitism gone wild for vengeance." It was under his tenure as secretary of state that the racist National Origins Act went into effect and a new 1929 law impeded unwanted immigration even further by empowering U.S. consuls to deny visas to anyone likely to become a "public charge." During World War II, he staunchly defended that legislation as a solution to the "Jewish problem in this country." "Nowhere," as Godfrey Hodgson has written, "did Stimson express any strong personal feelings about the sufferings of European Jews."[84]

Attitudes in the upper echelons of the army had important implications for American policy regarding the fate of the Jews, which during the war was largely seen as a matter of military policy. The first policy decision the army faced regarding Jews was in the strategic regions of North Africa and the Middle East. These areas remained essential to securing communication and supply lines for the duration of the war.

While the army planned its first battlefield test against the Germans in North Africa, the Geopolitical Section of G-2 sponsored a conference at Yale University in July 1942 on the "Mohammedan World." Among the conference recommendations, G-2 singled out for serious consideration winning over the Muslims through a "very bold" propaganda campaign in which the "United States [would] promise the Arab world the end of Zionism." Jews would have only a "cultural home in Palestine," all immigration would cease, and some Jewish-occupied land would be returned to Arabs. The Near Eastern Section of the State Department concurred. Throughout the war, army policy and actions usually reflected this pro-Arab tilt at the expense of Jews in Europe and the Middle East.[85]

In order to facilitate the Allied landing in North Africa, Eisenhower made a deal with the French admiral Jean Darlan in November 1942. Since this agreement left the Vichyites in power, a public outcry in the United States almost ended Eisenhower's career. The press criticism intensified when anti-Semitic Vichy legislation remained in effect after the Allies occupied the area. Quite defensive about the entire incident, Eisenhower affirmed his belief in American idealism and democracy. But as one biographer noted, he had no commitment to spreading democracy. He saw his mission as purely military—to win the war, "not to improve the conditions of the Arabs or relieve the persecution of the Jews."

Eisenhower applied the occupation lessons learned in the Philippines: govern from above, leaving the indigenous elites to handle local populations; neither inquire nor interfere so long as stability is maintained. He worried that any Arab disturbance might weaken French control or disrupt military security. Demanding democratic reforms from Vichyites or alleviating restrictions on Jews could set off the "boiling kettle."[86]

On the Jewish question, Eisenhower's key generals in North Africa, George S. Patton and Mark Clark, were interesting contrasts. Patton proved to be the crudest sort of racist anti-Semite, whereas Clark had a Jewish mother. Patton greatly respected the Germans, while Clark believed that Nazi crimes reflected the inherent "cruelty . . . of the German people." GIs must, Clark exclaimed, abandon the "soft ideas of sportsmanship and fair play. . . . Our men must kill Germans as they would kill rattlesnakes or scorpions."[87]

Clark, however, was raised as a Protestant and apparently was so devoid of Jewish identity that many who served with him had no idea of his heritage. A racist and nativist, he associated un-Americanism and communism with unassimilated immigrants, whose "less desirable qualities of their former nationalities" had not been erased by the "melting pot." World War I had taught the country a hard lesson about these "hyphenates," "undigested groups" with "no knowledge of and respect for American institutions." They "enjoyed the benefits" of America while shunning any "obligations" and were among the most active "forces of disloyalty." A staunch segregationist, Clark wanted the "death sentence" imposed on African-American soldiers who assaulted white officers.[88]

Before Eisenhower dispatched Clark to negotiate with Darlan, he warned him against doing anything that might cause Arab dissension or loosen French control. But soon after the Allies landed in Morocco and Algeria in November 1942, Patton warned that "stirrings of the Jewish population" could create the very "internal unrest or trouble" Eisenhower desperately wanted to avoid. According to Patton, the French leader in Morocco, General Nogues, "stated that the Jews in Morocco were of the lowest order, that they expected to take over the country when and if an American Expeditionary Force would arrive, and that they are now agitating against French authorities."[89]

While criticism mounted back home against army occupation policies, Patton's G-2 staff (now including the German expert Colonel Black) emphasized wartime realities on the spot. "The reform of the Pro-Nazi French . . . can only be incidental to our main purpose," wrote Major Bernard Carter to Black; "this may sound cynical, but we can only face the facts." What was "far more important" was the "proper handling" of the Arab majority.[90]

At the same time that Eisenhower was under relentless public pressure for these policies, his fears of an Arab-Jewish explosion worsened. Perhaps this predicament explains why during a meeting in Gibraltar with Patton on November 17, Eisenhower suddenly asked "if Clark was a Jew," to which Patton responded, "at least one-quarter, probably one-half." Patton considered Clark a self-centered, opportunistic "s.o.b." who played Eisenhower for the "fool" and "spent his time cutting Ike's throat."[91]

Returning to Morocco, Patton wrote Eisenhower that the Jews did not face discrimination and recommended against interference with the policies of the sultan of Morocco. Because his stenographer was a Jew, Patton waited until the report was typed before adding the following in longhand:

> Arabs don't mind Christians, but they utterly despise Jews. The French fear that the local Jews knowing how high their side is riding in the U.S. will try to take the lead here. If they do the Arabs will murder them and there will be a local state of disorder. . . . I suggest that you write Gen. Marshall and inform him of the situation so that if some State Department fool tries to foist . . . Jews on Morocco we will stop it at the source. If we get orders to favor the Jews we will precipitate trouble and possibly civil war.[92]

Patton's suggestion quickly materialized into an Eisenhower message to Washington that created the framework through which the General Staff thereafter judged such issues. The question was framed not in terms of lifting discriminatory practices but rather in terms of avoiding favoritism toward Jews. As the General Staff interpreted Eisenhower's position, "to give the comparatively few Jewish Semites a preferred status over the vastly more numerous Semites of Islam would almost certainly provoke an unfortunate and dangerous reaction on the part of the Moslems." Even the status of Jewish refugees in North Africa should remain unaffected: "Allied headquarters are opposed at the present time to the mass release of internees due to the delicate military and political situation."[93]

After Eisenhower's report reached Stimson, he brought it to Roosevelt's attention two days after Christmas. Stimson endorsed Eisenhower's position on the North African "race problem," where 25 million Arabs confronted only 350,000 Jews and Nazi propaganda claimed the Allies would turn the area "over to the Jews." Stimson indicated that Darlan acted prudently in not enacting a "general emancipation" of the Jews, as that would cause civil war. Roosevelt then requested the entire report.[94]

Although Roosevelt sympathized with the plight of Jews, in the end he usually deferred to the judgment of his military advisers. This was especially so regarding conditions in theaters of operation. Thus, neither American nor French policy on Jews in North Africa changed considerably.

These early decisions set the tone for future American wartime policies on the entire Middle East.[95]

Policy Struggles over Palestine

The news from New York in the winter of 1943 greatly disturbed General Strong. The general feared that political activities in that city rather than decisions in Washington might determine American policy on Palestine. So the master memo writer took the bull by the horns, moving quickly to initiate action among War Department policymakers to preclude this result. Sitting in intelligence headquarters, he composed a long message to Marshall on March 4, regarding the "paramount . . . political and military repercussions" of recent events. In a grave and ominous tone, Strong referred to

> rioting and local uprisings which have prejudiced the military situation in the Middle East, especially Syria, Iraq and Palestine. A further spread of the difficulties to Iran will seriously jeopardize our supply line to Russia. Further, by throwing Ibn Saud into the Axis camp, the Allied oil and gas reserves in the Persian Gulf area would be jeopardized.

Strong attributed these dangerous developments to "an increasing amount of political agitation by highly organized militant minorities both in England and the United States." Jewish militants, who fanned the flames of "Arab-Jewish animosities," were responsible for these rising "tensions."[96]

Three days earlier, 75,000 Christians and Jews had crowded in and around Madison Square Garden in a "Stop Hitler Now" rally, responding to the government's recent confirmation of news of the Holocaust by demanding action to "halt the liquidation of Europe's Jews." Among the proposals advanced at the rally were revisions of U.S. immigration laws to create havens for refugees in America and demands that England "open the doors of Palestine—the Jewish homeland—for Jewish immigration."

The American Federation of Labor and various church groups joined the American Jewish Congress in urging the United Nations to act before all Europe's Jews were murdered. It was a cause with prominent political support; Governor Dewey addressed the rally by radio from Albany, while Justice William O. Douglas and Senator Robert Wagner spoke from Washington.[97]

Strong was determined to prevent another rally the following week. "A militant minority group in this country," he informed Marshall, "is organizing a mass meeting in Madison Square Garden . . . on March 9 [to support] the 'Proclamation On the Moral Rights of Stateless and Palestinian Jews.'" But their real purpose, Strong said, was "forcing an immediate statement by this Government espousing the Jewish cause in Palestine."

Strong endowed this single event with momentous significance:

> If allowed to take place, [it] will blow the lid on the Jewish-Arab question and align the Arabs in North Africa and the Middle East against us, possibly under the guise of a holy war. It will thereby not only adversely affect our present campaign in Tunisia but set the Middle East aflame with consequent jeopardy to the supply line to Russia, and immobilization of Allied naval forces in the Eastern Mediterranean and the Indian Ocean.

Whether the "political questions" had "any intrinsic merit" was irrelevant in Strong's calculation. The Jewish political activity in New York seriously interfered with "this war for national existence" and thus "cannot be allowed." Strong urged Marshall to have the Joint Chiefs of Staff (JCS) and Combined Chiefs of Staff develop the "military policy of the United States" along his line of argument. In the meantime, the upcoming meeting had to be stopped.

Strong condensed his original memo into a letter for the secretary of war to send to the secretary of state, noting that he was "gravely concerned at the possible, if not probable, results arising from such a meeting." An "almost inevitable holy war," would "wreck" the North African Campaign, endanger supplies to Russia and oil sources, and "immobilize Allied naval forces." The secret letter concluded, "In view of the serious military implications involved, I venture to suggest that every effort be made by this Government to prevent the projected meeting in Madison Square Garden."[98]

Despite Strong's sense of urgency, his memo apparently died a quiet death; it would be buried in the secret Palestine File for the next half century. Stimson still regarded such "alarmist" G-2 analyses with almost instinctive skepticism. After all, Strong's division had been overly pessimistic about the ability of England and Russia to withstand the German assault. By G-2 estimates, North Africa should have been lost and the Russian front should have collapsed, whereas by 1943, the war had actually turned against the Axis.[99]

The event that Strong dreaded took place on March 9, when 40,000 people gathered in Madison Square Garden. The meeting was a dramatic pageant, a "mass memorial to the 2,000,000 Jews killed in Europe . . . staged to stir the Allied nations to stop the slaughter of a people by the Germans." Participants called for intergovernmental action to end the "wholesale slaughter" and to assist Jews to reach "Palestine or any temporary refuge."[100] Needless to say, the dire consequences Strong had foreseen for the war effort never materialized.

Although threats to "operational security" were serious considerations, this concept, like that of the "war effort," often was, in the words of Richard Breitman and Alan M. Kraut, "an all-inclusive and elastic standard." Balancing military risks with the lives of European Jews usually required judgments and interpretations, and these were often conditioned by preconceived notions about Jews and the role of the military in wartime.[101] Strong, like the army generally, tended to exaggerate the detrimental military impact of any rescue efforts while rarely weighing in earnest the human cost of not taking such action.

There are indications that the effort to silence Zionist activity in the United States was motivated by politics as well as strategic necessity. Knowingly or unknowingly, Strong advanced the position on Palestine that the British had been proposing to the American government for several months. Britain's Foreign Office became quite anxious that the Holocaust and the plight of Jewish refugees might shift the opinion of the American government and people toward the Zionist cause. The British wanted to neutralize the influence that America might bring to bear by taking Palestine off the table. The primary British concern was not an outbreak of hostilities in the Middle East but rather "future policy" on postwar Palestine in the context of protecting British global imperial interests. As handled by the Foreign Office, "these were questions of 'high policy' divorced from the realities of the Middle East."[102]

To dissuade the U.S. government from any commitment to a Jewish state, the British emphasized the danger that Zionism posed for "Allied interests." The British fortified their case by greatly exaggerating Zionist armed strength in Palestine and the effects of Jewish agitation in America. Even while possessing accurate information on the strength of the Hagana and Irgun, British military intelligence in the Middle East inflated their estimates more than threefold. Among themselves, however, British officials in London and Palestine were not alarmed by any imminent Arab-Jewish hostilities jeopardizing the war effort. They did not anticipate an anti-British Zionist revolt ("followed by an Arab insurrection") before "the War ends in Europe, or possibly a few months earlier."[103]

British lobbying supported Strong's persistent efforts throughout 1943 to counteract Jewish activity in the United States. The British also influenced American officers in the Middle East, who continually prodded Strong to push the anti-Zionist position in Washington.

Most of these officers were attached to the Joint Intelligence Collection Agency, Middle East (JICAME) in Cairo, a branch of G-2 charged with coordinating regional intelligence activities. Older career officers and younger wartime recruits brought with them a distrust of Jews and hostility toward Zionism. Among them was General Russell A. Osmun, a 1934 War College graduate and intimate friend of Frank Mason—one of the few people Osmun "ever liked *and trusted*." During the war, Osmun made several high-level attempts to secure a position for Mason in military intelligence.

An abrupt "live-wire type," Osmun said after meeting with Zionist leaders Moshe Shertok and David Ben-Gurion: "They are tough boys. . . . If they'd been born in Chicago, they'd have been part of Al Capone's mob."[104] Perhaps Osmun's most valued G-2 man in Jerusalem was Lieutenant Nicholas Andronovich, a Russian Orthodox émigré who still spoke with an accent. Andronovich had "established excellent relationships . . . with many prominent and well placed British" and befriended the Arab elite. Both served as his key sources on Palestine.[105]

Jewish sources in the United States and Middle East usually met with immediate skepticism. Officers occasionally attached notes to reports indicating their Jewish "bias" and emphasizing they did "not subscribe to the Subject's opinions and convictions." Yet anti-Zionist "American" sources were rated "highly reliable" even when they made snide remarks about Jewish motives or capabilities. One "smilingly" stated that "a Jewish army in Palestine would require a British or American army to protect it."[106]

G-2's "authority" on Palestine was Major Edwin M. Wright, a Middle East scholar closely connected with the American University in Cairo and with Arab elites. Wright often delivered the orientation lecture on Palestine at the American University and certain military camps. As recalled by a Jewish-American officer, Wright's historical survey included "vicious references . . . reflected only in the tone of voice." Wright referred to Theodor Herzl, the father of Zionism, as a "crackpot" eventually "repudiated by his own people." Wright made "a huge joke" out of explaining how Poles and Germans retaliated by dumping Jews back and forth across their borders.

The Palestinian crisis was, Wright said, caused by Jewish repression in Europe and not a natural desire to return to Palestine. Politicians like Roosevelt only backed the Zionist cause to win Jewish votes, under "immense pressure" from well financed, "influential" Jews with a "powerful press." But such domestic politics stirred up serious trouble in the Middle East, where well-organized, well-armed Jews with "vast resources" were moving against disorganized, ill-armed Arabs with "no one to speak for them." After one such talk, an Office of War Information official joked about a proposed exchange of land by saying, "[W]hat Jew could pass up an opportunity like that!"[107]

Osmun and Wright's written reports from Palestine tend to substantiate these recollections. Examining "Jewish Psychology," they wrote that "Zionism in Palestine . . . amounts to an obsession." Through distorted perspectives emanating from "fears, real and imagined," the Jews "are beginning to persuade themselves . . . that they are being persecuted again as they were in Biblical times. This gives a tinge of the mystic martyrdom to their activities and explains the spiritual culture in which fanaticism and violence grow."[108]

Jews, Osmun and Wright argued, displayed deep emotional and "intense atavistic impulses" that create "national paranoia." It is "a new persecution complex revivifying . . . the endless martyrdom of the Jewish people by the injustices of others." The "modern Jew" cannot be understood "independent of his past." The lawyer or trader considers himself as part of a universal cosmic process woven about the Jews and is distinctly conscious that he is one of "a peculiar people." Anyone standing in the way "is looked upon with the same animus ancient Jews looked upon a Nebuchadnezzar or a Caesar."[109]

G-2 reports did not necessarily lack merit. The factual content was often accurate and useful; analyses were sometimes incisive. The difficulty was with the tone or peculiar interpretations interwoven throughout documents such as "The Zionist Problem Today." G-2 Palestine wrote it as "background for Security Officers in countries, other than Palestine, which have a Jewish population exposed to Zionist political influences." G-2 identified the Zionist "maximum program" as "immigration on a vast scale after the war, and the early establishment of the Jewish National State." However, G-2 characterized Zionism not only as a movement disrupting the war effort but as one contrary to the very principles for which the Allies fought.[110]

The "Zionist proper," G-2 asserted, only pays "lip service to democracy and representative institutions and [is] outwardly organized along democratic lines." Aside from moderate democratic types "like Dr. Weizmann," the "totalitarian tendency of all this is unmistakable":

[It] is reflected in the external apparatus of the Zionist machine—the wide-spread Youth Movement, organized in Zionist schools by Zionist teachers trained in the Zionist University with its blue shirts and national flag and national songs; the insistence on the speaking of Hebrew by Jews and . . . above all, the existence of a powerful para-military organization, the Hagana.[111]

British officials in the Middle East sent similar depictions of Zionists to their embassy in Washington. They wrote of the "completely totalitarian, militaristic and National Socialist outlook of modern Zionism." One British official argued "this Jewish Commonwealth (i.e. state) could only be established by force, and that as a political aim, it is indistinguishable from Hitler's claim for *Lebensraum* implemented by the subjugation of 'inferior' races."[112]

Although urging "objectivity," G-2 instructed officers "to treat Zionist activities as a security matter requiring thorough investigation." In this spirit, G-2 compiled intelligence on the leadership, membership, and financing of "Jewish Political Organizations in Palestine." Officers in Cairo and Washington exchanged similar data on Jewish activities in the United States and Palestine.[113]

G-2 believed that the Jewish Agency, the representative body for Jews in Palestine, was "particularly active in penetrating Allied Intelligence Agencies" and that it worked "against our interests." Officers "should be warned," wrote the chief of American counterintelligence in Cairo, "to be particularly discreet with their Jewish contacts in the Middle East."[114]

Suspecting a leak, British intelligence withheld "valuable information" from Americans, because they thought the Jewish Agency received intelligence "via American Headquarters personnel, both civilian and military." This fear revived the old issue of the loyalty of American Jews. The G-2 chief in Cairo, Colonel R. W. McClenahan, suggested that Americans should learn from the British, who suspect "any British officer, regardless of rank or station, who visits Palestine, if he is Jewish or has a Jewish wife." But the matter was touchy. An American officer's "indiscretion" caused "most unfavorable complications" at Cairo headquarters when the Office of Strategic Services (OSS) learned that he had said, "Persons of Jewish extraction are not suitable for intelligence work in Palestine."[115]

The issue involved much more than suspicions that Jews, American or otherwise, might be leaking information to advance the Jewish cause in Palestine. Specific charges surfaced of Jews intentionally collaborating with the enemy to the detriment of the Allied war effort. In 1944, the chief of

American counterintelligence officers in the Middle East insisted that he had definite "proof" that

> some representatives of the Jewish Agency have been used by the German Intelligence Service. . . . The greatest mistake made by Allied intelligence and security officials is the presumption that a Jew, any Jew, is perforce Anti-Nazi and Anti-Axis. . . . To serve the Jewish Agency, and to help Jews in Europe, [they] will and do deal with Nazi party officials and the German Intelligence Service, sometimes "selling out" allied contacts, agencies, and operations. . . . Their representatives buy Nazi support with their own funds and the funds of Allied intelligence agencies.[116]

Indeed, G-2 foresaw that Jews would be a problem for vital geopolitical interests long after the defeat of Nazi Germany. Officers already linked the Jewish question with postwar Soviet imperialistic expansion in the Middle East. They argued that Soviet incursions would threaten the survival of the British Empire by cutting off strategic sea-lanes and controlling the oil resources of the Persian Gulf. This threat conflicted with U.S. interests because "the end of western hemisphere oil reserves is in sight" and the "Joint Chiefs of Staff have decided we will start exploitation immediately" in the Middle East.[117]

The army held contradictory views on the Middle East–Soviet geopolitical equation. Supporting the Jewish cause would alienate the Arabs and drive them toward the Soviets. At the same time, officers worried about Communist penetration brought about by Jews in Palestine serving as the wedge for Soviet expansionism. Although recognizing the conflict between Zionism and Soviet communism, some officers noted that all "socialistic adventures . . . are deeply rooted in Hebrew tradition and culture."[118] In Palestine, one report stated, "[T]he people really live a communist life. . . . While these Jews are not active members of the Communist Party, their sympathies lie in that direction and it is quite reasonable to expect that their system may embrace more definite Party ideas in the future."[119] Another report claimed that the "local population in HAIFA . . . [shows] a definite interest in things Russian and communistic, and it will become a feeling to be reckoned with in the future."[120]

Of immediate concern in the spring of 1943, however, were G-2 predictions "that hostilities might commence at any time, if the Arabs can be maneuvered into an overt act." While both sides were "jockeying the other" into being the "aggressor," G-2 emphasized that "Jews, particularly

. . . are overtly and continuously trying to agitate their opponents." And "pro-Jewish" statements by American politicians only encouraged the Zionists and aggravated the Arabs.[121]

It was in this context that American and British officials secretly drafted a joint statement in July 1943 reiterating Strong's earlier proposal to postpone all discussions and activities on Palestine until after the war. When Jewish groups learned of this proposal, they lobbied the White House and State Department to prevent its release. To deflect criticism, Secretary of State Cordell Hull requested a firm statement by the army justifying the postponement policy on the basis of military necessity.[122]

In Stimson's absence, Acting Secretary of War Robert P. Patterson complied and stressed the "profound effect upon the war" of the Middle East and its "utmost importance in the attainment of our strategic objectives." Using Strong's strategic arguments and warnings about "increasing unrest there," Patterson stated "military requirements . . . are paramount . . . and must be accorded precedence over the adjustment of any political questions." Otherwise, "the course of the entire war" could be "affect[ed] adversely."[123]

Meanwhile, Secretary of the Treasury Morgenthau and others tried to stop the statement's release. Morgenthau argued that if the British were so worried about security in Palestine, they should ask for more U.S. troops and not seek suspension of the constitutional rights of free speech by American citizens. The proposal to suspend discussion was an unprecedented attempt to silence a minority of U.S. citizens.[124]

Although a staunch opponent of Zionism and immigration into Palestine, former secretary of war Patrick Hurley also understood the constitutional principle involved. Acting as Roosevelt's personal representative to the Middle East in early 1943, Hurley told King Ibn Saud that he and "a great majority" of American Jews opposed a Jewish State. "But there are certain very rich, powerful, influential Jews who are using America's freedom of speech . . . to conduct a great propaganda among the American people." Still, Hurley said, "as a free country the United States would not prohibit the Jews from stating their case. We have to rely on our citizens being intelligent enough to make a just decision on this subject."[125]

Silence, even in the face of the Holocaust, was, of course, precisely what Strong sought. A few days later, he launched a counteroffensive in a long memo to Marshall, supported by a five-page chronological summary of intelligence from officers in the Middle East. Their "startling facts" described a situation "full of dynamite" and "deteriorating rapidly." It was a distinctly one-sided picture of a crisis spawned and inflamed by Jewish immigration, Zionism, arms, and terrorism: "Ben Gurion remains fanatically nationalistic"; "the Jews, who are well armed, are more likely to disturb the peace than are the Arabs"; "violence possible at any time. The Jews may strike first."

Strong depicted Arabs as reactive to Jewish provocations in Palestine and incited by "pro-Zionist" statements of Senator Wagner, Wendell Wilkie, and other American politicians. There was "alarming currency to the belief that the policy of America is determined by a circle of Jewish advisers in the White House." Nazi agents exploited the situation to "precipitate civil war."[126]

Strong criticized Washington's "official silence" in the face of "militant Zionism." Although it "has not officially underwritten Zionist aspirations, it has inadvertently offered encouragement by having failed to clarify American policy." And Washington was "wink[ing]" at "high ranking military officers and government officials as well as prominent citizens sponsoring Zionist propaganda." To the Arabs, he asserted, this signified "official approval of Zionist aims."[127]

Strong wrote bluntly: "Arabs and Jews are of importance only in so far as security is concerned . . . There are only 16,000,000 Jews throughout the world. But there are 320,000,000 Moslems." To antagonize the latter "may well prove disastrous" to "supply routes to Russia" and "security in the rear" when full-scale offensives began in Europe and Asia. Providing security through more soldiers was "a wasteful employment of troops needed elsewhere."[128]

But Strong thought beyond immediate wartime security. "Certainly not least important," he wrote, were "the huge oil reserves in the Middle East. Since "U.S. reserves are adequate for only fourteen years . . . we should be interested in maintaining friendly relations with Middle Eastern peoples."[129] The "only logical and militarily safe course" was for Washington to announce that it "disclaims any commitments to either party" and to "insist that all partisan groups interested in Palestine cease propaganda activities for the duration."[130]

But Stimson remained unconvinced. Still wary of G-2's alarmism, he was more receptive to Morgenthau's arguments. Although not opposing the State Department–British joint statement on Palestine, Stimson withdrew War Department support. That decision undermined the military rationalizations for such a policy. Hull thereupon abandoned the initiative, citing Stimson's judgment that

the situation in Palestine is not serious enough from a military point of view
to warrant the issuance of a statement . . . [particularly] in as much as its
sole purpose was to ameliorate a condition which was thought to be dangerous in the military sense.[131]

Nonetheless, Strong's memorandum continued to influence the army's
response to the Holocaust. In late summer 1943, frustrated Jewish groups
organized the Emergency Committee to Save the Jewish People of Europe
to pressure the United States into a more active role in rescue efforts. Its
proposals included greater reliance upon Jewish manpower for military
service, evacuation of Jews from Axis satellites, and transfer of the "rescued Jews . . . to Palestine and other territories."

When the Operations Division (OPD) of the General Staff considered
the committee's proposals, its members knew what was at stake: "saving
the 4,000,000 Jews surviving in Europe from annihilation by the Axis." Yet
OPD evaded the issue, declaring, "[I]t is clearly evident that nothing
should be done by the War Department until the overall Jewish question
in the Middle East is clarified on the political level by announcement of a
U.S.-British policy."[132]

The chief of the Policy Section, Colonel J. K. Woolnough, wrote that
Strong had explained "very logically" the "military reasons why the U.S.
Government should intervene to solve this infectious problem" of a Jewish-Arab conflict. Given the Strong-Stimson policy differences, "it would
be unwise" for the army to meet with "the Jewish Committee on any aspects of this matter."[133]

The army was, however, by no means uninterested in the activity of such
Jewish organizations, for this period witnessed the birth of the "Jewish
lobby." Zionists in America had shifted to a program of "loud diplomacy"
and mass public action to promote their cause locally and nationally.
Through rallies, letter campaigns, meetings, and lobbying activities aimed at
the Jewish community, as well as at Congress and the public at large, the
Zionists were able to mobilize growing sympathy. By 1944, thousands of
non-Jewish associations would pass pro-Zionist resolutions.[134]

As American Jews increased their political activity in 1943, the army reacted accordingly. While the Nazis were exterminating millions of Jews on
the grounds that they constituted an insidious threat to civilization, G-2
launched investigations of "Jewish organizations" and their influence in
the United States. This effort extended from Yeaton in Washington to
Wright and Osmun in the Middle East. After outlining the nature and

purpose of various Jewish organizations, G-2 in Washington tried to measure "Jewish political power . . . and the practical ability of American Jews to attain their ends." In contrast to earlier assertions about "International Jewry," G-2 now assessed "American Jewry [as] a group potentially powerful but not yet possessed of an organization capable of delivering that potential force at a given time on a given issue." They are united only on "rescuing the Jews of Europe and aiding as many as possible of them to immigrate into Palestine, but there the unity stops."[135]

G-2 wondered, "What then, is the practical power of American Jewry?" Despite their divisive tendencies, there was reason for concern regarding the "effect of a 'Jewish vote' on a presidential election." Assessment of Jewish strength revealed that half of America's Jews "are concentrated in New York City alone and many of the rest are concentrated in other urban areas. This concentration facilitates the organization of an urban block to influence sizable groups of electoral votes." Moreover, "Jewish leaders exert an influence out of proportion to their numbers. A large number of these leaders are active in law and politics and are in a position to wield political power."

If Jews developed a unifying organization, they could, G-2 worried, exert considerable political influence. Equally troublesome was the possibility "that the Zionist program will so capture the imagination of the rank and file of American Jewry that the 'mass will' may force their leaders into a Zionist position."[136]

Unless forcefully counteracted, "Zionist Propaganda" could sway the Jewish community and the American public generally. Yeaton's division collected and forwarded to JICAME lists and samples of "Jewish propaganda advertising" in U.S. newspapers. From the scene, JICAME, in turn, furnished refutations of this "propaganda" attempt to capture American sympathies. Major Wright stated:

> The Zionists use every means known to U.S. advertising agencies: threats to newspapers for including unfavorable publicity; bought space; insertion of propaganda through news items; pressure on State legislatures; insertion in the Congressional Record of pro-Zionist material . . . large dinners at fashionable hotels with "important" guests, etc. etc. The Zionists are probably more active in "lobbying" than any other group.[137]

Wright's censorship intercepts indicated that "Zionists subsidize U.S. Senators and Congressmen"; this financial support "explains" Congressman Will Rogers's "activities on behalf of Zionism." While "Jewish spokesmen lack nothing in vehemence," wrote Wright, "cool analysis" cast doubt upon many of their claims regarding "rights to immigrate" and "territory."[138]

"The Jew is even more clearly working here to a purpose and goal," wrote Colonel Paul Converse, chief of the Beirut office. "His plea of persecution as to arms possession and security is neither justified by facts or actually desired by him for defense from Arabs—but to be ready to promote his real goal—a Jewish State. His accusation of unfairness or persecution by civil authorities (British) is generally unfounded and contrary to fact." The Arabs were "satisfactorily passive." They "seldom resist—and put forth no propaganda," which "refutes the Jewish assertion that they alone are thus persecuted while Arab offenders go free."[139]

All of Converse's contacts "agreed the Jew is too smart to risk any major action before the end of the war" and thereby "alienate all sympathy even in the U.S." The Jews, wrote Converse, believed that

> their best weapon is public opinion in the U.S. (and probably in other countries) in their favor—built up by persistent propaganda—along the lines of Jewish persecution in Palestine—so that the U.S. will when desired be prepared—to act morally or economically . . . because of their persistent and sensational publicity—however contrary to fact. . . . [O]ne sided propaganda . . . is intended to build up a sort of cash reserve of sentiment prejudiced to their cause—a reserve to be drawn on later when needed.[140]

The army, Converse warned, should "carefully watch" the situation and "counter . . . any accumulation of unbalanced and inflammatory Jewish propaganda." JICAME officers "very definitely agree[d] with the conclusions drawn by Colonel Converse," adding that "naturally no Jew would describe their propaganda in America as 'contrary to fact,' 'Sensational,' etc.—however much it may thus appear to the observer."[141]

In early 1944, the Zionists approached a major victory when the Wagner-Taft Resolution was introduced into Congress. The resolution called for lifting restrictions on Jewish immigration into Palestine and the creation of a Jewish commonwealth. Alarmed, the State and War Departments acted immediately to preclude a vote on the measure. A "deeply concerned" Hull called Marshall to complain that such measures "may 'play hell with' our oil interests in Saudi-Arabia" and militarily cause a "very damaging clash." Hull reminded Marshall that "General Strong at one time made a very forceful statement of the dangers of any agitation on the question during this war." The chief of staff should convey this to

Congress and the president, Hull said, and stress the "great military risks and hazards which cannot be discussed publicly . . . , urging defeat of the resolution."[142]

Stimson had also come round to the G-2 position that he had earlier rejected as alarmist. He now took the lead in dealing with Congress. As he expressed it privately, "I found that the Jews were raising trouble in Palestine again." After talking with a "very apprehensive" Marshall, Stimson felt the "danger was manifest," a "powder mine": "The Jews want to drive out the Arabs and take possession," which would surely cause immediate "hostilities and war."

Stimson tried not only to undermine the resolution but to squelch discussion of it. Writing to congressional leaders, he warned that "even any public hearings thereon, would be apt to provoke dangerous repercussions . . . [to] many vital military interests." An Arab-Jewish conflict would force the diversion of resources away from "combat against Germany . . . [and] our effort would be seriously prejudiced."[143]

Although Stimson felt his "warnings" persuaded the Senate committee to "take no action," the House committee would be more difficult because Congressmen Sol Bloom of New York had "promised important hearings to a large number of Jewish rabbis." By working behind the scenes with "moderates" like Bloom, however, Stimson restricted the matter to a letter from him and testimony from Assistant Secretary of War John J. McCloy.[144]

In preparation, McCloy "talked to some G-2 officers" and intended to use their reports about increasing tension and their assessment that any conflict would "greatly compromise our military capacities." It would "pin down troops . . . badly needed . . . for other operations," jeopardize "lines of communication" and "supply routes to Russia," and so on.[145]

McCloy also had the new G-2 Chief, General Clayton Bissell, ready to "buttress" the case with "factual data." Upsetting the "extremely delicate" situation in Palestine, Bissell wrote, could force the "diversion of two full divisions and substantial air power from employment against the Germans" and "prejudice the success of important military operations." Even more persuasive, the "Wagner-Taft Resolution . . . risks increased cost in American lives by prolonging the war." Therefore, "General Marshall strongly recommends against its passage."[146]

Although McCloy argued the army's case before Congress, McCloy personally did not share its pessimism; nor was he convinced of the inevitable dire outcome it predicted. To him, the army's position amounted essentially to a preferable option. As he told Marshall in private:

> I do not intend to exaggerate the consequences which would flow from . . .
> this resolution, as I can not be certain that all these results will flow, but . . .
> I think it is quite apparent that from a military point of view we would much
> prefer to let such sleeping dogs lie.[147]

McCloy had again deferred to the judgment of the army and the wishes of Stimson. They arranged with Congressmen Bloom and others not "to proceed with the matter now," and the resolution was dropped.

But the "repercussions," officers complained, "continue to stir up local animosities." Osmun and Wright wrote that recent "statements by some American Senators have persuaded Arabs that the U.S. is dominated by Jews and U.S. leaders are but 'cheap and irresponsible politicians.'" These American political leaders were "rapidly" creating the impression among the Arabs that "U.S. wealth, newspapers, and policies are operated by a small clique of Jews." Impervious to pleas that immigration to Palestine was a desperate attempt to deal with the ongoing extermination of millions of Jews, they added: "U.S. citizens wonder why this stirring up of hopes and fears could not better wait until the war is won rather than risk a 'Third Front in the rear,' immobilize more troops and endangering more lives."[148]

Since 1944 was an election year, the Zionists did in fact make some headway. Both party platforms contained strong pro-Zionist planks. Officers in the Middle East lost little time conveying the irreparable damage done to American interests for political expediency. "In the old days Arabs looked to Americans as their friends"; now they "regard President Roosevelt as . . . pro-Jewish," and "never has the good name of America sank so low in the esteem of the Arabs."[149]

Attempts to revive the Wagner-Taft Resolution in September 1944 quickly met army opposition. By this time, the defeat of Germany was clearly inevitable. After liberating Paris, Allied armies in the west were rapidly approaching the German border, while Russian forces advanced from the east. Recalling that "strong military reasons" had been offered earlier for suspending the resolution, McCloy's office now requested "an opinion as to the present military implications of this resolution in light of the existing military situation."[150]

"War Department opinion," the army responded, "should remain unchanged." Since the "war is not yet won," General Bissell stated, "any disturbances in Palestine may definitely prejudice the success of military operations and thereby prolong the war at the cost of additional American lives." To bolster his position, Bissell appended G-2 "evidence" from the past four months on "terrorism by extremist Jews," "inflammatory" Zionist propaganda, Jewish arms, and the British divisions and air power "required to cope with civil war." Furthermore, "political stability" in the region had "deteriorated in recent months because of American support of Zionist aspirations in Palestine." As interpreted by G-2, the Arabs showed "restraint" but were aroused to "serious animosity" by "incessant agitation" by Jews in America and Palestine.[151]

A few weeks later, however, Stimson undermined the army's stance. He withdrew his opposition to the Wagner-Taft initiative in a statement that left "the impression that passage of the Resolution can now have no possible effect on the war effort." This reversal spawned a flurry of calls, meetings, and memos between the State and War Departments to iron out these contradictions between the army and the secretary of war. With victory in Europe perhaps only months away, the State Department recognized that earlier justifications of military necessity appeared less compelling. If called to testify before the Senate Foreign Relations Committee, Undersecretary of State Edward R. Stettinius Jr. would, therefore, concede Stimson's point that "political considerations now outweigh the military," while holding as much to the case of wartime necessity as current circumstances allowed.[152]

These institutional gambits had signified an important shift in policy justification. What had been repeatedly presented as almost inevitable grave consequences to operational security now became a qualified concern about possible interference. Stettinius would argue,

> I am sure that Mr. Stimson does not mean to imply that there would be no threat whatsoever to our war effort if the Resolution is passed. In fact, Mr. Stimson points out "there is still strong feeling on the part of many officers in my department that the passage of such a resolution would interfere with our military effort."[153]

In these political battles, the army sided with the State Department rather than its own secretary. While attempting to avoid having officers oppose Stimson in public testimony, Bissell tried to obstruct the resolution by privately furnishing the familiar litany of crucial "military considerations." Its passage would endanger access to the "oil . . . vital to the successful conduct of the war." Moreover, "every unit retained in Palestine . . . means that much less British participation on the battlefronts with the consequent greater burden on U.S. Troops and greater loss of American lives." But, warned Bissell, "this fact must not reach the Axis."[154]

The maneuvering by opponents within the State and War Departments proved fruitful. Even Roosevelt now favored postponing the resolution and intervened to prevent Stettinius's appearance before the Senate committee. As McCloy noted in his diary: "[T]he President . . . did not want . . . action to be taken at present—70 million Mohammedans against 500,000 Jews might mean serious trouble."[155]

While this issue was coming to a head in Washington, an elated Jewish-American GI wrote his wife from France expressing his renewed hope upon learning that the "Balkans are almost entirely lost to Hitler." This development, he thought, "ought surely [to] open up new avenues for saving some Jews into Palestine."[156]

Little did this soldier know that his own military leaders had played a crucial role in keeping the gates of Palestine closed. Indeed, the army had no interest in establishing routes through which Europe's Jews could escape annihilation.

Army Resistance to Rescue

In late 1943, 4,000 Yugoslavs evacuated by partisans to the Adriatic island of Rab anxiously awaited their fate. Most of them were Jews for whom recapture would mean deportation and probable extermination, since most Yugoslavian Jews had already been shipped to Nazi death camps. The World Jewish Congress and the Yugoslavian embassy in Washington had requested their transportation to Italy before the impending German reoccupation of the island. It was not an unusual request. Following the Allied invasion of Italy in September, a constant wave of refugees fled across the Adriatic into southern Italy. The British navy evacuated thousands of refugees from the Yugoslavian coast, relocating them in Italy and later Egypt.

In this instance, however, the American "Commanding General, North African Theater of Operations . . . determined that the military situation does not permit the military authorities to render any direct assistance to these refugees" on the island of Rab. "Operational needs" took precedence. He "recommended that no direct assistance or funds be provided."[157]

By the time Undersecretary of State Stettinius read the cablegram explaining this inaction, it was too late. Months had elapsed and the Germans had recaptured Rab. An exasperated Stettinius wrote to Secretary of State Hull on January 8, 1944, saying that the "philosophy of the military . . . concerns me greatly." Stettinius agreed fully that "we should acquiesce in practically all cases when the military refuses an undertaking on the grounds of operational reasons," but he suspected something else had influenced this negative decision. Stettinius cited the astounding statement by the theater commander: "[I]t is considered that to take such action might create a precedent which would lead to other demands and an influx of additional refugees."[158]

Stettinius wrote:

> If that is a true expression of military policy and I question if it can represent the considered opinion of high military leaders, we might as well "shut up shop" on trying to get additional refugees out of occupied Europe.

The military must be notified, he said, that arrangements already exist to care for refugees "from other than military resources." But the military must be willing to participate in positive rescue efforts. "The President should suggest to the military that the rescue of refugees is extremely important and something which should not be brushed aside in accordance with the philosophy recited above; in fact sufficiently important to require unusual effort on their part and to be set aside only for important military operational reasons."[159]

Roosevelt's issuance of Executive Order 9417, creating the War Refugee Board (WRB) later that month, should have forced the army to act, as Stettinius suggested. "It is the policy of this Government," the order declared, "to take all measures within its power to rescue the victims of enemy oppression who are in imminent danger of death and otherwise to afford such victims all possible relief and assistance consistent with the successful prosecution of the war." It obligated the War, Treasury, and State Departments "to execute at the request of the Board, plans and programs . . . [and] to extend to the board such supplies, shipping and other specified assistance and facilities as the Board may require in carrying out the provisions of this order."[160]

Yet Treasury Secretary Morgenthau's efforts to involve the army met with instant obstruction. He suggested notifying theater commanders about the WRB and that they "should do everything possible, consistent with the successful prosecution of the war in [their] theater, to effectuate this policy." To the president, "it was urgent that action be taken to forestall the plot of the Nazis to exterminate the Jews and other persecuted minorities of Europe." In essence, the army should assist in "immediate rescue and relief."[161]

Through indifference, evasion, and inaction, the army defied the spirit as well as the letter of this presidential directive. Referring Morgenthau's proposal to the general staff, McCloy stated, "I am very chary of getting the Army involved in this while the war is on." To which the deputy chief of staff, General Joseph T. McNarney, responded:

> We must constantly bear in mind . . . that the most effective relief which can be given victims of enemy persecution is to insure the speedy defeat of the Axis. For this reason I share your concern over further involvement of the War Department, while the war is on, in matters such as the one brought up by Secretary Morgenthau.

Within days, Assistant Chief of Staff Thomas T. Handy added:

> It is not contemplated that units or individuals of the armed forces will be employed for the purpose of rescuing victims of enemy oppression unless such rescues are the direct result of military operations conducted with the objective of defeating the armed forces of the enemy.[162]

Morgenthau's proposal was then booted down bureaucratic channels to a subcommittee of the Logistics Committee of the Joint Chiefs of Staff. The subcommittee met at 4 A.M. on February 9 to discuss what to cable theater commanders about the WRB. None but Colonel Harrison Gerhardt showed any concern for the plight of Europe's Jews; the others sought to thwart Morgenthau's initiative. The army's representative, Colonel J. C. Davis, was openly hostile to any army cooperation with the WRB: "I do not like the suggested cable. Do we have to send a cable to the theater commander at all? If so, keep it to a minimum. I had rather send no reply at all. Couldn't we get by with a reply here from the Secretary of War to the Secretary of Treasury?"[163]

Responded Gerhardt, McCloy's assistant: "I don't think we could get away with it, politically or otherwise. The War Refugee Board Representatives have a copy of the executive order which says contact government agencies. . . . Read from the executive order, in which it is stated . . . cooperate to the fullest extent."

Davis said: "All right, then, we have to send a cable, but . . . I do not see how the theater commander can do anything new. . . . I cannot see why the Army has anything to do with it whatever."

When Gerhardt noted that theater commanders might provide shipping, Davis balked. Without inquiring whether transport might be found,
Davis dismissed the idea out of hand—the ships, he said, "are all in use."

Gerhardt then suggested communications. Davis immediately rejected
this as well: "I see no necessity of their using our communication facilities."

While Gerhardt probed for some type of cooperation, other committee
members resisted involving theater commanders in rescue under any circumstances. Lieutenant J. D. Rockefeller III (U.S. Naval Reserves) argued,
"The island of Rab came up several months ago. In that instance the theater commander said they couldn't take care of the refugees, even if they
obtained their own transportation; that they were already flooded with
them." Davis agreed: "I think that this proposal is shoving too much on the
theater commander. . . . [T]he cable ought to be worded so that the theater
commander doesn't have to do anything at all if he doesn't feel he should."

To defend against pressure for expanded army involvement, Davis
wanted to make its "position fairly inelastic." The subcommittee revised
the cable accordingly.

Davis then said: "This cable as it is written has all the hedges in it. If you
want to read it from an objectionist point of view, you could throw it away
and it wouldn't mean anything. We are over there to win the war and not
to take care of refugees."

To which Gerhardt replied: "The President doesn't think so. He thinks
relief is a part of winning the war."

Conceding that point, Davis then invoked a literal interpretation of the
president's directive which undermined its intent: "The Preamble refers to
a group of people near death, but [Morgenthau's suggested] cable starts
out by stating the President has instructed the Secretaries of War, Treasury, and State to rescue the Jews and other people who are in danger of
death. The executive order doesn't specify any race or color."

Gerhardt concurred: "That is an excellent point. In the revision of the
cable the wording should follow the wording of the executive order rather
than the Morgenthau cable."

The urgency and pressure for action in Morgenthau's memo were then
replaced by a general message that also reversed the thrust of the presidential order. "This is not," it emphasized, "a directive to establish a special project; that specific instances where relief can be effected will be
referred to the appropriate theater commander for such action as he deems
possible in the light of military operations and resources available to him."

As late as April, officers in Italy were still unaware of the WRB, whereas General Benjamin Caffey at Allied headquarters in Algiers adamantly rejected any military assistance to the WRB. When military facilities in Italy became overcrowded, the army instituted a policy of discouraging refugees from fleeing across the Adriatic; the refugee flow dropped by two-thirds.[164]

By this time, the army had precise information on the "perilous conditions of Jews." G-2 knew that a substantial portion of Latvian and Lithuanian "Jews have been massacred" and that in Hungary, "the 'final settlement' of the Jewish question has begun." Regarding the rescue of European Jews, G-2 reported in May that it had no information "as to what steps could be taken to bring them needed security and relief." The only exception to a hopeless situation G-2 cited was Yugoslavia, which made the island of Rab tragedy all the more appalling: The "evacuation of refugees from [the] Dalmatian coast has been for the most part successful," as "Allied boats visit the coast frequently and pin points are possible along the coast."[165]

Although the War Department consistently maintained that it lacked sufficient transport, in spring 1944 it finally conceded that it had "'ample shipping' available for evacuating refugees." But the army then defended its opposition to rescue and its policy of discouraging refugee flight into its zones by arguing that no havens existed for resettling such people. The army was steadfastly against transporting even small numbers of Jews to North Africa or Palestine, even though tens of thousands of other people had been evacuated to these areas.[166]

When John Pehle, WRB executive secretary, proposed establishing temporary refugee camps for Central European Jews in the United States, Stimson balked. Without so much as an allusion to the suffering or extermination of the Jews, Stimson presented the "danger" as the possibility that "so many Jews" might stay after the war. Stimson then lectured Pehle on the historical background of the "Jewish problem in this country" and why a quota system had been introduced to prevent the "unrestricted immigration of Jews."

None of Stimson's objections related to military necessity or resources. He disapproved of any plan "at variance" with immigration laws which he "believe[d] in," especially if instituted without the consent of Congress. Stimson still exhibited the nativist mentality that had justified the racist quota system enacted in 1924. As he explained to Pehle:

> Our present immigration laws were the result of a very deeply held feeling
> of our people that the future immigration of racial stocks should be so lim-

ited as to coincide with the existing ratio of such stocks already within the country. Furthermore these laws were adopted at the close of the last war . . . for the purpose of preventing the entrance into this country of large blocks of immigrants who were likely to come from the very countries in which most of the present refugees with whom we are concerned originate. Our people then showed that they strongly feared that an uncontrolled immigration from such countries would modify the proportion of the racial stocks already existing in our own population and would introduce into the United States many people who would with difficulty be assimilated into our own population and brought into conformity with our own institutions and traditions.[167]

By the end of May, Stimson would acquiesce in a WRB plan relocating 1,000 Jewish refugees in a "temporary haven" at Fort Ontario, New York, but only with the assurance they would definitely be repatriated after the war. Within the legal quota system so steadfastly upheld by Stimson, there were still over 50,000 unfilled openings for immigrants from Axis-occupied Europe. America never opened its gates any further for the duration of the war.[168]

With refugee "congestion" somewhat relieved, Pehle won another concession from the Civil Affairs Division. The "Army would do nothing to discourage the flow of refugees into Italy" and commanders would be instructed "accordingly, mentioning the President's desire in this regard."[169]

Resistance to Bombing Auschwitz

While various government and military agencies negotiated the fate of a few thousand refugees, Adolf Eichmann was directing the deportation of hundreds of thousands of Hungarian Jews to the gas chambers in Poland. Leaders of Jewish rescue organizations in Switzerland received urgent pleas from Jews in Budapest to bomb the rail lines to the camps, which included a strategic Axis military junction. For a month, Jewish leaders repeated these pleas to the U.S. military attaché in Bern for transmission to New York. Inexplicably, these messages were never delivered.[170]

By mid-June, Pehle had received a request from Jacob Rosenheim of the Agudas Israel World Organization in New York "to bomb the railroad line . . . used for the deportation of Jews from Hungary to Poland." Pehle presented this request to the War Department on June 21, and on June 24, he "mentioned the matter" to McCloy "for whatever exploration might be appropriate by the War Department." But Pehle had "several doubts about . . . whether it would be appropriate to use military planes and personnel for this matter . . . [and] whether it would help the Jews of Hungary." Mc-Cloy then instructed his aide, Colonel Gerhardt, "to 'kill' this."[171]

McCloy responded only after Pehle forwarded a report from Roswell McClelland, WRB representative in Bern, confirming that "all sources in Slovakia and Hungary" urged that "vital sections of these lines . . . be bombed as the only possible means of slowing down or stopping future deportations." McClelland submitted this message "as a proposal of these agencies and . . . [could] venture no opinion on its utility." He did, however, add force to the appeal by noting "that many of these Hungarian Jews are being sent to the extermination camps . . . where . . . since early summer 1942 at least 1,500,000 Jews have been killed."[172]

Meanwhile, the Operations Division quickly considered and dismissed the request. It recommended informing Morgenthau that the "air operation is impracticable for the reason that it could be executed only by diversion of considerable air support essential to the success of our forces now engaged in decisive operations."[173]

At the time, this argument appeared self-evident and compelling, for these requests coincided with the Normandy invasion, where the future of the Allied war effort hung in the balance. The army was understandably preoccupied with this enormous and crucial offensive whose success was far from certain. During the very days OPD dealt with the bombing question, the invasion had been jeopardized by sudden powerful gales that seriously disrupted Allied supply of the 700,000 soldiers who had landed in France. The War Department expressed its regrets, stating that it "fully appreciates the humanitarian importance of the suggested operation. However, after due consideration of the problem, it is considered that the most effective relief to victims of enemy persecution is the early defeat of the Axis, an undertaking to which we must devote every resource at our disposal."[174]

Although Pehle and Morgenthau were temporarily persuaded, the army had not been candid. It had neither displayed any semblance of empathy with the "humanitarian" aspects of rescue nor given "due consideration to the problem." The army merely followed its earlier decision not to adhere to the intent of the presidential order. Unknown to Pehle and Morgenthau, the army's confidential memorandum cited as the reason for not bombing the railroad lines the February 7 decision by General Hull:

It is not contemplated that units of the armed forces will be employed for the purpose of rescuing victims of enemy oppression unless such rescues are the direct result of military operations conducted with the objective of defeating the armed forces of the enemy.[175]

The Operations Division had not even looked into the availability of resources or the effectiveness of the proposed air operations. It simply asserted that resources would be diverted and, as McCloy averred, that the operation "would in any case be of such very doubtful efficacy." On June 26, the very day the army finalized its response, a fleet of Flying Fortresses on a bombing mission flew near the very rail lines that needed to be bombed. Moreover, the Fifteenth Air Force stationed in Italy was available, since it did not participate in the French theater of operations. Less than two weeks later, 452 of its bombers crossed two of these rail lines while on a mission to attack oil refineries near Auschwitz.[176]

For the rest of the summer, pressure mounted from various groups for bombing not only the deportation lines but the extermination center at Auschwitz as well. Besides pleas from Europe, requests came from the Emergency Committee to Save the Jewish People and the World Jewish Congress in New York. In his response of August 14, McCloy reiterated his earlier memo to Pehle, with a few additions to enhance its persuasiveness. In McCloy's version, the army's quick decision suddenly became "a study" that showed the operation would divert "considerable air support essential . . . to decisive operations elsewhere" and would be of "doubtful efficacy." As a new twist, McCloy inserted that "considerable opinion" believes "such an effort, even if practicable, might provoke even more vindictive action by the Germans."[177]

According to David S. Wyman, a few days later, on August 20, "127 Flying fortresses, escorted by 100 Mustang fighters, dropped 1,336, 500-pound high explosive bombs on the factory areas of Auschwitz, *less than five miles* to the east of the gas chambers." In early September, heavy bombers hit the factory areas of Auschwitz. These missions were an integral part of the army's strategic warfare against the vital industrial and oil installations around the extermination center. The entire area had long been designated a significant military target.[178]

The army continually reassured petitioners it was "desirous of taking all possible measures to improve the condition" of these "unfortunate people." But in its private memos concerning its responses to inquiries about rescue, the army candidly noted that its "letters ma[d]e no commitment by the War Department," yet gave the authors "a satisfactory reply."[179]

This attitude was exemplified in the army's handling of requests to warn the Germans to cease exterminations or face punishment after the war. Roosevelt had issued a warning in March, which the WRB had spread across Europe throughout the year. In late 1944, additional warnings were requested as fears spread that the Germans were accelerating the exterminations.

When Agudas Israel World Organization proposed a warning on September 17, the adjutant general's office initially drafted a brief bureaucratic reply, essentially stating, "Your comments have been carefully noted." But recognizing this response "as being too stereotyped, and too much of an evident 'brush off,'" the OPD recommended inserting that

> the War Department continues to do everything in its power to rescue and relieve all victims of enemy persecution in Europe. However, it is believed that no advantage will be gained by repetition of previous warnings to German leaders, as their reiteration may be construed as threats and may react to the detriment of American prisoners of war in the custody of the German Government.[180]

However, a few weeks later the WRB and State Department prepared just such a warning. Believing that a statement from Eisenhower would carry additional weight, the WRB favored its release by the supreme commander. An internal army memo for Eisenhower stated that the Operations Division "has no objection to the proposed statement. . . . [I]t can do no harm and the threat may prevent the commission of some atrocities."[181]

Eisenhower agreed, "provided the words 'or religious faith' are substituted for the words 'and whether they are Jewish or otherwise.'" On November 7, Eisenhower's message told Germans to "disregard any order . . . to molest, or otherwise harm or persecute any . . . persons in forced-labor battalions and in concentration camps," warning that "severe penalties will be inflicted upon anyone who is responsible." The message concluded, "Those now exercising authority, take heed!"[182]

Reliable reports from the Polish underground that the Germans were "increasing their extermination activities" soon revived the bombing issue. Although the WRB had informed those advocating bombing that the army had already found it "impractical," Jews in Europe knowledgeable of conditions in the camps continued to insist on both its necessity and its feasibility. When he related the renewed pleas to McCloy in early October, Pehle stated that he understood that "the matter is now in the hands of appropriate theater commanders." But the assumptions of Pehle, the WRB, and others concerned with rescue about the involvement of theater commanders were certainly erroneous. Up to this date, theater commanders had never been asked to consider any proposal. And McCloy again took the advice of Gerhardt that "no action be taken on this, since the matter has been fully presented several times previously."[183]

When OPD became independently aware of these renewed requests, it sent a brief radiogram to General Carl Spaatz, commander in chief of U.S. Strategic Air Forces in Europe. It referred Spaatz to an earlier dispatch regarding "BOMBARDMENT INSTALLATIONS NEAR POLISH CONCENTRATION CAMPS." These four lines constituted the only message on such bombing the War Department ever submitted to "operational forces in Europe for consideration" throughout the entire war. And it emphasized: "THIS IS ENTIRELY YOUR AFFAIR. WE HAVE NOT MODIFIED MILITARY NECESSITY AS FUNDAMENTAL REQUIREMENT IN OUR VIEW."[184]

Within a day, Spaatz's staff had dismissed the request. His deputy commander, General Frederick I. Anderson, added another twist:

> I do not consider that the unfortunate Poles herded in these concentration camps would have their status improved by the destruction of the extermination chambers. There is also the possibility of some of the bombs landing on the prisoners as well, and in that event, the Germans would be provided a fine alibi for any wholesale massacre that they might perpetrate. I therefore recommend that no encouragement be given to this project.[185]

Implicit in Anderson's objection was a serious moral dilemma confronting all advocates of concentration-camp bombing. But Anderson's emphatic declaration that bombings would only inflict more suffering indicated no attempt to weigh the consequences of various alternatives. Deciding whether to risk killing a portion of concentration-camp prisoners to stop the mass murders was an agonizing burden for Jewish leaders in America and abroad. Some resisted the idea; the majority, however, ultimately judged it to be an urgent, necessary, and morally justifiable act. By this point in the war, almost all Jews arriving at Auschwitz faced immediate extermination. The risk was that some of those already condemned to a certain death would be killed, whereas bombing might destroy the machinery of systematic mass killings, saving tens, if not hundreds of thousands of Jews.[186]

In early September, G-2 Middle East intercepted a report from Europe vividly describing the genocide. Through a well-planned and executed process, the report said:

> 12,000 people are being deported daily . . . in hermetically closed trucks . . . who have to stand during the whole voyage. . . . When they have arrived . . . many are already dead from lack of air, food, and unhygienic conditions. The rest . . . are suffocated by cyanide gas. 2,000 people thus perish every day in each hall. . . . The corpses are burned in special incinerators which reduce to ashes twelve bodies in one hour . . . there were 36 incinerators. . . . Those brought from the trains straight into the death chambers . . . constitute about 95% of the people.

"The writer," G-2 stated, "continues with a passionate appeal. . . . To bomb from the air the death chambers."[187]

In early November, the "eye-witness accounts" of two escapees from Auschwitz finally prompted Pehle to pressure the War Department to conduct the long-requested bombing. Urging McCloy to read them, Pehle wrote that "no report of Nazi atrocities . . . has quite caught the gruesome brutality of what is taking place in these camps of horror as have these sober, factual accounts of conditions in Auschwitz and Birkenau." Since the Germans had devoted "considerable technological ingenuity and administrative know-how, . . . the elaborate murder installations, [if] destroyed," could not be easily reconstructed. Abandoning his earlier reluctance, Pehle wrote:

> Until now, despite pressure from many sources, I have been hesitant to urge the destruction of these camps by direct, military action. But I am convinced that the point has now been reached where such action is justifiable if it is deemed feasible by competent military authorities. I strongly recommend that the War Department give serious consideration to the possibility of destroying the execution chambers and crematories in Birkenau through direct bombing action.[188]

Pehle strengthened his argument by citing the strategic advantages of such a mission. It would destroy the "Krupp and Siemens factories . . . all within Auschwitz" and kill "German soldiers"; moreover, the "morale of underground groups might be considerably strengthened by such a dramatic exhibition of Allied air support." Emphasizing the "urgency of the situation," Pehle requested a War Department response "as soon as possible."[189]

Unknown to Pehle, the Operations Division characterized his proposal as "largely humanitarian" with only "incidental military advantages." OPD opposed it as "of very doubtful feasibility and unacceptable from a military standpoint," since "it would be a diversion from our strategic bombing effort and the results would not justify the high losses likely to result."

For the first time, OPD furnished specific data substantiating its objections. "The target is beyond the range of medium bombardment, dive bombers and fighter bombers located in United Kingdom, France, or Italy." Further, "use of heavy bombardment from United Kingdom bases would necessitate a round trip flight [McCloy added the word "hazardous" to his version] unescorted of approximately 2000 miles over enemy territory." The best solution, OPD reiterated, remained the quick defeat of Germany, to which "we should exert our entire means." Thus ended the last WRB effort to have the death camps bombed.[190]

This final rejection had not come after "careful consideration," as McCloy informed Pehle. And humanitarian sympathy aside, the objectives and justifications for the mission Pehle outlined did fall within the scope of the three "Target Priorities . . . selected by the Combined Chiefs of Staff (Washington)," those being "Economic," "Strategic," and "Political." A political target priority was defined as "what will be most damaging to enemy morale & helpful to occupied countries." As an example of a political factor justifying target priority, an army report in General Anderson's papers cited bombing a certain city to "boost Norwegian morale." Later, Stimson and McCloy intervened against the army's desire to bomb Kyoto, Japan, and Rothenburg, Germany, so as to spare these beautiful cities from the ravages of war.

The bombing of Auschwitz and its railroad lines remains a provocative subject of hostile historical debate. David S. Wyman and others have long argued that air strikes against Auschwitz were not at all unfeasible and would not have required a major diversion in the strategic bombing campaign. Since early 1944, the Fifteenth Air Force in Italy had sufficient range and power for a successful mission. "From July through November 1944, more than 2,800 bombers struck . . . targets close to Auschwitz. The industrial area of Auschwitz itself was hit twice."[191]

More recently, however, critics have raised operational objections about the efficacious use of air power for such missions. In retrospect, they contend that faulty intelligence, operational constraints, and strategic asset allocation precluded any successful strikes from the air.[192] But these criticisms have themselves been called into question by further research into intelligence, German defenses, and bombing scenarios. It appears that the bombing of Auschwitz, in the words of Stuart G. Erdheim, "was no more complicated from an operational standpoint than was bombing any of numerous other targets during the war." It was the "mindset" and "motives of those involved in the decision-making process," not any "military assessment," that accounted for the failure to bomb the camp. The army had the required intelligence and operational capability to launch a raid on Auschwitz in early 1944, and could thereby have saved many more lives than could have been expected from later bombings. The crucial factor was the absence of a will to act.[193]

Whatever path this controversy takes, the fact remains that at the time, the army never attempted to acquire intelligence or make the necessary operational assessments to determine whether such bombing was feasible. The army never pursued any systematic examination of the proposals presented to it; nor did it ask theater commanders what might be done. The quick and repetitious responses from the army without much inquiry into the intelligence or technical and operational aspects later interjected by critics of bombing suggest other reasons for these policy decisions, including indifference among highly placed officers to the plight of Jews.

While attempting to sway the army to bomb the camps, Pehle encountered similar resistance to publicizing the reports of the exterminations at Auschwitz. Upon learning that the WRB had released the escapee reports to the press, the director of the Office of War Information (OWI), Elmer Davis, summoned Pehle to his office in late November for a meeting with his staff. Davis chastised Pehle for disregarding an earlier instruction requiring OWI clearance for news releases "relating significantly to the war effort." Since the entire OWI staff "viewed with alarm" Pehle's action, Davis went around the room asking each of his associates to express their varied objections.

The OWI staff questioned the stories as "being concerned with a multiplicity of 'mean little things'" and raised the issue of "reprisals on American prisoners" as well as the "inadvisability of timing" given the recent War Loan drive. "All expressed fears of the reaction" of the public, though upon questioning Davis's staff admitted that a favorable press response was likely. Davis inquired whether the extermination stories were authentic. Someone else asked "whether the reports had not been planted by anti-Semites (because of the reference to Jews being cruel to Jews)."[194]

While demolishing "their objections one by one," Pehle read a WRB letter vouching for the authenticity of the death-camp reports. Several times during the conference, Davis acknowledged that his own Polish desk "had stated that the events . . . might well have happened." Pehle said he had consulted Jewish organizations, Congressman Emanuel Celler, and Henry Morgenthau, none of whom "had felt any fears such as those voiced by OWI."[195]

Confronted by a fait accompli, Davis was quite annoyed, though helpless. In light of what was happening to the Jews, one of Pehle's staff wrote sarcastically, "The enormity of the crimes which the WRB had perpetrated against the OWI was so great that Mr. Davis admitted there was practically nothing to be done at this late date."[196] Davis refused to give up. The next day he tried to have Pehle attach a statement to the news release essentially hedging their bets if the report's "credibility" did not hold up. Davis then conjured up the possibility that the reports might even be a clever plot by the German Propaganda Ministry to try to lessen the blame on the Germans by "smear[ing] other nationalities" with crimes committed in the camps.[197]

Given the role of authority and legal orders in the Nazi system of genocide, Davis's final statements have, in retrospect, an eerie tone. He reasserted his bureaucratic prerogatives of prior approval of news releases "as required by Paragraphs 5 and 7 of Executive Order 9182, and by Regulation No. 1 issued in pursuance to Paragraph 5 of that order . . . [and] our Regulations No. 3 and 5." He added: "See that your staff complies with these rulings hereafter."[198]

Pehle had similar difficulties with the editors of *Yank: The Army Weekly*. At the end of October, a *Yank* reporter, Sergeant Richard Paul, approached Pehle about serving as an "official source" for a "German atrocity story to show our soldiers the nature of their enemy." Pehle provided Paul with the reports on the "notorious extermination camps at Auschwitz and Birkenau," from which *Yank* would publish excerpts. The article included an interview in which Pehle stated:

These reports give facts which none of us want to believe and which Americans naturally refuse to believe until overwhelming evidence has been presented. We on the War Refugee Board have been very skeptical. . . . But Hitler's program of extermination has now been clearly substantiated . . . from reliable and corroborated sources.[199]

Paul's editors turned down the article, because the "reports were too Semitic and they had asked him to get a story from other sources." They wanted a story that "did not deal principally with Jews."

Paul also ran into a bureaucratic roadblock at the Pentagon when he sought clearance for overseas publication. "Sent from one officer to another in quick order," he encountered "a very negative attitude," since this "hell of a hot story" required approval at the "highest military channels." By this time, the American press had already received the information on the camps from Pehle. A week later, McCloy's office certified there was "no military security involved" and "no reason why the War Department should object to its release."[200]

Meanwhile, Paul had again been told by *Yank* editors "to get a less Jewish story." He then made another unsuccessful effort to explain the arguments favoring publication, including the fact that the WRB had already released the reports to the press. Still, he was told "that because of latent anti-Semitism in the Army, he ought, if possible, to get something with a less Semitic slant."[201]

The other major Army publication, *Stars and Stripes*, apparently had a similar editorial policy. Only in late April 1945 did *Stars and Stripes* first publish articles on Nazi concentration camps and atrocities, even though their existence had been verified years before. Now, as the camps were liberated, this paper finally informed soldiers of the gruesome details through photographs, testimony, and editorials under startling headlines:

> "Nazi Horror Stories Unfold"; "Pictures Don't Lie"; "Officials, Editors Tour Death Camps"; "Himmler's Death Factories."

These stories in *Stars and Stripes* covered some of the most infamous concentration camps: Bergen-Belsen, Buchenwald, Dachau, Ohrdruf, and Mauthausen. Conspicuous by its absence in these stories and editorials was the word "Jew." One could not detect the slightest hint that Jews had been the prime target of Nazi genocide or indeed that they had been victims at all.[202]

On May 18, 1945, a week after the German surrender, and seven months after Pehle offered confirmation, *Yank* finally published a story titled "German Atrocities." Although it focused on the barbaric brutality toward American POWs, intermixed were "first hand" reports on extermination centers accompanied by photos of thousands of emaciated corpses strewn in piles. Soldiers in the photos gazed at mounds of skulls and bones, while others peered into crematorium ovens full of human ashes.

A section on Buchenwald described the horrors of concentration-camp existence and the system of death and cremation—"too enormous a crime to be accepted fully." But here, too, the relationship between this system of mass murder and Jews was completely ignored. Instead, the article emphasized that "[a]ll the peoples of Europe were represented here among the survivors and the dead." Throughout this lengthy piece, there was only one reference to Jews inserted among a general listing of death tolls: "At the Oswiecm camp near Erfurt, Germany, 3,500,000 Jews were killed."[203]

Yank's belated minimal acknowledgment of the mass murder of Jews was typical of the army's entire response to the Holocaust. From the beginning of the war, the army resisted every major initiative or proposal for rescuing or assisting European Jewry. It was the tragic story of missed opportunities of momentous proportions, complicated by concerns officers had about operational security or essential military objectives. But it was also the story of indifference, refusal to seriously examine the feasibility of proposals, and outright hostility to any kind of involvement. These aspects of the stance taken by many officers indicate the role of factors other than the cold military calculations necessitated by war. Generations of racial thinking and anti-Semitism in the officer corps surely had an impact. The attitudes and positions of many officers right up to the outbreak of war reinforce such conclusions. The prejudice exhibited during the war by many officers, particularly in the senior ranks, likewise strongly suggests that long-standing attitudes toward Jews affected wartime decisions, sometimes consciously and even overtly, and sometimes in other ways.

Indeed, army intelligence, advice, and decisions on such matters were among the most important elements in determining America's response to the Holocaust. In many respects, the army held the trump card over those individuals, groups, and agencies advocating American action. The necessity of avoiding anything that might interfere with quickly winning the war was a powerful argumentative weapon. This was especially true when the army wielded such arguments, for it held responsibility for conducting the war, provided information on conditions in the theaters of war, and controlled the forces and resources required for relief and rescue.

This troublesome story, however, did not end with the defeat of Germany in May 1945. Immediately after the war in Europe, the army found new military and geopolitical arguments to justify inaction or strong opposition to the various solutions to the plight of Holocaust survivors.

CHAPTER 10

Survivors, Refugees, and the Birth of Israel, 1945–1949

A s MAJOR CHARLES ROBERTSON'S UNIT moved rapidly through the Alps into Austria in the last days of the war, he was immediately struck by two clashing images. He experienced the breathtaking, panoramic beauty of the snow-capped mountain range and the Austrian countryside. Then he came face to face with the emaciated, dying inmates of the Nazi concentration camps. Robertson truly empathized with the terrified children and starving men who ate right through cellophane food packaging; many continued to die "like flies." Disgusted by the sight of well-fed Austrians, he was bewildered that the inhabitants of this beautiful country could be "so damn mean."[1]

Within a matter of months Robertson's sympathies were completely reversed. In the course of his service as a public safety officer with the occupation forces, his fondness for the Austrians increased while his initial empathy for Nazi victims turned into visceral repulsion. He lived in a large villa with plenty of food and liquor, celebrated Christmas with Austrians he now admired, and complained of the hardships caused by denazification. The destitute Displaced Persons (DPs), particularly Jews, he treated as a contemptible unwanted burden.

The major never understood why DPs might loot surrounding areas. "These people," he wrote, "think that once they have been in a concentration camp they are eligible for all good things in life, and can confiscate & grab anything they like." Neither could he grasp why DPs refused to obey

the Austrian police, whom the army rearmed with carbine rifles. This former liberator now told the Austrian police "to shoot all they like if they
don't comply [since] that's the only kind of language they understand."[2]

American soldiers generally shared Robertson's initial shock upon encountering the concentration camps. Officers and enlisted men alike felt that
nothing "published to date begins to paint the picture in the horrible terms
of the reality as it exists." Soldiers showed sincere compassion and generosity toward survivors. Recalled one Jewish-American officer: "I saw their lib-
erators kissing and embracing those they had rescued. I found American
officers and GIs bringing their PX rations as gifts to those in the camps."[3]

Unfortunately, many American soldiers would soon undergo the same
rapid transition from sympathy to indifference and disdain that Major
Robertson had experienced. When confronted with Holocaust survivors
and refugees, many American officers displayed the kind of anti-Semitism,
and sometimes the racialist thought, characteristic of earlier generations of
the officer corps. Once again there was a tendency to integrate the question of Jewish survivors into various facets of the larger "Jewish Problem"
supposedly facing America. Some officers connected Jews with a whole
host of other issues, ranging from the spread of communism to vengeance
against Germans. On racial, anti-Semitic, and national security grounds,
many army officers opposed postwar Jewish immigration into the United
States with the same determination the officer corps had resisted it from
1918 through World War II. For similar reasons, the army just as
staunchly fought against Jewish immigration into Palestine and the establishment of Israel.

The Army and Jewish Survivors

Initially, the "evidence of bestiality and cruelty" in the liberated camps
prompted Eisenhower to order all available units to tour a concentration
camp. He also arranged visits by congressmen and journalists from America. "We are told," he said, "the American soldier does not know what he
is fighting for. Now, at least, he will know what he is fighting against."[4]

The army, however, was unwilling to deal with the problem of survivors. For years, the army had continually expressed its sympathy for
Jews in Nazi-occupied Europe while adamantly opposing rescue attempts
on the grounds that they would interfere with the war effort. Its standard
response to pleas for assistance had been that winning the war quickly was

the best means of saving the Jews of Europe. These wartime arguments against army involvement became irrelevant as the Allies emerged as masters of the continent. Now the army did not need to mount any rescue efforts, as surviving remnants of Europe's Jews were already in Western Allied areas or soon trying to move into the American occupation zone. Caring for these people did not compromise any military mission, conflict with grand wartime strategy, or risk the lives of American soldiers. Yet while pointing out to the world the unparalleled inhumanity of the camps, the army was reluctant to undertake even this limited mission.

Nonetheless, the burden soon fell to the army, for the United Nations Relief and Rehabilitation Administration (UNRRA) proved unable to care for and repatriate millions of DPs. Providing food and shelter, even communicating with DPs speaking various Eastern European languages, was an unprecedented task of immense logistical complexity that the army was compelled to undertake as it simultaneously coped with the difficulties of establishing an occupation government in Germany. The army carried it out while plagued by chronic shortages of food, fuel, shelter, and transportation.

In most respects, the army rose to the occasion, earning well-deserved recognition and praise for its humanitarian assistance to DPs and the repatriation of millions to their native lands. But the army also faced severe criticism for its treatment of those who could not be repatriated, including Jewish inmates of concentration camps.[5]

Very soon, Jewish survivors felt the brunt of attitudes that severely qualified the sympathies of officers and enlisted men alike. "About June of 1945," wrote Albert Hutler, a Jewish-American officer in charge of DPs, "I began to feel and see a change in attitudes in the American military towards refugees and displaced persons, especially towards Jews." He still witnessed compassion and generosity among American officers who did their best to help survivors, but many more "carried their homegrown prejudices against Jews and Eastern Europeans with them." They regarded DPs "as scum and dirt while treating the German[s] as . . . the salt of the earth." Even some UNRRA members viewed DPs, especially Jews, as "scum, dirty, filthy people, undisciplined, dangerous, troublesome scavengers." One UNRRA truck driver remarked: "Hitler should have killed all the Jews."

Hutler observed Jews placed in filthy, inhumane conditions in former concentration camps still surrounded by barbed wire and armed guards. "I have seen American officers who think nothing of hitting a DP, who tell the Germans that DPs are scum, who treat DPs as inferior people."[6]

In the eyes of the old officer corps, the behavior of survivors after liberation only confirmed their long-held racist stereotypes of Jews and Eastern Europeans. Prominent among that military generation was General George S. Patton, whose zone now contained the largest segment of Jewish DPs. In that region, Patton set the tone for army policies and behavior toward these emaciated and traumatized people. His attitude and racial worldview predisposed him to favor the Germans and detest Holocaust survivors.

Patton's biographer, Martin Blumenson, traced his views to his upbringing and Southern heritage, which created a mindset in which Mexicans, Indians, and African-Americans constituted inferior races. As a conquering general, Patton perhaps naturally extended these prejudices to include Arabs and Sicilians. But this racism also reflected the Darwinism within the old army, which for decades had reinforced the notion of a hierarchy of inferior and superior races.[7]

Patton greatly admired the Germans and despised peoples from further east. Upon entering bombed-out Berlin, the general felt depressed, lamenting that "Berlin marks the final epitaph of what should have been a great race." He would try to salvage their society.[8]

To Patton, Soviet communism posed a racial threat to white Western civilization. Russians were a Mongolian race of "savages," inherently "barbaric" with "no regard for human life." The Russian "is not a European, but an Asiatic, and therefore thinks deviously. We can no more understand a Russian than we can understand a Chinaman or a Japanese." Patton's only interest in Russians was "how much lead or iron it takes to kill them."[9]

From the liberation of the camps until his removal, Patton similarly invoked degrading racist terminology to describe Jewish DPs. They were "animals," he wrote repeatedly, "a sub-human species without any of the cultural or social refinements of our time."

Patton completely discounted the explanation that many concentration-camp survivors had taken on certain behaviors merely to stay alive and that recovery from unspeakable trauma and dehumanization would be long and difficult. To him, their wretched appearance, lethargy, and unsanitary habits were manifestations of their hereditary racial traits of "mental, moral and physical" inferiority and degeneracy. To explain their lack of "intelligence and spirit," he wrote: "Practically all of them had the flat brownish gray eye common among the Hawaiians which, to my mind, indicates very low intelligence." Dismissing "internment by the Germans" as a cause, he stated: "My personal opinion is that no people could have sunk to the level of degradation these have reached in the short space of four years."[10]

Although no doubt lacking the theoretical racial framework of the older officers, average American soldiers frequently drew similar conclusions about Germans and DPs. Spreading out quickly over Germany and Austria, most soldiers never saw a concentration camp, and their replacements never fought a German. Soldiers also had difficulty reconciling the horrors they read about with the "beautiful country" and "simple, pleasant" German people, so many of whom had "religious pictures" on their walls. Some GIs were definitely perplexed about "whether you can condemn a whole people for allowing such things to exist." One soldier wrote: "Thank Heaven, it is not my problem to solve."[11]

To American soldiers, the Germans, as well as the members of Baltic nationalities living in DP camps, were paradigms of cleanliness, orderliness, and the work ethic. Although the cities had been bombed and lay in ruins, Germans in the towns and countryside tended to be "well dressed, better fed, and living in a home." Deferential and obedient to military authority, proper in speech and mannerism, they eagerly cooperated in reestablishing an economic and legal system. They were adept at pursuing their own interests through bureaucratic and legal manipulations. Despite nonfraternization policies, they accommodated in whatever way they could the social needs and wishes of soldiers.

The DP, in stark contrast, lived in

> a barracks, schoolhouse or barn and usually with common sanitary facilities. His wardrobe is usually what he wears plus a few pieces of clothing stuffed in a bag. He had developed a defensive attitude as protection against German brutality. He had learned to steal to supplement his German starvation diet. He has learned to distrust promises and pieces of paper. His world revolves around food and shelter. In American slang, he looks and acts like a "bum."

It was no wonder, stated this UN observer, that officers placed "more credence in the German's complaint about looting than in the DP's complaint about inadequate food."[12]

Freed from the dehumanizing concentration camps, Jews were initially herded into crowded areas while still suffering from psychological trauma and physical deprivation. When officers inspected these centers, they found not only disorder but filth and human excrement in hallways and kitchens. These "unsanitary conditions," wrote one Jewish soldier, convinced GIs that "Jews as a whole were a dirty lot"; as a result, soldiers developed a "feeling of disgust and sometimes contempt" for Jews. When camp authorities were criticized for allowing intolerable overcrowding, some soldiers responded that "living conditions of this kind are what the displaced persons are 'used to.'" As one officer said:

> The DPs have food and clothes and a camp to live in. What more do they want? They should be grateful. If they are not satisfied let them go back where they came from.[13]

Some DPs also engaged in looting and general criminality, which the army could not tolerate. Soldiers could not understand why Jewish DPs in particular found nothing wrong with stealing from Germans or violating their laws or why they reacted as they did to armed German policeman. The refusal or inability of survivors to work also conjured up old images of Jews as weak, lazy parasites. Jews supposedly escaped from Poland so "they could live off the American army without working" and "they sure are playing us for suckers." A British UNRRA investigator, however, attributed the unwillingness to work, like the "looting and raiding exploits," partly to "an inadequacy of diet."[14]

Jewish involvement in the black market also revived latent anti-Semitism. The black market was quite alluring to Jews who lacked employment, property, money, family, or social networks. With "legitimate means of making a living closed to them," those who had become conditioned to survive by their wits and now found "authority of any kind repugnant" engaged in an illegal activity that attracted many DPs as well as American soldiers. To Jews, violating German law was "more of a virtue than a crime." Still, "some Americans . . . concluded that all Jews are cheating traders."[15]

By July 1945, distressing press accounts of wretched DP camps and ill-treatment of Jews prompted President Truman to appoint an investigatory committee led by Earl Harrison, U.S. representative to the Inter-Governmental Committee on Refugees. The army was now the subject of an official investigation into how it was carrying out its unwanted mission.

No doubt the Harrison committee reminded some older officers of the commission headed by Henry Morgenthau Sr. that investigated the predicament of Jews in Eastern Europe after World War I. Some officers believed that his son, Henry Morgenthau Jr., was behind criticism of the army's occupation policy in Germany. Once again the issue was perceived in terms of an opposition between Jewish and national interests. Harrison's senior assistant, Joseph Schwartz, European director of the Joint Distribution Committee, probably fueled such suspicions. From 1919 through attempts at rescuing Europe's Jews in World War II, the army had suspected the Jewish-American JDC of various activities contrary to American interests, ranging from circumventing U.S. immigration laws to facilitating the infiltration of Communist agents. The significant difference from 1919 was that the American army rather than the Poles had now become the target.[16]

Up to this point, Eisenhower apparently saw no serious problems with army policy or its implementation. In his mind, the army was doing its best. Ignoring the fact that the debilities of Jewish DPs stemmed from a Nazi policy of singling them out for brutalization, starvation, and extermination, Eisenhower agreed with the army policy of treating Jews like other DPs, without recognizing their special needs. As late as August, he refused to appoint a Jewish chaplain as a "special advisor on affairs dealing with displaced persons." Only years later did Eisenhower acknowledge that the concentration-camp trauma had left Jewish survivors psychotically hopeless, passive, and apathetic, "in some instances, no longer capable of helping themselves." Yet even then, he vigorously denied that American soldiers were indifferent, negligent, or callous. "Generally," he wrote, "these stories were lies."[17]

Harrison's report shocked Truman and caught Eisenhower by surprise. Its devastating critique would force the general into defensive explanations and belated policy changes:

> Many Jewish displaced persons . . . are living under guard behind barbed-wire fence, in camps of several descriptions, (built by the Germans for slave-laborers and Jews) including some of the most notorious concentration camps, amidst crowded, frequently unsanitary and generally grim conditions, in complete idleness, with no opportunity, except surreptitiously, to communicate with the outside world.[18]

The language and imagery in Harrison's accusations would stun any reader:

> We appear to be treating the Jews as the Nazis treated them except that we do not exterminate them. They are in concentration camps in large numbers under our military guard instead of S.S. troops. One is led to wonder whether the German people . . . are not supposing that we are following or at least condoning Nazi policy."[19]

"More severely victimized" than other DPs, Jews had special needs, Harrison stated. Yet they continued to suffer deprivation in housing, clothing, and shelter while the Germans lived well. He accused many American officers of "utmost reluctance or indisposition . . . about inconveniencing the German population." The military government, he charged, employed Germans rather than qualified DPs. Harrison called for the classification of "Jews as Jews" and for giving special consideration to their needs, including the requisition of housing from Germans. Furthermore, since most Jewish DPs desired to emigrate to Palestine, the United States should convince the British to open Palestine to refugees.[20]

After reading the Harrison report, Truman essentially ordered Eisenhower to establish separate DP centers for Jews, requisition necessary housing from Germans, and ensure that these policies were carried out. Reversing himself, Eisenhower appointed a Jewish adviser and toured the camps. In responding to Truman, Eisenhower conceded little to Harrison's accusations. No DPs still lived in the "horror" camps, he maintained. Only in one camp were living conditions "less than satisfactory"; officers were not reluctant to take over German housing; and he encountered a "distinct lack of cooperation" from DPs in one camp. The DP problem was serious, but conditions had greatly improved and would continue to improve. Overall, the "Army here has done an admirable and almost unbelievable job."[21]

When Harrison publicly challenged the accuracy of Eisenhower's letter to Truman, the general vented his frustration to Marshall: "I see that Mr. Harrison is still shouting from the housetops to get the Jews out of the centers in which we are taking care of them. I wonder whether he knows that we are giving these people every ounce of food they eat and how he would possibly distribute it if we had them scattered all over Germany." Eisenhower later wrote that "because perfection could not be achieved some so-called investigators saw a golden chance for personal publicity."[22]

Eisenhower's Jewish adviser, Rabbi Judah Nadich, later said that the general "was forced into action, but once acting, he cooperated 100%." Although he had to be pressured by Washington, Eisenhower saved the "lives not only of the Jews in the DP camps" but also of the "approximately 80,000 Jews . . . who came in across the borders from Eastern Europe."[23]

But Patton and other subordinates were indignant over policies that they considered inspired by American Jews. Such changes—"promulgated by Morgenthau"—were "unrealistic," "undemocratic," and "practically Gestapo methods." Patton balked at giving "Jews special accommodations. If for Jews, why not for Catholics, Mormons, etc.?"

After failing to convince Eisenhower, Patton wrote privately to Stimson complaining about the "pro-Jewish influence in the Military Government of Germany" and mistreatment of the Germans. He trusted Stimson, because the secretary had earlier shown him his correspondence with Morgenthau. To Patton, nothing less than the freedoms for which America had fought its revolution and civil war were at stake. Patton was also reluctant to institute denazification policies that called for purging Nazi members and sympathizers from public offices and institutions. But on September 11, Eisenhower forcefully reminded Patton that despite the wishes of officers to modify denazification policy, that "question had long since been decided. We will not compromise with Nazism in any way."[24]

Patton remained outraged by the new policies toward Germans and Jews, writing about a "virus" of "Semitic revenge against all Germans" spread by "Morgenthau and Baruch":

> Harrison and his ilk believe that the displaced person is a human being, which he is not, and this applies particularly to the Jews, who are lower than animals.

Patton relished the opportunity of taking Eisenhower through a model camp inhabited by the "best" DPs—the "Baltic people"—followed by a Jewish camp, "packed by the greatest stinking bunch," with "no sense of human relationships."[25]

Under press criticism over denazification, Patton finally caused his own downfall in late September. During a press conference, an irritated Patton supposedly compared Nazis to Democrats and Republicans. Doubts about Patton's commitments to denazification appeared validated, and editorial condemnation set the stage for his removal.

Even before this incident, Patton saw webs of intrigue woven about him. Not immune to conspiracy theories, he had in the past shown himself sympathetic to an in-laws' discussion of the *Protocols of the Elders of Zion*. Now, he wrote: "There is a very apparent Semitic influence in the press. They are trying . . . to implement Communism."

Immediately after Patton's showdown with the press, the journalist and member of the "Secret Americans" clique Frank Mason told him that "Jews and Communist elements" conspired to get rid of him. In Germany on a secret mission for Herbert Hoover, Mason recounted that he had learned this insidious plan from Colonel Percy Black of G-2. Black allegedly suggested that the attacks on Patton were a plot by "radical journalists" to help establish a Russian puppet government in Germany. Mason noted in his diary that Patton "talked like a Christian" and labeled denazification a "lot of B.S." Upon returning to America, Mason was debriefed privately by Marshall.[26]

The mounting controversy culminated in a dramatic, closed-door shouting match between Patton and Eisenhower. Soon, under immense pressure from Washington, Eisenhower removed his old friend. For the next several weeks, Patton wrote repeatedly about the plot by "Jews and Communists" to remove him and any other officer who stood in the way of their destructive plans for Germany. Ironically, Patton received a letter of support from an admiring Bernard Baruch. Patton responded: "I cannot understand who had the presumption to attribute to me anti-Semitic ideas which I certainly do not possess."[27]

Eisenhower instructed Patton's replacement, General Lucian K. Truscott, to be "stern" in implementing denazification and to give preferential treatment to Jewish displaced persons. Significant changes followed immediately as separate centers were set up for Jewish refugees, their food and clothing were improved, and Germans were dispossessed to house them. Generals issued strict instructions to their subordinates, while the military brass displayed a very accommodating attitude to Jewish advisers and organizations.

On October 26, 1945, *Yank* published an editorial titled "Short Memories and Nice People," urging soldiers to "wise up and wise up quickly." It cited as "frivolous and dangerous" an American general's comment that most Germans were forced into the Nazi Party, the denial by a major in Munich of concentration-camp atrocities, and the widespread feeling among enlisted men that the Germans were nice people—"more like us." Soldiers "must remember" that ending the hatred of the battlefield does not mean "excusing and apologizing to their late enemies. . . . A concentration camp cancels a clean bathroom and attempted mass extermination of a race overbalances a sunny disposition."[28]

Despite such efforts, widespread disagreement with the new policies continued. Except to avoid trouble by saying or doing the wrong thing, most officers had little interest in their humanitarian mission. A few days after the *Yank* article, John Herz, a Jewish refugee working on the Nuremberg Trials, wrote to his wife:

> In the countryside, the Nazis still appear to be in full possession of their positions of power. The Americans don't do anything, despite all the directives

from above; the average GI "griped" and wants to go home, and so long as he can't, "fraternizes" . . . and has an easy life. Anti-Nazis consequently are very fearful that the occupation might end and then the Nazis will come out of their mouse-holes and take revenge.[29]

Meanwhile, Professor James Pollock, political adviser to General Lucius Clay, military governor of Germany, traveled across Germany consulting officers. Upon returning to Berlin in early November 1945, he wrote in his diary:

> Everywhere the DP problem is brought up as a real headache. I can't see how we can continue to make these displaced people into another huge WPA project. If they don't want to work, they shouldn't be given rations. If they don't want to go home, they should be absorbed into the German population and treated accordingly. . . . The Balts are very clean and orderly. . . . The Poles are a serious problem.[30]

As late as December, a UNRRA official publicly resigned to protest the fact that officers frequently ignored the "letter or spirit of General Eisenhower's directives." The army "tends to protect and coddle the Germans," the official charged, while it "callously neglects elementary human needs" of the DPs. Army chaplains alerted Frank Mason to "an alarming spread of anti-Semitism particularly among our officers." The army generally, the chaplains remarked, "showed callous indifference to the misery of Jewish concentration camp victims" and when "Truman publicly ordered our command in Europe to improve relief measures for Jews still in Germany, obedience to these orders was often grudgingly given."[31]

The specter of supposed Jewish power also made officers cautious. As one British official described it, American officers were "haunted by the fear of Jewish opinion in the United States" and its "possible political reactions."[32] After Patton's removal, observed Mason, "American generals are highly sensitive to criticism from home that they are treating the Germans softly." But that was a matter of politics, not a change in heart. Generals and other officers complained about the "Truscott School of Brutalization." The draconian "eye-for-an-eye" policies toward Germany demanded by the politicians and press at home, complained certain officers, forced American soldiers "to act like Nazis": "Look at the way they persecuted Patton, simply because he was intent on keeping his area from becoming a starvation center [for Germans] like Buchenwald" had been for

Jews. One general confided that although most of the civilian German population consisted of women, children, and old men, "we are under constant
pressure to kick the Germans around."[33]

Another general considered it un-American to search German homes
without warrants, incarcerate civilians without trial, or pursue denazification against those who merely belonged to the Nazi Party. To evict Germans "from their homes to put in people displaced here at their own
volition whose living standards are little above animals" violated the
"golden rule." To him, "Patton was right and his approach more nearly the
American way than these people who have to listen to the Morgenthau direction from America."[34]

"Officers and men returning from the European Theatre," wrote
Colonel Bonner Fellers to his close friend General MacArthur, "condemn
certain features of our occupation, including the treatment of German
POWs, torture, trials, and requisitioning of homes." Fellers, another "Secret American," stated that "our officers in Europe are fearful lest they
incur disfavor and be relieved." Fellers cited the commanding general in
Austria, Mark Clark, as the exception—"being half Jew, he is not afraid."[35]

In actuality, the new policies appeared more strictly enforced in Austria
under Clark. According to army reports, Jews there "were housed in superior facilities and adequately cloth[ed] and fed." The army appointed Jewish liaison officers and cooperated with the Joint Distribution Committee.
The army's proactive engagement in Austria was probably due to Clark,
who insisted that his officers vigorously implement the new policies. Their
reports indicated a conscientious concern with anything that might elicit
criticism of Jewish treatment.[36] Judge Simon H. Rifkind, an adviser on
Jewish affairs, was impressed "with the zeal and spirit of the Army officers
engaged in working with the Jewish displaced persons and the well-mer-
ited pride they took in their accomplishments." He attributed this to the
"superior" leadership of Clark and his staff.

But the situation in Austria differed from that in Germany because the
number of Jewish DPs was initially quite limited. Further, beneath the surface, officers in Austria were perhaps not so different from those in Germany. A Jewish-American officer with the occupation forces in Vienna in
1945 claimed that the military government had done little to "restore the
losses" to Jewish displaced persons or "to improve their living conditions."
Another officer cited Austrian DP camps as "heavenly hell," where Jews
were humiliated and "totally stripped of their dignity." By 1946, conditions had "gone from bad to worse" for Jews, who saw "how wonderfully

things" were for the Austrians, including former Nazis, who cleverly ingratiated themselves with Americans. The problem became especially acute as noncombatant replacements took over from the wartime soldiers. The replacements were "completely disinterested in their work and interested only in having a good time" until relieved.[37]

OSS officers in Austria also had the impression that army officers in charge of the military government in Upper Austria were "pretty much on the wave-length of Patton." When two OSS officers reported in August 1945 that "top German Nazis remain at their posts" and that the military government had the "reputation of being indifferent to . . . de-nazification," they found themselves "in the doghouse." The report made such a "big stink in high quarters" that "all copies" were confiscated. The OSS men were more hopeful in October: "Now that Eisenhower has given Patton the boot, perhaps they can get up enough steam to kick out a certain Upper Austrian crew. At last!"[38]

At least some officers believed that Jewish influence and power accounted for the harsh occupation policies. Major Robertson, the American public safety officer in Wels who proudly advised the Austrian police to shoot DPs, was motivated by more than the need for law and order. To him, America was the "Jewnited States," where Jews manipulated the press and public opinion to the country's detriment. Merely to please "the blessed Jews" the "great hero!" Patton "had to be sacrificed." He believed that Jews, exercising tremendous power in America and Europe, actually undermined the ideals for which the country had fought World War II.

As Robertson interpreted events around him, the sacrifices of American soldiers only opened up postwar Europe to Jewish exploitation. To him, the Austrians were victims of intruding alien Jews who were ready to capitalize on every opportunity, especially currency reform, to enhance their power.[39] Watching the returning Jews, he said, "turns your stomach." American soldiers fought "to restore liberty & justice to these people," sacrificed life and limb, and "now the Jews are back." Jews seized businesses and property from Austrians merely because they were Nazi Party members. Although conceding that in some cases the property had originally been taken from Jews by the Nazis, he felt the Jews were "retaliating" unjustly.

Most "disgraceful" of all, Jews acted under protection of the American military government. As Robertson portrayed it, hundreds of earlier Jewish immigrants to the United States had returned in American army uniforms. No "more American than a local national" and still speaking

German, they exercised authority as Americans merely "because they have taken out the papers." Infiltrating the military government, they protected their fellow Jews no matter what the merits of the case.[40]

Just as Eisenhower's new policies on DPs started to deflect criticism of the army's earlier indifference, there occurred in early 1946 a mass migration of 40,000 Jewish refugees from Poland and other parts of Eastern Europe. Perhaps as many as 150,000 more waited to follow. This new wave of refugees was a nightmare for military and UNRRA officials lacking the resources to cope with it. Officers predicted outbreaks of "disease and famine" if budgets were not increased substantially.[41]

The army believed these "infiltrees" would also intensify the "ever increasing enmity" between Germans and Jewish DPs who were afforded special treatment, particularly if more German homes were requisitioned. The new refugees would accelerate the "steadily mounting tensions" and "ever increasing . . . incidents and clashes" between U.S. troops and DPs. Eisenhower attributed the latter to the "negative attitude shown by most displaced persons towards gainful employment or even the undertaking of work to help themselves."[42]

Whereas Jewish organizations explained the migration as a spontaneous flight for survival from anti-Semitic violence in Poland, army officials in Europe viewed it as a search for a better economic deal in the American Zone and a Zionist scheme to sneak Jews into Palestine. Although Jewish organizations denied it, there was in fact a well-financed program for Jewish refugees, as the army suspected. But much of the flight was a disorganized and spontaneous response to pogroms that killed several hundred Jews and terrified the rest. One British diplomat on the scene compared the new terror to anti-Semitic violence in Poland after World War I. And Clark recommended that the United States "secure the cooperation of appropriate governments in preventing attacks on Jews in Eastern Europe . . . [so as] to reduce Jewish refugee movements."[43]

In January 1946, the British director of UNRRA, Sir Frederick Morgan, revealed the Zionist involvement in the recent migrations. While Jewish denials of Zionist activity were indeed misleading, the demands for Morgan's resignation that ensued were also due to his denial of any danger to Jews in Poland. All the infiltrees, he said, were healthy "with plenty of money" and used the same unconvincing "monotonous story about pogroms." Although barely keeping his position, Morgan retained Eisenhower's confidence. Now chief of staff in Washington, Eisenhower hoped that no one would be "foolish enough" to remove this fine officer merely because "he said something about the 'Jewish migration' that doesn't sit well at all with the leaders of the Zionist Movement."[44]

By this point, the army had had enough of its humanitarian mission. The commander of the American zone, General Joseph T. McNarney, urged the army to close all the DP camps, with the exception of those for a small group of "persecuted" Jews. But Truman rejected the idea.[45]

Throughout the year, Jewish refugees by the tens of thousands moved westward, greatly taxing the army's resources and tolerance. In July, Eisenhower backed McNarney's proposal to "close all borders of the U.S. Zone of Germany and Austria to all displaced persons and to deny displaced persons care to all displaced persons infiltrating into the U.S. Zones after the in-camp population of Jewish displaced persons reaches 110,000." Again, Truman refused.[46]

In early August, McNarney repeated General Morgan's earlier charge of organized efforts to evacuate Jews from Poland. Since it cost taxpayers $84 million per year to care for them, the American Zone would remain open only for individual persecutees and closed to group entry. But McNarney quickly backtracked when General Morgan created another uproar by proclaiming that UNRRA served as a "cover for Soviet espionage, black marketeers and dope peddlers." Infuriated, UNRRA director general and former New York mayor Fiorello La Guardia had him removed on August 20.[47]

That very day, McNarney's Jewish adviser, Rabbi Philip S. Bernstein, suggested a "positive public relations program" to counteract impressions that the "Army is unsympathetic to Jewish DPs," that McNarney was "closing the borders to Jewish persecutees," and that he shared Morgan's attitude that "the Polish Jews are not fleeing out of genuine desperation, but as part of an organized movement . . . to Palestine." This "full publicity" campaign should include photographs with DPs, luncheon with Jewish leaders, articles on the "authorized movement of Jewish infiltrees," and so on.[48]

The next day, McNarney disassociated himself from Morgan's remarks and vigorously defended the army against La Guardia. Jewish refugees would not be turned back and would receive special treatment. In fact, his Jewish adviser had told him to expect 100,000 to 180,000 more Jewish refugees over the next year.[49]

The army's new public stance and the improved conditions of Jewish DPs between 1945 and 1947 apparently changed its image. In January 1947, the American Jewish Committee commended the government and army for treating DPs "consistent with the highest concepts of humanity and the best traditions of American democracy." It praised the army for providing a haven to those "fleeing before savage anti-Semitism . . . in Eastern Europe."[50]

Yet just a few months before, the perspective in "Analysis of the Jewish Situation in Poland" by Colonel James P. Abbott, Chief of the DP Division, differed little from Morgan's opinion. Abbott depicted Jewish refugees as people merely "dissatisfied with their present government and economic conditions." Jews left Poland to seek "better living conditions elsewhere rather than from fear of active Polish anti-Semitism." In fact, "terroristic activities in Poland have not been directed against the Jewish race as such and . . . where Jews were involved, the fact that individuals were Jews was merely incidental."

The United States should not, Abbott argued, "continue to offer a 'haven.'" To do so would create a "problem of such magnitude as to be both economically and internationally unsolvable within the foreseeable future." Opening Palestine to 100,000 Jewish settlers would only encourage an exodus of 3,000,000 European Jews eager "to benefit from the enormous funds now being raised by Jewish agencies" and from "a possible increase of immigration quotas" in America and elsewhere.[51]

In April 1947, the United States ended its lenient policy toward refugees by no longer allowing them to enter DP camps. The army would not stop the flow of infiltrees, but henceforth their care rested with private Jewish organizations.[52]

"Vengeful Semites"

The government's new policy did not end officers' concern with Jewish refugees. Many officers believed that they had a serious problem with members of an earlier generation of Jewish refugees now serving in their own ranks. Feeling inhibited from speaking publicly by alleged Jewish power, a number of officers, as well as some government officials, complained incessantly in private that Jewish "refugees in American uniforms," together with Jews in the U.S. government, unduly affected American policy toward Germany in a variety of detrimental ways.

Stimson described the problem as the "zeal of the Jewish American statesman seeking for vengeance." From Germany, Frank Mason wrote to Herbert Hoover that "to future generations [it will sound] very much as if Mr. Morgenthau learned his techniques from Herr Hitler's Mein Kampf." Colonel William Heimlich, then G-2 chief in Berlin, later wrote that much of Morgenthau's "foolish thinking spilled over into the Army and particularly the civilian staffs who made up the Occupation."[53]

Wherever Mason traveled—Berlin, Bremen, Frankfurt, Munich—officers confidentially criticized the nonfraternization and harsh occupation policies, which some considered, in large measure, Jewish inspired. The same was true of the Nuremberg Trials, especially the concept of "collective guilt" for Germans as a whole and the decision to try General Staff officers as criminals. James Pollock, General Clay's political adviser, had also noted that the "mention of Nürnberg made Clay a bit warm under the collar ... [since] Clay argued—like many Army men" against the trial of German generals.[54]

Mason sent home astonishing stories of "revenge" by some refugee officers "more versed in Gestapo methods than they are in American traditions." Among other things, they allegedly let Germans starve, treated German POWs with extreme cruelty, and sadistically beat SS officers. According to Mason, disapproving and disgusted officers felt helpless, given U.S. policy and the way the press was manipulated to mislead America about the truth in Germany.[55]

Criticism of press bias often involved charges of radicalism and communism. Colonel Heimlich later claimed that a number of naturalized refugees in the Military Government were Communist agents. He also referred to some members of the American press corps as "assistants to the USSR" who sacrificed great men like Patton in order to build their own reputations. After his own tour of Germany in early 1947, General Wedemeyer, the new Germanophile director of Plans and Operations (P&O), reported to Eisenhower that the "correspondents representing the various Allied news and radio agencies were biased or are tainted pink or red by the brush of Communism."[56]

Wedemeyer also made similar complaints to those related by Mason and others about returning refugees profiting from the suffering of Germans while under the protection of the American military umbrella. Although needed for their language skills and familiarity with Germany, they did not always represent "America creditably and effectively." Wedemeyer charged that "some of the civilians in Military Government or other agencies in Germany are there for their own self-aggrandizement"; they were among the "worst offenders in black market activities."

American officers speaking with Mason had long associated refugee officers and civilian officials with rampant bribery, corruption, and racketeering. On his return to Germany in 1948, General Loucks noted his encounter with a "disagreeable little Mil. Govt. man," "another carpetbagger." Loucks described the type as those "not otherwise successful . . . who are nonetheless mercenary, live by their wits, usually by means of their position come into possession of valuables . . . refusing to abide by any rules and demanding special consideration."[57]

In early 1947, Mason returned to Europe with Herbert Hoover and former ambassador to Poland Hugh Gibson as part of a food mission. While in Vienna, the trio informed Colonel Stanley J. Grogan of their distress over the behavior of the Counter Intelligence Corps (CIC) in Germany. As Grogan related the exchange to Clark:

> The President apparently believes, and with reason, that some of the new U.S. citizens who are used in CIC in Germany abuse individuals to get information and in many cases have private axes to grind. I got the impression from talking with him that he is extremely an American for Americans and that he does not think too well of the Austrians and Germans who became Americans in 1938, 39, 40, 41, etc.[58]

Perhaps unaware of Clark's heritage, Grogan also explained that among Hoover's party was a Dr. Stolper, a Vienna-born Jew and "one of the new American citizens such as we are using in CIC . . . and other places." Hoover supposedly included Stolper because he thought "it a good idea . . . to have a Jew arguing against" the "Morgenthau Plan," but since then Stolper had turned into the party's "problem child."

Mason told Grogan that CIC officers in Germany "believe they were recruited to implement the Morgenthau Plan" that called for the destruction of Germany as a modern industrial society. In reality, Mason said, "the Plan is not as dead as people think." This surprised Grogan, since he thought the plan had long been discounted. But Hoover told him, "[T]he question is so delicate, while the army and General Draper particularly would like to kill the Morgenthau Plan, that the pressure in America is too strong, even at this late date, to come out in the open on the matter."[59]

The need for German-speaking interpreters and administrators had brought many German Jews into the military government. Some probably agreed with Morgenthau's draconian idea of punishing Germany and preventing its future resurgence or even reconstruction of its industrial base. But most were simply persistent, even zealous, in pursuing Nazi war criminals and denazification at a time when U.S. military and civilian leaders shifted toward a more lenient German policy. Also, "their frequent sym-

General George S. Patton, Jr. with Secretary of War Henry L. Stimson in June 1945 shortly before the scandal regarding army treatment of Jewish Holocaust survivors. Referring to Jewish survivors as a "sub-human species" of animal, Patton, like many other officers, favored Germans and other northern Europeans over Jewish Displaced Persons. Patton believed that Jews were conspiring to undermine him and implement Communism in Europe.

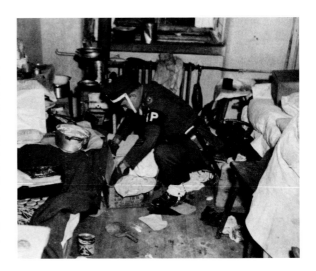

Searching for contraband, American soldiers launch a surprise raid on a Jewish Displaced Persons Camp in Germany in 1948. Anti-Semitism was quite strong among many officers who referred to Jewish DPs as "scum and dirt." Instead of eliciting sympathy, the traumatized behavior of Holocaust survivors merely reinforced the racial prejudices of many officers.

General Charles A. Willoughby, MacArthur's Intelligence Chief, at the Japanese surrender in August 1945. An advocate of racial geopolitical theory, Willoughby believed that eastern European Jews constituted a "fifth column" subverting America. He belonged to a coterie of prominent retired generals who struggled against alleged Jewish influence and power.

2 February 1948

SD

MEMORANDUM FOR THE SECRETARY OF THE ARMY:

SUBJECT: Palestine

1. There is submitted herewith a staff study on the probable consequences ensuing from the United Nations decision to partition Palestine.

2. This study was undertaken in order to explore and, if possible, amplify the argumentation contained in a draft of the paper currently being prepared by the Department of State for presentation to the National Security Council as a result of your action in early December placing this matter on the NSC agenda. It is believed that the conclusions reached in both papers are substantially identical.

3. It is recommended that you read the attached study as of possible value in the anticipated NSC deliberations but that you do not submit the paper to the NSC at this time. It would appear better policy for the Department of the Army not to take further initiative in this matter, at least until the direction of the Department of State's recommendations and NSC reactions thereto become more clearly apparent.

4. The enclosed has been informally coordinated at the working staff level with the Navy and Air Force and has met with their general approval.

FEB 9 48 AM   cy to c/S

A. C. WEDEMEYER
Lt General, GSC
Director of Plans & Operations

Incl
Staff Study,-Palestine.

TOP SECRET

See attached note
for dispatch record
of original memo.

efforts to raise their

This "Top Secret" study by the Plans and Operations Division of the army concluded that the partition of Palestine leading to the establishment of the State of Israel constituted a serious danger to the security of the United States. The Director of P & O privately attributed American support for a Jewish state to the power of Jews over the American government and public opinion.

THE PROBLEM

1. To analyze the alternatives available to the United Nations in carrying out the Plan to Partition Palestine and the probable consequences of each with particular reference to their effect on the United States

FACTS BEARING ON THE PROBLEM

2. See Tab "B".

DISCUSSION

3. See Tab "A".

CONCLUSIONS

4. That the UN decision to partition Palestine cannot be implemented without jeopardizing the basic objectives of the foreign policy of the United States, nor without a wholly disproportionate hazard to the prestige,— possibly the very existence,— of the United Nations.

5. That for the United States to support the UN decision and further its implementation would be dangerously contrary to its own best interests in the certain consequences of its inevitable involvement.

6. Therefore, since it is inadmissable that the United States should withhold continuing leadership in a situation for which it is largely responsible, that the United States should move now toward effecting at the earliest appropriate time a reversal of the UN decision.

7. That, by proper and complete prior education of the U.S. and world public of all the factors involved in the recent decision and in carrying it out, the public support essential to such a reversal would be forthcoming.

8. That such reversal should not be in the nature of a substitute final solution to the problem, but specifically to afford an opportunity to develop an ultimate practicable solution by providing the time and more conciliatory atmosphere required.

TOP SECRET

2

General Albert C. Wedemeyer (1943). Between the 1930s and 1980s Wedemeyer believed that Jews constituted a serious threat to America's national interests. His "Top Secret" reports in 1948 strongly opposed the creation of Israel as endangering national security and condemned an insidious Jewish manipulation of the American government and public.

Generals Charles A. Willoughby, Edward M. Almond, and George E. Stratemeyer (left to right), MacArthur's top commanders, during a meeting with Chiang Kai-Shek in 1950. After the Korean War, Willoughby, Almond, and Stratemeyer belonged to the clique of retired prominent generals known as the "Secret Americans," struggling against alleged insidious Jewish forces undermining America and the West.

General George E. Stratemeyer, a decorated and respected Air Force commander in World War II and Korea, attributed America's loss in Korea to secret alien forces. A member of the coterie of politically active retired generals and a confidant of General Moseley, Stratemeyer became a prominent promoter of Jewish conspiracy theories in the 1950s.

THE JEWISH SITUATION IN THE EAST

We have refrained for a long period of time to deal with the Jewish people in connection with the situation here in the East. At the present time there are many peculiar things going on; and our contacts with the Jews over the past 26 yrs. makes us wonder just what is in the making.

In the first place, the Jewish groups are raising tremendous amounts of money. We mean by that a "kitty" of over 150 million dollars is being raised—some out in the open, other amounts on the quiet; but they are holding dinners at $100 per plate and these affairs are being held in small towns. We know of one community of 6,000 where the Jewish quota was $12,500 and they raised $17,000.

Most of our readers are fully aware of the activities of the Jewish Information Service and the activities of Dave Prince and also the connections with Sidney Hillman and Dave Dubinsky. It seems rather strange right now that John Lewis is making one great attempt to invade the jurisdiction rights of Dubinsky's lady garment workers union.

Also it seems strange that Dubinsky should have a Communist setup on his payroll that contains some of the real brains of the Party movement in the years gone by. On the other hand, Sidney Hillman and the CIO and the PAC are cooperating in Hillman's efforts to enlarge his organization by taking in most everything along the same lines as John Lewis is doing with his District 50. Hillman has only recently absorbed some of the AFL Pocketbook Workers.

For sometime Dubinsky has been shouting that this country needs a new political party. Hillman thought he had that setup all created with the help of Leo Pressman and R. J. Thomas of the Auto Workers. But we believe that Henry Wallace thinks he stands a far better chance to go along with the Democratic Administration. He seems to feel that public opinion would be against a third party that is sponsored by the PAC.

Now the Jewish elements are beginning to look with favor on Claude Pepper of Florida and Governor Arnall of Georgia. Right at the present time, the Jewish movement in the US, which is practically at war with England over Palestine, is recruiting former members of the Abraham Lincoln Brigade which fought in Spain. They have a wonderful underground movement started; and according to the outspoken press releases, they could use the underground to slip a Jew into Palestine at a cost of $250.

Now let's get back to the Jews in the labor movement. Several weeks ago, the Jewish Labor Council, which is Communist controlled from top to bottom, held a convention in Chicago. It was just one nice Communist meeting, but they had a large number of delegates and observers. We might mention that some of the meetings had 1200 to 1500 in attendance. One of the chief speakers at this convention was Rabbi Stephen Wise, the militant Jewish leader who is now fighting England for the cause of Palestine.

There were rumors making the rounds in 1938 to the effect that the Jewish race had set a program in this country whereby they were to bankrupt the country and

The Jewish Situation in the East *(1946). A post-Holocaust memo on subversive Jewish activities from one of retired general Ralph Van Deman's agents in his private secret surveillance network that functioned with the official sanction and cooperation of Military Intelligence and the FBI. Such "intelligence" was shared mutually between Van Deman and MID/FBI between 1932 and 1946, as well as with influential restrictionist organizations opposing Jewish immigration to the United States.*

BARBOURSVILLE, VIRGINIA

Dear Friend:

Recent events have shown in a startling way the timeliness of "The Iron Curtain Over America".

Confirming the accuracy of Chapter III, "The Khazars Join the Democratic Party", U.S. NEWS & WORLD REPORT (May 1, 1961 - p. 66) states that the Democrats' share of the total Jewish vote in 1960 was 88%. An article in the Jewish paper, HERITAGE (November 17, 1960 - p. 1) shows that the largely Jewish precincts in Los Angeles were carried by Kennedy over Nixon by such majorities as: 127 to 6; 159 to 10; 250 to 10; 231 to 6, etc.

Chapter VII, "Does the National Democratic Party Want War?" is rich in earlier parallels of current events and trends. Mr. Kennedy's promises to minority pressure groups, his constantly mentioned admiration for Franklin Roosevelt, and also the events of his first months in office raise the fear that the new President may, like his admired predecessor, find war the easiest way to fulfill his campaign promises.

There are many other instances of the current timeliness of "The Iron Curtain Over America". The remarks on immigration (pp. 38-39; 160-162, etc), censorship (Chapter IV), and our terrible policy of engaging in combats which we do not expect to win (p. 145) are topics of the hour as this letter is written (May, 1961). Very significant in 1961 is the background material (pp. 134-135) on the fantastic hoax that the Germans killed 6,000,000 Jews during World War II.

Because of its easy-to-read type, its complete documentation, and its index of approximately 4,000 entries, "The Iron Curtain Over America" has become a standard work. Despite powerful opposition, it recently reached its 18th printing. Even if you have a copy, will you not help to increase the book's influence by ordering an additional copy or copies as gifts for special occasions (graduations, holidays, birthdays) and for influential people among your acquaintances?

The reverse of this letter presents some representative testimonials to the value of "The Iron Curtain Over America" and also an order blank. Hoping to hear from you and with all good wishes, I am,

Sincerely yours,

John Beaty

Several well-known retired American generals enthusiastically endorsed John Beaty's Iron Curtain over America, *one of the most fantastic works alleging Jewish conspiracies since the* Protocols.

THE IRON CURTAIN OVER AMERICA

IS RECOMMENDED BY PEOPLE IN A POSITION TO KNOW

JUN 1 1961

Lt. Gen. George E. Stratemeyer, USAF (ret.), says: "I congratulate you on your book and the service you have performed for our country. If my health would permit it I would go on a continuous lecture tour gratis and preach your book and recommendations. My 'Iron Curtain Over America' will be on loan continuously and I intend to recommend its reading in every letter I write."

Lt. Gen. Edward M. Almond, USA (ret.), says: "It is an inspiration to me to find an author with the courage and energy to research and to secure the publication of such information as you have assembled in order that the poorly informed average American may know wherein the real threats to our Country lurk. Your book is a magnificent contribution to those who would preserve our American ideals."

Vice Admiral T. G. W. Settle, U.S.N. (ret.), says: "The Iron Curtain Over America' is a most pertinent and excellently presented treatise on the 'cancer' in our national set-up.

"I hope this book has had, and will have, the widest possible dissemination, particularly to our leaders—in Washington, and in industry and the press,—and that our leaders who are 'uncontaminated' will have their serious attention engaged by it."

Lt. General P. A. Del Valle, USMC (ret.), says: "I am impelled to write to you to express my admiration of your great service to the Nation in writing this truly magnificent book. No American who has taken the oath of allegiance can afford to miss it, and I heartily recommend it as an honest and courageous dispeller of the fog of propaganda in which most minds seem to dwell."

"I think it ought to be compulsory reading in every public school in America." Senator William A. Langer, former Chairman, Judiciary Committee.

"A fine book." Senator Pat McCarran, former Chairman, Judiciary Committee.

"It's the most revealing and frightening book that has come across my desk in ages." Hedda Hopper, syndicated columnist.

"The most startling, challenging, alarming writing of the past fifty years." J. M. Hazlitt, syndicated columnist.

WHO IS THE AUTHOR?

John Beaty, author and former professor, Southern Methodist University, Dallas, Texas, is a veteran of World War I and served nearly five years in World War II with the War Department General Staff. He wrote military studies, edited the daily intelligence summary, and headed several important sections in the Military Intelligence Service.

SCOPE AND SUBJECT MATTER

With its documentation and its great scope, which is shown by an index of some 4,000 entries, ICOA is the key to understanding recent developments in the vitally important fields of IMMIGRATION, ATOMIC ENERGY, FOREIGN AFFAIRS, and the FEDERAL JUDICIARY. OVER 60,000 COPIES IN PRINT.

FURTHER INFORMATION

We will send you 20 circulars of five or more kinds for $1.00. These will include photostats showing minority censorship; a paper on the Supreme Court, and some circulars on the ICOA and Col. Beaty's completely censored book, "Crossroads"—a novel of the twentieth century South.

CHESTNUT MOUNTAIN BOOKS, BARBOURSVILLE, VIRGINIA

IMPORTANT!

Please mail me .... copies of The Iron Curtain Over America at $4.00 per copy, and .... copies of "Crossroads" at $4.00 per copy. (If 10 copies are ordered, price is $24, if 40 copies are ordered, price is $80. A wholesale order may include both books.)

I enclose check for .... or money order for .... dollars.

Kindly give to friends any circulars you yourself don't use!

NAME ....

ADDRESS ....

Marine Corps General Pedro del Valle (left) with General Archibald Arnold at the flag raising ceremony after the capture of Okinawa in June 1945. Part of the clique of "Secret Americans," del Valle believed that an "invisible government" of international Jews controlled America and worked in conjunction with their coconspirators in Russia. As late as 1962, he still emphasized the significance of The Protocols of the Elders of Zion.

pathies with liberal causes had become suspect during the paranoia about Communists."[60]

Mason had discussed Morgenthau, the spread of communism, and occupation policies with his friend "Pinky" (General Withers A. Burress), who had just assumed command of the American Constabulary Force. A grateful Burress shared Mason's "accurate and good" advice with "others who could use it" but noted he was still "careful about expressing myself too freely."[61]

Upon returning to the United States in early March 1947, Mason went to the Pentagon to be debriefed. During this "usual weekend visit," he discussed at length the Morgenthau plan and other occupation problems. A few days later, Eisenhower alerted Clay to allegations about the occupation worth looking into that had come to his private attention:

> For instance, that many of our civilians are German-speaking people of a rather undesirable type. Among other things they say that many of these people have been citizens of the United States only two or three years and are using their present positions either to communize Germany or to indulge in vengeance. One very conservative man recommended that we should allow no one to be in our Military Government organizations unless he has been a citizen . . . for at least 10 years.[62]

On April 7, 1947, Clay issued a secret directive to purge German-Jewish refugees from service in the military government. In a classified "confidential" memorandum, his deputy military governor, General Frank L. Keating, wrote that Clay "has decided we shall not employ anyone or renew any contracts of anyone who has been naturalized since 1933." Even in those areas where their technical expertise was needed, "we should try to find a way out." But in taking this "necessary action," officers must "refrain from general discussion of the subject or issuance of any orders. It is not necessary for us to indicate why we do not intend to rehire anyone [but] see that diplomacy is used in handling each case." Keating also told officers to "keep this letter . . . highly confidential and not reveal its contents to your staff" except where absolutely necessary. Although a penciled note of "recalled" was found on this document, in the words of Guy Stern, the "damage had already been done." For all practical purposes, the policy had gone into effect, and a wave of sudden dismissals followed.[63]

In light of the war and the Holocaust, deep hatred of the Germans by Jews was not surprising. But antipathy toward Germans was by no means restricted to refugee Jews or to those of liberal or leftist persuasion. Some of the severest judgments of the Germans among the Office of Military Government, United States (OMGUS) personnel emanated from Colonel David "Mickie" Marcus, a 1924 West Point graduate and native-born son of Romanian Jewish immigrants. An American nationalist to the core, with strong conservative and antileftist views, he returned to service in 1940 and was later assigned to War Crimes. He detested "all Germans" with "extreme loathing," saying they "must *writhe* under Military Government," so that they will learn they are not a master race and will never again upset world peace.[64]

Still, Marcus knew that his harsh condemnations were not universally shared among German Jews. The fact that a considerable number of Jews wanted to stay in Germany disturbed him a good deal. Colonel Heimlich also cited several examples of Jewish officers in Berlin who did not blame and hate all Germans for Nazi atrocities, including refugees who favored a just and humane occupation so as not to punish the innocent along with the guilty.[65]

This division in Jewish opinion toward Germans paralleled that in the army. When the concentration camps were liberated, General P. S. Gage urged Patton "to make the German populace suffer" whenever possible; "don't ever go soft," he advised, for "nothing could ever be too bad for them." Among those initially seeking a stern peace stood Eisenhower, who wrote to his wife, Mamie, in late 1944 that "the German is a beast," exclaiming, "God, I hate the Germans!" Eisenhower favored the destruction of German war-making ability, war-crimes trials, and the concept of "collective guilt" for all Germans.[66]

An array of Eisenhower's generals held the same opinions during and immediately after the war. Some generals retained their mistrust of Germans long thereafter, whereas others quickly mellowed upon seeing the massive destruction of German cities and the suffering of the urban population of women, children, and old men.

By early 1946, Eisenhower himself had started to soften. He wrote to Clay about the "slow but steady change in the public attitude towards the German problem." At a meeting with prominent newspapermen, he had received "not a single question about 'de-nazification,'" as most interest concerned Germany's economic recovery. By 1947, this altered frame of mind, combined with growing fear of Russia, led Eisenhower and others to pursue German industrial revival as the key to general European economic rebirth. While demilitarization and war-crimes trials continued, a pro-German tilt began to be evident among officers. Eisenhower denied he had ever favored Morgenthau's objective of permanently debilitating Germany.[67]

The perspectives of some of the old guard toward Germany were still affected by the convergence of geopolitics and racial thought. General Loucks, who returned to Germany in 1948, praised the new softer trend in U.S. policy toward Germany as necessary and democratic. This officer, who had personally witnessed Germany's invasion of France eight years before, now spoke of "fairness to poor Germans" as opposed to the "enslavement" desired by France and others. Despite abundant resources and a worldwide empire, the French were an undependable hopeless case, a decadent power without military or athletic prowess that no longer created anything "noteworthy" in politics, science, technology, or even the arts. Commenting upon the numerous Algerians and other immigrants, Loucks attributed French decline to the dilution of their best stock by the "predatory types from in and out of France." Through their liberalism, they had "admitted too many irresponsible and anti-social elements," thereby replacing progress with the "cancer of communism."

Loucks expressed similar fears that U.S. policies pandering to African-Americans, especially to "colored soldiers," might destroy America's military power. Germans, by contrast, retained their vibrancy and laudable technological ability. Americans "had better get the Germans on their side now in case the Eastern peoples decide to march again."[68]

Nor had the tension between Jewish DPs and American soldiers abated. As General Clay said in retrospect:

> The Jewish people obviously were our major concern because we had so many of them, and no place for them to go. . . . They were completely unwilling to take their place in the German economy, so they were living in camps, and they were really quite a disciplinary problem. They were not responding to German law. They hated soldiers. Soldiers were a sign of oppression to them, and we were the only people, our MPs, that could control them. We had quite a problem. . . . If we sent an MP in to arrest them, why it would be in every headline in the United States—"US Soldiers Invading Jewish Camp," and so forth just as if the Nazis were back at work, and so on.[69]

General Burress wrote Mason that "we are still having our same troubles with the DPs and especially those of a certain variety." After a meeting with a Jewish liaison officer regarding U.S. constabulary forces visiting "Jewish installations," Burress told General P. E. Gallagher he was "convinced" that this officer "had voiced the issue with the view of using it at a later date as a basis for claiming persecution of the Jews."[70]

On July 23, 1947, about 2,500 "local" Jews living in Munich staged a protest parade targeted at the British consulate to urge opening the "gates to Palestine." Although Burress acknowledged that the demonstration was "orderly" and without serious incident, he investigated the leading participants. In response to his report, Deputy Commander in Chief General C. R. Huebner immediately issued an order "requiring the arrest and trial of all persons suspected of, or found, leading or inciting any such demonstrations which might be attempted, or held, in the future."[71]

As late as March 1948, Burress was still insisting on the necessity of soldiers using unsheathed bayonets during "raids" on Jewish DP camps. He strongly resisted efforts by General Clay's new Jewish adviser, William Haber, to change this practice. After taking up his new position, Haber wrote home about how shocked he was by army attitudes. Throughout his tour, Haber often remarked that "anti-Semitism is a very serious problem among [American soldiers] and . . . our troops will return to the United States more critical of Jews at home than they have ever been before."[72]

When Haber asked Clay to assist in dealing with increasing German anti-Semitism, Clay responded that "anti-Germanism among the Jewish DPs is, perhaps, far stronger than the anti-Semitism among the Germans." Although Clay understood this Jewish reaction, he urged Haber to encourage greater understanding between the two groups. Nonetheless, like his predecessors, Haber praised Clay's sympathy, understanding, and efforts concerning Jewish DPs. Haber admired Clay as a "liberal American" who might actually be used to advance progressive causes in the United States.[73]

Unknown to Haber, however, it seems that Clay had handled him and others rather cautiously, being cooperative without revealing his true sentiments. When Pollock asked Clay in confidence about Haber, the general said:

> All right, but you can't trust him! I knew him from Washington and when anything Jewish comes up he is utterly unscrupulous. I am convinced that he inspired an ugly news story recently and just this morning he wanted me to admit Rumanians— Jews of course—simply because I was admitting Czechs who were slipping across the border to save their lives. I told him no.

Clay's other political adviser, Robert Murphy, concurred, stating that Haber was "just like all the other Jewish advisers—no better, and worse than two of them!"[74]

Meanwhile, the old conservative coterie of active and retired officers back home still complained that the "Morgenthau-Frankfurter clique" and their New Deal allies were determined to prevent German recovery. In private, Wedemeyer and Fellers continued to blame both such "misguided" policies as "unconditional surrender" and war-crimes trials on powerful Jewish forces, which they occasionally referred to as subversive and disloyal. In the face of expected opposition from Morgenthau et al., Truman Smith and Robert Wood tried, by working behind the scenes, to redirect America's policy toward increased German production and prosperity. Since 1945, Smith had believed that the mistake of disarming the Germans would have to be reversed to meet the Russian threat. Fellers pursued a public relations campaign through radio and 10,000 VFW posts to rally support for the new German policy.[75]

In early 1949, the spirits of this group were suddenly raised by rumors that one of their own would become military governor of Germany. Certain that he possessed all the necessary qualities for dealing with Germans and enjoying their confidence, Wedemeyer waited hopefully for an appointment that never came. The new high commissioner for Germany was John J. McCloy, whom Wedemeyer's supporters distrusted and believed to be influenced by Morgenthau. In fact, the only obstacle to his own appointment that Wedemeyer had foreseen was the "Jews and any other elements" whose "personal hatreds and selfish plans of aggrandizement" he would oppose "vigorously."[76]

Officers and Postwar Immigration

Powerful feelings and vivid memories were evoked when Congressman Emanuel Celler of New York launched his hostile examination of a familiar witness testifying before Congress in 1947. Unprecedented historical changes had irreversibly altered America and the world over the quarter century these antagonists had continually clashed. Yet on immigration matters, many traditional beliefs and biases retained their emotional strength; and old issues remained unresolved. Although revelations about the Holocaust had generated enormous sympathy, attempts to revise the 1924 Immigration Act to admit 400,000 displaced persons to the United States elicited strenuous opposition from the nativist restrictionist lobby.

Celler had little patience with the father of the 1924 law, John Trevor, who now sat before him, resurrecting old anti-Communist and racist objections to any changes. Said Celler:

I felt then and I feel now, that the Johnson Act set up what was called superior classes and advocated Nordic supremacy, and among Nordics included
the Germans, who also developed a theory . . . of Herrenvolk and Slaven-
volk, superior people and slave people. See what the Hitler theory of "superior people" brought us. All the Aryans and Nordics were to be superiors,
and all the rest of the people were to be slaves.

Congressman Gossett, a restrictionist, rose indignantly to Trevor's defense: "The gentleman is not contending that our immigration laws embody those principles?" Celler retorted: "It certainly does, because . . . the
present immigration laws . . . discriminated deliberately against the peoples from southern and eastern Europe and favored unduly the people
from northern and western Europe, and therefore . . . some peoples were
better or superior than others."

For his part, Trevor denied racial bias but argued nonetheless that "this
country could not stand further dilution of its basic stock or our political
institutions would be doomed." Trevor explained that because they had
been conditioned by centuries of authoritarian paternalism, Southern and
Eastern Europeans lacked the "individual initiative" of the basic stock that
made America great. As one restrictionist congressman added, few of Mr.
Celler's kind had participated in fighting the American Revolution and
Civil War, writing the Constitution, or "building this country." Since those
different stocks could not "assimilate into American institutions, American Ideals, and American life," it was logical to continue to prefer English,
Swedes, Dutch, and similar newcomers.[77] The commander of the Regular
Veterans Association similarly contrasted "hard-working, honest, and industrious" Northern European immigrants with the "mentally fogged"
new "undesirables" who would never become "real Americans."

These undesirable immigrants, Trevor argued, were predisposed toward
communism and crowded into big cities, the breeding grounds of radicalism. He spoke of how as "an officer in the Military Intelligence" he was
disgusted by the "mother of revolutions" and "curse of civilization"—the
slum. Restriction was absolutely necessary to eliminate "the constant influx of people who naturally gravitate into the slum." To clinch his argument, Trevor said he had "discussed the matter with Army officers . . . who
have been over there who are afraid to come to this committee and testify
because they think reprisal will be made against them."[78]

In light of Nazi racism and the Holocaust, restrictionists avoided directly raising the Jewish question, but it remained a central, though often

unspoken, point of contention. Trevor himself complained about the high percentage of Jewish refugees taken in by the United States compared to other countries. Although the leadership of the American Legion eventually backed the new legislation, its Americanization Committee worried about having "this country flooded with Jews."[79]

But this was not 1924, when anti-Semites and restrictionists enjoyed the public backing of the president as well as the State and War Departments. Noting America's humanitarian obligations and traditions, Truman took the lead in requesting legislation to open the United States to hundreds of thousands of DPs. The military men now serving in his administration fell in line and supported the legislation. Restrictionist arguments about subversive threats ran up against assurances from two of America's most revered military leaders—Secretary of State George Marshall and Chief of Staff Dwight Eisenhower.[80]

Many officers, however, privately never ceased thinking along racial lines when considering the army's institutional interests and those of America vis-à-vis DPs and immigration. Given such officers' hostile attitude toward Jewish DPs, they generally opposed their immigration to America. While favoring rapid resettlement to solve the army's DP problem, many officers probably shared General Holbrook's opinion regarding "Jewish Refugees." He wrote home, "Personally I feel that we have our share. I would suggest South and Central America."[81]

This attitude became abundantly clear when the army anticipated a postwar manpower shortage. That this gap between needs and volunteers occurred just as the Communist threat emerged accentuated its seriousness. In response, the War Department engaged in extensive "Top Secret" planning to consider enlisting DPs of certain desirable nationalities. Through service in the army or an American Foreign Legion, they would earn American citizenship.

In this atmosphere, there were laments that the refusal of American youth to volunteer, like dependence on foreigners, resembled the "national decadence" that had caused Rome's decline and fall. The issues of Communist infiltration, loyalty, and dependability all surfaced as well. General Clay worried lest "'skimming off the cream' of the DPs might leave a residue incapable of resettlement whose care would remain a U.S. problem indefinitely." Ultimately, though, numerous senior officers on the General Staff, as well as in Personnel, Plans and Operations, and other divisions dealing with this issue in Europe and Washington, preferred this option to an increased use of blacks, Puerto Ricans, or women. And Koreans made "poor risks," due to "their poor physical condition, poor sanitary habits, cruelty, emotional instability, low educational level, and un-American social background." Recruitment of Europeans, on the other hand, would also "ease the long drawn out Army responsibilities towards DPs."[82]

In pursuing this course, these officers deliberately involved the army in restrictive immigration, protecting America from undesirables as officers had done in the 1920s. Since the United States "seems obligated to accept fairly large numbers of these DPs," argued General W. S. Paul, director of personnel, America should quickly practice "selective immigration" rather than wait until it is forced to "accept less desirable . . . DPs." And most senior officers agreed that the pool of "most desirables" was quickly being siphoned off by other countries. Here, General Carter B. Magruder, director of procurement, suggested, the army could play a crucial role:

> The interests of the United States demand we screen any displaced persons whom we accept for United States citizenship carefully so only the best qualified are admitted. The quality of personnel now being secured under the immigration quotas indicates that no political agency will perform an acceptable screening. The Army can do this screening.[83]

The desirables consisted essentially of the "Balts and Poles," who could provide at least 50,000, perhaps eventually as many as 100,000 fine soldiers and good citizens. In contrast to the demeaning, dehumanizing terminology applied to Jewish DPs, American officers in Europe had from the beginning regarded the Balts and Poles as "outstanding human beings." Officers who used Baltic and Polish guard units to assist them in occupation duty worried about their "pitiful" situation and "hopeless" future, wishing that something could be done for them.[84]

The very anticommunism that made Baltic and Polish repatriation impossible also endeared them to most officers handling DPs, as did the fact that most Poles fell into the desired immigration classification of "agriculturalists." But the Balts embodied the most desirable characteristics. An educated and cultured group, their DP camps were often lauded as models compared to the filth, disorder, and apathy in Jewish camps. To Patton and others, such differences proved Jewish racial inferiority.

Of course, few Balts had undergone the degradation or suffering that Jews had. Considered Nordics by Nazi racial ideology, the Balts—many of whom were actually ethnic Germans—did rather well under Nazi occupation, and about 200,000 of those ending up in DP camps had earlier applied for German citizenship. Some visiting American diplomats and congress-men identified them as "most desirable immigrants"; coming as they did "from good stock and good breeding," they would "make excellent set-tlers."[85] Overall, a colonel on the General Staff evaluated the Balts and Poles as:

> a hardy lot, the survivors of a terrific elimination contest. A great many of them have had military training and service and are, within their limits ex-cellent soldiers . . . [known for] industriousness, adaptability, hardihood and loyalty to the hand that feeds them. I emphasize this rather strongly. This group also has no racial or religious barrier to assimilation.[86]

The pool of desirable immigrants and recruits generally excluded Jew-ish DPs. At first, though, the Germanophile Wedemeyer, now director of Plans and Operations in Washington, worried that the DP recruitment plan would bring too many Jews into the army and ultimately the United States. He wrote to MacArthur, "It must be apparent to you at once that we will obtain a disproportionately large number of Jews if this is done, and the minority groups in our country, particularly the Jewish one, can exert considerable pressure."

Wedemeyer made several inquiries to allay his fears of "an increase in immigration of any one nationality, race or religious group." Apparently these categories did not apply to the highly recruited Balts and Poles.[87]

After several surveys and analyses, the army estimated that of the ap-proximately 40,000 Jewish males of military age in Germany and Austria only about 7,000 would be both qualified and willing to serve. Other na-tionalities would together comprise a pool of almost 70,000 willing and able to enlist. The low Jewish percentage was based upon the army's cal-culation that only one-third of qualified Jews would join, compared to 75 to 98 percent of desirable non-Jewish DPs. This "estimate" was affected by factors other than the desire of many Jewish DPs to emigrate to Palestine. There were doubts about the kinds of soldiers Jews make, reinforced by the sense that Jewish DPs eschewed anything requiring work or discipline.[88]

The original Jewish pool had already been substantially reduced by the criterion of "political reliability." Balts rated "100% political reliability," with the Poles a close second at 80 percent, whereas Jews rated only 50 per-cent, with particular reservations about Hungarian and Romanian Jews. The presence of Jewish soldiers among the occupation forces revived the old question about Jews' loyalty. In objecting to the enlistment plan, G-2 director general S. J. Chamberlain cited "much difficulty recently with CIC personnel recruited from foreign elements in the U.S." because of their language ability. Lacking a "firm footing in the American tradition," they "have a tendency to forget where their principal allegiance lies."[89]

Within an emerging Cold War atmosphere, the long-standing Jewish-Communist association increased the significance of the loyalty issue. At European Command Headquarters in Frankfurt, General C. R. Huebner questioned whether the 50-percent political reliability of Jewish DPs was too high an estimate, saying, "It is also believed that Jewish groups form a coverage and vehicle for the presence of Communist planted personnel." Huebner cautioned that "the type of screening adequate to uncover [the] politically non-reliable or . . . gauge political reliability does not exist."[90]

Subsequent estimates reduced the total potential pool of DPs to 19,000, including about 3,500 Jews. By that point, the entire issue was moot, since in early 1948, Congress rejected proposals for enlisting foreigners.[91]

Meanwhile, army opinions on DPs continued to influence pending immigration legislation. The Truman administration sent Marshall and General John H. Hilldring, assistant secretary of state, among others, to testify in favor of the Displaced Persons Act. Hilldring had earlier complained about the problem that the DPs caused the army and thus, like Clay and other officers, saw the legislation as a way to relieve the military of this burden by admitting more refugees into the United States. He now rebuffed charges of Communists among the DPs, but his testimony was not very effectual. Perhaps most influential was Colonel Jerry M. Sage, who had been called from Europe. Since he supposedly expressed the army's views on DPs, his testimony supporting the legislation carried substantial weight in congressional committees.

However, the reports of William Haber, Clay's adviser on Jewish affairs, show that concerns about Jews and communism remained strong even among those now testifying in favor of the new DP law. According to Haber, upon returning to Germany, Sage sought assurances that "Jews applying for admission to the United States under the new legislation are not Communists or agents of Russia." Sage told Haber that whereas careful screening had cleared non-Jewish DPs, no such screening and assurances were possible for "Jewish camps." Assuming a natural inclination toward communism among Jews, the colonel argued that "many might actually be 'leaning' ideologically toward the Russian view. As a result, Russian agents can more readily be placed in Jewish camps and detection would be more difficult." Haber concluded that this influential officer reflected the general "antagonistic" army attitude prevailing in Germany: "[I]n spite of what he may say publicly about DPs in general, he probably believes that Jewish DPs represent a very real immigration hazard to the United States."[92]

Ultimately, the Displaced Persons Act of June 1948 discriminated against Jews by excluding the 100,000 refugees, essentially Jews, who had fled into DP camps in 1946–1947. The law also gave priority to Baltic peoples, Eastern Poles, and agriculturalists. It would be two more years before an amendment eliminated such preferences and indirect restrictions on Jews and initiated a more equitable admission policy for DPs.[93]

Few high-ranking officers had been so keenly interested in the selection of immigrants as Wedemeyer at Plans and Operations. After passage of the 1948 act, he wrote to his good friend General Huebner in Frankfurt for assistance in identifying two immigrating "German or Baltic peasant" families for his tenant farm in Maryland. Wedemeyer's only criteria were that they be the "right kind of German" or from a nationality of "good peasant stock."[94]

Oil, Reds, and Jews: The Birth of Israel

Although senior officers in the army desperately wanted to rid the army of the burden of Jewish DPs in Europe and yet keep the bulk of them out of the United States, they simultaneously tried to block the other major outlet, for the army steadfastly resisted opening Palestine to Jewish immigration. As the Nazi danger dissipated in the last months of the war, the army's rationale for this opposition quickly shifted from wartime necessity to anticommunism and containment of the Soviet Union.

In early 1945, Captain Nicholas Andronovich, G-2 in Jerusalem, reported that the Soviets sought a Middle East "sphere of influence" and that in Palestine "the only Communist Party is Jewish." Another G-2, Mordecai Allen, offered a contrasting assessment, pointing out Russia's anti-Zionism and the anticommunism of most Jews in Palestine. But for the next several years, senior officers in Europe and Washington believed that the Soviets, "seeking control of the Middle East," pressured Poland to facilitate the mass migration of Polish Jews to Palestine.[95]

When the Harrison report advocated freer Jewish immigration to Palestine, Colonel A. D. Reid in Plans and Operations anticipated a "violent Arab reaction" and estimated the effort would require 400,000 men to protect the Jews. Reid's secret report representing the War Department's position to the secretary of state envisaged a "heavy concentration of forces and consistently severe repression of all opposition" through air power, armor, and the "execution of Arab leaders." This would delay U.S. demobilization while severely impeding the occupation of Germany and Japan. More troublesome, the "imposition of the Jews on the Arabs by force of U.S. and British arms would quite inevitably . . . throw the majority of Arabs . . . into the arms of Soviet Russia."[96]

In 1946, the army, including Chief of Staff Eisenhower, opposed diplomatic maneuvers toward a joint U.S.-British trusteeship for Palestine. "Neither the U.S. nor the U.S.S.R. should be included"; certainly, the United States must not commit to sending American forces there. Owing to the vital importance of Mideast oil, nothing should be done to turn Arabs toward "Russia and against the United States." But to the dismay of probably all senior officers, in October Truman called for immediate immigration of 100,000 Jews into Palestine and an eventual Jewish state.[97]

In May 1947, Judge Simon H. Rifkind informed Eisenhower that the Truman request was in America's strategic interest. Once again the army balked. Rifkind, a former army Jewish adviser on DPs, saw an Arab reaction of limited scope and duration. Jews would be the "bulwark of democracy" in the region and an effective industrial, military ally of the West, while the Arabs would not. But to General Lauris Norstad and his staff in Plans and Operations, these were "specious" arguments unworthy of consideration by the secretary of state. P&O seriously doubted that "Jews would be more inclined to develop a democratic state" than the Arabs. "On the contrary," Norstad wrote on the original draft of the report, "it appears that the Arabs are more anti-Communist than the Jews." Rifkind had also "overstated" Jewish potential "as a military factor" as well as their contributions to the war in the Middle East. "Without the impetus of the British, it is unknown to what extent these contributions would have been made," and their potential in the next war remained highly questionable. That Rifkind was Jewish almost automatically weakened his case. As one military observer in the Middle East noted about Jews and Palestine: "[F]anatic desire to aid cause so strong that personal integrity is disregarded."[98]

At the end of August, a United Nations committee recommended partitioning Palestine into a Jewish and Arab state. Against strong opposition by the War and State Departments, Truman endorsed partition, as did the Soviet Union. Since the exact nature of the partition and the means of implementing it were sketchy at best, the army could still exert influence on American policy. Of particular importance here was the P&O and its new director, Wedemeyer.

Since his 1930s tour in Germany, Wedemeyer had developed a broad geopolitical view of world events that embodied racial dimensions and suspicions of Jewish motives. Even after the war, he continued to discuss politics, especially communism, with the anti-Semitic racial theorist Lothrop Stoddard. On December 3, 1947, Wedemeyer reminded Patrick Hurley that the American government had long been warned "about the implications of the Jewish influence, not only in our country, but in all 'money-making' areas of the world."[99]

The very next day, Wedemeyer had his division prepare a "Top Secret" report on forces available for implementing the UN resolution. The secretary of the army wanted to know whether a voluntary force could be recruited in the United States or Europe. Emphasizing the "dangerous implications . . . to U.S. security interests," Wedemeyer explained the serious dilemma for America caused by its commitment to partition. Israel could not survive long unless bolstered from outside, so that to not provide such support would undermine UN and U.S. prestige; on the other hand, furnishing it would alienate the Arabs and further the Soviet cause.

A U.S. volunteer force was out of the question, Wedemeyer argued, as the army was falling seriously short of its own recruitment goals. Also, screening out the "plethora of Jewish candidates and malcontent adventure-seekers . . . might result in a counter-problem of vociferous charges of discrimination." Although Poles and Balts could serve the purpose, the Soviets would never acquiesce in these American surrogates without their own presence. But America's security dictated keeping U.S. and Soviet troops out of the region.[100]

With the army anxious and pessimistic ever since the government's decision to support partition, P&O devoted considerable attention to Palestine over the next several months. In early January 1948, Wedemeyer sent Eisenhower an unnamed book to "quickly clarify" his "mind concerning the development of Judaism as well as Zionism." He also recommended an "enlightening document" on Zionism versus Judaism by the anti-Zionist American Council for Judaism.

On January 24, General Alfred M. Gruenther informed one of the staunchest opponents of Zionism, navy secretary James Forrestal, that due to Palestinian developments, the Joint Chiefs of Staff had drastically altered their strategic plans. JCS had not only "spiked" any idea of U.S. military intervention, he stated, but virtually conceded the loss of American access to Middle East oil.[101]

A week later, Wedemeyer's old friend and fellow German specialist, retired colonel Percy Black, confirmed his own pessimistic estimates. Black
and retired admiral W. S. Anderson, former chief of Naval Intelligence,
now worked for an American firm with interests in the Middle East. After
consulting State Department, Egyptian, and Saudi Arabian officials, as well
as Aramco and Bechtel, Black and Anderson called partition one of the
most "tragic mistakes" in American foreign policy.

America was totally to blame for its completely indefensible position
because, Black alleged, under Zionist pressure it threatened to cut off aid
to Europeans unless their delegates voted for partition. Thus, America undercut its own security and essential oil interests. Indeed, implementation
would inevitably require U.S. intervention, because the Arabs were
preparing to "annihilate" the Jews. Despite dubious assurances of their
military capability, the Jews were "now screaming for help." If the U.S. intervened, even through surrogates, it would lose that region and possibly
face a larger war.

Black revived the old charge of Jewish influence on policy, bemoaning
the stupidity of an America that sold out its national security "for New
York votes." America must reverse itself in favor of some alternative resolution (perhaps "trusteeship"). But he expected such a reversal only after
Congress and the American public learned of the dire consequences of current policy and counteracted the relentless "Zionist pressure" on the Truman administration.[102]

Within days, Wedemeyer provided the secretary of the army with an
updated "Top Secret" P&O study on Palestine. The study argued that it
was "imperative" to seek a "reversal" of "ill-advised and insufficiently
thought-through" support for partition. That plan was "dangerously contrary" to "basic U.S. interests; i.e., the avoidance of introducing U.S. troops
and the prevention of legalized intrusion of Soviet forces." "Trusteeship"
offered the United States an escape from its self-imposed dilemma.
Though earlier swayed by the uncontested "powerful voice . . . of Zionism," Americans would readily accept this reversal once they learned the
consequences of partition. Pubic opinion would certainly change dramatically when the "ventriloquism and unethical pressures used [by Jews] in
their earlier persuasion were authoritatively exposed."[103]

Reversal, the study argued, was even in the best interests of Jews. The
"overwhelming" disadvantages of a Jewish state extended beyond American
foreign policy to "the Jews themselves, by whom the U.S. position was primarily maneuvered." Without "strong and continuing external aid," Israel

would inevitably collapse under an Arab onslaught, culminating in "the probable extermination of a vast number of human beings, among whom will be thousands of blindly-trusting Jewish colonists." Since "the required aid means the involvement of U.S. troops," guaranteeing Israel's survival, though perhaps benefiting "world Jewry," spelled impending danger for domestic Jews as well, since American losses in Palestine would unleash an "almost certain surge of violent anti-Semitism in this country."[104]

Average Americans, the study continued, instinctively sympathized with the "plight of the unfortunate," calls for justice, and efforts to alleviate their "distress." Unaware of the Arab side and the real repercussions for U.S. interests, Americans accepted the partition of Palestine as a just and "attractive" solution to the predicament of the displaced Jews of Europe. Nonetheless, the average American

> has not yet acquired much more than a thin veneer of race-tolerance and, if the surface is lightly scratched, will be found to harbor latent antipathy to "the Jew." He makes no distinction between the racial, national and religious connotations of the term, largely because the Zionists for a long time have been deliberately confusing them.[105]

With the deployment of U.S. troops, Americans would learn the truth about Palestine, especially the "questionable practices and procedures whispered about the UN decision." Should national prestige or loss of American lives result, the country would react with a backlash of acute "resentment" and "blame": "Being no better able then than now to distinguish between pro and anti-Zionist, his animosity will be directed against Jews in general; anti-Semitism will have grown from today's unfortunate minor problem into a national calamity."[106]

The State Department had likewise been working to reverse the partition decision without undermining UN credibility. As pessimistic as the army, State invoked similar security concerns to convince Truman of the utmost necessity of noninvolvement in implementing partition. Alienation of the Arabs would result in loss of strategic air bases and access to oil, Soviet penetration of the Middle East, and so on. With Marshall's concurrence, the State Department devised various strategies to nullify the earlier U.S. vote and guide the UN away from a partition imposed by force.[107]

In a draft report of the National Security Council on February 17, 1948, State rejected as dangerous to U.S. security any solution that involved the Soviets or created Arab hostility toward America. The government "should continue support" for partition while opposing the "use of outside force to impose the Plan." But military staff members disapproved; they urged that the United States "alter its previous policy of support for partition and seek another solution." America should propose a UN trusteeship for Palestine.[108]

The next day, General Gruenther of JCS briefed Truman and Marshall, as well as State and Defense officials, at the White House on available military forces and potential commitments. Using force to implement partition, Gruenther reported, required 80,000 to 160,000 U.S. troops, reducing "our reserve to a dangerous degree." The partition plan was simply unworkable.[109]

Thereafter, America's UN representative, Warren Austin, carefully redirected America's Palestine stance. His proposal for a UN commission to study implementing partition signaled a weakening in the U.S. commitment to a Jewish state.[110]

On February 26, G-2, with Carter Clarke as its deputy director, completed a "Top Secret" estimate of the Palestine situation. The estimate asserted that Arabs and Jews were irrelevant to American, British, and Soviet interest in Palestine; there was merely a strategic engagement in a vital region. The United States must block Soviet exploitation of the partition resolution to penetrate the Middle East and convince the UN of an alternative. Accordingly, the United States should embargo all arms shipments to Palestine and oppose intervention by any outside forces.

G-2 criticized the "two non-Americanisms, Zionism and Jewish Nationalism," as contrary to American interests. Publicly, the Zionists' appeal was humanitarian—"to protect and aid a defenseless race and nation." But the American public remained unaware of "their 'behind-the-scene' solicitations and maneuvering," since in reality, by furnishing "huge amounts of money" and vocal political support for partition, American Zionists virtually precipitated the crisis in Palestine. "If United States Jewry could be prevented from forcing the issue by sending assistance to Palestinian Jews," the "more moderate" Arabs and Jews could work out a settlement among themselves.[111]

G-2 also considered the "Jewish Underground" in Germany and Austria as "security threats" to the U.S. occupation. It fostered "illegal migrations," undermining "law and order" and promoting "bribery, smuggling, and black market activities." "Undesirable" refugees from the East "refuse to become engaged in gainful or productive work" or to obey the law.

G-2 was convinced that some Jewish underground leaders were "Communist propagandists, agitators and terrorists." Since the army was not allowed to screen Jewish DPs, it estimated that hundreds of "low-level" and "high-level" Soviet agents had infiltrated the Jewish refugees. Equally ominous, "a considerable portion of Polish DPs . . . have been thoroughly indoctrinated with Communism" and their "views are beginning to pervade those Jewish DPs who had not been in the Soviet Union." As G-2 saw it:

> The Soviet Union and Soviet satellite states may be expected to select for emigration to Palestine those Jews who will be most useful in furthering Soviet expansion in the Middle East. The majority who have not already accepted communist ideology will be indoctrinated before their departure.

Of the 100,000 Polish and Romanian Jews "who passed through Vienna in 1946–47," a "large majority were pro-Russian," and among them were "many former Soviet military personnel."[112]

Zionists, G-2 maintained, knew the true intentions behind Soviet support for a Jewish state and realized that Communist-indoctrinated immigrants and Soviet agents would "form an influential and powerful group within the new state." But the Zionists tolerated this infiltration so long as the Soviets continued to facilitate Jewish immigration into Palestine.

The Arabs, G-2 argued, resisted a Jewish state, in part because they "fear infiltration of Communist influences." "Thoroughly opposed to communism and fearful of Soviet tactics," Arab security interests coincided with those of the United States and Britain. Unless driven away by a Western-imposed partition, Arab League states would remain "definitely oriented toward the Western Powers." Dedicated to peace and UN principles, the Arab League was amenable to an alternative, such as Jewish "autonomy within an independent Arab state of Palestine."[113]

If the UN failed to adopt an alternative before the British withdrew, G-2 warned, a power vacuum would be created in Palestine. Amid bitter Arab-Jewish fighting, the Soviets would certainly "take advantage of this vacuum to further expand their subversive activities." And once the Soviet Union got a foothold in the region, "any attempt to displace it might touch off World War III."[114]

A few weeks later, Wedemeyer expressed the same concern to the British admiral Lord Mountbatten, whom he had befriended in the Far East. The Soviet Union had proven quite adept at filling power vacuums, wrote Wedemeyer; "Will she not go for Palestine?" As a result of the mess created by America's "stupid actions," Wedemeyer envisaged a scenario in which "the Jews might first announce that they have set up a sovereign

State and then ask for Russian help." "What," he queried, "do we do under the circumstances?"[115]

Recent events in Europe had added some substance to assumptions of an impending Communist threat. A pro-Communist government had emerged in Czechoslovakia, while the hardening of the Soviet stance on Germany (soon to culminate in the Berlin blockade) became increasingly obvious. In mid-March, Truman proposed that Congress reinstate universal military training and selective service.[116]

Meanwhile, the administration shifted its UN position further away from partition. Under the urging of Secretary of State Marshall and the Defense Department, Truman apparently acquiesced in the U.S. delegation's taking the lead in reconsidering the plan. The United States then proposed a UN trusteeship and a truce in Palestine.

The army and State Department had achieved their goal of reversing the U.S. position; yet the crucial issue of U.S. or Soviet military intervention was unresolved. On April 19, Navy Secretary Forrestal informed Marshall that any American commitment of troops to enforce trusteeship or a truce would deplete "substantially our entire ground reserves." American intervention in Palestine would "render meaningless" U.S. strategic commitments to Italy, Iran, Greece, China, and Turkey.[117]

Events, however, outpaced UN discussions as the May 15 deadline for British withdrawal quickly approached. Realizing that the Jews intended to declare a sovereign Israeli state at that time, Truman finally resolved in favor of U.S. recognition of the new state. Historians still debate the relative weight in this decision of Truman's sincere sympathy for the Jewish cause and his desire to retain Jewish-American support in a difficult election campaign.

Truman decided on recognition against vocal opposition from Marshall and the State Department during a heated May 12 meeting at the White House. To Marshall, the decision was essentially "based on domestic political considerations." As he expressed it during and after this confrontational session, recognition would undermine U.S. international interests in "a transparent dodge to win a few votes." But in the end, despite urging from friends to resign, Marshall loyally accepted the decision of his president.[118]

On May 15, the United States announced its recognition of Israel. The upper echelons of the army were certainly dismayed, as this policy undermined all of their efforts to thwart such an outcome. With partition an apparent fait accompli, it anticipated the alienation of the Arab states and concurrent loss of oil and strategic bases. Would not the Soviets, despite their own recognition of Israel, somehow exploit the situation to split the Arabs from the West or to introduce troops into the region? Had not the likelihood of U.S. military intervention greatly increased? The gloomy mood within the army was probably captured by the sentiments of a retired military attaché, who ten years before had argued against U.S. attempts to relocate Jewish refugees in Central America. Upon hearing of U.S. and British recognition, he wrote:

> I doubt the wisdom of this hair trigger action by these two great Anglo-Saxon Christian Nations & fear that the Jews have led us into a trap, which may involve us in another war.[119]

After the declaration of the Jewish state, widespread fighting broke out between Jewish and Arab forces in Palestine. Marshall attributed this development to the "evident aggressive tendencies of the Israel government to capitalize to the limit on military advantages, real and anticipated." A "more conservative course," he felt, would have led to a more advantageous settlement for Israel, whereas the current aggressive one was "bound to have unfortunate results."[120]

Throughout the summer of 1948, America's admirals and generals, including Gruenther and Wedemeyer, worked hard to block any U.S. military commitments to a settlement in Palestine. They became alarmed when the United States supported a UN cease-fire resolution in July, fearing the "unacceptable eventuality" of U.S. military intervention. Their various planning sessions came to fruition in a report to the National Security Council in which Forrestal forcefully argued the case for the Joint Chiefs of Staff. Inadequate forces to meet U.S. security needs in other vital areas and the possibility of Soviet domination of the Middle East clearly meant that U.S. intervention in Palestine would "jeopardize our global strategy." The JCS urged that no armed forces of the United States, the Soviet Union, or the Soviet satellites should be permitted to enter Palestine. Therefore, the United States must prevent any "decision by the United Nations to employ military enforcement measures in Palestine."[121]

These same military leaders soon saw an "opportunity . . . to the U.S. to recover lost prestige and to better our future relations with the Arab world." From commanders in the Mediterranean to upper echelons in Washington came pleas for "generous aid" to the approximately 300,000 Arab refugees who fled during the establishment of Israel and related fighting. The same military institution that had earlier either shown reluctance or resistance to aiding Jewish refugees now urged the JCS to convince Forrestal of the "strategic benefits . . . of immediate aid to Arab refugees." Only the Logistic Division raised objections due to lacks of funds and authority. These considerations, Wedemeyer told the army chief of staff, were overridden by the chance for "the U.S. to strengthen the friendship of the Arab people . . . [by] providing succor for these Arab displaced persons."[122]

Hoping to prompt urgent action, Forrestal conveyed this JCS proposal to Truman and the secretary of state with his concurrence. Adding its support, the State Department informed Truman that U.S. failure to provide assistance was already further "jeopardizing" its Middle Eastern position. Truman apparently turned it over to the attorney general for a legal ruling.[123]

In January 1949, when Congress took up the issue of appropriations for Palestine refugees, Forrestal urged passage of the pending legislation. But in his request to Congressman Bloom, the chairman of the House Committee on Foreign Affairs, Forrestal significantly altered the wording and substance of his arguments. He depicted the refugee question in terms of an obstacle to peace and stability, as well as to the "health and welfare" of Arabs and Jews. Totally eschewing the original rationale of winning back Arab friendship, Forrestal created the impression that the JCS were concerned only with the general instability created by the refugee problem and favored "prompt and generous aid" to alleviate "this dangerous situation." Assistance would also be consistent with America's "traditional humanitarian role."[124]

In March, Congress passed a bill on financial support for Palestinian refugees to be channeled through the UN. Through the summer of 1949, the Joint Chiefs continued privately to justify such assistance as necessary for maintaining and improving relations with Arab states. The "primary significance . . . of the Arab refugee problem" remained oil, geopolitical strategy, and Soviet penetration.[125]

By 1949, the unexpected survival of Israel forced the military to reassess the infant state's strategic value. Israel, concluded the Joint Chiefs, could be "a danger or an asset," depending upon whether it shifted toward the West or the Soviet Union. Access to Israel would grant either side important advantages in "any contest for control of the Eastern Mediterranean–Middle East area." U.S. policy must now seek to draw Israel to the West, while at the same time reconciling Israel and the Arab states at least to the extent they could cooperate in resisting "Soviet Aggression."[126]

Despite Israel's policy of neutrality in the "cold war," the JCS saw the possibility of a future tilt toward the West. Contrary to earlier army doubts about Zionist sympathies with democracy or the West, the JCS now more readily accepted Israeli leaders' private assurances that "their sympathies lie with the West." America had supported establishment of Israel and the new state "had close ties with the United States," the JCS stated, "because of our large and influential Jewish minority." Israel's public neutrality was merely a necessary expedient to ensure the continued flow of Jewish immigrants from Iron Curtain countries.[127]

It was, however, with these very immigrants that the JCS saw the danger to its new policy toward Israel, for these immigrants provided the "opportunity for Communist penetration" and "domination of Israel by the USSR." After all, "there are indications that significant numbers of immigrants who have passed through Communist indoctrination courses have already entered Israel."[128] This familiar concern with the supposed connection between Jews and communism represented one of the threads of continuity in the attitudes of senior officers, even as the birth of Israel, the changing geopolitical landscape, and generational change within the army itself combined to mitigate anti-Semitism in the officer corps in the postwar era.

CHAPTER 11

Change and Continuity
in the Postwar Era,
1945–1960

W HAT STARTED OUT AS A ROUTINE LUNCH for General C. T. Lanham at the officer's mess in the Pentagon on August 27, 1946, ended with the general being publicly embarrassed and privately infuriated. While dining with two fellow officers, Lanham, chief of the War Department's Information and Education Division, was approached by Colonel Frederick S. Doll of G-2. Before Lanham could introduce any of his guests, Doll immediately "spewed" out that the Army Information School at Carlisle, Pennsylvania was "full of subversive elements." Caught "completely off balance" by this public airing of a security matter, Lanham was truly stunned when Doll began blurting out the name of the primary suspect—"Herzberg." Lanham quickly interrupted Doll and introduced him to his seated guests, among whom was Colonel Fred Herzberg. Doll then left, and Lanham laughed off his charge as a "ridiculous statement."[1]

Doll's behavior was, however, a "serious matter" that Lanham had watched get progressively worse throughout the year. Not long before, he had witnessed a similar outburst at a private dinner, where an officer friend had "launched into a tirade about the 'communists' at the school," repeatedly stating that Herzberg and others "were all communists." These accusations rested solely on the claim that a respected officer "had the goods on Herzberg" and the other officers had worked for *Stars and Stripes*. These "slanderous" accusations apparently originated with Doll.[2]

Within days, Lanham related these events to General Williston B. Palmer, commander of the Army Information School at Carlisle, for whom they were the last straw. Since assuming his post in January 1946, Palmer had been relentlessly beseeched by Doll to purge the subversive threat, especially Herzberg. Palmer's commanding officer, General Manton S. Eddy (Second Army Headquarters, Baltimore), had earlier asked him to discuss the security problems at the school with Doll, who enjoyed the confidence and trust of Eddy and many others. A 1936 graduate of the Army War College with forty years of service, Doll had spent the war running the G-2 operations from Baltimore. But his wartime penchant of hunting for subversives had become an "obsession."[3]

During that initial meeting, Palmer later admitted that Doll had "scared me badly" about the "subversive elements." "Thoroughly alarmed," Palmer rushed to G-2 in Washington, which curiously enough had no information. Back in Baltimore, he read every page of Doll's files on the school without discovering the slightest trace of subversive activity. When Palmer asked for the Herzberg file, he was told: "We have nothing on Colonel Herzberg."[4]

In March, Palmer refused Doll's demand for loyalty investigations of instructors, but Palmer still worried about subversion. He carefully observed his instructors for months, while Doll continually complained and spread rumors about them. Yet Palmer never discovered anything "remotely subversive." In every conversation, Doll brought up Herzberg, whereas Palmer came to admire Herzberg as a devoted officer and gifted instructor. Palmer gradually realized that Doll suffered from a "strong personal prejudice" toward Herzberg "which seemed to obsess him."[5]

Although Doll failed to produce a single piece of evidence substantiating his ceaseless accusations against Herzberg, he acted as if he knew something others did not. Moreover, Doll retained the confidence of his superior. After the dining-room fiasco, when Palmer and Lanham related the serious details of this affair, General Eddy responded:

> I would like to say on Doll's behalf that I have always found him to be an extremely conscientious and honest officer. He has been completely wrapped up in his work, and while I would agree with you that he has given the impression of being overzealous, I am not so sure from what is going on nowadays but what it is not a good thing to have a man like him in the job. I think his only desire is to do the best he can and I feel that his motives are entirely patriotic.[6]

The truth was finally revealed in a heated two-hour conference between Doll, Lanham, and Palmer on September 9, 1946. As Palmer had long suspected, what upset Doll most about Herzberg was his deep interest in "better treatment for racial minorities, with special emphasis on the Negro."[7] Since the end of the war, G-2 had been watching groups involved in "interracial agitation and subversive activities." Organizations and coalitions active in fighting anti-Semitism, as well as "discriminatory practices" against blacks in the armed forces and public life, had, G-2 believed, the "earmarks of being Communist infiltrated." Among its long list of suspects were the NAACP, the National Conference of Christians and Jews, and the American Jewish Congress. G-2 tended to impugn the real motives of those fostering progressive ideas on race or view them as Communist dupes.[8]

To Doll, advocacy of the "Negro" cause was inherently "subversive of American institutions." He suspected anyone who complied with existing War Department policies regarding the fair treatment of black soldiers. The very presence of African-Americans at the school upset Doll, particularly when they "intermingled with whites."[9]

Lanham and Palmer pressed on. What were the grounds for his relentless charges that Herzberg was subversive? Could he provide any information or sources? As Lanham later attested, when finally "pinned down," Doll "had absolutely no facts on which to rest his suspicion other than the fact that Fred was a Jew."[10]

Seemingly, that ended the affair. General Eddy promised that no similar instances would ever reoccur, while Doll appeared broken by his chastisement at the hands of Palmer and Lanham. In December, Herzberg retired to civilian life, completely in the dark about the yearlong campaign against him, and held reserve officer rank for another ten years. Palmer sincerely regretted his departure, expressing praise and gratitude for his devoted service. Earlier that year, Herzberg had received an Army Commendation Ribbon for "outstanding meritorious performance of duty."[11]

This incident was symbolic of the gradual changes that had taken place in the officer corps. Gone were the days when unfounded suspicions of Jewish Communist subversion would go unchallenged within the army. By 1944, in fact, G-2 in Boston regularly reported on anti-Semitism in its region. The war against Nazism, the shocking truth of the Holocaust, and the continued plight of Jewish survivors in Europe had definitely altered the perspectives through which many officers would view such issues. These new attitudes were also in line with progressive changes in general societal sentiments regarding Jews in the United States.

The Herzberg affair illustrated as well that the attitudes of some officers were not appreciably affected by the Holocaust or gradually changing American sentiments. Like the response of many officers to the larger questions of DPs, immigration, and Palestine, this personal incident had again demonstrated the persistence of anti-Semitism. In this regard, the story of the postwar officer corps does reflect positive change, but it also demonstrates significant continuity of attitude. Through the late 1940s, senior officers in G-2 and other divisions remained suspicious of Jews, particularly regarding Communist subversion. At home and abroad, these officers pursued the Jewish-Communist issue with the same zeal that Doll had pursued Herzberg.

Indeed, an important aspect of the story of the anti-Semitic politics of the officer corps extends beyond the active duty years of some officers. Even after many of the senior officers holding such views retired around the early 1950s, the significance of their strong suspicions and antipathies toward Jews did not end. For decades to come, several prominent retired generals remained politically active in support of racist and anti-Semitic causes. Some well-known retired officers would, in fact, continue to interrelate racial anti-Semitism and geopolitics with the kind of theoretical sophistication expressed by army officers in the 1920s.

"Subversives" in the Cold War Era

The old Jewish-Communist link took on ominous dimensions in the context of the emerging Cold War and postwar civil rights movement. It was a time and mood in which national security dictated the careful observation of potentially "subversive" groups.

Until 1946, G-2 assigned several officers to the domestic surveillance of "labor, the Negro population and minority groups," among whom "unrest is increasing." Originally justified by the need to maintain domestic tranquillity and unimpeded production in wartime, G-2's domestic intelligence shifted toward emerging postwar concerns. G-2 classified not only "the foreign born" but also the "majority of first generation residents" as "fertile ground for Communist agitation" and subversion. This characterization kept G-2 focused on "Jewish-Americans" and Palestine, with intelligence officers noting in December 1945 that given America's "abandonment of its former role as Jewish advocate, stronger protests may be expected . . . from embittered American Zionists."[12]

G-2 calculated that of the "4,770,647 Jews in the United States . . . 924,440 [were] foreign born," and a considerable number of the rest were first generation. These relative newcomers clearly constituted a "counter-intelligence problem." Increasing "anti-Semitic feeling" could "disrupt domestic tranquility," as indicated by a revival of anti-Semitic hate groups in the civilian sector, while "anti-Semitic feeling among white soldiers is reflected frequently in reports of verbal altercations." Equally important, Jews were "subjected to Communist agitation and many Communist leaders are Jewish."[13]

In December 1945, while the army struggled to recover from the political uproar and public-relations fiasco over Jewish DPs, Secretary of War Robert P. Patterson suggested that Eisenhower terminate investigations on subjects like "Negroes," "Jewish-Americans," and "Labor." Although Eisenhower concurred, G-2 had the new policy revised by early 1946 to allow such intelligence in "specific cases" where "the army may become involved."[14]

Using this loophole, G-2 Boston resumed its surveillance and media surveys of "Foreign Pressure Groups," including Zionists. Few meetings, articles, or radio programs on Palestine escaped its attention. Agent B-2 showed particular interest in Senator Claude Pepper, whose advocacy of a Jewish state was the subject of regular reports. Occasionally surveillance extended to such "Jewish" activity as meetings dealing with anti-Semitism or eyewitness accounts of the Warsaw ghetto. "Communist suspects" and "pro-Soviet" speakers were observed at certain other gatherings. The amounts collected by the United Jewish Appeal and other fund-raising drives caused similar unease within G-2.[15]

These confidential intelligence summaries were still sent to retired general Ralph Van Deman in San Diego, whose private investigative network, in turn, fed its surveillance to G-2 and the FBI. In July 1946, Van Deman forwarded an agent's report titled "The Jewish Situation in the East," whose opening set the tone for what followed:

> [T]here are many peculiar things going on; and our contacts with the Jews over the past 26 yrs. makes us wonder just what is in the making. . . . [T]he Jewish groups are raising tremendous amounts of money.

Jews and communism in the labor movement, the "Jewish element" courting Senator Pepper and other politicians, "Rabbi Stephen Wise, the militant Jewish leader," and "Emanuel Celler and . . . his ilk" were all drawn into the web of suspicion. In essence, "organized Jewry is out to control organized labor either by the liberals or the Communists."

Since 1938, the "Jewish race" had pursued a plan to "bankrupt the country" in order to capitalize on "chaotic conditions," especially the black market. Despite their denials, Jews "made an awful poor showing in World War II"; they were "powerful enough to pull the strings" necessary to keep them out of combat. The "re-appointment by Truman of a great many Jews" showed that Jews continued "to pull a lot of strings in the background." Meanwhile, "wealthy and influential Jews" sponsored Jewish refugees "coming in here by the shiploads," who always have homes, "plenty of money," and "good jobs."

"Jewish activities are so numerous," the Van Deman report complained, that even a small staff could not keep up with them. With "unlimited funds," Jewish organizations "dwarfed . . . honest, patriotic groups into insignificance." Hollywood and the New York stage—"practically controlled by the Jewish race"—provided their "finest outlets for propaganda," which "followed the Party line from top to bottom." For "out in Hollywood, Communism and the Jewish group seem to play hand in hand."[16]

Such correlations were sufficiently disturbing to prompt G-2's deputy director to request a study in late 1946 "showing the relationship between Jews and Communism." Written in G-2's U.S. branch by officers and civilians, the sober tone and balanced conclusions of the resulting report contrasted sharply with the 1919 study "The Power and Aims of International Jewry." Absent were the alarmist fears that motivated, as well as blinded, many earlier analysts, convinced as they were of real conspiracies.[17] A great deal of progress had obviously occurred in institutional thinking over the decades. The new study clearly refuted the theory that "Communism was one of the manifestations of alleged Jewish ambitions to destroy Christianity and establish Jewish rule the world over."[18] On the other hand, it is astonishing that as late as 1946, an official study had to address such absurd anti-Semitic claims.

There had never been in the twentieth century, the study began, any organization or movement capable of uniting Jews internationally. General patterns showed Western European and U.S. Jews undergoing assimilation. They assumed the national consciousness of an American, Englishman, and so on and were loyal to the interests of their countries. They remained divided from Eastern European Jews, whose Jewish nationalism, intensified by the Nazi exterminations, had fueled the fires of Zionism. Although American Jews furnished generous assistance to Jews around the world, "little support [could] be expected from them for the two-non-Americanisms: Zionism and Jewish Nationalism." And all strands of Judaism were antithetical to communism.[19]

Although the Bolshevik leadership included prominent Jews (Trotsky, Radek, Litvinov), the masses of Russian Jews had been "either indifferent or hostile to the Party of Lenin." Only the "threat of complete physical extermination" in the Russian Civil War by White Russians, "whose campaigns were marked by countless pogroms," led many Jews "to accept Bolshevism as the lesser evil." The "ruthlessness" of Communists toward the economic system and their "merciless . . . persecution of orthodox Hebrews" eventually turned the "bulk of the Jewish population" against the Soviets. Moreover, the Stalinist purges of the 1930s "brought about the disappearance of most of the old-line [Bolshevik] leaders and executives of Jewish origin."[20]

In the United States, the Communist Party initially recruited a substantial portion of its numbers from Russian-born Jews, especially among its leaders, but gradually the party "became predominantly non-Jewish." Although some Jews still held positions of authority, there were "no Jews . . . on the National Board of the Communist Party." With "little appeal to Jews in general," communism in America was thought to be "violently opposed by the great majority of Jewish organizations." Conversely, most Jewish Communists rejected Judaism, since they identified with the international Communist movement, not the Jewish cause. While the Communist Party had "initiated an all-out drive . . . among the Jewish masses," attempts to infiltrate legitimate Jewish movements had failed.

Similarly, "no direct evidence" existed of a relationship between "the world-wide Jewish movement and world-wide Communism." Soviet anti-Zionism, condemned by the World Zionist Congress, illustrated the wide gap between Jewish and Communist interests and aspirations.[21] The small numbers of Jews who accepted communism had a "negligible influence." Communists would, of course, "exploit fully the unrest inherent in the Jewish Problem." And in areas of mutual self-interest ("political liberties, opposition to war and fascism, aid and relief to oppressed peoples"), Jewish-Communist cooperation could be anticipated. But the study found that "there is little likelihood, so long as Communism maintains its totalitarian and anti-religious tenets, that there will be full-fledged fusion between Judaism and Communism."[22]

What, if any, circulation this study had within the army is unknown. Of twelve copies, only the one in Wedemeyer's private papers has apparently survived; a search revealed no army references to the study. The attitudes and activities of various officers around the globe indicated, in fact, that suspicions of some Jewish-Communist link lingered on. Within a month of this report, G-2 officers in Washington reactivated their collection of data on "Jewish Groups," using published articles as well as FBI and MID sources. They then filed these under classification 000.2436, "Subversives."[23]

Although quantitatively minuscule compared to earlier MID records on Jews, the twenty-five or so cards in this file were highly suggestive. Throughout 1947, officers cut out newspaper articles and typed brief intelligence summaries on Jewish organizations and individuals ranging from the United Jewish Appeal to groups that were allegedly outright Communist organizations as well as those suspected as covers. The American Jewish Congress, for example, "participated in a Rent Rally held in Wash DC" and "has frequently sponsored Party fronts and causes." Interspersed were an equal number of entries dealing with Palestine and Zionism, always identifying groups believed to be Communist controlled or influenced.[24]

These postwar concerns extended beyond America, Germany, and Palestine to the Pacific theater. In occupied Japan, MacArthur's intelligence chief, General Charles A. Willoughby, instigated a yearlong investigation of "Leftist Infiltration" of subversive "foreign elements" in his own headquarters and in Washington. Willoughby's pursuit had an ironic twist, since he himself was foreign born. In his mind, though, there was a crucial difference. Whereas those who caused him so much apprehension had "Russian and Russian-satellite backgrounds," his pedigree was that of a German baron.[25]

After attending various European schools, Willoughby came to the United States in 1910 and joined the American army as a private. Finishing his education at Gettysburg College, he was commissioned as a major in 1914. He served in the air corps in World War I and as military attaché to Latin America in the 1920s, attended the War College in 1935–1936, and was promoted to general in World War II. He proudly stated that unlike certain other immigrants, he was never accused of either divided loyalties or unwillingness to fight for his adopted country.

Early on, Willoughby had renounced his aristocratic title of von Tschepps-Weidenbach in favor of his American mother's name and subsequently strove to portray himself as American to the core by identifying himself with her deep family roots in Pennsylvania. Nevertheless, his German lineage followed him for the rest of his life, and he complained about "sinister germanophobe innuendoes." Others seemed to think he elicited these epithets by his own mannerisms and behavior. Irritated by his "intolerant arrogance," even officers who shared his extremist views referred to him disparagingly as "the Prussian." After all, he was a demanding superior who had not taken a vacation in ten years.[26]

After World War II, Willoughby emerged as a staunch anti-Communist crusader with few equals. That avocation brought him into the confidence and friendship of Wedemeyer, Senator Arthur H. Vandenberg, and Robert McCormick of the *Chicago Tribune*. Willoughby earned a special place in the hearts of Catholic anti-Communist circles; Monsignor Fulton J. Sheen confided in him in long letters about politics and the decline of Western culture. In Sheen's lofty estimate, Willoughby had distinguished himself as a profound thinker and one of the greatest Americans; he prayed for him often.

For his part, Willoughby lavished accolades upon Francisco Franco, whom he considered a military genius, the savior of Spain from communism, and a defender of traditional Christian Western values and moral principles. The two men expressed their mutual admiration through an exchange of gifts; Franco received a Colt automatic pistol and Willoughby a sixteenth-century Spanish sword. Willoughby became a champion of U.S. recognition of Franco's regime.[27]

Willoughby's thought represented a clear continuity from early twentieth-century racial geopolitical theory into the Cold War era. He was a devotee of the German geopolitical theorist Karl Haushofer, from whom the Nazis borrowed the concept of *Lebensraum* (living space), the cornerstone of Hitler's foreign policy. According to Haushofer, a nation had the intrinsic right to conquer territory necessary to support its population. His "heartland" theory emphasized the decisive importance of land mass and strategic distances in the grand historical struggles for economic and military survival. Willoughby's mixture of such geopolitical ideas with racial perspectives created analyses almost identical to the Darwinian ones articulated by MID chief Churchill after World War I.[28]

Willoughby's world was one in which the "white race," with special talents for administration and leadership as well as a "genius" for technology and complex machinery, confronted the "teeming millions of the Orient and the Tropics." Foolishly and tragically armed by whites, the nonwhite masses now presented the "greatest international menace since Genghis Khan." An "expensive and limited commodity," the superior white man was not only "outnumbered a hundred-to-one" by masses of "oriental cannon fodder" but killed by his own technological creations. Behind it all stood the "Eurasian" intellectuals and ideologues who incited artificial nationalism among the nonwhite races in order to turn them against the colonial empires of the West.[29]

Although an integral part of the Cold War, Third World national liberation movements did not represent a new conflict. Only the means and ideological slogans had changed in what was actually a long, arduous racial struggle. The Soviet Union's quest for world domination, Willoughby argued, signified merely the "historical continuity" in the aggressive assault of "Mongoloid-Panslavism" against Western civilization under the new "guise of Communism." It was the age-old battle between "Saxon and Cossack," "antagonistic exponents of freedom and absolutism," wherein the Communists merely continued where the czars left off.[30]

The present world situation had left the West in a very precarious defensive position, Willoughby believed. Misguided, foolish policies had led to America's destruction of Germany and Japan, the two historical "buffer-states" against Mongoloid-Panslavism. The "punitive" postwar treatment of Germany only compounded the problem through "irresponsible de-Nazification" and war crimes trials. Dropping the atomic bomb and attempting to purge Japan's traditional society and government were likewise gargantuan mistakes. Both countries had to be resurrected quickly to resume their roles as Western civilization's "front lines" of defense.[31]

America also had to contend with the internal threat of "fifth column" infiltration and native treachery. Cultural decadence and a susceptibility to alien ideologies offered fertile soil for subversion. A sense of duty, professionalism, and principles had given way to "cynical materialism" and declining "moral values" most evident along the Eastern seaboard. Meanwhile, American democracy committed "national suicide" with its "legalistic protection" of "traitors and alien saboteurs."[32]

The circles in which Willoughby traveled often associated Jews with these foreign and domestic problems. He himself believed that "unassimilated" aliens, particularly those from Russia and Eastern Europe, constituted the bulk of the "fifth column" in America: "There appears to be a racial and geographical affinity for Communism and uncontrolled immigration has become a channel for subversion."

Upon retirement, Willoughby would become more explicit in identifying Jewish influences. He once complained to MacArthur that an unprincipled Eisenhower had removed Patton "at the behest of Frankfurter, Bnai Brith and the Jewish Conspirators."[33]

Throughout his 1946–1947 investigations of leftist infiltration of MacArthur's occupation government in Japan, Willoughby was repeatedly frustrated by the unpersuasive reports of his subordinates. They "mixed weak cases with strong ones," yet without the "weak cases," the "force of the list shrinks considerably"; only eleven cases would remain. In his own heart, he knew that all the suspected personnel in the military government were indeed subversives, but he had difficulty convincing commanders outside G-2. Two "strong cases" had already been rejected for inadequate evidence. Undeterred, Willoughby ordered his subordinates to strengthen the study's content and "dollup" the format and presentation for effectiveness. They must also emphasize a very "significant factor" so far neglected. "Bring up and list," he told them, "the ex-Russian nationalities of many, if not most of these people."[34]

After criticizing several drafts, Willoughby finally alerted the chief of staff in late January 1947 that G-2 investigations "had revealed an unusually large percentage of leftist-inclined personnel among individuals with Russian or Russian-satellite backgrounds." Occupying "exceedingly responsible positions" through which they exercised "direct influence" on policymaking, they constituted "a dangerous security risk" to the United States and threatened the "success of the Occupation." Out of 3,877 civilians employed by headquarters, G-2 identified 199 as either Russian or satellite-born or first-generation Americans with families from these areas. Eleven of these currently under investigation "disclosed a relatively high degree of leftist activity." The entire case was reinforced with bar graphs, which Willoughby especially liked, as well as statistical correlations on nationality and citizenship percentages, and the like.[35]

Discouraged that his report did not reach the top brass, Willoughby revived his efforts a few weeks later. It was a "good time psychologically," he noted, since "the newspapers are full of the anti-Communist investigations and purges now going on in the States, especially in Congress." This time he aimed to get a report "upstairs." But again, he was "disappointed in the small number of cases"—ten cases instead of twenty-one. The whole thing had to be "doctored up a bit" to create the right "punch line" and strengthen the "statistical statements."[36]

The limited quantity of cases could be offset, Willoughby decided, by listing all other "suspects" under investigation. And subsequent versions emphasized that G-2, FBI, and local surveillance yielded "extensive dossiers" on all them. The "potential effect" was also greater if the 199 Russian types employed at headquarters were combined with all foreigners, thus raising the percentage from 5 to 13.2. "That's more convincing," he thought. So his mind worked.[37]

The key was the "pattern" employed by this leftist "fifth column." The "genus Tokyo," as Willoughby labeled infiltrators in Japan, shared identifiable characteristics: They were of Russian or satellite origin; they might be "stateless" persons who had entered through "relaxed entry quotas"; they were either intelligentsia or had acquired an "academic cover"; and they were affiliated with Communist front organizations. Further, they showed "a marked tendency to avoid military service by securing positions as 'experts' in various civilian agencies, or, if entering military service, to seek out such non-combatant branches as headquarters, intelligence offices, information services, or military publications like *The Stars and Stripes*."[38]

In fact, Willoughby's cases lacked substance, resting solely on unfounded conjecture and unspecified charges of leftist "reputations," "associations," or "tendencies." Still, Willoughby warned his superiors of their "relentless effort to subvert the occupation" through "their pro-leftist and pro-Communist acts and expressions." These apparently stemmed from their efforts to purge government officials and police of the old regime and to develop a Japanese labor movement. This offended Willoughby's antidemocratic and antilabor sympathies and impeded his geopolitical goal of resurrecting Japan as a bulwark against Communist expansionism in the Far East.[39]

The final reports Willoughby sent upstairs never raised the Jewish angle. Only once was an individual even briefly identified as Jewish, even though all probably were. But the issue lurked in the background of Willoughby's thinking and in the minds of others. The characteristics attached to these alleged subversives of foreign heritage or birth were those often utilized in categorizing Jews.

Most revealing was Willoughby's personal intervention in constructing the case against one Beate Sirota. A Viennese-born émigré and naturalized citizen of Russian-Jewish parentage, Sirota worked in the administration division of the occupation government. Willoughby charged that she used her office to advance the Communist cause within the new government of Japan. To him, she presented a danger to the occupation's success and "the ultimate security of the United States." Upset over the "weak" case against Sirota, Willoughby immediately sprung into action, exclaiming, "Where are my own notes. Get this stuff up to me. . . . Something must be said about her parents. That's the *punch line*."[40]

After writing his own interpretation, he told his subordinates to "work this into your report of the Sirota case," which they did after sanitizing his actual comments to eliminate the Jewish references. But Willoughby's original rendition of her and her musician parents disclosed his true thoughts:

> Her English is initially the kind that is spoken in a foreign household. . . . [She is] certainly not American; and her familiarity with American standards, thoughts and ideals are those hastily acquired. . . . [Her] parents are state-less persons. . . . They are Jewish. Nevertheless, they appear in Japan . . . [which] has never been a haven of refuge for foreigners. . . . At this time, we run into a small Jewish clique. . . . One Jew recommends the other; so here we find strange characters drift into Tokyo . . . where they work mysteriously and precariously. . . . [Later] we find the "expert" [daughter] almost psychopathic in her hatred of the [Japanese] police and authority . . . able to vent her fury [by] purging neighborhood Japanese officials. . . . [A] stateless Jewess, a hastily acquired citizenship, wielding the power of the United States and the prestige of General MacArthur.[41]

By summer of 1947, not only had Willoughby failed to win support for cleansing the subversive network at headquarters, but he had stirred up a hornet's nest. His study had "caused [such] resentment" in the Government Section (the focus of his "attack") that parts of the report were actually destroyed. Dismissing the uproar as a misunderstanding due to "faulty or tactless phraseology," he held firm to the conviction about these "subversive elements." Whatever actually happened thereafter, mutual suspicion and resentment apparently endured. Among Willoughby's friends it was believed that a certain officer who had worked on this investigation later failed to earn a citation, though highly worthy, because "he ran afoul of . . . [his] Italian-Jew enemy" at headquarters.[42]

Willoughby's investigations of subversives and the uproar it caused occurred almost simultaneously with the Doll-Herzberg affair in G-2 back home. Like Colonel Doll, Willoughby now also encountered unexpected and frustrating opposition from within his own ranks unlike any he had experienced or would even have anticipated in earlier times. But the struggle between the old guard and those with different attitudes went on. Willoughby's persistence in this case and for years thereafter again indicated how deeply rooted such biased convictions were.

A year later, the *Tribune's* "Colonel" McCormick, en route from Paris to Madrid, wrote to Willoughby about the Jewish hindrance to maintaining anti-Communist bulwarks in Europe. McCormick had supposedly "confidentially confirmed," through American diplomatic officials and others, that the Jews were preventing U.S. recognition of Franco's Spain as revenge for the Inquisition. Vengeful Jews were also responsible for America's physical destruction of Germany. McCormick, however, dismissed gossip that a certain American prominent in diplomatic circles was Jewish. Willoughby found the reference to the Inquisition "very intriguing"; the Jews, he noted, must have a "long memory."[43]

In fact, the same year that Willoughby's crusade was thwarted also witnessed Colonel's Doll quick recovery from his castigation over the Herzberg affair. Bouncing back vigorously, Doll resumed his anti-Communist crusade with the "whole-hearted backing and sympathetic leadership" of his new commanding officer—for in early 1947, Wedemeyer had taken over the Second Army at Baltimore. He urged Doll to proceed with his endeavors to preserve the "'American Way of Life' and a tranquil Service."[44]

Besides their mutual admiration and respect, Doll and Wedemeyer thought similarly on the Communist-Jewish-Negro linkage that had so disturbed Doll in the Herzberg case. While in China as chief of staff to Chiang Kai-shek, Wedemeyer had had his own run-in with a Jewish-American journalist whom he believed exploited the "racial problems" of blacks in the army to fit the Communist "party line." To Wedemeyer, Communists generally proved quite supple in adjusting recruitment tactics. While they pursued one angle in China and another in Canada, their "Fifth Column penetration" in the United States centered on "racial discrimination" because of the "large negro population and the important Jewish group."[45]

In his swan song in 1948, Doll passed on the benefits of his counterintelligence experience to Wedemeyer in a final assault on the army's Information Service. Doll related his "deep concern" with that branch's "stress on sociological programs . . . [which] lend themselves to distortion and inevitably to the introduction of socialistic and communistic theories." These "dangerous subjects" must be replaced by training in "fundamental Americanism," because "in these critical times our military personnel should not be exposed to indoctrination." Unfortunately, the serious damage already caused by wartime army Information and Education programs was "still discernible among many of our veterans."[46]

Without identifying Doll, Wedemeyer extracted the essentials of the colonel's letter and forwarded them to several generals for consideration with his own strong endorsement. Wedemeyer had known this unnamed officer for years, valued his experience, and had "confidence in his judgment and unselfish interest in the welfare of his country."[47]

Wedemeyer's patronage aside, however, the tide had already turned against the old guard. The year of Doll's retirement marked the realization of what many officers of his generation would have considered unthinkable national catastrophes—the army's racial desegregation and U.S. recognition of Israel. Further, the institutional parameters wherein officers like Doll could find a receptive audience had greatly narrowed. With the departure of Wedemeyer, Willoughby, and others over the next several years, they would narrow even further. Yet the old guard's attitudes and concerns would still not completely depart with them.

In late 1949, the military attaché in Switzerland sent under "special handling" a report outlining the "financial activities by Jewish agents not only in Italy but also Switzerland, England, the United States and Yugoslavia—all in the interest of the Communist Party." Through an international Jewish network, millions of dollars had supposedly been transferred to finance "Communist terrorists . . . and Palestine interests." After requesting information from commanders, attachés, and the FBI, G-2 headquarters could not, however, find any substantiation.[48] As General Palmer grumbled several years later, "[T]he gnomes down in the mines of G2 always keep bringing up those same old spurious nuggets . . . no matter how many times the subject has been disposed of previously."[49]

Even the Herzberg affair did not remain buried. In 1954, Herzberg found himself in the midst of a "nightmarish experience" during the national hysteria of the McCarthy era. While McCarthy viciously attacked the army in the fall of that year, Herzberg was suddenly caught in the rash of anti-Communist security checks. Like a character in a Kafka novel, Herzberg was shocked when "accused of subverting the Army." He had retired in 1946 with commendations and continued exemplary reserve service since then. Yet he now faced an immediate dishonorable discharge. With no knowledge of Doll's 1946 investigations, the charges remained "unintelligible" to him. While these accusations threatened and damaged him, he could only deny them; he could mount no defense.[50]

But Herzberg did not stand alone. In an admirable hour for the American officer corps, Generals Lanham and Palmer courageously rose to his defense as they had years before. Despite the risks involved as Senator McCarthy's attack on the army reached its peak, these officers never hesitated in forcefully refuting the "untrue and unfounded" charges. Whereas throughout the institutions of government many others sheepishly retreated to protect themselves, Lanham and Palmer did the honorable thing. They knew that the baseless case against Herzberg had emanated from Doll's anti-Semitic prejudice and "existed only in his own mind."

Palmer and Lanham's unflinching stand triumphed over bigotry, hysteria, and injustice, as their testimony led to Herzberg's full exoneration the following year. He retired from the reserves with an honorable discharge.

To these officers, defending Herzberg had been simply a matter of honesty and integrity, of standing by a "friend" in serious trouble. As Lanham modestly said, Herzberg "is as good an American as you or I. . . . Therefore, regardless of any embarrassment that might accrue to me either personally or officially I intend to stand by Fred."[51]

Officers such as Lanham and Palmer either never shared the anti-Semitism of many of their contemporaries and earlier generations of officers or they had risen above it at some point. The officer corps that fought World War II was generally less homogeneous in its social, political, and racial makeup and outlook than its predecessors. The Pattons, Dolls, and Wedemeyers were mixed with the Lanhams, Palmers, and Herzbergs; few would now agree publicly with Moseley.

For some officers, racism and anti-Semitism were simply no longer acceptable, while for others, overt manifestations gave way to more subtle forms of prejudice. Although there would still be the occasional revelation that certain high-ranking officers had concerns about Jewish loyalty, as well as about the financial and political influence of Jews, this would be the exception. What had also apparently changed within the army through the passing of the generations of senior officers trained before World War II was the gradual disappearance of theoretical racial thinking. Newer generations of officers probably remained unaware that their predecessors had ever embraced such political biology or Darwinian geopolitical thought.

This prewar racial thinking, however, remained very much alive among certain politically active retired officers. They also showed that even at this stage in America's history, they could be as susceptible to Jewish conspiracy theories as MID officers had been after World War I. In retirement, they lent the prestige of their distinguished ranks and reputations to radical conservative causes, including anti-Semitic ones. In doing so, they added credibility to extremist political ideas and groups, for several of these retired generals commanded such respect that their advice was sought by politicians, congressional committees, and the army. Prominent among such men was Charles Willoughby, Albert C. Wedemeyer, and George E. Stratemeyer. During the Korean War, Willoughby had, in fact, worked closely with Stratemeyer and Edward M. Almond, two of MacArthur's other top generals who shared Willoughby's racial thinking and commitment to political action to save America.

Retired Officers and the Battle for America

By coincidence, the very day that General Lanham rose to Herzberg's defense, retired general George E. Stratemeyer testified before the Senate Internal Security Subcommittee on America's failure in Korea. A well-known air force commander, Stratemeyer (West Point, 1915; War College, 1939) said he had been relatively uninformed of the "political situation" at home and abroad. Of course, he distrusted Communists, but beyond such gut reactions, he was a commander preoccupied with day-to-day military operations.

When the committee probed about policy, Stratemeyer expressed bewilderment regarding the political decisions made in Washington. "We were not permitted to win" in Korea, he said; U.S. actions were "not American." In exasperation, he remarked:

> There is something going on, has been going on since World War II ended. . . . There is some hidden force or some hidden power or something that is influencing our people. They don't act like Americans. Americans are supposed to have guts, and our policy . . . is wishy-washy and appeasing. . . . [T]here is something wrong. Good old Americanism doesn't exist as it did when I came to West Point as a youngster. What it is, I don't know. . . . Why we do it? Who is the force? What does that? I don't know.[52]

About two weeks later, Stratemeyer found "the answers" in a book revealing that hidden force of "traitors." A grateful Stratemeyer immediately wrote the author, retired colonel John Beaty, praising his service to America; only ill health prevented Stratemeyer from touring the country to spread the lessons of this "great book." Still, Beaty could rest assured that Stratemeyer would be relentless in recommending *The Iron Curtain over America*.[53]

An English professor and former chairman at Southern Methodist University in Dallas, Beaty was a G-2 officer in Washington between 1941 and 1947, where he edited secret daily intelligence reports. He claimed to have acquired many of his insights while inside G-2. In *Iron Curtain*, Beaty picked up where Stoddard left off, resuscitating the old story that Eastern European Jews were Khazars not the Semitic Hebrews of ancient Israel who gave Christians the Old Testament.[54]

Had Beaty's book been a run-of-the-mill Cold War piece on Communist subversion, Stratemeyer's accolades would have held little significance. But Beaty's *Iron Curtain* ranks among the most vicious anti-Semitic diatribes of the postwar era, one that enjoyed very considerable success. The book went through seventeen printings during the 1950s, propelled by its inflammatory promotional flyers that posed provocative rhetorical questions about the "inassimilable minority," secret "Forces," the "relationship between war dead and immigration," and "[h]ow the Truman Administration helped the Communists who are killing our men in Korea."

Beaty's diatribe was nothing if not sensational. It attributed America's "problems" to "Judaized Khazars," a "powerful and rapidly growing minority—closely knit and obsessed with its own objectives, which are not those of Western Christian civilization." Driven by an "ideology alien to our traditions," they infiltrated the Democratic Party and other institutions through which they were secretly leading America to "ruin." This "restless aggressive minority" was involved with "international Communism, the seizure of power in Russia, Zionism, and continued migration to America."[55]

The Khazars, Beaty argued, were a "mixed non-Russian stock" from Southern Russia who converted to Judaism in the Middle Ages but who became known as "Russian Jews." They remained "an indigestible mass in the body politic . . . [a] state within a state [and] a formidable anti-government force" against the Westernized Russian ruling classes of Nordic blood. Dictatorial and immoral in everything from trade to politics, these Khazar Jews assassinated czars and founded Bolshevism. Since the Russian Revolution, they had been the "masters of Russia"; "Stalin, Kaganovich, Beria, Molotov, and Litvinoff all have Jewish blood or are married to Jewesses." The same was true of Communist leaders in Russia's Eastern European satellites.[56]

According to Beaty, the Khazars had created Zionism to acquire the mineral wealth and strategic advantages of the Middle East. Communist subversion was "principally" Jewish, as shown by the U.S. "atomic espionage" of spies like Harry Gold, David Greenglass, and Julius and Ethel Rosenberg; 91.4 percent of militant U.S. Communists were of "foreign stock."[57]

The infiltration of unassimilable Jews had begun, Beaty wrote, with the new immigration of the 1880s. Unlike earlier nativists, Beaty no longer perceived Italians and Slavs as a problem. They could assimilate, since they stemmed from the "same parent Indo-Germanic racial stock as the

English-German-Irish majority, and above all by their being Christian." The "vast hordes" of Jewish immigrants, however, were "strikingly different." Through "sheer weight of numbers" and "aggressiveness," they pushed aside the original assimilated American Jews, the real descendants of ancient Israel. Believing themselves to be a "superior people," the newcomers had no intention of assimilating. Unknown to the average American, they pursued their own selfish aims "covertly by infiltration, propaganda, and electoral and financial pressure" until they became a powerful force economically and politically.[58]

The Democratic Party and liberalism were convenient vehicles to advance the ends of these Jewish immigrants. "For reasons not yet fully known," President Wilson had appointed Louis Brandeis, the "Harvard Jew of Prague stock," to the Supreme Court; under the influence of Frankfurter and Morgenthau, Roosevelt had recognized the Soviet Union; and gradually the newcomers were "infiltrated . . . into the State Department, presidential coterie, and other sensitive spots." The "so-called refugees" from Nazi Germany also immediately took over "sensitive government positions," while Frankfurter exercised unparalleled sway over Roosevelt's policies. The essential question was whether the "ratio of *appointed* persons of Eastern European origin . . . in *strategic positions* reflect the will of the U.S. people? If not, what controlling *will* does it reflect?"[59]

World War II, Beaty charged, was an unnecessary war fostered within Roosevelt's Democratic Party by the "dominant Eastern European element," who bore responsibility for the dead sons "beneath the white crosses." He quoted Eisenhower's statement that 90 percent of American soldiers did not know why they were fighting Germans. Nazi Germany was a country "strangled" economically, politically, and militarily by international powers that forced it down the tragic path to war. Germany had made "sincere efforts" to accommodate the United States, "only to be rebuffed."

The real Jewish goal was not victory over a dictatorship but "killing as many as possible of the world-ruling and Khazar-hated race of 'Aryans,'" both German and American, by prolonging the war through demands for unconditional surrender and the Morgenthau Plan. By these means, and through the uncivilized bombing of German cities, they sought to destroy the "race which next to the English gave America most of its life-blood." While American boys died in this unnecessary fratricidal racial war, Eastern European refugees were brought into America by the hundreds of thousands. "Our alien-dominated government fought the war for the annihilation of Germany, the historic bulwark of Christian Europe."

After the war, the Khazars sought vengeance against the Germans through starvation, economic dismantling, unjust and illegal war-crimes trials, and general inhumanity, all designed to alienate the German people and drive them toward communism. Jewish refugees in American uniforms and the military government often implemented these policies directly. Beaty also decried the "hideous atrocities perpetrated upon the German people by displaced persons after the surrender."[60]

To Beaty, the Holocaust was a "fantastic hoax" used to burden the Germans with reparations for Israel. America's support of "bloody little Israel" ranked with China, Korea, and Germany as a crucial policy fiasco of the Truman era. Immigrant Khazar Jews from Russia spearheaded Soviet penetration of the Middle East while alienating Muslims from the previously admired "Anglo-Saxon powers." Morality, justice, and "vital oil reserves" demanded that America win back Arab friendship. Meanwhile, involving America in constant foreign occupations or wars depleted the "native stock" that made America great by killing off its young men or preventing them from procreating by keeping them abroad. This demographic gap was filled by faster-breeding Jewish refugees. As Beaty summed up the "present peril": "Could it be that *those* who pull the strings from hidden seats behind the scenes, *want* Americans to be killed in Korea," the Middle East, and Germany?[61]

Beaty, who always flaunted his "five years in Military Intelligence" to establish credibility, created a scandal by including Stratemeyer's letter praising him in promotional material for his book.[62] Certain that a general of Stratemeyer's prominence would never endorse such a book, Jewish-American groups expected him to disassociate himself from Beaty. However, after an entire year passed without Stratemeyer taking such action, Henry Schultz, national chairman of the Anti-Defamation League, wrote the general on October 4, 1955. In a highly deferential tone, he informed Stratemeyer that the anti-Semitic Beaty and the notorious "anti-Jewish hatemonger" Gerald K. Smith had misused him as an endorsement. A "compilation of anti-Jewish lies and distortions," *Iron Curtain* had become the "primer for lunatic fringe groups" across America. The book had been condemned by a variety of Christian writers and publications, and Beaty had been censured by Southern Methodist University. Schultz respectfully asked Stratemeyer to "consider the advisability" of repudiating "religious hatred" and misuse of his name.

American Jews were as stunned by Stratemeyer's scathing reply as anti-Semites were elated. "Forcefully resenting" the implications of Schultz's letter, he decried it as the "most outrageous communication" he had ever received. Anti-Semitism was a "meaningless expression"; neither he nor the book was "anti-Jewish"; he had "many Jewish friends," all "loyal honest Americans." He questioned not Beaty's credibility but the real "purpose" of the Anti-Defamation League, assailing its "veiled threat" against his own "free expression and thoughts." He compared the league's efforts to repression in the Soviet Union. In truth, he owed Beaty a great debt, since it was from him that he finally learned what really occurred back home while he was fighting overseas. Every "loyal citizen" should read *Iron Curtain over America*.[63]

Thereafter, Stratemeyer actively promoted the book and publicized what he believed was a Jewish attempt to silence him. He encouraged Beaty to use his letter and was highly gratified to find that it was "hurting" his Jewish critics. For the next ten years, Stratemeyer worked with Beaty and helped to recruit other retired officers to the cause.[64]

Stratemeyer sent copies of *Iron Curtain* to old military friends, who welcomed them enthusiastically. Retired general Robert Wood praised his rare "courage and patriotism" in standing up to Schultz. To Wedemeyer, Stratemeyer's "righteous stand" helped preserve America's freedoms. Surely his old friend was not anti-Semitic just because he opposed a Jewish organization and endorsed a book, particularly when it "was not written in a destructive vein." Real Americans like he and Stratemeyer opposed any kind of bigotry and intolerance. It was the Zionists who created a problem by inducing a "self conscious" nationalist movement among Jewish Americans.[65]

Beaty's new flyers portrayed Stratemeyer as the courageous hero of Korea resisting Jewish coercion. Additional endorsements followed. Senator Pat McCarran called it a "fine book," while Senator William Langer favored making it "compulsory reading in every public school."

Soon other former officers lent their support. Next to Stratemeyer, Beaty printed the pictures of three retired officers in full uniform, beneath which stood their long and ardent endorsements. To General Edward M. Almond, this "magnificent contribution" showed "wherein the real threats to our Country lurk." For Vice Admiral T. G. W. Settle, it exposed the real "cancer" in America and deserved the "widest possible dissemination." General Pedro A. del Valle felt compelled to admire the "great service" of this "magnificent book," which courageously dispelled the "fog of propaganda" under which the country existed.[66]

When retired general George Van Horn Moseley received Stratemeyer's material, he enthusiastically joined Beaty's efforts to warn America about the Jewish danger and the "vile State of Israel." Considering the
publicity surrounding Moseley's earlier notorious politics and vehement
anti-Semitism, he enjoyed a surprising degree of respect and trust among
certain retired officers and in their political circles. "Disillusioned and frustrated" that they were losing control of America in its time of "peril,"
Stratemeyer, Wedemeyer, and other retired officers shared in his tirades
against the disastrous Roosevelt-Truman era and the country's resulting
decadence and decline.[67]

The *Tribune*'s "Colonel" McCormick made special stops in Atlanta to
speak with Moseley, while Wedemeyer commended Moseley's "outstanding contribution . . . as a dedicated public servant, both in and out of uniform." In 1959, General Wood and Moseley organized Americans for
Constitutional Action, a new version of America First. When rumors
spread that an admiral in line for its leadership might be Jewish, Wood told
Moseley, "You are quite right . . . that it is a strategic mistake to start out
with a president who is a Jew."

Wood usually introduced Moseley as a "very distinguished" officer, as
"patriotic a man as I know, he sincerely loves his country." To Wood,
Moseley's controversial past was an unfortunate misunderstanding: "He
got in bad with our Jewish people, though to the best of my knowledge he
never told anything but the exact truth."[68]

Although Moseley vented his malicious anti-Semitism as frankly as
ever, his correspondents often relied on euphemisms. "Internationalists,"
"subversive pressure groups," "treacherous termites in our midst," "alien
groups," and "minorities," all were invoked to identify what Moseley
called Jews. But some of Moseley's generation were not so circumspect.
Retired general William D. Connor, a former War College commandant
and West Point superintendent, stated that Moseley was right in identifying the problematic "pressure group" as "Jews." The same characteristics
that made Jews a "menace" 2,000 years ago, Connor wrote, made them a
danger today.[69]

Most Americans really agreed with Moseley, said Connor, but were reluctant to state so openly. Assumptions about Jewish influence and power
did make many former military men wary of saying what they truly felt.
In public talks, Wedemeyer identified those usurping American liberties
simply as "minority groups, interested only in their own aggrandizement." His autobiographical book on American foreign and military pol-

icy, *Wedemeyer Reports*, intentionally eschewed the Jewish question. A friend had advised him, he wrote in his private fragmentary notes on communism, to exclude the material on Jews; otherwise, Jewish influence and boycotts would ensure the book's failure. Even the powerful J. Edgar Hoover had supposedly "whitewashed" his coverage of Jews in return for their support of *Masters of Deceit*.[70] But Wedemeyer's letters left no doubt that by minority groups he meant Jews. Until the end of his life, he saw Jews as aggressive, obnoxious, and insidious.

The old wartime clique of "secret Americans" showed amazing endurance in the 1950s and beyond. These retired officers never abandoned their quest to awaken America to the dangers at home and abroad. In retirement, Fellers, Ralph Smith, Truman Smith, Stratemeyer, Wedemeyer, Willoughby, Wood, and others not only maintained their close personal relationships but remained politically active as a group. They provided legitimacy to right-wing intellectual thought and politics, thereby contributing publicly to the anti-Communist paranoia of the period and privately to the perpetuation of political anti-Semitism.

To the old civilian members of their circle such as Lindbergh, Colonel McCormick, and Frank Mason were added controversial conservative publicists like John Flynn. While still working through the right wing of the Republican Party, where Fellers served as assistant to the national chairman, at times they considered forming a new party. They also developed their own "right-wing organization" called For America to fight the likes of New Dealers, Communists, and internationalists.[71]

At other times, they associated with an assortment of right-wing organizations, individuals, and publications. Truman Smith supported Joseph McCarthy; Willoughby tried to convince the John Birch Society to publish a new edition of his *MacArthur*. Wedemeyer circulated an edition of the *Williams Intelligence Summary* that read like the anti-Semitic diatribes of Secret Agent B-1 after World War I. It portrayed Zionism as a Communist movement, described the controlling power of international Jewish bankers (Kuhn, Loeb; Schiff; and so forth), and even intimated that Dean Acheson and Alger Hiss were Jews.[72]

Among the most extreme activists was retired Marine Corps general Pedro del Valle, who founded Defenders of the American Constitution to protect "Christ and country" against treason. A close Beaty collaborator and confidant, the Catholic del Valle believed that Christians had an instinctive distrust of Jews and that no Jew could ever be a "good American" because America was inherently a Christian civilization.

Initially, del Valle tried to work within the Republican Party, but then he became convinced that both major political parties were secretly manipulated by an "invisible government" of international Jewish bankers. A Jewish oligarchy had basically run the country for almost half a century, while their fellow conspirators did likewise in Russia and now the UN. Del Valle uncovered their influence in Eisenhower's policies, in the NAACP and the civil rights movement, in Supreme Court decisions on desegregation and race mixing, and in the Federal Reserve system. They had maneuvered Truman into prolonging the war with Japan (unnecessarily killing tens of thousands of American boys) and dropping the atomic bomb just so Russia could move into China.

Del Valle provided Beaty with a list of current and retired American generals who would be sympathetic to their cause. But he preferred that Beaty do the recruiting because he himself had supposedly been unjustly smeared by the Anti-Defamation League as a dangerous anti-Semitic "crack-pot." As late as 1961, del Valle still enlightened others about the power of the Rothschilds and the "significance" of *The Protocols of the Elders of Zion*.[73]

Truman Smith, Willoughby, and Wood also associated with the National Economic Council, whose president, Merwin K. Hart, waged a relentless battle against Jews and the Anti-Defamation League. Willoughby served as a director while Wood provided financial support.

In his council's newsletters, Hart singled out the Jews as a primary cause of the country's current "plight." While conceding that a "multitude of useful citizens" were Jews, Hart believed that most had betrayed a country that had given them so much. These "alien-minded" Jews with "completely un-American" ideas and goals were a "mighty force in this land." Through "deceit," "trickery," and intimidation, they hid their actual numbers and power from other Americans, while their numbers swelled by millions through decades of massive legal and illegal immigration. They secretly undermined any congressmen who refused to "do their bidding"; Burton Wheeler, the restrictionist senator from Montana, and others were defeated by a "stealthy campaign" orchestrated from the apartment of a prominent New York Jew.[74]

Working closely with Communists, left-wing Jews had, Hart argued passionately, a "dominating part" in forming "vital" policies. They threatened the "complete destruction" of America's constitutional government and involved the country in wars. He held them "largely responsible" for fulfillment of such horrendous Communist goals as Supreme Court decisions on desegregation and congressional civil rights legislation. General Wood considered Hart's efforts in exposing and counteracting such trends "among the best" work of his council: "I admire you for your courage in speaking out on the Jewish question, in fighting the immigration battle, and in denouncing the present Supreme Court."[75]

Hart argued further that Jewish power and Communist collaboration had forced the United States to make the "most tragic mistake" in its history by partitioning Palestine. That decision cost America oil, alienated its natural Arab allies, and handed the Middle East to the Soviets.

The Middle East was a perennial sore point within this military-civilian circle. Stratemeyer could conceive of nothing worse than turning Arab allies into enemies. Returning from Jerusalem, retired general Connor told Moseley of the great pity he felt for the "dreadful plight" of displaced Arabs; by supporting Israel, the United States had destroyed Arab friendship. The Jews, Connor stated, were doing to the Arabs exactly what Hitler had done to them.[76]

This comparison between Zionists and Nazis also surfaced in *Will the Middle East Go West?* by Freda Utley, another member of this circle. Utley thought that American policy must no longer be decided by Jewish influence on elections but by the need to block Communist expansion through more evenhanded treatment of Arabs. The Arabs should not be forced to pay for the European persecution of the Jews, especially since "Israel's exaggerated pretensions . . . recall Nazi claims to 'Aryan' superiority." Utley wrote:

> I do not here mean to imply that Israel has perpetrated any such great crimes against humanity as Hitler. There is, nevertheless, a basic similarity in kind, although not in degree, between her treatment of the Arabs and the Nazi attitude toward the Jews. In both cases the conception of themselves as a "master race" or "chosen people" has led to the perpetration of injustices and crimes against "inferior" races.[77]

Israel, Utley wrote, is not a democracy. With "oppressive and discriminatory laws similar to those of the Nazis," Israel is more "completely based on a racial myth" than any state in history. Moreover, backed by the "massive supernational organization" of Zionism, it is a menace to its Arab neighbors. "Like Japan and Germany of yesterday, [Israel] proclaims her need for more *Lebensraum* to accommodate" world Jewry.[78]

In this book, read and recommended by Fellers, Wedemeyer, and Wood, Utley retained a veneer of scholarly detachment. Her invidious comparisons failed to disclose the depth of her animosity toward what she called the "Nazi-like Israelis and Zionists." She found Jewish behavior in general "egregiously bad"; noisy, inconsiderate, and clannish, these "chosen people" felt the right to disregard all other people. Utley, ironically herself a naturalized citizen, complained that Jews lacked deep roots in America; even after several generations, they retained their foreignness and "linguistic peculiarities." Their loyalty was suspect; moreover, since they usually acted in concert, could it be "pure coincidence" that so many atomic spies were Jews?[79]

The counterpart to criticism of Israel was sympathy for the plight of postwar Germany. These retired officers had much to say about the supposed lingering damage of Morgenthau's policies and little, if anything, about the suffering and extermination of Europe's Jews at the hands of the Nazis. In certain important relevant contexts, they never even mentioned the Holocaust.

When Truman Smith returned to Germany, he remarked how the "absence" of Jews had dramatically changed the atmosphere of the country from what he had known as attaché in the interwar era. Referring only to the "exodus" and "disappearance" of German Jews, Smith noted the great loss for German cultural life but pointed out that financially and economically the country still thrived without them. Of greater consequence, German politics was far more tranquil than during the chaos of Weimar. Smith attributed the tumultuous and hostile party politics of the 1920s to the "ever 'fermenting' Jew." The Jews were "always agitating some special radical cause or other" and took the lead in "all political melees." As a result of their disappearance, contemporary Germany was dull but stable.[80]

When sincere admiration for German culture merged with Cold War geopolitics, the restoration of German "pre-war power" appeared imperative. Smith and Wedemeyer reestablished their relationships with German officers they had known before the war. Most prominent among these was General Hans Speidel, NATO ground forces commander, who had taught at the Kriegsakademie when Wedemeyer was a student. The Americans often lamented the disappearance of the old military spirit among German youth and "deplored" the destruction of Germany during the war. As a result, the American soldier now had to replace the German in defending civilized Europe from "Asiatic barbarism."[81]

Willoughby envisaged a restored Germany that included all of its lost Eastern territories and the repatriation of the millions of German expellees. Only then could Germany regain its place as the historic buffer zone against the threat to Western civilization from "Mongoloid-Panslavism." But anti-German groups impeded this goal by using the mass media to harp on the Nazi past, while neglecting the accomplishments of the new Germany. They needed to be counteracted by publications, films, and organizations sympathetic to Germany.[82]

Several members of the clique, including Wedemeyer, sent "good wishes and apologies" to Admiral Karl Dönitz upon his completion of the "illegal" ten-year prison sentence received at the Nuremberg Trials. Willoughby also told the press director of the Krupp industries that he had opposed the trial of Krupp on "moral" grounds and that he and MacArthur had resisted the war-crimes trials in Japan. Willoughby described Krupp and others as "martyrs." He intended to publish an article aimed at creating a "new tolerant" attitude toward Krupp so as to eliminate this divisive point in the Western alliance.[83]

Some of those Germans with whom Willoughby maintained a political relationship had highly dubious pasts. One of them was a Sudeten German, Dr. Walter Becher, who as a Nazi Party editor in occupied Czechoslovakia had attacked "Jewish cultural warts," "fat Jewesses," "Ghetto hams," and "Jewish cultural destruction." After World War II, Becher belonged to various neo-Nazi parties and groups; he organized the Witiko-Bund, a racist, neoromantic movement of expelled Sudeten Germans, many of whom were unrepentant Nazis. A spokesman for millions of German refugees and expellees from the East, Becher won election to the Bavarian legislature. In the early 1950s, he set up a very effective lobby in Washington, where his anti-Communist crusade found a sympathetic ear among right-wing senators and congressman; he then used this Washington success to advance his political career in Germany.[84]

One of Becher's close confidants, George Brada, told Willoughby that Americans were defenseless against communism because they still saw it as "some abstract evil." In reality, it was a conspiracy of a specific "Asiatic race, internationally dispersed among all nations."

Brada explained this "back-bone" of international communism with exactly the same ideas and terminology used by Nazi racist ideologues. They were a parasitic "dark race" incapable of the "creative thinking" inherent in "White Men." Their "deceit," "slyness," and "great energy" nonetheless permitted them to "infiltrate," and then dominate societies according to a predetermined plan. While manifesting themselves in diverse forms—rich businessmen as well as Communists—they were united in common cause by the "deep unwritten instinct of their race." Through "intrigue," they mobilized the "abnormal" and "subnormal" elements in society against its unsuspecting citizens.[85]

America must act now, Brada warned, to protect itself against "alien domination." So long as the "Anglo-Saxon" permits this "Asiatic race" to exist within its land, America will be "menaced" by the dual threat of either Communist subversion or racial bastardization ("half-Asiatic") of its leadership through intermarriage. America must act like Perón in Argentina: ban the Communist press, including the *New York Times*, and win back the working classes through "National Socialism." The "ultimate aim" must be, Brada proclaimed,

> *the definitive removal of all members of the Communist race from the public life* and from the country. They have an inborn inferior slyness. You are not going to change the Asiatic character. . . . [T]heir inborn instinct of conspiracy can overthrow every American President in the future and enslave the future generations again. They must be removed once and for ever from the public life and the country. Do not act superficially. This is a serious matter of death or life.[86]

Brada left no doubt that he meant Jewish Communists. They were so insidious, he informed Willoughby and Senator McCarran, that they had taken over Radio Free Europe.

Rather than disassociating himself from such racist extremism, Willoughby maintained contact with the Becher-Brada circle for the next twenty years. Perhaps this is not surprising, since Willoughby himself had referred to "the Jewish Conspirators" and had also traced subversion in America to those of Eastern European and Russian "ancestry," emphasizing their "racial affinity for Communism."[87]

Willoughby attended conferences of expellee groups in Germany into the 1960s. Over these years, Becher spent weeks touring the United States, courting high State Department officials as well as influential senators, congressmen, and journalists. How many of these Americans were aware of the racist ideology of this group is not known. But after one trip, Brada told Willoughby that "every second word" from the American politicians with whom Becher spoke dealt with the Jews and that Americans were finally realizing the real source of the Communist threat. He added that racial segregation South African style was America's only hope, because distinctive races cannot survive together.

The political capital accruing from Becher's American liaisons facilitated his rise at home. By the late 1960s, Becher had won a seat in the Bundestag as a member of the Christian Socialist Union Party and went on to serve on the foreign-relations committee.[88]

The Becher circle pinned its hopes for international recognition on the Nixon administration, which would also solidify collaboration between the German and American conservative movements. After three White House visits in March 1969, Becher and Brada played host to several administration officials in Austria and Bonn over the next two years. But their desired international conservative alliance never materialized.[89]

Despite the decades-long preoccupation with the Jewish question, the coterie of retired officers reacted indignantly to the slightest insinuation of their anti-Semitism. They habitually prefaced critical remarks about Jews with defensive statements about their close Jewish friends, who, in fact, thought as they did. Indeed, over the decades relationships did exist among certain officers and several conservative public figures of Jewish heritage. Wedemeyer and other retired officers worked closely and occasionally socialized with Alfred Kohlberg, the central figure in the anti–Communist China lobby. And some older members of the clique had the highest regard for the right-wing journalists Isaac Don Levine and George Sokolsky, whose works they read and supported.

Bound together by deep-seated American nationalism, paranoid anticommunism, and usually anti-Zionism, these officers and conservative Jews displayed extraordinary unanimity on most political issues. They believed the New Deal had undermined America at home, while Roosevelt's foreign policy had betrayed the country's interest abroad. Kohlberg proved as susceptible to conspiracy theories about Communist and liberal subversion as had MID since 1918. They all suspected anyone lacking a longstanding reputation for 100 percent Americanism and anticommunism.[90]

Still, the Jewish question remained a chronic complication in otherwise harmonious and mutually supportive affiliations. Perhaps most ironic was the case of Isaac Don Levine, whose publication *Plain Talk* articulated so well the views of these right-wing circles. Unknown to Levine, important progenitors of his political and ideological circle had earlier targeted him as the very type of subversive he now condemned and warned America about.

For several years after World War I, MID, Naval Intelligence, and the State Department had kept the "dangerous" Levine under "constant investigation." Secret files emphasized the Russian Jewish origin of this naturalized citizen, pointing out his "pronounced Jewish nose" and depicting his articles as "typical bolshevik propaganda." MID urged cancellation of his passport and the blocking of his readmission to the United States. Basically, MID regarded Levine as an unscrupulous Jew of the international type so much in evidence in all questionable dealings in Europe today. He is the type that will make great pogroms occur in Russia and possibly in Germany in the years to come.[91]

It is doubtful whether Levine and other right-wing Jews ever fully grasped the depth and persistence of general anti-Semitic feelings within the circle of retired officers and their allies. Even these conservative Jews were mistrusted by some who spurned their cooperation. Del Valle waged a private campaign to keep Kohlberg out merely because he was, as a Jew, an inherent enemy of America no matter what he said or did.[92]

Levine and Sokolsky vigorously contested those manifestations of anti-Semitism that occasionally surfaced. Levine quickly challenged Utley's loose statements about Germans, Jews, and Nazis. Sokolsky tried to eliminate anti-Semites from the right-wing American Jewish League Against Communism. Within officer circles, that organization represented loyal American Jews who put "their country's interest above every other." It also provided a convenient defense against charges of anti-Semitism, and certain officers flaunted their affiliation with the league as proof of their toleration. Yet, when attending league functions, Sokolsky was "shocked" to discover "not only very few Jews" but also participants who were "publicly anti-Semitic."[93]

Kohlberg, on the other hand, bent over backward to accommodate anti-Semites if they had sound conservative credentials, while extending no similar understanding to nonconservative Jews. Jewish leaders had, Kohlberg said, "led the Jews of Europe from 19th Century Conservative Liberalism to the gas chambers and the ghetto of Israel."

Kohlberg did not assail Beaty's extreme anti-Semitism in *Iron Curtain over America*. He simply criticized Beaty's "inaccuracies and false generalizations" regarding Jews and communism. This was "not an attack on Mr. Beaty," who had otherwise written "a good and useful" book about Communist infiltration of the American government. Kohlberg seriously considered publishing a scholarly version of the book excluding the sections on Jews.[94]

Even Kohlberg, however, could not stomach the vicious anti-Semitism that suddenly filled the pages of *American Mercury* throughout 1959. Since 1945, Kohlberg had been closely affiliated with the magazine, for which he collected material and published articles. Like the retired conservative officers, he enthusiastically encouraged its extreme rightist editorial policy, fully supporting its propagation of not only Communist but liberal conspiracy theories. Then, in 1959, the magazine launched a barrage of exposes linking communism and liberalism to alleged Jewish conspiracies.[95]

Since the late nineteenth century, the magazine claimed, a "world wide betrayal" on the part of Zionists and powerful international Jewish bankers (behind the guise of liberalism, communism, and internationalism) had pursued a "master plan for world domination." Through an "unseen empire" of political and economic power, the Rothschilds, Warburgs, Schiffs, and the like exercised control over major nations, including the United States, where Baruch, Brandeis, and Frankfurter played major conspiratorial roles. They launched the Russian Revolution, forced America "foolishly" into war in 1917, and stole Palestine.

Insidious "termites of the cross" and "enemies of Jesus," these Zionist-Communist conspirators were out to destroy Christianity. Massive immigration, legally and illegally, by Khazar Jews from Eastern Europe spearheaded "large scale Communist exploitation of the United States." Was anyone "naive enough to believe ... that Jews who are American citizens would not work tirelessly for the USSR to destroy their own country?"[96]

"In fairness to the Germans," *American Mercury* also engaged in Holocaust denial, claiming that although the Nazis did kill Jews, they never exterminated millions in gas chambers. Zionism, however, did originate with a "fantastic creed of violence ... conceived, carried out, and preserved intact ... to this very day." As recorded in the Book of Deuteronomy, Jews were a "master race" out to "exterminate other peoples ... particularly the Gentiles." Here were the "seeds of a racial totalitarianism" surpassing the "savage chauvinism of the Japanese" and Hitler's racial doctrines.[97]

To substantiate these claims, the magazine's writers not only cited Beaty's *Iron Curtain over America* but conjured up the works of the infamous Jew-baiting MID informant Boris Brasol, Ford's *International Jew,* and even the Nazi-inspiring *Foundations of the Nineteenth Century.* When the magazine came under attack for its anti-Semitism, it clarified that it never intended to include "loyal American Jews," only the Communist-Zionists seeking "world conquest."[98]

The *American Mercury* episode was a watershed. By the late 1950s, this brazen expression of paranoid anti-Semitism was clearly out of step with much of mainstream conservatism. Whatever individuals might say privately, the time had passed when such beliefs could be publicly displayed with impunity. The series met with broad and harsh condemnation from even previously sympathetic quarters. Kohlberg abruptly cut all ties with *American Mercury.* William F. Buckley Jr., representing a younger generation of conservatives at the *National Review,* called it "reprehensible and irresponsible" and dropped anyone affiliated with the *American Mercury.*[99]

Whether things had changed much among the old guard is another question. Willoughby, the magazine's military editor and a frequent contributor, was reluctant to break with *American Mercury.* When Buckley pressured him to resign, Willoughby chastised the "insolent youngsters" at the *National Review* for their "stupid intolerance." As his magazine affiliation hurt his reputation, Willoughby became defensive. He told the American Jewish Committee that despite its "frictional situation" with the *American Mercury,* he needed this journalistic outlet for his campaign to save America. He protested that, rather than an anti-Semite, he was a "good friend" of Israel.[100]

Impressed by Israeli troops during the Suez Crisis of 1956, Willoughby had indeed become a champion of the Jewish state in articles and congressional hearings. From a geopolitical perspective, he assessed Israel and Turkey as the only viable military bulwark against Russian penetration of the Middle East. He now buttressed this argument with the "moral" justification that the Diaspora Jews had a "legitimate" claim to Palestine.[101]

Willoughby eventually disassociated himself from *American Mercury,* and in 1963, sought financial support from the American Jewish Committee for his *Foreign Intelligence Digest.* When some of his loyal anti-Semitic readers accused him of betrayal, he charged them with prejudice against Jews.

Yet this was the same retired officer who a few years earlier had asserted the "communist leadership is Jewish." As late as 1957, Willoughby had declared certain Jewish speakers "unsuitable" for a conservative club. Their "names are not Anglo-Saxon; they rather suggest the mass migrations from Central and Eastern Europe, Poland and Russia, that have deluged this unfortunate country in the last decades." To him, New York especially was a "cesspool of international subversion," where some would "sell their grandmother's gold teeth."[102]

For at least ten years thereafter, Willoughby maintained a working relationship with the anti-Semitic Becher-Brada circle. They considered him their most treasured political contact in America. And Willoughby continued to warn other Germans that New York—"40% Jewish"—remained "a center of anti-German activity." The "crypto-communist" *New York Times* and its Jewish readership were, he complained, still unnecessarily keeping the Hitler era "alive artificially."[103]

Throughout the 1950s, Willoughby's name and reputation commanded respect within the army, Congress, and the general public. Colonel Frederick D. Sharp, G-2 executive officer, "so valued" Willoughby's "vast experience and background" that he called upon his assistance with a major reorganization of Military Intelligence. In 1955, Chief of Staff General Maxwell D. Taylor personally wrote Willoughby, "a distinguished alumnus of the Army," to enlist his help "in interpreting the Army to the American people." Through his articles in *American Mercury Magazine* and his own *Foreign Intelligence Digest*, Willoughby definitely influenced conservative thought and politics. As late as 1958, Willoughby articulated his racial geopolitical theory of the Cold War before the Senate Foreign Relations Committee.[104]

As a whole, the members of the coterie to which Willoughby belonged used the prestige of the officer corps to bolster the cause of paranoid anti-communism. They were the heroes of the triumphant war against Nazi totalitarianism now warning against the immediate threat of Soviet totalitarianism. Since many of these retired officers had served in MID, their presumed expertise and experience in secret matters only enhanced their importance and credibility.

Like MID officers and attachés after World War I, these retired officers helped to create and sustain a Red Scare atmosphere of fear and suspicion in which intolerance and prejudice thrive. Although the nature and intensity of anti-Semitism varied among these individual retired officers, most related Jews to one or more important political or geopolitical questions facing America. In doing so, they helped perpetuate prejudice against Jews in society generally. Perhaps more important, they ensured that suspicions about Jewish interests and influence would remain issues in American foreign and domestic politics as well as in public discourse.

The persistence or absence of similar attitudes among active duty officers after the older generation retired around 1950 is difficult to determine. By World War II there was already more diversity of opinion about Jews among officers than previously. And it appears that the pattern of continuity and change characteristic of officer corps thinking after that war continued over the next several decades. The disappearance of the 1920s and 1930s variety of racial theory from postwar officer thinking and army educational institutions undoubtedly eliminated political biology as a framework for geopolitical assessments. On the other hand, during the Korean War and well into the Vietnam era, certain anti-Semitic attitudes, like widespread racism toward nonwhites, could still be found among many officers. Similarly, suspicions about the connection between Jews and communism probably lingered for a long time. Yet over that same Cold War period, the army gradually came to regard Israel as a bulwark against the spread of communism in the Middle East.

All indications are that over time, the changes in attitudes within the officer corps toward Jews were substantial. But the nature, extent, and pace of such progress will never be adequately understood until the army files and private papers for postwar generations of officers become available for examination. What can be established beyond doubt, however, is that into the late 1970s and beyond, certain retired officers pursued their crusade to save America from a Jewish threat.

Epilogue

It was an unusually cold November 1976 when Frank Mason made plans for Wedemeyer to drive him from Leesburg, Virginia, to the Army and Navy Club in Washington. The two men were really looking forward to this luncheon of the Military Order of the World Wars. Over the past twenty years, the aging coterie of "true Americans" to which they belonged had relished every opportunity to socialize with each other and confer on the country's problems.

Historical recollections and contemporary events fueled many fiery discussions at such gatherings. The America they watched evolve over these decades would have been unimaginable when Mason had joined the Army and Navy Club in the 1920s. Then, America had been a society run by the descendants of those Anglo-Saxons who had created the country and its system of government. Passage of the 1924 Immigration Act had been a watershed victory through which officers thought the country's future had been secured against alien subversion and racial degeneracy.[1]

But by the time America celebrated its bicentennial, the social and political preeminence these officers had known in their prime had long been lost. Ever since the New Deal, they had felt themselves increasingly on the defensive, struggling to hold back the powerful tide of socialism and insidious minority influence in America. The current volatile global and domestic situation (a "Frankenstein monster") they attributed to the "jaded mind and sinister soul of FDR and his henchmen." This old guard, in stark contrast, perceived of themselves as in the "selfless traditions of the early Americans." In their old age, they were as convinced of the righteousness of their cause as they had been a half century before. It was still necessary to man the ramparts to defend America's great heritage as a "Christian nation" against the "powerful," secret "forces" undermining it.[2]

Inevitably, the drastic changes the country had been experiencing in their final years of life caused these men much consternation. Particularly during the upheavals of the 1960s, they envisaged a Spenglerian scenario of national decline into anarchy. Old dangers—Communist subversion and Soviet power—were exacerbated by the civil rights movement, race riots, and antiwar activism, as well as by the general vicissitudes of momentous social and cultural transformations.

The coterie of conservative retired officers saw "ominous decay" everywhere. Despite its inherent wealth and strength, America was being sapped by increasing socialization and national bankruptcy. Meanwhile, degenerate hippies, nauseating pornography, and narcotics exemplified a "moral collapse" among the country's youth, reminiscent of the decadence that had caused Rome's fall. Disrespect for authority—in government, churches, and family—drew foreboding comparisons with events preceding the French Revolution. Words like "morality" and "discipline" retained their meaning and value only for "WASPs." And given the Vietnam War's domestic divisiveness, some feared American democracy could not survive a defeat. Naturally, international communism exploited all of this. In its critical hour, the country cried out for a leader with old American ideals and the "guts" to stand up and save civilization from inevitable collapse.[3]

In this turbulent atmosphere, they also began to focus on issues that had captivated the old officer corps in the uncertain aftermath of World War I. As the self-appointed guardians of America's heritage and future, they, like their nativist predecessors, took up the fight against immigration and racial degeneration. There was even an institutional continuity with the past provided by retired captain Trevor's American Coalition, now headed by his son, John B. Trevor Jr. This group was reinforced by the American Committee on Immigration Policies, headed by retired rear admiral Charles S. Stephenson, and later by Conservatives for Immigration Reform, both supported by Wedemeyer.

Initially, the fight was to preserve the 1924 "national origins quota system." After 1960s immigration legislation eliminated those quotas, this alliance of retired officers and conservative civilians concentrated on reversing such reforms. These "true Americans" portrayed immigration as an "invasion" endangering the "future of our children and grandchildren" through escalating "crime, disease, unemployment, overcrowding, racial discord, and welfare abuse." Beneath the surface of a host of actual problems associated with immigration, however, stood the perennial issue of race. As Frank Mason told Trevor Jr.:

> I am a fervent follower of your father's belief that our country's safety and
> future will depend on maintaining to the extent we can the homogeneity of

the American people and avoidance of unnecessary dilution of the strains that made our country great and a world leader.[4]

Since the new immigration laws had for the first time opened up America to all nonwhite people of the globe, the danger appeared far greater than in the 1920s. The immigration fight shifted from the supposedly inferior races of Eastern and Southern Europe to the significantly lower races inhabiting the Third World. The anticipated massive influx of "orientals" under new immigration laws was in itself a danger to the country's "security and well-being." This argument revived the century-old image of the "Yellow Peril," the teeming masses looming across the Pacific waiting to overwhelm the West. To this circle of retired officers and conservative civilians, "no greater calamity could now befall the United States than to have the Pacific slope fill up with a Mongolian population."[5]

Bringing the Third World to America would immeasurably aggravate the existing burdensome and unsolvable racial problem of the country's black population. To a group of "true Americans" believing passionately in the inherent racial inferiority of blacks, the very presence of the descendants of African slaves within the nation caused perpetual embarrassment. When the civil rights movement and urban riots of the 1960s seriously advanced the country toward integrating this marginalized and segregated population into the rest of society, these circles reacted predictably. The arguments once created to deter the assimilation of Eastern and Southern Europeans were now mustered against racial integration. The new "permissiveness" had already resulted in crime, riots, radicalism, and a race war among American troops. Meanwhile, mixing whites and blacks seriously risked racial degeneracy as miscegenation greatly lowered the overall intelligence level of Americans. One heard the familiar refrain—the country's institutions, culture, and entire way of life were at stake.

Among themselves, some of the "true Americans" spoke of "militant blacks" as "our sun-tanned brethren," while circulating stories of huge "Zulu girls" attacking "little white girls" at school. To alert the American public, they resurrected the racial wisdom of Theodore Roosevelt. Archibald A. Roosevelt, the president's son and a good friend of Mason and Wedemeyer, published a collection of his father's statements on the unalterable centrality of "racial differences," the inherent superiority of the white race, and the necessity of preserving "racial purity."

In *Race-Riots-Reds-Crime*, the dead president proclaimed that "ape-like African savages [were] 50 to 100 thousand years behind whites in development" and that the "Negro population grew only under white rule." Here was a Darwinian worldview in which "conquest by inferior barbarian races brings sheer evil," whereas the "displacement of an inferior race [through] armed settlement or conquest by a superior race" represented the progress of mankind.[6]

This was the kind of "truth" an appreciative Wedemeyer sought to popularize about the "race problem." He and his cohorts soon discovered further confirmation of their racial dogma in Dr. William Shockley's controversial claims that the inborn and immutable intelligence of blacks was substantially inferior to that of whites. Wedemeyer, Mason, and others quickly seized upon Shockley's "scientific genetic truths" as proof of what they had always known. They did what they could to support Shockley's research and promote his ideas.[7]

Meanwhile, retired general Edward Almond continued his decades-long struggle against desegregation and the "naive" belief that "race is only skin deep." He urged public figures not to forget that there was a "persistent gap between negroes and whites in mental test performances" and that the "genetic basis for those differences" in "native abilities" is as strong as any "scientific case can be made."[8]

This concern about African-Americans and Asians had not supplanted the perennial Jewish question but merely transformed its dimensions. Significant responsibility for the racial integration threatening American society and the white gene pool was laid at the feet of Jews. Supposedly, Jews had facilitated the rise of blacks to "infamous heights" in America. And Jewish influence in American society and government generally was reaching the stage of manipulation and control.[9]

Richard Nixon's 1968 presidential victory temporarily relieved such worries. Initially, some members of the Wedemeyer-Mason circle believed American Jews had lost their "strong leverage on the White House" and the country was about to embark on a "balanced" (i.e., more pro-Arab) Middle Eastern course. Jewish attempts to pressure the Nixon administration on Israel would cause an American backlash; Jewish leaders were supposedly troubled by the renewed "prospect of anti-Semitism." Some of the "true Americans" interpreted this as proof that a "persecution complex" was a "congenital inheritance" of Jews.[10]

But the great hope Nixon originally symbolized soon dissipated, as his policies at home and abroad deviated from the expected staunch conservatism. Rather than resisting steadfastly Soviet and Chinese power, as well as domestic movements for change, Nixon sought accommodation; he, too, appeared to sell out. The gradual disillusionment felt by these "true Americans" turned to suspicion as Henry Kissinger rose to prominence in the administration and on the world scene.

Certain the real policies were implemented behind the scenes, some in the Wedemeyer-Mason circle subscribed to the line preached by the right-wing *Washington Observer Newsletter*, which they circulated among themselves. Replete with titles like "Kosher Diplomacy," this newsletter carried highly evocative stories of "mysterious international doings" involving Kissinger's shuttle diplomacy: Through secret midnight flights to London, Kissinger conferred with "Victor Louis . . . the mysterious Jew who holds a position in Russia roughly equivalent to the position Kissinger has in the U.S."[11]

By the early 1970s, some of the "true Americans" suspected that "international Jewry" was part of a far broader worldwide intrigue. These ideas received their fullest articulation in *None Dare Call It Conspiracy*, in which Gary Allen linked the centers of world communism with the centers of international capitalism, and the Bolshevik Revolution with the White House. Allen modified Brasol's post–World War I theory of an international Jewish conspiracy by excluding average Jews from the century-long machinations of wealthy Jewish and Anglo-Saxon bankers. Besides the newly added Rockefellers and Morgans, however, most prominent conspirators remained essentially the same as in earlier versions (and basically Jewish).

In Allen's view, the Rothschild, Kuhn-Loeb, Schiff, and Warburg concerns used their international financial power to control the economies and governmental policies of major countries. In pursuit of their insidious plans, they created the Federal Reserve system, intentionally started World War I, and later manipulated America into an unnecessary war with Germany in 1941; after financing Lenin and Trotsky, they controlled world communism; they even financed Hitler. In essence, they sought to control all sides.

Presently, they also worked through the United Nations and the U.S. Council on Foreign Relations, to which "Henry Kissinger, Nixon's chief foreign policy adviser" belonged. Secretly dominating the mass print and electronic media, as well as the Democratic and Republican parties, they kept the public in the dark. The ultimate goal was "One World Socialism" in the hands of these power-hungry international financial families.[12]

After a thorough reading of *None Dare Call It Conspiracy*, Wedemeyer acknowledged his agreement with many of its ideas. Years later, he still complained that the "parasitic" Warburg and "people of his ilk" undermined the Constitution and U.S. interests. Despite Allen's claim this was not a "Jewish plot," the pervasiveness of rich Jews throughout the book ensured that at least for some readers, the Jewish angle retained its significance. For Wedemeyer's "good friend" and confidant, William LaVarre, the logical associations remained as clear as ever: the Rothschilds, Wall Street, Zionists, and international Jewry.[13]

Grand conspiracy theories aside, Wedemeyer believed that Jews increasingly exercised tremendous influence in the White House and halls of Congress. With Kissinger still dominating the scene, they worried that current foreign policy, especially regarding Israel, ran contrary to America's real interests. Who would ever have believed, exclaimed Wedemeyer, that a "German Jew" could acquire such power that leaders from Congress to the Middle East and China would kneel before him?[14]

The grumbling of aging retired officers was one thing. But when the chairman of the Joint Chiefs of Staff invoked age-old anti-Semitic clichés in criticizing Jewish influence in the United States, his remarks caused a mini-scandal for the Ford administration. Responding to questions following a lecture at Duke Law School on October 10, 1974, General George S. Brown complained that the power of the Israeli lobby was "so strong you wouldn't believe it." Had he restricted his comments to Jewish-American and Israeli political pressure on Congress, they probably would have passed without much notice. What he said thereafter, however, revealed such biased assumptions about Jews, it sent shock waves across the country. The Israelis, Brown stated, say:

> "Don't worry about the Congress. We'll take care of the Congress." Now this is somebody from another country, but they can do it. They own, you know, the banks in this country, the newspapers, you just look at where the Jewish money is in this country.[15]

Once again, an important public figure had conjured up deeply rooted suspicions about international Jewish solidarity, doubtful loyalty to America, hidden financial power, and media control. Brown speculated further that if Americans really suffered in a future oil crisis, they might finally "get tough-minded enough to set down the Jewish influence in this country and break that lobby."

Reactions ranged from outrage to bewilderment. Congressmen and Jewish organizations chastised the JCS chairman's "appalling ignorance" and the "prejudice and malice" of his "contemptible" comments. For many

American Jews, the incident reawakened the anxiety about latent anti-Semitism lurking behind the veil of acceptance and government protection. To them, the general's resignation appeared certain.[16]

Others, Jews and non-Jews alike, seemed perplexed that such statements could emanate from the country's top officer. Many had assumed that anti-Semitic expressions by public figures belonged to an earlier age of bigotry and intolerance that was now dead and buried. Such opinion ran counter to the image many Americans had of their country and its government as the embodiment of democratic and humanitarian ideals. And despite the damage done to the reputation and prestige of the army as a result of Vietnam and antiwar movements, many believed the army still represented those ideals. Was not this the institution that had defeated Nazism, manned the ramparts against communism around the globe, and supported Israel as its dependable ally in the Middle East? Moreover, fellow officers attested there had never been the slightest hint of anti-Semitism in this highly regarded officer; he had, in fact, enthusiastically orchestrated the U.S. arms airlift to Israel during the Yom Kippur War. The public they sought to reassure remained unaware of the earlier history of pervasive anti-Semitism in the officer corps.[17]

With demands spreading for investigations and Brown's dismissal, Ford personally reprimanded the general in the Oval Office. Brown publicly apologized for his "unfortunate" and "unfounded" remarks, stating they did not reflect his real convictions. After a month of controversy, the Senate Armed Services Committee refused to hold hearings on Brown and the flap suddenly died a quiet death. A country torn by domestic strife, the interminable Vietnam War, a volatile Middle East, and sweeping repercussions from Watergate was not anxious to risk yet another political scourging.[18]

Although Brown survived relatively unscathed, some of the "true Americans" interpreted the very controversy itself as further evidence of Jewish power. Rumors spread among Wedemeyer's friends that American soldiers and their German allies were furious over the Brown reprimand. General Brown had performed a patriotic act by stating a "truth" that others should have revealed to Americans long ago—Zionists really controlled Congress.[19]

Wedemeyer and Mason were so convinced of this that they kept a check on which senators had "sold out" to the pro-Israel lobby. They also tried to discover the "real" number of Jews and blacks in the United States. In words sounding very similar to General Brown's original statement, an exasperated Mason told Wedemeyer that Jewish "penetration" was "incredible" in American society, economics, and politics. Jews certainly sowed "corruption" on Capitol Hill.[20] Wedemeyer believed that the president and public were captives of a Jewish-controlled mass media, which insidiously manipulated the minds of Americans and actually determined the policies of their government. Only some truly drastic political action could break this perilous grip on the country. Wedemeyer concluded that it was imperative to ship the Jews back to Russia and blacks back to Africa.[21]

Most dangerous of all was Kissinger, whose foreign policy sacrificed U.S. security while advancing Soviet and Red Chinese aims. In July 1975, Wedemeyer and Mason circulated the accusations of Frank Capell, author of *Henry Kissinger—Soviet Agent*, that the secretary had been recruited by the KGB while an intelligence officer in Germany after the war. The charge made perfect sense to old G-2 hand Ivan Yeaton, a retired colonel and active member of this coterie.

Yeaton represented fifty years of continuity in the attitudes, thoughts, and activities of older intelligence officers. Starting his anti-Communist crusade as a novice G-2 in Siberia in 1919, Yeaton participated in the domestic surveillance of radicals in the 1920s and 1930s. An ardent New Deal opponent, he truly believed there were subversive forces in the Roosevelt administration that advanced Soviet interests. These suspicions were confirmed in his mind while he served as military attaché to Moscow in 1939–1941. In Washington during World War II, Yeaton was involved in G-2's efforts to counteract Zionist attempts at opening Palestine to Jewish refugees.

Having fought subversive specters all his life, in his old age Yeaton never displayed the slightest reservation in believing Kissinger might very well be a KGB operative. After all, as a "German Jew" Kissinger was a likely target, Yeaton argued, since the Soviets had long realized that Jews and homosexuals were most susceptible to recruitment or blackmail. If not under Soviet control, Kissinger must then surely be a sincere Socialist.[22]

Into the late 1970s, this shrinking coterie of aging men continued their pessimistic fuming about Jewish power and America's future. "Wandering Jews" (Javits, Kissinger, Ribicoff), together with the manipulated media, kept America subservient to Israel and vulnerable to Communist expansion. The penetration of the government by the "Chosen People" proceeded at a steady pace, even reaching into the military itself. There was trepidation that the sacred ground of West Point might be violated and the army's future compromised if a Jewish general were appointed superintendent of the military academy.[23]

Occasionally, they would backslide into the fantastic notions of earlier generations. Even the same argument MID had invoked after World War I to establish the authenticity of *The Protocols of the Elders of Zion* reappeared. It was suggested that recent events (particularly Israel's domination of U.S. policy) and the goals of the country's leading newspapers paralleled the scheme embodied in the *Protocols*. How many of this vanishing breed could still attach any credibility to the *Protocols* will never be known. Perhaps such comments were merely intended (and taken) as historical allusions interjected in frustration for dramatic effect.[24]

Nonetheless, the underlying assumptions of international Jewish collaboration and insidious power were apparently sincerely held. Indeed, this coterie of retired officers continued to receive correspondences from LaVarre on which were printed the words of Benjamin Disraeli:

> So you see, my dear Coningsby, the world is governed by different personages from what is imagined by those who are not behind the scenes.

It is tempting to dismiss the ravings of these men as the residue of a sadly benighted period that one might be relieved to think had expired years before. But to assume this would be a false comfort. That well-educated officers with such distinguished careers would go to their graves believing in long-refuted anti-Semitic ideas is in itself telling. It demonstrates how susceptible even educated elites with worldwide experiences and distinguished service in high levels of responsibility can be to the most incredible and crude forms of anti-Semitism normally associated only with the fringes of society. Far from the genteel cultural and social prejudice usually associated with American elites, this brand of anti-Semitism was often of the racist variety. This component of the officers' worldview had theoretical roots, intellectual progenitors, and characteristics similar to the teachings of racial ideologues and extremists. Contrary to current expert opinion, American racial anti-Semitism endured long after it had supposedly died out when the progressive New Deal era replaced the nativist 1920s.

Even after the horrors of World War II and the Holocaust, some of the old guard, who themselves had just waged war against Nazi Germany, held firmly to such racist beliefs; other officers retained more general perceptions of presumed problematic Jewish characteristics, behavior, and influence. The Nazis had used the charges of "Jewish-Bolshevism" to justify their repressive measures; presumably this might have been enough to discredit the old charge. Nonetheless, a year after the Nazi defeat, top-ranking intelligence officers felt the need to commission a study examining the "relationship between Jews and Communism." Although there is some consolation in the fact that the report ultimately questioned such close linkage, the continued surveillance of Jews, like the analyses on Jewish immigration to the United States and Palestine, indicated that such biased political perspectives continued to affect decisionmaking on important international and domestic issues. Once such notions are entrenched in individuals and institutional cultures, they prove to be enduring and very difficult to alter or eradicate, even in the face of new evidence or revelations of the horrendous human consequences of such ideas.

This significant and consequential dimension of the history of the U.S. Army during the first half of this century has, for the most part, been neglected. Yet without understanding the thoughts and biases underlying the attitudes and decisions of such officers regarding racism generally and the Jewish question in particular, we cannot have an accurate, complete, and balanced picture of this important governmental institution. This aspect of the army's history certainly clarifies the long-disputed and previously clouded response of the U.S. military to the Holocaust. For it is now clearly established that anti-Semitism was a significant factor in the army's decisions and actions regarding relief and rescue.

Moreover, we now know that the Nazi era was not the first time the U.S. Army had to deal with the question of Jewish persecutions, pogroms, refugees, and immigration. After World War I, officers personally observed such problems across Europe. Officers kept the top military and political leadership in Washington fully informed, though they often tried to downplay or deny pogroms. But even when they acknowledged pogroms and, in fact, actually anticipated the massive slaughter of Jews following an expected anti-Bolshevik reaction in Russia, the army did not favor U.S. involvement. While occasionally condemning anti-Semitic violence, the army usually attributed this aggression to a reaction against the characteristics and behavior of the Jews themselves.

Officers and their State Department counterparts after World War I did not justify U.S. inaction on logistical grounds or with arguments over technical feasibility, as would the army in World War II. Diplomatic, economic, or military interference with the new Polish state or with an emerging counterrevolutionary movement in Russia, they argued, would undermine attempts to contain and destroy communism. The army would tolerate pogroms in Poland and a possible slaughter in Russia rather than compromise what senior officers perceived as an important American foreign policy interest. Indeed, officers' beliefs in the Jewish nature of Bolshevism at home as well as abroad further strengthened the case for nonintervention.

It was this Jewish-Communist link, together with eugenic arguments of inherent Jewish racial inferiority, that likewise convinced the army to mount such a vigorous campaign against Jewish immigration to the United States in the 1920s. This campaign coincided with the surveillance of Jews in Europe and America. The army had, in essence, established the fundamental arguments and institutional precedents that would condition its later response to the Nazi persecution of Jews. The continuity in thinking and policy decisions into the Nazi era is equally clear regarding personnel. Many officers who were a part of this institutional culture or participated directly in anti-Jewish activity in the 1920s rose to high-ranking positions in the army during the 1930s, including the two future chiefs of MID, Majors Warner McCabe and Sherman Miles. This generation of intelligence officers played an important part in justifying and sustaining restrictionist immigration policies at a time when Jews were desperately seeking refuge.

Outside of MID, this same generation of officers provided many of the army's decisionmakers after World War II. Generals such as Patton in Europe, Wedemeyer at Plans and Operations, and Gruenther on the General Staff likewise proved instrumental in determining policies concerning the treatment of Holocaust survivors as well as Jewish immigration to America and Palestine. They all had been socialized into military culture at a time when anti-Semitism was not only prevalent and open but considered morally, politically, and even scientifically warranted.

Neglecting this earlier history, defenders of the army's response to the plight of Jews during World War II have recently relied upon technical arguments to explain its inaction. They have strongly rejected either indifference or anti-Semitism within the army as possible motives. The impression created by these historians resembles closely the official line the army used during the war. At that time, the army claimed that it sympathized with the plight of Jews and truly desired to assist with relief and rescue but that logistical obstacles or strategic wartime necessity unfortunately precluded any assistance. In the absence of realistic alternatives, officers argued, the greatest humanitarian action the army could take for the sake of Jews would be to win the war as quickly as possible and not divert resources away from that objective by unfeasible rescue efforts or bombings.

However, that official line, then and now, is an inaccurate rendition of the reality of the army's attitude. Many officers, including those in decisionmaking positions, did not view the persecuted Jews of Europe as a suffering group of people they truly wished to help. Instead, they saw a continuation of the same "Jewish Problem" that the army and America had been dealing with for half a century. It was a perpetual troublesome question interrelated with a whole host of problems and supposed threats the army had confronted for decades. These ranged from racial degeneration and communism to presumed Jewish influence in the American government, especially under Roosevelt. Between World War I and the immediate post–World War II era, the U.S. Army, in attitude and policy, consistently stood against efforts to assist Jews. More often than not, the army actively aligned itself against what it perceived to be a serious Jewish threat to American interests.

After World War II, the persistent "Jewish Problem" became linked to new geopolitical concerns over the containment of Soviet power generally, and especially in the vital area of Middle East oil. And once again, perceptions of these new circumstances were colored by old perspectives and assumptions within the officer corps. Supposedly under Jewish influence, the U.S. government was losing both its access to oil and its anti-Communist Arab allies by supporting Israel. This misguided policy was ensuring Communist domination of the Middle East by driving the Arabs into the Soviet camp while simultaneously facilitating the penetration of Jewish-Communist immigration into Israel. Although army policy toward Israel gradually began to shift in a more sympathetic direction around the time the old guard was retiring, the careers of several prominent retired generals indicate no such change in their views. The postwar attitudes and activities of such officers revealed that racism and anti-Semitism had played a vital role in their thinking all along and had remained unaffected by events.

Not all officers shared the views or intensity of concern and commitment of the extremists within the army. Throughout the first half of the twentieth century, examples can also be found of officers at all levels who were free of anti-Semitism or manifested it in the form of some vague bias. Such officers were more numerous by World War II and after, when more officers were willing to openly oppose anti-Semitism within the corps. However, anti-Semitism continued to be pervasive, influential, and enduring. Even those officers, who, like Eisenhower, cannot be characterized as anti-Semitic, were influenced in more or less subtle ways. Racialist anti-Semitism, planted, nourished, and institutionalized in the officer corps in the early part of the century, in fact became so deeply rooted that it survived decades of momentous historical change, bearing fruit well into the postwar era.

Notes

Abbreviations

ALL American Legion National Headquarters Library, Indianapolis, IN
AJCA American Jewish Committee Archives, New York City
AWCA U.S. Army War College Archives, in MHI
CMH U.S. Army Center for Military History Archives, Washington, DC
DDEL Dwight D. Eisenhower Library, Abilene, KS
DMMA Douglas MacArthur Memorial Archives, Norfolk, VA
DUL Duke University Library, Manuscript Department, Durham, NC
ECMC East Carolina Manuscript Collections, East Carolina University, Greenville, NC
FDRL Franklin D. Roosevelt Library, Hyde Park, NY
GC Gettysburg College, Gettysburg, PA
GRFL Gerald R. Ford Library, Ann Arbor, MI
HHL Herbert Hoover Library, West Branch, IA
HIA Hoover Institution Archives, Stanford, CA
HSTL Harry S. Truman Library, Independence, MO
LBI Leo Baeck Institute, New York City
JWV Jewish War Veterans Papers, in MHI
LC Library of Congress, Washington, DC
MHC Michigan Historical Collections, Bentley Historical Library, University of Michigan, Ann Arbor, MI
MHI U.S. Military History Institute Archives, Carlisle, PA
MID Military Intelligence Division, in NACP
MIDRF MID Regional File, in NACP
NACP U.S. National Archives, College Park, MD
NADC National Archives, Washington, DC
NYHS New York Historical Society, New York City
OMGUS Office of Military Government, United States, in NACP
ONI Office of Naval Intelligence, in NADC
UOL University of Oregon Library, Eugene, OR
USMA U.S. Military Academy, West Point, NY
VHS Virginia Historical Society, Richmond, VA
WRB Records of the War Refugee Board, in FDRL
YV Yad Vashem Central Archives, Jerusalem, Israel

Prologue

1. "Plans for the Protection of New York in Case of Local Disturbances," May 2, 1919, National Archives, College Park, MD (hereafter NACP), RG 165, Military Intelligence Division (hereafter MID), Records of the War Department General and Special Staffs, 10110-920 (538).

2. Ibid.; Colonel K. C. Masteller to intelligence officer New York, May 3, 1919, NACP RG 165, MID 10110-920 (550).

3. NACP, RG 165, MID 10110-920 (538).

4. Inspector C. L. Converse to Captain John B. Trevor, May 2, 1919, NACP RG 165, MID 10110-920 (547).

5. "Trip to Vilna and Warsaw," May 15, 1919, NACP, RG 165, MID 2067-85.

6. Ibid.

7. Colonel William Godson to Major Sherman Miles, February 21, 1921, NACP, RG 165, MID 245-48 (41).

8. Military Intelligence Subject Index, "Jews: Race," March 1918–August 1941, NACP, RG 165, MID.

9. NACP, RG 165, MID 245-1/151.

10. "The Power and Aims of International Jewry," August 1919, MID 245-1, pp. 1–28.

11. General military histories do not indicate the slightest hint of anti-Semitism in the American army. See such standard works as Russell F. Weigley, *History of the United States Army* (New York, 1967) and *Towards an American Army: Military Thought from Washington to Marshall* (Westport, CT, 1962). The same is true of the bibliographical guides to military literature. See Robin Higham, ed., A *Guide to the Sources of United States Military History* (Hamden, CT, 1975); and *Supplement 1* (1981) and *Supplement 2* (1986), which Higham edited with Donald J. Mrozek. Most specialized studies of military intelligence likewise completely neglect this issue. See Bruce W. Bidwell, *History of the Military Intelligence Division, Department of the Army General Staff: 1775–1941* (Washington, DC, 1954); and Joan M. Jensen, *Army Surveillance in America, 1775–1980* (New Haven, 1991) and *Military Intelligence of Civilians in America* (Morristown, NJ, 1975). The two exceptions are Roy Talbert, *Negative Intelligence: The Army and the American Left, 1917–1941* (Jackson, MS, 1991) and Richard D. Challener, ed., *United States Military Intelligence, 1917–1927*, 30 vols. (New York, 1978). However, although both Talbert and Challener identify the existence of anti-Semitism in military intelligence at certain points, they treat it as prejudice expressed in a few specific instances. Neither is aware of the extensive documentation of anti-Semitism in MID or other parts of the army. Not only do they fail to understand the magnitude, persistence, and impact of anti-Semitism, but what they do identify has not worked its way into studies of the American army, anti-Semitism, or the Holocaust.

12. For examples of two excellent studies that argue for the decline of racism, see Robert Singerman, "The Jew as Racial Alien: The Genetic Component of American Anti-Semitism," in David Gerber, ed., *Anti-Semitism in American History*

(Urbana and Chicago, 1986), pp. 103–128; and John Higham, *Send These to Me: Immigrants in Urban America* (Baltimore, 1984).

13. For an excellent discussion, see David Gerber, "Anti-Semitism and Jewish-Gentile Relations in American Historiography and the American Past," in Gerber, *Anti-Semitism*, pp. 3–54. See also the more recent work by Leonard Dinnerstein, *Antisemitism in America* (New York, 1994).

14. See David S. Wyman, *Paper Walls: America and the Refugee Crisis, 1938–1941* (Amherst, MA, 1968) and *The Abandonment of the Jews: America and the Holocaust, 1941–1945* (New York, 1984); and Richard Breitman and Alan M. Kraut, *American Refugee Policy and European Jewry, 1933–1945* (Bloomington, IN, 1987).

15. Gerber, "Anti-Semitism," pp. 18–20.

16. The scholarly debate between Wyman and Breitman and Kraut illustrates this difficulty quite well. Although supported by a tremendous amount of research and new documentation, their studies still lack the kind of evidence needed to resolve this question about the documentation of anti-Semitism expressed by individuals involved in policymaking or implementation. In the absence of such documentation, Breitman and Kraut contend that political and bureaucratic factors, together with indifference, were the major determinants. They relegate anti-Semitism to a far less significant role, whereas Wyman infers from indirect evidence that it was of central importance, even though he could actually document only two explicit examples of anti-Semitism in the State Department. See Breitman and Kraut, *American Refugee Policy*, pp. 9–10; and Wyman, *Paper Walls*, pp. 10–20, and *Abandonment of the Jews*, pp. 190–191.

Chapter 1

1. Colonel William A. McCain to Colonel Gordon Johnston, May 20, 1920, NACP, RG 165, MID 9684-268.

2. Richard Hofstadter, *Social Darwinism in American Thought* (New York, 1959), pp. 171–184.

3. Bradford G. Chynoweth, *Bellamy Park: Memoirs by Bradford Grethen Chynoweth* (Hicksville, NY, 1975), p. 13. John B. Trevor, House, *Exclusion of Immigration from Philippine Islands*, 71 Cong., 2d sess., 1930, H-559-9, p. 19; Truman Smith, *Berlin Alert: The Memoirs and Reports of Truman Smith*, ed. Robert Hessen (Stanford, 1984), p. 5. General George Van Horn Moseley, "One Soldier's Story" (unpublished manuscript), vol. 1, chap. 1, p. 1, George Van Horn Moseley Papers, Library of Congress, Washington, DC (hereafter LC); Major Martin C. Shallenberger to Colonel Sherman Miles, April 8, 1921, NACP, RG 165, MID 2511-72.

4. General Amos A. Fries to John Briggs, June 6, 1950, Amos A. Fries Papers, box 3, University of Oregon Library, Eugene, OR (hereafter UOL). Smith, *Berlin Alert*, pp. 5–6.

5. Brigadier General John W. Clous, "The Army as a Pioneer of Civilization," *Journal of the Military Service Institution*, vol. 49 (1911), pp. 44–55. General Con-

rad S. Babcock to George C. Marshall, December 11, 1941, George C. Marshall Papers, box 13, fol. 29, George C. Marshall Foundation, Lexington, VA.

6. Jack Bales, *Kenneth Roberts: The Man and His Works* (Metuchen, NJ, 1989), pp. 3, 16–17; Colonel Joy Dow to Douglas MacArthur, July 2, 1946, RG 10, MacArthur Private Correspondence, Douglas MacArthur Memorial Archives, Norfolk, VA (hereafter DMMA).

7. Fries to H. M. Warner, August 28, 1934, Fries Papers, box 3, UOL.

8. John G. Clifford, *The Citizen Soldiers: The Plattsburg Training Camp Movement, 1913–1920* (Lexington, KY, 1972), pp. 39, 57–58.

9. Richard C. Brown, *The Social Attitudes of American Generals, 1898–1940* (New York, 1979), pp. 34–39, 87–97.

10. Moseley, "One Soldier's Story," vol. 1, chap. 1, pp. 1–2; Chynoweth, *Bellamy Park*, p. 14.

11. "Internal Stability of Nations," February 1, 1936, pp. 11–12, U.S. Military History Institute Archives, Carlisle, PA (hereafter MHI), U.S. Army War College Archives (hereafter AWCA) 6-1936-8.

12. Major Ralph Pennell, "Bolshevik Influence and Its Importance," February 5, 1927, pp. 1–2, MHI, AWCA 332A-28; General Eli A. Helmick, "Correct Human Relations: The Practical Application of the Golden Rule," May 13, 1927, Eli A. Helmick Papers, East Carolina Manuscript Collections, East Carolina University, Greenville, NC (hereafter ECMC).

13. Clous, "Army as Pioneer," pp. 45, 55; "Americanism," *Infantry Journal*, vol. 16 (March 1920), p. 796.

14. "Publicity and Censorship in a Red-Orange War," December 16, 1931, pp. 4–6, MHI, AWCA, 382-2; 276-18; General Joseph S. Kuhn, "Thoughts," September 1919, Joseph E. Kuhn Papers, box 5, U.S. Military Academy, West Point, NY (hereafter USMA); Eichelberger, "Notebooks," November 12, 1956, pp. 305–306, Robert Eichelberger Papers, box 175, Duke University Library, Manuscript Department, Durham, NC (hereafter DUL).

15. Dr. Elmer Hess to Colonel Benjamin M. Bailey, August 14, 1921, General Benjamin M. Bailey Papers, box 3, Atlanta Historical Society, Atlanta, GA.

16. Johnson Hagood, Diary, August 17, 1918, pp. 151–152, General Johnson Hagood Papers, box 2, MHI.

17. Chynoweth, *Bellamy Park*, pp. 38–39; Fries to wife, November 14, 1918, Fries Papers, box 3, UOL.

18. "Germany—1920," October 1, 1920, NACP, RG 165, MID 2656-B-9.

19. Fries to Captain George Chandler, March 1, 1927, Fries Papers, box 3, UOL; Arthur Wellesley Kipling, "God and the Soldier," *Infantry Journal*, vol. 9 (November–December 1912), p. 313; Clous, "Army as a Pioneer," p. 48.

20. Ibid.

21. Major Herbert E. Pace, "An Estimate of the Dangers of the So-Called Pacifistic Activities," February 4, 1927, MHI, AWCA 332A-26.

22. Bailey, Miscellaneous Manuscripts, Bailey Papers, box 3.

23. Charles E. Woodruff, *Expansion of Races* (New York, 1909), pp. 123–127; Arthur Kipling, "God and the Soldier," *Infantry Journal*, vol. 9 (November–De-

cember 1912), p. 305; Major Robert J. Halpin, "Group Psychology," *Infantry Journal*, vol. 19 (October 1921), p. 412.

24. Bailey, Miscellaneous Manuscripts; General Johnson Hagood, unpublished autobiography, vol. 3, p. 353, Hagood Papers, MHI.

25. Bailey, "Americanism and Guts," Miscellaneous Manuscripts.

26. NACP, RG 165, MID 9684-268.

27. General Kenyon A. Joyce, unpublished memoirs, chap. 14, p. 232, Kenyon A. Joyce Papers, MHI; Moseley, "One Soldier's Story," vol. 2, chap. 4, pp. 84–88.

28. McCain to Colonel Alexander Coxe, January 14, 1920, Coxe Sr. Papers, ECMC. "Emergency Plans White" Report, October 17, 1932, pp. 6–8, MHI, AWCA 391-1.

29. Brown, *American Generals*, pp. 87–94, 120–121, 147–148; Kuhn, "Thoughts"; Edward W. Bok, "The Young Man and the Small Town," *American Legion Weekly*, May 13, 1921, pp. 5–6. Thomas E. Campbell, "Americanism," *American Legion Weekly*, July 18, 1919, p. 29. Captain William Wallace, "Our Military Decline," *Infantry Journal*, vol. 9 (March–April, 1913), pp. 625–644.

30. Brown, *American Generals*, pp. 87, 94, 216, 226–227; "Americanism," *Infantry Journal*, vol. 16 (March 1920), pp. 795–796.

31. United States Army, *Training Manual*, no. 2000-25 (Washington, DC, 1928), as cited in Brown, *American Generals*, p. 162.

32. Colonel Gordon Johnston to Colonel William A. McCain, April 21, 1920, NACP, RG 165, MID 9684-268 (5); "Estimate on Russia," September 28–29, 1921, p. 1, MHI, AWCA 225-B; "Study of Military Attaché System," "Comments on Intelligence Work," 1938, p. 7, MHI, AWCA 2-1938-12; "Influence of Public Opinion on the Conduct of War," Discussion, February 26, 1940, pp. 1–8, MHI, AWCA 6-1940-6.

33. General William D. Connor to George Van Horn Moseley, May 2, 1949, Moseley Papers, vol. 15.

34. "Captain John B. Trevor Report on Radical Situation in the United States," January 1920, p. 3, NACP, RG 165, MID 10110-1665; "Estimate on the United States," October 22, 1919, pp. 1–2, MHI, AWCA 57-3; "Estimate on the United States," October 21, 1919, MHI, AWCA 57-31, p. 5; "Estimate on the United States," October 18, 1919, pp. 9–10, MHI, AWCA 57-31/c; "Anti-War Societies," December 20, 1924, pp. 6–7, MHI, AWCA 287-8; "Internal Stability of Nations," February 1, 1936, pp. 6, 11–15, MHI, AWCA 6-1936-8.

35. Major Gilbert Marshall to Colonel Edwards, November 5, 1920, NACP, RG 165, MID 242-29 (2).

36. John Higham, *Strangers in the Land: Patterns of American Nativism, 1860–1925* (New Brunswick, NJ, 1955); Frank Donner, *The Age of Surveillance: The Aims and Methods of America's Political Intelligence System* (New York, 1980), pp. 9–20.

37. General Eli A. Helmick, "Undermining the Youth of the Nation," February 23, 1925, Helmick Papers, ECMC; General Amos Fries, *Communism Unmasked* (published privately, 1937); "Gen. Fries Says Communists Use Pacifists," press clipping, January 17, 1924, NACP, RG 165, MID 10314-526 (92).

38. Hofstadter, *Social Darwinism*; Higham, *American Nativism*, pp. 136–156; Thomas F. Gossett, *Race: The History of an Idea in America* (Dallas, 1963), pp. 144–175; Daniel J. Kevles, *In the Name of Eugenics: Genetics and the Uses of Human Heredity* (New York, 1985).

39. Higham, *American Nativism*, pp. 136–156; Gossett, *Race*, pp. 144–175; Kevles, *Eugenics*, pp. 44–58, 78–83.

40. Ibid.

41. William Z. Ripley, *The Races of Europe: A Sociological Study* (New York, 1899); Higham, *American Nativism*, pp. 154–155.

42. "Poland: Psychologic Factor," May 5, 1921, pp. 5–9, NACP, RG 165, MID 2656-DD-18.

43. William McDougall, *The Group Mind: A Sketch of the Principles of Collective Psychology* (New York, 1920), and *An Introduction to Social Psychology* (London, 1908), pp. 15–19; G. R. Searle, *Eugenics and Politics in Britain, 1900–1914* (Leyden, Netherlands, 1976), pp. 12, 43, 52, 88; William Trotter, *Instincts of the Herd in Peace and War* (London, 1916); Higham, *American Nativism*, p. 151; Gossett, *Race*, pp. 375–380.

44. McDougall, *Group Mind*, pp. 159, 306, 317.

45. William McDougall, *Is America Safe for Democracy?* (New York, 1921), pp. 26–29, 172–173, 194–195.

46. Gustave Le Bon, *The Crowd: A Study of the Popular Mind* (New York, 1896) and *The Psychology of Peoples* (New York, 1923); Higham, *American Nativism*, p. 142.

47. NACP, RG 165, "General References, G-2 Course," Course at the Army War College, 1922–1923, MID 238-B-3 (62); "G-2 Factors in War Planning," Course at Army War College, 1927–1928, pp. 13–22, MID 238-B-11 (113); "Compilation of Book Reviews," Course at Army War College, 1927–1928, pp. 57–60, 238-B-11 (154). "Publicity and Censorship in a Red-Orange War," December 16, 1931, pp. 3–4, MHI, AWCA, 382-2. Arthur Wellesley Kipling, "God and the Soldier," *Infantry Journal*, vol. 9 (November–December 1912), p. 310. Major Robert J. Halpin, "Group Psychology," *Infantry Journal*, vol. 19 (October 1921), pp. 411–413.

48. Woodruff, *Expansion of Races*, pp. v–vi, 122–137, passim.

49. Ibid., pp. 132–133.

50. Ibid., pp. 118–119, 125, 127–129.

51. Ibid., p. vi.

52. Ibid., pp. 268–271, 379–387.

53. Ibid., pp. 268–273.

54. Moseley, "One Soldier's Story," vol. 4, chap. 1, pp. 3–4.

55. Henry L. Stimson Diaries, February 10, 1942, (microfilm) LC; Russell F. Weigley, *Towards an American Army: Military Thought from Washington to Marshall* (Westport, CT, 1962), pp. 153–155; General George S. Patton, "The Causes of War: A Comparative Study of the Similarity of Conditions Existing in 1913 and 1935" (unpublished manuscript, 1935), George S. Patton Jr. Papers, LC, box 12, p. 10; Captain Matthew E. Hanna, "The Valor of Ignorance," *U.S. Cavalry Journal*, vol. 20 (1910), pp. 1025–1026; Charles A. Willoughby, *MacArthur, 1941–1951* (New York, 1954), pp. 1–3, 19–22, 33.

56. Charles E. Van Loan, "General Homer Lea," *Harper's Weekly*, vol. 57 (1913), p. 7; Higham, *American Nativism*, p. 146.

57. Homer Lea, *The Day of the Saxon* (New York, 1912), pp. 129–133, 146, 218–219, passim; and *The Valor of Ignorance* (New York, 1909).

58. Weigley, *Military Thought*, p. 155; Robert C. Kemble, *The Image of the Army Officer in America: Background for Current Views* (Westport, CT, 1973), pp. 166–171.

59. Higham, *American Nativism*, p. 155; Gosset, *Race*, pp. 356–359.

60. Gosset, *Race*, pp. 394–398.

61. Lothrop Stoddard, *The Rising Tide of Color Against White World-Supremacy* (New York, 1920), pp. xxix–xxx, 305; and *The Revolt Against Civilization: The Menace of the Under-Man* (New York, 1922); Madison Grant, *The Passing of the Great Race: Or the Racial Basis of European History* (New York, 1916), p. 197.

62. Grant, *Passing of the Great Race*, pp. 150–165; Stoddard, *Rising Tide of Color*, pp. xiv–xxvii; Major Charles E. Woodruff, *The Effects of Tropical Light on White Men* (New York, 1905), pp. 129–134, 159–164, 224–250.

63. Grant, *Passing of the Great Race*, p. 198; Stoddard, *Rising Tide of Color*, pp. 148–149; Woodruff, *Effects of Tropical Light on White Men*, pp. 165–168, 252–267.

64. Madison Grant, *The Conquest of a Continent or the Expansion of Races in America* (New York, 1933), pp. ix, 15, 222–227; and *Passing of the Great Race*, p. 228; Stoddard, *Rising Tide of Color*, pp. xxix–xxxi, 145–149.

65. Grant, *Passing of the Great Race*, pp. 86, 166; Stoddard, *Rising Tide of Color*, pp. 154–155, 162–167; Woodruff, *Effects of Tropical Light on White Men*, pp. 276–300.

66. Grant, *Conquest of a Continent*, pp. 356–357; Stoddard, *Rising Tide of Color*, pp. 219–221.

67. James Dealey, *The Development of the State: Its Governmental Organization and Its Activities* (New York, 1909), pp. 14–25, 45, 76–79, 304–314.

68. William Swinton, *Outlines of the World's History* (New York, 1874), pp. 2–4, 72. George Fisher, *Outlines of Universal History* (New York, 1885), pp. 9, 19, 55, 71–72, 622. George Fisher, *A Brief History of the Nations* (New York, 1896), pp. 3–5, 48–58. Victor Duruy, *General History of the World* (New York, 1898), pp. 1–6, 38–44. Raymond Gettell, *Introduction to Political Science* (Boston, 1910), pp. 33–39.

69. Ferdinand Schwill, *A Political History of Modern Europe* (New York, 1908); James Harvey Robinson and Charles Beard, *The Development of Modern Europe* (Boston, 1908); Charles Hazen, *Europe Since 1815* (New York, 1910).

70. NACP, RG 165, MID 238-B-11 (154), p. 111; MID 235-B-11 (47), p. 3; MID 238B-11 (115), p. 12.

71. Foreword to *Psychology of the Filipino*, ed. Headquarters Philippine Department, U.S. Army, NACP, RG 165, MID 2656-Z-3.

72. Colonel William A. McCain to Colonel Gordon Johnston, May 20, 1920, NACP, RG 165, MID 9654-268; Moseley, "One Soldier's Story," vol. 4, chap. 6, "The Passing of the Great Race."

73. Colonel Johnson Hagood, Diary, April 26, 1919, p. 127; and Autobiography, pp. 336–337, MHI, Hagood Papers.

74. Weigley, *Military Thought*, pp. 147–155; Clifford, *Citizen Soldiers*, pp. 38–39, 57; Brown, *American Generals*, p. 186; Hagood, Autobiography, pt. 3, pp. 353–363, MHI, Hagood Papers.

75. Hagood, Autobiography, pt. 3, p. 335.

76. Moseley, "One Soldier's Story," vol. 2, preface.

77. General William Durward Connor, concluding remarks to lecture by Robert Kelley, "The Bolshevik Regime in Russia," G-2 Course at Army War College, 1931–1932, vol. 2, pp. 29–30, MHI, AWCA.

78. Henry C. Emery, "Some Economic Aspects of War," *Infantry Journal*, vol. 10 (May–June 1914), pp. 795–818; Major Evan M. Johnson, "The Philosophy of War," *Infantry Journal*, vol. 8 (May–June 1912), pp. 783–794; Captain Arthur P. S. Hyde, "The Evolution of Warfare," *Journal of the Military Service Institution*, vol. 46 (1910), pp. 103–104; Major C.A.P. Hatfield, "The Tendency of Evolution in the Army," *Journal of the Military Service Institution*, vol. 21 (1897), p. 441.

79. Emery, "Economic Aspects of War," p. 818; Johnson, "Philosophy of War," pp. 791–795.

80. NACP, RG 165, MID 2656-Z-3, pp. 28–29.

81. General Albert C. Wedemeyer to Ernst von Helms, August 29, 1968, Albert C. Wedemeyer Papers, box 66, Hoover Institution Archives, Stanford, CA (hereafter HIA).

82. "Anatomical Type of Head and Brain," November 1, 1920, NACP, RG 165, MID 2656-H-10, p. 2; "Translation of Psychological Data Referring to Brain Weights, Etc.," MID 2656-H-11.

83. "France: Psychological," NACP, RG 165, MID 2656-C; "Swiss Psychology," October 13, 1921, MID 2656-R-2. "Strategical Estimate of Italy: Psychological," December 17, 1931, MHI, AWCA 382-3B. Woodruff, *Effects of Tropical Light on White Men*, pp. 206–207.

84. "Summary of Estimate on European Russia: Psychological Situation," September 30, 1919, pp. 7–8, MHI, AWCA 57-15; "Estimate on Russia: B. National Psychology," September 28, 1921, p. 3, AWCA 225b; "Strategic Estimate of USSR: 4. Psychological Factors," December 20, 1932, p. 30, AWCA 392-5B; "Strategic Survey of the USSR: B. Psychological and Military Factors," January 10, 1935, p. 2, AWCA 2-1935-7; "Survey USSR: II. Conclusions," pp. 3–4, "Discussion," p. 2, January 23, 1939, AWCA 2-1939-5.

85. "Strategic Survey of Germany: Psychologic," January 8, 1935, p. 3, MHI, AWCA 2-1935-6.

86. Retired General William Lassiter to Representative John J. McSwain, Chairman, House Committee on Military Affairs, February 8, 1936, DUL, John J. McSwain Papers, box 12; Major Preston Brown, lecture for "Course on Intelligence, General Staff College Course," September 6, 1919, MHI, AWCA *Intelligence, Lectures, 1919–1920*, vol. 2, pp. 61–62; Walter C. Sweeney, *Military Intelligence: A New Weapon of War* (New York, 1924), pp. 60–61; Colonel C. A. Seone, "Military Aspects of Economic Recovery," Army Industrial College, March 15, 1936, pp. 2–3, 44–46, MHI, AWCA 221-37-31.

87. Patton, "Causes of War," pp. 6, 10. Johnson, "Philosophy of War," pp. 790–794.

88. Bailey, Miscellaneous Manuscripts; Sweeney, *Military Intelligence*, p. 65; Emery, "Economic Aspects of War," pp. 801–803.

89. General Robert E. Wood to John J. McSwain, February 24, 1936, McSwain Papers, box 12; Hagood, Autobiography, vol. 3, p. 363, Hagood Papers; Woodruff, *Expansion of Races*, pp. 268–271.

90. General Edward M. Almond to Vermont Royster, March 11, 1970, MHI, Edward M. Almond Papers, box "A Voice for Conservatism."

91. Brown, *American Generals*, p. 186; Bailey, Miscellaneous Manuscripts.

92. "Estimate on the United States: Racial Characteristics," October 21, 1919, pp. 3–4, MHI, AWCA 57-31.

93. "Estimate on the United States: Psychological Situation," October 18, 1919, pp. 9–10, MHI, AWCA 57-31/c; "Internal Stability of Nations: (3) Measures to Increase Stability," February 1, 1936, p. 6, AWCA 6-1936-8.

94. "Strategic Estimate of Italy: Psychological," pp. 4–5, AWCA 382-3B; "Strategic Survey of USSR," p. 2, AWCA 2-1935-7. See also Alfred P. Schultz, *Race or Mongrel: A Brief History of the Rise and Fall of the Ancient Races of the Earth* (Boston, 1908); Clinton S. Burr, *America's Race Heritage* (New York, 1922), pp. 6, 291; Higham, *American Nativism*, p. 155.

95. "Internal Stability of Nations," February 16, 1935, pp. 8, 19, 25, MHI, AWCA 17-A; Lieutenant Roy W. Winton, "The Problem of Patriotism," *Infantry Journal*, vol. 9 (May–June 1913), pp. 773–777; Stoddard, *Rising Tide of Color*, pp. 166, 232.

96. Major Henry S. Kilbourne, "The Physical Proportions of the American Soldier," *Journal of the Military Service Institution*, vol. 22 (1898), pp. 50–61.

97. Gerber, *Anti-Semitism*, p. 5; Higham, *Immigrants*, pp. 95–116, and *American Nativism*, pp. 277–286.

98. Higham, *Immigrants*, pp. 99–104.

99. Melvin I. Urofsky, *American Zionism from Herzl to the Holocaust* (New York, 1975), pp. 53–78.

100. Ibid., pp. 56–71; Gerber, *Anti-Semitism*, pp. 22–28.

101. Edward A. Ross, *The Old World in the New: The Significance of Past and Present Immigration to the American People* (New York, 1914); Hofstadter, *Social Darwinism*, pp. 160–161.

102. Ross, *Old World in the New*, pp. 146–157.

103. Ibid., pp. 289–292.

104. Ibid., pp. 145–149, 290–293.

105. Ibid., pp. 282–289.

106. Colonel John Dunn to Captain John B. Trevor, February 1, 1919, NACP, RG 165, MID 10110-581; Colonel John R. Thomas to military observer, Berlin, January 4, 1921, MID 10214-625 (15); "The Jew, the Lett, and the Russian," December 14, 1920, MID 2656-D-17.

107. NACP, RG 165, MID 2656-D-17; "National Faults of the Hungarians," May 2, 1921, NACP, RG 165, MID 2656-GG-9; "Plans of German Propaganda in America Against Poles," May 9, 1919, NACP, RG 165, MID 10059-102 (4); "Hungary," May 26, 1921, NACP, RG 165, MID 2656-GG-14.

108. "Hungary," May 26, 1921, NACP, RG 165, MID 2656-GG-9-14.

109. Helmick, "Golden Rule," pp. 1–5.

110. General Amos Fries to James Chandler, April 25, 1950, Fries Papers, box 3.

111. Woodruff, *Expansion of Races*, p. 386.

112. Major Thomas W. Hollyday, "Jewish Migration to U.S.A.," November 27, 1920, NACP, RG 165, MID 245-71; "Notes on Foreigners in the United States," February 11, 1921, pp. 12–13, NACP, RG 165, MID 239-64.

113. Bailey, "Aliens," Miscellaneous Manuscripts, Bailey Papers, box 3.

114. Ibid.; NACP, RG 165, MID 239-64.

115. NACP, RG 165, MID 245-71.

116. Bailey, "Aliens"; General George Van Horn Moseley Note, 1947, Moseley Papers, vol. 13.

117. American Jewish Committee Archives, New York City (hereafter AJCA), AJC General Correspondence, 1906–1932, "Discrimination in Armed Forces."

118. Louis Marshall to Harry Schneideman, March 4, 1918, AJC, "Discrimination in Armed Forces."

119. Major M. D. Wheeler to MID Director, March 19, 1919, NACP, RG 165, MID 10560-152 (88).

120. Major J. S. Richardson, "Contre-Espionage in the A.E.F.," January 26, 1920, NACP, RG 165, MID 10560-328 (162).

121. Smith, *Berlin Alert*, p. 11.

122. General Joseph Dickman to Colonel Alexander Coxe, September 2, 1917, Alexander B. Coxe Sr. Papers, ECMC.

123. NACP, RG 165, MID 245-71; Bailey, Miscellaneous Manuscripts.

124. McDougall, *Group Mind*, pp. 155–156, and *Is America Safe?* p. 127; Ripley, *Races of Europe*, pp. 373, 382–383, 400. See also Robert Singerman, "The Jew as Racial Alien: The Genetic Component of American Anti-Semitism," in David Gerber, ed., *Anti-Semitism in American History* (Urbana and Chicago, 1986).

125. Ripley, *Races of Europe*, pp. 372–373.

126. Woodruff, *Expansion of Races*, pp. 379, 381–387, and "The Complexion of the Jews," *American Journal of Insanity*, vol. 62 (1905–1906), pp. 327–333.

127. Woodruff, *Expansion of Races*, pp. 384–385.

128. Ibid., p. 382.

129. Ibid., pp. 385–387.

130. Stoddard, *Rising Tide of Color*, pp. xxii, 75, 165; Grant, *Conquest of a Continent*, p. 225; Burr, *America's Race Heritage*, pp. 27, 121, 195–196, 290–291; Singerman, "Jew as Racial Alien," pp. 116–117.

131. "Poland: Psychologic Factor," May 5, 1921, pp. 2–7, NACP, RG 165, MID 2656-DD-18.

132. Grant, *Conquest of a Continent*, pp. 226–227; Burr, *America's Race Heritage*, pp. 121, 194–196, 235, 293, 310.

133. Burr, *America's Race Heritage*, p. 194.

134. Grant, *Passing of the Great Race*, pp. 16–18.

135. General Edward M. Almond to Vermont Royster, March 11, 1970, MHI, Almond Papers, box "A Voice of Conservatism."

136. Estimate of the United States: Psychological Situation," October 18, 1919, pp. 9–10, MHI, AWCA, 57-31/c.

137. "Hungary: (18) Racial," May 26, 1921, NACP, RG 165, MID 2656-GG-14.

138. "The Jew, the Lett, and the Russian."

139. Ibid.

140. Hofstadter, *Social Darwinism*, pp. 171–172.

141. John M. Gates, *Schoolbooks and Krags: The United States Army in the Philippines, 1898–1902* (Westport, CT, 1973), p. 286, passim.

142. Stanley Karnow, *In Our Image: America's Empire in the Philippines* (New York, 1989), pp. 212–215, passim.

Chapter 2

1. Colonel Ralph Van Deman to General Marlborough Churchill, "Bolshevism and Semitism," July 5, 1919, NACP, RG 165, MID 10058-396 (2).

2. Ibid.

3. Ibid.

4. Ibid.

5. Marc Powe and Edward Wilson, *The Evolution of American Military Intelligence* (Fort Huachuca, AZ, 1973), pp. 12–13.

6. Ibid., pp. 12–13; Rhodri Jeffreys-Jones, *American Espionage: From Secret Service to CIA* (New York, 1977), pp. 48–49.

7. Powe and Wilson, *Military Intelligence*, pp. 18–19; Jeffreys-Jones, *American Espionage*, pp. 49–50.

8. General Marlborough Churchill, "The Military Intelligence Division," January 15, 1920, p. 17, NACP, RG 165, MID 10560-328, and "The Military Intelligence Division," *Journal of the United States Artillery*, vol. 52 (April 1920), pp. 293–315; Powe and Wilson, *Military Intelligence*, p. 31.

9. Churchill, "Military Intelligence Division," pp. 9–12, MID 10560-328; Oliver Edwards, "The Military Intelligence Division," lecture at General Staff College, September 2, 1920, MHI, pp. 2–4.

10. Churchill, "Military Intelligence," pp. 311–313; Edwards, "Military Intelligence," pp. 12–13; Roy Talbert, *Negative Intelligence: The Army and the American Left, 1917–1941* (Jackson, MS, 1991), pp. 22–23.

11. Churchill, "Military Intelligence," MID 10560-328, pp. 3–5; Powe and Wilson, *Military Intelligence*, pp. 18–19; Jeffreys-Jones, *American Espionage*, p. 50; Frank Donner, *The Age of Surveillance: The Aims and Methods of America's Political Intelligence System* (New York, 1980), pp. 9–29, 290–291, 416–420; Talbert, *Negative Intelligence*, pp. 30–35.

12. Edwards, "Military Intelligence," p. 12; see also Talbert, *Negative Intelligence*.

13. Ibid., pp. 5–7; Churchill, "Military Intelligence," pp. 301–307, and "Military Intelligence," MID 10560-32, pp. 20–23.

14. Letter from American Legation, Copenhagen to Secretary of State, June 27, 1918, and Lieutenant Norman C. Stinnes, "The Role of the Russian Jew in the Great War," NACP, RG 59, Records of Department of State, 861.4016/243.

15. Ibid.

16. Ibid.

17. Ibid.

18. See marginal notes on Stinnes report by State Department official in Washington, in ibid.

19. See MID file on Alex M. de Lochwitzky-Luxembourg, NACP, RG 165, MID 10110-2756 (8–12).

20. See Boris Brasol Papers, LC; Robert Singerman, "The American Career of the Protocols of the Elders of Zion," *American Jewish History*, vol. 71 (September 1981); and John Higham, *Strangers in the Land: Patterns of American Nativism, 1860–1925* (New Brunswick, NJ, 1955), p. 280.

21. NACP, RG 165, MID 10058-285 (84), 10058-208. See also the file on Casimir Pilenas, AJCA, Cyrus Adler Papers, Chronological File.

22. Marlborough Churchill to Colonel K. C. Masteller, November 30, 1918, NACP, RG 165, MID 10110-920.

23. B-1, memorandum, August 14, 1918, NACP, RG 165, MID 10110-920.

24. Ibid.

25. B-1, Report 5, November 25, 27, 1918, NACP, RG 165, MID 10110-920.

26. B-1, "Bolshevism and Judaism" (undated but written after late October 1918), NACP, RG 165, MID 10110-920.

27. Ibid.

28. B-1, Report 11, December 17, 1918, NACP, RG 165, MID 10110-920.

29. Captain Carlton J. H. Hayes memorandum for Major Brown, December 19, 1918, NACP, RG 165, MID 101110-920 (127).

30. Ibid.

31. Captain Edwin P. Grosvenor memorandum for Colonel Dunn, December 20, 1918, NACP, RG 165, MID 10110-920 (128).

32. Colonel Masteller's handwritten note to Major Brown (undated), NACP, RG 165, MID 10110-920 (129).

33. Colonel Dunn memorandum to Colonel Masteller, December 24, 1918, NACP, RG 165, MID 10110-920 (129).

34. See surviving B-1 reports, NACP, RG 165, MID 10110-920 (101–148).

35. Captain Hayes memoranda, January 25, 27, 1919, NACP, RG 165, MID 10110-920 (142–148).

36. Casimir Pilenas memorandum for Captain Hayes, and Nathan Isaacs' Supplement, February 19, 1919, NACP, RG 165, MID 10058-285 (83–84).

37. A. E. Stevenson to Captain John B. Trevor, December 23, 1918, NACP, RG 165, MID 171-79 (8).

38. See summaries of dispatches from abroad in MID subject index cross-reference cards, "Jews: A. Race" NACP, RG 165, MID, throughout 1918, but especially June 5, October 26, 28, 1918. See also: "Russia," *Weekly Intelligence Summary* (Washington, September 14, 1918), Richard D. Challener, ed., *United States Military Intelligence, 1917–1927*, 30 vols. (New York, 1978), vol. 5, p. 29.

39. Colonel S. L. Slocum to MID director, November 27, 1918, NACP, RG 165, MID 2070-1073; and "Bolshevism: Developments in Russia," MID *Weekly Intel-*

ligence Summary (January 4, 1919), Challener, *Military Intelligence*, vol. 6, pp. 376–379.

40. British secret agent report, "The Perils of Bolshevism," submitted to MID November 27, 1918, NACP, RG 165, MID 2070-1073 pp. 1–7.

41. Ibid.

42. Philip Brown, "Zionism and Anti-Semitism, *North American Review*, vol. 210 (January 1919), p. 656.

43. Ibid., pp. 660–662.

44. Melvin I. Urofsky, *American Zionism: From Herzl to the Holocaust* (New York, 1975), pp. 224–232.

45. Jerry Z. Muller, "Communism, Anti-Semitism, and the Jews," *Commentary*, vol. 86 (August 1988), pp. 31–32.

46. Singerman, "American Career of the Protocols," pp. 50–53.

47. Ibid., pp. 48–51; Captain John B. Trevor to MID director, April 3, 1919, NACP, RG 165, MID 99-75 (5).

48. Colonel John M. Dunn, cover memorandum to "Protocols of the Meeting of the Zionist Men of Wisdom," September 1, 1918, NACP, RG 165, MID 99-75.

49. NACP, RG 165, MID 99-75.

50. Dunn, September 1, 1918 memo, MID 99-75.

51. W. Nelson to Captain Henry G. Pratt, March 3, 1919, MID 99-75 (4).

52. MID 99-75 (5).

53. Ibid.

54. Ibid.

55. See files in NACP, RG 165, MID 10110-920; Higham, *American Nativism*, pp. 280–281, 314–315.

56. Churchill telegram to Colonel Dunn, January 22, 1919, NACP, RG 165, MID 10110-920 (141).

57. Captain John B. Trevor to MID director, February 19, 1919, NACP, RG 165, MID 245-18 (5).

58. Trevor to MID director on "Justice Brandeis and the 'Jewish International Movement,'" February 19, 1919, MID 245-18 (6).

59. Colonel H. A. Parkenham to M.I.4, January 22, 1919, NACP, RG 165, MID 10058-309 (1).

60. "Plans of German Propaganda in America Against the Poles," and Captain Nathan Isaacs to Major Brown, June 13, 1919, NACP, RG 165, MID 10059-102 (4).

61. Casimir Pilenas to Churchill, June 14, 1919, NACP, RG 165, MID 9961-5427.

62. Ibid.

63. Colonel Ralph Van Deman to Churchill, July 5, 1919, NACP, RG 165, 10058-396 (2).

64. Military attaché, London, to Washington, July 8, 1919, cited in William L. Hurley–L. Lanier Winslow Correspondence, Office of the Counselor, Department of State, NACP, RG 59, Entry 538, 861.0-628.

65. Ibid.

66. Ibid.

67. NACP, RG 165, MID 245-1 (1).

68. DeWitt Clinton Poole Oral History, Columbia University Manuscript Library, New York City, pp. 1–3, 27–28, 74–75.

69. Ibid, pp. 274–275; George F. Kennan, *Russia Leaves the War* (Princeton, 1956), pp. 17, 74, 180–183, 472.

70. "Judaism and the Present World Movement—A Study," September 29, 1919, NACP, RG 165, MID 245-15 (1), pp. 1–2.

71. Ibid., pp. 3–4.

72. Ibid., pp. 5–8.

73. Ibid., pp. 9–13, 17. Italics in original.

74. Ibid., pp. 15–16.

75. Ibid., p. 6; and "Appendix-A Comparison of Protocols and Jewish Writings"; "Appendix-B Fulfillment of Protocols by World Events"; "Appendix-C Jewish Principles and Ideals"; "Appendix-D Miscellaneous Extracts and Quotations Including Statements by Louis Marshall, Israel Cohen, and Others"; "Appendix-E Photographs of Bolshevik Commissars of Bela Kun's Regime in Hungary."

76. Ibid., pp. 18–19.

77. Ibid., p. 18.

78. "Summary Report of Progress of Radicalism in the United States and Abroad," December 27, 1919, p. 9; and L. Lanier Winslow to Churchill, December 11, 1919, NACP, RG 165, MID 10058-452.

79. "Zionist Men of Wisdom," October 11, 1919; "The Jews" December 27, 1919, *Weekly Intelligence Summary*, Challener, *Military Intelligence*, vol. 10, p. 1998, vol. 11, p. 2592.

Chapter 3

1. Colonel William A. Castle, "Situation in Russia and the Near East," April 27, 1920, NACP, RG 165, MID 10560-328 (180).

2. "Bolshevism in Cartoon," May 3, 1922, NACP, RG 165, MID 10058-U-122 (2).

3. Zosa Szajkowski, *Kolchak, Jews, and the American Intervention in Northern Russia and Siberia, 1918–1920* (New York, 1977), pp. 74–78; State Department relay of telegram to MID, October 13, 1919, NACP, RG 59, Entry, 861.00/5346.

4. William S. Graves, *America's Siberian Adventure* (New York, 1931), pp. 100–102, 110, 296–297; George F. Kennan, *The Decision to Intervene* (Princeton, 1958), pp. 413–417; Szajkowski, *Kolchak*, pp. 18–19.

5. John Ward, *With the "Die Hards" in Siberia* (London, 1920), pp. 277–286.

6. Graves, *America's Siberian Adventure*, pp. 108–113, 198–199; Szajkowski, *Kolchak*, pp. 78–79.

7. Eichelberger to wife, December 2, 1918, October 7, 1919, DUL, Eichelberger Papers, box 17, box 1B.

8. Eichelberger to wife, August 28, October 21, December 19, 1918, January 2, 7, 28, 1919, box 1A, DUL, Eichelberger Papers; Paul Chwialkowski, *In Caesar's Shadow: The Life of General Robert Eichelberger* (Westport, CT, 1993), p. 24.

9. Eichelberger to wife, April 10, 1919, May 14, 1919, box 1A, DUL, Eichelberger Papers.

10. "Report to Colonel Eichelberger Re Cook and Forsythe," 1919, box 54; Major Robert L. Eichelberger, "Final Report on the Operations of the Intelligence Section AEF Siberia," October 20, 1920, pp. 2–3, box 56, DUL, Eichelberger Papers.

11. "Siberia: The Jewish Question," *Weekly Intelligence Summary*, March 15, 1919, Richard D. Challener, ed., *United States Military Intelligence, 1917–1927*, 30 vols. (New York, 1978), vol. 7, pp. 682–683.

12. Paraphrase of Harris cable of September 20, 1919, and Churchill to chief of staff, September 17, 1919, NACP, RG 165, MID 245-4 (18).

13. Ronald Sanders, *Shores of Refuge: A Hundred Years of Jewish Immigration* (New York, 1988), pp. 328–358; Salo W. Baron, *The Russian Jew Under the Tsars and Soviets* (New York, 1976), pp. 183–186; Zvi Y. Gitelman, *Jewish Nationality and Soviet Politics: The Jewish Section of the CPSU, 1917–1930* (Princeton, 1972), pp. 158–168.

14. Szajkowski, *Kolchak*, pp. 126–132.

15. Major H. H. Slaughter, "Secret Report from Czech Agent," September 8, 1919, NACP, RG 165, MID 245-4.

16. Telegrams to Churchill, June 20, July 11, 1919, NACP, RG 256, American Commission to Negotiate the Peace, 184.01602/66; 184.01602/83.

17. Baron, *Russian Jew*, p. 184; Gitelman, *Jewish Nationality*, pp. 160–161.

18. American Consul Constantinople to American Mission to Negotiate Peace, Paris, July 25, 1919, NACP, RG 256, 861.00/888.

19. "The Jews," "Another Jewish Mission Demanded," "Alleged Pogroms," and "Russia," 1919; "The Jewish Question," 1920, *Weekly Intelligence Summary*, Challener, *Military Intelligence*, vol. 9, pp. 1530, 1790, 1873, 1905–1906, vol. 11, p. 2685.

20. "The Ukraine," "Polish Sketch of Deniken's Army," 1919, *Weekly Intelligence Summary*, Challener, *Military Intelligence*, vol. 11, pp. 2504–2505, vol. 10, pp. 2340–2341.

21. Digest of Jadwin's Report, NACP, RG 256, 186.3111/470A.

22. Ibid.; "The Jews," *Weekly Intelligence Summary*, 1919, Challener, *Military Intelligence*, vol. 11, p. 2592.

23. See Jadwin, "Report on Ukraine," October 23, 1919, NACP, RG 165, 60-167 (9), pp. 3, 9–11.

24. Churchill to secretary of war, January 13, 1919, NACP, RG 165, MID 10059-118 (4), p. 3.

25. Ibid., pp. 1–2.

26. Ibid., p. 2.

27. Ibid., p. 3.

28. Sanders, *Shores of Refuge*, pp. 316–320.

29. Major Ernest H. Schelling, "The Advance of the Red Army," February 3, 1919, NACP, RG 165, MID 2067-52.

30. Hugh S. Gibson Diary, January 11, 29, March 27, 1919, HIA, Hugh S. Gibson Papers, box 69.

31. American Commission to Negotiate Peace, April 24, May 1, 1919, NACP, RG 256, 860C.4016/19-20; Henry Morgenthau, "Mission of the United States to Poland," October 3, 1919, pp. 5–6, NACP, RG 165, MID 60-167.

32. Morgenthau, "Poland," p. 7.

33. Biographical Sketches of Military Attachés, July 31, 1925, NACP, RG 165, MID 2355-329 (33); Bruce W. Bidwell, *History of the Military Intelligence Division, Department of the Army General Staff: 1775–1941* (Washington, DC, 1954), pp. 162–163.

34. NACP, RG 165, MID 2067-85.

35. Ibid.

36. Ibid.

37. Gibson Diary, May 5, 1919, HIA, Gibson Papers, box 69.

38. Hugh Gibson to Robert Lord, May 25, 1919, NACP, RG 256, 184.019/3.

39. Ibid.

40. Gibson Diary, May 29–30, June 1, 1919, HIA, Gibson Papers, boxes 69–70.

41. Hugh Gibson telegram to AmMission, Paris, June 2, 1919, AJCA, Louis Marshall Papers, Correspondence, Peace Conference, 1919 (1).

42. Ibid.

43. Anson Conger Goodyear Diary, July 17, 1919, HIA, Anson Conger Goodyear Papers, box 2.

44. General Ralph H. Van Deman to Churchill, June 6, 1919, Van Deman Diary, pp. 19–22, MHI, Ralph H. Van Deman Papers.

45. HIA, Gibson Papers, State Department telegram to AmMission, Paris, June 23, 1919, box 92; Gibson Diary, June 24, 1919, box 70.

46. HIA, Gibson Papers, Gibson to William Phillips, July 6, 1919, box 92; Gibson Diary, June 24, 1919, box 70.

47. Ibid.

48. Morgenthau, "Mission of the United States to Poland," pp. 3–4.

49. General Edgar Jadwin, Memorandum on Situation in Minsk, Warsaw, August 17, 1919, NACP, RG 165, MID 60-167 (3).

50. Ibid.

51. Ibid.

52. Ibid.

53. William Phillips to Gibson, November 25, 1919, HIA, Gibson Papers, box 56.

54. Louis Marshall to William Phillips, December 5, 1919; Stephen Wise to Phillips, November 29, 1919; Captain George M. Russell to Captain Sherman Miles, July 7, 1920, NACP, RG 165, MID 60-167.

55. Morgenthau Report, "Mission of the United States to Poland," pp. 3–12.

56. Ibid.

57. Jadwin-Johnson Report, pp. 13–23.

58. Ibid.

59. "Jewish Bolsheviks in Poland," July 8, 1919, NACP, RG 165, MID 2067-109.

60. "The Jews," "Poland," "Poland," "Bolsheviks and Jews," "Poland Critical Conditions," "The Jews," and "The Jews Again," *Weekly Intelligence Summary*, 1919, Challener, *Military Intelligence*, vol. 7, p. 886, vol. 8, pp. 1199, 1226–1227, vol. 9, pp. 1691–1693, vol. 11, pp. 2502–2503, 2813–2814.

61. "Suspected Jewish Propaganda Against Poland," 1919, *Weekly Intelligence Summary*, Challener, *Military Intelligence*, vol. 9, pp. 1724–1725.

62. Churchill to chief, Positive Branch, October 2, 1919, NACP, RG 165, MID 245-3.

63. "Internationality," MHI, Castle Papers, box 2.

64. Churchill to Colonel Sherman Miles, March 30, 1921, NACP, RG 165, MID 2610-37 (74).

65. Churchill to Miles, February 4, 1921, NACP, RG 165, MID 2610-37 (47).

66. Martin Weil, *A Pretty Good Club: The Founding Fathers of the U.S. Foreign Service* (New York, 1978), pp. 15–21; Robert D. Schulzinger, *The Making of the Diplomatic Mind: The Training, Outlook, and Style of United States Foreign Service Officers, 1908–1931* (Middletown, CT, 1975), p. 52; Waldo H. Heinrich, "Bureaucracy and Professionalism in the Development of American Career Diplomats," in *Twentieth-Century American Foreign Policy*, ed. John Braeman, Robert H. Bremmer, and David Brody (Columbus, OH, 1971), pp. 147–155.

67. HIA, Gibson Papers, Phillips to Gibson, October 22, 1920, box 56; William L. Hurley to Gibson, October 1, 1920, box 46.

68. HIA, Gibson Papers, Hurley to Gibson October 1, 1920, box 46; and Gibson's files on "Jewish Question," box 92.

69. Weil, *Pretty Good Club*, pp. 24–34.

70. Ibid., pp. 34–45; HIA, Gibson Papers, Allen Dulles to Gibson, August 27, 1920, box 22; William R. Castle to Gibson, June 2, 1921, and July 13, 1922, box 17; William L. Hurley to Gibson, February 5, 1920, box 45; Jay Pierrepont Moffat to Gibson, April 19, 1920, box 54; Gibson to Colonel William F. Godson, June 7, 1924, box 42.

71. Castle to Churchill, February 26, 1921, MHI, William A. Castle Papers, box 2; Allen Dulles to Gibson, May 6, 1921, HIA, Gibson Papers, box 22.

72. HIA, Gibson Papers, Gibson Diary, May 27, June 17, 1919, boxes 69–70; Gibson to secretary of state, November 10, 1922, p. 7, box 100.

73. HIA, Gibson Papers, Gibson to secretary of state, February 9, November 10, 1922, boxes 100–101; *Naval Intelligence:* "Conditions in Russia, 1921–22," February 23, 1922, National Archives, Washington, DC (hereafter NADC), RG 38, Naval Attaché Reports, 1886–1939, Office of Naval Intelligence (hereafter ONI) C-10-L: 14230C.

74. Colonel Elbert E. Farman to Colonel Sherman Miles, January 10, February 10, 1920, NACP, RG 165, MID 2476-18, 2632-DD-1; HIA, Gibson Papers, Gibson Diary, May 19, 1919, box 69.

75. Farman to Miles July 28, 1919, NACP, RG 165, MID 2476-17; "The Political Jewish Factor," December 9, 1919, MID 245-9.

76. *Report by Sir Stuart Samuel on His Mission to Poland* (London, 1920), NACP, RG 165, MID 10059-153 (2).

77. Captain P. Wright Report, ibid., pp. 17–20, 24–25. See also Nathan Isaacs, "The International Jew," *Menorah Journal* (December 1920), pp. 355–357.

78. Wright Report, pp. 18–19, 35–36.

79. Ibid., pp. 23, 26, 34–35.

80. Ibid., pp. 21, 25–29.

81. Farman, "Poland. Jewish Problem," November 24, 1920, NACP, RG 165, MID 10059-153 (3), 10059–90; "Poland. Psychological Factor," MID 2656-DD-18, p. 9. "The Jewish Problem in Poland," *Weekly Intelligence Summary,* November 13, 1920, Challener, *Military Intelligence,* vol. 16, pp. 5766–5773; Allen Dulles to Gibson, October 14, 1920, HIA, Gibson Papers, box 22.

82. Farman, "Poland. Psychological Factor," May 5, 1921, NACP, RG 165, MID 2656-DD-18.

83. Farman, "Poland Psychological Factor, July 1, 1921, NACP, RG 165, MID 2656-DD-23; "Present State of the Polish Jews," January 26, 1921, MID 245-68.

84. Ibid.

85. Ibid.

86. Ibid.

87. Ibid.; Gibson to Hurley, February 9, 1920, NACP, RG 165, MID 60C-36.

88. See Gibson-Hurley February 1920 Correspondence, MID 60C-36.

89. Farman to Miles, January 5, 1920, Miles–Colonel William M. Colvin Correspondence, February–March, 1920, NACP, RG 165, MID 245-10 (1–4).

90. "Bolshevism and Its Possibilities," *Weekly Intelligence Summary,* April 3, 1920, Challener, *Military Intelligence,* vol. 12, pp. 3456–3458.

91. "The Jewish Problem," *Weekly Intelligence Summary,* February 1, 1919, Challener, *Military Intelligence,* vol. 6, pp. 502–503.

92. Colonel Arthur Poillon to Churchill, March 5, 1920, NACP, RG 165, MID 2632-V-2.

93. Poillon to Churchill, January 20, 1920, and Churchill's related memos, NACP, RG 165, MID 245-8.

94. "Jewism," May 18, 1921, NACP, RG 165, MID 245-98.

95. Ibid.

96. Ibid.

97. Colonel Matthew C. Smith to Hurley, June 28, 1921, NACP, RG 165, MID 245-98.

98. "Bolshevik Russia," July 15, 1921, NACP, RG 165, MID 10058-1174 (1).

99. General Harry H. Bandholtz Diary, January 4, 1920, MHI, Harry H. Bandholtz Papers.

100. Ibid., August 27, 31, September 9, 1919. See also Joan M. Jensen, *Army Surveillance in America, 1775–1980* (New Haven, 1991), pp. 88–108.

101. "Hungary," November 29, 1919, "Anti-Jewish Feeling," January 10, 1920, *Weekly Intelligence Summary,* Challener, *Military Intelligence,* vol. 10, pp. 2353–2355, vol. 11, p. 2690.

102. Bandholtz Diary, October 29, December 6, 10, 1919, MHI, Bandholtz Papers.

103. "National Faults—Indolence," July 14, 1921, NACP, RG 165, MID 2656-GG-18; "Central Europe—the Tribal Instinct," January 18, 1922, MID 2656-B-4.

104. Ibid.; "Religion," October 13, 1920; "National Faults of the Hungarians," May 2, 1921, NACP, RG 165, MID 2656-GG-2, 2656-GG-9.

105. Ibid.; "Hungarian Social Customs," May 1, 1921, "Hungary Not to Be Judged from Budapest Experience Alone," May 26, 1921, NACP, RG 165, MID 2656-GG-13/14.

106. Ibid.; "The Jewish Question," June 3, 1921, NACP, RG 165, MID 245-100; "National Faults . . . Racial," May 2, 1921, MID 2656-GG-9.

107. "Awakening Hungarians," September 28, 1920, NACP, RG 165, MID 245-40 (3).

108. Churchill to John Gade, October 8, 1919; Colonel Oscar Solbert, January 30, 1920; Colonel T. Bentley Mott, March 8, 1922; Colonel E. R. Warner McCabe to Baron Leopold Plessen, May 28, 1923, NACP, RG 165, MID 2475-30, 46, 117, 150.

109. "Jewish Migration to U.S.A.," November 27, 1920, NACP, RG 165, MID 245-71 (1).

110. Colonel T. Worthington Hollyday to Churchill, August 17, 1921, NACP, RG 165, MID 2632-BB-3 (1).

111. Hollyday to McCabe, September 9, 1922, NACP, RG 165, MID 2475-128 (1).

112. "Bolshevism: A Jewish Clique in Marienlyst," August 14, 1919, NACP, RG 165, MID 245-2 (1); "Political," April 9, 1919, MID 2059-1334; "The Northwest," *Weekly Intelligence Summary,* September 27, 1919, Challener, *Military Intelligence,* vol. 9, pp. 1891–1892; Norman Hapgood to secretary of state, October 25, 1919, NACP, RG 59, Purport Lists for the Department of State Decimal File, 1910–1944, NA Microfilm M973, 861.4016/282.

113. "Jewish Emigration to the United States," December 11, 1920, NACP, RG 165, MID 245-71 (2).

114. Naval Intelligence: "Conditions in Russia," 1920, NADC, RG 38, ONI C-10-K: 13180.

115. "Russia—Jewry" January 11, 1921, NACP, RG 165, MID 245-82 (1); "Bolshevik Propaganda," October 10, 1922, MID 10058-747 (73); "Activity of International Jews," December 6, 1920, MID 10058-863 (12); "Alien Policies—Estonia" November 2, 1920, HIA, Gibson Papers, box 92.

116. "Jewish Emigration to the United States," December 11, 1920, MID 245-71 (2); memo for file, January 20, 1921, MID 245-4 (24).

117. "International Jews," January 8, 1921, NACP, RG 165, MID 245-4 (23); "Bolshevism," September 28, 1920, MID 10058-450 (4); "Jewish Activities," December 21, 1920, MID 245-4 (22).

118. Churchill–Arthur H. Frazier and Churchill–Colonel Allan L. Briggs Correspondence, August–November 1921, NACP, RG 165, MID 2684-28-32.

119. "Austria, Psychological, Ethics," March 5, 1921, NACP, RG 165, MID 2656-FF-11.

120. "Racial Character of the Austrians," October 10, 1920, NACP, RG 165, MID 2656-FF-1.

121. Ibid.

122. "Germany and Anti-Semitism," April 6, 1920, NACP, RG 165, MID 2656-B-2; "Growth of Anti-Semitism in German Circles," March 31, 1920, MID 245-21 (2); "Anti-Semitism in Germany," May 20, 1919, MID 124-284 (1); "Anti-Semitism in Germany," March 11, 1919, MID 2059-1206.

123. Biographical Sketch, October 23, 1925, NACP, RG 165, MID 2215-158; Bidwell, *Military Intelligence,* p. 162.

124. Colonel Edward Davis, "Military Attaché" (unpublished memoirs), MHI, Edward Davis Papers, box 1, pp. 43, 211–212, 214, 257–258, and passim.

125. Miles to Davis, October 29, 1920; Davis, "Jews," January 6, 1921, NACP, RG 165, MID 245-74 (1–4).

126. "Jews," January 12, 1921, NACP, RG 165, MID 245-83 (1); "Emigration of Undesirables to America," January 3, 1921, MID 245-71 (3).

127. "The Jew, the Lett, and the Russian. Their Relative Roles in Soviet Russia," December 14, 1920, NACP, RG 165, MID 2656-D-17.

128. Ibid.

129. Major Ivens Jones to Churchill, October 11, 1921, NACP, RG 165, MID 2632-R-8 (4); Ronald Steel, *Walter Lippmann and the American Century* (Boston, 1980), pp. 142–154, 166–167, 186–196.

130. Churchill to Jones, November 12, 1921, NACP, RG 165, MID 2632-R-8 (6).

131. Colonel Matthew Smith to William L. Hurley, March 10, 1921, NACP, RG 165, MID 245-87; Colonel William F. Godson to Colonel Sherman Miles, January 10, 1920, MID 2632-R-2; "Jews with Bolshevik Tendencies," June 23, 1919, MID 10102-489 (146–147); "Various Bolshevists Residing in Switzerland," February 5, 1919, MID 10102-489 (31); "Bolshevism in Switzerland," January 29, 1919, MID 10102-489 (26).

132. Godson to MID Director, December 11, 1919, Miles to Godson, January 26, 1920, NACP, RG 165, MID 10214-571 (1). See also MID 10214-580 (1), 10214-600 (3), 10214-625 (13–16).

133. "Jewry," November 20, 1920, NACP, RG 165, MID 245-6 (1); Colonel Matthew Smith to William L. Hurley, December 21, 1920, MID 245-65.

134. Godson, "The Jewish Mondiale Movement," December 6, 1920, NACP, RG 165, MID 245-70 (1).

135. Ibid.

136. Ibid.; Smith to Hurley, December 30, 1920, NACP, RG 59, 000-1472.

137. "Racial-Russia," January 5, 1921, NACP, RG 165, MID 245-85 (1); "The Jew, the Lett, and the Russian," December 14, 1920, MID 2656-D-17; "Relations Between Jews and Russians Strained," *Weekly Intelligence Summary*, May 29, 1920, Challener, *Military Intelligence*, vol. 13, pp. 3740–3741.

138. Naval Intelligence: "Conditions in Russia, 1922," NADC, RG 38, ONI C-10-M:15533-B; "Anti-Semitism," August 23, 1921, NACP, RG 165, MID 245-127; "Russia (Anti-Semitism)," August 20, 1921, MID 245-107; Major Philip H. Bagby to MID director, January 8, 1921, MID 10058-956 (8).

139. Ibid.

140. *General Intelligence Bulletin*, no. 43, March 26, 1921, p. 18; no. 58, July 9, 1921, pp. 3–15; in *U.S. Military Intelligence Reports: Surveillance of Radicals in the United States, 1917–1941*, microfilm (Frederick, MD, 1984). See also Athan G. Theoharis and John Stuart Cox, *The Boss: J. Edgar Hoover and the Great American Inquisition* (Philadelphia, 1988), pp. 43–81.

141. "Report on Bolshevism," pp. 1, 9, 26; and *General Intelligence Bulletin*, July 9, 1921.

142. "Report on Bolshevism," p. 11; and "Russia," *General Intelligence Bulletin*, November 13, 1920, p. 24.

143. "Jews in Roumania," February 21, 1921, NACP, RG 165, MID 245-8 (6).

Chapter 4

1. "Bolsheviki," *Weekly Intelligence Summary*, January 26, 1918, Richard D. Challener, ed., *United States Military Intelligence, 1917–1927*, 30 vols. (New York, 1978), vol. 3, p. 32; and military attaché, The Hague, telegram to Washington, December 29, 1918; NACP, RG 165, MID 2266-X-316.

2. Special Agent R. B. Spencer, Chicago, to Bielaski, chief, Bureau of Investigation, October 29, 1918, NACP, RG 165, MID 10058-65 (4).

3. Sergeants John C. Dillon and William J. Gillen to CO, MID Intelligence Police NYC, November 26, 1918; Inspectors C. L. Converse and L. F. Dixon to Captain John B. Trevor, November 29, 1918; Trevor to MID director, November 29, 1918, NACP, RG 165, MID 10110-920 (29–30, 35).

4. "Says Mass of Jews Oppose Bolsheviki," *New York Times*, February 15, 1919, AJCA, AJC.

5. Major Thwaites to Colonel H. A. Parkenham, MID Washington, May 22, 23, 1918, and cablegram July 2, 1918, "Confidential File on Louis Brandeis" maintained by Office of Counselor, Department of State, NACP, RG 59, Entry 538, Brandeis-173.

6. Melech Epstein, *The Jew and Communism: The Story of Early Communist Victories and Ultimate Defeats in the Jewish Community, U.S.A.* (New York, 1959), pp. 27–29, 61–64.

7. Robert K. Murray, *Red Scare: A Study in National Hysteria, 1919–1920* (Minneapolis, 1955), pp. 45–49; 58–66; Epstein, *The Jew and Communism*, pp. 28–30.

8. Murray, *Red Scare*, pp. 31–32, 47–56.

9. Captain John B. Trevor, "Ethnic Map of New York City," February 27, 1919, NACP, RG 165, MID 10110-920 (290).

10. Trevor, "Plans for the Protection of New York in Case of Local Disturbances," May 2, 1919, NACP, RG 165, MID 10110-920 (538), p. 4.

11. Trevor, "Ethnic Map," MID 10110-920 (290); Colonel K. C. Masteller to Trevor, March 7, 1919, MID 10110-920 (315).

12. Trevor, March 1919 Correspondence, NACP, RG 165, MID 110110-920 (347) (391–392).

13. Jerry Z. Muller, "Communism, Anti-Semitism, and the Jews," *Commentary* 86 (August 1988), pp. 32–33.

14. Ibid., pp. 31–32.

15. Murray, *Red Scare*; *New York Times*, May 1–3, 1919.

16. Inspectors C. L. Converse and John D. Purdie to Trevor, May 2, 1919, NACP, RG 165, MID 10110-920 (543) (547).

17. Lieutenant Albert B. Pattou, Report, Chicago, May 21, 1919, NACP, RG 165, MID 10110-853 (333).

18. "1,700 Police Guard Mooney Meeting," *New York Times*, May 2, 1919.

19. Purdie Report, May 2, 1919, NACP, RG 165, MID 10110-920 (543).

20. Converse Report, May 2, 1919, NACP, RG 165, MID 10110-920 (547).

21. Trevor to MID director, May 2, 1919, NACP, RG 165, MID 10110-920 (548).

22. Trevor, "Plans for the Protection of New York," MID 10110-920 (538).

23. Colonel K. C. Masteller to Trevor, May 3, 1919, NACP, RG 165, MID 10110-920 (550).

24. Trevor, "Jewish Influences in the Radical Movement," NACP, RG 165, MID 10058-285 (176).

25. Inspector George Starr to Lieutenant William Moffat, and Trevor to MID director, May 23, 24, 1919, NACP, RG 165, MID 10110-920 (638–639).

26. Major Thomas B. Crockett to Churchill, September 22, 1919, NACP, RG 165, MID 10566-281 (2). On Crockett's earlier surveillance activities, see Roy Talbert, *Negative Intelligence: The Army and the American Left, 1917–1941* (Jackson, MS, 1991), pp. 184–196.

27. Colonel William McCain to Colonel Gordon Johnston, May 20, 1920, NACP, RG 165, MID 9684-268.

28. See September 1919 correspondence between Churchill, Colonel Nicholas Biddle, and Major H. A. Strauss, NACP, RG 165, MID 10566-281 (3–11), 10566-297 (10).

29. Colonel E. R. Warner McCabe to Churchill, October 9, 1919, NACP, RG 165, MID 10566-281 (6).

30. Churchill to McCabe, October 11, 1919, NACP, RG 165, MID 10566-281 (7).

31. Joan M. Jensen, *Army Surveillance in America, 1775–1980* (New Haven, 1991), pp. 178–195; Talbert, *Negative Intelligence*, pp. 182–207.

32. RG 165, 10560-152 (104).

33. Murray, *Red Scare*.

34. Colonel Alexander B. Coxe Memorandum, January 21, 1920, NACP, RG 165, MID 10566-291 (3); Coxe–H. A. Vivian Correspondence, August 1920, MID 10566-297 (1–2); Joseph H. Defrees–Newton D. Baker Correspondence, October 1919, MID 10566-297.

35. Churchill Memorandum, December 8, 1921, NACP, RG 165, MID 10566-308 (1–6); see also Trevor files listed in "Name Index to Correspondence of the Military Intelligence Division," NA microfilm M1194, roll 235.

36. Trevor Report, NACP, RG 165, MID 10110-1665 (1–2).

37. Talbert, *Negative Intelligence*, pp. 197–207.

38. Colonel Charles H. Mason, "Policies Governing Alterations in M.I.D.," May 15, 1920, NACP, RG 165, MID 255-54 (1).

39. "International Movements or 'Isms,'" June 10, 1920, NACP, RG 165, MID 10058-586 (1); revised policy, October 14, 1920, and "A Brief Sketch of the Important International Movements or 'Isms' and Certain Combinations of These Movements (Intrigues) with Which the Military Intelligence Division Is Concerned," NACP, RG 165, MID 10110-2048 (1).

40. NACP, RG 165, MID 10110-2048 (1).

41. Ibid.

42. Ibid.

43. Captain W. L. Moffat to MID director, March 8, 1920, NACP, RG 165, MID 10565-115; August 19, 1919, MID 10110-1194 (157–159).

44. See March 1920 correpondence between Captain W. L. Moffat and Captain Robert T. Snow on "Justice Brandeis and the 'Jewish International Movement'"; Major H. A. Strauss, "Zionist Movement," September 13, 1919, NACP, RG 165,

MID 245-18 (3–8); Captain Henry Frothingham to MID director, February 19, 1920, MID 10110-1727; "Bolshevik Activities," February 5, 1920, NACP, RG 165, MID 10110-1194 (300).

45. L. Lanier Winslow to William L. Hurley, March 7, and Hurley to J. Edgar Hoover, March 15, 1921; NACP, RG 59, 000-1612; Department of Justice, *General Intelligence Bulletin*, no. 44 (April 2, 1921), p. 6, NACP, RG 165 MID 10110-4283; Colonel Gordon Johnston to MID director, April 17, 1920, MID 10110-1534.

46. J. Edgar Hoover to William L. Hurley, June 10, 1920, NACP, RG 59, 800.11-97; J. Edgar Hoover to Churchill, June 15, and Colonel Sherman Miles to military attaché London, June 22, 1922, NACP, RG 165, MID 245-26 (1–2); J. Edgar Hoover to General Dennis E. Nolan, November 18, 1920, MID 245-18.

47. Johnston-McCain Correspondence, May 20, April 21, 1920, NACP, RG 165, MID 9684-268 (5).

48. Johnston-McCain-Cox Correspondence, February–April 1920, NACP, RG 165, MID 269-1 (3–11); Johnston to Charles Davis, March 18, 1920, MID 8028/2.

49. "Situation Report," Chicago, January 17, 1920, NACP, RG 165, MID 10110-1649, pp. 1–2; Report on "All Chicago Liberty Demonstration," January 11, 1920, MID 10110-1627 (7).

50. Memo, January 29, 1920, and McCain to Johnston on "Russo-German Jews" May 10, 1920, NACP, RG 165, MID 245-23 (1–2).

51. Ibid.

52. Johnston to MID director on "Russo-German Jews," May 26, 1920, and Report of Secret Agent No. 8, "Jewry—Zionist Movement," NACP, RG 165, MID 245-23 (3–4).

53. Ibid.

54. Colin Holmes, *Anti-Semitism in British Society, 1876–1939* (London, 1979), pp. 141–160; Gisela Lebzelter, *Political Anti-Semitism in England, 1918–1939* (New York, 1978), pp. 13–28.

55. See William L. Hurley–L. Lanier Winslow Correspondence, January and March, 1920, and "Most Secret Memorandum," on "Bolshevism and Judaism" and the *Protocols*, February 17, 1920, NACP, RG 59, Entry 538, 861.0-628.

56. Churchill–Dr. Harris A. Houghton Correspondence, February 27, 29, 1920, NACP, RG 165, MID 99-75 (10–13).

57. Churchill telegram, March 5, 1920; Colonel Oscar N. Solbert to Churchill, March 8, 1920, MID 99-75 (9, 16).

58. See "Extracts from Protocols," circulated within MID, March 1920, MID 99-75 (22).

59. Captain Robert T. Snow's note to Colonel William W. Hicks, MID 99-75 (22).

60. Leo Ribuffo, "Henry Ford and *The International Jew*," *American Jewish History*, vol. 69 (June 1980), pp. 437–477.

61. *The Dearborn Independent*, May 22, 1920, p. 1.

62. Ibid.; Ribuffo, "Henry Ford," pp. 446–454.

63. Ribuffo, "Henry Ford," pp. 446–447; Robert Singerman, "The American Career of the Protocols of the Elders of Zion," *American Jewish History*, vol. 71 (September 1981), pp. 71–74.

64. Ribuffo, "Henry Ford," pp. 457–459.

65. NACP, RG 165, MID 10110-KK-8 (7–8).

66. See articles on "The Causes of World Unrest" in copies of *Morning Post* in NACP, RG 165, MID 245-29.

67. *The Protocols and World Revolution* (Boston, 1920); Singerman, "American Career of the Protocols," pp. 60–66.

68. MID Washington to intelligence officer Boston, August 23, 1920, MID 99-75 (29), Colonel William B. Graham to chief, Negative Branch, September 24, 1920, MID 99-75 (35). For drafts of Brasol's work, see MID 99-75 (6).

69. Colonel John M. Dunn to MID Boston, October 12, Major Theodore Spencer to chief, Negative Branch, October 18, 1920, MID 99-75 (41); Dunn to corps area intelligence officers, October 22, 1920, MID 99-75 (45).

70. Major Iven Jones to MID Washington, December 8, 1920; Colonel Sherman Miles to military attaché, Bern, January 5, 1921; Colonel William F. Godson to MID, January 29, 1921; MID 99-75 (67, 70, 75).

71. Godson to Miles, February 21, 1921, NACP, RG 165, MID 245-48 (41).

72. Miles to military attaché, Paris, November 24, 1920, NACP, RG 165, MID 2347-C-5 (3).

73. Miles to Churchill, January 15, 1921, NACP, RG 165, MID 2610-37 (330).

74. Miles to Godson, February 25, 1921, MID 99-75 (76).

75. Colonel Raymond Sheldon Letters, October 2, 21, 1920, and "Protocols of the Zionists," MID 99-75 (34, 42).

76. See MID Protocol File 99-75 (61, 67, 71, 87–88); Singerman, "American Career of the Protocols," pp. 68–70.

77. *The "Protocols," Bolshevism, and the Jews: An Address to Their Fellow-Citizens by American Jewish Organizations* (New York, 1921), especially pp. 11–14.

78. Ibid., pp. 15–16. Cyrus Adler to Lucien Wolf, February 8, 1921, AJCA, Adler Papers, Chronological File. Allan K. Kage, "The American Jewish Committee's Attitude Towards Anti-Semitism," Columbia University Center for Israel and Jewish Studies Working Papers (New York, 1979), pp. 41, 47, 51–61.

79. *"Protocols," Bolshevism, and the Jews*, p. 14.

80. Alexander Sachs–Newton D. Baker Correspondence, July 20, 30, 1920, NACP, RG 165, MID 245029; Colonel Alexander B. Coxe to chief of staff, July 30, 1920, NACP, RG 165, MID 9683-42 (33); Singerman, "American Career of the Protocols," pp. 66–69.

81. See Adler-Wolf Correspondence, June–July 1920; Adler to Herman Bernstein, January 21, 1921; Adler to Wolf, February 8, 1921; AJCA, Adler Papers, Chronological File.

82. Miles to Godson, March 17, 1921, NACP, RG 165, MID 245-48 (42).

83. Senate, *Emergency Immigration Legislation*, 66 Cong., 3d sess., 1921, S164-3, pp. 290–295.

84. John B. Trevor Testimony, in ibid., pp. 295–305.

85. Anson Conger Goodyear Lecture before University Club, November 29, 1919, pp. 4–5, HIA, Goodyear Papers; Robert D. Schulzinger, *The Making of the Diplomatic Mind: The Training, Outlook, and Style of United States Foreign Service Officers, 1908–1931* (Middletown, CT, 1975), pp. 62–63, 126–134.

86. "The Passport Office," HIA, John A. Stader Papers, box 1; Stader to Anson C. Goodyear, April 28, 1921, HIA, Goodyear Papers, box 2.

87. Memo to Colonel McCain, May 1920, MID 10058-61 (5–7) in MID files on Hebrew Sheltering and Immigrant Aid Society, NA microfilm, 1984.

88. "Immigration Report," January 29, 1920, NACP, RG 165, MID 245-8.

89. House, *Temporary Suspension of Immigration*, 66th Cong. 3d sess., 1920, H.R. 1109, pp. 3–11.

90. Colonel T. Worthington Hollyday, November 27, 1920, NACP, RG 165, 245-71 (1); Colonel Matthew C. Smith to William L. Hurley, January 12, 1921, MID 245-75; Hollyday, January 14, 1921, MID 245-71 (4); "Emigration of Undesirables to the United States," February 7, 1921, MID 10058-972; "Jewism in Roumania," February 21, 1921, MID 245-8 (6).

91. Hollyday, January 3, 1921, NACP, RG 165, MID 10110-2127; Colonel Edward Davis, January 3, 1921, MID 245-71 (3).

92. Ibid.; Hollyday December 11, 1920, January 26, 1921, NACP, RG 165, MID 245-71 (2–6).

93. Ibid.

94. Ibid.; "Notes on Foreigners in the United States," February 11, 1921, NACP, RG 165 MID 239-64; Davis, February 17, 1921, MID 245-71 (13).

95. Colonel John M. Dunn–Colonel Raymond Sheldon Correspondence, November 4, 14, 1920, NACP, RG 165, MID 245-53 (1–2); Parker Hitt, June 15, 20, 1921, MID 10058-P-14, 10110-1585.

96. Unidentified handwritten cover memo to Colonel Graham D. Fitch; Colonel Charles H. Mason to Fitch; Major Gilbert Marshall to Fitch, January 17, 1921, NACP, RG 165, MID 245-70; Parker Hitt–Major James L. Collins Correspondence, February 1, 11, 1921, MID 245-82 (2).

97. NACP, RG 165, MID 245-70.

98. Colonel Matthew C. Smith to William L. Hurley, May 10, 1921, NACP, RG 165, MID 245-95 (2).

99. "The World," *Weekly Intelligence Summary*, May 10, 1921, Challener, *Military Intelligence*, vol. 18, p. 7900.

100. John Higham, *Strangers in the Land: Patterns of American Nativism, 1860–1925* (New Brunswick, NJ, 1955), pp. 308–311; E. P. Hutchinson, *Legislative History of American Immigration Policy, 1798–1965* (Philadelphia, 1981), pp. 171–180.

101. "Coblenz Conference of Military Attachés," June 1921, NACP, RG 165, MID 2580-47 (29).

102. Ibid., pp. 4–5.

103. Ibid.

104. J. Edgar Hoover to MID director, January 20, 1921, NACP, RG 165, MID 10058-949 (2); "Monograph Report Roumania: Jewish, Revolutionary," May 18, 1921, and Colonel Matthew C. Smith to Hurley on "Jewism," June 28, 1921, MID 245-98 (1, 10); Colonel Elbert E. Farman, September 3, 1921, MID 245-25 (4); Chief Special Agent Bannerman of the State Department to Hurley on JDC and Jews, June 30, 1921, NACP, RG 59, 861.0-1559; DeWitt C. Poole to Secretary of State, October 28, 1921, RG 59, 861.4016/299.

105. *The Truth About "The Protocols": A Literary Forgery: From the* Times *of August 16, 17, and 18, 1921* (London, 1921), AJCA, Protocols File; Captain Hamilton E. Maguire, "Jewish World Plot," August 18, 1921, NACP, RG 165, MID 99-75 (85).

106. *The Protocols, Bolshevism, and the Jews* (New York, 1921); "The English Press on the Exposé of the Protocol Forgery by the *London Times*" typescript, AJCA, Protocols Files.

107. Churchill memorandum, August 27, 1921, NACP, RG 165, MID 245-89.

108. Harris A. Houghton File, NACP, RG 165, MID 9683-42.

109. William F. Godson–MID Correspondence, NACP, RG 165, MID 2243-113-120, 2257-B-61 (11–12).

110. Congressman Albert Johnson–John B. Trevor Correspondence, NADC, RG 233, Records of U.S. House of Representatives, Committee on Immigration and Naturalization, H.R. 69A-F20.1; Higham, *American Nativism*, pp. 314–315; Trevor MID File; Churchill–Trevor Correspondence 1922, NACP, RG 165, MID 10525-815 (3–5), 9771-245 (18–21).

111. See the 16 boxes of American Defense Society Papers, New York Historical Society, New York City (hereafter NYHS); Higham, *American Nativism*, pp. 313–314.

112. Daniel J. Kevles, *In the Name of Eugenics: Genetics and the Uses of Human Heredity* (New York, 1985), pp. 79–83, 129–130; "Testing the Army's Intelligence: Psychologists and the Military in World War I," *Journal of American History*, vol. 55 (December 1968), pp. 565–581.

113. Madison Grant, *The Passing of the Great Race: Or the Racial Basis of European History* (New York, 1916); Lothrop Stoddard, *The Rising Tide of Color Against White World-Supremacy* (New York, 1920) and *The Revolt Against Civilization: The Menace of the Under-Man* (New York, 1922); Clinton Stoddard Burr, *America's Race Heritage* (New York, 1922); Higham, *American Nativism*, pp. 270–277.

114. Stoddard, *Revolt Against Civilization*, preface, pp. 28–31, 86–87, 133, 224–225.

115. Ibid., pp. 113, 151–153, 191; Stoddard, *Rising Tide of Color*, pp. xxxii, 165, 218–221.

116. Kenneth Roberts, *Why Europe Leaves Home* (Indianapolis, IN, 1922).

117. Ibid., pp. 47–51, 120; Jack Bales, *Kenneth Roberts: The Man and His Works* (Metuchen, NJ, 1989), pp. 16–18.

118. "1st Immigration," Notebooks, LC, Kenneth L. Roberts Papers, box 1.

119. Ibid.; "1920: Berlin/Warsaw," "Kaluszyn, Warsaw," "Germany, Denmark, Norway, Sweden," "1921: Chapira (Paris) Airplane Trip, Antwerp, Rotterdam, Danzig," Notebooks, LC, Roberts Papers, box 2.

120. Roberts, "Kaluszyn," pp. 1–3, "Germany," pp. 3–7; *Why Europe Leaves Home*, pp. 13–18.

121. Roberts, "1920: Berlin/Warsaw," p. 24; "Germany," p. 24; *Why Europe Leaves Home*, pp. 76–79, 122–123.

122. Roberts, "1921: Chapira," p. 14.

123. Ibid., pp. 14–15.

124. Bales, *Kenneth Roberts*, p. 19; Higham, *American Nativism*, pp. 262, 265, 271, 273, 316.

125. Bales, *Kenneth Roberts*, p. 19; Higham, *American Nativism*, p. 313.

126. Colonel Amos A. Fries to Senator George E. Chamberlain, June 7, November 6, 1920; Colonel W. C. Sweeney to Fries, March 28, 1923; Fries to General John J. Bradley, November 12, 1923; UOL, Fries Papers, box 3; Brown, *American Generals*, pp. 296–302.

127. Colonel Benjamin M. Bailey lectures on "Americanism and Guts," "Aliens," and untitled lecture manuscript, Bailey Papers.

128. *Infantry Journal*, vol. 18 (January 1921), pp. 89–90, (March 1921), pp. 291–293; vol. 21 (August 1922), p. 219; vol. 22 (April 1923), pp. 371–386; vol. 24 (March 1924), pp. 639–642.

129. "History of the World Revolution," *Infantry Journal*, vol. 19 (August 1921), pp. 174–188.

130. *American Legion Weekly*, August 8, 22, November 21, 1919, January 12, November 2, 1923.

131. *American Legion Weekly*, July 20, August 3, 1923.

132. Roscoe Baker, *The American Legion and American Foreign Policy* (New York, 1954), pp. 28–32, 51–57; Robert A. Divine, *American Immigration Policy, 1924–1952* (New York, 1972), pp. 6–8; Higham, *American Nativism*, pp. 224, 256, 313.

133. House, *Restriction of Immigration: Minority Report*, H.R. 350, pt. 2, 68th Cong., 1st sess., 1924, pp. 3–5, 16; *Restriction of Immigration Hearings*, 68th Cong., 1st sess., H344-2, 1923/1924, pp. 288–291, 341–345; *Views of the Minority, Restriction of Immigration and Revision of Quota Act*, 67th Cong., 4th sess., H.R. 1621, 1923, pp. 39–43.

134. *Restriction of Immigration*, 68th Cong., 1st sess., H.R. 350, 1924, pp. 13–17; Higham, *American Nativism*, pp. 316–319.

135. Albert Johnson, "Immigration: A Legislative Point of View," *Nation's Business*, vol. 11 (July 1923), pp. 26–28.

136. Higham, *American Nativism*, pp. 321–324. See also John B. Trevor, *An Analysis of the American Immigration Act of 1924* (New York, 1924).

137. Johnson to Trevor, April 15, 1924, NADC, RG 233, HR-68A-F18.3.

Chapter 5

1. Colonel H. A. Smith to Charles B. Davenport, September 29, 1921, Davenport to Smith, October 3, 1921, MHI, AWCA 215-39.

2. Daniel J. Kevles, *In the Name of Eugenics: Genetics and the Uses of Human Heredity* (New York, 1985), pp. 44–56.

3. Charles B. Davenport, "Racial Features in War," October 29, 1921, pp. 2–3, MHI, AWCA 215-39.

4. Ibid, pp. 3–7; Kevles, *Eugenics*, pp. 80–83.

5. Davenport, "Racial Features in War," pp. 7–8.

6. Ibid., pp. 8, 17–18.

7. Ibid., pp. 18–19.

8. Ibid., pp. 20–21.

9. George S. Pappas, *Prudens Futuri! The U.S. Army War College, 1901–1967* (Carlisle, PA, 1968), pp. 40–45, 86, 124; "Personnel of the Army War College, 1925–1926," NACP, RG 165, MID 238-B-11 (57).

10. Pappas, *Army War College*, pp. 93–111, 127–132; MHI, AWCA, "Course at Army War College," 1919–1920, 1921–1922, 1923–1924, 1924–1925; NACP, RG 165, MID 238-B-3.

11. D.K.R. Crosswell, *The Chief of Staff: The Military Career of General Walter Bedell Smith* (New York, 1991), pp. 60–68.

12. Ibid., pp. 66–68; Pappas, *Army War College*, pp. 136–137; Henry G. Gole, "War Planning at the War College in the Mid-1930s," *Parameters, Journal of the U.S. Army War College*, vol. 15, no. 1 (Spring 1985), pp. 55–56, 63.

13. Clark Wissler, "Racial Problems Involved in International Relations," November 2, 1921, pp. 7, 19–22, MHI, AWCA 215-40.

14. Ibid., pp. 24–28.

15. William McDougall, *Is America Safe for Democracy?* (New York, 1921), pp. 27–35, 78–81, 100–101, 172–174, 194–195, and *The Group Mind: A Sketch of the Principles of Collective Psychology* (New York, 1920), pp. 149–169, 256, 306, 317.

16. William McDougall, "Race as a Factor in Causation of War," April 15, 1924, pp. 1–2, 6, MHI, AWCA 274A-37.

17. Ibid., pp. 4–6.

18. Ibid., pp. 2–4.

19. Ibid., pp. 5–7; John Higham, *Strangers in the Land: Patterns of American Nativism, 1860–1925* (New Brunswick, NJ, 1955), p. 273.

20. Henry Pratt Fairchild, "Problems of Population," October 14, 1932, pp. 1–2, MHI, AWCA G-1, 10. See also Fairchild, "Population," 1935, AWCA G-1, 6, 1936, and "Population," October 29, 1936, MHI, Frank J. McSherry Papers, box 1936-37; Robert A. Divine, *American Immigration Policy, 1924–1952* (New York, 1972), p. 26; Higham, *American Nativism*, p. 327.

21. Fairchild, "Problems of Population," October 14, 1932, pp. 2–6, 10.

22. Clayton Lane, "Functions of the Department of Commerce," February 2, 1927, pp. 5–6, MHI, AWCA 332A-14.

23. Herbert Adams Gibbons, *The New Map of Asia (1900–1919)* (Chautauqua, NY, 1919), preface, passim, and *An Introduction to World Politics* (New York, 1923), pp. 535–547.

24. Herbert Adams Gibbons, "General Aspects of the World Situation," November 5, 1931, MHI, AWCA G-2 Course 1931–1932, vol. 2, p. 20.

25. Robert F. Kelley, "The Bolshevik Regime in Russia," MHI, AWCA G-2 Course, 1931–1932, vol. 2, pp. 18, 28.

26. Bradford G. Chynoweth, *Bellamy Park: Memoirs by Bradford Grethen Chynoweth* (Hicksville, NY, 1975), p. 133; Pappas, *Army War College*, pp. 125–127; Merle Miller, *Ike the Soldier As They Knew Him* (New York, 1987), pp. 236–238, 258, 298.

27. See General William D. Connor's monologue, MHI, AWCA G-2 Course, 1931–1932, vol. 2, pp. 29–30.

28. Ibid., p. 30.

29. William D. Connor, "Some Aspects of the Foreign Policies of the United States," January 25, 1929, pp. 13–15, MHI, AWCA Course at AWC, 1928–1929, G-2 Doc Nos. 1–18, vol. 2.

30. General George Van Horn Moseley, "War Department General Staff and General Council," September 2, 1932, p. 20, MHI, AWCA 393-A-14; Colonel Preston Brown, "Political Situation," September 13, 14, 1920, pp. 1, 14, MHI, AWCA G-2, 20–21.

31. Major Preston Brown, "Population and Food," September 6, 1919, MHI, AWCA Course in Intelligence, 1919–1920, vol. 2, *Intelligence, Lectures*, p. 61.

32. Ibid., p. 62.

33. Major Williams W. Hicks, "Estimate of the Radical or Revolutionary Situation in the United States," December 16, 1920, pp. 1–2, 22, NACP, RG 165, MID 10058-984 (1).

34. Ibid.

35. See MHI, McSherry Papers, box 1936-37; HIA, Ralph C. Smith Papers, box 14.

36. "G-2 Orientation and Outline of the Course," January 3–February 5, 1927, "Section V: Individual Reports," MHI, AWCA 332A-4; Pappas, *Army War College*; Chynoweth, *Memoirs*, pp. 135–136.

37. "General References, G-2 Course," 1922–1923, NACP, RG 165, MID 238-B-3 (325).

38. Ibid.; "Compilation of Book Reviews," G-2 Course, 1927–1928, NACP, RG 165, MID 238-B-11 (154).

39. Ibid.; "Selections from Library Accessions," May and December 1924, NACP, RG 165, MID 238-B-3 (95), 238-B-11 (47); Walter C. Sweeney, *Military Intelligence: A New Weapon of War* (New York, 1924), pp. vii, 59–65, 74–75.

40. "G-2 Factors in War Planning," pp. 14–22, NACP, RG 165, MID 238-B-11 (113).

41. Ibid.

42. Earnest Sevier Cox, *White America* (Richmond, VA, 1923), pp. 5–10, 22–23; "Compilation of Book Reviews," p. 92, NACP, RG 165, MID 238-B-11 (154).

43. McDougall, *Group Mind*, pp. 159, 256, 306, 317.

44. Lothrop Stoddard, *Racial Realities in Europe* (New York, 1924), foreword, pp. 26–27, 144–145.

45. Ibid., pp. 171–172, 231–246.

46. Leon Dominion, *The Frontiers of Language and Nationality in Europe* (New York, 1917), pp. xiii–xvi, 124–127, 301; "Significant Factors in World Political and Social Conditions," January 20, 1928, pp. 4–6, 12, NACP, RG 165, MID 238-B-11 (115).

47. Isaiah Bowman, *Supplement to the New World Problems in Geography* (Yonkers, NY, 1924), pp. 12–17, 25–30; "European Colonization," February 6, 1926, bibliography, MHI, AWCA 315-A/35.

48. Isaiah Bowman, *The New World Problems in Political Geography* (Yonkers, NY, 1921), pp. 380–382, 420–421.

49. Ibid., pp. 220–222, 286–287, 354–360, 380–382.

50. Archibald and Ethel Colquhoun, *The Whirlpool of Europe: Austria-Hungary and the Habsburgs* (New York, 1914), pp. 154–156, 173–176, 223; "Restrictive Measures in the Treaty of Versailles and Significant Factors in the Problems of the So-Called European Minorities," January 20, 1928, MHI, AWCA 342-5.

51. Colquhoun, *Whirpool of Europe*, pp. 109–111, 174–175, 223, 301.

52. Herbert Adams Gibbons, *The Reconstruction of Poland and the Near East* (New York, 1917), pp. 52–53, 212–218. Although Gibbons's *Introduction to World Politics* was also recommended reading at the War College and reveals his general anti-nativist stand, it contained nothing on the Jewish question.

53. Herbert Adams Gibbons, *The New Map of Europe (1911–1914): The Story of the Recent European Crises and Wars and of Europe's Present Catastrophe* (New York, 1914), pp. 107–108.

54. Gibbons, *New Map of Asia*, pp. 192–228.

55. John Spargo, *The Jew and American Ideals* (New York, 1921), foreword, pp. 6–13, 40–47, 60–71, 76, 90–91, 136–137. Army War College, "Selections from Library Accessions," May 1924, p. 4, NACP, RG 165, MID 238-B-3 (95).

56. Pappas, *Army War College*, pp. 132–133; "General References, G-2 Course, 1922–1923," NACP, RG 165, MID 238-B-3 (62); "G-2 Factors in War Planning," MID 238-B-11 (113); "Significant Factors in World Political and Social Conditions," MID 238-B-11 (115).

57. C. H. Mason, *Military Intelligence: Strategic Index* (August 1917), NACP, RG 165, MID 2665-1-A; Joseph W. Bendersky, "Psychohistory Before Hitler: Early Military Analyses of German National Psychology," *Journal of the History of the Behavioral Sciences*, vol. 24 (April 1988), pp. 166–182. Donald S. Napoli, *Architects of Adjustment: The History of the Psychological Profession in the United States* (Port Washington, NY, 1981), pp. 13–25, 32–33; Robert M. Yerkes, "Psychology in Relation to War," *Psychological Review*, vol. 25 (1918), pp. 85–115; Daniel J. Kevles, "Testing the Army's Intelligence: Psychologists and the Military in World War I," *Journal of American History*, vol. 55 (December 1968), pp. 565–567.

58. Churchill and Major Sherman Miles to military attachés, November 20, 1920, August 18, 1921, and to attaché, Bern, November 15, 1921, NACP, RG 165, MID 2665-1-17-19; *The Psychological Sub-Section M.I.2*, MID 2665-9, p. 6; Bendersky, "Early Military Analyses," pp. 170–173.

59. Ibid.

60. *Psychological Sub-Section*.

61. Ibid., pp. 9–18.

62. Ibid., pp. 9–10.

63. Ibid.

64. Churchill to military attaché, Bern, November 15, 1921, NACP, RG 165, MID 2665-19 (2).

65. Ibid.; *Psychological Sub-Section*, pt. 4, "The Strategic Estimate," p. 1.

66. Major Gilbert Marshall to Colonel Edwards, November 5, 1920, and Major T. C. Cook to chief, Positive Branch, November 8, 1920, NACP, RG 165, MID 255-29.

67. Bendersky, "Early Military Analyses," pp. 171–176.

68. "Anatomical Type of Head and Brain," and Major Charles Burnett to MID director, November 1, 1920, NACP, RG 165, MID 2656-H-10-11.

69. "Psychology of the German People," "German Hypocrisy," "Influence of Environment on German Mentality," "German National Brain," "Germany—Sexual Perversion," 1920–1921, NACP, RG 165, MID 2656-B; "Central Europe—the Tribal Instinct," January 18, 1922, MID 2656-B-4; "France," 1920–1921, MID 2656-C-7-10; "Japan-Psychologic," October 12, 1921, MID 2656-H-25.

70. See entire files on MID psychological reports from attachés, NACP, RG 165, MID 2656; Bendersky, "Early Military Analyses," p. 172.

71. Bendersky, "Early Military Analyses," p. 176; Churchill to Colonel McKenney, "Information re Jewry," December 27, 1919, NACP, RG 165, MID 245-6; Churchill memorandum for executive officers, May 19, 1922, MID 2610-G-10.

72. "Estimate of Strategic Situation, Germany," December 18, 1930, p. 17, MHI, AWCA 372-4A; "Strategical Estimate of Italy," December 17, 1931, pp. 4–7, AWCA 382-3B.

73. "European Colonization," February 6, 1926, p. 16, MHI, AWCA 315-A/35; "Strategic Survey of Union of Socialist Soviet Republics," December 20, 1932, p. 30, AWCA 392-5B; "Intelligence Summary of Estimate on European Russia," September 30, 1919, pp. 7–8, AWCA 57-15; "Summary of Estimate on Russia," October 14, 1922, pp. 1–3, 13, AWCA 251-9.

74. "Current Estimate of Comparative Military Power . . ." January 14, 1927, p. 5, MHI, AWCA 332-2.

75. "Poland" October 1, 1919, in *General Staff College, 1919–1920*, vol. 2, *Intelligence*, pt. 2, "Committee Reports," pp. 174–178, MHI, AWCA; "Summary of Estimate of Poland," September 20, 1921, p. 3, AWCA 225-3; "Significant Factors in World Political and Social Conditions," January 20, 1928, pp. 4–6, 12, NACP, RG 165, MID 238-B-11 (115).

76. "Austria-Hungary," in *General Staff College 1919–1920*, vol. 2, *Intelligence*, pt. 2, September 24, 1919, p. 81, MHI, AWCA; "Succession States of the Austro-Hungarian Empire," September 20–21, 1921, pp. 2–3, 10, 17, 34; and appendix, September 20, 1921, p. 16, AWCA 225-2 and 225-2A.

77. Ibid.

78. Ibid.

79. "Summary of Estimate on Russia," September 30, October 1–2, 1920, pp. 9–11, MHI, AWCA 83-12/B; "Bolshevism," October 1, 1920, pp. 3–6, 9, 12, 25–26, NACP, RG 165, MID 10058-910-1; "Summary of Estimate on Russia," September 28, 29, 1921, pp. 1–3, MID 238-B-11 (5); "Summary of Estimate on Russia," October 14, 1922, pp. 1–2, MHI, AWCA 251-9; "Bolshevik Influence and Its Importance," February 5, 1927, pp. 1–2, AWCA 332A-28.

80. "Bolshevism," pp. 9–12, 25–27, NACP, RG 165, MID 10058-910-1.

81. "Estimate on the United States," pt. 3, "Military Situation," October 21, 1919, p. 5, MHI, AWCA 57-31; "United States Political Situation," October 19, 1921, p. 35, AWCA 225-16; "Anti-War Societies," December 20, 1924, pp. 6–7, AWCA 287-8.

82. "United States Political Situation," October 19, 1921, pp. 33–34, MHI, AWCA 225-16. See also Edward A. Ross, *The Old World in the New: The Significance of Past and Present Immigration to the American People* (New York, 1914), pp. 154–157.

83. "Estimate of the United States: Psychological Situation," October 18, 1919, pp. 9–10, MHI, AWCA 57-31/c; "United States," pt. 3, "Military Situation," October 21, 1919, p. 5, AWCA 57-31.

84. Ibid.; "Estimate on the United States," pt. 4, "General Situation," October 22, 1919, pp. 1–2, MHI, AWCA 57-3; "Anti-War Societies," December 20, 1924, pp. 6–7, AWCA 287-8.

85. "Estimate on the United States," pt. 3, "Military Situation," October 21, 1919, pp. 3–4, MHI, AWCA 57-31; "Strategic Survey of the United States," September 17, 1927, p. 13, AWCA 346-3; "Citizen and Army Espionage," February 6, 1926, AWCA 315-A/30.

86. "Estimate on the United States," pt. 3, "Military Situation," October 21, 1919, pp. 3–5, MHI, AWCA 57-31.

87. Stephen Ambrose, *Eisenhower: Soldier, General of the Army, President-Elect, 1890–1952* (New York, 1983), p. 90.

Chapter 6

1. Colonel William F. Godson to Colonel N. E. Margetts, August 31, 1925, NACP, RG 165, MID 10058-1271 (2).

2. Roy Talbert, *Negative Intelligence: The Army and the American Left, 1917–1941* (Jackson, MS, 1991), p. 224; Rhodri Jeffreys-Jones, *American Espionage: From Secret Service to CIA* (New York, 1977), pp. 120–123; Russell F. Weigley, *History of the United States Army* (New York, 1967), pp. 400–405.

3. "Radicalism in the United States," NACP, RG 165, MID 10110-2512, p. 7.

4. Colonel William B. Graham–Colonel Walter O. Boswell Correspondence, February 17, 20, 1926, NACP, RG 165, MID 99-75 (87–88).

5. Memo to Patrick J. Hurley, March 1, 1933, and "A Survey of the Caucasian in the Territory of Hawaii," January 1930, NACP, RG 165, MID 9605-97 (1–3).

6. "Report on May Day Celebration," May 1, 1926, NACP, RG 165, MID 10110-2562; "Radical and Anti-Military Speakers," March 18, 1926, MID 10314-556 (137); General S. D. Sturgis to adjutant general, April 2, 1925, MID 10110-2452 (114); Colonel William B. Graham–Colonel Walter O. Boswell Correspondence, May 16, 27, 1925, MID 2774-19 (23–24); "Developments in Radical Activities in the United States Since 1923," February 7, 1924, MID 10110-2512 (2); Organized Reserve Lieutenant Harold Printz to Colonel Charles Allen, January 16, 1924, NADC, RG 394, U. S. Army Continental Commands, 1920-42, box 172, 350.05.

7. Colonel Raymond Sheldon to Major John S. Pratt, January 31, 1927, NACP, RG 165, MID 290-13 (11); Leo Ribuffo, "Henry Ford and *The International Jew*," *American Jewish History*, vol. 69 (June 1980), pp. 445–469.

8. General Amos Fries to Senator David Ferguson, January 2, 1951; Fries to Captain George Chandler, March 1, 1927; Fries to General Clarence Edwards, Sep-

tember 30, 1926; UOL, Fries Papers, box 3; "General Fries Says Communists Use Pacifists," *Providence Journal* clipping, MID 10314-526 (92); Joan M. Jensen, *Army Surveillance in America, 1775–1980* (New Haven, 1991), pp. 199–200.

9. General Amos Fries to Colonel C. Seymour Bullock, February 16, 1928; H. E. West, American Defense Society to Fries, June 1, 1926; UOL, Fries Papers, box 3; Fries to Colonel J. H. Reeves, August 21, 1926, NACP, RG 165, MID 2314-D-51 (1).

10. Captain Trevor W. Swett to Colonel Nelson Margetts, October 4, 1926, NACP, RG 165, MID 2314-D-51 (4).

11. J. A. Moss to Colonel W. K. Wilson, July 30, 1926, NACP, RG 165, MID 10314-586; Colonel Stanley H. Ford, "Radical Situation in the United States," July 13, 1927, and Wilson to Ford, July 12, 1927, MID 10110-2512 (3); Talbert, *Negative Intelligence*, pp. 224–225.

12. General Eli A. Helmick, "Correct Human Relations," "Loyalty and Obedience," "Undermining the Youth of the Nation," ECMC, Helmick Papers.

13. Joyce, Memoirs, chap. 14, pp. 214–215, 233–235, MHI, Joyce Papers.

14. Talbert, *Negative Intelligence*, pp. 235–236; Jensen, *Army Surveillance*, pp. 202–203.

15. Colonel Roy C. Kirkland to commanding general, Third Corps Area, April 9, 1932, adjutant general, "Sabotage, Langley Field," April 29, 1932, Colonel J. C. Pegram to adjutant general, June 22, 1932, NADC, RG 394, box 1, A.G.000.24, 000.51 Sabotage; Pegram to G-2 director, June 27, September 7, 1932, Officer John Schnir, Police Department Report, November 13, 1932, NACP, RG 165, MID 10110-2663 (12–13, 20).

16. Joyce, Memoirs, pp. 178, 214–215, 232–235, MHI, Joyce Papers.

17. "General Subversive Situation," February 3, 1932, NACP, RG 407, Adjutant General Office, A.G.0000.24 (2-2-32), pp. 1–6. "Communist Party USA," July 1932, NACP, RG 165, MID 10110-2662 (12), pp. 1–5.

18. Daniel J. Lisio, *The President and Protest: Hoover, Conspiracy, and the Bonus Riot* (Columbia, MO, 1974), pp. 89–111, 194; Talbert, *Negative Intelligence*, p. 237; Jensen, *Army Surveillance*, pp. 203–204. See also Roger Daniels, *The Bonus Marches: An Episode of the Great Depression* (Westport, CT, 1971).

19. General George Van Horn Moseley to Herbert Corey, May 24, 1932, pp. 557–564, LC, Moseley Papers, container 9.

20. Ibid.

21. Ibid.

22. Joyce, Memoirs, chap. 14, pp. 233–235, MHI, Joyce Papers; Talbert, *Negative Intelligence*, pp. 237–238; Jensen, *Army Surveillance*, p. 203.

23. Lisio, *President and Protest*, pp. 90–111, 194–225, 240, 310–311.

24. Colonel J. T. Conrad to adjutant general, June 15, 1932, NADC, RG 98, U.S. Army Command Third Corps Area, General Correspondence 1920-39, box 2, 240-Bonus 1932; Major William Nalle to G-2 chief, Fort Sam Houston, June 25, 1932; Colonel James Totten to Adjutant General Washington, June 27, 1932; Colonel Robert Morris to Major Alexander Weyand, August 1, 1932, NADC, RG 94, Office of the Adjutant General Central Files, 1926-39, Bonus Marchers, box 1181.

25. Major Sherman Miles, "Army Composed of Russian Jews," February 19, 1923, and similar correspondence from Major A. L. Loustalot (Latvia) and Major El-

bert E. Farman (Poland), NACP, RG 165, MID 245-135 (1–8); "Russia," *Weekly Intelligence Bulletin*, February 23–March 7, 1924, Richard D. Challener, ed., *United States Military Intelligence, 1917–1927*, 30 vols. (New York, 1978), vol. 23, p. 10083.

26. "Special Report: Palestine," December 10, 1925, NACP, RG 165, MID 2568-83.

27. "Anti Jewish Riot in Stadtpart Vienna," July 18, 1925; "Serious Trouble Expected When Zionist Congress Meets," July 31, 1925; "Disturbances During Zionist Congress," August 19, 1925, NACP, RG 165, MID 2657-FF-124 (1–3).

28. "Races and Languages in Hungary," June 2, 1925, NACP, RG 165, MID 2542-120; "Religions in Hungary," August 29, 1925, MID 2542-121; "The Numerus Clausus Law," November 15, 1925, MID 2657-GG-117.

29. "The Jewish Problem in Poland," April 26, 1926, NACP, RG 165, MID 2657-DD-490, pp. 1–5.

30. Ibid., p. 4; "Jews in Poland," September 11, 1925, NACP, RG 165, MID 2657-DD-475, p. 1; "Jews in Poland—Facts and Fancies," December 21, 1928, MID 2657-DD-490 (2), p. 5.

31. "Jews in Poland," p. 2; "Jews in Poland—Facts and Fancies," p. 2.

32. "Jewish Problem in Poland," p. 3; "Jews in Poland," pp. 2–3.

33. "Jews in Poland—Facts and Fancies," p. 5.

34. Ibid., pp. 4–6.

35. Major Emer Yeager to Colonel Robert C. Foy, February 10, 1930, NACP, RG 165, MID 2632-DD-21 (1); Yeager to Colonel Joseph A. Baer, March 6, 1931, MID 2610-72 (292).

36. Ibid.

37. "Jewish Influences in Soviet Russia," March 28, 1931, NACP, RG 165, MID 2657-D-999 (1).

38. Ibid., and "Suggested Organization of an Information Service on Soviet Russia," NACP, RG 165, MID 2610-DD-69.

39. "Jewish Influences in Soviet Russia."

40. Major Gordon R. Young Diary, June 1, 2, 1931, pp. 44–47, MHI, Gordon R. Young Papers.

41. Ibid., June 6, 18, 23, July 10, 1931, pp. 73, 89–90, 118, 167.

42. Ibid., July 20–21, 1931, pp. 176–178; Ludwig Lewisohn, *The Last Days of Shylock* (New York, 1931), pp. 192–193, 216–217, passim.

43. Ibid.

44. Colonel Herman Beukema to Professor William Myers, September 28, 1933, September 7, 1938, USMA, Program of Instruction Files; General Johnson Hagood, "Autobiography" (unpublished), pt. 3, p. 416, MHI, Hagood Papers; General Benjamin Bailey to wife, August 18, 1938, Bailey Papers, box 4; Katherine Smith, "Memoirs" (unpublished), MHI, folder 1939-46, p. 126.

45. Bradford G. Chynoweth, *Bellamy Park: Memoirs by Bradford Grethen Chynoweth* (Hicksville, NY, 1975), p. 139; Richard C. Brown, *Social Attitudes of American Generals, 1898–1940* (New York, 1979), pp. 330–333; "Subversive Activities: G-2 Contribution to White Plan, January 25, 1937," MHI, AWCA 2-1937-12, pp. 75–76; Colonel Herman Beukema to Professor F. R. Fairchild, July 17, 1935, USMA, Programs of Instruction Files.

46. Merle Miller, *Ike the Soldier As They Knew Him* (New York, 1987), pp. 269–270; Talbert, *Negative Intelligence*, pp. 249–250.

47. James D. Clayton, *Years of MacArthur, 1880–1941* (Boston, 1970), pp. 415–443; General George Van Horn Moseley to MacArthur, September 26, 1938, LC, Moseley Papers, container 9, pp. 537–540.

48. Hagood, "Autobiography," pt. 3, pp. 445–446, MHI, Hagood Papers; Brown, *American Generals*, pp. 345–353.

49. Ibid.

50. Ibid., pp. 339–353.

51. See extensive collection of letters from retired officers to McSwain on defense and preparedness, 1936, DUL, MacSwain Papers, boxes 12–13.

52. General Johnson Hagood, "White Faced Cattle," "White Man's Country," and "Race Prejudice," South Carolina Historical Society, Charleston, SC, Johnson Hagood Papers, 11/192/22.

53. Hagood, "White Faced Cattle," pp. 5–6.

54. Ibid., p. 4.

55. General George Van Horn Moseley to MacArthur, August 10, 1934; MacArthur to Moseley, August 13, 1934, LC, Moseley Papers, MacArthur File, box 31.

56. Talbert, *Negative Intelligence*, pp. 242–243.

57. Letters of June 5, 1934, NACP, RG 165, MID 10314-556 (304).

58. Ibid.

59. Colonel John H. Fulmer to commanding general Governor's Island, NY, June 19, 1934; Major A. C. Sandeford to G-2 chief Washington, July 2, 1934, MID 10314-556 (304).

60. General George Van Horn Moseley to MacArthur, September 26, 1938; MacArthur to Moseley, March 9, 1938, LC, Moseley Papers, container 9.

61. Jensen, *Army Surveillance*, pp. 205–207; Talbert, *Negative Intelligence*, pp. 250–251.

62. "Subversive Activities: G-2 Contribution to White Plan," MHI, AWCA 2-1937-12, pp. 75–79; Brown, *American Generals*, pp. 356–358.

63. Colonel C. R. Clark to G-2 Chief, February 24, 1937, NACP, RG 165, MID 10110-2663 (129).

64. "Meeting of American League Against War and Fascism," January 11, 1936, NACP, RG 165, MID 10110-2663 (119).

65. MHI, AWCA 2-1937-12, pp. 75–76.

66. Jensen, *Army Surveillance*, p. 205; Talbert, *Negative Intelligence*, pp. 234–235; Frank Donner, *The Age of Surveillance: The Aims and Methods of America's Political Intelligence System* (New York, 1980), pp. 417–419; "Senate Panel Holds Vast 'Subversives' Files Amassed by Ex-Chief of Army Intelligence," *New York Times*, September 7, 1971, p. 35.

67. J. Edgar Hoover to General Ralph H. Van Deman and General Sherman Miles, June 7, 1941, NACP, RG 165, MID 10110-2550 (52). See also NADC, RG 46, Van Deman Collection, Investigative Files, Records of U.S. Senate Internal Security Subcommittee of the Senate Judiciary Committee, 1951–1975.

68. Major Thomas J. Betts to General Ralph Van Deman, July 25, 1936, RG 46, Van Deman, box 7, R-1588a; Colonel A. M. Jones to Van Deman, September 3, 1935, box 4, R-1063.

69. Office of Naval Intelligence Report, February 2, 1937, RG 46, Van Deman, box 8, R-1843; G-2 Ninth Corps Area Report, October 31, 1935, box 4, R-1102; Major Thomas J. Betts to Van Deman, October 19, 1936, box 7, R-1697; San Diego Police Department Report "Communist Activities," June 24, 1940, box 16, R-3598; and letter of February 21, 1938, box 10, R-2390.

70. "Communism in California," RG 46, Van Deman, box 1, R-58; letter of January 6, 1937, box 8, R-1810; Commander Hartwell C. Davis, U.S. Navy, to Van Deman, June 9, 1936, box 6, R-1525a; commander Eleventh Naval District, Los Angeles, to Van Deman, August 6, 1934, box 2, R-499.

71. F. W. Cole to Van Deman, October 8, 1935, RG 46, Van Deman, box 4, R-1087; "Communistic Activities," November 1934, box 3, R-695; "Russian Sound-Film," December 22, 1934, box 3, R-754a; San Diego Police Department Report, "Radical Activities," November 11, 1935, box 5, R-1153; Office of Naval Intelligence Report, "Hollywood Anti-Nazi League," October 23, 1936, box 7, R-1709.

72. "Radical Activities, Aircraft Industry," December 18, 1936, RG 46, Van Deman, box 7, R-1790; undated report, R-946, box 4; copy of November 15, 1937, report forwarded by Van Deman to G-2 Ninth Corps Area, November 16, 1937, box 9, R-2248.

73. John Merrick Church, "B'nai B'rith: An International Anti-Christian, Pro-Communist Jewish Power" (pamphlet), RG 46, Van Deman, box 11, R-2547.

74. Ibid.

75. Report from Better America Foundation on "Bolshevist Brotherhood Masonry and Jewry," May 12, 1937, RG 46, Van Deman, box 8, R-2000; Talbert, *Negative Intelligence*, p. 247.

76. Colonel F. H. Lincoln memorandum, October 18, 1933, NACP, RG 165, MID 10110-2550 (10).

77. Margaret A. Kerr to MacArthur, November 18, 1933, February 6, 1934, MID 10110-2550 (15, 33).

78. General Ralph Van Deman to MacArthur, MID 10110-2550 (43).

79. Margaret A. Kerr–General Amos Fries Correspondence, February 5, 15, May 6, 1932; Fries to Irene DuPont, September 18, 1934, and Captain R. L. Queisser, December 18, 1934, UOL, Fries Papers, box 2.

80. MHI, Jewish War Veterans Papers (hereafter JWV), boxes 5, 8, especially "Memo to All Commanders," June 21, 1938.

81. "The Jewish War Veterans' Attitude on Communism," *Jewish War Veteran* (February 1939), pp. 10–12.

82. Ibid.; "The American Legion and the Jews," *Jewish War Veteran* (April 1939), pp. 8–9, 14.

83. Ibid.; and memorandum, October 7, 1940, MHI, JWV, box 5.

84. Amos Fries, *Communism Unmasked* (privately published, 1937), pp. 119–125.

85. Ibid., pp. 125–126.

86. See Robert E. Herzstein, *Roosevelt and Hitler: Prelude to War* (New York, 1989), pp. 82–83, 256–270; Godfrey Hodgson, *The Colonel: The Life and Wars of Henry Stimson, 1867–1950* (New York, 1990), pp. 170–175.

Chapter 7

1. Captain Hugh W. Rowan and Major John H. Hineman, "Attitude of the Foreign Press Towards the Hitler Government," May 8, 1933, NACP, RG 165, MID 2657-B-760 (1).

2. Captain James C. Crockett to Major Truman Smith, March 2, 1935, HIA, Truman Smith Papers, box 1.

3. General Robert C. Richardson to George B. Conrad, October 9, 1937, USMA, George B. Conrad Papers, box 4.

4. See drafts of "Wedemeyer Reports," chap. 12, p. 116, HIA, Freda Utley Papers, box 79.

5. Martin Weil, *A Pretty Good Club: The Founding Fathers of the U.S. Foreign Service* (New York, 1978), pp. 56–63; Jeffrey M. Dorwart, *Conflict of Duty: The U.S. Navy's Intelligence Dilemma, 1919–1945* (Annapolis, MD, 1983), pp. 78–80; Richard C. Brown, *Social Attitudes of American Generals, 1898–1940* (New York, 1979), pp. 333–334.

6. Colonel Jacob Wuest, "Germany: Current Political Events," April 10, 1933, NACP, RG 165, MID 2657-B-735 (20); "Sterilization of the Unfit, Germany: Political Developments," July 28, 1933, NACP, RG 319, Army Intelligence, Project Decimal, ACSI-G-2 (1941–1945) (1941–1948), 350.05; Wuest, "Address to War Department," May 10, 1935, MHI, AWCA 132-18.

7. William E. Dodd, *Ambassador Dodd's Diary, 1933–1938* (New York, 1941), p. 149.

8. Ret. colonel Truman Smith, "Memo to G-2 Historical Section," n.d., pp. 4–5, HIA, Truman Smith Papers, box 1; Weil, *Pretty Good Club*, pp. 60–61.

9. Weil, *Pretty Good Club*, pp. 60–61; MHI, Smith Memoirs, folder 1935-39, p. 13, folder 1939-46, p. 3.

10. Truman Smith, *Berlin Alert: The Memoirs and Reports of Truman Smith*, ed. Robert Hessen (Stanford, 1984), pp. 43–66.

11. "Strategic Survey of Germany," December 20, 1932, pp. 23–25, 34, MHI, AWCA 392-5A.

12. Major Truman Smith, "Germany and Hitler," April 29, 1933, pp. 1–4; HIA, Truman Smith Papers, "War College Monographs," box 1.

13. Major Truman Smith to Colonel Raymond E. Lee, February 7, 1936, HIA, Truman Smith Papers, box 1.

14. Smith, "Memo to Historical Section," pp. 2–8; Smith to Colonel John B. Coulter, July 26, 1937, NACP, RG 165, MID 2632-B-23; Smith to General George C. Marshall, November 20, 1938, Marshall Papers, box 43, folder 18.

15. Albert C. Wedemeyer, *Wedemeyer Reports* (New York, 1958), pp. 10–11.

16. Ibid.; Keith Eiler, "Memo for the Record," March 7, 1988, and Albert C. Wedemeyer to Eiler, March 7, 1988, copies in possession of author. See also Kurt

Eiler, ed., *Wedemeyer on War and Peace* (Stanford, 1987); and drafts of "Wedemeyer Reports," p. 18, HIA, Utley Papers, box 80.

17. Wedemeyer, *Wedemeyer Reports*, pp. 10–11, 14.

18. See HIA, Ralph C. Smith Papers, box 27.

19. See Ralph and Madeleine Smith notes on travels, August 3–September 7, 1936, HIA, Ralph C. Smith Papers, box 18.

20. Ibid.

21. Ibid.

22. Ibid.; Colonel Sumner Waite, "Conditions in Germany," April 9, 1937, NACP, RG 165, MID 2655-B-391.

23. Captains H. A. Sears and Lowell M. Riley to chief, European Information Center American Embassy Paris, September 24, 1935, May 9, 1936, NACP, RG 165, MID 2610-166 (36, 51).

24. Colonel Joseph A. Baer, "Comments on Central European Affairs," October 14, 1933, pp. 1–6, NACP, RG 165, entry 181, box 934.

25. Ibid.

26. Ibid.

27. "The Jewish Problem," November 16, 1933, pp. 1–2, NACP, RG 165, MID 2657-FF-165 (2); "Resolution of the World Congress of Jewish War Veterans," July 11, 1936, MID 2657-FF-168 (2); "Nazi Agitation," March 11, 1937, p. 1, MID 2657-GG-142 (1); "The Jewish Question," December 18, 1933, p. 2; "Jews," March 12, 1934, p. 4; "Jews," May 31, 1934, p. 2, NACP, RG 165, entry 181, box 932.

28. "Jewish Program of the Heimwehr," March 22, 1934, NACP, RG 165, MID 2657-FF-168 (1).

29. Smith, "Memo to Historical Section," pp. 1–4; "Germany and Hitler," pp. 1–5.

30. Smith, "Germany and Hitler," pp. 2–3.

31. Colonel Truman Smith to John O. Beaty, March 24, May 22, 1955, UOL, John O. Beaty Papers, Incoming Correspondence.

32. Ibid.; and Houston Stewart Chamberlain, *Die Grundlagen des Neunzehnten Jahrhunderts*, vol. 1 (Munich, 1904), pp. 320–459.

33. General Albert C. Wedemeyer to Ernst von Helms, June 19, 1975, HIA, Wedemeyer Papers, box 66.

34. General Albert C. Wedemeyer to Robert H. Goldsborough, May 23, 1978, HIA, Wedemeyer Papers, box 38.

35. Captain Albert C. Wedemeyer to Paul, July 2, 1937, and Helen and Guy, November 11, 1937, HIA, Wedemeyer Papers, box 114.

36. Hugh Wilson, Diary, November 12, 1938, Franklin D. Roosevelt Library, Hyde Park, NY, box 4.

37. Robert E. Herzstein, *Roosevelt and Hitler: Prelude to War* (New York, 1989), pp. 234–237; Herbert Hoover broadcast, November 14, 1938, Herbert Hoover Library (hereafter HHL), West Branch, IA, Herbert Hoover Papers, Post-Presidential, Subject, box 204.

38. Smith, "Memo to Historical Section," pp. 6–8.

39. Colonel Truman Smith, "Foreign Political Aspects of the Recent Anti-Semitic Measures of Germany," December 16, 1938, NACP, RG 165, MID 2657-B-801 (2); "Anti-Semitism in Germany," January 12, 1939, MID 2657-B-801 (5).

40. Ibid.

41. Smith, "Anti-Semitism in Germany," p. 1

42. Ibid., p. 2.

43. Ibid., pp. 2–4.

44. Ibid., p. 5.

45. Herzstein, *Roosevelt and Hitler*, pp. 235–239.

46. *New York Times*, March 27, 28, 1933.

47. "Estimate of Subversive Situation," April 7, 1933, NACP, RG 165, MID 10110-2662 (46).

48. Colonel Fred T. Cruse, "Immigration: Polish Peddlers," January 10, 1931, NACP, RG 165, MID 2655-P-23 (6); Major Arthur R. Harris, "Campaign Against Jews Started," December 20, 1934, MID 2657-P-509 (1).

49. Harris, "Campaign Against Jews Started."

50. Herzstein, *Roosevelt and Hitler*, pp. 239–257; David S. Wyman, *Paper Walls: America and the Refugee Crisis, 1938–1941* (Amherst, MA, 1968), pp. 10–20; John Higham, *Send These to Me: Immigrants in Urban America* (Baltimore, 1984), pp. 58–59.

51. Herzstein, *Roosevelt and Hitler*, pp. 235–236, 239, 256–257, 265; Richard Breitman and Alan M. Kraut, *American Refugee Policy and European Jewry, 1933–1945* (Bloomington, IN, 1987), pp. 58, 88–89; Wyman, *Paper Walls*, pp. 21–23.

52. House, *Deportation of Aliens*, 74 Cong., 1st sess., 1935, H714-2, pp. 87–89, and Senate, 75 Cong., 1st sess., 1937, S549-6, pp. 166–169; House, *Prompt Deportation of Certain Aliens*, 75 Cong., 1st sess., 1937, H801-4, pp. 14–16; House, *Supervision and Detention of Certain Aliens*, 77 Cong., 1st sess., 1941, H929-7, pp. 76–79; General Amos Fries's unsent letter to Congressman Samuel Dickstein, March 21, 1933, UOL, Fries Papers, box 3. See also the file on the American Coalition in archives of the American Jewish Committee.

53. House, *Nonquota Status to Certain Alien Relatives*, 74 Cong., 1st sess., 1935, H772-6, pp. 36–37.

54. Senate, *Regulating Status of Aliens*," 74 Cong., 2d sess., 1935–1936, S516-10, pp. 45–54.

55. John B. Trevor to Van Deman, October 18, 1934, NADC, RG 46, Ralph H. Van Deman Papers, box 2, R-498a; "Report on the Importation of Jewish Children," November 20, 1934," box 3, R-685; Military Intelligence Report "091-Mexico," June 1, 1939, box 12, R2858a.

56. "Report on Samuel Untermeyer," NADC, RG 46, Van Deman Papers, box 2, R-408.

57. Russell Cook, National Director, American Legion, to Lieutenant Theodore G. Holcombe, August 10, 1934; Stephen F. Chadwick, national commander, American Legion, to Alfred Maier, May 2, 1939, American Legion National Headquarters Library (ALL), Indianapolis, IN, "American-Naturalization 1935–1939," microfilm 89-2031.

58. Higham, *Immigrants*, p. 58; Robert A. Divine, *American Immigration Policy, 1924–1952* (New York, 1972), pp. 93–94.

59. Breitman and Kraut, *American Refugee Policy*, pp. 58–67; Wyman, *Paper Walls*, pp. 34–63; Divine, *American Immigration Policy*, pp. 95–96.

60. Colonel Joseph B. Pate Diaries, April–August 1937, March 1, 1939, May 17–18, September 23, November 5–6, 1946, March 17, May 14, 1948, February 11, 1952, UOL, Joseph B. Pate Papers.

61. Colonel Joseph B. Pate, "Attitude on Jewish Refugee Question," March 15, 1939, NACP, RG 165, MID 2657-P-540 (3); "Government Opposition to Jewish Immigration and Colonization," September 30, 1937, MID 2655-P-73 (15).

62. "Agitation Against Illegal Immigration," March 18, 1938, "Mexico's Attitude Toward Immigration of Jews," "Presence of Jews in Mexico," and "Campaign Against Jews in Mexico," October 11, 17, 21, 1938, NACP, RG 165, MID 2655-G-188 (5–9); "Jewish Immigration in Chile," January 23, 1940, 2657-G-185 (5), MID Subject Index: Jews.

63. Major Lowell M. Riley, "Hitler to Chvalkovsky," and "The Jewish Question," February 1, 1939, "Anti-Jewish Legislation" January 16, 1939, NACP, RG 165, MID 2493-84 (4–5).

64. Riley, "Jewish Question," March 14, 1939, MID 2493-84 (6); "Anti-Jewish Legislation."

65. Riley, memo, December 11, 1936, p. 4, NACP, RG 165, MID 2610-166 (64); John C. Wiley to Robert Kelley, July 12, 1935, Franklin D. Roosevelt Library, Hyde Park, NY (hereafter FDRL), John C. Wiley Papers, box 1.

66. Major John S. Winslow, "Poland: Domestic Issues and Problems," May 11, 1937, "Domestic Politics," October 18, 1937, NACP, RG 165, MID 2657-DD-589 (2–4).

67. Ibid.; Winslow, "Poland: Recent Political Incidents," July 30, 1937, p. 2, NACP, RG 165, MID 2657-DD-589 (3).

68. Colonel Sumner Waite, "France: Jews," October 11, 1938, pp. 1–2, NACP, RG 165, MID 2015-1049 (56).

69. Ibid.

70. General George Van Horn Moseley to General Malin Craig, May 18, 1938, LC, Moseley Papers, box 9.

71. Ibid.

72. *Atlanta Constitution*, May 24; *New York Herald Tribune*, May 14, *New York Sun*, May 14, 1938.

73. See extensive Moseley files on incident, LC, Moseley Papers, box 9; General Campbell B. Hodges to mother, May 29, 1938, USMA, Campbell B. Hodges Papers, box 11.

74. General Lorenzo D. Gasser to Moseley, May 16, 1938, LC, Moseley Papers, box 34.

75. General Malin Craig to Moseley, May 16, 1938, LC, Moseley Papers, box 9.

76. Moseley to Craig, May 18, 1938, LC, Moseley Papers, box 9.

77. Colonel E.R.W. McCabe to adjutant general, June 17, 1938, NACP, RG 165, MID 2659-B-799 (1).

78. See E.R.W. McCabe Papers and McCabe-Tenant Correspondence, Tenant Collection, Virginia Historical Society (hereafter VHS), Richmond, Virginia; Colonel E.R.W. McCabe, "The Military Intelligence Division," January 4, 1938, MHI, AWCA G-235 (1938).

79. "The Ukrainian Question," December 22, 1938, NACP, RG 165, entry 182, G-2 Eastern European Intelligence Reports and Memoranda, 1935-44, War Department General Staff, box 802; Colonel E.R.W. McCabe to Colonel Bradford Chynoweth, April 18, 1939, MHI, Bradford Chynoweth Papers, box 5; McCabe to General George Van Horn Moseley, March 27, 1941, LC, Moseley Papers, box 9.

80. Moseley press release, September 30, 1938, HHL, Hoover Papers, Post-Presidential-Individual, box 156.

81. Woodring press release, September 30, 1938, LC, Moseley Papers, box 5.

82. *New York Times*, October 1, 1938; *Army Navy Journal*, October 8, 1938; General Johnson Hagood to Moseley, October 26, 1938, LC, Moseley Papers, box 5; Herbert Hoover to Moseley, October 1, 1938, HHL, Hoover Papers, Post-Presidential-Individual, box 156.

83. Editorial, *Army Navy Journal*, October 8, 1938, p. 108.

84. General Malin Craig to Moseley, October 3, 1938, LC, Moseley Papers, box 9.

85. General Lorenzo Gasser to Moseley, March 6, 1938, LC, Moseley Papers, box 9.

86. Colonel Benjamin Bailey to wife, August 18, October 3, 1938, Bailey Papers, box 4.

87. *Army and Navy Journal*, November 19, 1938; *New York Times*, December 15, 1938.

88. "Moseley of the Fifth Column," *New Republic*, vol. 99 (June 7, 1939), pp. 119–122.

89. Moseley to Tiffany Blake, March 30, 1939, LC, Moseley Papers, box 5.

90. Moseley, "One Soldier's Story" (unpublished manuscript), vol. 3 (1940), pp. 100–115, 136–138, 215–219.

91. Ibid., pp. 22–24, 37–38, 155, 215–219, passim; vol. 4, preface, and passim.

92. Ibid., vol. 3, pp. 155–162; "Moseley's Fears," *Newsweek*, June 12, 1939, p. 15; Senator Robert P. Reynolds to Moseley, June 2, 10, 1939, LC, Moseley Papers, box 31; Brown, *American Generals*, pp. 336–338; Herzstein, *Roosevelt and Hitler*, pp. 262–270.

93. Moseley, "One Soldier's Story," vol. 3, p. 20.

94. "Moseley of the Fifth Column," p. 20.

95. "Moseley Loses His Horse," *The Nation*, vol. 148, June 10, 1939, pp. 662–663.

Chapter 8

1. Henry P. Fairchild, "Population," October 29, 1936, pp. 1–14, MHI, McSherry Papers, box: Army War College 1936–37.

2. Lothrop Stoddard, "The Pedigree of Juda," *Forum*, vol. 75, no. 3 (March 1926), pp. 321–333.

3. Lothrop Stoddard, "The Racial Factor as a Determinant in National Policies," April 26, 1937, pp. 1–4, 15–16, MHI, AWCA 221-37-30.

4. Ibid., p. 3.

5. Ibid., pp. 17–19.

6. Lothrop Stoddard, "An Impressionistic Survey of World Affairs," May 17, 1938, p. 2, MHI, AWCA 221-38-46.

7. Ibid., pp. 3, 7, 12.

8. Lothrop Stoddard, "An Impressionistic Survey of World Affairs," May 22, 1939, pp. 4–6, NACP, RG 165, MID 248-86 (206).

9. Ibid., pp. 1–4, 12–13.

10. Stefan Kühl, *The Nazi Connection: Eugenics, American Racism and German National Socialism* (New York, 1994), pp. 38, 53, 61–63, 73, 99–100.

11. Carl N. Degler, "Culture Versus Biology in the Thoughts of Franz Boas and Alfred L. Kroeber," German Historical Institute Annual Lecture Series no. 2 (Washington, DC, 1989), and *In Search of Human Nature: The Decline and Revival of Darwinism in American Social Thought* (New York, 1991); Daniel J. Kevles, *In the Name of Eugenics: Genetics and the Uses of Human Heredity* (New York, 1985), pp. 113–146.

12. Colonel C. A. Seone, "Military Aspects of Economic Recovery: A Political-Economic Paper," March 15, 1936, pp. 2–3, 44–46, MHI, AWCA 221-37-31; "Survey of Soviet Socialist Republics," January 24, 1940, p. 16, MHI, AWCA 2-1940-7.

13. "Strategic Survey of the USSR," January 10, 1935, p. 2, MHI, AWCA 2-1935-7.

14. "Survey of USSR," January 23, 1939, pp. 3–4, and discussion section, p. 2, MHI, AWCA 2-1939-5.

15. "Strategic Survey of Poland and the Little Entente," January 7, 1935, pp. 1–3, 17–18, 85–86, MHI, AWCA 2-1935-4.

16. "Russia, Political Estimate," June 15, 1935, pp. 12, 17, MHI, AWCA 236-D-Russia (4-2).

17. General Peyton C. March, "Reminiscences," April 6, 1934, pp. 1–2, Dwight D. Eisenhower Library (hereafter DDEL), Abilene, KS, General Courtney H. Hodges Papers, box 3; "The Influences of Public Opinion on the Conduct of War," February 26, 1940, pp. 1–3, MHI, AWCA 6-1940-6.

18. "Surveys—Austria, Hungary, Poland," January 27, 1937, pp. 75–78, MHI, AWCA 2-1937-8; "Surveys—Austria, Hungary, Poland," January 29, 1938, p. 80, MHI, AWCA 2-1938-11.

19. "Poland-Political," August 1, 1939, pp. 25–28, 47–48, MHI, AWCA 236-D-Poland.

20. Ibid.

21. Ibid.

22. Ibid.

23. "Internal Stability of Nations," February 16, 1935, pp. 8, 19, 25, MHI, AWCA 17-A; "Internal Stability of Nations," February 1, 1936, pp. 6, 11–12, 15, AWCA 6-1936-8.

24. Ibid.

25. "War Department Procedure in Mobilization," December 23, 1938, pp. 1, 8, MHI, AWCA 8-1939-10; "Survey of United States," February 26, 1938, pp. 45–46, 58–59, AWCA 6-1938-7.

26. "Strategic Survey of Germany," December 14, 1935, pp. 52–56, MHI, AWCA 2-1936-5; "Strategic Survey of Germany, Austria, Hungary," January 8, 1935, pp. 3, 29–33, AWCA 2-1935-6; "Survey of Germany," January 26, 1938, pp. 64–68, AWCA 2-1938-4.

27. Ibid.

28. Ibid.

29. MHI, AWCA 2-1938-4, p. 23; 2-1935-6, p. 43.

30. MHI, AWCA 2-1938-4, p. 23.

31. "Survey of Germany," January 31, 1940, p. 34, MHI, AWCA 2-1940-6.

32. Ibid., p. 66; MHI, AWCA 1935-6, pp. 43; "Survey of Germany," January 20, 1939, pp. 8, 34, 40, AWCA 2-1939-2.

33. MHI, AWCA 2-1938-4, p. 70.

34. "Survey of Germany," January 25, 1937, p. 34, MHI, AWCA 2-1937-5.

35. MHI, AWCA 2-1939-2, p. 39.

36. Ibid., pp. 39–40.

37. MHI, AWCA 2-1938-4, pp. 5–6, 70; 2-1937-5, pp. 13–14; "Strategic Survey of Germany," December 16, 1933, pp. 1–2, AWCA 402-7.

38. AWCA 2-1938-4, pp. 5–6, 37–38; AWCA 2-1935-6, pp. 1–2; AWCA 402-7, pp. 1–2; "Estimate of European Situation," January 11, 1935, p. 25, MHI, AWCA 2-1935-10.

39. Colonel E.R.W. McCabe, "The Military Intelligence Division," January 4, 1939, discussion section, pp. 5–6, MHI, AWCA cg-2#6, 1939.

40. Ibid., pp. 5–6, 13–14.

41. William L. Langer, "The German Situation," January 6, 1938, MHI, AWCA G-2#10, 1938; and January 7, 1939, G-2#8, 1939; Gole, "War Planning," pp. 60–62.

42. Gole, "War Planning," pp. 52–60.

43. "A Survey of Germany," January 26, 1938, pp. 37–38, MHI, AWCA 2-1938-4.

44. Bonner F. Fellers, "Monroe Doctrine," February 25, 1939, pp. 1–3, MHI, AWCA 7-1939-83; AWCA 2-1938-4, pp. 37–38; Robert E. Herzstein, *Roosevelt and Hitler: Prelude to War* (New York, 1989), pp. 94–105, 218–231.

45. AWCA 2-1935-10, p. 25.

46. "Report of War Plans Group No. 4," April 17, 1935, pp. 2–5, 172–174, MHI, AWCA 5-1935-20.

47. AWCA 2-1939-2, p. 11; AWCA 2-1937-5, p. 49.

48. "Germany, Political Estimate," November 7, 1938, pp. 1, 9–12, MHI, AWCA 236-D-Germany.

49. AWCA 2-1936-5, pp. 4–7, 37; question and answer section, p. 20.

50. AWCA 2-1940-6, p. 71; AWCA 402-7, p. 30.

51. AWCA 2-1939-2, p. 11.

52. Ibid.

53. Handwritten commentary on 1920 Nazi Party Program, pp. 3–4, MHI, AWCA 2-1935-6.

54. AWCA 236-D-Germany, pp. 11–12; AWC 402-7, p. 30.

55. Commentary on 1920 Nazi Party Program, AWCA 2-1935-6, pp. 3–7.

56. AWCA 2-1939-2, pp. 8, 12.

57. AWCA G-2#8, 1938–1939.

58. AWCA cg-2#6, 1939, p. 12.

59. General Albert C. Wedemeyer to Colonel Truman Smith, April 19, 1949, HIA, Wedemeyer Papers, box 101; Wedemeyer, "Fragments: Notes on W.W.II," pp. 14–15, box 6.

60. Major Percy Black, "Present Disorders in Czechoslovakia," March 13, 1939, NACP, RG 165, MID Regional File (1929–44) (hereafter MIDRF), box 690, 2059-1914 (10).

61. Colonel Raymond Lee to Colonel E. R. Warner McCabe, April 13, 1939, NACP, RG 165, MID 2632-A-27.

62. General Stanley Embick to General George C. Marshall, April 12, 1939, Marshall Papers, box 67, folder 36; Harold I. Ickes, *The Secret Diary of Harold I. Ickes* (New York, 1953–1955), vol. 1, p. 313, vol. 2, pp. 336–337.

63. Embick to Marshall, April 12, 1939.

64. Marshall to Embick, April 14, 1939, Marshall Papers, box 67, folder 36. Ronald Schaffer, "General Stanley D. Embick: Military Dissenter," *Military Affairs*, vol. 37 (October 1973), pp. 89–95.

65. Forrest C. Pogue, *George C. Marshall: Ordeal and Hope, 1939–1942* (New York, 1986), vol. 2, pp. 120–127.

66. Justus D. Doenecke, ed., *In Danger Undaunted: The Anti-Interventionist Movement of 1940–1941 as Revealed in the Papers of the America First Committee* (Stanford, 1990), pp. 1–6; Leo P. Ribuffo, *The Old Christian Right: The Protestant Far Right from the Great Depression to the Cold War* (Philadelphia, 1983), pp. 179–189; Herzstein, *Roosevelt and Hitler*, pp. 326–343, 389–396.

67. Charles A. Lindbergh, *The Wartime Journals of Charles A. Lindbergh* (New York, 1970), vol. 3, pp. 244–245, 498–499.

68. Charles Lindbergh, "Aviation, Geography, and Race," *Reader's Digest* (November 1939), pp. 64–67.

69. Lindbergh, *Wartime Journals*, vol. 3, pp. 200–201, 218–219, 242–245.

70. Ibid., pp. 126–137. Major Truman Smith to Colonel John Coulter, October 27, Lindbergh to Smith, October 29, 1937, NACP, RG 165, MID 2257-ZZ-216 (5–7); Truman Smith, *Berlin Alert: The Memoirs and Reports of Truman Smith*, ed. Robert Hessen (Stanford, 1984), pp. xvi–xviii, 29–30, 75–165; Herzstein, *Roosevelt and Hitler*, pp. 389–391.

71. General George C. Marshall to General James G. Harbord, February 17, 1940, Larry I. Bland, ed., *The Papers of George Catlett Marshall*, 2 vols. (Baltimore, 1981, 1986), vol. 2, p. 161; Smith, *Berlin Alert*, pp. 30–32.

72. Lindbergh, *Wartime Journals*, vol. 3, pp. 242–243.

73. Ibid., pp. 256–261.

74. "Germany," notes of lecture by Major Percy Black, December 8, 1939, pp. 1–4, MHI, AWCA G-2#28, 1940.

75. General George C. Marshall to General Lorenzo Gasser, December 14, 1939, Marshall Papers, box 14, folder 35; "U.S. Military Aide Back from Berlin," *New York Times*, November 30, 1939, p. 11.

76. Bland, *Papers of George Marshall*, vol. 2, pp. 120–121, 161.

77. Herzstein, *Roosevelt and Hitler*, pp. 326–327, 336–343; Joan M. Jensen, *Army Surveillance in America, 1775–1980* (New Haven, 1991), pp. 211–212; Ribuffo, *Old Christian Right*, pp. 178–188.

78. Lindbergh, *Wartime Journals*, vol. 3, p. 352.

79. Smith, *Berlin Alert*, pp. 31–35; Katherine Smith Memoirs, vol. 3, folder 1939-46, pp. 28–30; Anne Morrow Lindbergh, *The War Within and the War Without: Diaries and Letters of Anne Morrow Lindbergh, 1939–1944* (New York, 1980), vol. 3, p. 121; Colonel Truman Smith to Beaty, March 27 [post–World War II, year unknown], UOL, Beaty Papers; Bernard Baruch to General George C. Marshall, June 13, 1945, Marshall Papers, box 57, folder 15.

80. General Sherman Miles to chief of staff, February 1, 1941, NACP, RG 165, MID 2657-C-314 (1).

81. "Monograph on Domestic Subversion," January 23, 1941, NACP, RG 165, MID 10110-2723 (89–93); Colonel Robert Snow to Colonel Manton S. Eddy, October 10, 1940, MID 9140-7183; "Fifth Column Preparations in Germany," October 5, 1940, MID 2801-445 (44). See also MID File 10261-351. Roy Talbert, *Negative Intelligence: The Army and the American Left, 1917–1941* (Jackson, MS, 1991), pp. 252–266.

82. "Subversive Literature, Anti-Semitic Circular, Crucifixion of Uncle Sam," May 21, 1941, NACP, RG 165, MID 245-149 (9); Colonel S. V. Constant Reports, January 26, March 18, 1941; J. Edgar Hoover to Miles, April 5, 1941, MID 10261-351 (12–14); "Anti-Semitic Propaganda," March 27, 1941, MID 245-147 (1); Constant Report on Anti-Semitic Meeting, March 7, 1941, MID 2801-14441 (3); Major Cornelius O'Leary to quartermaster general, January 7, 1941, MID QM 300.5.

83. "Report on Subversive Activities Among Civilians (Christian Front)," August 28, 1940, NACP, RG 165, MID 10110-2826 (4).

84. Major David G. Erskine letter, September 30, 1941, NACP, RG 319, Project Decimal, MID 000.24, box 11; J. Edgar Hoover to G-2 chief, June 13, 1941, NACP, RG 165, MID 2801-445 (159); Lawrence Dennis to Truman Smith, March 15, 20, 1940, June 14, 1957, HIA, Lawrence Dennis Papers, box 5.

85. Colonel W. C. Crane to G-2 chief, September 5, 1940, NACP, RG 165, MID 2483-117 (112); General Sherman Miles–Colonel Oscar Solbert Correspondence, April–July 1941, MID 2474-111; Miles to Colonel Elbert E. Farman, February 17, 1941, NACP, RG 319, Project Decimal, MID 350.05; Major Trevor Swett to G-2 chief, October 1, 1941, NACP, 165, entry 182, box 802; Colonel Ralph C. Smith letter, July 21, 1941, NACP, RG 165, MID 10110-2723.

86. *War Department Index Guide for Military Information* (Washington, DC, 1940), pp. 5–6, 12, 16.

87. Miles–Alexander B. Coxe Sr. Correspondence, May–August 1940, ECMC, Coxe Sr. Papers, box 3; Miles to General Ralph Van Deman, September 29, 1941, NADC, RG 46, Van Deman Papers, box 20; "German-American Bund," Van Deman Papers, R-2622, box 11; Talbert, *Negative Intelligence*, pp. 256–260.

88. "American White Guardsmen," NADC, RG 46, Van Deman Papers, R-351, box 2; "Moseley" and "I.P.A. Meeting," R-3011, box 13; Reports R-3251, R-3255-

56, R-3260, box 14; R-3547, box 15; MID Report on Solomon Berlin, September 5, 1941, R-5195, box 20; Colonel L. R. Forney to Van Deman, October 16, 1941, R-5427, box 21.

89. "Special Report on Subversive Situation," November 20, 1940, NACP, RG 165, MID 10110-2662 (362).

90. Ibid.

91. Ibid.

92. Doenecke, *Anti-Interventionist Movement*, pp. 2–51.

93. Lindbergh, *Wartime Journals*, vol. 3, pp. 381–382; Captain Bonner Fellers to Herbert Hoover, June 20, 1940, HHL, Hoover Papers PPI: Fellers; unpublished memoirs of Ivan D. Yeaton, pp. 75–76, HIA, Yeaton Papers; Columbia University Manuscript Library, New York City, General Robert E. Wood Oral History, p. 90.

94. Doenecke, *Anti-Interventionist Movement*, pp. 8–10, 396–397; Wood Oral History, pp. 44, 90–99; "Jewish Welfare Fund," HHL, Robert E. Wood Papers, box 38.

95. Wood–Sidney J. Weinberg Correspondence, 1940, HHL, Wood Papers, box 19; Wood to Lawrence Dennis, January 14, 1942, HIA, Dennis Papers, box 5; Wood Oral History, p. 32.

96. Robert R. McCormick to General Charles Willoughby, July 20, 1948, Willoughby to McCormick, March 18, 1950, Gettysburg College, Gettysburg, PA [hereafter GC], Charles A. Willoughby Papers; Jerome E. Edwards, *Foreign Policy of Colonel McCormick's Tribune, 1929–1941* (Reno, 1971), pp. 12, 127, 153, 166; Frank C. Waldorf, *McCormick of Chicago: An Unconventional Portrait of a Controversial Figure* (Englewood Cliffs, NJ, 1966), pp. 8, 42.

97. Lindbergh, *Wartime Journals*, vol. 3, pp. 405–406.

98. LC, Stimson Diaries, March 28, 1941, p. 122; "General Miles's Estimate of Colonel Ratay," January 10, 1941, Marshall Papers, box 39, folder 31.

99. LC, Stimson Diaries, April 15, 17, 1941, pp. 160, 167; Pogue, *Marshall*, vol. 2, pp. 130–131.

100. Lindbergh, *Wartime Journals*, vol. 3, pp. 499–500; Anne Morrow Lindbergh, *Diaries, 1939–1944*, pp. 184–185.

101. Herbert Hoover memorandum on Smith briefing, June 1, 1941, HHL, PPI: Truman Smith, box 216.

102. Ibid.

103. Anne Morrow Lindbergh, *Diaries, 1939–1944*, pp. 220–229.

104. Doenecke, *Anti-Interventionist Movement*, pp. 37–40.

105. General Thomas S. Hammond to Robert E. Wood, September 16, 1941, in ibid., pp. 396–397; "Comments on Current Events," October 2, 1941, NACP, RG 319, Project Decimal, MID Seventh Corps Area, box 26.

106. Lindbergh, *Wartime Journals*, vol. 3, pp. 550–551, 556–557; Lawrence Dennis to General Robert E. Wood, October 10, 1941, HHL, Wood Papers, box 3; Wood–Colonel Truman Smith Correspondence, November–December 1941, Wood Papers, box 15.

107. John C. O'Laughlin–Wood Correspondence, October 1941, HHL, Wood Papers, box 12; USMA, Conrad Papers, box 2; "General Krueger's Speech—San Antonio—November 10, 1941," DDEL, Dwight D. Eisenhower Papers, Pre-Presi-

dential Principles Files, box 67: Krueger; Schaffer, "General Stanley B. Embick," pp. 93–94.

108. Smith, *Berlin Alert*, pp. viii, 36–42.

109. Richard Breitman and Alan M. Kraut, *American Refugee Policy and European Jewry, 1933–1945* (Bloomington, IN, 1987), pp. 167–173.

Chapter 9

1. Charles E. Loucks Diaries, June 17–20, 1940, MHI, Charles E. Louckes Papers.

2. Ibid.; and December 6, 1940.

3. Ibid.

4. Ibid.

5. Robert E. Herzstein, *Roosevelt and Hitler: Prelude to War* (New York, 1989), pp. 338–341; Richard Breitman and Alan M. Kraut, *American Refugee Policy and European Jewry, 1933–1945* (Bloomington, IN, 1987), pp. 118–123.

6. "Roosevelt Presidential Press Conferences," no. 649-A (June 5, 1940), *Complete Presidential Press Conferences of Franklin D. Roosevelt*, vol. 15 (New York, 1972).

7. NACP, RG 165, MID 28010-445 (13), 10214-675 (1), 10525-821.

8. Breitman and Kraut, *American Refugee Policy*, pp. 123–125.

9. Ibid.

10. Ibid.; David S. Wyman, *Paper Walls: America and the Refugee Crisis, 1938–1941* (Amherst, MA, 1968), pp. 144–149; Colonel John T. Bissell to General Sherman Miles, March 5, 1941, NACP, RG 165, MID 106602-240; Major Charles R. Mabee, "War Department Policy for Consideration of Visa Applications of Aliens," August 16, 1941, NACP, RG 165, entry 192, G-2, Visa and Passport Control Branch Correspondence, 1941–46, box 900.

11. Mabee to Bissell, August 29, 1941, NACP, RG 165, entry 192, G-2, box 900.

12. Mabee to Mr. Warren, Visa Division, State Department, September 11, 24, 1941, NACP, RG 165, entry 192, G-2, box 900.

13. Colonel George D. Dorroh to Colonel John T. Bissell, April 16, September 4, 1942, NACP, RG 165, entry 192, G-2, box 901.

14. Director of Naval Intelligence, "The Refugee Problem," October 22, 1942, NACP, RG 319, Project Decimal, MID 383.7.

15. Ibid., pp. 1–6, 9–11.

16. Ibid., pp. 6–8.

17. Captain Frank Broadbent to Colonel John T. Bissell, July 16, 1941, NACP, RG 165, entry 192, G-2, box 900.

18. See file on "Julius Steinfeld Case," 1942–1944, NACP, RG 165, entry 192, G-2, box 902.

19. Wyman, *Paper Walls*, pp. 203–204.

20. Ibid.; John W. Pehle to Abrahamson, April 25, 1944, FDRL, Records of the War Refugee Board (WRB), box 26; memorandum [1944?], FDRL, WRB, box 49, folder: Department of Justice.

21. See "Comments on Current Events," January 4, 1943, NACP, RG 319, Project Decimal, MID 350.05, First Service Command, Boston; "Political Refugees," January 3, 1941, NACP, RG 165, MID 10602-218.

22. "Jewish Unity," May 4, 1943, NACP, RG 319, Project Decimal, MID 291.2: Jews; Daily Report, November 19, 1942, MID 319.1: First Service Command; "Pilgrimage of Jewish Rabbis to Washington," October 7, 1943, MID 291.2: Jews; File: "Jewish Groups," RG 319, Decimal File 1941–48, MID 000.2436, box 15; Weekly Intelligence Reports, 1943–1944, Second Service Command, New York, NACP, RG 165, entry 189, box 1033.

23. NADC, RG 46, Van Deman Papers, R6053, R6116, box 27; R6382, box 30; R6601, box 32.

24. Report of Army Intelligence Officers' Conference, New Orleans, November 1943, pp. 37–39, NACP, RG 165, entry 189, G-2, box 1009.

25. Colonel Dean Hutnutt, "Political and Racial Reasons for the Collapse of the Polish Army," January 31, 1940, p. 2 and appendix, MHI, AWCA 7-1940-76.

26. Ibid.

27. Charles Katz to A. W. Rosenthal, October 5, 1940, YIVO, Waldman Archives, "Selective Service," box 40.

28. Morris Stone to J. George Fredman, September 19, 1940 and memorandum of April 25, 1942, YIVO, Waldman Archives, "Selective Service," box 40; "Weekly Estimate of Subversive Situation," March 14, 1942, NACP, RG 319, Project Decimal, MID 000.24: Third Corps Area, box 6; David S. Wyman, *The Abandonment of the Jews: America and the Holocaust, 1941–1945* (New York, 1984), pp. 10–13.

29. YIVO, Autobiographies of Jewish American Soldiers in World War II, no. 16, p. 3; "Anti-Semitic Rumors Within Seventh Service Command," March 18, 1944, NACP, RG 319, Project Decimal, MID 091.412, box 25.

30. YIVO, Autobiographies, no. 18, p. 42; no. 34, pp. 2–3.

31. Wyman, *Abandonment of the Jews*, p. 11; Frederick S. Harris, general chairman, Jewish War Veterans, to General Douglas MacArthur, April 15, 1947, DMMA, RG 10 P.C.; MHI, Senior Officers' Oral History Project, 85-B, General Gerd S. Grombacher; YIVO, Autobiographies, no. 50, p. 1.

32. YIVO, Autobiographies, no. 3, p. 6.

33. General Philip E. Brown to Deputy Chief of Staff, March 10, 1944, NACP, RG 165, ACS 1944–45, WDCSA 291.2: Jews.

34. YIVO, Autobiograhies.

35. Ibid.

36. YIVO, Autobiographies, no. 3, pp. 1–5; no. 7, p. 3; no. 12, p. 16; no. 16, p. 3; no. 39, p. 1; no. 52, p. 8.

37. YIVO, Autobiographies, no. 10, p. 10; no. 13, p. 21; no. 34, p. 2.

38. YIVO, Autobiographies, no. 10, p. 10; no. 39, p. 1; no. 29, pp. 5–6.

39. YIVO, Autobiographies, no. 16, p. 2; no. 22, pp. 19–20, 33; no. 29, p. 7; no. 42, p. 5.

40. YIVO, Autobiographies, no. 10, p. 4; no. 16, p. 5; no. 21, p. 7; no. 43; no. 48, p. 8; no. 50, p. 16.

41. YIVO, Autobiographies: no. 13, p. 20; no. 22, p. 33; no. 34, p. 4; no. 47; no. 49, p. 17.

42. *Command of Negro Troops* (Washington, DC, 1944), pp. 7–8; Colonel James H. Shoemaker to General John H. Hildring, December 15, 1943, NACP, RG 165, Civil Affairs Division (1943–1944), entry 463, 291.2, box 67.

43. Colonel Benjamin A. Dickson, "G-2 Journal" (unpublished manuscript); Letters from Siberia, June 31, July 10, August 25, 1919, April 4, 1920, USMA, Benjamin A. Dickson Papers.

44. General Floyd L. Parks letter of March 26 (no year), DDEL, Floyd L. Parks Papers, box 4; General Malin Craig to Parks, November 12, 1943, January 7, April 13, April 21, 1944, box 8; Hersh Livazer to Parks, July 11, 1944, box 5.

45. General Albert C. Wedemeyer to General George C. Marshall, January 17, 1944, Marshall Papers, box 90, folder 16.

46. McClean Diaries, vol. 1, May 9–10, 1940, NYHS, Henry C. McClean Papers.

47. Ibid., vol. 2, October 3, 1942, March 1, 1943, vol. 4, December 1945.

48. Ibid., vol. 4, August 31, September 29, 1945.

49. Ibid., vol. 2, November 11, 1942.

50. Ibid., vol. 3, March 25, 1945.

51. Ibid., vol. 4, December 11, 1943.

52. Bonner F. Fellers–Frank Murphy Correspondence, 1943, Michigan Historical Collections, Bentley Historical Library, University of Michigan, Ann Arbor, MI (hereafter MHC), Frank Murphy Papers, boxes 39–41; General Charles Willoughby–Robert E. Wood Correspondence, 1943–1944, HHL, Wood Papers, box 19; Vandenberg to Willoughby, August 17, 1943, MacArthur Papers, RG 10, P.C.; Anne Morrow Lindbergh, *The War Within and Without: Diaries and Letters of Anne Morrow Lindbergh, 1939–1944* (New York, 1980), June 4, 1943, January 20, 1944, pp. 357, 403; Charles A. Lindbergh, *The Wartime Journals of Charles A. Lindbergh* (New York, 1970), vol. 4, November 18, 1942, August 21, 1944.

53. Frank E. Mason to General Albert C. Wedemeyer, June 14, August 29, 1975, HHL, Frank E. Mason Papers, boxes 24–25; Mason–Ivan D. Yeaton Correspondence, HIA, Yeaton Papers, box 5.

54. William LaVarre to Patrick J. Hurley, December 8, 1945, University of Oklahoma Library, Norman, OK, Patrick J. Hurley Collection, box 98, folder 6; LaVarre to Yeaton, January 3, 1977, January 10, 1978, HIA, Yeaton Papers, box 5; William LaVarre Papers, box 6.

55. Lindbergh, *Wartime Journals*, vol. 4, November 1942, p. 748; Herbert Hoover memorandum, June 24, 1943, HHL, Hoover Papers PPI, box 216: T. Smith.

56. Colonel Ivan D. Yeaton memorandum, March 29, 1943, NACP, RG 165, entry 182, G-2, box 804; Bonner Fellers Report, April 23, 1943, Fellers to Colonel William J. Donovan, February 2, 1943, MHC, Murphy Papers, boxes 39–40; Fellers to Herbert Hoover, May 26, 1943, HHL, Hoover Papers PPI, box 57.

57. Fellers to Donovan, April 8, 1943, HIA, Bonner F. Fellers Papers, box 5; "Chronology . . . on Arab-Jewish Controversy," June 7, 1943, NACP, RG 319, Project Decimal, MID 092.Palestine.

58. Colonel Ivan D. Yeaton memoranda (1942–1943), NACP, RG 165, entry 182, G-2, boxes 803–805; "Memoirs of Colonel Ivan D. Yeaton (1919–1953)" (unpublished manuscript), HIA, Yeaton Papers, box 1; Yeaton–William LaVarre Correspondence (1970s); Yeaton–General John V. Grombach Correspondence, boxes 2,

5; Yeaton to Frank Mason, July 10, 1975, HHL, Mason Papers, box 27; Yeaton to General Albert C. Wedemeyer, July 14, 1975, August 24 1976, HIA, Wedemeyer Papers, box 70.

59. Thomas Parrish, *The Ultra Americans: The U.S. Role in Breaking the Nazi Codes* (New York, 1986), pp. 33–37, 83, 86, 204; General John V. Grombach to Yeaton, February 10, 1977, HIA, Yeaton Papers, box 5.

60. Bonner Fellers to Bernice Miller, September 28, 1943, HHL, Hoover Papers PPI, box 57; Frank Mason to Carter Clarke and Ralph Smith, April 26, 1977, HHL, Mason Papers, box 23: Strauss, Lewis L. (1977); Mason to Wedemeyer, June 23, 1976, HIA, Wedemeyer Papers, box 51; Fellers to Douglas MacArthur, August 21, 1943, DMMA, RG 10 P.C.

61. "Estimate of the Palestine Situation in 1948," February 26, 1948, pp. 1–3, 6, 31, NACP, RG 319, entry 154, 091.Palestine TS, box 24.

62. Anthony C. Brown, *The Last Hero: Wild Bill Donovan* (New York, 1982), pp. 304–315, 342; Colonel George V. Strong to Colonel L. P. Gerow, February 5, 1936, NACP, RG 165, entry 418, Operations Division (OPD), box 24.

63. Strong–Hugh Gibson Correspondence (1928–1931), HIA, Gibson Papers, box 61.

64. General George V. Strong memorandum, July 11, 1940; G-2 Governor's Island, NY, to G-2 chief Washington, July 18, 1940; "Biographical Sketch Dr. Albert Einstein," NACP, RG 165, MID 8930-B-254 (17–19). Italics in original.

65. Ibid.

66. Ibid.

67. Rabbi Judah Nadich Oral History Interview, April 18, 1977, pp. 9–11, Ben-Gurion Research Institute, Sde Boker, Israel.

68. Alfred M. Gruenther to Williston B. Palmer, June 14, 1935, USMA, Williston B. Palmer Papers, box 2; U.S. Army Center for Military History Archives, Washington, DC, Biographical File: Alfred M. Gruenther.

69. General George C. Marshall to General George Van Horn Moseley, September 9, 1938, in Larry I. Bland, ed., *The Papers of George Catlett Marshall* (Baltimore, 1981, 1986), vol. 3, p. 626; Forrest C. Pogue, *George C. Marshall: Ordeal and Hope, 1939–1942* (New York, 1986), vol. 2, pp. 12–13; Ed Cray, *General of the Army: George C. Marshall, Soldier and Statesman* (New York, 1990), pp. 6–7, 118, 479.

70. Marshall to Moseley August, October 1940, January 9, 1945, Marshall Papers, box 77, folders 6–7.

71. Charles H. Martin to Marshall, November 21, 1944, Marshall Papers, box 75, folder 27.

72. Pogue, *Marshall*, vol. 3, pp. 96–99, 538–539, 664; Cray, *Marshall*, pp. 168–169, 751.

73. Colonel George C. Marshall, "The Development of the National Army," U.S. Army War College Lecture (1920), p. 6, Marshall Archives; Marshall to General Hugh A. Drum, February 27, 1941, Marshall Papers, box 66, folder 24.

74. Bland, *Papers of George Marshall*, vol. 2, pp. 640–641.

75. Pogue, *Marshall*, vol. 4, pp. 336–378, 430–434; Cray, *Marshall*, pp. 627, 655–663, 687–688.

76. "Moseley," Eisenhower Diaries, DDEL, Kevin McCann Papers, box 1; Stephen E. Ambrose, *Eisenhower: Soldier, General of the Army, President-Elect, 1890–1952* (New York, 1983), pp. 90–98; Merle Miller, *Ike the Soldier As They Knew Him* (New York, 1987), p. 249.

77. Eisenhower Diary, February 28, October 29, 1933. Miller, *Ike the Soldier*, p. 269.

78. Eisenhower to General George Van Horn Moseley, January 24, 1934, DDEL, Eisenhower Papers, PPP, box 84.

79. Eisenhower to Moseley, April 26, 1937, DDEL, Eisenhower Papers, box 84; Eisenhower Diaries, 1935–1938, box 1.

80. Eisenhower to Moseley, August 27, 1942, DDEL, Eisenhower Papers, PPP, box 84; Eisenhower to Colonel Mark W. Clark, September 17, 1940, box 23; Eisenhower-Moseley Correspondence, LC, Moseley Papers, box 13; Miller, *Ike the Soldier*, p. 249.

81. Ambrose, *Eisenhower*, pp. 113–114; Miller, *Ike the Soldier*, p. 297.

82. Daniel E. Holt, ed. *Eisenhower: The Prewar Diaries and Selected Papers, 1905–1941* (Baltimore, 1998), pp. 445–446.

83. John J. McCloy to General George C. Marshall, June 9, 1944, WDI-19l; Mc-Cloy, Personal Affairs File, PAI-52; McCloy Diaries, 1941–1944, Amherst College Library Archives, Amherst, MA, John J. McCloy Papers; Breitman and Kraut, *American Refugee Policy*, p. 221; Godfrey Hodgson, *The Colonel: The Life and Wars of Henry Stimson, 1867–1950* (New York, 1990), p. 251; Truman Smith, *Berlin Alert: The Memoirs and Reports of Truman Smith*, ed. Robert Hessen (Stanford, 1984), pp. 38–39.

84. Hodgson, *Stimson*, p. 121–129, 172, 250–251, 372–373; LC, Stimson Diaries, January 17, 24, February 10, 1942, July 2, 1945.

85. Colonel William S. Culbertson memorandum, August 14, 1942, NACP, RG 59, 740.0011 European War/26651.

86. Ambrose, *Eisenhower*, pp. 206–210; Miller, *Ike the Soldier*, pp. 421–427.

87. General Mark W. Clark to General Charles W. Ryder, December 12, 1943; DDEL, Charles W. Ryder Papers, box 1.

88. Mark W. Clark to Eric F. Goldman, April 24, 1956, box 12, folder 6; Clark to Eisenhower, October 28, 1942, box 1, folder 8; Chautauqua speech (undated), box 1, folder 10; The Citadel Archives, Charleston, SC, General Mark W. Clark papers; Martin Blumenson, *Mark Clark* (New York, 1984), pp. 9–13, 272–273.

89. General George S. Patton memorandum, November 15, 1942, LC, Patton Papers, box 24; Ambrose, *Eisenhower*, p. 205.

90. Major Bernard S. Carter to Colonel Percy Black, December 29, 1942, USMA, Bernard S. Carter Papers, box 3.

91. General George S. Patton Diary, November 16–17, 1942, January 10, 1943, LC, Patton Papers, box 3.

92. Breitman and Kraut, *American Refugee Policy*, pp. 169–170.

93. General Thomas T. Handy to undersecretary of war, December 13, 1942, LC, Robert P. Patterson Papers, box 154.

94. LC, Stimson Diary, December 27, 1942.

95. Breitman and Kraut, *American Refugee Policy*, p. 170.

96. "Jewish-Arab Situation in the Middle East," NACP, RG 319, Project Decimal, MID 092.Middle East, 3-4-43.

97. Moritz N. Penkower, *The Jews Were Expendable: Free World Diplomacy and the Holocaust* (Urbana, IL, 1983), pp. 105, 111; *New York Times*, March 2, 1943, p. 1.

98. NACP, RG 319, Project Decimal, MID 092.Middle East, 3-4-43.

99. Peter Grose, *Israel in the Mind of America* (New York, 1983), p. 180.

100. *New York Times*, March 10, 1943.

101. Breitman and Kraut, *American Refugee Policy*, pp. 180–181.

102. Ronald W. Zweig, *Britain and Palestine During the Second World War* (London, 1986), pp. 148–157, 164–170.

103. Ibid., pp. 172–176.

104. General Russell A. Osmun to Frank Mason, September 21, 1945 and General Clayton Bissell, April–June 1944, HHL, Mason Papers, box 20; Archie Roosevelt, *For Lust of Knowing: Memoirs of an Intelligence Officer* (Boston, 1988), p. 122.

105. Colonel Harold E. Pride, "Intelligence Coverage of Palestine," October 1, 1944, RG 319, Project Decimal, MID 350.05 Palestine; Lieutenant Thomas J. Nokes, "CIC Agent in Palestine," August 22, 1944, NACP, RG 226, OSS, Research and Analysis Branch, Palestine, entry 120, box 31; Roosevelt, *Lust of Knowing*, pp. 9, 49–50, 120, 355.

106. "Jewish Political Aspirations in Palestine," November 6, 1943, NACP, RG 226, OSS, entry 120, box 31; "Current Events," May 6, 1942, NACP, RG 19, Project Decimal, MID 350.05 Palestine.

107. YIVO, Autobiographies, no. 5, pp. 10–18; Roosevelt, *Lust of Knowing*, p. 124.

108. "Palestine—Jewish Psychology and Attitudes," April 30, 1944; NACP, RG 319, Project Decimal, MID 092.Middle East, box 885.

109. Ibid.

110. "Palestine-Zionist Problem Today," October 3, 1943; "Palestine-Background of Recent Bombing Incidents," March 4, 1944; NACP, RG 319, Project Decimal, MID 092.Middle East, box 885.

111. Ibid.; "Betar: Revisionist Youth Organization," October 1, 1943, RG 226, entry 120, box 31.

112. Zweig, *Britain and Palestine*, p. 167.

113. "Zionist Problem Today"; "Jewish Political Organizations in Palestine," October 22, 1943, NACP, RG 319, Project Decimal, MID 092.Middle East.

114. Major C.T.S. Keep to Mr. Penrose and Captain Edward P. Barry to G-2, June 13, 1944, NACP, RG 226, OSS, entry 190, box 172.

115. "General Security," September 1, 1943, NACP, RG 319, Project Decimal, MID 092.Middle East; "Alleged Indiscretion by CIC Agent," March 31, 1945, NACP, RG 226, OSS, entry 120, box 31.

116. "Jewish Agency," August 7, 1944, NACP, RG 226, OSS, entry 190, box 172.

117. "British-Russian-American Interests in the Middle East"; "Soviet Interests in the Middle East," July 24, 1944, NACP, RG 165, entry 182, box 805.

118. "Jewish Psychology," p. 5.

119. MID New York Office Report on Palestine, December 14, 1943, NACP, RG 319 Project Decimal, MID 350.05 Palestine.

120. "Summary Report on Palestine," September 14, 1944, NACP, RG 226, entry 120, box 32.

121. "Potential Arab-Jewish Civil Strife," April 9, 1943, NACP, RG 319, Project Decimal, 092.Middle East.

122. Grose, *Israel in the Mind of America*, pp. 178–181.

123. Robert P. Patterson to Cordell Hull, July 27, 1943, NACP, RG 165, ABC 383.7 (28 Jan 44).

124. Grose, *Israel in the Mind of America*, pp. 180–182.

125. Patrick J. Hurley to Franklin D. Roosevelt, May 5, 1943; "Notes on Conference Between . . . King Ibn Saud and General Hurley," Hurley Collection, box 81, folder 9, box 82, folder 3.

126. General George V. Strong to Marshall, August 5, 1943, NACP, RG 319, MID 092.Palestine.

127. Ibid.

128. Ibid.

129. Ibid.

130. Ibid.

131. Cordell Hull to Henry L. Stimson, August 18, September 1, 1943, NACP, RG 165, ABC 383.7 (28 Jan 44); Grose, *Israel in the Mind of America*, pp. 180–182.

132. Colonel J. K. Woolnough to Colonel Roberts, September 23, 1943, NACP, RG 165, ABC 383.7 (28 Jan 44).

133. Ibid.

134. Wyman, *Abandonment of the Jews*, pp. 150–170; Grose, *Israel in the Mind of America*, pp. 169–176.

135. Colonel Ivan D. Yeaton to JICAME, Cairo, December 2, 1943; "Table of Organizations," "The American Jewish Conference," NACP, RG 319, Project Decimal, MID 291.2 Jews.

136. Ibid.

137. Colonel Ivan Yeaton to JICAME, Cairo, January 1, 1944; "Palestine-Zionist Propaganda Methods," NACP, RG 319, Project Decimal, MID 092.Middle East, box 885.

138. Ibid.; "Palestine-Jewish Claims—Pro and Con," April 14, 1944, NACP, RG 319, Project Decimal, MID 092.Middle East.

139. "Palestine-Political," December 8, 1943, NACP, RG 319, Project Decimal, MID 092.Middle East, box 885.

140. Ibid.

141. Ibid.

142. Colonel Frank McCarthy to George C. Marshall, February 5, 1944, Marshall Papers, box 78, folder 15; Wyman, *Abandonment of the Jews*, pp. 172–173.

143. Stimson Diaries, February 14, 1944; Stimson to Senator Tom Connally, February 7, 1944, Marshall Papers, box 78, folder 15.

144. Stimson Diaries, March 2, 8, 17, 1944.

145. John J. McCloy to George C. Marshall, February 22 1944, McCloy Papers, WDI-19.

146. General Clayton Bissell memorandum, February 21, 1944, NACP, RG 319, Project Decimal, MID 092.Middle East.

147. McCloy to Marshall, February 22, 1944.

148. "Repercussions of Terrorism in Palestine"; "Palestine Bombings," April 4, 12, 1944, NACP, RG 319, Project Decimal, MID 092.Middle East, box 885.

149. "Palestine Jewish and Arab Opinion Concerning Approaching American Presidential Elections"; "Arab Reaction to the United States," August 10, 16, 1944, NACP, RG 226, OSS, entry 120, box 31; Grose, *Israel in the Mind of America*, pp. 183–183; Wyman, *Abandonment of the Jews*, p. 173.

150. Colonel Harrison A. Gerhardt to G-2 chief, September 16, 1944, NACP, RG 319, Project Decimal, MID 092.Middle East.

151. General Clayton Bissell to John J. McCloy, "Present Military Implications of Senate Resolution 247," September 19, 1944, NACP, RG 319, Project Decimal, MID 092.Middle East.

152. Major Harry R. Snyder to General Clayton Bissell, December 1, 1944, NACP, RG 319, Project Decimal, MID 092.Middle East; Wyman, *Abandonment of the Jews*, p. 173.

153. Ibid.

154. Ibid.

155. John J. McCloy Diaries, December 1, 1944, McCloy Papers; Wyman, *Abandonment of the Jews*, p. 173.

156. Kieve Skidell to wife, October 10, 1944, Kieve Skidell Papers, 048/44-3, Yad Vashem Central Archives, Jerusalem, Israel (hereafter YV).

157. Airgram, January 3, 1944, in David Wyman, ed., *America and the Holocaust* (New York, 1989–1991), vol. 12, pp. 203–204; Wyman, *Abandonment of the Jews*, pp. 227–228, 293–294.

158. Edward R. Stettinius to Hull, January 8, 1944, LC, Breckinridge Long Papers, box 202.

159. Ibid.

160. Wyman, *Abandonment of the Jews*, pp. 209–210.

161. Henry Morgenthau to McCloy, January 28, 1944; Wyman, *America and the Holocaust*, vol. 12, pp. 115–116.

162. McNarney to McCloy, February 4, 1944; Wyman, *America and the Holocaust*, vol. 12, p. 120; General Thomas T. Handy to George C. Marshall, February 8, 1944, NACP, RG 165, entry 418, OPD 334.8 War Refugee Board; Wyman, *Abandonment of the Jews*, p. 292.

163. Memorandum, Joint Logistics Committee, February 9, 1944, NACP, RG 107, ASW 400.38 WRB (B151).

164. Colonel Harrison Gerhardt subcommittee memorandum, February 11, 1944. Wyman, *America and the Holocaust*, vol. 12, p. 129; Wyman, *Abandonment of the Jews*, pp. 227–228, 292–294, 407.

165. General Clayton Bissell–Adolf Berle Correspondence on Refugees, May 1944, NACP, RG 165, entry 182, G-2, box 805.

166. Wyman, *Abandonment of the Jews*, pp. 227–228, 293–294.

167. Stimson to Pehle, March 31, 1944, NACP, RG 107, General Correspondence of John J. McCloy, assistant secretary of state (ASW) 400.38 (Jews); LC, Stimson Diaries, March 9, 21, 31, May 8, 1944.

168. Wyman, *Abandonment of the Jews*, pp. 265–276.

169. Conference memorandum, May 27, 1944, FDRL, WRB, War Department, box 50.

170. Wyman, *Abandonment of the Jews*, pp. 291–292.

171. Pehle memorandum, June 24, 1944; Gerhardt to McCloy July 3, 1944, Wyman, *America and the Holocaust*, vol. 12, pp. 104, 151.

172. McClelland to secretary of state, June 24, 1944; Pehle to McCloy, June 29, 1944; Wyman, *America and the Holocaust*, vol. 12, pp. 147–150.

173. General J. E. Hull memorandum, "Proposed Air Action to Impede Deportation of Hungarian and Slovak Jews," June 26, 1944, NACP, RG 165, entry 418, OPD 383.7 (23 Jun 44).

174. Ibid.

175. Ibid.

176. McCloy to Pehle, July 4, 1944, Wyman, *America and the Holocaust*, vol. 12, p. 152; Wyman, *Abandonment of the Jews*, pp. 298–299.

177. McCloy to A. Leon Kubowitski, Wyman, *America and the Holocaust*, vol. 12, p. 165; Wyman, *Abandonment of the Jews*, pp. 294–295.

178. Wyman, *Abandonment of the Jews*, pp. 298–300.

179. Memo, "Saving of Jews, Poles, Czechs, etc.," September 21, 1944, NACP, RG 165, entry 418, OPD 383.7 (20 Sept 44).

180. Ibid.; Wyman, *Abandonment of the Jews*, pp. 254–257.

181. Joint Chiefs of Staff "Statement on Treatment of Persons in Forced-Labor Battalions and in Concentration Camps in Germany," October 18, 1944, NACP, RG 165, MIDRF, 387-Germany, sec. 7B.

182. Ibid.

183. Winant cable, September 29, 1944, NACP, RG 165, entry 418, OPD 383.7 (22 Sep 44); Pehle to McCloy, October 1, 1944, NACP, RG 107, ASW 400.38 Jews; Wyman, *Abandonment of the Jews*, pp. 296–297.

184. Arnold to Spaatz, October 4, 1944, LC, Carl Spaatz Papers, box 19; David S. Wyman, "Why Auschwitz Was Never Bombed," *Commentary* (May 1978), p. 41, and *Abandonment of the Jews*, pp. 297, 307.

185. Anderson to Spaatz, October 5, 1944, Wyman, *America and the Holocaust*, vol. 12, p. 174.

186. Wyman, *Abandonment of the Jews*, pp. 302–303.

187. "Jewish Refugees in Hungary," September 8, 1944, NACP, RG 226, OSS, entry 191, TC 091 (Hungary), box 1.

188. Pehle to McCloy, November 8, 1944, NACP, RG 165, ABC 383.6 (8 Nov 44) sec. 1A.

189. Ibid.

190. General J. E. Hull to McCloy, November 14, 1944, NACP, RG 165, ABC 383.6 (8 Nov 44) sec. 1A.

191. "Sequence to Conduct a Mission," Headquarters 8 Bomber Command, HIA, General Frederick J. Anderson Papers, box 2; Wyman, *Abandonment of the Jews*, pp. 305–307.

192. William Rubinstein, *The Myth of Rescue: Why the Democracies Could Not Have Saved More Jews from the Nazis* (London, 1997), pp. 157–181; Richard H. Levy, "The Bombing of Auschwitz Revisited: A Critical Analysis," *Holocaust and Genocide Studies*, vol. 10, no. 3 (winter 1996), pp. 267–298; Richard Foregger, "Two Sketch Maps of the Auschwitz-Birkenau Extermination Camps," *Journal of Military History*, vol. 59 (October 1995), pp. 687–696; James H. Kitchens III, "The Bombing of Auschwitz Re-examined," *Journal of Military History* vol. 58 (April 1994), pp. 233–266; Richard Foregger, "Technical Analysis of Methods to Bomb the Gas Chambers at Auschwitz," and Frank W. Brecher, "David Wyman and the Historiography of America's Response to the Holocaust: Counter-Considerations," *Holocaust and Genocide Studies*, vol. 5, no. 4 (1990), pp. 403–446.

193. Stuart G. Erdheim, "Could the Allies Have Bombed Auschwitz?" *Holocaust and Genocide Studies*, vol. 11, no. 2 (Fall 1997), pp. 129–170; Richard Breitman, "Allied Knowledge of Auschwitz-Birkenau in 1943–1944," in *FDR and the Holocaust*, ed. Verne W. Newton (New York, 1996), pp. 175–182.

194. Virginia M. Mannon memorandum, November 22, 1944, FDRL, WRB, box 6.

195. Ibid.

196. Ibid.

197. Elmer Davis to Pehle, November 23, 1944, FDRL, WRB, box 6.

198. Ibid.

199. Virginia M. Mannon to Pehle, November 16, 1944; Pehle Interview, *Yank's* Washington Bureau, November 7, 1944, FDRL, WRB, box 6.

200. Ibid.; Colonel Harrison A. Gerhardt to Pehle, November 23, 1944, FDRL, WRB, box 6.

201. Ibid.

202. *Stars and Stripes* (London edition), April 23, 26, May 1, 12, 30, 1945.

203. "German Atrocities," *Yank: The Army Weekly*, vol. 3, no. 48 (May 18, 1945).

Chapter 10

1. Major Charles A. Robertson Correspondence, May 1945, HIA, Charles A. Robertson Papers.

2. Ibid., September 12, October 4, 1945.

3. Albert Hutler, "The Agony of Survival: An Untold Story of World War II Forty Years After" (unpublished manuscript, 1986), p. 314, YV, Albert A. Hutler Papers, B/60-1.

4. General Frank J. McSherry to Julius Holmes, April 24, 1945, MHI, McSherry Papers, box 13; Eisenhower to Marshall, April 19, 1945, Alfred Chandler, Stephen Ambrose, and Louis Galambos, eds. *The Papers of Dwight D. Eisenhower* (Balti-

more, 1970), vol. 4, p. 2623; Robert H. Abzug, *Inside the Vicious Heart: Americans and the Liberation of Nazi Concentration Camps* (New York, 1985), pp. 130–139.

5. Leonard Dinnerstein, *America and the Survivors of the Holocaust* (New York, 1982), pp. 9–15

6. Hutler, "Agony of Survival," pp. 2, 26–27, 140–141, 250–254, 298, 314, YV, Hutler Papers.

7. Martin Blumenson, ed., *The Patton Papers* (Boston, 1974), vol. 2, p. 759.

8. Ibid., p. 731.

9. Ibid., p. 734.

10. Patton Diaries, September 21, October 1, 1945, LC, Patton Papers, box 4; Patton to Charles Codman, October 4, 1945, box 31.

11. Thomas R. Brush to Kay, May 5, 1945, MHI, Thomas R. Brush Papers; Dinnerstein, *America and the Survivors of the Holocaust*, pp. 47–48.

12. "D.P.s Versus German Authorities," August 29, 1945, UNRRA Headquarters, HIA, Margaret E. Fait Papers, box 5; Mark Wyman, *DP: Europe's Displaced Persons, 1945–1951* (Philadelphia, 1989), pp. 173–175; Dinnerstein, *America and the Survivors of the Holocaust*, pp. 14–15, 33, 54–56.

13. "Displaced Persons Report No. 43," September 30, 1945, appendix A, pp. 3–5, NACP, RG 165, entry 463, Civil Affairs Division (CAD), 1945–1946, box 212; YIVO, Autobiographies, no. 34, pp. 20–22, no. 43; Abzug, *Inside the Vicious Heart*, p. 152; Dinnerstein, *America and the Survivors of the Holocaust*, p. 56.

14. Ibid.

15. YIVO, Autobiographies, no. 29, pp. 20–24, no. 46, pp. 17–19. See also the autobiographical work by Anton A. Pritchard, "The Social System of a Displaced Persons Camp" (unpublished honors thesis), Marion Pritchard Private Papers, Vershire, VT; Wyman, *DP*, pp. 132–134; Dinnerstein, *America and the Survivors of the Holocaust*, pp. 50–54.

16. Abzug, *Inside the Vicious Heart*, pp. 161–163; Wyman, *DP*, p. 135; Dinnerstein, *America and the Survivors of the Holocaust*, pp. 39–71.

17. Eisenhower to Stimson, August 10, 1945, DDEL, Eisenhower Papers, PP Principle File, box 111; Dwight D. Eisenhower, *Crusade in Europe* (New York, 1948), pp. 439–441.

18. Report of Earl G. Harrison, August 1945, p. 2, Harry S. Truman Library, Independence, MO (hereafter HSTL), Harry S. Truman Papers, Official Files, box 127.

19. Ibid., p. 12.

20. Ibid., pp. 12–13, 18.

21. Truman to Eisenhower, August 31, Eisenhower to Truman September 18, 1945, HSTL, Truman Papers, Official Files, box 127.

22. Eisenhower to Marshall, October 27, 1945, Marshall Papers, box 67, folder 30; Eisenhower, *Crusade in Europe*, p. 440.

23. Judah Nadich, Oral History Interview, April 18, 1977, Ben-Gurion Research Institute, Sde Boker, Israel, pp. 8–12.

24. Patton Diaries, August 27–31, 1945, LC, Patton Papers, box 4; Patton to Stimson, September 1, 1945, box 16; Eisenhower to Patton, September 11, 1945, box 31.

25. Patton Diaries, September 15–21, 1945.

26. Ibid., September 22–25, 1945; Frank Mason to Roy Howard, September 26, 1945, HHL, Mason Papers, General Correspondence, 1945, box 4; Blumenson, *Patton Papers*, vol. 2, pp. 760–780.

27. Patton to wife, September 29–October 19, 1945, LC, Patton Papers, box 16; Patton-Baruch Letters, November 8, December 3, 1945, box 29; Chandler, *Papers of Dwight D. Eisenhower*, vol. 6, pp. 394–395.

28. "Short Memories and Nice People," *Yank: The Army Weekly*, October 26, 1945.

29. John Herz to wife, November 1, 1945, Herz-Aschaffenburg Collection, Leo Baeck Institute, New York City.

30. Pollock Diary, November 8, 1945, MHC, James K. Pollock Papers, box 58.

31. Chandler, *Papers of Dwight D. Eisenhower*, vol. 6, p. 394; USFET Release no. 804, December 5, 1945, HIA, Fait Papers, box 2; Frank E. Mason, untitled draft, HHL, Mason Papers, Germany Articles, box 5; Dinnerstein, *America and the Survivors of the Holocaust*, pp. 14, 47–55; Judah Nadich, *Eisenhower and the Jews* (New York, 1953).

32. Ibid.

33. Ibid.

34. General Willard A. Holbrook to wife, October 18, 23, 1945, USMA, Willard A. Holbrook Jr. Papers, box 40.

35. Bonner Fellers to MacArthur, January 19, 1946, DMMA, RG 10, VIP Files: Fellers.

36. General Edgar Erskine Hume to General Mark Clark, September 18, 29, 1945; Simon H. Rifkind to Clark, January 2, 1946, Clark Papers, box 40; Hume to General John Hildring, October 30, 1945, NACP, RG 165, entry 463, CAD, box 211; Martin Blumenson, *Mark Clark* (New York, 1984), pp. 252–253; Nadich, *Eisenhower and the Jews*, pp. 177, 191.

37. YIVO, Autobiography, no. 15; Hutler, "Agony of Survival," pp. 248–249, YV, Hutler Papers.

38. Oliver Rathkolb, ed., *Gesellschaft und Politik am Beginn der Zweiten Republik: Vertrauliche Berichte der US-Militäradministration aus Österreich 1945* (Vienna, 1985), pp. 228–247; former OSS officer in Austria, Professor Paul R. Sweet to author, May 18, 1992.

39. Major Charles Robertson letters, December 26, 30, 1945, February 14, 26, April 19, 1946, HIA, Robertson Papers.

40. Ibid.

41. "Factors and Costs Involved in Caring for DPs," August 21, 1946, NACP, RG 319, entry 153, Plans and Operations, 383.7, box 397; Dinnerstein, *America and the Survivors of the Holocaust*, pp. 111–112.

42. Ibid.

43. Dinnerstein, *America and the Survivors of the Holocaust*, pp. 108–110; Wyman, *DP*, pp. 144–148; General Lauris Norstad to secretary of war, July 16, 1946, NACP, RG 165, entry 15, Chief of Staff (1946) Top Secret, box 2.

44. See documents on Morgan, HIA, Fait Papers, box 2; Chandler, *Papers of Dwight D. Eisenhower*, vol. 7, pp. 722–723.

45. Ibid.; Patton Diaries, November 13, 1945; Dinnerstein, *America and the Survivors of the Holocaust*, p. 53.

46. "Factors and Costs of DPs."

47. HIA, Fait Papers, box 2.

48. Rabbi Philip S. Bernstein to General McNarney on "Public Relations and the Jewish Displaced Persons Problem," August 20, 1946, HIA, Fait Papers, box 2.

49. Fait Papers, box 2.

50. Joseph M. Proskauer to Robert P. Patterson, January 29, 1947, NACP, RG 165, entry 463, CAD, box 344.

51. "Analysis of Jewish Situation in Poland," October 18, 1946, HIA, Fait Papers, box 2.

52. Wyman, *DP*, p. 149.

53. LC, Stimson Diaries, July 2, 1945; Mason to Herbert Hoover, August 27, 1945, HHL, Mason Papers, Germany Correspondence 1945, box 4; William F. Heimlich, "The Eagle and the Bear, Berlin 1945–50" (unpublished memoir), p. 53, HIA, William F. Heimlich Papers.

54. Pollock Diary, January 9, 1946, MHC, Pollock Papers, box 58.

55. Mason to Herbert Hoover, August 31, September 18; to wife, October 5; to Patton, November 4; memorandum to Neil, November 22, 1945; and various Mason manuscripts on Germany 1945; HHL, Mason Papers, boxes 4–5, 17.

56. Heimlich, "Berlin," pp. 104–105; Wedemeyer to Eisenhower, June 23, 1947; HIA, Wedemeyer Papers, box 94.

57. Wedemeyer to Eisenhower, June 23, 1947; Loucks Diary, June 23, 1948, MHI, Loucks Papers.

58. Colonel Stanley J. Grogan to Clark, February 13, 1947, Clark Papers, box 45, folder 8.

59. Ibid.

60. Guy Stern, "The Jewish Exiles in the Service of U.S. Intelligence: The Post-War Years," *Leo Baeck Institute Year Book*, vol. 40 (1995), pp. 51–62; and "In the Service of American Intelligence: German-Jewish Exiles in the War Against Hitler," *Leo Baeck Institute Yearbook*, vol. 37 (1992), pp. 461–477.

61. Burress-Mason Correspondence, MHI, Withers A. Burress Papers, box 6.

62. Eisenhower to Clay, March 4, 1947, DDEL, Eisenhower Papers, PP Principle, box 24.

63. Keating to directors, OMGUS, April 7, 1947, NACP, RG 260, U.S. Occupation HA, World War II, OMGUS, AG, General Correspondence (1945–1949), box 558; Stern, "Jewish Exiles," pp. 60–62.

64. Marcus to wife, August 22, 1942, February 6, May 2, 26, June 27, July 12, 25, September 15, October 16, December 10, 1945, January 10, 25, 1946, USMA, David Marcus Papers, boxes 1–2.

65. Marcus to wife, October 1, 4, 1945, box 1; Heimlich, "Berlin," pp. 68–71.

66. General P. S. Gage to Patton, April 20, 1945, LC, Patton Papers, box 30; DDEL, Eisenhower Papers, "Morgenthau Plan" File, box 151; Ambrose, *Eisenhower*, pp. 421–425; General Lucius Clay to General Daniel Noce, February 16,

1948, NACP, RG 165, entry 463, CAD (1948), box 416; McCloy Diary, April 10, 1945, Amherst College Library Archives, Amherst, MA, McCloy Papers.

67. General William B. Palmer to Frederick Herzberg, November 9, 1948, USMA, Palmer Papers, box 5; General Floyd Parks to wife, May 29–30, 1945, DDEL, Parks Papers, box 4; Eisenhower to Clay, March 4, 1946, DDEL, Eisenhower Papers, PP Principle, box 24; Ambrose, *Eisenhower*, pp. 422–423.

68. Loucks Diary, July 31, Oct 29, 1948, July 15, September 29, 1949, MHI, Loucks Papers.

69. Oral History Interview with Lucius D. Clay (February 9, 1971), Columbia University Oral History Project, DDEL.

70. Burress-Mason Correspondence and General P. E. Gallagher, memo for the record, May 24, 1947, MHI, Burress Papers, box 6.

71. Burress-Huebner Correspondence, MHI, Burress Papers, box 6.

72. William Haber to Lillian, May 6, 1948, MHC, William Haber Papers, box 20.

73. Haber, notes, January–December, 1948, MHC, Haber Papers, box 20.

74. James K. Pollock to wife, May 16, 1948, MHC, Pollock Papers, box 113.

75. Wedemeyer to General Hans Speth, March 11, 1948; Wedemeyer-Truman Smith Correspondence 1950; Wedemeyer to Alfred Vagts, April 29, 1955; HIA, Wedemeyer Papers, boxes 98, 135; Truman Smith to Herbert Hoover, March 24, 1947, HHL, Hoover Papers, PPI, box 216; Truman Smith–Freda Utley Correspondence, HIA, Utley Papers, box 11; Truman Smith to Robert Wood, November 27, 1948, HHL, Wood Papers, box 15; Truman Smith, *Berlin Alert: The Memoirs and Reports of Truman Smith*, ed. Robert Hessen (Stanford, 1984), p. 42; Fellers to commander-in-chief, October 27, 1945, DMMA, RG 5, Records of Headquarters, SCAP, 1945–1951; Fellers to Mason, March 11, 1947, HHL, Hoover Papers, PPI, box 57.

76. Wedemeyer to Ivan D. Yeaton, October 22, 1947, MHI, Yeaton Papers, box 6; Charles Lindbergh to Robert E. Wood, May 14, 1949, HHL, Wood Papers, box 9; Wedemeyer to Freda Utley, February 21, 1949, HIA, Utley Papers, box 13.

77. Trevor's testimony, Congress, House, Committee on Immigration, *Admission of 400,000 Displaced Persons* (1947), 80th Cong., 1st sess., pp. 85–114; see also John B. Trevor, *Refugees 1944* (American Coalition pamphlet, 1944).

78. Ibid.

79. Dinnerstein, *America and the Survivors of the Holocaust*, pp. 145, 158–159.

80. Ibid., pp. 113–115, 144–145.

81. General Willard A. Holbrook to wife, November 1, 1945, USMA, Holbrook Papers, box 40.

82. Colonel C. R. Kutz to General George A. Lincoln, June 27, 1947; "Gains and Losses During FY 1949," September 30, 1947; "Possible Enlistment of Foreign Nationals," August 20, 1947; "Enlistment of Displaced Persons in U.S. Army," November 15, 1947; Secretary of Army Kenneth C. Royal to secretary of defense, March 19, 1948; NACP, RG 319, entry 154, 091.714 TS, box 29; Truman Smith to Herbert Hoover, February 27, 1948, HHL, Hoover Papers PPI, box 217.

83. "Possible Enlistment of Foreign Nationals," July 4, 1947; "Recruitment of Non-Enemy Aliens," November 6, 1947; "Possible Enlistment of Displaced Per-

sons in U.S. Army," November 21, 1947, NACP, RG 319, entry 154, 091.714 TS, box 29.

84. General William A. Burress–Colonel Richard D. Prather Correspondence, 1947–1948, MHI, Burress Papers, box 6.

85. Ibid.; Dinnerstein, *America and the Survivors of the Holocaust*, pp. 19–21, 159.

86. Colonel John G. Hill, assistant to chief of staff to General Arthur G. Trudeau, General Staff, November 19, 1947, NACP, RG 319, entry 153, 320.2, box 258.

87. Wedemeyer to MacArthur, December 11, 1947, DMMA, RG 10: P.C. VIP Files, Wedemeyer. Memorandum for Wedemeyer, February 12, 1948, NACP, RG 319, entry 154 091.714 TS, box 29.

88. "Recruitment of DPs in U.S. Army," January 5, 1948, NACP, RG 319, entry 154, 091.714 TS, box 29; "Displaced Persons Who Are Qualified for U.S. Army Service," March 2, 1948, NACP, RG 319, entry 153, 320.2, box 258; "Displaced Persons Who Are Qualified for U.S. Army Service," March 20, 1948, NACP, RG 165, entry 463 CAD (1948), box 480.

89. Ibid.; Chamberlain to General J. Lawton Collins, Deputy Chief of Staff, November 15, 1947; NACP, RG 319, entry 153, 091.714, box 111.

90. General C. R. Huebner to CAD, February 11, 1948, NACP, RG 165, entry 463 CAD (1948), box 480.

91. "Training in Army Ground Forces, 1 September 1945–10 March 1948," Historical Section (1948), pp. 65–66, U.S. Army Center for Military History Archives, Washington, DC (hereafter CMH), 6-1 CA5 C1.

92. Haber Notes, April 1948, MHC, Haber Papers, box 20.

93. Dinnerstein, *America and the Survivors of the Holocaust*, pp. 159, 247; Divine, *American Immigration Policy*, pp. 116–145.

94. Wedemeyer to Huebner, September 3, 1948, HIA, Wedemeyer Papers, box 98.

95. "Communist Activities in Palestine," February 15, March 3, 1945; "Jewish Agency and Russia," April 15, 1945, NACP, RG 226 OSS, entry 120, boxes 31–32; "Jewish Situation in Poland," HIA, Fait Papers, box 2.

96. Reid Report, September 13, 1945, NACP, RG 165, ABC 383.7; Bissell Report, September 7, 1945, NACP, RG 319, MID 291.2 Jews.

97. Chandler, *Papers of Dwight D. Eisenhower*, vol. 8, pp. 1137–1138, 1778.

98. P&O 091.Palestine (23 Jun 47) and (13 Jul 48), NACP, RG 319, entry 153, box 93.

99. Wedemeyer to Hurley, May 25, 1946, November 26, 1947, HIA, Wedemeyer Papers, boxes 81, 98.

100. "Study on Palestine Situation," December 8, 1947, NACP, RG 319, entry 154, 091.Palestine TS, box 24.

101. Wedemeyer to Eisenhower, January 8, 1948, DDEL, Eisenhower Papers, PPP, box 123; *Foreign Relations of the United States*, vol. 5 (1948) (Washington, DC, 1976), pp. 631–633; Walter Millis, ed, *The Forrestal Diaries* (New York, 1951), pp. 361–363.

102. Black to Wedemeyer, January 30, 1948, HIA, Wedemeyer, box 99.

103. "Palestine," February 2, 1948, NACP, RG 319, entry 154, 091.Palestine TS, box 24.

104. Ibid.

105. Ibid.

106. Ibid.

107. Forrest C. Pogue, *George C. Marshall: Statesman, 1945–1959* (New York, 1987), vol. 4, pp. 345–358.

108. *Foreign Relations of the United States* (1948), vol. 5, pp. 631–633.

109. *Forrestal Diaries*, pp. 374–377.

110. Pogue, *Marshall*, vol. 4, pp. 359–360.

111. "Estimate of the Palestine Situation in 1948," February 26, 1948, pp. 1–3, 6, 31, NACP, RG 319, entry 154, 091.Palestine TS, box 24.

112. Ibid., pp. 10–18, 22, 42.

113. Ibid., pp. 29–33.

114. Ibid., pp. 41–44.

115. Wedemeyer to Mountbatten, March 18, 1948, HIA, Wedemeyer Papers, box 98.

116. Pogue, *Marshall*, vol. 4, p. 367.

117. *Foreign Relations of the United States* (1948), vol. 5, pp. 832–833; Pogue, *Marshall*, vol. 4, pp. 361–370; Grose, *Israel in the Mind of America* (New York, 1983), pp. 274–278.

118. Pogue, *Marshall*, vol. 4, pp. 370–378; Grose, *Israel in the Mind of America*, pp. 281–298; Cray, *Marshall*, pp. 657–662.

119. Pate Diary, May 14, 1948, UOL, Pate Papers.

120. Grose, *Israel in the Mind of America*, p. 299.

121. Wedemeyer memorandum, July 16, 1948, and Forrestal memorandum, August 18, 1948, NACP, RG 319, entry 154, 091.Palestine TS, box 24.

122. "Relief of Arab Refugees," September 1, 1948, NACP, RG 319, entry 153, 383.7, box 397.

123. *Foreign Relations of the United States* (1948), vol. 5, pp. 1427–1428, 1444, 1478–1480.

124. Ibid. (1949), vol. 6, pp. 697–698.

125. Ibid. (1949), vol. 6, pp. 899, 1134–1135, 1202–1203.

126. Secretary of defense, "United States Strategic Interests in Israel," May 17, 1949, Marshall Papers, Xerox 1574.

127. Ibid.

128. Ibid.

Chapter 11

1. Herzberg File, USMA, Palmer Papers, box 2.

2. Ibid.

3. Ibid.

4. Ibid.

5. Ibid.

6. Ibid.

7. Ibid.

8. "Inter-Racial Agitation," July 4, 1945, NACP, RG 319, Project Decimal, MID 000.2412, box 6.

9. "Doll File," USMA, Palmer Papers.

10. Ibid.

11. Ibid.

12. "Estimate of Domestic Intelligence Situation," June 18, 1945, NACP, RG 165, ACS 1941-45, 350.05.

13. Ibid.

14. Memorandum for the secretary of war, December 7, 1945, NACP, RG 165, ACS 1941-45, 350.05; Alfred Chandler, Stephen Ambrose, and Louis Galambos, eds., *The Papers of Dwight David Eisenhower*, 9 vols. (Baltimore, 1970, 1978), vol. 7, pp. 597–598.

15. Army Service Forces, *Weekly Intelligence Summaries*, 1946, NADC, RG 46, Van Deman Papers, box 45.

16. "The Jewish Situation in the East," June 29, 1946, NADC, RG 46, Van Deman Papers, box 45.

17. "Study Showing the Relationship Between Jews and Communism," December 18, 1946, HIA, Wedemeyer Papers, box 94.

18. Ibid., p. 5.

19. Ibid., pp. 1–3.

20. Ibid., pp. 5–7.

21. Ibid., pp. 7–11.

22. Ibid., p. 12.

23. Jewish Groups: Jewish Activities, May 15, 1944, NACP, RG 319, Decimal File 1941–1948, 000.2436: Subversives, box 15.

24. Ibid.

25. "Leftist Infiltration into SCAP," May 30, 1947, DMMA, Major General Charles A. Willoughby Papers.

26. Undated Willoughby biography; Willoughby to editor of *Time*, November 4, 1946; Willoughby to Edwin W. Pauley, November 10, 1949; GC, Willoughby Papers; Ivan D. Yeaton to William LaVarre, January 14, 1978, HIA, Yeaton Papers, box 5.

27. See Willoughby Correspondence with Don Alberto Artajo, Francisco Franco, Reverend Monsignor Fulton J. Sheen, Arthur Vandenberg, and Wedemeyer, GC, Willoughby Papers.

28. "The Communist Threat in the Far East," May 5, 1958, GC, Willoughby Papers.

29. Ibid.; Willoughby to Vandenberg, February 4, 1945, and McCormick, March 18, 1950, GC, Willoughby Papers.

30. Ibid.

31. Ibid.

32. Willoughby to McCormick, March 13, 1948, to Franco, January 14, 1949, to Frank S. Tavenner, Committee on Un-American Activities, March 7, 1950, GC, Willoughby Papers.

33. Undated Willoughby lecture on "Kremlin-Directed Espionage, Sabotage and National Subversion," DMMA, RG 23, Willoughby Correspondence, Addresses; Willoughby to MacArthur June 1952, RG 10: P.C. VIP File, Willoughby.

34. "Leftist Classification of Civilian Employees of GHQ," September 18, 1946, DMMA, RG 23.

35. Willoughby to chief of staff, January 28, 1947, DMMA, RG 23.

36. Leftist Investigation memoranda, February 9, 20, 1947, DMMA, RG 23.

37. "Foreigners Employed in General Headquarters," February 25, "Leftist Infiltration into SCAP," February 27, 1947, DMMA, RG 23.

38. Willoughby to commander-in-chief and chief of staff, April 23, 1947, DMMA, RG 23.

39. Ibid.; "Leftist Infiltration into SCAP."

40. "Leftist Investigation," February 20, 1947.

41. "G-2 Comment" (undated), DMMA, RG 23.

42. Willoughby to General Whitney, June 7, 1947, DMMA, RG 23; Holmes to Willoughby, September 10, 1952, GC, Willoughby Papers.

43. Willoughby-McCormick Correspondence, July 30, September 14, 1948, GC, Willoughby Papers.

44. Doll to Wedemeyer, December 1, 1948, HIA, Wedemeyer Papers, box 99.

45. "African-American Soldiers," HIA, Wedemeyer Papers, box 87; "Communist Fifth-Column Penetration in China" (undated speech), box 5.

46. Doll to Wedemeyer, December 1, 1948.

47. Wedemeyer memorandum, December 13, 1948, HIA, Wedemeyer Papers, box 99.

48. "Jewish Financial Activities for Communist Account," August 30, September 9, 1949, NACP, RG 319, G2, 291.2:Jews.

49. Herzberg File, USMA, Palmer Papers.

50. Ibid.

51. Ibid.

52. "Stratemeyer Testifies," U.S. News and World Report, September 3, 1954, pp. 81–86.

53. General George E. Stratemeyer to John Beaty, September 14, 1954, LC, Moseley Papers, vol. 21.

54. John Beaty, The Iron Curtain over America (Barboursville, VA, 1958), pp. ix–xii. AJCA, John O. Beaty File. HIA, Alfred Kohlberg Papers, Beaty File, box 16.

55. Beaty, Iron Curtain over America, pp. 25, 42–43.

56. Ibid., pp. 18–29.

57. Ibid., pp. 30–33.

58. Ibid., pp. 36–39.

59. Ibid., pp. 46–59. Italics in original.

60. Ibid., pp. 60–78.

61. Ibid., pp. 123–156, 163–169, 216–218. Italics in original.

62. Hurley Papers, box 151, folder 13.

63. HHL, Wood Papers, Stratemeyer File, box 16.

64. UOL, Beaty Papers, Stratemeyer-Beaty Correspondence.

65. Ibid.; HIA, Wedemeyer Papers, box 62; Utley Papers, box 11.

66. AJCA, Beaty File.

67. Moseley-Stratemeyer Correspondence, October 1955; Moseley-Beaty Correspondence, September 1958; LC, Moseley Papers, vols. 21–22. Wedemeyer-Moseley Correspondence, November-December 1958, HIA, Wedemeyer Papers, box 52.

68. Robert McCormick to Moseley, April 1, 1954, LC, Moseley Papers, vol. 20; Stratemeyer to Moseley, April 30, J. B. Pate to Moseley, April 6, 1959, Robert E. Wood to Moseley, July 15, 23, 1959, vol. 27.

69. General Stanley D. Embick–Moseley Correspondence, September 1954, LC, Moseley Papers, box 34; General William B. Graham–Moseley Correspondence, June 1959, vol. 26; General William D. Connor–Moseley Correspondence, October 1954, vol. 20.

70. Wedemeyer, Address at the Bohemian Grove, July 22, 1951, HHL, Hoover Papers, PPI, box 249: Wedemeyer. "Untitled Fragments on Communism," HIA, Wedemeyer Papers, box 6.

71. HHL, Hoover Papers, PPI, box 57: Bonner Fellers File. Truman Smith–Flynn Correspondence, Wedemeyer-Flynn Correspondence, UOL, John T. Flynn Papers, box 20. Wedemeyer-Willoughby Correspondence, HIA, Wedemeyer Papers, box 69. UOL, Merwin K. Hart Papers, box 8. General Ralph C. Smith to General Charles A. Willoughby, DMMA, RG 23, Willoughby Papers, Miscellaneous Correspondence; RG 10, MacArthur Papers, P.C., V.I.P. Fellers, Wedemeyer.

72. Senator Joseph McCarthy to Truman Smith, November 20, 1952, MHI, Truman Smith Papers. DMMA, RG 23, Willoughby Papers, American Opinion. Victor Emanuel to Wedemeyer, September 11, 1952, HIA, Wedemeyer Papers, box 105.

73. General Pedro del Valle–Beaty Correspondence, UOL, Beaty Papers.

74. UOL, Hart Papers, boxes 3, 8.

75. General Robert E. Wood to Merwin Hart, April 22, 1958, UOL, Hart Papers, box 8.

76. General William D. Connor to Moseley, April 24, 1953, LC, Moseley Papers, vol. 19.

77. Freda Utley, *Will the Middle East Go West?* (Chicago, 1957), pp. 34–35, 134–138, 158.

78. Ibid., pp. 64, 140–147.

79. HIA, Utley Papers, boxes 8, 13.

80. Truman Smith Report from Germany, September 9, 1955, HHL, Wood Papers, box 15. Truman Smith Report from Germany, September 25, 1963, HHL, Truman Smith Papers, box 6.

81. Wedemeyer to Truman Smith, November 27, 1950, HHL, Smith Papers, box 5. Truman Smith to General Robert E. Wood, August 6, 1955, HHL, Wood Papers, box 15. Wedemeyer, "Observations on Trip in Europe, February 22 to March 7, 1957," HHL, Hoover Papers, PPI, boxes 249–250: Wedemeyer.

82. DMMA, RG 23, Willoughby Papers, German Correspondents, 1959–1961; Central Intelligence Agency.

83. H. Keith Thompson to Wedemeyer, January 29, 1957, Wedemeyer to Grand Admiral Dönitz, February 2, 1957, HIA, Wedemeyer Papers, box 34. General

Charles A. Willoughby to Sven Hasselblatt, January 14, 1963, DMMA, RG 23, Willoughby Papers, German Correspondents.

84. Abraham Ashkenasi, *Modern German Nationalism* (New York, 1976), pp. 170–173. Hans W. Schoenberg, *Germans from the East: A Study of Their Migration, Resettlement, and Subsequent Group History Since 1945* (The Hague, 1970), pp. 99–100, 141. T. H. Tetens, *The New Germany and the Old Nazis* (London, 1962), pp. 122–124, 136–138.

85. George Brada, "Analysis of the Political Situation in the United States of America in the Year 1952," GC, Willoughby Papers. DMMA, RG 23, Willoughby Papers, German Correspondents: Brada File.

86. Brada, "Analysis of the Political Situation." Italics in original.

87. Willoughby to MacArthur, June 1952, DMMA, RG 10: P.C., V.I.P. Files: Willoughby. Undated Willoughby lecture on "Kremlin-Directed Espionage, Sabotage and National Subversion."

88. Brada to Willoughby, September 1, 1967, DMMA, RG 23, Willoughby Papers, German Correspondents.

89. Ibid. Detlef Bischoff, *Franz Josef Strauss, die CSU und die Aussenpolitik: Konzeption und Realität am Beispiel der Grossen Koalition* (Meisenheim, 1973), pp. 25–27, 208–213.

90. HIA, Kohlberg Papers, box 64: Flynn; box 77: Heimlich; box 104: Klein; box 199: Wedemeyer. UOL, Flynn Papers, box 20.

91. NACP, RG 165, MID 10175-563.

92. General Pedro del Valle–Beaty Correspondence, UOL, Beaty Papers.

93. Isaac Don Levine to Freda Utley, September 15, 1949, HIA, Utley Papers, box 8. Wedemeyer to Herbert Hoover, March 12, 1956, HHL, Hoover Papers PPI, boxes 249–250. George Sokolsky to Arthur Kohlberg, August 2, 1956, HIA, Kohlberg Papers, box 160.

94. Kohlberg to Sokolsky, January 10, 1957, HIA, Kohlberg Papers, box 160; Kohlberg to Dr. James W. Fifield, April 7, 1952, box 16.

95. HIA, Kohlberg Papers, box 10: *American Mercury* File.

96. *American Mercury*, 1959: Stephen Paulsen, "Frankfurter and Brandeis" (January); "Termites of the Cross" (October); "Termites of the Cross" and John Benedict, "The Reign of the Lehman Brothers: The Intriguing Story of the Financial "Elders" and their Political Powers" (November).

97. *American Mercury*, 1959: John Lines, "Jewish Population of the United States (September); "Termites of the Cross" (December).

98. *American Mercury*, 1959: Stephen Paulsen, "The World Wide Betrayal" (September); "Termites of the Cross" (December).

99. "The *American Mercury* and Russell Maguire," *FACTS* (Anti-Defamation League, October–November 1959), vol. 13, no. 7. HIA, Kohlberg Papers, box 10: *American Mercury* File.

100. DMMA, RG 23, Willoughby Papers: American Jewish Committee.

101. Charles A. Willoughby, "Korea and the Middle East: Last Chance?" *Foreign Intelligence Digest*, no. 135 (February 1957), pp. 1–8.

102. Willoughby to Lawrence Speckman, March 27, 1956; Willoughby to General Hans Speidel, March 22, 1959, DMMA, RG 23, Willoughby Papers: "S" and

"German Correspondents." Willoughby Report (February–March 1952), RG 10, MacArthur, P.C.: Willoughby.

103. DMMA, RG 23, Willoughby Papers: "German Correspondent"; Willoughby to Ruediger von Wechman, Correspondence: "W".

104. General Frederick D. Sharp to Willoughby, July 26, September 12, 19, 1952; Willoughby to Theodore F. Green, Chariman, Foreign Relations Committee, April 30, 1958, GC, Willoughby Papers. General Maxwell D. Taylor to Willoughby, November 28, 1955, DMMA, RG 23, Willoughby Papers, Correspondence.

Epilogue

1. Frank Mason to Colonel Ivan Yeaton, November 30, 1976, HIA, Yeaton Papers, box 5.

2. Wedemeyer to T. Coleman Andrews, November 21, 1960, UOL, T. Coleman Andrews Papers, box 8. Wedemeyer to Truman Smith, February 10, 1964, HIA, Truman Smith Papers. Wedemeyer to Ezra Benson, September 20, 1980, HIA, Wedemeyer Papers, box 26.

3. Ibid. Truman Smith to Carter Clarke, November 20, 1967, HIA, Truman Smith Papers, box 1. DMMA, RG 23, Willoughby Papers, Correspondence: *American Opinion*. HIA, Wedemeyer Papers, box 52/12.

4. HHL, Mason Papers, box 24: Trevor File. DMMA, RG 23, Willoughby Papers: Trevor Correspondence. HIA, Wedemeyer Papers, box 115: Immigration.

5. HIA, Wedemeyer Papers, box 115: Immigration. Theodore Roosevelt, *On Race-Riots-Reds-Crime,* ed. Archibald B. Roosevelt (West Sayville, NY, 1968), pp. 89–90.

6. HIA, Wedemeyer Papers, boxes 52/6, 58/28. Roosevelt, *On Race,* pp. 77–92.

7. HHL, Mason Papers, box 24: Trevor File.

8. General Edward Almond to Vermont Royster, March 11, 1970, MHI, Almond Papers, box "A Voice of Conservatism."

9. HIA, Wedemeyer Papers, box 52/12.

10. HHL, Mason Papers, box 24, Trevor File.

11. *Washington Observer Newsletter,* no. 124, August 15, 1971, DMMA, RG 23, Willoughby Papers, Correspondence "C."

12. Gary Allen, *None Dare Call It Conspiracy* (Rossmoor, CA, 1971), pp. 38–51, 62–75, 86–91.

13. HIA, Wedemeyer Papers, boxes 70/1–4, 115. UOL, A. G. Heinsohn Papers, box 2: LaVarre File; box 3: Wedemeyer File.

14. HIA, Wedemeyer Papers, box 66/12–14.

15. "Head of Joint Chiefs Criticizes Jewish Influence in the U.S.," *Washington Post,* November 13, 1974, pp. 1, 9.

16. Letters to editor, *New York Times,* November 21, 1974. "Brown's Bomb," *Time,* November 25, 1974. Meg Greenfield, "The General and the Jews," *Newsweek,* December 9, 1974.

17. Joseph Alsop, "What General Brown Said," *Washington Post,* November 15, 1974. "The General and the Jews," *Newsweek,* November 25, 1974.

18. "Ford Scores General on Jewish Remarks," *Washington Post,* November 14, 1974, pp. 1, 8. "Chairman of Joint Chiefs Regrets Remarks on Jews," and "Sen-

ate Panel Declines to Query General Who Criticized Jews," *New York Times*, November 26, 1974.

19. HIA, Wedemeyer Papers, box 66/12–13.

20. HIA, Wedemeyer Papers, box 51/12–13. HHL, Mason Papers, box 25: Wedemeyer File.

21. HHL, Mason Papers, box 24: Wedemeyer File.

22. HIA, Wedemeyer Papers, boxes 51/12–13, 70/1–4. HHL, Mason Papers, box 27: Yeaton File.

23. HIA, Wedemeyer Papers, boxes 54/3–5, 57/18. HIA, Yeaton Papers, box 5.

24. HIA, Wedemeyer Papers, box 51/12–13.

Bibliography

Archival Material

U.S. National Archives (NADC), Washington, DC

RG 38, Naval Attaché Reports, 1886–1939, Office of Naval Intelligence (ONI)
RG 46, Van Deman Collection, Investigative Files, Records of U.S. Senate Internal Security Subcommittee of the Senate Judiciary Committee, 1951–1975
RG 94, Office of the Adjutant General Central Files, 1926–1939, Bonus Marchers
RG 98, U.S. Army Command III Corps Area, General Correspondence 1920–1939, Bonus March 1932
RG 233, Records of U.S. House of Representatives, Committee on Immigration and Naturalization
RG 394, U.S. Army Continental Commands, 1920–1942

U.S. National Archives (NACP), College Park, MD

RG 59, Entry 538, Office of the Counselor, General Records of the Department of State
RG 59, Records of the Department of State Relating to the Problems of Relief and Refugees in Europe Arising from World War II and Its Aftermath, 1938–1949 (NA Microfilm M1284)
RG 59, Purport Lists for the Department of State Decimal File, 1910–1944 (NA Microfilm M973)
RG 84, "American Mission Riga" (Latvia), Foreign Service Post of Department of State
RG 107, General Correspondence of John J. McCloy, Assistant Secretary of War (ASW) 400.38 (Jews)
RG 107, Entry 74A, Stimson "Safe File" (1940–1945), "War Refugee Board"
RG 165, Military Intelligence Division (MID), Records of the War Department General and Special Staffs
RG 165, Military Intelligence, Regional File (1929–1944) (MIDRF)
RG 165, Entry 15, Chief of Staff
RG 165, Entry 181, G-2 Intelligence Division Central European Branch

RG 165, Entry 182, G-2 Eastern European Intelligence Reports and Memoranda, 1935–1944, War Department General Staff

RG 165, Entry 192, G-2, Visa and Passport Control Branch Correspondence, 1941–1946

RG 165, Entry 418, Operations Division (OPD)

RG 165, Entry 463, Civil Affairs Division (CAD)

RG 200, Duker/Dwork Papers, OSS Research and Analysis Branch, Jewish Desk

RG 226, OSS, Research and Analysis Branch, Palestine

RG 256, American Mission to Negotiate Peace

RG 260, U.S. Occupational Headquarters, World War II, OMGUS, Office of Adjutant General, Correspondence (Decimal File) 1945–1949

RG 319, Army Intelligence Project Decimal, ACSI-G-2 (1941–1945), (1941–1948)

RG 319, Records of the Army Staff

RG 319, Entries 152-154, Plans and Operations Division

RG 407, Adjutant General Office (AGO)

U.S. Army Center for Military History Archives (CMH), Washington, DC

U.S. Military History Institute Archives (MHI), Carlisle, PA

U.S. Army War College Archives (AWCA)

Jewish War Veterans Papers (JWV)

Senior Officers Oral History Project
    85-B, Gerd S. Grombacher

Katherine Smith Memoirs (unpublished manuscript)

Private Collections

Edward M. Almond Papers

Harry H. Bandholtz Papers

William S. Biddle Papers

Thomas R. Brush Papers

Withers A. Burress Papers

William A. Castle Papers

Bradford G. Chynoweth Papers

Edward Davis Papers

William J. Donovan Papers

Hugh A. Drum Papers

Philip R. Faymonville Papers

Johnson Hagood Papers

Kenyon A. Joyce Papers

Morris W. Kolander Papers

Raymond E. Lee Papers

Joseph B. Longuevan Papers

Charles E. Loucks Papers

Frank J. McSherry Papers

John Paul Ratay Papers
Truman Smith Papers
Ralph H. Van Deman Papers
Leory W. Yarborough Papers
Ivan D. Yeaton Papers
Gordon R. Young Papers

U.S. Military Academy (USMA), West Point, NY

Archives

Department of Economics, Government, and History, Organizational History and
    Programs of Instruction Files, 1921–46, Series 83, 5b

Special Collections

West Point Historical Collection
USMA Textbook Collection

Manuscript Collection

Bernard S. Carter Papers
George B. Conrad Papers
Benjamin A. Dickson Papers
Randle Elliott Papers
Campbell B. Hodges Papers
Willard A. Holbrook Jr. Papers
Walter Krueger Papers
Joseph E. Kuhn Papers
John J. Maginnis Memoirs
Peyton C. March Papers
David Marcus Papers
Thomas B. Mott Papers
Daniel Noce Papers
Williston B. Palmer Papers
Charles G. Stevenson Papers
USMA, Letters: 1894–1902
USMA, Booklists: 1902–1940

U.S. Library of Congress (LC), Washington, DC

Boris Brasol Papers
Breckinridge Long Papers
William E. Dodd Papers
George Van Horn Moseley Papers
John C. O'Laughlin Papers

Robert P. Patterson Papers
George S. Patton Jr. Papers
Kenneth L. Roberts Papers
Carl Spaatz Papers
Henry L. Stimson Diaries (Microfilm)

DWIGHT D. EISENHOWER LIBRARY (DDEL), ABILENE, KS

Oral History Interview Lucius Clay (February 9, 1971), Columbia University Oral
    History Project
Dwight D. Eisenhower Papers
Alfred M. Gruenther Papers
Courtney H. Hodges Papers
Frank A. Keating Papers
Kevin McCann Papers
Floyd L. Parks Papers
Charles W. Ryder Papers

GERALD R. FORD LIBRARY (GRFL), ANN ARBOR, MI

Files on General George E. Brown

HERBERT HOOVER LIBRARY (HHL), WEST BRANCH, IA

William R. Castle Papers
Herbert Hoover Papers
Frank E. Mason Papers
Truman Smith Papers
Lewis Strauss Papers
Robert E. Wood Papers

HOOVER INSTITUTION ARCHIVES (HIA), STANFORD

Frederick L. Anderson Papers
Lawrence Dennis Papers
Margaret E. Fait Papers
Bonner F. Fellers Papers
Hugh S. Gibson Papers
Anson Conger Goodyear Papers
William F. Heimlich Papers
Stanley K. Hornbeck Papers
Alfred Kohlberg Papers
William LaVarre Papers
Charles A. Robertson Papers
Ralph C. Smith Papers
Truman Smith Papers
James A. Stader Papers

Freda Utley Papers
Albert C. Wedemeyer Papers
Ivan D. Yeaton Papers

Douglas MacArthur Memorial Archives (DMMA), Norfolk, VA

RG 5, Records of Headquarters, Supreme Commander for the Allied Powers, 1945–1951
RG 10, General Douglas MacArthur Private Correspondence
RG 23, Major General Charles A. Willoughby Papers

Franklin D. Roosevelt Library (FDRL), Hyde Park, NY

Records of the War Refugee Board (WRB)
Henry Morgenthau Jr. Papers
Franklin D. Roosevelt Papers
John C. Wiley Papers

Harry S. Truman Library (HSTL), Independence, MO

Harry S. Truman Papers

Private Collections

American Jewish Committee Archives (AJCA), New York City

AJC Chronological File
AJC General Correspondence, 1906–1932
Cyrus Adler Papers
American Coalition File
John O. Beaty File
Louis Marshall Papers
Protocols Files

American Legion National Headquarters Library (ALL), Indianapolis, IN

Americanization-Naturalization, and Investigation 1935 to Refugees 1939, Microfilm 89-2031 to 89-2033

Amherst College Library Archives, Amherst, MA

John J. McCloy Papers

Atlanta Historical Society, Atlanta, GA

General Benjamin M. Bailey Papers

Ben-Gurion Research Institute, Sde Boker, Israel

Judah Nadich Oral History Interview

The Citadel Archives, Charleston, SC

General Mark W. Clark Papers

Columbia University Manuscript Library, New York City

DeWitt Clinton Poole, Oral History
General Robert E. Wood, Oral History

Duke University Library, Manuscript Department (DUL), Durham, NC

Robert Eichelberger Papers
John J. McSwain Papers

East Carolina Manuscript Collection (ECMC), East Carolina University, Greenville, NC

Alexander B. Coxe Jr. Papers
Alexander B. Coxe Sr. Papers
Eli A. Helmick Papers

Gettysburg College (GC), Gettysburg, PA

Charles A. Willoughby Papers

George C. Marshall Foundation, Lexington, VA

George C. Marshall Papers
Francis Pickens Miller Papers

Leo Baeck Institute (LBI), New York City

Herz-Aschaffenburg Collection

Michigan Historical Collections, Bentley Historical Library, University of Michigan (MHC), Ann Arbor, MI

William Haber Papers
Frank Murphy Papers
James K. Pollock Papers

New York Historical Society (NYHS), New York City

American Defense Society Papers
Henry C. McClean Papers

South Carolina Historical Society, Charleston, SC

Johnson Hagood Papers

University of Oklahoma Library, Norman, OK

Patrick J. Hurley Collection

University of Oregon Library (UOL), Eugene, OR

T. Coleman Andrews Papers
Kendall Banning Papers
John O. Beaty Papers
John T. Flynn Papers
General Amos A. Fries Papers
Merwin K. Hart Papers
A. G. Heinsohn Jr. Papers
Lee J. Levinger Papers
Joseph B. Pate Papers
Walter M. Pierce Papers

University of Virginia Library, Charlottesville, VA

Edwin M. Watson Papers

Virginia Historical Society (VHS), Richmond, VA

E.R.W. McCabe Papers
T. Bentley Mott Papers
Tenant Collection

Yad Vashem Central Archives (YV), Jerusalem, Israel

John B. Coulston Papers
Albert A. Hutler Papers
Kieve Skidell Papers

YIVO Institute for Jewish Research, New York City

American Jewish Committee, Waldman Archives
Autobiographies of Jewish American Soldiers in World War II

Published Documents

Bland, Larry I., ed. *The Papers of George Catlett Marshall*. 2 vols. Baltimore, 1981, 1986.

Blumenson, Martin, ed. *The Patton Papers*. 2 vols. Boston, 1972, 1974.

Challener, Richard D., ed. *United States Military Intelligence, 1917–1927*. 30 vols. New York, 1978.

Chandler, Alfred, Stephen Ambrose, and Louis Galambos, eds. *The Papers of Dwight David Eisenhower*. 9 vols. Baltimore, 1970, 1978.

Complete Presidential Press Conferences of Franklin D. Roosevelt. Vol. 15. New York, 1972.

Doenecke, Justus D., ed. *In Danger Undaunted: The Anti-Interventionist Movement of 1940–1941 as Revealed in the Papers of the America First Committee*. Stanford, 1990.

Eiler, Keith, ed. *Wedemeyer on War and Peace*. Stanford, 1987.

Foreign Relations of the United States (FRUS). Vol. 5 (1948), vol. 6 (1949). Washington, DC, 1976, 1977.

Holt, Daniel D., ed. *Eisenhower: The Prewar Diaries and Selected Papers, 1905–1941*. Baltimore, 1998.

Rathkolb, Oliver, ed. *Gesellschaft und Politik am Beginn der Zweiten Republik: Vertrauliche Berichte der US-Militäradministration aus Österreich 1945*. Vienna, 1985.

U.S. Congress. House. Committee on Immigration and Naturalization. *Temporary Suspension of Immigration*. 66th Cong., 3d sess. House Report no. 1109. 1920.

_____. House. Committee on Immigration and Naturalization. 67th Cong., 4th sess. House Report no. 1621. 1923.

_____. House. Committee on Immigration and Naturalization. Hearings: Restrictions of Immigrations. 68th Cong., 1st sess. House Report no. 350. 1924.

_____. Senate. Committee on Immigration. Hearings: Emergency Immigration Legislation. 66th Cong., 3d sess. 1921.

_____. Senate. Committee on Immigration. Hearings: Selective Immigration Legislation. 68th Cong., 1st sess. 1924.

U.S. Military Intelligence Reports: Surveillance of Radicals in the United States, 1917–1941. Microfilm. Frederick, MD, 1984.

Wyman, David, ed. *America and the Holocaust*. 13 vols. New York, 1989–1991.

Published Diaries and Memoirs

Chynoweth, Bradford G. *Bellamy Park: Memoirs by Bradford Grethen Chynoweth*. Hicksville, NY, 1975.

Collins, J. Lawton. *Lightning Joe: An Autobiography*. Baton Rouge, LA, 1979.

Dodd, William E. *Ambassador Dodd's Diary, 1933–1938*. New York, 1941.

Eisenhower, Dwight D. *At Ease: Stories I Tell to Friends*. New York, 1967.

_____. *Crusade in Europe*. New York, 1948.

Graves, William S. *America's Siberian Adventure*. New York, 1931.

Hayes, Carlton J. H. *Wartime Mission in Spain, 1942–1945*. New York, 1945.

Heinsohn, A. G. *One Man's Fight for Freedom*. Caldwell, ID, 1957.

Ickes, Harold I. *The Secret Diary of Harold I. Ickes*. 3 vols. New York, 1953–1955.

Israel, Fred L., ed. *The War Diaries of Breckinridge Long*. Lincoln, NE, 1965.

Leutze, James, ed. *The London Journal of Raymond E. Lee, 1940–1941*. Boston, 1971.

Lindbergh, Anne Morrow. *The Flower and the Nettles: Diaries and Letters of Anne Morrow Lindbergh, 1936–1939*. New York, 1976.

_____. *The War Within and Without: Diaries and Letters of Anne Morrow Lindbergh, 1939–1944*. New York, 1980.

Lindbergh, Charles A. *The Wartime Journals of Charles A. Lindbergh*. New York, 1970.

Mills, Walter, ed. *The Forrestal Diaries*. New York, 1951.

Mott, Thomas Bentley. *Twenty Years as Military Attache*. New York, 1937.

Murphy, Robert. *Diplomat Among Warriors*. New York, 1964.

Pelley, William Dudley. *The Door to Revelation: An Intimate Autobiography*. Asheville, NC, 1936.

Roosevelt, Archie. *For Lust of Knowing: Memoirs of an Intelligence Officer*. Boston, 1988.

Smith, Truman. *Berlin Alert: The Memoirs and Reports of Truman Smith*. Edited by Robert Hessen. Stanford, 1984.

Truscott, Lucian K. *The Twilight of the U.S. Cavalry: Life in the Old Army, 1917–1942*. Lawrence, KS, 1989.

Ward, John. *With the "Die-Hards" in Siberia*. London, 1920.

Wedemeyer, Albert C. *Wedemeyer Reports*. New York, 1958.

Published Primary Sources

Allen, Gary. *None Dare Call It Conspiracy*. Rossmoor, CA, 1971.

Beaty, John. *The Iron Curtain over America*. Barboursville, VA, 1958.

Bernstein, Herman. *The History of a Lie: "The Protocols of the Wise Men of Zion." A Study*. New York, 1921.

Bogardus, Emory S. *Immigration and Race Attitudes*. Boston, 1928.

Bouton, S. Miles. "The Persecution of the Jews in Europe: The Problem of Anti-Semitism." *Forum* 75 (June 1926):820–828.

Bowman, Isaiah. *The New World Problems in Political Geography*. Yonkers, NY, 1921.

_____. *Supplement to the New World Problems in Geography*. Yonkers, NY, 1924.

Brasol, Boris. *The Elements of Crime (Psycho-Social Interpretation)*. New York, 1927.

_____. *The Protocols and World Revolution*. Boston, 1920.

Burr, Clinton Stoddard. *America's Race Heritage*. New York, 1922.

The Causes of World Unrest. New York, 1920.

Colquhoun, Archibald, and Ethel Colquhoun. *The Whirlpool of Europe: Austria-Hungary and the Habsburgs*. New York, 1914.

Cox, Earnest Sevier. *White America*. Richmond, VA, 1923.

Dilling, Elizabeth. *The Red Network: A "Who's Who" and Handbook of Radicalism for Patriots*. Kenilworth, IL, 1934.

Dominion, Leon. *The Frontiers of Language and Nationality in Europe*. New York, 1917.

East, Edward M. *Heredity and Human Affairs*. New York, 1929.

_____. *Mankind at the Crossroads*. New York, 1923.

Ford, Henry. *The International Jew*. Dearborn, MI, 1920.

Gibbons, Herbert Adams. *An Introduction to World Politics*. New York, 1923.

_____. *The New Map of Asia (1900–1919)*. Chautauqua, NY, 1919.

_____. *The New Map of Europe (1911–1914): The Story of the Recent European Crises and Wars and of Europe's Present Catastrophe*. New York, 1914.

_____. *The Reconstruction of Poland and the Near East*. New York, 1917.

Goddard, H. H. *Human Efficiency and Levels of Intelligence*. Princeton, 1920.

Grant, Madison. *The Conquest of a Continent, or the Expansion of Races in America*. New York, 1933.

_____. *The Passing of the Great Race: Or the Racial Basis of European History*. New York, 1916.

Heald, Howard T. *Witness to Revolution: Letters from Russia, 1916–1919*. Edited by James B. Gidney. Kent State, OH, 1972.

Isaacs, Nathan. "The International Jew." *Menorah Journal* (December 1920):355–360.

The Jewish Peril: Protocols of the Elders of Zion. London, 1920.

Johnson, Albert. "Immigration: A Legislative Point of View." *Nation's Business* 11 (July 1923):26–28.

Johnston, Robert M. *Arms and the Race: The Foundations of Army Reform*. New York, 1915.

LaVarre, William. "Moscow's Red Letter Day in American History." *American Legion Magazine* 51 (August 1951):11–13, 50–54.

Lea, Homer. *The Day of the Saxon*. New York, 1912.

_____. *The Valor of Ignorance*. New York, 1909.

Lindbergh, Charles. "Aviation, Geography, and Race." *Reader's Digest* (November 1939):65–67.

McDougall, William. *The Group Mind: A Sketch of the Principles of Collective Psychology*. New York, 1920.

_____. *An Introduction to Social Psychology*. London, 1908.

_____. *Is America Safe for Democracy?* New York, 1921.

McSweeney, Edward F. *The Racial Contribution to the United States*. New Haven, n.d.

Muir, Ramsay. *The Expansion of Europe: The Culmination of Modern History*. Port Washington, NY, 1917.

Osborn, Henry Fairchild. "Facts of the Evolutionists." *Forum* 75 (June 1926):842–851.

Protocols of the Wise Men of Zion: Translated from the Russian to the English Language for the Information of all TRUE AMERICANS & to Confound Enemies of Democracy and the Republic also to Demonstrate the Possible Fulfillment of Biblical Prophecy as to World Domination by the Chosen People. New York, 1920.

Ripley, William Z. "Races in the United States." *Atlantic Monthly* (December 1908):745–759.

_____. *The Races of Europe: A Sociological Study.* New York, 1899:

Roberts, Kenneth. *Why Europe Leaves Home.* Indianapolis, IN, 1922.

Roosevelt, Theodore. *On Race-Riots-Reds-Crime.* Edited by Archibald B. Roosevelt. West Sayville, NY, 1968.

Ross, Edward A. *The Old World in the New: The Significance of Past and Present Immigration to the American People.* New York, 1914.

_____. *Russia in Upheaval.* New York, 1918.

Schultz, Alfred P. *Race or Mongrel: A Brief History of the Rise and Fall of the Ancient Races of the Earth.* Boston, 1908.

Spargo, John. *Bolshevism: The Enemy of Political and Industrial Democracy.* New York, 1919.

_____. *"The Greatest Failure in All History": A Critical Examination of the Actual Workings of Bolshevism in Russia.* New York, 1920.

_____. *The Jew and American Ideals.* New York, 1921.

Stoddard, Lothrop. "The Pedigree of Judah." *Forum* 75 (March 1926):321–333.

_____. *Present-Day Europe: Its National States of Mind.* New York, 1917.

_____. *Racial Realities in Europe.* New York, 1924.

_____. "Racial Realities in Europe." *Saturday Evening Post* 1906 (March 22, 1924):14–16.

_____. *The Revolt Against Civilization: The Menace of the Under-Man.* New York, 1922.

_____. *The Rising Tide of Color Against White World-Supremacy.* New York, 1920.

Sweeney, Walter C. *Military Intelligence: A New Weapon of War.* New York, 1924.

Trevor, John. *Refugees 1944.* Washington, DC, 1944.

Weyl, Nathaniel, *The Jew in American Politics.* New Rochelle, NY, 1968.

Woodruff, Charles E. "The Complexion of the Jews." *American Journal of Insanity* 62 (1905–1906):327–333.

_____. *The Effects of Tropical Light on White Men.* New York, 1905.

_____. *Expansion of Races.* New York, 1909.

Periodicals and Newspapers

American Legion Weekly
American Mercury
Forum
Infantry Journal
Journal of Military History

Journal of the Military Service Institution
Journal of U.S. Artillery
Journal of U.S. Cavalry Association
New York Times
Newsweek
North American Review
Parameters: Journal of the U.S. Army War College
Quartermaster Review
Saturday Evening Post
Stars and Stripes
Time
U.S. News and World Report
Washington Post
Yank

Books

Abzug, Robert H. *Inside the Vicious Heart: Americans and the Liberation of Nazi Concentration Camps.* New York, 1985.

Ambrose, Stephen E. *Citizen Soldier: The U.S. Army from the Beaches of Normandy to the Bulge to the Surrender of Germany.* New York, 1997.

_____. *Duty, Honor, Country: A History of West Point.* Baltimore, 1966.

_____. *Eisenhower: Soldier, General of the Army, President-Elect, 1890–1952.* New York, 1983.

_____. *Ike: Abilene to Berlin.* New York, 1973.

Baker, Roscoe. *The American Legion and American Foreign Policy.* New York, 1954.

Bales, Jack. *Kenneth Roberts: The Man and His Works.* Metuchen, NJ, 1989.

Baron, Salo W. *The Russian Jew Under the Tsars and Soviets.* New York, 1976.

Bidwell, Bruce W. *History of the Military Intelligence Division, Department of the Army General Staff: 1775–1941.* Washington, DC, 1954.

Blumenson, Martin. *Mark Clark.* New York, 1984.

_____. *Patton: The Man Behind the Legend, 1885–1945.* New York, 1985.

Braeman, John, Robert Bremmer, and David Brody, eds. *Twentieth-Century American Foreign Policy.* Columbus, OH, 1971.

Breitman, Richard, and Alan M. Kraut. *American Refugee Policy and European Jewry, 1933–1945.* Bloomington, IN, 1987.

Brown, Anthony. *The Last Hero: Wild Bill Donovan.* New York, 1982.

Brown, Richard C. *Social Attitudes of American Generals, 1898–1940.* New York, 1979.

Calavita, Kitty. *U.S. Immigration Law and the Control of Labor, 1820–1924.* Orlando, FL, 1984.

Chwialkowski, Paul. *In Caesar's Shadow: The Life of General Robert Eichelberger.* Westport, CT, 1993.

Clayton, James D. *The Years of MacArthur, 1880–1941*. Boston, 1970.

Clifford, John G. *The Citizen Soldiers: The Plattsburg Training Camp Movement, 1913–1920*. Lexington, KY, 1972.

Corson, William R. *The Armies of Ignorance: The Rise of the American Intelligence Empire*. New York, 1977.

Cowen, Ida. *Jews in Remote Corners of the World*. Englewood Cliffs, NJ, 1971.

Cray, Ed. *General of the Army: George C. Marshall, Soldier and Statesman*. New York, 1990.

Crosswell, D.K.R. *The Chief of Staff: The Military Career of General Walter Bedell Smith*. New York, 1991.

Curran, Thomas J. *Xenophobia and Immigration, 1820–1930*. Boston, 1975.

Daniels, Roger. *The Bonus Marches: An Episode of the Great Depression*. Westport, CT, 1971.

Davies, Norman. *God's Playground: A History of Poland*. Vol. 2. New York, 1982.

Degler, Carl N. *In Search of Human Nature: The Decline and Revival of Darwinism in American Social Thought*. New York, 1991.

Dinnerstein, Leonard. *America and the Survivors of the Holocaust*. New York, 1982.

_____. *Antisemitism in America*. New York, 1994.

Divine, Robert A. *American Immigration Policy, 1924–1952*. New York, 1972.

Donner, Frank. *The Age of Surveillance: The Aims and Methods of America's Political Intelligence System*. New York, 1980.

Dorwart, Jeffrey M. *Conflict of Duty: The U.S. Navy's Intelligence Dilemma, 1919–1945*. Annapolis, MD, 1983.

Edwards, Jerome E. *The Foreign Policy of Col. McCormick's Tribune, 1929–1941*. Reno, NV, 1971.

Epstein, Melech. *The Jew and Communism: The Story of Early Communist Victories and Ultimate Defeats in the Jewish Community, U.S.A.* New York, 1959.

Forman, Sidney. *West Point: A History of the United States Military Academy*. New York, 1950.

Fussell, Paul. *The Great War and Modern Memory*. New York, 1975.

_____. *Wartime: Understanding and Behavior in the Second World War*. New York, 1989.

Gerber, David, ed. *Anti-Semitism in American History*. Urbana, IL, 1986.

Gies, Joseph. *The Colonel of Chicago*. New York, 1979.

Gitelman, Zvi Y. *Jewish Nationality and Soviet Politics: The Jewish Sections of the CPSU, 1917–1930*. Princeton, 1972.

Gossett, Thomas F. *Race: The History of an Idea in America*. Dallas, 1963.

Grose, Peter. *Israel in the Mind of America*. New York, 1983.

Herzstein, Robert E. *Roosevelt and Hitler: Prelude to War*. New York, 1989.

Higham, John. *Send These to Me: Immigrants in Urban America*. Baltimore, 1984.

_____. *Strangers in the Land: Patterns of American Nativism, 1860–1925*. New Brunswick, NJ, 1955.

Higham, Robin, ed. *A Guide to the Sources of United States Military History*. Hamden, CT, 1975. *Supplement 1* (1981), *Supplement 2* (1986).

Hodgson, Godfrey. *The Colonel: The Life and Wars of Henry Stimson, 1867–1950*. New York, 1990.

Hofstadter, Richard. *Social Darwinism in American Thought*. New York, 1959.

Holmes, Colin. *Anti-Semitism in British Society, 1876–1939*. London, 1979.

Hutchinson, E. P. *Legislative History of American Immigration Policy, 1798–1965*. Philadelphia, 1981.

Janowicz, Morris. *The Professional Soldier*. New York, 1960.

Jeffreys-Jones, Rhodri. *American Espionage: From Secret Service to CIA*. New York, 1977.

Jensen, Joan M. *Army Surveillance in America, 1775–1980*. New Haven, 1991.

_____. *Military Surveillance of Civilians in America*. Morristown, NJ, 1975.

Karsten, Peter, ed. *The Military in America from the Colonial Era to the Present*. New York, 1980.

Katz, Barry M. *Foreign Intelligence: Research and Analysis in the Office of Strategic Services, 1942–1945*. Cambridge, MA, 1989.

Kemble, C. Robert. *The Image of the Army Officer in America: Background for Current Views*. Westport, CT, 1973.

Ketchum, Richard M. *The Borrowed Years, 1938–1941: America on the Way to War*. New York, 1989.

Kevles, Daniel J. *In the Name of Eugenics: Genetics and the Uses of Human Heredity*. New York, 1985.

Kirkpatrick, Charles E. *An Unknown Future and a Doubtful Present: Writing the Victory Plan of 1941*. Washington, DC, 1990.

Kühl, Stefan. *The Nazi Connection: Eugenics, American Racism, and German National Socialism*. New York, 1994.

Kushner, Tony. *The Persistence of Prejudice: Antisemitism in British Society During the Second World War*. Manchester, England, 1989.

Lebzelter, Gisela. *Political Anti-Semitism in England, 1918–1939*. New York, 1978.

Lee, Albert. *Henry Ford and the Jews*. New York, 1980.

Levine, Isaac Don. *Eyewitness to History: Memoirs and Reflections of a Foreign Correspondent for Half a Century*. New York, 1973.

Lisio, Daniel J. *The President and Protest: Hoover, Conspiracy, and the Bonus Riot*. Columbia, MO, 1974.

Ludmerer, Kenneth M. *Genetics and American Society: A Historical Appraisal*. Baltimore, 1972.

Lyons, Gene, and John Masland. *Education and Military Leadership: A Study of the R.O.T.C.* Princeton, 1959.

Mayo, Louise A. *The Ambivalent Image: Nineteenth-Century America's Reception of the Jew*. Rutherford, NJ, 1988.

McFarland, Keith. *Harry H. Woodring: A Political Biography of FDR's Controversial Secretary of War*. Lawrence, KS, 1975.

Mendelsohn, Ezra. *The Jews of East Central Europe Between the World Wars*. Bloomington, IN, 1983.

Miller, Merle. *Ike the Soldier As They Knew Him*. New York, 1987.

Millett, John D. *The Organization and Role of the Army Service Forces.* Washington, DC, 1954.

Murray, Robert K. *Red Scare: A Study in National Hysteria, 1919–1920.* Minneapolis, 1955.

Nadich, Judah. *Eisenhower and the Jews.* New York, 1953.

Newton, Verne W., ed. *FDR and the Holocaust.* New York, 1996.

Pappas, George S. *Prudens Futuri: The U.S. Army War College, 1901–1967.* Carlisle Barracks, PA, 1968.

Parrish, Thomas. *The Ultra Americans: The U.S. Role in Breaking the Nazi Codes.* New York, 1986.

Patton, Gewald W. *War and Race: The Black Officer in the American Military, 1915–1941.* Westport, CT, 1981.

Penkower, Moritz N. *The Jews Were Expendable: Free World Diplomacy and the Holocaust.* Urbana, IL, 1983.

Pogue, Forrest C. *George C. Marshall: Ordeal and Hope, 1939–1942.* Vol. 2. New York, 1986.

_____. *George C. Marshall: Organizer of Victory, 1943–1945.* Vol. 3. New York, 1976.

_____. *George C. Marshall: Statesman, 1945–1959.* Vol. 4. New York, 1987.

Powe, Marc, and Edward Wilson. *The Evolution of American Military Intelligence.* Fort Huachuca, AZ, 1973.

Powers, Richard. *Secrecy and Power: The Life of J. Edgar Hoover.* New York, 1987.

Ribuffo, Leo P. *The Old Christian Right: The Protestant Far Right from the Great Depression to the Cold War.* Philadelphia, 1983.

Rubinstein, William D. *The Myth of Rescue: Why the Democracies Could Not Have Saved More Jews from the Nazis.* London, 1997.

Sanders, Ronald. *Shores of Refuge: A Hundred Years of Jewish Immigration.* New York, 1988.

Sayen, Jamie. *Einstein in America: The Scientist's Conscience in the Age of Hitler and Hiroshima.* New York, 1985.

Schulzinger, Robert D. *The Making of the Diplomatic Mind: The Training, Outlook, and Style of United States Foreign Service Officers, 1908–1931.* Middletown, CT, 1975.

Searle, G. R. *Eugenics and Politics in Britain, 1900–1914.* Leyden, Netherlands, 1976.

Shortal, John F. *Forged by Fire: General Robert L. Eichelberger and the Pacific War.* Columbia, SC, 1987.

Steel, Ronald. *Walter Lippmann and the American Century.* Boston, 1980.

Stouffer, Samuel A., et al. *The American Soldier: Combat and Its Aftermath.* Princeton, 1949.

Szajkowski, Zosa. *The Impact of the 1919–1920 Red Scare on American Jewish Life.* New York, 1974.

_____. *Jews, Wars, and Communism: The Attitude of American Jews to World War I, the Russian Revolution, and Communism.* New York, 1972.

_____. *Kolchak, Jews, and the American Intervention in Northern Russia and Siberia, 1918–1920.* New York, 1977.

Talbert, Roy. *Negative Intelligence: The Army and the American Left, 1917–1941.* Jackson, MS, 1991.

Taylor, Maxwell D. *Swords and Plowshares.* New York, 1972.

Theoharis, Athan, and John Cox. *The Boss: J. Edgar Hoover and the Great American Inquisition.* Philadelphia, 1988.

Urofsky, Melvin I. *American Zionism: From Hertzl to the Holocaust.* New York, 1975.

Volkman, Ernest. *A Legacy of Hate: Anti-Semitism in America.* New York, 1982.

Waldrop, Frank C. *McCormick of Chicago: An Unconventional Portrait of a Controversial Figure.* Englewood Cliffs, NJ, 1966.

Weigley, Russell F. *The American Way of War: A History of United States Military Strategy and Policy.* New York, 1973.

_____. *History of the United States Army.* New York, 1967.

_____. *Towards an American Army: Military Thought from Washington to Marshall.* Westport, CT, 1962.

Weil, Martin. *A Pretty Good Club: The Founding Fathers of the U.S. Foreign Service.* New York, 1978.

Willoughby, Charles A., and John Chamberlain. *MacArthur, 1941–1951.* New York, 1954.

Wolfe, Robert, ed. *Americans as Proconsuls: United States Military Government in Germany and Japan, 1944–1952.* Carbondale, IL, 1984.

Wyman, David S. *The Abandonment of the Jews: America and the Holocaust, 1941–1945.* New York, 1984.

_____. *Paper Walls: America and the Refugee Crisis, 1938–1941.* Amherst, MA, 1968.

Wyman, Mark. *DP: Europe's Displaced Persons, 1945–1951.* Philadelphia, 1989.

Zweig, Ronald W. *Britain and Palestine During the Second World War.* London, 1986.

Articles

Bendersky, Joseph W. "Psychohistory Before Hitler: Early Military Analyses of German National Psychology." *Journal of the History of the Behavioral Sciences* 24 (April 1988):166–182.

Brecher, Frank W. "David Wyman and the Historiography of America's Response to the Holocaust: Counter-Considerations." *Holocaust and Genocide Studies* 5 (1990):423–446.

Cooling, Benjamin F. "Dwight D. Eisenhower at the Army War College, 1927–1928." *Parameters: The Journal of the U.S. Army War College* 5 (1975):26–36.

Degler, Carl. "Culture Versus Biology in the Thoughts of Franz Boas and Alfred L. Kroeber." *German Historical Institute Annual Lecture Series,* no. 2. Washington, DC, 1989.

Erdheim, Stuart G. "Could the Allies Have Bombed Auschwitz?" *Holocaust and Genocide Studies* 11 (Fall 1997):129–170.

Foregger, Richard. "Technical Analysis of Methods to Bomb the Gas Chambers at Auschwitz." *Holocaust and Genocide Studies* 5 (1990):403–421.

_____. "Two Sketch Maps of the Auschwitz-Birkenau Extermination Camps." *Journal of Military History* 59 (October 1995):687–696.

Gole, Harry. "War Planning at the War College in the Mid-1930s." *Parameters: The Journal of the U.S. Army War College* 15, 1 (Spring 1985):52–63.

Kage, Allan K. "The American Jewish Committee's Attitude Towards Anti-Semitism, 1919–1921." *Columbia University Center for Israel and Jewish Studies Working Papers* 2 (New York, 1979):33–64.

Kevles, Daniel J. "Testing the Army's Intelligence: Psychologists and the Military in World War I." *Journal of American History* 55 (December 1968):565–581.

Kitchens III, James H. "The Bombing of Auschwitz Reexamined." *Journal of Military History* 58 (April 1994):233–266.

Langer, John. "The Red General: Philip R. Faymonville and the Soviet Union, 1917–1952." *Prologue* 8 (Winter 1976):89–95.

Levy, Richard H. "The Bombing of Auschwitz Revisited: A Critical Analysis." *Holocaust and Genocide Studies* 10 (Winter 1996):267–298.

Muller, Jerry Z. "Communism, Anti-Semitism and the Jews." *Commentary* 86 (August 1988):28–39.

Ribuffo, Leo. "Henry Ford and *The International Jew*." *American Jewish History* 69 (June 1980):437–477.

Schaffer, Ronald. "General Stanley D. Embick: Military Dissenter." *Military Affairs* 37 (October 1973):89–95.

Schapiro, Leonard, "The Role of the Jews in the Russian Revolutionary Movement." *Slavonic Review*:149–167.

Singerman, Robert. "The American Career of the Protocols of the Elders of Zion." *American Jewish History* 71 (September 1981):48–78.

Stern, Guy. "In the Service of American Military Intelligence: German-Jewish Exiles in the War Against Hitler." *Leo Baeck Institute Year Book* 37 (1992):461–477.

_____. "The Jewish Exiles in the Service of U.S. Intelligence: The Post-War Years." *Leo Baeck Institute Year Book* 40 (1995):51–62.

Van Loan, Charles E. "General Homer Lea." *Harper's Weekly* 57 (1913):7.

Vaughn, Stephen. "Prologue to *Public Opinion*: Walter Lippmann's Work in Military Intelligence." *Prologue* 15 (Fall 1983):151–163.

Williams, David. "The Bureau of Investigation and Its Critics, 1919–1921: The Origins of Federal Political Surveillance." *Journal of American History* 68 (December 1981):570–571.

Wyman, David S. "Why Auschwitz Was Never Bombed." *Commentary* (May 1978):37–46.

Index

About the Author

Joseph W. Bendersky is professor and director of graduate studies in history at Virginia Commonwealth University. He is the author of *Carl Schmitt: Theorist for the Reich* and *A History of Nazi Germany*.